An Introduction to Database Systems

Second Edition

An Introduction to Database Systems

Second Edition

C. J. DATE
IBM (UK) Laboratories Ltd.

ADDISON-WESLEY PUBLISHING COMPANY
Reading, Massachusetts • Menlo Park, California
London • Amsterdam • Don Mills, Ontario • Sydney

ISBN 0-201-14456-5
CDEFGHIJ-HA-7987

For Lindy

THE SYSTEMS PROGRAMMING SERIES

Foreword

The field of systems programming primarily grew out of the efforts of many programmers and managers whose creative energy went into producing practical, utilitarian systems programs needed by the rapidly growing computer industry. Programming was practiced as an art where each programmer invented his own solutions to problems with little guidance beyond that provided by his immediate associates. In 1968, the late Ascher Opler, then at IBM, recognized that it was necessary to bring programming knowledge together in a form that would be accessible to all systems programmers. Surveying the state of the art, he decided that enough useful material existed to justify a significant publication effort. On his recommendation, IBM decided to sponsor The Systems Programming Series as a long term project to collect, organize, and publish principles and techniques that would have lasting value throughout the industry.

The Series consists of an open-ended collection of text-reference books. The contents of each book represent the individual author's view of the subject area and do not necessarily reflect the views of the IBM Corporation. Each is organized for course use but is detailed enough for reference. Further, the Series is organized in three levels: broad introductory material in the foundation volumes, more specialized material in the software volumes, and very specialized theory in the computer science volumes. As such, the Series meets the needs of the novice, the experienced programmer, and the computer scientist.

The Editorial Board

Preface
to the
First Edition

Computers have already had a considerable impact on many aspects of our society. Medicine, law enforcement, government, banking, education, transportation, planning—these are only some of the fields in which computers are already playing a highly significant role. Over the next few years we can expect a vast increase in the range of computer applications and a corresponding increase in the effect computers will have on our daily lives. The two areas of computer technology that will make the new applications possible—indeed, in most cases they are absolutely fundamental—are telecommunications and the integrated database.

In the years ahead, then, database systems will become increasingly widespread and increasingly important. At present, however, they represent a new and relatively unexplored field, despite the fact that the number of systems installed or under development is growing at considerable speed. There is a real need for a good basic textbook that covers the fundamental concepts of such systems in a clear and concise manner. This book represents an attempt to meet the need.

The reader is assumed to be professionally interested in some aspect of data processing. He or she may, for example, be a systems analyst or designer, an application programmer, a systems programmer, a student following a university or similar course in computer science, or a teacher of such a course. (The book is in fact based on an intensive course in the subject that the author has been teaching to professional staff within IBM over a considerable period of time.) Generally speaking, the reader is expected to have a reasonable appreciation of the capabilities of a modern computer system, with particular reference to the file-handling features of such a system. He or she should also have some knowledge of at least one

high-level programming language. Since these prerequisites are not particularly demanding, I am hopeful that the book will prove suitable as an
introductory text for anyone concerned with using or implementing a
database system, or for anyone who simply wishes to broaden a general
knowledge of the computer science field.

The book is divided into six major parts:

1. Database System Architecture
2. The Relational Approach
3. The Hierarchical Approach
4. The Network Approach
5. Security and Integrity
6. Review, Analysis, and Comparisons

Each part in turn is subdivided into a number of chapters. Part 1 provides
a general introduction to the concepts of a database system, and in
particular outlines three distinct approaches to the design of such a
system, namely, the relational, hierarchical, and network approaches.
Part 2 then examines the relational approach in considerable detail; Part 3
performs the same function for the hierarchical approach; and Part 4 does
the same for the network approach. Part 5 presents a discussion of the
problems of security and integrity in a database system. Part 6 draws
together some of the more important themes introduced earlier in the
book and considers them in somewhat more depth.

The structure just outlined requires some justification. As explained,
Part 2 is concerned with the relational approach. In fact, it is largely
devoted to an exposition of the ideas of Dr. E. F. Codd, the recognized
authority in the relational database field. It is only fair to point out,
however, that most commercial systems currently available (1977) are
based on one of the other two approaches. Why, then, the emphasis on
the relational approach? There are at least two answers to this question.

1. The relational approach may be viewed as the beginnings of a theory
of data; as such, it provides an excellent basis for understanding and
comparing the other two approaches, and a convenient measure or
yardstick against which any existing system can be judged. The sound-
ness and permanence of the theory would make it an ideal vehicle for
tutorial purposes, even if it possessed no other advantages.

2. The fact that most existing systems are not relational may be viewed
as the natural outcome of the way in which computing technology itself
has developed. The comparatively small capacity and high access times of
early direct-access devices, the traditional emphasis on sequential media
such as tape and cards, the limited amount of storage available in the

computer itself—these and similar considerations had significant repercussions on the original design of most early systems. With modern
hardware and techniques, however, it seems possible to design and build
a system that does not have the shortcomings of earlier designs. To be
more specific, many authorities now believe that the future will see the
implementation of one or more large-scale systems based on the relational
approach. (Since this was first written, in fact, a number of commercial
systems incorporating relational concepts have begun to appear on the
scene.)

From these remarks the reader will conclude, quite rightly, that the
text is somewhat biased throughout in favor of the relational approach.
Obviously the author believes that such a bias is justified; but it would be
dishonest not to warn the reader that the bias is there.

Despite the views just expressed, however, the hierarchical and
network approaches are obviously extremely important, and they possess
the advantage of having several years' experience behind them. Parts 3
and 4 therefore deal with these approaches in some detail (and I hope
fairly, in spite of my prejudices). Part 3 is based entirely on an existing
system, IBM's Information Management System (IMS), which is already
operating successfully in a number of computer installations. This system
has been chosen as the basis for Part 3 both because it is a good example
of the hierarchical approach and, of course, because it is an important
system in its own right. For similar reasons, Part 4 is based on the
proposals of the Data Base Task Group (DBTG) of the CODASYL
Programming Language Committee. I hope, therefore, that Parts 3 and 4
will serve not only as a general introduction to the hierarchical and
network approaches, but also specifically as a tutorial on the IMS and
DBTG systems. However, teaching specific systems is not the major aim
of the book; rather, the object is to describe some general concepts, using
specific systems primarily for purposes of illustration. (For this reason
many otherwise important systems are little more than just mentioned.)
Even so, the descriptions of IMS and DBTG, in particular, do go into a
fair amount of rather specific detail. The reader who is not too interested
in the finer detail of these systems may omit certain portions of the text if
he or she wishes—principally Chapters 16–18, and certain sections (appropriately indicated) of Chapters 20 and 22. In any case it may be as well
to omit these portions on a first reading.

A note on terminology. Like many other new subjects, the field of
database systems possesses as yet no commonly agreed nomenclature. In
particular, the terminology of IMS differs in many respects from that of
DBTG. This book attempts to reconcile the differences by relating both
IMS and DBTG terminology to a "neutral" terminology defined in Parts 1

and 2. (Once this has been done, however, the "correct" terminology for each system is generally employed in subsequent discussions.) The terminology of Parts 1 and 2, in turn, is an amalgam derived from many sources.

A few further points about the structure of the book:

1. I have tried to write a textbook, not a reference work. Of course, these two objectives are not wholly incompatible—indeed, I hope that to a large extent both are achieved—but whenever they clash, I have aimed at the first rather than the second. To this end I have not hesitated to omit minor points in the interests of clarity, nor to simplify others for the same reason, although as a general rule I have attempted to be as thorough as possible. (The reader is referred elsewhere for further details where appropriate.)

2. Since it is a textbook, most chapters are followed by a set of exercises, of which the reader is strongly urged to attempt at least a few. Answers, sometimes giving additional information about the subject of the question, will be found at the end of the book.

3. Each chapter is followed by a list of references, many of them annotated. References are identified in the text by numbers in brackets. For example, [1.3] refers to the third item in the list of references at the end of Chapter 1, namely, a paper by the CODASYL Systems Committee published in the *BCS Computer Bulletin,* Vol. 15, No. 4, and also in *Communications of the ACM,* Vol. 14, No. 5.

There remains only the pleasant task of acknowledging the help I have received in writing this book. I am grateful, first, to Dr. Codd for a great deal of encouragement, for permission to make use of much of his published material, particularly in Part 2, and for his helpful comments on the initial draft. The following people also very kindly read that draft and produced many valuable criticisms and suggestions: Joel Aron, Jan Hazelzet, Roger Holliday, Paul Hopewell, Larry Lewis, Salah Mandil, Bill McGee, Herb Meltzer, John Nicholls, Terry Rogers, and Tom Work. I would also like to thank Professor Julius T. Tou, the organizer of the 4th International Symposium on Computers and Information Science (Miami Beach, Florida, 14–16 December 1972), and Plenum Publishing Corporation (publishers of the proceedings) for permission to use a paper I presented at that symposium as the basis for Chapters 3 and 11. Thanks should also be given to the many IBM students whose comments on the original course from which this book is derived have been most helpful. Finally, I am grateful to IBM for allowing much of the work of preparing the book to be done using company time and resources. I must emphasize, however, that I am entirely responsible for the contents of the book; the views expressed are my own and in no way represent an official statement on the part of IBM.

Palo Alto, California   C. J. D.
November 1974 (revised January 1977)

Preface
to the
Second Edition

Many changes have occurred in the field of database development since the first edition was written. The DBTG data manipulation language and sub-schema data description language have been accepted by the CODASYL Programming Language Committee for incorporation into COBOL, and a number of DBTG-based systems are now commercially available. Secondary indexing and various other features have been added to IMS. Commercial systems based on relational concepts have started to become available. Various standardization activities are under way. Perhaps most significant of all, universities and similar institutions throughout the world are displaying an unprecedented level of interest in the subject. The present edition is an attempt to reflect some of this activity. It includes a great deal of new material, which is of course its primary raison d'être; however, the opportunity has also been taken to correct some errors from the first edition and to improve the presentation in many places. Many new references have also been included, most of them with annotation.

Some of the more significant differences between this edition and the previous one are summarized below.

Part 1: The overall systems architecture (Chapter 1) has been revised to incorporate ANSI/SPARC terminology. The comparative presentation of the three approaches (Chapter 3) has been unified and extended.

Part 2: Treatment of the relational data model has been expanded into a separate chapter (Chapter 4); chapters on SEQUEL and Query By Example have been added (Chapters 7 and 8); and Chapter 9 (Further Normalization) has been totally rewritten and includes an improved treatment of third normal form and the new fourth normal form. All other chapters have been considerably revised.

Part 3: Secondary indexing has been introduced (Chapter 18). Other chapters have been revised in accordance with the latest version of IMS.

Part 4: All chapters have been revised to incorporate changes made by the Data Description Language and Programming Language Committees of CODASYL.

Part 5: Both chapters have been revised to incorporate IMS and DBTG changes. Additional relational systems have been included. The treatment of integrity constraints and concurrency (Chapter 24) has been greatly expanded.

Part 6: This section is completely new.

Once again it is a great pleasure to acknowledge the assistance I have received in producing this book. I am particularly pleased to have the chance to thank the many people who commented favorably on the first edition and encouraged me to expand it into its present form. In this regard, I would especially like to mention Ted Codd, Frank King, Ben Shneiderman, and Mike Stonebraker. I am also deeply indebted to the following people for helping me over numerous technical questions and for reviewing and criticizing various portions of the draft of this edition: David Beech, Don Chamberlin, Rod Cuff, Bob Engles, Ron Fagin, Peter Hitchcock, Roger Holliday, Bill Kent, Bill Lockhart, Ron Obermarck, Vern Watts, and Moshe Zloof. As with the previous edition, I am extremely grateful to IBM for supporting me in this work. I would also like to thank Technical Publishing Company, publishers of *Datamation,* for permission to base the revisions in Chapter 3 on an article that appeared in that journal in April 1976; and ACM, for permission to base portions of Chapter 25 on material from three papers (references [22.2], [25.3], and [25.8]) for which ACM holds the copyright. Last but not least, I would like to express my appreciation to the staff of Addison-Wesley for the tremendous enthusiasm, encouragement, and patience they have shown throughout the production of both editions.

San Jose, California   C. J. D.
June 1977

Contents

PART 1
DATABASE SYSTEM ARCHITECTURE

CHAPTER 1
BASIC CONCEPTS

1.1	What Is a Database?	3
1.2	Why Database?	6
1.3	Data Independence	9
1.4	An Architecture for a Database System	13
	Exercises	21
	References and Bibliography	22

CHAPTER 2
STORAGE STRUCTURES

2.1	Introduction	27
2.2	Possible Representations for Some Sample Data	30
2.3	The Physical Record Interface: Indexing Techniques	37
2.4	General Indexing Techniques	40
	Exercises	43
	References and Bibliography	44

CHAPTER 3
DATA MODELS AND DATA SUBLANGUAGES

3.1	Introduction	51
3.2	The Relational Approach	52

3.3   The Hierarchical Approach   55
3.4   The Network Approach   58
3.5   Higher-Level Data Sublanguages.   62
3.6   Summary   66
       Exercises   67
       References and Bibliography   68

**PART 2
THE RELATIONAL APPROACH**

**CHAPTER 4
THE RELATIONAL DATA MODEL**

4.1   Relations   73
4.2   Domains and Attributes   75
4.3   Keys   77
4.4   Summary   79
       Exercises   81
       References and Bibliography   81

**CHAPTER 5
A DATA SUBLANGUAGE BASED ON RELATIONAL CALCULUS**

5.1   Introduction   83
5.2   Assumptions and Definitions   84
5.3   Retrieval Operations   86
5.4   Storage Operations   96
5.5   Library Functions   98
5.6   Summary   103
       Exercises   104
       References and Bibliography   107

**CHAPTER 6
A DATA SUBLANGUAGE BASED ON RELATIONAL ALGEBRA**

6.1   Introduction   113
6.2   Traditional Set Operations   114
6.3   Special Relational Operations   115
6.4   Retrieval Examples   118
6.5   Storage Examples   119
6.6   Summary   119
       Exercises   120
       References and Bibliography   120

CHAPTER 7
THE DATA SUBLANGUAGE SEQUEL

7.1	Introduction	123
7.2	Retrieval Operations	124
7.3	Storage Operations	131
7.4	Library Functions	132
7.5	Summary	134
	Exercises	134
	References and Bibliography	134

CHAPTER 8
QUERY BY EXAMPLE

8.1	Introduction	137
8.2	Retrieval Operations	138
8.3	Retrieval Operations on Tree-Structured Relations	143
8.4	Storage Operations	146
8.5	Library Functions	148
8.6	Retrieval Operations on the Dictionary	149
8.7	Summary	151
	Exercises	152
	References and Bibliography	152

CHAPTER 9
FURTHER NORMALIZATION

9.1	Introduction	153
9.2	Functional Dependence	154
9.3	First, Second, and Third Normal Forms	156
9.4	Relations With More Than One Candidate Key	163
9.5	Fourth Normal Form	167
9.6	Summary	169
	Exercises	170
	References and Bibliography	172

CHAPTER 10
THE EXTERNAL MODEL

10.1	Introduction	179
10.2	External Relations	180
10.3	External Domains	183
10.4	Data Sublanguage Operations	185
10.5	Changes to the Conceptual Schema	186
10.6	Summary	188
	Exercises	190
	References and Bibliography	190

CHAPTER 11
SOME RELATIONAL SYSTEMS

11.1   Introduction 191
11.2   Early Systems 191
11.3   Recent Systems 193
        References and Bibliography 196

PART 3
THE HIERARCHICAL APPROACH

CHAPTER 12
THE ARCHITECTURE OF AN IMS SYSTEM

12.1   Background 205
12.2   Architecture 206
        References and Bibliography 208

CHAPTER 13
THE IMS DATA MODEL

13.1   Physical Databases 209
13.2   The Database Description 212
13.3   Hierarchical Sequence 215
13.4   Some Remarks on the Education Database 216
        Exercise 217
        References and Bibliography 218

CHAPTER 14
THE IMS EXTERNAL MODEL

14.1   Logical Databases 219
14.2   The Program Communication Block 221
        Exercise 223
        References and Bibliography 223

CHAPTER 15
THE IMS DATA SUBLANGUAGE

15.1   Defining the Program Communication Block (PCB) 225
15.2   The DL/I Operations 227
15.3   DL/I Examples 229
15.4   Constructing the Segment Search Argument (SSA) 234
15.5   SSA Command Codes 234
        Exercises 239
        References and Bibliography 239

CHAPTER 16
IMS STORAGE STRUCTURES

16.1   Introduction 241
16.2   HSAM 243
16.3   HISAM 244
16.4   HD Structures: Pointers 249
16.5   HDAM 251
16.6   HIDAM 254
16.7   Secondary Data Set Groups 255
16.8   The Mapping Definition 260
16.9   Reorganization 264
16.10   Data Independence 265
16.11   Summary 267
        Exercises 268
        References and Bibliography 268

CHAPTER 17
IMS LOGICAL DATABASES

17.1   Logical Databases (LDBs) 269
17.2   An Example 270
17.3   Terminology 273
17.4   The Database Descriptions (DBDs) 274
17.5   Loading the Logical Database 277
17.6   Processing the Logical Database 278
17.7   Bidirectional Logical Relationships 280
17.8   A Note on the Storage Structure 286
17.9   Logical Databases Involving a Single Physical Database 286
17.10   Some Rules and Restrictions 290
17.11   Summary 291
        Exercises 291
        References and Bibliography 292

CHAPTER 18
IMS SECONDARY INDEXING

18.1   Introduction 293
18.2   Indexing the Root on a Field Not the Sequence Field 295
18.3   Indexing the Root on a Field in a Dependent 298
18.4   Indexing a Dependent on a Field in That Dependent 301
18.5   Indexing a Dependent on a Field in a Lower-Level Dependent . . 303
18.6   Additional Features 304
18.7   Summary 304
        Exercises 306
        References and Bibliography 306

PART 4
THE NETWORK APPROACH

CHAPTER 19
THE ARCHITECTURE OF A DBTG SYSTEM

19.1   Background 309
19.2   Architecture 311
       References and Bibliography 313

CHAPTER 20
THE DBTG DATA MODEL

20.1   Introduction 315
20.2   The Set Construct: Hierarchical Examples 316
20.3   The Set Construct: Network Examples 323
20.4   Singular Sets 326
20.5   Areas 327
20.6   Database-Keys 328
20.7   A Sample Schema 329
20.8   Membership Class 335
20.9   LOCATION MODE 338
20.10 SET SELECTION 339
20.11 Source and Result Data-Items 343
20.12 DDL/COBOL Terminology 344
       Exercises 345
       References and Bibliography 346

CHAPTER 21
THE DBTG EXTERNAL MODEL

21.1   Introduction 349
21.2   Differences between the Sub-Schema and Schema 349
21.3   A Sample Sub-Schema 351
       Exercise 351
       References and Bibliography 352

CHAPTER 22
THE DBTG DATA SUBLANGUAGE

22.1   Introduction 353
22.2   Currency 353
22.3   GET 356
22.4   MODIFY 357
22.5   CONNECT 359
22.6   DISCONNECT 359
22.7   ERASE 360
22.8   STORE 361

22.9   FIND 361
22.10   Miscellaneous Statements 368
        Exercises   369
        References and Bibliography 371

PART 5
SECURITY AND INTEGRITY

CHAPTER 23
SECURITY

23.1   Introduction   375
23.2   Identification and Authentication 377
23.3   Access Control 378
23.4   Security in IMS 385
23.5   Security in DBTG 386
23.6   Bypassing the System 388
        Exercise 389
        References and Bibliography 390

CHAPTER 24
INTEGRITY

24.1   Introduction   395
24.2   Integrity Constraints 396
24.3   Data Sharing 405
24.4   Support Routines 408
24.5   Integrity in IMS 410
24.6   Integrity in DBTG 412
        References and Bibliography 418

PART 6
REVIEW, ANALYSIS, AND COMPARISONS

CHAPTER 25
THE THREE APPROACHES REVISITED

25.1   The ANSI/SPARC Architecture 425
25.2   The External Level 429
25.3   The Conceptual Level 443
25.4   Conclusion 456
        References and Bibliography 457

        Answers to Selected Exercises 463

        Index 525

Part 1
Database System Architecture

Part 1 consists of three introductory chapters. Chapter 1 sets the scene by explaining what a database is and defining an outline architecture for a database system. This architecture serves as a framework on which all later chapters of the book will build. Chapter 2 is a brief introduction to some techniques for physically arranging the data in the stored database. Chapter 3 is the longest and most important chapter; it concerns a problem which is central to the design of any database system, namely, the problem of how the database is to be viewed by the users. (It is normal to shield users from details of how the data is physically stored and to allow them to view the database in a form more suited to their requirements.) Chapter 3 introduces the three major approaches to this problem, namely, the relational, hierarchical, and network approaches, and thus paves the way for the next three parts of the book.

1
Basic
Concepts

1.1 WHAT IS A DATABASE?

Even if they have never studied the subject before, many readers will already have formed a general impression—from articles in data processing magazines, news items, advertisements, and similar sources—as to what constitutes a database system. Their impression probably looks something like Fig. 1.1.

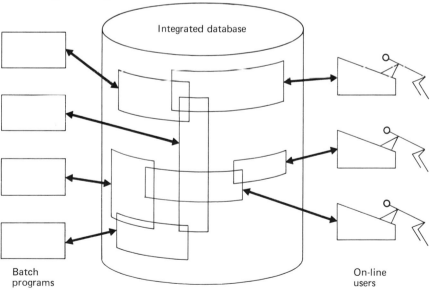

Fig. 1.1 Simplified view of a database system

First of all, there is the database itself—a (probably large) collection of data stored on disks, drums, or other secondary storage media. Second, there is a set of ordinary batch application programs which run against this data, operating on it in all the usual ways (retrieving, updating, inserting, deleting). Additionally (or alternatively), there may be a set of on-line users who interact with the database from remote terminals— again, in general, performing all the functions of retrieving, updating, inserting, and deleting, although it is probably true to say that retrieval is the most common and most important function in this case. Third, the database is "integrated." This means that the database contains the data for many users, not just for one, which in turn implies that any one user (batch or on-line) will be concerned with just a small portion of it; moreover, different users' portions will overlap in various ways—that is, individual pieces of data may be shared by many different users.

This picture of a database system is in fact reasonably accurate so far as it goes. The rest of the present chapter is an attempt to make the picture more precise. We start with a working definition of *database* (based on one given by Engles [1.6]).

■ A database is a collection of stored operational data used by the application systems of some particular enterprise.

This definition requires some explanation.

"Enterprise" is simply a convenient generic term for any reasonably large-scale commercial, scientific, technical, or other operation. Some examples are:

Manufacturing company

Bank

Hospital

University

Government department

Any enterprise must necessarily maintain a lot of data about its operation. This is its "operational data." The operational data for the enterprises listed above would probably include the following:

Product data

Account data

Patient data

Student data

Planning data

Note, however, that operational data does *not* include input or output data, work queues, or indeed any purely transient information. "Input data" refers to information entering the system from the outside world (typically on cards or from a terminal); such information may cause a change to be made to the operational data but is not itself part of the database. Similarly, "output data" refers to messages and reports emanating from the system (printed or otherwise displayed at a terminal); again, such a report contains information derived from the operational data, but it is not itself part of the database.

As an illustration of the concept of operational data, let us consider the case of a manufacturing company in a little more detail. Such an enterprise will wish to retain information about the *projects* it has on hand; the *parts* used in those projects; the *suppliers* who supply the parts; the *warehouses* in which the parts are stored; the *employees* who work on the projects; and so on. These are the basic entities about which data is recorded in the database. See Fig. 1.2.

It is important to note that in general there will be *associations* or *relationships* linking the basic entities together. These are represented by connecting arrows in Fig. 1.2. For example, there is an association between suppliers and parts: Each supplier supplies certain parts, and conversely, each part is supplied by certain suppliers. Similarly, parts are used in projects, and conversely, projects use parts; parts are stored in warehouses, and warehouses store parts; and so on. Note that the relationships are all bidirectional. The significant point is that relationships such as these are just as much a part of the operational data as are the associated entities. They must therefore be represented in the database. (This may be done by means of pointers, by physical adjacency, or by any other method that seems suitable, but it must be done.)

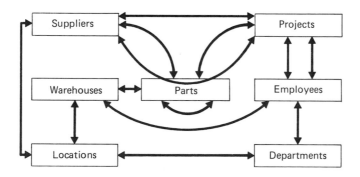

Fig. 1.2 An example of operational data

Figure 1.2 also illustrates a number of other points.

1. Although most of the relationships in the diagram associate *two* types of entity, this is by no means always the case. In the example there is one arrow connecting three types of entity (suppliers–parts–projects). This could represent the fact that certain suppliers supply certain parts to certain projects. This is *not* the same as the combination of the suppliers–parts association and the parts–projects association (in general). For example, the information that "supplier S2 supplies part P4 to project J3" tells us *more* than the combination "supplier S2 supplies part P4" and "part P4 is used in project J3"—we cannot deduce the first of these three associations knowing only the second and third. More explicitly, we can deduce that S2 supplies P4 to some project Jx, and that some supplier Sy supplies P4 to J3, but we cannot infer that Jx is J3 or that Sy is S2. A false inference such as this is an example of what is sometimes referred to as the *connection trap*.

2. The example also shows one arrow involving only *one* type of entity (parts). This represents an association between one part and another: for example, the fact that some parts are components of other parts (a screw is a component of a hinge assembly, which is also considered as a part).

3. In general, the same entities may be associated in any number of relationships. In the example, projects and employees are linked in two relationships. One might represent the relationship "works on" (the employee works on the project), the other the relationship "is the manager of" (the employee is the manager of the project).

Many database texts (and systems) consider entities and relationships as two fundamentally dissimilar types of object. However, an association between entities may itself be considered as an entity. If we take as our definition of entity "an object about which we wish to record information," then an association certainly fits the definition. For example, "part P4 is stored in warehouse W8" is an entity about which we may wish to record information, e.g., the appropriate quantity. Thus in this book we shall tend to view relationships merely as special types of entity.

1.2 WHY DATABASE?

Why should an enterprise choose to store its operational data in an integrated database? There are many answers to this question. One general answer is that it provides the enterprise with *centralized control* of its operational data—which, as Meltzer [1.9] points out, is its most valuable asset. This is in sharp contrast to the situation that prevails in

most enterprises today, where typically each application has its own
private files—quite often its own private tapes and disk packs, too—so
that the operational data is widely dispersed, and there is little or no
attempt to control it in a systematic way.

The foregoing implies that in an enterprise with a database system
there will be some one identifiable person—the *database administrator*, or
DBA—who has this central responsibility for the operational data. In
fact, we may consider the DBA as part of the database system (that is, the
system is more than just data plus software plus hardware—it includes
people, too). We shall be discussing the role of the DBA in more detail
later; for the time being, it is sufficient to note that the job will involve
both a high degree of technical expertise and the ability to understand
and interpret management requirements at a senior level. (In practice the
DBA may consist of a team of people instead of just one person.) It is
important to realize that the position of the DBA within the enterprise is
a very senior one.

Let us now consider the advantages that accrue from having centralized control of the data, as discussed above.

- The amount of redundancy in the stored data can be reduced.

In most current systems each application has its own private files.
This can often lead to considerable redundancy in stored data, with
resultant waste in storage space. For example, a personnel application
and an education-records application may each own a file containing
name, number, and department for every employee. With central control,
however, the DBA can identify the fact that the two applications require
essentially the same data, and hence can integrate the two files; that is,
the data can be stored once only and can be shared by the two applications.

- Problems of inconsistency in the stored data can be avoided (to a
  certain extent).

This is really a corollary of the previous point. If the "same" fact
about the real world—say, the fact that employee E3 works in department D8—is represented by two distinct entries in the database, then at
some time the two entries will not agree (i.e., when one and only one has
been updated). The database is then inconsistent. If, on the other hand,
the information is represented by a single entry—if the redundancy has
been removed—such an inconsistency cannot arise.

- The stored data can be shared.

This point has already been made in passing but is worth stating here as an important advantage in its own right. It means not only that all the files of existing applications are integrated, but also that new applications may be developed to operate against the existing database.

- Standards can be enforced.

With central control of the database, the DBA can ensure that installation and industry standards are followed in the representation of the data. This simplifies problems of maintenance and data interchange between installations.

- Security restrictions can be applied.

Having complete jurisdiction over the operational data, the DBA (a) can ensure that the only means of access to the database is through the proper channels, and hence (b) can define authorization checks to be carried out whenever access to sensitive data is attempted. Different procedures can be established for each type of access (retrieve, update, delete, etc.) to each type of data field in the database. [Perhaps it should also be pointed out that without such procedures the security of the data may actually be *more* at risk in a database system than in a traditional (dispersed) filing system.]

- Data integrity can be maintained.

The problem of integrity is the problem of ensuring that the database contains only accurate data. Inconsistency between two entries representing the same "fact" is an example of lack of integrity (which of course can only occur if redundancy exists in the stored data). Even if redundancy is eliminated, however, the database may still contain incorrect data. For example, an employee may be shown as having worked 200 hours in the week, or a list of employee numbers for a given department may include the number of a nonexistent employee. Centralized control of the database helps in avoiding these situations (insofar as they can be avoided) by permitting the DBA to define validation procedures to be carried out whenever any storage operation is attempted. (Here, as elsewhere, we use the term "storage operation" to cover all the operations of updating, inserting, and deleting.)

- Conflicting requirements can be balanced.

Knowing the overall requirements of the enterprise—as opposed to the requirements of any individual user—the DBA can structure the database system to provide an overall service that is "best for the enterprise." For example, a representation can be chosen for the data in storage that gives fast access for the most important applications at the cost of poor performance in some other applications.

Most of the advantages listed above are fairly obvious. However, one other point, which is not so obvious—although it is implied by several of the foregoing—must be added to the list, namely, *the provision of data independence.* (Strictly speaking, this is an *objective* rather than an advantage.) This concept is so important that we devote a separate section to it.

1.3 DATA INDEPENDENCE

Data independence may be most easily understood by first considering its opposite. Most present-day applications are data-dependent. This means that the way in which the data is organized in secondary storage and the way in which it is accessed are both dictated by the requirements of the application, *and moreover that knowledge of the data organization and access technique is built into the application logic.* For example, it may be decided (for performance reasons) that a particular file is to be stored in indexed sequential form. The application, then, must know that the index exists and must know the file sequence (as defined by the index), and the internal structure of the application will be built around this knowledge. In addition, the precise form of the various accessing and exception-checking procedures within the application will depend very heavily on details of the interface presented by the indexed sequential software.

We say that an application such as this one is *data-dependent* because it is impossible to change the storage structure (how the data is physically recorded) or access strategy (how it is accessed) without affecting the application, probably drastically. For example, it would not be possible to replace the indexed sequential file above by a hash-addressed file without making major modifications to the application. It is interesting to note, incidentally, that the portions of the application requiring alteration in such a case are the portions that communicate with the file-handling software, and that the difficulties involved are quite irrelevant to the problem the application was written to solve—they are difficulties *introduced* by the structure of the file-handling software interface.

In a database system, however, it would be extremely undesirable to allow applications to be data-dependent. There are two major reasons.

1. Different applications will need different views of the same data. For example, suppose that before the enterprise introduces its integrated database, we have two applications, A and B, each owning a file containing the field "customer balance." Suppose, however, that application A records this value in decimal, whereas application B records it in binary.

It will still be possible to integrate the two files and to eliminate the redundancy, provided that the database software performs all necessary conversions between the stored representation chosen (which may be decimal or binary or something else again) and the form in which each application wishes to see it. For example, if the decision is to hold the value in decimal, then every access from B will require a conversion to or from binary.

This is a fairly trivial example of the sort of difference that may exist in a database system between an application's view of the data and what is physically stored. Many other possible differences are considered later.

2. The DBA must have the freedom to change the storage structure or access strategy (or both) in response to changing requirements, without the necessity of modifying existing applications. For example, the enterprise may adopt new standards; application priorities may change; new types of storage device may become available; and so on. At present such changes involve corresponding alterations to applications, thus tying up programmer effort that would otherwise be available for the creation of new applications. For example, one large installation has approximately 25 percent of the programming staff working full-time on this sort of maintenance activity [1.6]. Clearly this is a waste of an extremely valuable resource.

It follows that the provision of data independence is a major objective of database systems. We can define data independence as the *immunity of applications to change in storage structure and access strategy*—which implies, of course, that the applications concerned do not depend on any one particular storage structure and access strategy. In Section 1.4, we present an architecture for a database system that provides a basis for achieving this objective. Before then, however, let us consider in more detail the types of change that the DBA may wish to make (and that we wish applications to be immune to).

We start with some definitions.

A *stored field* is the smallest named unit of data stored in the database. The database will in general contain many *occurrences* of each of several *types* of stored field. For example, a database containing information about parts would probably include a stored field type called "part number," and there would be one occurrence of this stored field for each distinct part.

A *stored record* is a named collection of associated stored fields. Again we distinguish between type and occurrence. A stored record *occurrence* consists of a group of related stored field occurrences (and represents an association between them). For example, a stored record occurrence might consist of an occurrence of each of the following stored fields: part number, part name, part color, and part weight. The association between them is of course that they all represent properties of some particular part. We can say that the database contains multiple occurrences of the "part" stored record *type* (again, one occurrence for each distinct part). The stored record occurrence is the unit of access to the database—i.e., the unit that may be retrieved or stored in one access by the database software (see Chapter 2).

A *stored file* is the (named) collection of all occurrences of one type of stored record.[1]

In most present-day systems an application's logical record is identical to a stored record. However, as we have already seen, this is not necessarily so in a database system, because the DBA may make changes to the storage structure—that is, to the stored fields and records—while the corresponding logical fields and records do *not* change (this is what data independence means). For example, the "part weight" field mentioned above could be stored in binary to economize on storage space, whereas a given COBOL application might see it as a PICTURE item (i.e., as a character string). A difference such as this—involving data type conversion on a particular field on each access—is comparatively minor, however; in general, the difference between what the application sees and what is actually there can be very considerable. This fact is illustrated by the following subsections describing aspects of the database storage structure which may be subject to variation. (A more complete list will be found in Meltzer [1.9].) The reader should consider in each case what is required of the database software in order to provide an application with a constant picture of the data.

Representation of numeric data

A numeric field may be stored in internal arithmetic form (e.g., in packed decimal) or as a character string. In each case the DBA must choose an appropriate base (e.g., binary or decimal), scale (fixed or floating point), mode (real or complex), and precision (number of digits). Any of these aspects may be changed to improve performance, to conform to a new standard, or for many other reasons.

Representation of character data

A character string field may be stored in any of several character codes (e.g., EBCDIC, ASCII).

---

[1] For simplicity we ignore the possibility of a stored file containing more than one type of stored record. This simplifying assumption does not materially affect any of the subsequent argument.

Units for numeric data

The units in a numeric field may change—from inches to centimeters, for example, during the process of metrication.

Data coding

In some situations it may be desirable to represent data in storage by coded values. For example, the "part color" field, which an application sees as a character string ('RED' or 'BLUE' or 'GREEN'...), may be stored as a single decimal digit, interpreted according to the table 1 = 'RED', 2 = 'BLUE', and so on.

Data materialization

Normally the logical field seen by an application corresponds to some unique stored field (although as we have already seen, there may be differences in data type, units, and so on). In such a case the process of materialization—that is, constructing an occurrence of the logical field from the corresponding stored field occurrence and presenting it to the application—may be said to be direct. Occasionally, however, a logical field will have no single stored counterpart; instead, its values will be materialized by means of some computation performed on a set of several stored field occurrences. For example, values of the logical field "total quantity" may be materialized by summing a number of individual quantity values. "Total quantity" here is an example of a *virtual* field, and the materialization process is said to be indirect. (Note, however, that the user may see a difference between real and virtual fields, inasmuch as it would probably not be possible to create or update an occurrence of a virtual field.)

Structure of stored records

Two existing types of stored record may be combined into one. For example, the record types (part number, color) and (part number, weight) may be integrated to give (part number, color, weight). This commonly occurs as pre-database applications are brought into the database system. It implies that an application's logical record may consist of some subset of a stored record (that is, some of the stored fields may be invisible to that particular application).

Alternatively, a single type of stored record may be split into two. For example, (part number, color, weight) may be broken down into (part number, color) and (part number, weight). Such a split would allow less frequently used portions to be stored on slower devices, for example. The implication here is that an application's logical record may contain fields from several stored records.

Structure of stored files

A given stored file may be physically implemented in storage in a wide variety of ways. For example, it may be entirely contained within one storage volume (e.g., one disk pack), or it may be spread across several volumes of several different types. It may or may not be physically sequenced according to the values of some stored field. It may or may not be sequenced by some other means, e.g., by one or more associated indexes or by means of embedded pointers. It may or may not be accessible via hash-addressing. The stored records may or may not be blocked. But none of these considerations should affect applications in any way (other than in performance, of course).

The list above implies that the database is (or should be) able to *grow* without affecting existing applications. Indeed, enabling the database to grow without impairing existing applications is the major single reason for providing data independence. For example, it should be possible to extend an existing stored record type by the addition of new field types (representing, typically, further information concerning some existing type of entity or relationship; e.g., a "unit cost" field might be added to the part stored record). These new fields will simply be invisible to all previous applications. Similarly, it should be possible to add entirely new types of stored record to the database, again without requiring any change to existing applications; such records would typically represent completely new types of entity or relationship (e.g., a "supplier" record type could be added to the parts database).

1.4 AN ARCHITECTURE FOR A DATABASE SYSTEM

We conclude Chapter 1 by outlining an architecture for a database system (Fig. 1.3). Our aim in presenting this architecture is to provide a framework on which we can build in subsequent chapters. Such a framework is extremely useful for describing general database concepts and for explaining the structure of individual systems; but we do not claim that every database system can be neatly matched to this particular framework, nor do we mean to suggest that this particular architecture provides the only possible framework. However, the architecture of Fig. 1.3 does seem to fit a large number of systems reasonably well; moreover, it is in broad agreement with that proposed by the ANSI/SPARC Study Group on Data Base Management Systems [1.14]. (We choose not to follow the ANSI/SPARC terminology in every detail, however.)

The architecture is divided into three general levels: internal, conceptual, and external. Broadly speaking, the *internal* level is the one closest to physical storage, that is, the one concerned with the way in which the

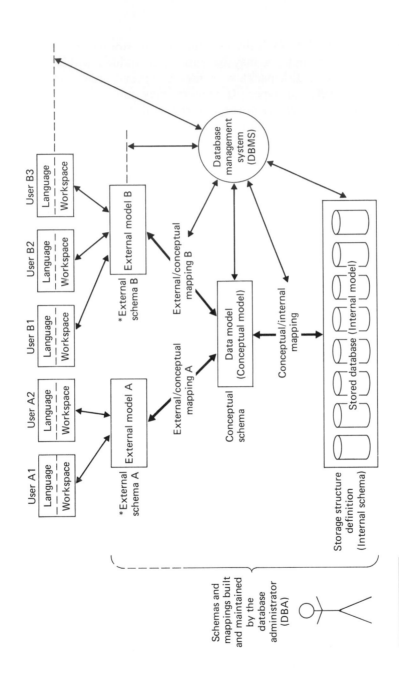

Fig. 1.3   An architecture for a database system

data is actually stored; the *external* level is the one closest to the users, that is, the one concerned with the way in which the data is viewed by individual users; and the *conceptual* level is a "level of indirection" between the other two. If the external level is concerned with *individual* user views, the conceptual level may be thought of as defining a *community* user view. In other words, there will be many "external views," each consisting of a more or less abstract representation of some portion of the database, and there will be a single "conceptual view," consisting of a similarly abstract representation of the database in its entirety.[2] (Remember that most users will not be interested in the total database, but only in some restricted portion of it.) Likewise, there will be a single "internal view," representing the total database as actually stored.

Now let us examine the various components of the system in somewhat more detail.

The *users* are either application programmers or remote terminal users of any degree of sophistication (they may include dispatch clerks, personnel officers, design engineers—anyone, in fact, who needs access to some portion of the database). Each user has a *language* at his or her disposal. For the application programmer it will be a conventional programming language, such as COBOL or PL/I; for a terminal user it will probably be a special-purpose language tailored to that user's requirements. For our purposes the important thing about the user's language is that it will include a *data sublanguage* (DSL), which is that subset of the language concerned with retrieval and storage of information in the database. We talk about the data sublanguage as being embedded in a *host language*, although to the user the two are not really separable. (Actually, so far as present-day *programming* languages are concerned, the data sublanguage frequently consists of nothing more than calls to standard subroutines.)

Each user is (conceptually at least) provided with a *workspace*, which acts as the receiving or transmitting area for all data transferred between the user and the database. For an application programmer this workspace is simply an input/output area. For a terminal user it may consist of the working storage assigned to the terminal, or perhaps a video screen.

As already indicated, an individual user will generally be interested only in some portion of the total database; moreover, the user's view of that portion will generally be somewhat abstract when compared with the way in which the data is physically stored. In ANSI/SPARC terms the user is said to view the database by means of an *external model*.[3] An

---

[2] When we describe some representation as abstract we merely mean that it involves user-oriented constructs (such as logical records and fields) rather than machine-oriented constructs (such as bits and bytes).

[3] External models were called data submodels in the first edition of this book.

external model is thus the information content of the database as it is viewed by some particular user (that is, to that user the external model *is* the database). For example, a user from the personnel department may regard the database as a collection of department record occurrences plus a collection of employee record occurrences (and may be quite unaware of the supplier and part record occurrences seen by users in the purchasing department). In general, then, an external model consists of multiple occurrences of multiple types of *external record.*[4] An external record is *not* necessarily the same as a stored record. The user's data sublanguage operates in terms of external records; for example, a DSL "get" operation will retrieve an external record occurrence, rather than a stored record occurrence. (We can now see, incidentally, that the term "logical record" used in Section 1.3 actually refers to an external record. From this point on we shall generally avoid the term "logical record.")

Each external model is defined by means of an *external schema,* which consists basically of descriptions of each of the various types of external record in that external model. For example, the employee external record type may be defined as a 6-digit employee number field plus a 20-character name field, and so on. In addition there must be a definition of the *mapping* between the external schema and the underlying conceptual schema (described below). We shall return to this topic later.

We turn now to the conceptual level. The *conceptual model* (in this book frequently referred to as simply the *data model*) is a representation of the entire information content of the database, again in a form that is somewhat abstract in comparison with the way in which the data is physically stored. (It may also be quite different from the way the data is viewed by any particular user. Broadly speaking, it is intended to be a view of the data "as it really is," rather than as users are forced to see it by the constraints of [for example] the particular language or hardware they are using.) The conceptual model consists of multiple occurrences of multiple types of *conceptual record;*[5] for example, it may consist of a

---

[4] For the time being we assume that all information is represented in the form of records. Later we shall see that information may be represented in other ways as well, e.g., in the form of "links" (see Chapter 3). For a system employing such alternative methods, the definitions and explanations given in this section will require suitable modification.

[5] Footnote 4 applies to the conceptual level also. It should also be stressed that there may well be other, preferable ways of modeling the operational data of the enterprise at the conceptual level. For example, instead of dealing in terms of "conceptual records" it may be more desirable to consider "entities," and perhaps "relationships" too, in some more direct fashion. The ANSI/SPARC Interim Report [1.14] uses "conceptual records," however. The reader is referred to [1.11] for an interesting discussion of such questions.

collection of department record occurrences plus a collection of employee record occurrences plus a collection of supplier record occurrences plus a collection of part record occurrences .... A conceptual record is not necessarily the same as either an external record, on the one hand, or a stored record, on the other. The conceptual model is defined by means of the *conceptual schema*, which includes definitions of each of the various types of conceptual record. If data independence is to be achieved, these definitions must not involve any considerations of storage structure or access strategy—they must be definitions of information content *only*. Thus there must be no reference to stored field representations, physical sequence, indexing, hash-addressing, or any other storage/access details. If the conceptual schema is made truly data-independent in this way, the external schemas, which are defined in terms of the conceptual schema (see below), will, a fortiori, be data-independent too.

The conceptual model, then, is a view of the total database content, and the conceptual schema is a definition of this view. However, it would be misleading to suggest that the conceptual schema is nothing more than a set of definitions much like the simple record definitions in a COBOL program today. The definitions in the conceptual schema are intended to include a great many additional features, such as the authorization checks and validation procedures mentioned in Section 1.2. Some authorities would go so far as to suggest that the ultimate objective of the conceptual schema is to describe the complete enterprise—not just its operational data, but also how that data is used: how the data flows from point to point within the enterprise, what the data is used for at each point, how accuracy and other controls are to be applied at each point, and so on. It must be emphasized, however, that few systems today—if any—actually support a conceptual level of anything approaching this degree of comprehensiveness; in most existing systems the conceptual model is really little more than a simple union of all individual users' views, possibly with the addition of some simple authorization and validation procedures. But it seems clear that database systems of the future will eventually be far more sophisticated in their support of the conceptual level. Our reason for using "data model" rather than "conceptual model" in this book is primarily to avoid giving the impression that existing systems already support a conceptual level in the full ANSI/SPARC sense.

The third level of the architecture is the internal level. The *internal model* is a very low-level representation of the entire database; it consists of multiple occurrences of multiple types of *internal record*.[6] "Internal record" is the ANSI/SPARC term for the construct that we have been

---

[6] Footnote 4 applies to the internal level also.

calling a *stored* record (and we shall generally continue to use this latter term); the internal model is thus still one remove away from the physical level, since it does not deal in terms of *physical* records or blocks. The internal model is described by means of the *internal schema*, which not only defines the various types of stored record but also specifies what indexes exist, how stored fields are represented, what physical sequence the stored records are in, and so on. In this book we shall tend to use the term "stored database" in place of "internal model," and "storage structure definition" in place of "internal schema." Also, we shall generally (but not invariably!) use the unqualified term "database" as a synonym for "stored database," thus reserving it to mean what is actually stored; but the reader should be warned that this latter interpretation is by no means universal.

Referring again to Fig. 1.3, the reader will observe two levels of *mapping*, one between the external and conceptual levels of the system and one between the conceptual and internal levels. The *conceptual/internal mapping* defines the correspondence between the data model and the stored database; it specifies how conceptual records and fields map into their stored counterparts. If the structure of the stored database is changed—i.e., if a change is made to the storage structure definition—the conceptual/internal mapping must be changed accordingly, so that the conceptual schema may remain invariant. (It is the responsibility of the DBA to control such changes.) In other words, the effects of such changes must be contained below the conceptual level, so that data independence can be achieved.

An *external/conceptual mapping* defines the correspondence between a particular external model and the data model. In general, the same sort of differences may exist between these two levels as may exist between the data model and the database. For example, fields may have different data types, records may be differently sequenced, and so on. Any number of external models may exist at the same time; any number of users may share a given external model; different external models may overlap. Incidentally, some systems permit the definition of one external model in terms of others, rather than always requiring an explicit definition of the mapping to the conceptual level (a very useful feature if several external models are closely related to one another).

Turning again to Fig. 1.3, we see that there still remain three topics for discussion: the database management system, the database administrator, and the user interface. The *database management system* (DBMS) is the software that handles all access to the database. Conceptually what happens is the following: (1) A user issues an access request, using some particular data sublanguage; (2) the DBMS intercepts the request and interprets it; (3) the DBMS inspects, in turn, the external schema, the external/conceptual mapping, the conceptual schema, the conceptual/internal mapping, and the storage structure definition; and (4) the DBMS performs the necessary operations on the stored database. (This brief description assumes that the entire process is interpretive, with the usual implication of very poor performance. In practice, of course, it is frequently possible for access requests to be *compiled* in advance, thus avoiding the interpretive overheads.) For example, consider what is involved in the retrieval of a particular external record occurrence. In general, fields will be required from several conceptual record occurrences. Each conceptual record occurrence, in turn, may require fields from several stored record occurrences. Conceptually, at least, then, the DBMS must retrieve all required stored record occurrences, construct the required conceptual record occurrences, and then construct the required external record occurrence. At each stage data type or other conversions may be necessary.

The DBMS is also responsible for applying the authorization checks and validation procedures mentioned in Section 1.2.

The *database administrator* (DBA), who has already been discussed to some extent, is the person (or group of persons) responsible for overall control of the database system. The DBA's responsibilities include the following.

Deciding the information content of the database

It is the DBA's job to decide exactly what information is to be held in the database—in other words, to identify the entities of interest to the enterprise and to identify the information to be recorded about those entities. Having done this, the DBA must then define the content of the database by writing the conceptual schema (using a specially provided language). The object (compiled) form of this schema is used by the DBMS in responding to access requests. The source (uncompiled) form acts as a reference document for the users of the system.

Deciding the storage structure and access strategy

The DBA must also decide how the data is to be represented in the database, and must specify the representation by writing the storage structure definition. In addition, the associated mapping between the storage structure definition and the conceptual schema must also be specified. Again appropriate languages will be provided for these purposes. (In practice, a single *data definition language* will probably include the means for writing all three definitions—conceptual schema, mapping, and storage structure—but the three aspects should be clearly separable.)

Liaising with users

It is the business of the DBA to liaise with users, to ensure that the data they require is available, and to write the external schemas and associated mapping definitions (with the users' assistance). Since the function of an external schema is to present the user with a view of the data that is compatible with the appropriate data sublanguage, there will in general be many distinct languages for writing such schemas. For example, the language for writing a schema to be used by a PL/I application must allow the definition of PL/I structures. Of course, these various languages will bear a strong family resemblance. Each external schema, like the conceptual schema, will exist in both source and object form.

Defining authorization checks and validation procedures

As already suggested, authorization checks and validation procedures may be considered as logical extensions of the conceptual schema. The data definition language referred to earlier will include facilities for specifying such checks and procedures.

Defining a strategy for back-up and recovery

Once an enterprise is committed to a database system, it becomes critically dependent on the successful operation of that system. In the event of damage to (any portion of) the database—caused by human error, say, or a failure in the hardware or supporting operating system—it is essential to be able to repair the data concerned with a minimum of delay and with as little effect as possible on the rest of the system. (For example, the availability of data that has *not* been damaged should not be affected in any way.) The DBA must define and implement an appropriate recovery strategy, involving, for example, periodic dumping of the database to a backup tape and procedures for reloading the relevant portions of the database from the latest tape.

Monitoring performance and responding to changes in requirements

The DBA is responsible for so organizing the system as to get the performance that is "best for the enterprise," and for making the appropriate adjustments as requirements change. As already mentioned, any change to details of storage and access must be accompanied by a corresponding change to the definition of the mapping to storage, so that the conceptual schema may remain constant.

It is clear that the DBA will require a number of utility programs to help in this job. Such utilities would be an essential part of a practical database system, although they have not been shown in Fig. 1.3. Below are some examples of the sort of utilities that would be necessary.

- Loading routines (to create the initial version of the database).
- Reorganization routines (to rearrange the database to reclaim space occupied by deleted data, for example).
- Journaling routines (to note each operation against the database, together with identification of the user performing the operation and a record of the before and after states).
- Recovery routines (to restore the database to an earlier state after a hardware or program failure).
- Statistical analysis routines (to assist in monitoring performance).

The single most important DBA tool is the *data dictionary* (not shown explicitly in Fig. 1.3). The data dictionary is really a database in its own right—a database that contains "data about data," in other words, *descriptions* of other entities in the system, rather than simply "raw data." For example, all the various schemas (external, conceptual, internal) are physically stored, in both source and object form, in the dictionary; so too are mapping definitions, authorization checks, and validation procedures (if not already included as part of the conceptual schema), and so on. A comprehensive dictionary will also include cross-reference information, showing, for instance, which programs use which pieces of data, which departments require which reports, and so on. It should be clear that the dictionary is a vital component of the system, provided, of course, that it is kept up to date at all times. In particular, it is crucial to the DBA in the task of maintaining overall control of the system, as outlined in Section 1.2. For example, the impact of any proposed change in the system can be quickly determined by means of a query to the dictionary.

Finally we come to the *user interface*. This may be defined as a boundary in the system below which everything is invisible to the user. By definition, therefore, the user interface is at the *external* level. However, as we shall see later—in Chapter 10, in particular—there are some situations in which the external model cannot differ very significantly from (the relevant portion of) the underlying conceptual model.

EXERCISES

It is scarcely possible at this early point in the book to set particularly searching questions. However, the questions below cover the most important concepts introduced so far, and you are urged to attempt them. Try to answer the questions in your own terms before looking back at the discussions in the chapter.

1.1 Draw a diagram of the database system architecture, as presented in Section 1.4.

1.2 Define the following terms.

database	external schema
data independence	external model
data model (conceptual model)	data sublanguage
conceptual schema	database administrator
storage structure definition	database management system

REFERENCES AND BIBLIOGRAPHY

1.1 CODASYL Systems Committee. "A Survey of Generalized Data Base Management Systems." Technical Report (May 1969). Available from ACM and IAG.

1.2 CODASYL Systems Committee. "Feature Analysis of Generalized Data Base Management Systems." Technical Report (May 1971). Available from ACM, BCS, and IAG.

These monumental works (over 900 pages between them) complement each other in the following sense: [1.1] consists of independent descriptions of a number of systems (that is, a separate chapter is devoted to each system); [1.2] consists of feature-by-feature comparisons of a (slightly different) set of systems. [1.1] is particularly recommended. The following systems are covered: ADAM ([1.1] only), COBOL ([1.2] only), DBTG ([1.2] only), GIS, IDS, ISL-1 ([1.1] only), IMS ([1.2] only), MARK IV, NIPS/FFS, SC-1, TDMS, UL/1.

1.3 CODASYL Systems Committee. "Introduction to 'Feature Analysis of Generalized Data Base Management Systems'." *Comp. Bull.* **15,** No. 4 (April 1971); also *CACM* **14,** No. 5 (May 1971).

Adapted from the initial section of [1.2] and published separately. A useful introduction to some of the basic concepts of a database system.

1.4 GUIDE/SHARE Data Base Task Force. "Data Base Management System Requirements" (November 1971). Available from SHARE, Suite 750, 25 Broadway, New York, N.Y., 10004; also published as Appendix A of [19.4].

A detailed statement by representatives of the IBM users' associations of the features required of an ideal database system.

1.5 R. G. Canning. "Trends in Data Management." Part 1, *EDP Analyzer* **9,** No. 5 (May 1971); Part 2, *EDP Analyzer* **9,** No. 6 (June 1971).

These two issues of *EDP Analyzer* contain outline descriptions of the following systems: TOTAL, DBOMP, MARS III, CZAR, Disk Forte, SERIES, IMS (Version 2) and dataBASIC. In each case notes are included on some actual users' experience of the system. A brief tutorial on database is also included.

1.6 R. W. Engles. "A Tutorial on Data Base Organization." *Annual Review in Automatic Programming,* Vol. 7, Part 1 (eds., Halpern and McGee). Elmsford, N.Y.: Pergamon Press (July 1972).

A good introduction to the database problem. The major topics included are a theory of operational data, a survey of storage structures and accessing techniques, and a discussion of data independence.

1.7 G. C. Everest. "The Objectives of Database Management." *Information Systems: COINS IV* (ed., J. T. Tou). New York: Plenum (1974).

An attempt to bridge the gap between management and technical specialists by explaining in simple terms both how management would like to use a database system and some of the technical problems involved in implementing such a system.

1.8 W. C. McGee. "Generalized File Processing." *Annual Review in Automatic Programming*, Vol. 5 (eds., Halpern and Shaw). Elmsford, N.Y.: Pergamon Press (1969).

The paper that first introduced the term "schema" (though not with quite the ANSI/SPARC meaning [1.14]). A most readable survey of the features that a generalized DBMS should provide to the user, with examples taken from a number of early database systems.

1.9 H. S. Meltzer. "Data Base Concepts and an Architecture for a Data Base System." Presentation given to SHARE Information Systems Research Project, SHARE XXXIII, Boston, Mass. (20 August 1969).

1.10 D. A. Jardine (ed.). "Data Base Management Systems: Proceedings of the SHARE Working Conference on Data Base Management Systems, Montreal, Canada, July 23–27, 1973." North-Holland (1974).

This book includes papers on user requirements, future trends, user experience with a number of systems (IMS, TOTAL, IDS, DMS 1100, and EDMS), and statements of plans and intentions by a number of vendors (Burroughs, Cincom, CDC, Honeywell, IBM, UNIVAC, and XDS).

1.11 W. Kent. "Describing Information." IBM Technical Report TR 03.012 (May 1976).

A stimulating and thought-provoking discussion of the nature of information; recommended. Paraphrasing the author's own introduction slightly, the aims of the paper are:

- To advocate the usefulness of a descriptive model based on entities, naming, relationships, and attributes.

- To emphasize the special importance of relationships in information.

- To illustrate the slippery and elusive nature of real information, and the consequent difficulty of applying any model to it.

- To attempt to influence the design, evaluation, and teaching of descriptive systems, user interfaces, and design and usability aids.

- To provide a source of examples, as a test bed of situations which any descriptive model is challenged to deal with.

1.12 I. R. Palmer. "Data Base Systems: A Practical Reference." Q.E.D. Information Sciences Inc., 141 Linden Street, Wellesley, Mass. 02181 (June 1975).

Contains a useful outline of over 20 implemented systems, as well as a checklist including about 50 more, and some interesting case studies. The author was active in the CODASYL Data Description Language Committee (see Part 4 of this book).

1.13 M. R. Stonebraker. "A Functional View of Data Independence." *Proc. 1974 ACM SIGMOD Workshop on Data Description, Access and Control*. Available from ACM.

This paper is an attempt to provide a precise framework for dealing with the problem of data independence. Seven classes of transformation of a stored database from one representation to another are identified and rigorously defined. The following examples give some idea of the types of transformation in each of the seven classes.

1. Physical relocation of stored files
2. Conversion of stored field values from one data type to another
3. Replacement of one hashing algorithm by another
4. Addition of indexes
5. Duplication of stored data
6. Splitting one stored record into two
7. Combining two stored records into one

It is suggested that a measure of the degree of data independence provided by a particular system may be obtained by considering the transformations supported (in a data-independent fashion) in each of the seven classes. The paper concludes with a brief examination of three specific systems in the light of these ideas: RDMS [11.20], ISAM [16.2], and IMS [12.1].

1.14 ANSI/X3/SPARC Study Group on Data Base Management Systems: Interim Report. *FDT (Bulletin of ACM SIGMOD)* **7,** No. 2 (1975).

An extremely important document (though the reader is cautioned that it is an interim report, not a final position paper). The ANSI/X3/SPARC Study Group on Data Base Management Systems was established in late 1972 by the Standards Planning and Requirements Committee (SPARC) of ANSI/X3. ANSI/X3 is the American National Standards Committee on Computers and Information Processing. The objectives of the Study Group were to determine the areas, if any, of database technology for which standardization activity was appropriate, and to produce a set of recommendations for action in each such area. To meet these objectives the Study Group has taken the view that *interfaces* are the only aspect of a database system that may possibly be suitable for standardization, and has expended a great deal of effort in defining a generalized architecture or model for a database system and in identifying the corresponding interfaces. The Interim Report provides a detailed description of this architecture and of some of the 41 interfaces so far identified.

1.15 P. P. Uhrowczik. "Data Dictionary/Directories." *IBM Sys. J.* **12,** No. 4 (1973).

> An introduction to the basic concepts of a data dictionary system. An implementation using IMS physical and logical databases is suggested (see Part 3 of this book).

1.16 E. H. Sibley. "The Development of Data Base Technology." Guest Editor's Introduction to *ACM Computing Surveys* **8,** No. 1: Special Issue on Data Base Management Systems (March 1976).

1.17 J. P. Fry and E. H. Sibley. "Evolution of Data Base Management Systems." *ACM Computing Surveys* **8,** No. 1.

1.18 B. Sundgren. "Conceptual Foundation of the Infological Approach to Data Bases." *Proc. IFIP TC-2 Working Conference on Data Base Management Systems* (eds., Klimbie and Koffeman), April 1974. North-Holland (1974).

> The work of Langefors [1.19] and Sundgren has many points in common with the ANSI/SPARC proposals, which they anticipated by a number of years. Until recently, however, their ideas did not receive much general acceptance except in Scandinavia.

1.19 B. Langefors. "Theoretical Analysis of Information Systems." Lund, Sweden (1966, 1973).

1.20 Data Dictionary Systems Working Party of the British Computer Society. Interim Report (1976).

> An excellent description of the role of the data dictionary; includes a brief but good discussion of the conceptual schema.

1.21 B. Shneiderman (ed.). "Database Management Systems." Vol. I of the Information Technology Series (from the National Computer Conferences). Montvale, N.J.: AFIPS Press (1976).

> A useful collection of papers from the Fall and Spring Joint Computer Conferences of 1972, the National Computer Conferences of 1973–1975, and the USA/Japan Computer Conferences of 1972 and 1975. The papers are grouped under the following headings: Management and Utilization Perspectives; Implementation and Design of Database Management Systems; Query Languages; Security, Integrity, Privacy, and Concurrency; and Specification, Simulation and Translation of Database Systems. The editor contributes an informative introduction to each section, as well as a brief historical review of the entire subject.

2
Storage
Structures

2.1 INTRODUCTION

The purpose of this chapter is to provide an introduction to the way in which data may be organized in secondary storage. By "secondary storage" here we really mean present-day direct access media, such as disk packs, drums, and so on. In other words, the following limitations apply.

- We are not considering purely sequential media, such as tape, since such media in general impose far too many restrictions to be useful in a database system[1] (for example, it is not generally possible to perform "update in place" on tape).

- We make no attempt to predict what future media may be like. Note, however, that if a new device—say, a large-capacity associative memory—were to be produced, the enterprise could take immediate advantage of it, provided data independence had been achieved.

One other introductory remark: In this chapter we are not concerned with specific systems. The storage structures provided in individual systems are considered to some extent in later chapters.

We start with a simplifying assumption: The database management system makes use of an *access method* to handle the details of physical

---

[1] Tapes do have a use in database systems as a medium for journaling and dumping operations. This use was mentioned briefly in Section 1.4, and is discussed in a little more detail in Chapter 24. However, tapes are not normally used for storing the operational database itself.

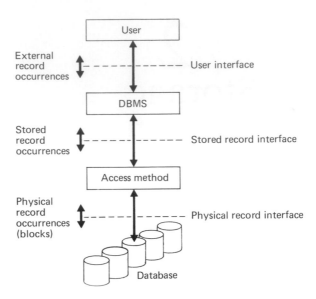

Fig. 2.1 The stored record interface

access to the database (Fig. 2.1). The access method consists of a set of
routines whose function is to conceal all device-dependent details from
the DBMS and to present the DBMS with a *stored record interface.*[2]

The stored record interface permits the DBMS to view the storage
structure as a collection of stored files, each one consisting of all
occurrences of one type of stored record (see Chapter 1). Specifically, the
DBMS knows what stored files exist, and for each one (a) the structure of
the corresponding stored record; (b) the stored field(s), if any, on which it
is sequenced; and (c) the stored field(s), if any, that can be used as search
arguments for direct access. This information will all be specified as part
of the storage structure definition. Note that points (b) and (c) amount to
saying that the DBMS knows what access statements it can issue against
the stored file. Note, too, that the unit that crosses the stored record
interface is one stored record occurrence.

---

[2] Many existing access methods actually do rather more. Thus many of the
functions attributed in what follows to the DBMS may in practice be performed
by the access method; for example, the access method may provide secondary
indexes of its own. However, we choose to assume a rather elementary access
method as a more suitable basis for describing possible storage structures. The
existence of more complex access methods does not invalidate any of the
subsequent discussion.

The DBMS does *not* know (a) anything about physical records (blocks); (b) how stored fields are associated to form stored records (although in practice this will almost invariably be via physical adjacency); (c) how sequencing is performed (e.g., it may be by means of physical contiguity, an index, or a pointer chain); or (d) how direct access is performed (e.g., it may be via an index, a sequential scan, or hash-addressing). This information is also part of the storage structure definition, but it is a part used by the access method, not the DBMS.

As an illustration, let us suppose that the storage structure includes a stored file of PARTs, where each stored record occurrence consists of a part number (P#), a part name (PNAME), a color (COLOR) and a weight (WEIGHT). Part of the storage structure definition might then go as follows:

<u>STORED</u> <u>FILE</u> PART (P#, PNAME, COLOR, WEIGHT)

<u>SEQUENCED</u> <u>ASCENDING</u> P#

<u>INDEXED</u> P#

This definition is intended to convey the following information.

- The stored file of PARTs exists.
- The corresponding stored record has a particular structure.
- The stored record occurrences are sequenced on ascending P# values (note that the sequencing mechanism is *not* specified).
- The P# stored field is indexed, so that direct access may be performed by quoting a value for this field.

(Of course, many other aspects of the storage structure—the representation of each stored field, for example—will have to be specified, too.)

We make one other assumption: When a new stored record occurrence is first created and entered into the database, the access method is responsible for assigning it a unique *stored record address* (SRA). This value distinguishes that stored record occurrence from all others in the database. It may, for example, be simply the physical address of the occurrence within the storage volume (together with a volume identification), or alternatively an identification for the appropriate stored file together with an offset within that file (considering the file as a linear string). The SRA for a particular occurrence is returned to the DBMS by the access method when the occurrence is first created, and it may be used by the DBMS for subsequent direct access to the occurrence concerned. We assume here that the SRA for a given occurrence is fairly static; that is, its value does not change until the occurrence is physically moved as part of a database reorganization (if then).

The SRA concept permits the DBMS to build its own access mechanisms (indexes, pointer chains, etc.), over and above those maintained by the access method. This is illustrated by many of the examples in Section 2.2.

2.2 POSSIBLE REPRESENTATIONS FOR SOME SAMPLE DATA

In this section we take a simple collection of sample data and consider some of the many ways it could be represented in storage (at the level of the stored record interface). The sample data is shown in Fig. 2.2. It consists of information about five suppliers; for each supplier we wish to record a supplier number (S#), a supplier name (SNAME), a status value (STATUS), and a location (CITY). Note that Fig. 2.2 is actually a very simple conceptual model of the data.

S#	SNAME	STATUS	CITY
S1	Smith	20	London
S2	Jones	10	Paris
S3	Blake	30	Paris
S4	Clark	20	London
S5	Adams	30	Athens

Fig. 2.2 Sample data

In what follows, the assumption, unless we explicitly state otherwise, will be that each stored file is sequenced by the access method on its *primary key*. (This term will be defined rigorously in Chapter 4; for the present we assume that it is well understood. Basically it corresponds to the traditional concept of a record identifier.) The mechanism by which this sequencing is performed will not be shown.

The first (and simplest) representation consists of a single stored file containing five stored record occurrences, one for each supplier. Figure 2.2 may be considered as an illustration of this. This representation has the advantage of simplicity but would probably be inadequate for various reasons in a realistic situation. Suppose, for example, that we had 10,000 suppliers instead of just five, but that they were located in only 10 different cities. If we assume that the amount of storage required for a *pointer* is less than that required for a city name, the representation illustrated in Fig. 2.3 will clearly save some storage space in such a situation.

SUPPLIER file   CITY file

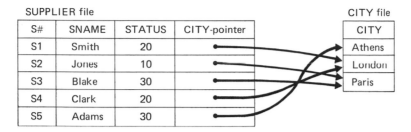

S#	SNAME	STATUS	CITY-pointer
S1	Smith	20	
S2	Jones	10	
S3	Blake	30	
S4	Clark	20	
S5	Adams	30	

CITY
Athens
London
Paris

Fig. 2.3 Factoring out the CITY values

Here we have two stored files, a supplier file and a city file, with pointers out of the former into the latter. These pointers are SRAs. The *only* advantage of this representation (compared with the previous one) is the saving in space. For example, a request to find all properties of a given supplier will require at least one more access than before; a request to find all suppliers in a given city will involve several more accesses. Note, incidentally, that it is the DBMS, not the access method, that maintains the pointers; the access method is not aware of the connection between the two files. (The connection must be stated in the definition of the mapping from the conceptual schema to storage.)

If the query "Find all suppliers in a given city" is an important one, the DBA may choose the alternative representation shown in Fig. 2.4.

Here again we have two stored files, a supplier file and a city file, but this time there are pointers out of the latter into the former (each city stored record occurrence contains pointers to all corresponding supplier stored record occurrences). It should be obvious that this is better than the previous representation for queries asking for all suppliers in a given city but worse for queries asking for all attributes of a given supplier. The storage requirement is exactly the same.

CITY file

SUPPLIER file

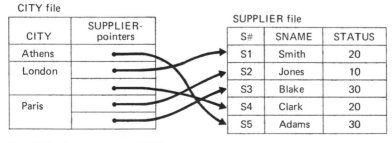

CITY	SUPPLIER-pointers
Athens	
London	
Paris	

S#	SNAME	STATUS
S1	Smith	20
S2	Jones	10
S3	Blake	30
S4	Clark	20
S5	Adams	30

Fig. 2.4 Indexing on CITY

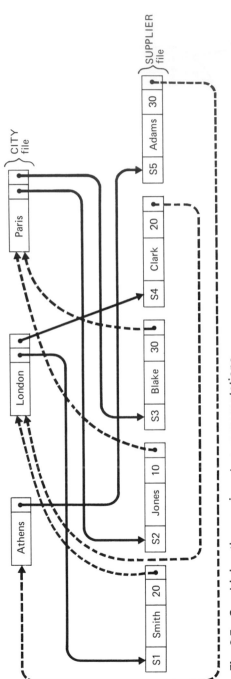

Fig. 2.5   Combining the previous two representations

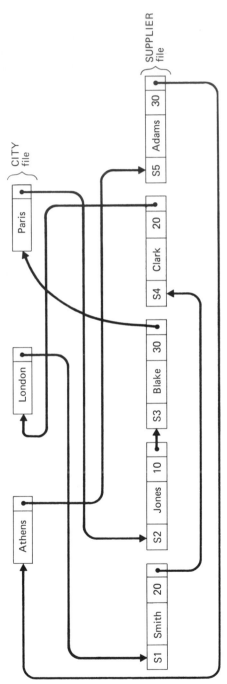

Fig. 2.6   Using pointer chains

The interesting thing about this representation is that the city file is an *index* to the supplier file (an index controlled by the DBMS, not the access method). It is in fact a *dense, secondary* index. "Dense" means that it contains an entry for every stored record occurrence in the indexed file; note that this means that the indexed file does not have to contain the indexed field (in the example, the supplier file no longer includes a city field). (We shall consider *non*dense indexing in Section 2.4.) "Secondary" means that it is an index on a field other than the primary key.

We can combine the two previous representations to obtain the advantages of each, at the cost of requiring slightly more storage space and (probably more significant) having more pointer maintenance to do when changes occur. Figure 2.5 shows such a representation. To illustrate the maintenance problem, consider what the DBMS must do if supplier S3 moves from Paris to London.

A disadvantage of secondary indexes in general is that each index entry—i.e., each stored record occurrence in the index—must contain an unpredictable number of pointers (because the indexed field will not usually contain a distinct value for each stored record occurrence in the indexed file). This fact complicates the job of the DBMS in applying changes to the database. An alternative to the previous representation that avoids this problem is illustrated in Fig. 2.6.

In this representation each stored record occurrence (supplier or city) contains just one pointer. Each city points to the first supplier in that city. That supplier then points to the second supplier in the same city, who points to the third, and so on, up to the last, who points back to the city. Thus for each city we have a *chain* of all suppliers in that city. The advantage of this representation is that it is easier to apply changes. The disadvantage is that, for a given city, the only way to access the nth supplier is to follow the chain and access the 1st, 2nd, ..., $(n - 1)$th suppliers, too. If each access involves a seek operation, the time taken to access the nth supplier may be quite considerable.

As an extension of the foregoing representation, we could make the chains two-way (so that each stored record occurrence contains exactly *two* pointers). The DBA might choose such a representation if deleting a supplier is a common operation, for example, since it simplifies the process of pointer adjustment necessitated by such an operation. Another extension would be to include a pointer in each supplier direct to the corresponding city, to cut down on the amount of chain-traversing required for certain types of query.

The representation shown in Fig. 2.6 (using pointer chains) is a simple example of *multilist organization*. In Fig. 2.6 we chained together all suppliers in the same city; in other words, for each city we had a *list* of

SNAME index		STATUS index		CITY index		SUPPLIER file
SNAME	Pointers	STATUS	Pointers	CITY	Pointers	S#
Smith	↑ S1	10	↑ S2	Athens	↑ S5	S1
Jones	↑ S2	20	↑ S1, ↑ S4	London	↑ S1, ↑ S4	S2
Blake	↑ S3	30	↑ S3, ↑ S5	Paris	↑ S2, ↑ S3	S3
Clark	↑ S4					S4
Adams	↑ S5					S5

Fig. 2.7 Inverted organization

corresponding suppliers. In exactly the same way (by means of additional pointers) we could also have a list of suppliers for each distinct status value, for example. The reader should try sketching this representation for the sample data. In general, a multilist organization can clearly contain any number of such lists.

To return to secondary indexing: Just as it is possible to provide any number of lists in the multilist organization, it is also possible to provide any number of secondary indexes in an indexing organization. In the extreme case we have the situation illustrated in Fig. 2.7: an index on every secondary field, or *inverted organization*. (The symbol ↑ is used to mean "pointer to.")

However, although inverted organization will give good performance in response to a request for all suppliers with a given property (say, a status of 20), a request for all properties of a given supplier will take a long time to answer. In practice, therefore, we frequently compromise by providing a *regular* organization (as shown in Fig. 2.2) together with secondary indexes on those fields deemed important by the DBA. (Note that this involves redundant storage of the indexed field values.) This is one of the most common storage structures in current use.

Another representation that should be mentioned is the *hierarchical* organization, illustrated in Fig. 2.8.

Here we have one stored file containing three (hierarchical) stored record occurrences, one for each city. Part of each stored record occur-

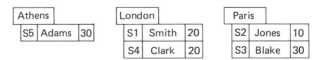

Fig. 2.8 Hierarchical organization

rence consists of a variable-length list of supplier entries, one for each supplier in that city, and each supplier entry contains supplier number, name, and status. As in many previous examples, we have here factored out the CITY values, but we have chosen this time to represent the association between a city and its suppliers by making the city and suppliers all part of one stored record occurrence (instead of using pointers, as in Fig. 2.4, for example). Incidentally, a secondary index, such as that in Fig. 2.4, is in fact a hierarchical file.

The last representation we shall consider is a *hash-addressing organization*. The basic idea of hash-addressing is that each stored record occurrence is placed in the database at a location whose address (SRA) may be computed as some function (the hash function) of a value that appears in that occurrence—usually the primary key value. Thus, to store the occurrence initially, the DBMS computes the SRA and instructs the access method to place the occurrence at that position; and to retrieve the occurrence subsequently, the DBMS performs the same computation as before and then requests the access method to fetch the occurrence at the computed position. The advantage of this organization is that it provides very fast direct access on the basis of values of the hashed field.

As an example of hash-addressing, let us assume that the S# values are S100, S200, S300, S400, S500 (instead of S1, S2, S3, S4, S5), and let us consider the hash function:

SRA = remainder after dividing (numeric part of) S# value by 13

(a simple example of a fairly common class of hash function— "division/remainder").[3] The SRAs for the five suppliers are then 9, 5, 1, 10, 6, respectively, giving us the representation shown in Fig. 2.9 (where we have assumed that these SRA values simply represent record positions within the stored file).

In addition to showing how hashing works, the example also shows why the hash function is necessary. It would be theoretically possible to use an "identity" hash function, i.e., to use the (numeric) primary key value for any given occurrence directly as the SRA for that occurrence. However, this is usually inadequate in practice, because the range of primary key values is generally much wider than the range of available SRAs. For example, suppose that supplier numbers are in fact three digits wide, as specified above. This allows a theoretical maximum of 1000 different suppliers, whereas in practice there may be a maximum of only ten. To avoid a colossal waste of storage space, we ideally require a hash

---

[3] For reasons that are beyond the scope of this text, the divisor is usually chosen to be prime.

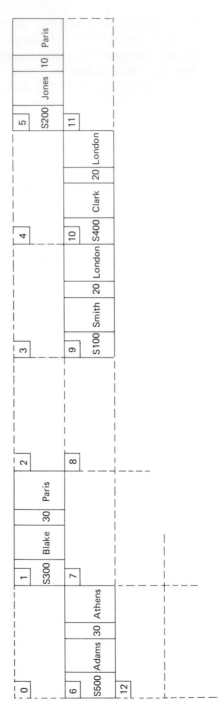

Fig. 2.9 A hash-addressing organization

function that will reduce any value in the range 0–999 to one in the range 0–9. To allow a little room for future growth, it is usual to extend the target range by 20 percent or so; thus in the example, we actually choose a function that generates values in the range 0–12 rather than 0–9.

The example also illustrates one of the disadvantages of hash-addressing: The sequence of stored record occurrences within the stored file will almost certainly not be the primary key sequence (in addition, there may be gaps of arbitrary size between consecutive occurrences). In fact, a stored file in a hash-addressing organization is usually (not invariably) considered to have no particular sequence.

Another disadvantage of hash-addressing is the possibility of *collisions*—that is, two distinct stored record occurrences whose keys hash to the same SRA. For example, suppose that the sample data also included a supplier with an S# value of S1400. This supplier would collide (at SRA 9) with supplier S100, given the same hash function as before. The implication is that the hash function has to be made more complicated to handle this sort of situation. One possibility is to make the SRA (derived as above) the start point for a sequential scan. Thus to insert supplier S1400 (assuming that suppliers S100–S500 already exist), we go to SRA 9 and search forward from this position for the first free location. The new supplier will be stored at SRA 11. To retrieve supplier S1400 subsequently, we go through a similar process.

Our survey of some storage structures permitted by the stored record interface is now complete. In conclusion we should perhaps point out that there is no such thing as a "best" storage structure. What is "best" depends on what is important to the enterprise. It is the responsibility of the DBA to balance a large number of conflicting requirements in choosing a storage structure. The considerations that must be taken into account include retrieval performance, the difficulty of applying changes, the amount of storage space available, the ease with which the database may be reorganized and the desired frequency of such reorganization, problems of recovery, and so on.

2.3 THE PHYSICAL RECORD INTERFACE: INDEXING TECHNIQUES

The physical record interface is the interface between the access method and the physical database. The unit that crosses this interface is one physical record occurrence (one block). The really significant difference between this interface and the stored record interface discussed in Section 2.2 is that here the concept of physical contiguity becomes significant. Physical contiguity provides an important means of representing the sequence of stored record occurrences within their stored file, making use of (a) the physical sequence of stored record occurrences within one block, and (b) the physical sequence of blocks on the medium. This has two implications in the area of index design.

First, it is possible to construct *nondense* indexes. The idea here is that the file being indexed is divided into groups, with several stored record occurrences in each group, such that the following conditions hold.

- For any two groups, all the stored record occurrences in one precede all those in the other (with respect to the sequencing being imposed on the file).
- Within any one group, the file sequence is represented by physical contiguity.

(In practice a group may be one block, one track, or any other convenient unit of storage space.) The index then contains one entry per group, giving (typically) the highest value of the indexed field occurring in the group and a pointer to the start of the group. The sequence of groups is represented by the sequence of entries in the index.

The term "nondense" refers to the fact that the index does *not* contain an entry for every stored record occurrence in the indexed file. Thus the stored record occurrences *must* contain the indexed field (contrast the situation with a dense index—Fig. 2.4). Figure 2.10 illustrates the situation in which the group is one track.

The second point arising from the availability of physical sequencing is the possibility of constructing *multilevel* (tree structure) indexes. The reason for providing an index in the first place is to remove the need for sequential scanning of the indexed file. However, sequential scanning is still necessary in the *index*. If the index gets very large, that fact in itself can cause a significant performance problem. The solution is to construct an index to the index. For one common example, see Fig. 2.11.

Here the indexed file is divided into groups of one track each. The *track index* contains an entry for each such track (as in Fig. 2.10). The track index in turn is divided into groups, each of which consists of the entries

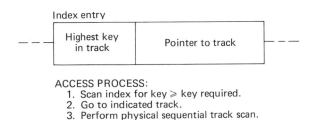

Index entry

| Highest key in track | Pointer to track |

ACCESS PROCESS:
1. Scan index for key ⩾ key required.
2. Go to indicated track.
3. Perform physical sequential track scan.

Fig. 2.10   An example of nondense indexing

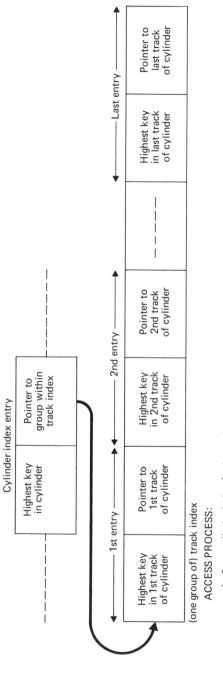

Fig. 2.11 An example of multilevel indexing

for all tracks of one cylinder in the indexed file, and a *cylinder index* contains an entry for each such group in the track index. (Each group within the track index is normally recorded at the beginning of the appropriate cylinder of the indexed file, to cut down on seek activity.)

In general, a multilevel index can contain any number of levels, each of which acts as a nondense index to the level below. (It *must* be nondense: otherwise nothing is achieved.) If we were to take the technique to its logical conclusion, the top level would contain a single entry; in practice, however, a top level consisting of a single block (containing many entries) is the most that can be required.

2.4   GENERAL INDEXING TECHNIQUES

In the previous section we presented two techniques, nondense indexing and multilevel indexing, that can be applied at the physical record interface. In theory these techniques *could* be applied at the stored record interface too, but such application would be unlikely in practice since the techniques depend so much on the concept of physical contiguity. By way of contrast, the following techniques may be used in indexes at either level.

Indexing on field combinations

Selectivity in the index

Compression techniques

Symbolic pointer representation

Indexing on field combinations

It is possible to construct an index on the basis of the values of two or more fields in combination. For example, Fig. 2.12 shows an index to the sample data of Fig. 2.2 on the field combination CITY and STATUS (in that order).

With such an index we can respond to such queries as "Find all suppliers in Paris with status 10" in one scan of the index. If the

CITY/STATUS	Pointers
Athens/30	↑ S5
London/20	↑ S1, ↑ S4
Paris/10	↑ S2
Paris/30	↑ S3

Fig. 2.12   Indexing on CITY/STATUS

combined index did not exist, this query would involve (a) finding all suppliers in Paris, (b) finding all suppliers with status 10, and (c) extracting the suppliers common to both lists. Since steps (a) and (b) could perfectly well be performed in the reverse order, moreover, we would have a strategy problem (i.e., deciding which to do first).

Note that the combined index also acts as an index on the CITY field, inasmuch as all the entries for a given city are at least consecutive within the index. (A separate index will have to be provided if indexing on STATUS is required, however.) In general, an index on the combination of n fields $F_1, F_2, \ldots, F_n$ (in that order) will also serve as an index on F_1, as an index on the combination F_1F_2 (or F_2F_1), as an index on the combination $F_1F_2F_3$ (in any order), and so on. Thus the total number of indexes required to provide complete indexing in this way is not so large as might appear at first glance.

Selectivity in the index

The reader should realize that it is not necessary to provide access via the index to every record occurrence in the indexed file. In some situations it may be useful to have index entries for selected values only of the indexed field. For example, consider an employee file in which 95 percent of the employees have a status of exempt, 5 percent have a status of nonexempt. It would scarcely be worth providing a general index on the status field. On the other hand, it might be very useful to have an index pointing to all nonexempt employees—in other words, to select a subset of the set of possible values to be indexed.

Compression techniques

Compression techniques are ways of reducing the amount of storage required for a piece of stored data by replacing the data with some representation of the difference between it and the data next to it. In general, these techniques can be used wherever the data will be accessed *sequentially*—for example, within an index or within one "group" of a file for which a nondense index exists (see Section 2.3).

To fix our ideas, let us take as an example a single block of an index to an employee file. We suppose that the first four entries in this block are for the following employees.

```
ROBERTON
ROBERTSON
ROBERTSTONE
ROBINSON
```

Employee names are 12 characters long (so that each of these names may be considered—in its uncompressed form—to be padded at the right with the appropriate number of blanks).

The first compression technique we can apply is to replace those characters at the front of each entry which are the same as those in the previous entry by a corresponding count: *front compression*. This gives us

```
0-ROBERTONbbbb
b-SONbbb
7-TONEb
3-INSONbbbb
```

(The trailing blanks are now shown explicitly as b.)

The second compression technique is *rear compression*. One way to apply rear compression in the example would be to eliminate all trailing blanks (again, replacing them by an appropriate count). Further compression can be achieved by dropping all characters to the right of the one required to distinguish this entry from its two adjacent entries. This gives us

```
0-7-ROBERTO
b-2-SO
7-1-T
3-1-I
```

where the second number is a count of the number of characters recorded. (We have assumed that the next entry does not have ROBI as its first four characters when decompressed.) Note, however, that we have actually lost some information from this index. That is, when decompressed, it looks like this:

```
ROBERTO?????
ROBERTSO????
ROBERTST????
ROBI????????
```

(where ? represents an unknown character). This is permissible only on the assumption that the values are recorded in full *somewhere* (in this case, in the indexed file).

Symbolic pointer representation

So far we have assumed that all pointers are SRAs. As we pointed out in Section 2.1, however, SRA values are apt to change when a stored file is reorganized. If a given stored file is reorganized, therefore, all files pointing into it—in particular, all indexes—will have to be updated to contain the revised SRA values. This can be a major problem. To avoid it we can replace all pointers by the corresponding primary key values—all pointers, that is, except those (if any) used in the access method's fundamental sequencing mechanism for the file. For example, if the access method sequences a stored file by means of an index on its primary key, it is clearly not sufficient for that index to contain only the primary key values (there would still be no direct way of getting from the index to the file). Apart from this case, however, the technique of *symbolic pointer representation* can be used wherever pointers are used (not only in indexes but also in chains, for example). Figures 2.13 and 2.14 show the result of applying this technique to the representations of Figs. 2.4 (indexing on CITY) and 2.7 (inverted organization), respectively. In Fig. 2.14, note that the need for the supplier stored file has disappeared entirely.

CITY file

CITY	S#
Athens	S5
London	S1
	S4
Paris	S2
	S3

SUPPLIER file

S#	SNAME	STATUS
S1	Smith	20
S2	Jones	10
S3	Blake	30
S4	Clark	20
S5	Adams	30

Fig. 2.13 Indexing on CITY (symbolic pointers)

SNAME index

SNAME	S#
Smith	S1
Jones	S2
Blake	S3
Clark	S4
Adams	S5

STATUS index

STATUS	S#
10	S2
20	S1, S4
30	S3, S5

CITY index

CITY	S#
Athens	S5
London	S1, S4
Paris	S2, S3

Fig. 2.14 Inverted organization (symbolic pointers)

EXERCISES

Exercises 2.1–2.3 may prove suitable as a basis for group discussion; they are intended to lead to deeper consideration of various design problems. Exercises 2.5 and 2.6 have rather a mathematical flavor.

2.1 A company database is to contain information about the divisions, departments, and employees of the company. Each employee works in one department;

each department is part of one division. Invent some sample data and sketch some possible storage structures for this data. Where possible, state the relative advantages of each structure.

2.2 Repeat Exercise 2.1 for a database that is to contain information about customers and items. Each customer may order any number of different items; each item may be ordered by any number of customers.

2.3 Repeat Exercise 2.1 for a database that is to contain information about parts and components (a component is itself a part and may have further components).

2.4 The first ten values of the indexed field in a particular indexed file are as follows.

```
ABRAHAMS,GK
ACKERMANN,LZ
ACKROYD,S
ADAMS,T
ADAMS,TR
ADAMSON,CR
ALLEN,S
AYRES,ST
BAILEY,TE
BAILEYMAN,D
```

(Each is padded with blanks at the right to a total length of 15 characters.) Show the values actually recorded in the *index* if the compression techniques described in Section 2.4 are applied. What is the percentage saving in space? Show the steps involved in retrieving (or attempting to retrieve) the stored record occurrence for ACKROYD,S and ADAMS,V. Show also the steps involved in inserting a stored record occurrence for ALLINGHAM,M.

2.5 Suppose that we have a multilevel index such that the lowest level contains an entry for each of N stored data record occurrences, and each level above the lowest contains an entry for every block in the level below. Suppose also that each block in the index contains n index entries, and that the index is extended up to a single block at the top level. Derive expressions for the number of *levels* in the index and the number of *blocks* in the index.

2.6 Let us define "complete indexing" to mean that an index exists for every distinct field combination in the indexed file. How many indexes will be necessary to provide complete indexing for a file defined on (a) 3 fields; (b) 4 fields; (c) N fields?

REFERENCES AND BIBLIOGRAPHY

See also [1.6].

2.1 W. Buchholz. "File Organization and Addressing." *IBM Sys. J.* **2,** No. 2 (June 1963).

2.2 C. J. Date and P. Hopewell. "Storage Structure and Physical Data Independence." *Proc. 1971 ACM SIGFIDET Workshop on Data Description, Access and Control.* Available from ACM.

An investigation into possible storage structures to support the relational model (see Chapter 3). A given storage structure is said to be a "conformable representation" of a given relational model if there exists a 1–1 onto mapping between the two. Several examples of conformable and nonconformable representations of a sample data model are given, and it is demonstrated by example that (a) the class of conformable representations for a given model is very large, and (b) it is difficult to implement even very simple relational operations in terms of a nonconformable representation. It is therefore suggested that in practice only conformable representations should be considered if the data model is relational.

2.3 M. E. D'Imperio. "Data Structures and their Representation in Storage." *Annual Review in Automatic Programming.* Vol. 5 (eds., Halpern and Shaw). Pergamon Press (1969).

The paper that first emphasized the distinction between data structures (or data models) and storage structures. A method is described for representing both data structures and storage structures in diagrammatic form. A most interesting paper, although discussion is restricted to primary rather than secondary storage.

2.4 G. G. Dodd. "Elements of Data Management Systems." *Computing Surveys* **1**, No. 2 (June 1969).

Despite the title, this paper is primarily concerned with storage structures (at the level of the stored record interface).

2.5 B. J. Dzubak and C. R. Warburton. "The Organization of Structured Files." *CACM* **8**, No. 7 (July 1965).

Compares and contrasts ten methods of storing and accessing a "structured file" (i.e., a collection of information in the form of a linear graph, for example, a parts explosion).

2.6 D. Hsiao and F. Harary. "A Formal System for Information Retrieval from Files." *CACM* **13**, No. 2 (February 1970).

This paper is an attempt to unify the ideas of various storage structures— inverted organization, indexed sequential organization, multilist organization, and so on—into a "generalized file structure," and so to form a basis for a theory of storage structures. A "general retrieval algorithm" is presented for retrieving occurrences satisfying an arbitrary Boolean combination of "attribute = value" conditions from the generalized structure. The paper is marred slightly by some confusing terminology (perhaps not too important); also, anyone reading the paper should be warned that Figs. 5 and 9 have been interchanged, as have Figs. 6 and 7.

2.7 D. Lefkovitz. *File Structures for On-Line Systems.* Spartan Books (1969).

A comprehensive and detailed survey. Essential for anyone seriously concerned with this aspect of database systems.

2.8 V. Y. Lum. "Multi-attribute Retrieval with Combined Indexes." *CACM* **13,** No. 11 (November 1970).

The paper that introduced the technique of indexing on field combinations. See also [2.12] and [2.25].

2.9 V. Y. Lum, P. S. T. Yuen, and M. Dodd. "Key-to-Address Transform Techniques: A Fundamental Performance Study on Large Existing Formatted Files." *CACM* **14,** No. 4 (April 1971).

An investigation into the performance of several different hashing algorithms. The conclusion is that the division/remainder method seems to be the best all-round performer.

2.10 B. A. Marron and P. A. D. de Maine. "Automatic Data Compression." *CACM* **10,** No. 11 (November 1967).

Detailed descriptions are presented of two algorithms for automatically compressing and decompressing data (and hence reducing secondary storage space requirements): NUPAK, which operates on numeric data, and ANPAK, which operates on alphanumeric or "any" data (i.e., any string of bits).

2.11 R. Morris. "Scatter Storage Techniques." *CACM* **11,** No. 1 (January 1968).

This paper is primarily concerned with hashing techniques as they apply to the symbol table of an assembler or compiler. However, it is a useful survey of the techniques available and should prove valuable to anyone concerned with the problems of storage structure design.

2.12 J. K. Mullin. "Retrieval-Update Speed Tradeoffs Using Combined Indices." *CACM* **14,** No. 12 (December 1971).

A sequel to [2.8] that gives performance statistics for the combined index scheme for various retrieval/storage ratios.

2.13 W. W. Peterson. "Addressing for Random-Access Storage." *IBM J. R&D* **1,** No. 2 (April 1957).

A classic paper on the subject. Its primary concern is the amount of searching required to locate a particular record in a number of different storage structures.

2.14 Storage Structure Definition Language Task Group (SSDLTG) of CODASYL Systems Committee. "Introduction to Storage Structure Definition" (by J. P. Fry); "Informal Definitions for the Development of a Storage Structure Definition Language" (by W. C. McGee); and "A Procedural Approach to File Translation" (by J. W. Young, Jr.). *Proc. 1970 ACM SICFIDET Workshop on Data Description and Access.* Available from ACM.

An introduction to the work of the SSDLTG. The objective of this group is to define a storage structure definition language that could be used to describe any existing or planned storage structure, with a view to tackling the data interchange problem.

2.15 M. R. Vose and J. S. Richardson. "An Approach to Inverted Index Maintenance." *Comp. Bull.* **16,** No. 5 (May 1972).

Describes a multilist approach to the construction and maintenance of secondary indexes. This method avoids some of the problems of variable-length index entries. Each data record occurrence is represented within the system by a "sequential index number" (SIN), assigned when the occurrence is first stored. SIN values are assigned in ascending sequence. The "basic index" contains an entry for every data record occurrence, giving its SIN and its physical address, and it is in this index that multilist organization is used. For each indexed field, each basic index entry gives the SIN of the next occurrence having the same value in that field. For each value of each indexed field, pointers are maintained to the start and the end of the chain within the basic index.

2.16 E. Wong and T. C. Chiang. "Canonical Structure in Attribute Based File Organization." *CACM* **14,** No. 9 (September 1971).

A novel storage structure that has a number of advantages is proposed. It is assumed that all retrieval requests are expressed as a Boolean combination of elementary "attribute = value" conditions, and that these elementary conditions are known. Then the file can be partitioned into disjoint subsets for storage purposes; the subsets are the atoms of the Boolean algebra which is the set of all sets of record occurrences retrievable via the Boolean access requests. The advantages of this technique include the following.

a) Set intersection (of atoms) is never necessary.

b) An arbitrary request can easily be converted into a request for (the union of) one or more atoms.

c) Such a union never involves elimination of duplicates.

2.17 J. Martin. *Computer Data-Base Organization.* Englewood Cliffs, N.J.: Prentice-Hall (1975).

This book is divided into two major parts: Logical Organization and Physical Organization. Part II consists of an extensive description (over 300 pages) of storage structures and associated access strategies.

2.18 D. E. Knuth. *The Art of Computer Programming. Vol. III*: *Sorting and Searching.* Reading, Mass.: Addison-Wesley (1973).

Volume III of Knuth's outstanding series includes a comprehensive analysis of search algorithms (Chapter 6). For *database* searching, where the data resides in secondary storage, the most directly applicable sections are 6.2.4 (Multiway Trees), 6.4 (Hashing), and 6.5 (Retrieval on Secondary Keys).

2.19 W. D. Maurer and T. G. Lewis. "Hash Table Methods." *Computing Surveys* **7,** No. 1 (March 1975).

A tutorial survey of hashing techniques.

2.20 D. G. Severance. "Identifier Search Mechanisms: A Survey and Generalized Model." *Computing Surveys* **6,** No. 3 (September 1974).

2.21 R. E. Wagner. "Indexing Design Considerations." *IBM Sys. J.* **12,** No. 4 (1973).

A good description of indexing concepts, with details of the techniques—including compression algorithms—used in IBM's Virtual Storage Access Method, VSAM [16.4].

2.22 M. E. Senko, E. B. Altman, M. M. Astrahan, and P. L. Fehder. "Data Structures and Accessing in Data-Base Systems." *IBM Sys. J.* **12,** No. 1 (1973).

This paper is in three parts, as follows.

   I. Evolution of Information Systems.

  II. Information Organization.

 III. Data Representations and the Data Independent Accessing Model.

Part I consists of a short historical survey of the development of database systems. Part II describes the entity set model, which corresponds to the conceptual level in the ANSI/SPARC architecture [1.14]. Part III is probably the most interesting—it forms an introduction to the Data Independent Accessing Model (DIAM), which is an attempt to describe a database in terms of four successive levels of abstraction: the entity set (highest), string, encoding, and physical device levels. These four levels may be thought of as a more detailed, but still abstract, definition of the lower portions of the architecture in Fig. 1.3. We may characterize the three lower levels of the four as follows.

- *String level.* Access paths to data are defined as ordered sets or "strings" of data objects. Three types of string are identified: atomic strings (example: a string connecting field values to form a PART stored record occurrence), entity strings (example: a string connecting PART record occurrences for red parts), and link strings (example: a string connecting a SUPPLIER record occurrence to PART occurrences for parts supplied by that supplier).

- *Encoding level.* Data objects and strings are mapped into linear address spaces, using a single simple representation primitive known as a basic encoding unit.

- *Physical device level.* Linear address spaces are allocated to formatted physical subdivisions of real recording media.

The aim of DIAM is to provide a framework in which a variety of system design problems can be addressed in a controlled and structured manner.

2.23 G. D. Held. "Storage Structures for Relational Data Base Management Systems." (Ph.D. thesis). Berkeley: University of California, Electronics Research Laboratory Memorandum ERL-M533 (August 1975).

See also the shorter related paper [5.10].

2.24 D. G. Severance and G. M. Lohman. "Differential Files: Their Application to the Maintenance of Large Databases." *ACM Transactions on Database Systems* **1,** No. 3 (September 1976).

This paper discusses the many advantages that follow from the use of a "differential file" to hold updates. The basic idea is that updates are not made directly to the database itself—instead, they are recorded in a physically distinct file (the differential file) and are merged with the actual database at some suitable subsequent time. The following advantages are claimed for this approach. Note that the first six of these relate to database integrity and recovery (see Part 5), while the remaining four are operational advantages.

- Database dumping costs are reduced.

- Incremental dumping is facilitated.

- Both dumping and reorganization may be performed concurrently with updating operations.

- Recovery after a program error is fast.

- Recovery after a hardware failure is fast.

- The risk of a serious data loss is reduced.

- "Memo files" are supported efficiently.

- Software development is simplified.

- The main file software is simplified.

- Future storage costs may be reduced.

One problem not discussed is that of supporting key-sequenced access to the data when some records are in the real database and some are in the differential file.

2.25 B. Shneiderman. "Reduced Combined Indexes for Efficient Multiple Attribute Retrieval." *Information Systems* **2,** No. 4 (1976).

Proposes a refinement of Lum's combined indexing technique [2.8] that considerably reduces the storage space and search time overheads. For example, the index combination ABCD, BCDA, CDAB, DABC, ACBD, BDAC—see the answer to Exercise 2.6(b)—could be replaced by the combination ABCD, BCD, CDA, DAB, AC, BD. If each of A, B, C, D can assume 10 distinct values, then in the worst case the original combination would involve 60,000 index entries, the reduced combination only 13,200 entries.

3
Data Models
and Data
Sublanguages

3.1 INTRODUCTION

It should be clear from the architecture of Section 1.4 that the heart of
any database system is the data model (or conceptual model). The range
of data structures supported in the conceptual model is a factor that
critically affects just about every other component of the system. In
particular it dictates the design of the corresponding data sublanguage(s),
since each data sublanguage operation must be defined in terms of its
effect on these data structures.[1] Hence a crucial question is: What form
should the data model and accompanying data sublanguage take?

We may conveniently categorize database systems according to the
approach they adopt to this central question. The three best-known
approaches are

- the relational approach;
- the hierarchical approach; and
- the network approach.

---

[1] It is more accurate to say that each data sublanguage operation is defined in
terms of its effect on the data structures in the relevant *external* model. However,
just as the external model must be mapped into the data model, so operations on
the external model must be transformed into operations on the data model; and it
is really these latter operations that concern us here. In effect, we are simply
assuming that the external model and the data model are identical for the
purposes of this chapter. Moreover, we shall continue to make this assumption
throughout the next few chapters.

This fact accounts for the overall structure of this book—Parts 2, 3, and 4 consist of detailed examinations of each of these three approaches. The purpose of the present chapter is to pave the way for these later chapters by providing a brief introduction to, and comparison of, the three approaches. This chapter may accordingly be viewed as the key to the entire book; however, the reader is cautioned that we shall make no attempt at rigor or completeness until we reach the later chapters.

3.2 THE RELATIONAL APPROACH

This section and the following two are based on a sample database concerning suppliers, parts, and shipments. Figure 3.1 shows the sample data in relational form; that is, it represents a *relational model* of the data.

It can be seen that the data is organized into three tables: S (suppliers), P (parts), and SP (shipments). The S table contains, for each supplier, a supplier number, name, status code, and location; the P table contains, for each part, a part number, name, color, weight, and location where the part is stored; and the SP table contains, for each shipment, a supplier number, a part number, and the quantity shipped. We shall assume that circumstances are such that no more than one shipment can exist at any given time for a given supplier/part combination. (The S table, incidentally, consists of the first three rows of the table in Fig. 2.2, which we can now see is a relational view of the data used as the basis of the examples in Chapter 2.)

S

S#	SNAME	STATUS	CITY
S1	Smith	20	London
S2	Jones	10	Paris
S3	Blake	30	Paris

P

P#	PNAME	COLOR	WEIGHT	CITY
P1	Nut	Red	12	London
P2	Bolt	Green	17	Paris
P3	Screw	Blue	17	Rome
P4	Screw	Red	14	London

SP

S#	P#	QTY
S1	P1	300
S1	P2	200
S1	P3	400
S2	P1	300
S2	P2	400
S3	P2	200

Fig. 3.1 Sample data in relational form

Each of the three tables closely resembles a traditional sequential file, with rows of the table corresponding to records of the file and columns corresponding to fields of the records. The table P, for example, contains four rows or records, each consisting of five fields. However, there are certain significant differences—to be explained in detail in Chapter 4—between tables such as those of Fig. 3.1 and traditional sequential files. Each of these tables is actually a special case of the construct known in mathematics as a *relation*—a term that has a much more precise definition than the more traditional data processing term "file," or "table" for that matter. (However, in this book we shall frequently use "table" as if it were synonymous with "relation.") The relational approach to data is based on the realization that files that obey certain constraints may be considered as mathematical relations, and hence that elementary relation theory may be brought to bear on various practical problems of dealing with data in such files.

In much of the relational literature, therefore, tables such as those of Fig. 3.1 are referred to as relations. Rows of such tables are generally referred to as *tuples* (usually pronounced to rhyme with "couples"), again because the term has a more precise definition than "row" or "record." In this book, however, we shall tend to use the terms "tuple" and "row" interchangeably. Likewise, columns are usually referred to as *attributes;* again we shall use the two terms interchangeably.

One concept that relational theory emphasizes and for which there does not seem to be an established data processing term is the concept of the *domain.* A domain is a pool of values from which the actual values appearing in a given column are drawn. For example, the values appearing in the P# column of both the P table and the SP table are drawn from the underlying domain of all valid part numbers. This domain itself, while it may not be explicitly recorded in the database as an actual set of values, will be defined in the conceptual schema and will have a name of its own; columns based upon this domain may or may not have the same name. (Obviously they must have a different name if any ambiguity would otherwise result; e.g., if two columns in the same table were drawn from the same domain. An example of such a situation is given in Chapter 4.)

Observe that relations S and SP have a domain (supplier numbers) in common; so do P and SP (part numbers), and so do S and P (locations). A crucial feature of relational data structure is that *associations between tuples (rows) are represented solely by data values in columns drawn from a common domain.* The fact that supplier S3 and part P2 are located in the same city, for example, is represented by the appearance of the same value in the CITY column for the two tuples concerned. It is a characteristic of the relational approach, in fact, that all information in the database—both "entities" and "associations," to use the terminology of Section 1.1—is represented in a single uniform manner, namely, in the form of tables. As we shall see later, this characteristic is not shared by the hierarchical and network approaches.

We shall not discuss any further aspects of relational structure at this point; a more complete treatment will be found in Chapter 4. It is clear, however, that relational structure is very easy to understand. But simplicity of data representation is not the end of the story. From the user's point of view the data sublanguage—i.e., the set of operators provided to manipulate data in relational form—is naturally at least as important. Before discussing relational operators in any detail, we observe that the uniformity of data representation leads to a corresponding uniformity in the operator set: Since information is represented in one and only one way, we need only one operator for each of the basic functions (insert, delete, etc.) that we wish to perform. This contrasts with the situation with more complex structures, where information may be represented in several ways and hence several sets of operators are required. As we shall see in Part 4 of this book, for example, the network-based DBTG system provides two "insert" operators: STORE to create a record occurrence, and CONNECT (originally called INSERT) to create a link between an "owner" and a "member."

Now let us consider some specific operations. For retrieval the basic operator we need is "get next where," which will fetch the next row of a table satisfying some specified condition. "Next" is interpreted relative to the *current position* (normally the row most recently accessed; for the initial case we assume it to be just prior to the first row of the table). This operator is illustrated in the examples of Fig. 3.2, which shows in outline the code required to handle two specific queries against the database of Fig. 3.1. The two queries are intentionally symmetric (each is the inverse of the other).

Q1: Find supplier numbers for suppliers who supply part P2.	Q2: Find part numbers for parts supplied by supplier S2.
Next: Get next shipment where P# = P2. Shipment found? If not, exit. Print S#. Go to Next.	Next: Get next shipment where S# = S2. Shipment found? If not, exit. Print P#. Go to Next.

Fig. 3.2 Two sample queries against the relational model

As for storage operations, we content ourselves with considering three simple problems, one for each of the basic functions insert, delete, and update, and indicating briefly in each case a possible relational operation to handle it.

Insert.　Workspace W contains information concerning a new supplier S4. Insert this information into the database.

- Insert tuple from W into supplier relation.

Delete.　Delete the shipment connecting part P2 and supplier S3.

- Delete shipment tuple where P# = P2 and S# = S3.

Update.　Supplier S1 has moved from London to Amsterdam.

- Update supplier tuple where S# = S1 setting CITY to Amsterdam.

We shall return to the question of relational data sublanguages in Section 3.5. Before then, however, let us consider the hierarchical and network approaches.

3.3 THE HIERARCHICAL APPROACH

Figure 3.3 shows a possible *hierarchical model* for the suppliers-and-parts database. In this model the data is represented by a simple tree structure, with parts superior to suppliers. The user sees four individual trees, or

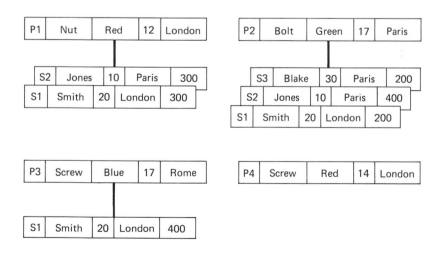

Fig. 3.3　Sample data in hierarchical form (parts superior to suppliers)

hierarchical occurrences, one for each part. Each tree consists of one part record occurrence, together with a set of subordinate supplier record occurrences, one for each supplier of the part. Each supplier occurrence includes the corresponding shipment quantity. Note that the set of supplier occurrences for a given part occurrence may contain any number of members, including zero (as in the case of P4).

The record type at the top of the tree—the part record type in our example—is usually known as the "root." Figure 3.3 is an example of the simplest possible hierarchical structure (other than the degenerate case of a hierarchy consisting of a root only), with a root and a single dependent record type. In general, the root may have any number of dependents, each of these may have any number of lower-level dependents, and so on, to any number of levels. Examples of more complex hierarchies will be found in Part 3 of this book.

In the previous section we likened the relational model of Fig. 3.1 to three simple files. We may similarly liken the hierarchical model of Fig. 3.3 to a *single* file, containing records arranged into four individual trees. The hierarchical data sublanguage discussed below may be thought of as a collection of operations on such files. Note, however, that such a file is a more complex object than the tables of Fig. 3.1. In the first place, it contains several types of record, not just one; in our example there are two, one for parts and one for suppliers. Second, it also contains *links* connecting occurrences of these records; in our example there are links between part occurrences and supplier occurrences, representing the associated shipments.

It is fundamental to the hierarchical view of data that any given record occurrence takes on its full significance only when seen in context—indeed, no dependent record occurrence can even exist without its superior. In the data sublanguage, therefore, the analogue of the relational "get next where" must include an additional operand (shown below via a "for" clause) to specify this context, i.e., to identify the superior of the target occurrence. Figure 3.4 shows in outline the code required to handle the two queries of Fig. 3.2 with the hierarchical model of Fig. 3.3. We have placed square brackets around "next" in those statements where we expect at most one occurrence to satisfy the specified conditions. Also, we have assumed that "where" may be omitted if we do not wish to specify any particular condition to be satisfied.

Although the original queries are symmetric, the two procedures shown in Fig. 3.4 are certainly not. (Contrast the relational case—Fig. 3.2—where the original symmetry is retained.) The loss of symmetry is a direct consequence of the model (Fig. 3.3), which is itself asymmetric, with parts being treated as superiors and suppliers as dependents. This

Q1: Find supplier numbers for suppliers who supply part P2.	Q2: Find part numbers for parts supplied by supplier S2.
Get [next] part where P# = P2. Next: Get next supplier for this part. Supplier found? If not, exit. Print S#. Go to Next.	Next: Get next part. Part found? If not, exit. Get [next] supplier for this part where S# = S2. Supplier found? If not, go to Next. Print P#. Go to Next.

Fig. 3.4 Two sample queries against the hierarchical model

asymmetry is a major drawback of the hierarchical approach, because it leads to unnecessary complications for the user. Specifically, the user is forced to devote time and effort to solving problems that are introduced by the model and are not intrinsic to the questions being asked. It is clear that matters will rapidly become worse as more types of record are introduced into the structure and the hierarchy becomes more complex. This is not a trivial matter. It means that programs are more complicated than they need be, with the consequence that program writing, debugging, and maintenance will all require more programmer time than they should.

On the other hand, it may fairly be claimed that hierarchies are a natural way to model truly hierarchic structures from the real world. The suppliers-and-parts example is not such a case, since there is a many-to-many correspondence between suppliers and parts. Departments and employees afford an example of a "genuine" hierarchical structure (if it is true that each employee belongs to exactly one department). But even in a "genuine" hierarchical situation the problem of asymmetry in retrieval still arises—consider the queries "Find employees in a given department" and "Find the department for a given employee," for example. Moreover, even "genuine" hierarchical situations tend to develop into more complex many-to-many situations with time. We shall return to the question of presenting a hierarchical view of a many-to-many situation in Section 13.4 and Chapter 17.

Turning now to storage operations, we find that the hierarchical model of Fig. 3.3 possesses certain further undesirable properties. Anomalies arise in connection with each of the basic storage operations (insert, delete, update). Unlike the retrieval problems discussed earlier, however, these anomalies are directly due to the fact that we are dealing with a many-to-many situation; they would not arise in a genuine hierarchical situation. The difficulties are illustrated by the three simple problems from the end of the previous section.

Insert.   It is not possible, without introducing a special dummy part, to insert data concerning a new supplier—S4, say—until that supplier supplies some part.

Delete.   Since shipment information is incorporated into the supplier record type, the only way to delete a shipment is to delete the corresponding supplier occurrence. It follows that, if we delete the only shipment for a given supplier, we lose all information on that supplier. (The insert and delete anomalies are really two sides of the same coin.) For example, deleting the shipment connecting P2 and S3 is handled by deleting the occurrence for S3 under part P2, which—since it is the only occurrence for S3—causes all information on S3 to be lost.

Incidentally, a similar problem arises if we want to delete a part that happens to be the only part supplied by some supplier, because deletion of any record occurrence automatically deletes all dependent occurrences too, in keeping with the hierarchical philosophy.

Update.   If we need to change the description of a supplier—e.g., to change the city for supplier S1 to Amsterdam—we are faced with either the problem of searching the entire model to find every occurrence of supplier S1 or the possibility of introducing an inconsistency (supplier S1 might be shown as being in Amsterdam at one point, and London at another).

3.4   THE NETWORK APPROACH

Figure 3.5 shows a *network model* for the suppliers-and-parts database. In this model, as in the hierarchical approach, the data is represented by *records* and *links*. However, a network is a more general structure than a hierarchy because a given record occurrence may have *any number* of immediate superiors (as well as any number of immediate dependents)— we are not limited to a maximum of one as we are with a hierarchy. The network approach thus allows us to model a many-to-many correspondence more directly than does the hierarchical approach, as Fig. 3.5 illustrates. In addition to the record types representing the suppliers and parts themselves, we introduce a third type of record which we will call the connector. A connector occurrence represents the association (shipment) between one supplier and one part, and contains data describing that association (in the example, the quantity of the part supplied). All

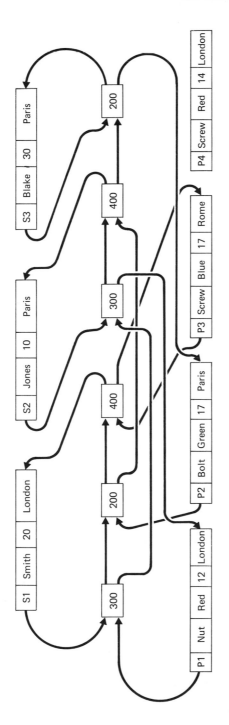

Fig. 3.5 Sample data in network form

Q1: Find supplier numbers for suppliers who supply part P2.	Q2: Find part numbers for parts supplied by supplier S2.
Get [next] part where P# = P2.	Get [next] supplier where S# = S2.
Next: Get next connector for this part.	Next: Get next connector for this supplier.
Connector found? If not, exit.	Connector found? If not, exit.
Get superior supplier for this	Get superior part for this
connector.	connector.
Print S#.	Print P#.
Go to Next.	Go to Next.

Fig. 3.6 Two sample queries against the network model

connector occurrences for a given supplier are placed on a chain[2] starting at and returning to that supplier. Similarly, all connector occurrences for a given part are placed on a chain starting at and returning to that part. Each connector occurrence is thus on exactly two chains, one supplier chain and one part chain. For example, Fig. 3.5 shows that supplier S2 supplies 300 of part P1 and 400 of part P2; similarly, it shows that part P1 is supplied in a quantity of 300 by supplier S1 and a quantity of 300 by supplier S2. Note, incidentally, that the correspondence between, say, one supplier and the associated connector records is one-to-many, which shows that hierarchies may easily be represented in a network system.

Again we may liken the data model to a file of records and links; the internal structure of this file is more complex than in the hierarchical case. As Fig. 3.6 illustrates, in the data sublanguage we now need not only the "get next for where" operator, but also a "get superior for" operator to fetch the unique superior in a specified chain of a specified connector occurrence.

The network model of Fig. 3.5 is more symmetric than the hierarchical model of Fig. 3.3; and the symmetry is reflected in the two procedures of Fig. 3.6. However, these procedures are significantly more complicated than both (a) their relational analogues (Fig. 3.2), on the one hand, and (b) the hierarchical solution to query Q1, at least (Fig. 3.4), on the other. Thus symmetry is not everything.

Another complication, not illustrated by Fig. 3.6, arises in connection with queries such as "Find the quantity of part P2 supplied by supplier S2." To answer this query we must fetch the (unique) connector occur-

---

[2] These chains may be physically represented in storage by actual chains of pointers or by some functionally equivalent method (see [18.9]). However, the user may always *think* of the chains as physically existing, regardless of the actual implementation.

rence that lies on both the chain for S2 and the chain for P2. The problem is that there are two strategies for locating this occurrence, one that starts at the supplier and scans its chain looking for a connector linked to the part, and one that starts at the part and scans *its* chain looking for a connector linked to the supplier. How does the user decide which strategy to adopt? (The choice could be significant.)

Similar remarks apply to storage operations. We find that the anomalies discussed in Section 3.3 for hierarchies do not arise with the network of Fig. 3.5.[3] However, the programming involved is not always as straightforward as it might be. In the delete case below, for example, we encounter precisely the strategy problem described in the previous paragraph.

Insert.   To insert data concerning a new supplier—S4, say—we simply create a new supplier record occurrence. Initially there will be no connector records for the new supplier; its chain will consist of a single pointer from the supplier to itself.

Delete.   To delete the shipment connecting P2 and S3 we delete the connector record occurrence linking this supplier and this part. The two chains concerned will need to be adjusted appropriately (such adjustments will probably be performed automatically).

Update.   We can change the city for supplier S1 to Amsterdam without search problems and without the possibility of inconsistency, because the city for S1 appears at precisely one place in the model.

We contend, therefore, that the prime disadvantage of the network approach is undue complexity, both in the model itself and in the associated data sublanguage. The source of the complexity lies in the range of information-bearing constructs supported in the data model (two have been illustrated in this chapter, namely, records and links, but many network systems support others in addition). In general, the more such constructs there are, the more operators are needed to handle them, and hence the more complicated the data sublanguage becomes. The range of data structures supported reflects the fact that the network model is really rather close to a storage structure (compare the data model of Fig. 3.5 with the storage structure of Fig. 2.6 in the previous chapter). We shall discuss these points at greater length later in this book.

---

[3] To be accurate, the difficulties do not disappear simply because of the network approach per se, but rather because of the particular form the network takes. A similar qualification applies to our discussion of storage operations in the relational approach (Section 3.2). The problem is really one of model design and normalization, details of which are beyond the scope of the present chapter; see Chapter 9.

3.5 HIGHER-LEVEL DATA SUBLANGUAGES

So far in our discussion of data sublanguages we have tacitly assumed that, as in traditional file programming, all operations should deal with essentially one record at a time. However, many problems are most naturally expressed, not in terms of individual records, but rather in terms of *sets*: Consider queries Q1 and Q2 of Fig. 3.2, for example. In this section we introduce the possibility of more powerful data sublanguages—languages in which the operators are capable of manipulating entire sets as single objects, instead of being restricted to one record at a time.

We consider retrieval operations first, and begin by looking at some sample queries against the relational model of Fig. 3.1.

3.5.1 Find CITY for supplier S1.

S	S#	SNAME	STATUS	CITY
	S1	Smith	20	London
	S2	Jones	10	Paris

→

RESULT	CITY
	London

The answer is "London." More accurately, the answer is a *table* (relation) with one row and one column, this column being based on the domain of locations (cities) and containing the single value "London."

3.5.2 Find S# and STATUS for suppliers in Paris.

S	S#	SNAME	STATUS	CITY
	S2	Jones	10	Paris
	S3	Blake	30	Paris

→

RESULT	S#	STATUS
	S2	10
	S3	30

The result is again a table, this time with two rows and two columns.

3.5.3 Find PNAME for parts supplied by supplier S1.

SP	S#	P#
	S1	P1
	S1	P2
	S1	P3

+

P	P#	PNAME
	P1	Nut
	P2	Bolt
	P3	Screw

→

RESULT	PNAME
	Nut
	Bolt
	Screw

Once again the result is a table. In fact the result of *any* retrieval operation may be considered as a table, and this point is of vital importance as we shall see later. In this particular example the result table is a subset of a single table, as it was in the two preceding examples, but *two* tables must be examined in constructing this result.

3.5.4 For each part supplied, find P# and names of all cities supplying the part.

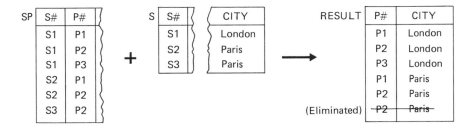

In this final example, not only is it necessary, again, to examine two tables, but the values in the result are actually derived from two tables. Note, incidentally, that a redundant duplicate row is eliminated from the final result; the reason for this is that, mathematically speaking, a table (relation) is a set—a set of rows—and sets by definition cannot contain duplicate elements. We shall discuss this point in more detail in Chapter 4.

In general, then, the result of any retrieval is a table, derived in some way from the tables in the database; any number of tables may be involved in forming the result, both in conditioning selection and in actually supplying result values. In other words, the process of retrieval is, precisely, a process of table construction. Recognizing this fact, we can define a set of *table construction operators* for use in retrieval. We will discuss briefly three such operators: SELECT, PROJECT, and JOIN.

The SELECT operator constructs a new table by taking a *horizontal subset* of an existing table, that is, all rows of an existing table that satisfy some condition. The PROJECT operator, in contrast, forms a *vertical subset* of an existing table by extracting specified columns and removing any redundant duplicate rows in the set of columns extracted. Using these two operators we may immediately write programs for the first two examples above.

3.5.1 Find CITY for supplier S1.

Step 1.   SELECT S WHERE S#='S1' GIVING TEMP.

This step gives us the following table.

TEMP	S#	SNAME	STATUS	CITY
	S1	Smith	20	London

Step 2.   PROJECT TEMP OVER CITY GIVING RESULT.

This step extracts the CITY column from TEMP, giving the desired result.

3.5.2 Find S# and STATUS for suppliers in Paris.

```
SELECT S WHERE CITY='PARIS' GIVING TEMP.
PROJECT TEMP OVER S#,STATUS GIVING RESULT.
```

The remaining two examples—the ones involving two tables—require the use of the JOIN operator. If two tables have a domain in common then they may be *joined* over that domain; the result of the join is a new, wider table in which each row is formed by joining together two rows, one from each of the original tables, such that the two rows concerned have the same value in the common domain. For example, tables S and P may be joined over their common location domain; the result is shown in Fig. 3.7.

S#	SNAME	STATUS	SCITY	P#	PNAME	COLOR	WEIGHT	PCITY
S1	Smith	20	London	P1	Nut	Red	12	London
S1	Smith	20	London	P4	Screw	Red	14	London
S2	Jones	10	Paris	P2	Bolt	Green	17	Paris
S3	Blake	30	Paris	P2	Bolt	Green	17	Paris

Fig. 3.7 Join of S and P over CITY

We have renamed the two CITY columns as SCITY and PCITY to avoid ambiguity. Note that if a row in one of the original tables has no counterpart in the other, it simply does not participate in the result; for example, P3 (stored in Rome) does not appear in the join in Fig. 3.7.

Now we can program the other two examples.

3.5.3 Find PNAME for parts supplied by supplier S1.

```
SELECT SP WHERE S#='S1' GIVING TEMP1.
JOIN TEMP1 AND P OVER P# GIVING TEMP2.
PROJECT TEMP2 OVER PNAME GIVING RESULT.
```

3.5.4 For each part supplied, find P# and names of all cities supplying the part.

```
JOIN SP AND S OVER S# GIVING TEMP.
PROJECT TEMP OVER P#,CITY GIVING RESULT.
```

In this last example the definition of PROJECT ensures that no duplicate rows will appear in the result.

The operators SELECT, PROJECT, and JOIN, along with others which will be discussed in Chapter 6, together constitute the *relational algebra*. Each operation of the relational algebra takes either one or two relations as its operand(s) and produces a new relation as its result. As we have illustrated, it is clearly possible to provide the user with a data sublanguage in which these operators are directly available; hence a higher-level (set-handling) data sublanguage is perfectly feasible, at least so far as retrieval is concerned. As for storage operations, we content ourselves at this point with the claim that it is indeed possible to define insert, delete, and update operators which, like the operators of the relational algebra, deal with entire sets as single operands. Examples of such operators will be shown in Part 2 of this book. Thus, for relational systems at least, a set-level data sublanguage is definitely achievable, and many relational systems do actually provide a language of this level. Indeed, it is one of the strengths of the relational approach that languages such as the relational algebra, which are very simple and yet extremely powerful, can so readily be defined.

What about the hierarchical and network approaches? It would be misleading to suggest that set-level languages cannot be defined for such systems. Once again, however, the fact that there is more than one way to represent information in the data model leads to the need for more than one set of operators in the data sublanguage. This statement is true regardless of language level. Without going into details, therefore, we claim that a set-level hierarchical or network language is necessarily more complex than a set-level relational language. Again we shall discuss this question in more detail later in the book.

In this section we have concentrated on relational algebra. Several relational systems (e.g., MacAIMS [11.13, 11.14], IS/1 [11.16]) provide a data sublanguage that is directly based on such an algebra. Since the algebra was first developed, however, a number of other languages have been designed for operating on relations, all at least as powerful as the algebra and many of them even easier to use. These languages include ALPHA and QUEL, both based on *relational calculus*; SQUARE and SEQUEL, based on an operation known as a "mapping"; and at least two highly ingenious graphic languages, Query By Example and CUPID, which are intended primarily for use with a visual display terminal. We shall describe some of these languages in subsequent chapters.

3.6 SUMMARY

At the end of Section 1.1 we pointed out that a database system must be able to represent two types of object, namely, "entities" and "associations." We also pointed out that fundamentally there is no real difference between the two; an association is merely a special kind of entity. The three approaches (relational, hierarchical, network) differ in the way in which they permit the user to view and manipulate *associations*.

In the relational approach associations are represented in the same way as other entities, i.e., as tuples in relations. In the hierarchical and network approaches certain associations[4] are represented by means of "links." Basically such links are capable of representing one-to-many associations; the difference between the network and hierarchical approaches is that with the former links may be combined to model more complex many-to-many associations, whereas this is not possible with the latter. Another difference, not emphasized in the present chapter, is that links are generally named in a network and anonymous in a hierarchy, for reasons that are beyond the scope of this chapter.

We conclude this chapter by identifying some systems that may be considered as representative of the three approaches. Some of the longest-established systems are *hierarchical*; as examples we may point to IBM's Information Management System, IMS [12.1]; Informatics' Mark IV [3.3]; MRI's System 2000 [3.4]; and the latter's distinguished forerunner, the Time-Shared Data Management System, TDMS, of SDC [3.5,

---

[4] Not all, however. In the hierarchical model of Fig. 3.3, for example, the association "shipments having the same part number" is represented by links, whereas the association "suppliers having the same location" is represented by equality of CITY values in the record occurrences concerned. This latter method of representing associations is the only method supported in the relational approach. See Chapter 25.

3.6]. IMS provides a record-at-a-time data sublanguage known as DL/I (Data Language/I), which we shall deal with in some detail in Part 3 of this book. System 2000 provides a powerful set-oriented language, which, however, does not possess the full generality of the relational algebra introduced in Section 3.5.

The most important example of a *network* system is provided by the proposals of the CODASYL Data Base Task Group, DBTG [18.1]. Several commercially available systems are based on these proposals, among them UNIVAC's DMS 1100 [3.7, 3.8] and Cullinane's IDMS [3.9]. Other network systems include Cincom's TOTAL [3.10]; IBM's DBOMP [3.11]; and the GE (now Honeywell) Integrated Data Store, IDS [3.12, 3.13], from which many of the DBTG ideas are derived. We shall discuss DBTG in depth in Part 4 of this book.

As for *relational* systems, we can identify Tymshare's MAGNUM [3.14] and IBM's ADL [3.15] among commercially available systems. MAGNUM provides a sophisticated record-at-a-time language, including full computational and report generation facilities, which can be used both in a command mode from an on-line terminal and in a more traditional batch programming mode. ADL provides a collection of simple set-oriented operators for use in an APL environment. Mention should also be made of the NOMAD system of NCSS [3.16], which is basically a hierarchical system but which includes several relational algebra operators—in particular, several forms of the join—among its report generation features. In addition to these (comparatively recent) commercial systems, a large number of experimental systems have been, and continue to be, developed at universities and similar institutions; several of these are described briefly in Chapter 11. In particular we mention here System R [7.6] and the Query By Example system [8.1], which will be dealt with more fully in Chapters 7 and 8, respectively. Both provide full set-handling languages that are actually *more* powerful than the relational algebra.

EXERCISES

A database is to contain information about persons and skills. At a particular time the following persons are represented in the database, and their skills are as indicated.

Person	Skills
Arthur	Programming
Bill	Operating and Programming
Charlie	Engineering, Programming, and Operating
Dave	Operating and Engineering

For each person the database contains various personal details, such as address. For each skill it contains an identification of the appropriate basic training course, an associated job grade code, and other information. The database also contains the date each person attended each course, where applicable (the assumption is that attendance at the course is essential before the skill can be said to be acquired).

3.1 Sketch a relational model for this data.

3.2 Sketch *two* hierarchical models for this data.

3.3 Sketch a network model for this data.

3.4 For each of your answers to the first three questions, give an outline procedure for finding the names of all persons having (a) a specified skill, (b) at least one skill in common with a specified person. In the relational case you should give solutions using both levels of language (tuple-at-a-time, set-at-a-time) introduced in this chapter.

REFERENCES AND BIBLIOGRAPHY

In addition to the references listed below, the reader's attention is drawn to *ACM Computing Surveys* **8,** No. 1 (special issue on database management systems), which includes tutorials on each of the three approaches [4.5, 12.3, 19.13].

3.1 C. J. Date. "Relational Database Systems: A Tutorial." *Information Systems: COINS IV* (ed., J. T. Tou). New York: Plenum Press (1974).

An early version of the present chapter.

3.2 C. J. Date. "Relational Database Concepts." *Datamation* **22,** No. 4 (April 1976).

An introduction to the basic ideas of relational systems. The relational sections of the present chapter are heavily based on this article.

3.3 Informatics Inc. Mark IV Reference Manual. Order No. SP-681810-1.

3.4 MRI Systems Corporation. System 2000 General Information Manual (1972).

3.5 R. E. Bleier. "Treating Hierarchical Data Structures in the SDC Time-Shared Data Management System (TDMS)." *Proc. ACM National Meeting* (1967).

Includes examples of the TDMS data sublanguage and schema language.

3.6 R. E. Bleier and A. H. Vorhaus. "File Organization in the SDC Time-Shared Data Management System (TDMS)." *Proc. IFIP Congress* (1968).

Describes the TDMS storage structure (an inverted organization).

3.7 Sperry-Univac. Univac 1100 Series Data Management System (DMS 1100): Schema Definition. Order No. UP-7907.

3.8 Sperry-Univac. Univac 1100 Series Data Management System (DMS 1100): Data Manipulation Language Programmer Reference Manual. Order No. UP-7908.

3.9 Cullinane Corporation. Integrated Database Management System (IDMS) Brochure (1975).

3.10 Cincom Systems Inc. TOTAL Users' Manual. Order No. AB65.

3.11 IBM Corporation. System/360 Data Base Organization and Maintenance Processor Application Description Manual. Form No. GH20-0771.

3.12 Honeywell Information Systems. Series 600/6000 Integrated Data Store Reference Manual. Order No. CPB-1565.

3.13 C. W. Bachman and S. B. Williams. "A General Purpose Programming System for Random Access Memories." *Proc. FJCC*, AFIPS Press (1964).

One of the earliest descriptions of IDS (forerunner of DBTG). Bachman was the original architect of IDS.

3.14 Tymshare Inc. MAGNUM Reference Manual (November 1975).

3.15 IBM Corporation. APL Data Language Program Description/Operations Manual. Form No. SB21-1805.

3.16 National CSS Inc. NOMAD Reference Manual. Form No. 1004 (April 1976).

Part 2
The Relational
Approach

The basic concepts of the relational approach were introduced in Chapter 3. Part 2 consists of a more detailed treatment of some of those ideas. Chapter 4 deals more thoroughly with the relational model of data, discussing such fundamental notions as domain, key, and normalized form in considerable detail. Chapters 5–8 describe four very high-level (set-oriented) relational data sublanguages: the ALPHA language, which is based on relational calculus; a language based on relational algebra; the SEQUEL language; and Query By Example. These four chapters are primarily intended to be read in sequence, but to a considerable extent each one does stand alone. The reader may choose to skip any or all of Chapters 6–8 on a first reading, but Chapter 5 is referenced in several later chapters and should not be omitted.

Chapter 9 (Normalization) is concerned with the problem of choosing the most appropriate set of relations to represent a given collection of data, i.e., the problem of data model design. Chapter 10 contains a detailed discussion of the concept of the external model, particularly as it applies to a relational system. Finally, Chapter 11 provides a brief summary of the major characteristics of some existing relational systems.

The reader will notice that we are primarily concerned with those parts of the system that appear above the user interface, i.e., those parts that have a direct effect on the user. However, Chapter 11 does contain a few details of the implementation techniques employed in one or two individual systems; also several of the references at the end of each chapter give implementation details. A general discussion of methods of representing a relation in storage has already been given in Chapter 2. (In particular, the reader's attention is drawn to reference [2.2].)

4
The Relational
Data Model

4.1 RELATIONS

Definition. Given a collection of sets $D_1, D_2, \ldots, D_n$ (not necessarily distinct), R is a *relation* on these n sets if it is a set of ordered n-tuples $\langle d_1, d_2, \ldots, d_n \rangle$ such that d_1 belongs to D_1, d_2 belongs to $D_2, \ldots, d_n$ belongs to D_n. Sets $D_1, D_2, \ldots, D_n$ are the *domains* of R. The value n is the *degree* of R.

Figure 4.1 illustrates a relation called PART, of degree 5, defined on domains P# (part number), PNAME (part name), COLOR (part color), WEIGHT (part weight), and CITY (location where the part is stored). The domain COLOR, for example, is the set of all valid part colors; note that there may be colors included in this domain that do not actually appear in the PART relation at this particular time.

As the figure illustrates, it is convenient to represent a relation as a table. (The table in Fig. 4.1 is actually an extended version of the table P

PART	P#	PNAME	COLOR	WEIGHT	CITY
	P1	Nut	Red	12	London
	P2	Bolt	Green	17	Paris
	P3	Screw	Blue	17	Rome
	P4	Screw	Red	14	London
	P5	Cam	Blue	12	Paris
	P6	Cog	Red	19	London

Fig. 4.1 The relation PART

73

of Fig. 3.1.) Each row of the table represents one n-tuple (or simply one *tuple*) of the relation. The number of tuples in a relation is called the *cardinality* of the relation; e.g., the cardinality of the PART relation is six.

Relations of degree one are said to be *unary;* for examples, see the result relations in Examples 3.5.1 and 3.5.3 (Section 3.5). Similarly, relations of degree two are *binary* (for examples, see the result relations in Examples 3.5.2 and 3.5.4), relations of degree three are *ternary,...,* and relations of degree n are *n-ary.*

We give another, equivalent, definition of relation that is sometimes useful. First we define the notion of a *Cartesian product.* Given a collection of sets $D_1, D_2, ..., D_n$ (not necessarily distinct), the Cartesian product of these n sets, written $D_1 \times D_2 \times \cdots \times D_n$, is the set of all possible ordered n-tuples $\langle d_1, d_2, ..., d_n \rangle$ such that d_1 belongs to D_1, d_2 belongs to $D_2, ..., d_n$ belongs to D_n. For example, Fig. 4.2 shows the Cartesian product of two sets S# and P#.

Now we define R to be a relation on the sets $D_1, D_2, ..., D_n$ if it is a subset of the Cartesian product $D_1 \times D_2 \times \cdots \times D_n$.

Strictly speaking, there is no ordering defined among the tuples of a relation, since a relation is a set and sets are not ordered. In Fig. 4.1, for example, the tuples of the relation PART could just as well have been shown in the reverse sequence—it would still have been the same relation. However, there are situations where it is very convenient to be able to guarantee some particular ordering, so that we know, for example, that the "get next" operator will fetch PART tuples in ascending part number sequence. In the relational model of data, therefore, we frequently consider relations to have an ordering—in fact, we must do so if "get next" is to have a meaning—but *either* (a) the ordering is system-defined, i.e., the user has no knowledge of the ordering and is independent of it, *or* (b) it is defined in terms of the values appearing in some

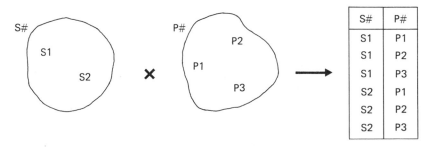

Fig. 4.2 An example of a Cartesian product

domain(s) within the relation, e.g., as ascending sequence by part number. All other types of ordering, e.g., first-in/first-out or program-controlled, are specifically excluded. We shall return to this subject in Chapter 25.

Referring back to the original definition, we can see that, by contrast, the domains of a relation do have an ordering defined among them (a relation is a set of *ordered n*-tuples, with the *j*th element in each *n*-tuple being drawn from the *j*th domain). If we were to rearrange the five columns of the PART relation (Fig. 4.1) into some different order, the resulting table would be a different relation, mathematically speaking. However, since users normally refer to columns by name rather than by their relative position, many systems relax this restriction and treat column order as if it were just as irrelevant as row order. In this book we shall generally assume that column ordering is insignificant unless we explicitly state otherwise.

4.2 DOMAINS AND ATTRIBUTES

It is important to appreciate the difference between a domain, on the one hand, and columns—or *attributes*—which are drawn from that domain, on the other. An attribute represents the *use* of a domain within a relation. To emphasize the distinction we may give attributes names that are distinct from those of the underlying domains; for example, see Fig. 4.3.

In this figure we have part of a conceptual schema, in which five domains (P#, PNAME, etc.) and one relation (PART) have been declared. The relation is defined with five attributes (PARTNO, PART-NAME, etc.), and each attribute is specified as being drawn from a corresponding domain.

```
DOMAIN      P#          CHARACTER (6)
DOMAIN      PNAME       CHARACTER (20)
DOMAIN      COLOR       CHARACTER (6)
DOMAIN      WEIGHT      NUMERIC (4)
DOMAIN      CITY        CHARACTER (15)
     . . . . .
RELATION    PART        (PARTNO     DOMAIN   P#,
                         PARTNAME   DOMAIN   PNAME,
                         COLOR      DOMAIN   COLOR,
                         WT         DOMAIN   WEIGHT,
                         LOC        DOMAIN   CITY)
```

Fig. 4.3 Sample schema declarations

COMPONENT

MAJOR_P#	MINOR_P#	QUANTITY
P1	P2	2
P1	P4	4
P5	P3	1
P3	P6	3
P6	P1	9
P5	P6	8
P2	P4	3

Fig. 4.4 The relation COMPONENT

We shall generally make use of the convention that allows us to omit the specification "DOMAIN name" from an attribute declaration if the attribute bears the same name. However, it is not always possible to do this, as the example of Fig. 4.4 shows.

In this example we have a relation with three attributes but only two distinct domains. (Note in the original definition, in Section 4.1, that domains are "not necessarily distinct.") The meaning of a tuple of the relation COMPONENT is that the major part includes the minor part, in the indicated quantity, as an immediate component. The two distinct domains are P# (part numbers) and QUANTITY. The example illustrates another common convention, that of generating distinct attribute names by prefixing a common domain name with distinct *role names* to indicate the distinct roles being played by that domain in each of its appearances.

At this point we introduce the idea of *normalization*. The only relations permitted in the relational model are those that satisfy the following condition.

- Every value in the relation—i.e., each attribute value in each tuple— is *atomic* (nondecomposable).

To put it another way, at every row-and-column position in the table there exists precisely one value, never a set of values. (We allow the possibility of null values, e.g., for "hours worked" for an employee on vacation.) A relation satisfying the foregoing condition is said to be *normalized*.

It is a trivial matter to cast an unnormalized relation into an equivalent normalized form. A single example will suffice to illustrate the procedure. Relation BEFORE (see Fig. 4.5) is defined on domains S# (supplier number) and PQ (part-quantity); the elements of PQ are themselves relations defined on domains P# (part number) and QTY (quan-

BEFORE	S#	PQ		AFTER	S#	P#	QTY
		P#	QTY				
	S1	P1	300		S1	P1	300
		P2	200		S1	P2	200
		P3	400		S1	P3	400
		P4	200		S1	P4	200
		P5	100		S1	P5	100
		P6	100		S1	P6	100
	S2	P1	300		S2	P1	300
		P2	400		S2	P2	400
	S3	P2	200		S3	P2	200
	S4	P2	200		S4	P2	200
		P4	300		S4	P4	300
		P5	400		S4	P5	400

Fig. 4.5 An example of normalization

tity), and thus BEFORE is unnormalized.[1] Relation AFTER is an equivalent normalized relation. (The meaning of each of these relations is that the indicated suppliers supply the indicated parts in the indicated quantities.)

Mathematically speaking, BEFORE *is* a relation, of degree two, but it is a relation for which not all the underlying domains are *simple*. (A simple domain is one in which all elements are atomic.) AFTER is a semantically equivalent relation of degree three, with the property that all its domains *are* simple—in other words, AFTER is normalized. We choose to support only normalized relations in the relational approach because (a) as the example shows, this choice imposes no real restriction on what can be represented, and (b) the resulting simplification in data structure leads to a corresponding simplification in the operators of the data sublanguage. Hereafter we shall assume that relations are always normalized.

4.3 KEYS

It is frequently the case that within a given relation there is one attribute with values that uniquely identify the tuples of the relation. For example,

---

[1] BEFORE is actually a hierarchy. See Fig. 3.3.

attribute P# of the PART relation has this property: Each PART tuple contains a distinct P# value, and this value may be used to distinguish that tuple from all others in the relation. P# is said to be the *primary key* for PART.

Not every relation will have a single-attribute primary key. However, every relation *will* have some combination of attributes that, when taken together, have the unique identification property; a "combination" consisting of a single attribute is merely a special case. In the relation AFTER of Fig. 4.5, for example, the combination (S#,P#) has this property; so does the combination (MAJOR_P#,MINOR_P#) in the relation COMPONENT of Fig. 4.4. The existence of such a combination is guaranteed by the fact that a relation is a set: Since sets do not contain duplicate elements, each tuple of a given relation is unique with respect to that relation, and hence at least the combination of *all* attributes has the unique identification property. In practice it is not usually necessary to involve all the attributes—some lesser combination is normally sufficient. Thus every relation does have a (possibly composite) primary key. We shall assume that the primary key is nonredundant, in the sense that none of its constituent attributes is superfluous for the purpose of unique identification; for example, the combination (P#,COLOR) is not a primary key for PART.

Occasionally we may encounter a relation in which there is more than one attribute combination possessing the unique identification property, and hence more than one *candidate key*. Figure 4.6 illustrates such a relation (SUPPLIER). Here the situation is that, for all time, each supplier has a unique supplier number *and* a unique supplier name. In such a case we may arbitrarily choose one of the candidates, say S#, as *the* primary key for the relation.

It is usual to impose the constraint that no component of a primary key value may be null.

We also introduce the concept of "foreign key." An attribute of relation R1 is a *foreign key* if it is not the primary key of R1 but its values

SUPPLIER	S#	SNAME	STATUS	CITY
	S1	Smith	20	London
	S2	Jones	10	Paris
	S3	Blake	30	Paris
	S4	Clark	20	London
	S5	Adams	30	Athens

Fig. 4.6 The SUPPLIER relation

are values of the primary key of some relation R2 (R1 and R2 not necessarily distinct). For example, attribute P# of relation AFTER is a foreign key, since its values are values of the primary key of the PART relation. Keys, primary and foreign, provide a means of representing associations between tuples; note, however, that not all such "associating" attributes are keys. For example, there is an association ("colocation") between parts and suppliers, represented by the CITY attributes of relations PART and SUPPLIER (see Figs. 4.1 and 4.6), but CITY is not a key. (It could *become* a foreign key if a relation with CITY as primary key were added to the database.)

To conclude our discussion of keys we should perhaps point out that access to a relation from a relational data sublanguage should not be restricted to "access by primary key." This point has already been illustrated in the examples of Chapter 3 (see, for example, Fig. 3.2 and Example 3.5.2).

4.4 SUMMARY

We can define the *relational model of a database* as a user's view of that database as a collection of time-varying, normalized relations of assorted degrees. It is necessary to specify "time-varying" to allow for the insertion, deletion, and update of tuples. Figure 4.7 shows a sample relational model; it consists of three relations, S (the SUPPLIER relation from Fig.

S

S#	SNAME	STATUS	CITY
S1	Smith	20	London
S2	Jones	10	Paris
S3	Blake	30	Paris
S4	Clark	20	London
S5	Adams	30	Athens

P

P#	PNAME	COLOR	WEIGHT	CITY
P1	Nut	Red	12	London
P2	Bolt	Green	17	Paris
P3	Screw	Blue	17	Rome
P4	Screw	Red	14	London
P5	Cam	Blue	12	Paris
P6	Cog	Red	19	London

SP

S#	P#	QTY
S1	P1	300
S1	P2	200
S1	P3	400
S1	P4	200
S1	P5	100
S1	P6	100
S2	P1	300
S2	P2	400
S3	P2	200
S4	P2	200
S4	P4	300
S4	P5	400

Fig. 4.7 The suppliers-and-parts database: Relational model

```
DOMAIN    S#        CHARACTER (5)
DOMAIN    SNAME     CHARACTER (20)
DOMAIN    STATUS    NUMERIC (3)
DOMAIN    CITY      CHARACTER (15)
DOMAIN    P#        CHARACTER (6)
DOMAIN    PNAME     CHARACTER (20)
DOMAIN    COLOR     CHARACTER (6)
DOMAIN    WEIGHT    NUMERIC (4)
DOMAIN    QTY       NUMERIC (5)


RELATION S (S#,SNAME,STATUS,CITY) KEY (S#)


RELATION P (P#,PNAME,COLOR,WEIGHT,CITY) KEY (P#)


RELATION SP (S#,P#,QTY) KEY (S#,P#)
```

Fig. 4.8 The suppliers-and-parts database: Relational schema

4.6), P (PART from Fig. 4.1), and SP (AFTER from Fig. 4.5). The model is an extension of the sample data of Fig. 3.1. Figure 4.8 shows the corresponding conceptual schema. We shall base most of our examples in the next few chapters on this sample data.

To sum up, we can say that, in traditional terms, a relation resembles a *file*, a tuple a *record* (occurrence, not type), and an attribute a *field* (type, not occurrence). These correspondences are at best approximate, however. To put it another way, relations may be thought of as *highly disciplined* files—the discipline concerned being one that results in a considerable simplification in the data structures the user has to deal with, and hence in a corresponding simplification in the operators needed to manipulate them (as Chapter 3 has demonstrated). We conclude by summarizing informally the major features of relational "files" which distinguish them from traditional, undisciplined files.

1. Each "file" contains only one record type.
2. Each record type has a fixed number of field types (in COBOL terms, OCCURS DEPENDING ON is outlawed).
3. Each record occurrence has a unique identifier.
4. Within a "file," record occurrences either have an unknown ordering or are ordered according to values contained within those occurrences. (The ordering field [combination] is not necessarily the primary key.) The relations defined in Fig. 4.8 are assumed to have unknown ordering.

EXERCISES

4.1 *Terminology.* A large number of new terms have been introduced in this chapter. In many cases the underlying concept will already be reasonably familiar to you, but in general the relational terms for these concepts have a more precise definition than do many more traditional data processing terms. We have arranged the new terms below in two columns; you should be able to provide definitions for at least those in the lefthand column.

relation	degree (of a relation)
domain	cardinality (of a relation)
attribute	unary relation
tuple	binary relation
normalized relation	Cartesian product
primary key	simple domain
relational model (of a database)	candidate key
foreign key	

A term not used in this chapter so far, but one that you will frequently encounter, is the term "relational database." This term is used, somewhat loosely, to mean a database for which the *user's view* is relational, and for which the operators available to the user are ones that operate on relational structures. It does *not* mean that the data is stored in the form of physical tables.

4.2 Define a schema for your solution to Exercise 3.1 (relational model for the persons-and-skills database).

4.3 Summarize the major differences between a relation and a traditional file.

REFERENCES AND BIBLIOGRAPHY

See also [3.1] and [3.2].

4.1 E. F. Codd. "A Relational Model of Data for Large Shared Data Banks." *CACM* **13,** No. 6 (June 1970).

> The current interest in the relational approach is largely due to the work of E. F. Codd, and this is the paper which triggered off much of the subsequent activity in the field. It contains an explanation of the relational model, definitions of some relational algebra operations, and a discussion of redundancy and consistency. A seminal paper.

4.2 E. F. Codd. "Derivability, Redundancy, and Consistency of Relations Stored in Large Data Banks." IBM Research Report RJ 599 (August 1969).

> An early version of [4.1].

4.3 E. F. Codd. "Understanding Relations." Continuing series of articles in *FDT* (quarterly bulletin of ACM Special Interest Group on Management of Data [SIGMOD, formerly SIGFIDET]), beginning with Vol. 5, No. 1 (June 1973).

4.4 E. F. Codd (ed.). "Relational Data Base Management: A Bibliography." IBM Research Laboratory, San Jose, CA 95193 (August 1975).

A comprehensive (but not annotated) list of references pertaining to the relational approach. The references are organized under the following headings.

- Models and theory
- Languages and human factors
- Implementations
- Implementation technology
- Authorization, views, and concurrency
- Integrity control
- Applications
- Deductive inference and approximate reasoning
- Natural language support
- Sets and relations prior to 1969

See also [4.5].

4.5 D. D. Chamberlin. "Relational Data Base Management: A Survey." *Computing Surveys* **8,** No. 1 (March 1976).

A comprehensive survey of many aspects of the relational approach. The paper is organized around the bibliography [4.4], which is included as an appendix.

5
A Data Sublanguage Based on Relational Calculus

5.1 INTRODUCTION

In Chapter 3 we introduced the *relational algebra* as a basis for an extremely high-level language for operating on relations. We also mentioned the existence of other languages having at least the same retrieval power as an algebraic language but having different theoretical foundations. In the present chapter we are concerned with one such language, Codd's "data sublanguage ALPHA" [5.1–5.4], which is based on *relational calculus.*

Recall from Chapter 3 that the result of any retrieval operation may be considered as a relation. The relational calculus is simply a notation for expressing the definition of some new relation in terms of some given collection of relations; in other words, it is a method of defining a relation that we wish to derive (the result of a query) in terms of the relations we already have (the relations in the database). As an example, consider the query of Example 3.5.4 (Section 3.5): "For each part supplied, find P# and names of all cities supplying the part." The following is a relational calculus definition of the result of this query.

$$\{(SP.P\#,S.CITY):SP.S\#=S.S\#\}$$

The braces { } indicate that the expression is a set (relation) definition; the colon stands for "such that" or "where"; the term preceding the colon represents a typical member (tuple) of the set; and the term following the colon is a qualification, or *predicate*, representing the "defining property" of the set. The value of the complete expression is the set of all (P#,CITY) pairs such that the P# value comes from an SP tuple, the CITY value comes from an S tuple, and the S# values in these two tuples are equal.

Note that this set definition is completely nonprocedural: It states merely what the result of the query is, not how to obtain it. An algebraic solution to the same problem, by contrast, does indicate how the result may be constructed—it involves a sequence of two operations, a join followed by a projection, which if actually executed will build the required relation. (A sophisticated implementation will not blindly execute the two operations without optimization, however.) Thus by comparison with the calculus, the algebra may be considered somewhat procedural, though the level of procedurality is still vastly above that of more traditional languages.

Data sublanguage ALPHA (DSL ALPHA) consists simply of the relational calculus in a syntactic form which more closely resembles that of a programming language. In fact the actual syntax used in this chapter is comparatively unimportant; it has been chosen for expository purposes only. In practice the syntax would have to be compatible with that of the host language, whatever that was. Reference [5.1] defines DSL ALPHA in detail; we shall restrict ourselves to consideration of its major features only.

INGRES [5.8–5.11] and DAMAS [5.6 and 5.7] are examples of systems that provide a calculus-based data sublanguage. However, the author knows of no system that supports DSL ALPHA in exactly the form described in this chapter.

5.2 ASSUMPTIONS AND DEFINITIONS

For simplicity we again assume that the external model is identical to the underlying data model (in fact, we shall continue to make this assumption throughout the next four chapters). We shall base all examples on the suppliers-and-parts data model (Figs. 4.7 and 4.8), both in this chapter and throughout the remainder of Part 2 of this book.

In Chapter 1 we mentioned the fact that each user owns a *workspace*, which forms the communication area between that user and the data model. In DSL ALPHA the user is assumed to own an arbitrary number of workspaces, so that it is possible (for example) to retrieve some S tuples into one and some P tuples into another, and have both sets of data concurrently available. To illustrate the format of such a workspace, we consider the retrieval statement

```
GET W (S.S#,S.STATUS):S.CITY='PARIS'
```

which is the DSL ALPHA equivalent of the relational calculus expression

$$\{(\texttt{S.S\#},\texttt{S.STATUS}):\texttt{S.CITY='PARIS'}\}$$

(see Example 3.5.2 in Section 3.5). W is the name of the workspace into which the data is to be retrieved. After the <u>GET</u> has been executed, W looks like this:

W	S#	STATUS
	S2	10
	S3	30

That is, W contains a *relation*, extracted (in the example) from the data model by means of a <u>GET</u> statement. This relation is in the form of a rectangular array, the first row of which consists of the appropriate *attribute names*. Once the <u>GET</u> has been executed, the contents of W can be manipulated in any way the host language may permit (e.g., by ordinary array-processing statements in a language such as PL/I).

Similarly, if data is to be transmitted from a workspace to the data model (e.g., by a <u>PUT</u> statement), the data must be organized in the workspace in the same fashion, that is, as the tabular representation of a relation.

The retrieval example also illustrates two other points that have already been made in passing, but to which we now explicitly draw the reader's attention. One is that the <u>GET</u> statement provides associative retrieval. Associative retrieval may be defined as direct retrieval by value; that is, the user identifies the data required by (some condition on) its value, not its address. The familiar "direct access by primary key" provided in many present-day systems is a limited form of associative retrieval. In DSL ALPHA all retrieval is direct in this sense; it is never "direct by address" or "sequential."[1]

The second point is that the idea of the "conceptual record occurrence" (or tuple) as the unit of access is de-emphasized: It is possible to retrieve any desired combination of attributes, from one relation or several, by simply indicating those required in the <u>GET</u> statement.

These two points also apply—but with some modification—to the case of storage operations.

---

[1] This statement ignores "piped mode" [5.1], in which "sequential access" does have a meaning. In piped retrieval, for example, the user may—at least conceptually—extract a relation from the data model associatively, but then proceed to retrieve the tuples of that relation one at a time in sequence. For simplicity we shall ignore piped mode from this point on.

We now proceed to illustrate the major features of DSL ALPHA by means of a carefully developed set of examples.

5.3 RETRIEVAL OPERATIONS

5.3.1 Simple retrieval.   Get part numbers for all parts supplied.

>   GET W (SP.P#)

Result:

W	P#
	P1
	P2
	P3
	P4
	P5
	P6

This example emphasizes the fact that redundant duplicate values are not delivered to the workspace. There are 12 values in the P# column of SP, but only 6 *distinct* values.

5.3.2 Simple retrieval.   Get full details of all suppliers.

>   GET W (S)

Result: The entire S relation is delivered to W. This GET statement is equivalent to

>   GET W (S.S#,S.SNAME,S.STATUS,S.CITY)

In general, the *target list* (the expression in parentheses) may contain relation names, attribute names, or both. Attribute names may be qualified by the appropriate relation name. They *must* be so qualified if the reference would otherwise be ambiguous, as would be true of S#, for example.

5.3.3 Qualified retrieval.   Get supplier numbers for suppliers in Paris with status > 20.

>   GET W (S.S#):S.CITY='PARIS'∧S.STATUS>20

Result:

W	S#
	S3

(a unary relation with just one tuple in it). As explained in the discussion of relational calculus in Section 5.1, the colon stands for "such that" (or "where"), and the expression following it is a qualification or predicate. The user can think of the predicate as defining a set of tuples (a relation) and of the target list as then specifying which attributes that relation is to be projected over (see the explanation of projection in Chapter 3). In general, a predicate may consist of an expression of arbitrary complexity, formulated according to the usual rules. The permitted operators are the comparison operators $=$, $\neq$, $<$, $\leq$, $>$, $\geq$, the Boolean operators $\wedge$ (and), $\vee$ (or), and $\neg$ (not), and of course parentheses ( ) to enforce a desired order of evaluation. We shall assume that comparison operators have higher priority than Boolean operators.

5.3.4   Retrieval with ordering.   Get supplier numbers and status for suppliers in Paris, in descending order of status.

<u>GET</u> W (S.S#,S.STATUS):S.CITY='PARIS' <u>DOWN</u> S.STATUS

Result:

W	S#	STATUS
	S3	30
	S2	10

In general, the result of <u>GET</u> is a relation and hence has no particular sequence. Here, however, the user has specified that the result is to be ordered in a particular way before being delivered to the workspace. Ordering may be specified as

<u>UP</u>   attribute <u>UP</u>   attribute ...
<u>DOWN</u>   <u>DOWN</u>

where the left-to-right order of naming attributes signifies major-to-minor sorting in the usual way. See the discussion of relation ordering in Section 4.1.

5.3.5   Retrieval with quota.   Get the supplier number of any one Paris supplier.

<u>GET</u> W (1) (S.S#):S.CITY='PARIS'

Result:

W	S#		W	S#
	S2	or		S3

The "(1)" is a *quota*. Its effect is to cause just one supplier tuple—presumably the first one encountered that satisfies the predicate—to participate in the retrieval.

5.3.6   Retrieval with ordering and quota.   Get the supplier number of a supplier such that no other supplier has a lower status.

GET W(1) (S.S#):UP S.STATUS

Result:

W	S#
	S2

Here, since there is no predicate, all S tuples will be initially selected; they will then (conceptually) be sequenced into ascending status order; then the S# value will be extracted from the first one.

5.3.7   Retrieval using a range variable.   Get supplier numbers for suppliers who supply part P2.

There are two ways of doing this. One is

GET W (SP.S#):SP.P#='P2'

Result:

W	S#
	S1
	S2
	S3
	S4

Alternatively we may write

RANGE SP X
GET W (X.S#):X.P#='P2'

These two statements together are precisely equivalent to the previous GET. Here X is a *range variable*, that is, a variable that ranges over the relation SP (in this case). Its permitted values are tuples of SP. In this example the use of a range variable has achieved very little. In general, a range variable can be used as a simple shorthand; for example, if relation SP were called SUPPLIERPART instead, abbreviating it to X would save a good deal of writing. However, a more important reason for introducing range variables is that some such facility is required—at least, in some circumstances—when we wish to use a *quantifier*. Since it is sometimes necessary, we impose the simple rule that a range variable must *always* be used if the variable in question is to be quantified. Most of the remaining examples illustrate the use of quantified range variables.

Incidentally, <u>RANGE</u> is a dynamically executable statement (like <u>GET</u>), not a static declaration. Thus the variable X could be subsequently given a different range, for example.

5.3.8   Retrieval using an existential quantifier.   Get supplier names for suppliers who supply part P2.

From the answer to the previous query, we can immediately see that the required set of supplier names is Smith, Jones, Blake, Clark. In general we want supplier names which are such that there exists an SP tuple linking the appropriate supplier number to part number P2. This is exactly what the following <u>GET</u> statement says.

> <u>RANGE</u> SP X
> <u>GET</u> W (S.SNAME):∃X(X.S#=S.S#∧X.P#='P2')

Result:

W	SNAME
	Smith
	Jones
	Blake
	Clark

The symbol ∃ represents the *existential quantifier;* it is read as "there exists." One way of thinking about the <u>GET</u> above is to consider each SNAME value in turn and to see whether it satisfies the predicate. Thus the first SNAME value (Fig. 4.7) is 'Smith'; the corresponding S# value is S1; does there exist an X (i.e., an SP tuple) with S# equal to S1 and P# equal to P2? If the answer is yes, 'Smith' is one of the values retrieved. Similarly for each of the remaining SNAME values.

The existential quantifier is so important in DSL ALPHA that we present a number of further examples of its use. The first two do not really illustrate any new points.

5.3.9   Retrieval using an existential quantifier.   Get part names for parts supplied by supplier S2.

> <u>RANGE</u> SP Y
> <u>GET</u> W (P.PNAME):∃Y(Y.P#=P.P#∧Y.S#='S2')

Result:

W	PNAME
	Nut
	Bolt

5.3.10 Retrieval using an existential quantifier. Get supplier cities for suppliers who supply part P2.

> RANGE SP Z
> GET W (S.CITY):∃Z(Z.S#=S.S#∧Z.P#='P2')

Result:

W	CITY
	London
	Paris

5.3.11 Retrieval using an existential quantifier. Get supplier numbers for suppliers who supply at least one red part.

We can answer this by considering the tuples of relation SP. For each such tuple, does the corresponding P tuple contain the value 'RED' for COLOR? That is, does there exist a P tuple with the same P# value and with COLOR value 'RED'?

> RANGE P PX
> GET W (SP.S#):∃PX(PX.P#=SP.P#∧PX.COLOR='RED')

Result:

W	S#
	S1
	S2
	S4

This example illustrates the fact that the quantified variable need not necessarily range over a "linking" relation such as SP.

5.3.12 Retrieval using several existential quantifiers. Get supplier names for suppliers who supply at least one red part.

One way of tackling this query is to break it down into smaller queries. First we get the appropriate supplier numbers into a workspace W1 (as in Example 5.3.11). Then we retrieve the corresponding supplier names by means of a separate GET.

```
RANGE W1 WX
GET W2 (S.SNAME):∃WX(WX.S#=S.S#)
```

Result:

W1	S#		W2	SNAME
	S1			Smith
	S2			Jones
	S4			Clark

This example illustrates the fact that a relation in a workspace may be used for retrieval purposes exactly as if that relation were itself part of the data model (so far as the owner of that workspace is concerned).

However, it is possible—and simpler—to express the whole query as a single <u>GET</u>.

```
RANGE P PX
RANGE SP SPX
GET W (S.SNAME):∃SPX(SPX.S#=S.S#
                    ∧∃PX(PX.P#=SPX.P#∧PX.COLOR='RED'))
```

The predicate here, though correct, is not unique. Two equivalent predicates follow:

```
∃PX(PX.COLOR='RED'∧∃SPX(SPX.P#=PX.P#∧SPX.S#=S.S#))
```

and

```
∃SPX(∃PX(SPX.S#=S.S#∧SPX.P#=PX.P#∧PX.COLOR='RED'))
```

It is usually true that many different predicates may be written to express the same qualification. In general, however, these different predicates are all *equivalent* to one another, in the sense that any one can be systematically converted into any other by a sequence of simple and well-understood operations (such as interchanging the two comparisons on either side of an "and" operator, or shifting a quantifier and its associated variable to the left). In particular, any predicate can be systematically reduced to an equivalent form in which all quantifiers (and associated variables) appear at the lefthand end: "prenex normal form." It is usual to omit any left parenthesis (and of course the corresponding right parenthesis) appearing in the middle of a sequence of quantifiers at the left of a prenex normal form predicate. Thus the following is a prenex normal form equivalent of the predicate above:

```
∃SPX∃PX(SPX.S#=S.S#∧SPX.P#=PX.P#∧PX.COLOR='RED')
```

Another equivalent prenex normal form would have the two quantifiers interchanged. In general, a sequence of *like* quantifiers can be written in any order.

5.3.13 Retrieval using several existential quantifiers. Get supplier names for suppliers who supply at least one part supplied by supplier S2.

```
RANGE SP SPX
RANGE SP SPY
GET W (S.SNAME):∃SPX(SPX.S#=S.S#
                ∧∃SPY(SPY.P#=SPX.P#∧SPY.S#='S2'))
```

Result:

W	SNAME
	Smith
	Jones
	Blake
	Clark

The first part of the predicate—∃SPX(SPX.S# = S.S# ... —specifies that the S supplier must supply *something*. The second part— ...∧∃SPY(SPY.P# = SPX.P# ∧ SPY.S# = 'S2'))—specifies that that something is supplied by supplier S2. Note that here we have two range variables, both ranging over the same relation.

The reader should consider (a) how this query could be broken down into smaller queries, and (b) how supplier S2 (Jones) could be excluded from the result if necessary.

5.3.14 Retrieval with multiple-relation target list. For each part supplied, get part number and names of all cities supplying the part.

```
GET W (SP.P#,S.CITY):SP.S#=S.S#
```

Result:

W	P#	CITY
	P1	London
	P1	Paris
	P2	London
	P2	Paris
	P3	London
	P4	London
	P5	London

The reader should consider what would be involved in answering this query if the target list were restricted to attributes from a single relation in each <u>GET</u>.

5.3.15 Retrieval with multiple-relation target list. Get all supplier-number/part-number pairs such that the indicated supplier and part are "colocated" (in other words, have the same value for the CITY attribute).

<u>GET</u> W (S.S#,P.P#):S.CITY=P.CITY

Result:

W	S#	P#
	S1	P1
	S1	P4
	S1	P6
	S2	P2
	S2	P5
	S3	P2
	S3	P5
	S4	P1
	S4	P4
	S4	P6

The point of this example is that linking expressions in a predicate do not necessarily involve key attributes.

5.3.16 Retrieval using a universal quantifier. Get supplier names for suppliers who do not supply part P1.

<u>RANGE</u> SP SPX
<u>GET</u> W (S.SNAME):∀SPX(SPX.S#≠S.S#∨SPX.P#≠'P1')

Result:

W	SNAME
	Blake
	Clark
	Adams

The symbol ∀ represents the *universal* quantifier; it is read as "for all." The predicate may be paraphrased as follows: For all SP tuples, either the supplier number is not the one we are currently interested in, or the part number is not P1.

An equivalent (and possibly clearer) predicate follows.

¬∃SPX(SPX.S#=S.S#∧SPX.P#='P1')

Note, however, that this is not in prenex normal form.

5.3.17 Retrieval using both types of quantifier. Get supplier names for suppliers who supply all parts.

RANGE P PX
RANGE SP SPX
GET W (S.SNAME):∀PX∃SPX(SPX.S#=S.S#∧SPX.P#=PX.P#)

Result:

W	SNAME
	Smith

The predicate here may be paraphrased as follows: For all parts there exists an SP tuple linking the S supplier number and the part number. Note that the sequence of quantifiers is important, because they are *unlike*.[2]

5.3.18 Retrieval using both types of quantifier. Get supplier numbers for suppliers who supply all parts.

RANGE P PX
RANGE SP SPX
GET W (S.S#):∀PX∃SPX(SPX.S#=S.S#∧SPX.P#=PX.P#)

Result:

W	S#
	S1

The point about this example is that the required S# values *cannot* be extracted from SPX. That is, the statement

GET W (SPX.S#):∀PX∃SPX(SPX.P#=PX.P#)

which at first glance might appear as a possible solution, is not "well formed." Variables appearing in the target list may not be quantified.

---

[2] As an illustration, if x and y are finite positive integers, the predicate $\forall x \exists y (y > x)$ has the value *true*, whereas the predicate $\exists y \forall x (y > x)$ has the value *false*; hence interchanging unlike quantifiers changes the meaning of the predicate.

5.3.19 Retrieval using implication. Get supplier numbers for suppliers who supply at least all those parts supplied by supplier S2.

```
RANGE P PX
RANGE SP SPX
RANGE SP SPY
GET W (S.S#):∀PX(∃SPX(SPX.S#='S2'∧SPX.P#=PX.P#)
            ⇒∃SPY(SPY.S#=S.S#∧SPY.P#=PX.P#))
```

Result:

W

S#
S1
S2

The symbol $\Rightarrow$ represents *implication;* thus $A \Rightarrow B$ can be read, "If A then B." The predicate here can therefore be read, "For all parts, if S2 supplies the part, then the S supplier supplies the part." The symbol $\Rightarrow$, though useful, is not actually necessary, since $A \Rightarrow B$ is precisely equivalent to $(\neg A) \vee B$; indeed, this is how implication is defined. Note that as a corollary, if S2 does not supply any parts at all, *all* S.S# values will be retrieved. The reader should consider how this query could be broken down into smaller queries.

We have now reached the end of our retrieval examples. It is clear that the retrieval language is very powerful. It is in fact *relationally complete* [5.5]. Relational completeness is a basic measure of the selective power of a data sublanguage. A language is said to be relationally complete if any relation derivable from the data model by means of an expression of the relational calculus can be retrieved using that language. What makes DSL ALPHA (and similar languages) so powerful is the economy with which this completeness is achieved: Any derivable relation can be retrieved using a *single statement* of the language. In fact, the term "relational completeness" is frequently taken to include this additional constraint (namely, that any derivable relation be retrievable via a single statement), and in this book we shall generally use the term in this more demanding sense. Most of the set-level relational languages discussed in this book are at least this powerful; lower-level languages, relational or otherwise, are certainly not. What relational completeness means to the user is that, *very* loosely speaking, if the information wanted is in the database, then it can be retrieved by means of a single self-contained request. (But see Section 5.5.) In lower-level languages the user must write quite complicated procedures to answer all but the simplest questions. Of course, most queries will be fairly simple in practice; but we know from the underlying theory that the user *can* ask arbitrarily complex questions if necessary.

5.4 STORAGE OPERATIONS

5.4.1 Simple update. Change the color of part P2 to yellow.

```
HOLD W (P.P#,P.COLOR):P.P#='P2'
W.COLOR='YELLOW' (host language)
UPDATE W
```

To modify a set of values from a relation, the user must retrieve them, using a HOLD statement, change them in the workspace, and then put them back via an UPDATE statement. The HOLD statement operates basically as a GET, but warns the DBMS of the user's intention to modify the data concerned. For example, it may prevent any concurrent user from accessing the relation—other than for retrieval—until the updating operation is complete (see Part 5 of this book).

If after issuing HOLD the user decides not to UPDATE after all, he or she may complete the operation by issuing

```
RELEASE W
```

where W is the workspace concerned.

Note, incidentally, that the target list in HOLD must include the primary key [5.3]. Notwithstanding this requirement, a HOLD-UPDATE sequence may not be used to change the primary key of a tuple. If such a change is required, the user must DELETE the old tuple and then PUT a new one (with the new primary key value) into the relation.[3] (See Example 5.4.6.)

5.4.2 Multiple-relation update. Suppose that relation P includes an extra column QOH (quantity on hand). Supplier S1 is now supplying 10 more of part P1 than before; add 10 to the quantity on hand for P1 and to the quantity of P1 supplied by S1.

```
HOLD W (P):P.P#='P1'
W.QOH=W.QOH+10
UPDATE W
HOLD W (SP):SP.S#='S1'∧SP.P#='P1'
W.QTY=W.QTY+10
UPDATE W
```

The point about this example is that HOLD, unlike GET, is restricted to a single relation in its target list. Hence modifying two relations requires two HOLD-UPDATE sequences. We therefore have a problem of *integ-*

---

[3] This restriction is part of the ALPHA language as originally defined. However, there are good reasons for not building such a restriction into the language itself, but rather allowing the DBA to impose it, if desired, by means of a separate *integrity assertion.* See Chapter 24.

rity: The data model is inconsistent as soon as the first UPDATE has been performed and remains so until the second is performed. We shall return to this point in Chapter 24.

Incidentally, the reason that HOLD is restricted to a single relation in its target list is that it is logically impossible to formulate a rule defining the effect of updating an *arbitrary* derived relation (even if all appropriate primary key values are retained). For example, suppose that the following HOLD were permitted.

HOLD W (SP.P#,S.S#,S.CITY):SP.S#=S.S#

Result:

W	P#	S#	CITY
	P1	S1	London
	P2	S1	London
	P3	S1	London

Now suppose that the first (only) of these tuples is modified to

P#	S#	CITY
P1	S1	Rome

What can the DBMS possibly do when the UPDATE is issued? (Supplier S1 is now apparently located in both Rome and London.)

5.4.3 Simple insertion. Add part P7 (name 'WASHER', color 'GREY', weight 2, city 'ATHENS') to relation P.

```
W.P#='P7'
W.PNAME='WASHER'
W.COLOR='GREY'
W.WEIGHT=2
W.CITY='ATHENS'
PUT W (P)
```

Note that workspace W must be previously structured in the appropriate tabular format. How this is done will depend on how workspaces are handled in the host language. The effect of the PUT is to insert *all* the tuples from the workspace into the nominated relation. (Like HOLD, PUT operates on just one relation.) The DBMS will reject any tuple whose primary key value is the same as that of a tuple that already exists.

5.4.4 Insertion with ordering. Workspace W contains a set of tuples in ascending P# sequence. Insert them into relation P.

```
PUT W (P) UP P.P#
```

The reason for specifying the sequence is simply to allow the DBMS to take advantage of it, if appropriate.

5.4.5 Deletion.[4]   Delete supplier S1.

```
HOLD W (S):S.S#='S1'
DELETE W
```

<u>DELETE</u> may be thought of as a special case of <u>UPDATE</u>. Its effect is to remove from the relation that was the object of the <u>HOLD</u> those tuples whose primary key values are given in the workspace. The contents of the workspace are left intact. Note in the example that SP tuples for S1 are *not* deleted; if this is required, the following statements would have to be executed.

```
HOLD W (SP):SP.S#='S1'
DELETE W
```

5.4.6 Primary key update.   Change the part number of P2 to P8.

```
HOLD W (P):P.P#='P2'
DELETE W
W.P#='P8'
PUT W (P)
```

5.4.7 Unqualified deletion.   Delete all parts.

```
HOLD W (P)
DELETE W
```

P is still a known relation but is empty.

5.5 LIBRARY FUNCTIONS

The retrieval power of DSL ALPHA, though "complete" as explained in Section 5.3, will in practice be inadequate for many queries. The user will quite often need to retrieve values that are *computed* in some way from

---

[4] We depart here from the language as defined by Codd [5.1]. Specifically, Codd does not require <u>HOLD</u> before <u>DELETE</u>; to delete supplier S1, for example, he would write simply

```
DELETE (S):S.S#='S1'.
```

However, we prefer our approach for reasons of integrity.

those in the data model. For example, we may wish to find the number of tuples currently appearing in a certain relation, or the total of all values currently occurring in a certain attribute of a certain relation. Similarly, we may wish to base the decision to retrieve other data on such computed values (in other words, to use such computed values within a predicate). For reasons such as these, the basic retrieval power of the language is enhanced by the provision of an open-ended library of standard functions that may be invoked within a <u>GET</u> statement, either in the target list or in the predicate.

5.5.1 Simple function in the target list. Get the total number of suppliers.

<u>GET</u> W (COUNT(S.S#))

Result:

W	COUNT_S#
	5

The effect of using COUNT in the target list is exactly as if (a) the <u>GET</u> were executed without any reference to the COUNT, forming an intermediate result relation, and then (b) COUNT were applied to that intermediate result. Thus the reader can think of the foregoing result as being achieved by (a) forming the intermediate relation

S#
S1
S2
S3
S4
S5

and then (b) applying COUNT to this relation. The effect of COUNT is simply to count the number of tuples in a relation.

Note the "attribute name" that appears in the workspace. (The user may ignore the COUNT_ prefix since there is no chance of ambiguity.)

5.5.2 Simple function in the target list. Get the total number of suppliers currently supplying parts.

<u>GET</u> W (COUNT(SP.S#))

Result:

W	COUNT_S#
	4

5.5.3 Simple function in the target list.
Get the total number of supplier cities.

GET W (COUNT(S.CITY))

Result:

W	COUNT_CITY
	3

5.5.4 Simple function in the target list, with a predicate.
Get the number of suppliers who supply part P2.

GET W (COUNT(SP.S#)):SP.P#='P2'

Result:

W	COUNT_S#
	4

Here the intermediate relation is the set of supplier numbers S1, S2, S3, S4.

5.5.5 Simple function in the target list, with a predicate.
Get the total quantity of part P2 supplied.

GET W (TOTAL(SP.QTY)):SP.P#='P2'

Result:

W	TOTAL_QTY
	1000

There is a significant difference in the manner of operation of the two functions COUNT and TOTAL: Whereas for COUNT the intermediate result is a relation, for TOTAL it is a *list* in which duplicate values have *not* been removed. Thus the intermediate result to which TOTAL is applied in the example above is the list of quantities (200, 400, 200, 200)—*not* the set of quantities {200, 400}.

Some other simple functions that should be available for use in target lists are the following:

MAX—to select the maximum value in a unary relation;

MIN—to select the minimum value in a unary relation; and

AVERAGE—to form the arithmetic mean of a list of values.

5.5.6 **Simple function in the predicate.**   Get the supplier numbers of all suppliers such that no other supplier has a higher status. (Contrast Example 5.3.6.)

GET W (S.S#):TOP(1,S.STATUS)

Result:

W	S#
	S3
	S5

The function reference TOP(n,S.STATUS) has the value *true* if the STATUS value in the current S tuple has a value that is the nth largest in the set of S.STATUS values; otherwise it has the value *false*. Similarly, we may define a function BOTTOM to pick out smallest values.

5.5.7 **Image function in the target list.**   For each part supplied, get the part number and a count of the number of suppliers who supply that part.

GET W (SP.P#,ICOUNT(SP,P#,S#))

Result:

W	P#	ICOUNT_S#
	P1	2
	P2	4
	P3	1
	P4	2
	P5	2
	P6	1

ICOUNT is an example of an *image function.* Applied to a particular SP tuple, the P# attribute and the S# attribute, it gives the count of the number of elements in the *image set* consisting of those S# values associated (in the SP relation) with the P# value from the specified SP tuple. Similarly, ICOUNT(SP,S#,P#) gives the count of the number of P# values associated with the S# value from the specified SP tuple.

5.5.8 Image function in the target list.   For each part supplied, get the part number and the total quantity supplied of that part.

<u>GET</u> W (SP.P#,ITOTAL(SP,P#,QTY))

Result:

W	P#	ITOTAL_QTY
	P1	600
	P2	1000
	P3	400
	P4	500
	P5	500
	P6	100

ITOTAL operates on the appropriate image *list* rather than on an image *set*. (The difference between ICOUNT and ITOTAL is analogous to that between COUNT and TOTAL.)

5.5.9 Image function in the target list, with a predicate.   Get the number of suppliers who supply part P2 (the same as Example 5.5.4).

<u>GET</u> W (ICOUNT(SP,P#,S#)):SP.P#='P2'

Result:

W	ICOUNT_S#
	4

5.5.10 Image function in the predicate.   Get part numbers for all parts supplied by more than one supplier.

<u>GET</u> W (SP.P#):ICOUNT(SP,P#,S#)>1

Result:

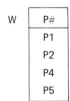

W	P#
	P1
	P2
	P4
	P5

Additional image functions that should be provided include IMAX, IMIN, and IAVERAGE (with definitions analogous to those of MAX, MIN, and AVERAGE).

5.6 SUMMARY

By way of summary we now present what we consider to be some of the advantages of DSL ALPHA when compared with lower-level languages, such as the tuple-at-a-time (or record-at-a-time) languages considered briefly in Chapter 3. Many of the following points apply equally well to other set-level relational languages, as we shall see in later chapters.

- Simplicity

   The simplicity of the language may not be immediately apparent to the reader who has just encountered it for the first time, especially if he or she is unfamiliar with mathematical notation. (Of course, a less mathematical syntax could be used in a real implementation, and probably would be.) It may be worth noting that in DSL ALPHA the complexity of a statement is generally in direct proportion to the complexity of the operation that the user is trying to perform (contrast the situation with lower-level languages); in particular, simple operations can be expressed very simply indeed. Language simplicity is a particularly important consideration for people concerned with application maintenance.

- Completeness

   The language is relationally complete, as explained in Section 5.3. This means that, for a very large class of queries, the user will never need to use loops or branching in extracting the data required.

- Nonprocedurality

   Many DSL ALPHA statements are simply descriptions of intent. For example, a GET statement is a statement of the data that is required; it does not specify how that data is to be retrieved. This simplifies all those aspects of implementation that depend on the ability of the DBMS to capture the user's intent: for example, search optimization, authorization control, integrity checking.

- Ease of extension

   Section 5.5 illustrates how the retrieval power of the basic language can be simply and indefinitely extended by the provision of library functions.

- Support for higher-level languages

   We do not really suggest that all users of the database should employ an ALPHA-like language. Many users will require their own special-purpose languages, involving, for example, terminology specific to their application area or a set of very simple interactive terminal facilities based on a menu approach [5.12, 5.13]. Indeed, some "casual" users may have no formal language at all for querying the system other than their own unrestricted natural language [5.14]. However, DSL ALPHA provides a common core of features that will be required in some shape or form in all such languages. It therefore seems reasonable to adopt DSL ALPHA—or some other language of comparable power—as a common target language for all such higher-level language translators.

EXERCISES

All the questions in this section are based on a data model defined as follows:

```
RELATION  S  (S#,SNAME,STATUS,CITY)
             KEY (S#)
          P  (P#,PNAME,COLOR,WEIGHT)
             KEY (P#)
          J  (J#,JNAME,CITY)
             KEY (J#)
        SPJ  (S#,P#,J#,QTY)
             KEY (S#,P#,J#)
```

(Domain definitions are not shown.) The significance of an SPJ tuple is that the specified supplier (S#) supplies the specified part (P#) to the specified project (J#) in the specified quantity. Some sample data values are shown in Fig. 5.1. You may find it helpful to interpret the questions in terms of this sample data; the process of working out the result values by hand for a given query may give you some insight into how to formulate an appropriate DSL ALPHA statement.

The questions are in approximate order of increasing complexity. It should not be necessary to tackle them all; as a guide to help you select some representative questions, we give a rough categorization, as follows.

5.1–5.5: No quantifiers

5.6–5.14: Existential quantifiers only

5.15–5.17: Existential quantifiers only (more complex)

5.18–5.20: Multiple-relation target lists

5.21–5.28: Both types of quantifier; most involve implication also

5.29–5.33: Storage operations

5.34–5.36: Library functions

As an additional exercise, you are strongly recommended to try converting some of the answers provided for the more complex retrieval questions back into their English equivalents.

S

S#	SNAME	STATUS	CITY
S1	Smith	20	London
S2	Jones	10	Paris
S3	Blake	30	Paris
S4	Clark	20	London
S5	Adams	30	Athens

P

P#	PNAME	COLOR	WEIGHT
P1	Nut	Red	12
P2	Bolt	Green	17
P3	Screw	Blue	17
P4	Screw	Red	14
P5	Cam	Blue	12
P6	Cog	Red	19

J

J#	JNAME	CITY
J1	Sorter	Paris
J2	Punch	Rome
J3	Reader	Athens
J4	Console	Athens
J5	Collator	London
J6	Terminal	Oslo
J7	Tape	London

SPJ

S#	P#	J#	QTY
S1	P1	J1	200
S1	P1	J4	700
S2	P3	J1	400
S2	P3	J2	200
S2	P3	J3	200
S2	P3	J4	500
S2	P3	J5	600
S2	P3	J6	400
S2	P3	J7	800
S2	P5	J2	100
S3	P3	J1	200
S3	P4	J2	500
S4	P6	J3	300
S4	P6	J7	300
S5	P2	J2	200
S5	P2	J4	100
S5	P5	J5	500
S5	P5	J7	100
S5	P6	J2	200
S5	P1	J4	1000
S5	P3	J4	1200
S5	P4	J4	800
S5	P5	J4	400
S5	P6	J4	500

Fig. 5.1 Sample data values

5.1 Get full details of all projects.

5.2 Get full details of all projects in London.

5.3 Get the part number for a part such that no other part has a smaller weight value.

5.4 Get S# values for suppliers who supply project J1.

5.5 Get S# values for suppliers who supply project J1 with part P1.

5.6 Get JNAME values for projects supplied by supplier S1.

5.7 Get COLOR values for parts supplied by supplier S1.

5.8 Get S# values for suppliers who supply both projects J1 and J2.

5.9 Get S# values for suppliers who supply project J1 with a red part.

5.10 Get P# values for parts supplied to any project in London.

5.11 Get S# values for suppliers who supply a London or Paris project with a red part.

5.12 Get P# values for parts supplied to any project by a supplier in the same city.

5.13 Get P# values for parts supplied to any project in London by a supplier in London.

5.14 Get J# values for projects supplied by at least one supplier not in the same city.

5.15 Get J# values for projects not supplied with any red part by any London supplier.

5.16 Get S# values for suppliers supplying at least one part supplied by at least one supplier who supplies at least one red part.

5.17 Get J# values for projects using at least one part available from supplier S1.

5.18 Get all pairs of CITY values such that a supplier in the first city supplies a project in the second city.

5.19 Get all ⟨CITY,P#,CITY⟩ triples such that a supplier in the first city supplies the specified part to a project in the second city.

5.20 Repeat Exercise 5.19, but do not retrieve triples in which the two CITY values are the same.

5.21 Get S# values for suppliers who supply the same part to all projects.

5.22 Get J# values for projects supplied entirely by supplier S1.

5.23 Get P# values for parts supplied to all projects in London.

5.24 Get J# values for projects supplied with at least all parts supplied by supplier S1.

5.25 Get J# values for projects which use only parts which are available from supplier S1.

5.26 Get J# values for projects supplied by supplier S1 with all parts that supplier S1 supplies.

5.27 Get J# values for projects which obtain at least some of every part they use from supplier S1.

5.28 Get J# values for projects supplied by all suppliers who supply some red part.

5.29 Change the name of project J6 to 'VIDEO'.

5.30 Change the color of all red parts to orange.

5.31 The quantity of P1 supplied to J1 by S1 is now to be supplied by S2 instead. Make all the necessary changes.

5.32 Add the tuples ('P7', 'WASHER', 'GREY', 1) and ('P8', 'SCREW', 'YEL-LOW', 2) to relation P.

5.33 Delete all red parts and the corresponding SPJ tuples.

5.34 Get the total number of projects supplied by supplier S3.

5.35 Get the total quantity of part P1 supplied by supplier S1.

5.36 For each part being supplied to a project, get the part number, the project number, and the corresponding total quantity.

REFERENCES AND BIBLIOGRAPHY

ADL [3.15] is an example of a commercially available system providing a calculus-based language. (The language is not relationally complete, however; basically it provides the existential quantifier but not the universal quantifier. Also all quantification is implicit.)

5.1 E. F. Codd. "A Data Base Sublanguage Founded on the Relational Calculus." *Proc. 1971 ACM SIGFIDET Workshop on Data Description, Access and Control.* Available from ACM.

5.2 E. F. Codd. Corrigendum to [5.1] (9 August 1971).

5.3 E. F. Codd. Private communication (14 March 1972).

5.4 E. F. Codd. Private communication (7 April 1972).

5.5 E. F. Codd. "Relational Completeness of Data Base Sublanguages." In *Data Base Systems*, Courant Computer Science Symposia Series, Vol. 6. Englewood Cliffs, N.J.: Prentice-Hall (1972).

> This paper includes a formal definition of the relational calculus underlying DSL ALPHA, and introduces the concept of relational completeness that was discussed briefly in Section 5.3. A language is said to be relationally complete if it possesses the property that any relation definable by means of calculus expressions may be retrieved via suitable statements in that language. (DSL ALPHA is actually *more* than complete, in that its retrieval expressions may include a quota, an ordering, and the use of library functions, none of which forms part of the relational calculus per se. As already indicated, our definition of relational completeness in Section 5.3 is more demanding than that of [5.5]: It stipulates that any relation definable via a *single* calculus expression be retrievable via a *single* statement of the language.)

> The paper also provides a formal definition of a relational algebra, and proves the completeness of this algebra by giving an algorithm ("Codd's reduction algorithm") for converting an arbitrary calculus expression into a semantically equivalent algebraic expression (and thus demonstrating a possible approach to implementing the calculus). The paper concludes with a brief section comparing and contrasting the calculus and algebra as candidates for a data sublanguage. Storage operations are not considered.

5.6 J. B. Rothnie, Jr. "Evaluating Inter-Entry Retrieval Expressions in a Relational Data Base Management System." *Proc. NCC* **44** (1975).

5.7 J. B. Rothnie, Jr. "An Approach to Implementing a Relational Data Management System." *Proc. 1974 ACM SIGMOD Workshop on Data Description, Access and Control.* Available from ACM.

These two papers [5.6, 5.7] describe some techniques used in the experimental system DAMAS (built at M.I.T.) for implementing a calculus-based retrieval language. [5.6] is more tutorial in nature; [5.7] gives some experimental results and more internal details. The papers discuss, specifically, the implementation of retrieval expressions involving a single existentially quantified range variable in terms of simpler expressions known as "primitive Boolean conditions" or PBCs. A PBC is a predicate that can be established as true or false for a given tuple by examining that tuple in isolation—i.e., it is a predicate involving no quantifiers. The "storage modules" of DAMAS, which are responsible for managing the stored database, support the following operations directly:

- get next tuple where P is true,

- test the existence of a tuple such that P is true,

- eliminate from consideration all tuples where P is true,

where P is a PBC. Using these operations, DAMAS handles a retrieval involving R1 (unquantified) and R2 (existentially quantified) as follows. Note that the target of the query must be some projection of R1.

Step 1.   In the original predicate, set all terms involving R2 to true and simplify. The result is a PBC, PBC1 say. Tuples of R1 not satisfying PBC1 may be eliminated from further consideration.

Step 2.   Get a (noneliminated) tuple from R1. Substitute values from this tuple in original predicate and simplify, yielding PBC2. Does there exist a tuple in R2 such that PBC2 is true?

Step 3.   (Yes) Fetch identified R2 tuple. Extract target values from the R1 tuple and add to result relation. Build PBC3, selecting all R1 tuples containing the same values for target attributes, and use it to eliminate from consideration all R1 tuples that would generate duplicates. (This elimination can be performed whenever a tuple is added to the result.) Also, substitute values from fetched R2 tuple in original predicate and simplify, yielding PBC4. Get all R1 tuples satisfying PBC4 and add target values to result.

Step 4.   (No) Build PBC5, selecting all R1 tuples that would yield (in Step 2) a PBC for which there cannot exist an R2 tuple to make it true (because no R2 tuple made PBC2 true). Eliminate these R1 tuples.

Step 5.   Repeat from Step 2 until no R1 tuples remain.

The design of the foregoing algorithm is based on the principle that as much information as possible should be derived from each database access. In practice, however, it may prove *more* expensive to eliminate tuples from consideration (for example) than simply to examine and reject them. For this reason certain steps of the algorithm may or may not be applied in a given situation. In DAMAS the choice of whether or not to apply them is left to the user, but some suggestions are given for automating this choice.

5.8 G. D. Held, M. R. Stonebraker, and E. Wong. "INGRES—A Relational Data Base System." *Proc. NCC* **44** (1975).

5.9 N. McDonald, M. R. Stonebraker, and E. Wong. "Preliminary Design of INGRES. Part I: Query Language, Data Storage and Access." Berkeley: University of California, Electronics Research Laboratory Memorandum ERL-M435 (April 1974).

5.10 G. D. Held and M. R. Stonebraker. "Storage Structures and Access Methods in the Relational Data Base Management System INGRES." *Proc. ACM Pacific Conference, San Francisco* (April 1975). Available from Mail Room, Boole and Babbage Inc., 850 Stewart Drive, Sunnyvale, CA 94086.

5.11 M. R. Stonebraker. "Getting Started in INGRES—A Tutorial." Berkeley: University of California, Electronics Research Laboratory Memorandum ERL-M518 (April 1975).

These four papers [5.8–5.11] are concerned with INGRES (Interactive Graphics and Retrieval System), which is being developed at Berkeley. Reference [5.8] gives an overall description of the system: It includes an introductory definition of the data sublanguage QUEL, an outline of the implementation algorithm, a survey of the access methods and storage structures supported, and an introduction to the technique of query modification which is used to deal with security, integrity, and the definition of views. More details on query modification are given in [23.13, 24.4, and 24.5].

QUEL is another relationally complete language that is based on the relational calculus. However, it does not include any explicit quantifiers. Instead, range variables are always considered to be existentially quantified if necessary. (Actually, Codd proposed a similar default rule for DSL ALPHA in [5.1]; for clarity all quantifiers were shown explicitly in the examples in this chapter.) As an illustration, the query of Example 5.3.12 ("Get supplier names for suppliers who supply at least one red part"), which requires two existential quantifiers, may be expressed in QUEL as follows.

```
RANGE OF SX IS S
RANGE OF PX IS P
RANGE OF SPX IS SP
RETRIEVE INTO W (SX.SNAME) WHERE SX.S#=SPX.S#
                          AND SPX.P#=PX.P#
                          AND PX.COLOR='RED'
```

Note that QUEL requires a range variable to be used even in the unquantified case (see SX above). The universal quantifier is not directly supported;

however, it is always possible to express a query that in ALPHA would require "for all" in some other terms. For example, the predicate "for all x, P is true" can be paraphrased as "the count of the number of x's where P is false is zero." QUEL includes a comprehensive set of library functions such as COUNT—in fact, the arithmetic and function-handling aspects of QUEL are more general than those of ALPHA.

QUEL also permits the user to specify attribute names for the result relation, as the following example illustrates. The query is "Get all supplier-number pairs such that the two indicated suppliers are located in the same city."

```
RANGE OF SX IS S
RANGE OF SY IS S
RETRIEVE INTO W (FIRST#=SX.S#,SECOND#=SY.S#) WHERE SX.CITY=SY.CITY
```

Here FIRST# and SECOND# are user-specified attribute names for the result. If no attribute names are specified, then names are generated automatically as in DSL ALPHA. Note, incidentally, that the name inheritance rules presented in this chapter for DSL ALPHA are inadequate for problems such as the one above.

5.12 N. McDonald and M. R. Stonebraker. "CUPID—The Friendly Query Language." *Proc. ACM Pacific Conference, San Francisco* (April 1975). Available from Mail Room, Boole and Babbage Inc., 850 Stewart Drive, Sunnyvale, CA 94086.

A short introduction to the CUPID language, which is implemented on top of QUEL (see also [5.13]). CUPID is a graphic language in which the user can construct queries of arbitrary complexity by simple light-pen manipulation of a small number of standard symbols. At the top of the following page, we show a possible CUPID representation of Example 5.3.12 to illustrate the language's ready comprehensibility.

5.13 N. McDonald. "Getting Started in INGRES with CUPID: A Tutorial." Berkeley: University of California, Engineering Research Laboratory Memorandum ERL-M546 (September 1975).

5.14 E. F. Codd. "Seven Steps to Rendezvous with the Casual User." *Proc. IFIP TC-2 Working Conference on Data Base Management Systems* (April 1974), North-Holland (1974).

This paper describes a system, already partially implemented, that permits an on-line "casual" user—i.e., one who has no knowledge of computers, programming, or artificial languages—to make queries against a relational database, using his or her own unrestricted natural language. Where necessary the system interrogates the user about the query, until it is able to synthesize an internal representation of it (in the form of a relational calculus expression) which it can then execute. The conversation between the system

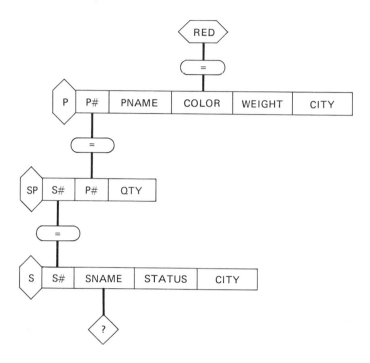

and the user includes the use of multiple-choice interrogation (menu selection) as a fallback, and a precise restatement of the user's query as the system understands it before any data is actually retrieved.

5.15 F. P. Palermo. "A Data Base Search Problem." *Information Systems: COINS IV* (ed., J. T. Tou). New York: Plenum Press (1974).

This paper presents a method of implementation for an arbitrary retrieval statement of the relational calculus. The method is based on Codd's reduction algorithm (described in [5.5]), but introduces a number of important optimization techniques. Specifically, the following improvements (among others) are made to the basic algorithm. (It is assumed that the tuple is the unit of access to the stored database.)

- No tuple is ever retrieved more than once.

- Unnecessary values are discarded from a tuple as soon as that tuple is retrieved ("unnecessary values" being either values corresponding to attributes not referenced in the query or values used solely for selection purposes—e.g., values of S.CITY in Example 5.3.4). This is equivalent to projecting the relation over the attributes concerned, and therefore not only reduces the space required for each tuple but may also reduce the number of tuples that have to be retained.

- The method used to build up the result relation is based on a "least growth principle," so that the result tends to grow slowly. This has the effect of reducing both the number of comparisons involved and the amount of intermediate storage necessary.

- An efficient technique is employed in the construction of joins, involving the dynamic factoring out of values used in "join terms" (such as S.S# = SP.S#) into "semi-joins" (which are effectively a kind of secondary index) and the use of an internal representation of each join called an "indirect join" (which makes use of internal tuple reference numbers to represent the tuples involved). These techniques are designed to reduce the amount of scanning necessary in the construction of a join, by ensuring for each join term that the tuples concerned are (logically) ordered on the values in the relevant attributes. They also permit the dynamic determination of a "best" sequence in which to access the required database relations.

5.16 E. Dee, W. Hilder, P. King, and E. Taylor. "Syntax for a COBOL-Based Data Manipulation Language." Report of BCS Advanced Programming Group Database Working Party 5 (October 1973). Available from BCS.

This report presents suggestions for a COBOL syntax for DSL ALPHA. The paper consists largely of the examples of reference [5.1], reworked in the proposed syntax.

5.17 E. Wong and K. Youssefi. "Decomposition—A Strategy for Query Processing." *ACM Transactions on Database Systems* **1,** No. 3 (September 1976).

Describes the strategy for processing queries in INGRES [5.8]. The general procedure is to break a query involving more than one range variable down into a sequence of queries involving one such variable each, using *reduction* and *tuple substitution* alternately to achieve the desired decomposition. *Reduction* is the process of removing a component of the query that has just one variable in common with the rest of the query. *Tuple substitution* is the process of substituting for one of the variables a tuple at a time. The paper gives algorithms for reduction and for selecting the variable for tuple substitution.

5.18 N. McDonald. "CUPID: A Graphics Oriented Facility for Support of Nonprogrammer Interactions with a Data Base." Memorandum No. ERL-M563 (Ph.D. thesis). Berkeley: University of California (November 1975).

5.19 M. Stonebraker, E. Wong, P. Kreps, and G. Held. "The Design and Implementation of INGRES." *ACM Transactions on Database Systems* **1,** No. 3 (September 1976).

6
A Data
Sublanguage
Based on
Relational Algebra

6.1 INTRODUCTION

Relational algebra is a collection of high-level operations on relations. Codd [5.5] defines a set of such operations and shows that this set is relationally complete, i.e., provides at least the retrieval power of the relational calculus. In this book we have already introduced three algebraic operations—SELECT, PROJECT, and JOIN—but we have not defined them in detail. In this chapter we shall describe a complete set of algebraic operators (and indicate a possible programming language syntax for them), without, however, going into quite as much detail as we did for the calculus in the previous chapter.

The complete algebra consists of two groups of operations: traditional set operations (union, intersection, difference, and a form of Cartesian product), and special relational operations (selection, projection, join, and division).[1] All these operators are involved in the retrieval language. Storage operations involve only union and difference.

All examples will be based on the suppliers-and-parts data model. We shall assume throughout the chapter that the order of attributes within a relation *is* significant, not because it is essential to do so but because it simplifies the definition of the operations.

---

[1] The algebra originally defined by Codd in [5.5] contained a restriction operation in place of selection.

6.2   TRADITIONAL SET OPERATIONS

For the operators union, intersection, and difference, the two relations concerned must be *union-compatible;* that is, they must be of the same degree, n say, and the jth attribute of the one must be drawn from the same domain as the jth attribute of the other $(1 \leq j \leq n)$. We shall not discuss the traditional set operations in any great detail, contenting ourselves with a definition and a simple example in each case.

Union

The union of two (union-compatible) relations A and B, A UNION B, is the set of all tuples t belonging to either A or B (or both).

Example.   Let A be the set of supplier tuples for suppliers in London, and B the set of supplier tuples for suppliers who supply part P1. Then A UNION B is the set of supplier tuples for suppliers who *either* are located in London *or* supply part P1 (or both).

Intersection

The intersection of two (union-compatible) relations A and B, A INTERSECT B, is the set of all tuples t belonging to both A and B.

Example.   Let A and B be as in the example under "Union" above. Then A INTERSECT B is the set of supplier tuples for suppliers who are located in London *and* supply part P1.

Difference

The difference between two (union-compatible) relations A and B (in that order), A MINUS B, is the set of all tuples t belonging to A and not to B.

Example.   Let A and B again be as in the example under "Union." Then A MINUS B is the set of supplier tuples for suppliers who are located in London and who do *not* supply part P1. (What is B MINUS A?)

Extended Cartesian Product

The extended Cartesian product of two relations A and B, A TIMES B, is the set of all tuples t such that t is the concatenation of a tuple a belonging to A and a tuple b belonging to B. The *concatenation* of a tuple $a = (a_1, \ldots, a_m)$ and a tuple $b = (b_{m+1}, \ldots, b_{m+n})$—in that order—is the tuple $t = (a_1, \ldots, a_m, b_{m+1}, \ldots, b_{m+n})$.

Example.   Let A be the set of all supplier numbers, and B the set of all part numbers. Then A TIMES B is the set of all possible supplier-number/part-number pairs.

6.3 SPECIAL RELATIONAL OPERATIONS

Selection

SELECT is an operator for constructing a "horizontal" subset of a relation—i.e., that subset of tuples within a relation for which a specified predicate is satisfied. The predicate is expressed as a Boolean combination of terms, each term being a simple comparison that can be established as true or false for a given tuple by inspecting that tuple in isolation. Some examples are shown in Fig. 6.1.

SELECT S WHERE CITY = 'LONDON'

S#	SNAME	STATUS	CITY
S1	Smith	20	London
S4	Clark	20	London

SELECT P WHERE WEIGHT < 14

P#	PNAME	COLOR	WEIGHT	CITY
P1	Nut	Red	12	London
P5	Cam	Blue	12	Paris

SELECT SP WHERE S# = 'S1'
                AND P# = 'P1'

S#	P#	QTY
S1	P1	300

Fig. 6.1 Three sample selections

Projection

PROJECT is an operator for constructing a "vertical" subset of a relation—i.e., a subset obtained by selecting specified attributes and eliminating others (and also eliminating duplicate tuples within the attributes selected). Since we are assigning significance to the order of attributes within a relation, projection provides us with a way to permute (reorder) the attributes of a given relation. See Fig. 6.2.

PROJECT S OVER CITY

CITY
London
Paris
Athens

PROJECT S OVER SNAME, CITY, S#, STATUS

SNAME	CITY	S#	STATUS
Smith	London	S1	20
Jones	Paris	S2	10
Blake	Paris	S3	30
Clark	London	S4	20
Adams	Athens	S5	30

Fig. 6.2 Two sample projections

Join

The join introduced in Section 3.5 was actually an *equi-join*, that is, a join based on equality of values in the common domain. We may define a *greater-than* join as follows. The greater-than join of relation A on attribute X with relation B on attribute Y—JOIN A AND B WHERE $X > Y$—is the set of all tuples t such that t is a concatenation of a tuple a belonging to A and a tuple b belonging to B, where $x > y$ (x being the X-component of a and y the Y-component of b). Similarly we may define joins for each of the other comparison operators $\neq$, $\geq$, $<$, $\leq$. (In all cases attributes X and Y should be based on the same domain.) Figure 6.3 shows a sample equi-join: JOIN S AND SP OVER S#. "OVER S#" here is an obvious shorthand for WHERE S# = S#. Unless we explicitly state otherwise, in this book we shall generally take the un-qualified term "join" to mean an equi-join.

S#	SNAME	STATUS	CITY	S#	P#	QTY
S1	Smith	20	London	S1	P1	300
S1	Smith	20	London	S1	P2	200
S1	Smith	20	London	S1	P3	400
S1	Smith	20	London	S1	P4	200
S1	Smith	20	London	S1	P5	100
S1	Smith	20	London	S1	P6	100
S2	Jones	10	Paris	S2	P1	300
S2	Jones	10	Paris	S2	P2	400
S3	Blake	30	Paris	S3	P2	200
S4	Clark	20	London	S4	P2	200
S4	Clark	20	London	S4	P4	300
S4	Clark	20	London	S4	P5	400

Fig. 6.3   Join of S and SP over S#

Division

In its simplest form, which is all that we consider here, division is defined as an operation between a binary relation (the dividend) and a unary relation (the divisor) which produces a unary relation (the quotient) as its result. Let the dividend A have attributes X and Y and let the divisor B have attribute Z, and let Y and Z be defined on the same underlying domain. Then the divide operation—DIVIDE A BY B OVER Y AND Z—produces a quotient defined on the same domain as X; a value x will appear in the quotient if and only if the pair ⟨*x, y*⟩ appears in A for *all* values *y* appearing in B. In other words, the quotient consists of those X-components of the dividend whose corresponding Y-components (in the dividend) include *every* component of the divisor. Figure 6.4 shows some examples of division: The dividend in each case (DEND) is the projection of SP over attributes S#, P#; the divisors (DOR) are indicated in the figure. We have used OVER P# as a simplification for OVER P# AND P#.

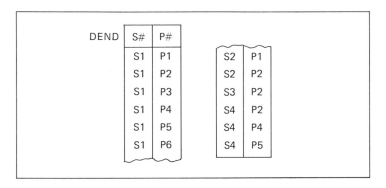

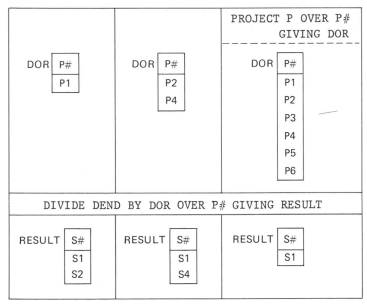

Fig. 6.4 Three sample divisions

6.4   RETRIEVAL EXAMPLES

6.4.1   Get supplier numbers for suppliers who supply part P2. (Example 5.3.7)

```
SELECT SP WHERE P#='P2' GIVING TEMP.
PROJECT TEMP OVER S# GIVING RESULT.
```

We have deliberately shown the two operations necessary in this example as two separate statements, for ease of understanding. However, since the result of any algebraic operation is itself a relation, we can extend the syntax of these operations so that wherever it is necessary to specify a relational operand, the user can specify *either* a simple relation name (such as SP or TEMP) *or* a relational algebra *expression* which evaluates to a relation. For example, we can combine the two statements above into one:

```
PROJECT (SELECT SP WHERE S#='S2') OVER S# GIVING RESULT.
```

In other words, relational algebra expressions may be nested; moreover such nesting may be carried to any depth. (There is an obvious analogy here with nested arithmetic expressions in ordinary programming languages.) In mathematical terms we express the fact that the result of any algebraic operation is itself a relation by saying that relations form a *closed system* under the algebra; and it is this property of closure that permits the nesting of expressions, and hence makes the algebra relationally complete.

6.4.2   Get supplier numbers for suppliers who supply at least one red part. (Example 5.3.11)

Unnested:

```
SELECT P WHERE COLOR='RED' GIVING TEMP1.
JOIN TEMP1 AND SP OVER P# GIVING TEMP2.
PROJECT TEMP2 OVER S# GIVING RESULT.
```

Nested:

```
PROJECT (JOIN (SELECT P WHERE COLOR='RED')
         AND SP OVER P#)
             OVER S#
                 GIVING RESULT.
```

6.4.3   Get supplier names for suppliers who supply all parts. (Example 5.3.17)

Unnested:

```
PROJECT SP OVER S#,P# GIVING TEMP1.
PROJECT P OVER P# GIVING TEMP2.
DIVIDE TEMP1 BY TEMP2 OVER P# GIVING TEMP3.
JOIN TEMP3 AND S OVER S# GIVING TEMP4.
PROJECT TEMP4 OVER SNAME GIVING RESULT.
```

Nested:

```
PROJECT (JOIN (DIVIDE (PROJECT SP OVER S#,P#)
                  BY (PROJECT P OVER P#) OVER P#)
              AND S OVER S#)
              OVER SNAME
                  GIVING RESULT.
```

6.5 STORAGE EXAMPLES

To *insert* a new tuple into a relation we can make use of the UNION operation. For example, to add part P7 (name 'WASHER', color 'GREY', weight 2, city 'ATHENS') to relation P, we might write

```
P UNION {('P7','WASHER','GREY',2,'ATHENS')} GIVING P.
```

Similarly, to *delete* a tuple from a relation we can make use of the MINUS operation. For example, to delete supplier S1, we might write

```
S MINUS {('S1','SMITH',20,'LONDON')} GIVING S.
```

although in practice it should not be necessary to specify every value in the tuple(s) to be deleted. To delete all SP tuples for supplier S1, for example, a possible notation could be

```
SP MINUS {('S1',?,?)} GIVING SP.
```

Here the question mark denotes an arbitrary value; any tuple containing the value 'S1' in the first attribute position is to be removed from the relation SP.

As for *update* operations, any update can be achieved by a suitable sequence of MINUS and UNION operations—although, in practice, a single operator would presumably be provided, for ease of use if for no other reason.

6.6 SUMMARY

To summarize the algebraic language, let us consider the advantages we claimed in Chapter 5 for DSL ALPHA and see in each case how the algebraic language compares.

■ Simplicity

The algebra, like the calculus, is fairly simple and very powerful; in fact, of course, it is exactly *as* powerful as the calculus. Which of the two is considered simpler is very much a matter of personal taste— programmers often seem to favor the algebra, nonprogrammers the calculus, probably because the algebra is closer to a procedural programming language (see below) while the calculus is closer to natural language.

■   Completeness

The algebra is relationally complete. A corollary of this fact is that to show that any given language L is relationally complete, it is sufficient to show that L includes analogues of each of the algebraic operations.

■   Nonprocedurality

Although fairly nonprocedural when compared with tuple-at-a-time languages, there is no doubt that the algebra is somewhat procedural in comparison with the calculus. For the DBMS this procedurality can be an advantage, in that implementation, on one level at least, can be reasonably straightforward: The DBMS can simply perform all the joins, projections, and other operations as specified in the expression that the user has written. On the other hand, such an implementation would not be very efficient, and would very likely result in the user having to expend time and effort in choosing the most efficient expression of the query—clearly an undesirable state of affairs. However, interesting work has been done on optimizing the implementation of algebraic expressions [6.4 and 6.5]; and thus this objection may cease to be valid in time.

■   Ease of extension

The algebra does not lend itself as readily as does the calculus to the inclusion of operations such as COUNT and TOTAL. See [5.5].

■   Support for higher-level languages

For essentially the same reasons as given under "Nonprocedurality" and "Ease of extension," the algebra seems less suitable than the calculus as a common target language for higher-level language translators.

EXERCISES

The reader should try to give algebraic solutions to some of the retrieval exercises of Chapter 5. N.B.: Several of the exercises require minor extensions to the language as presented in this chapter. In particular, an attribute-naming problem arises with some of the later, more complex questions. The answers at the back of the book give some indication as to the nature of the required extensions.

REFERENCES AND BIBLIOGRAPHY

Codd originally defined the special relational operations (join, etc.) in [5.1], and later refined the definitions in [5.5]. Examples of algebraic systems include IS/1, later renamed PRTV [11.16 and 11.17], and MacAIMS [11.13 and 11.14]. See also [5.14].

6.1 R. M. Pecherer. "Efficient Evaluation of Expressions in a Relational Algebra." *Proc. ACM Pacific Conference, San Francisco* (April 1975). Available from Mail Room, Boole and Babbage Inc., 850 Stewart Drive, Sunnyvale, CA 94086.

This paper begins by introducing a slightly revised version of the algebra, containing join and restriction operators that are more general than those of [5.5]. The revisions are motivated by efficiency considerations. The implementation of individual operators of this algebra is then discussed; it is assumed that relations are stored as sorted tables and may only be accessed according to their stored sequence. Performance bounds are given for each operator. Under the stated assumptions the operators requiring the most careful attention are projection and division. For these two it is concluded that the best approach is to sort the data before the operation; the paper shows that, for a large class of algebraic expressions, intermediate results can be obtained in the desired order at no extra cost. The paper also considers the transformation of expressions into an equivalent, more efficient form, using some of Palermo's techniques [5.14].

6.2 R. M. Pecherer. "Efficient Retrieval in Relational Data Base Systems." (PhD thesis). Berkeley: University of California, Electronics Research Laboratory Memorandum No. ERL-M547 (October 1975).

6.3 L. R. Gotlieb. "Computing Joins of Relations." *Proc. 1975 ACM SIGMOD International Conference on the Management of Data.* Available from ACM.

Presents and compares a number of algorithms for implementing "natural" joins. (A natural join is an equi-join with one of the two duplicate result columns projected out.)

6.4 J. M. Smith and P. Y.-T. Chang. "Optimizing the Performance of a Relational Algebra Database Interface." *CACM* **18,** No. 10 (October 1975).

An extremely clear paper explaining the algorithms used in the "Smart Query Interface for a Relational Algebra" (SQUIRAL). The optimization techniques employed include the following.

- Transforming the original algebraic expression into an equivalent but more efficient sequence of operations.

- Assigning distinct operations in the transformed expression to distinct tasks and exploiting concurrency and pipelining among them.

- Coordinating the sort orders of the temporary relations passed between these tasks.

SQUIRAL also seeks to exploit any indexes that may exist and to localize stored page references.

6.5 P. A. V. Hall. "Optimisation of a Single Relational Expression in a Relational Data Base System." IBM UK Scientific Centre Report No. UKSC 0076 (June 1975). Available from IBM UK Scientific Centre, Neville Rd., Peterlee, Co. Durham, England HA2 7HH.

This paper describes some of the optimizing techniques used in the system PRTV [11.17]. PRTV, like SQUIRAL [6.4], attempts to transform a given algebraic expression into a more efficient form before evaluating it. A feature of PRTV is that the system does not automatically evaluate each expression as soon as it receives it; rather, it combines each new expression with those it has already accepted to build a larger and more complex expression, and defers actual evaluation until the last possible moment. Thus the "single relational expression" of the paper's title may represent an entire sequence of end-user operations. The optimizations described resemble those of SQUIRAL but go further in some respects; briefly they are as follows (in order of application).

- Move SELECT operations so that they are performed as early as possible.

- Combine sequences of PROJECT operations.

- Eliminate redundant operations; simplify expressions involving empty relations and trivial predicates.

- Eliminate common subexpressions.

The paper concludes with some experimental results and some suggestions for further investigations.

6.6 M. W. Blasgen and K. P. Eswaran. "On the Evaluation of Queries in a Relational Data Base System." IBM Research Report RJ 1745 (April 1976).

Several techniques for handling queries involving projection, join, and restriction operations are compared on the basis of their cost in secondary storage access. The conclusions are that physical clustering of logically related items is a critical performance parameter, and that, in the absence of such clustering, methods that depend on sorting seem to be the most generally satisfactory.

6.7 A. L. Furtado and L. Kerschberg. "An Algebra of Quotient Relations." Dept. of Information Systems Management Technical Report No. 14, University of Maryland, College Park, Md. 20742 (February 1977).

Presents a revised relational algebra for operating directly on "quotient relations." Given an n-ary relation R, a corresponding quotient relation may be derived from R by grouping tuples on the basis of the values of some attribute of R (see the description of GROUP BY in Chapter 7). For example, the quotient relation derived from relation SUPPLIER (Fig. 4.6) on the basis of CITY values is a set of three groups of tuples: one containing two London tuples, one containing two Paris tuples, and one containing a single Athens tuple. The authors claim that operating directly on quotient relations leads both to more natural query formulation and to a potential for more efficient implementation.

7

The Data
Sublanguage
SEQUEL

7.1 INTRODUCTION

Since the relational algebra and relational calculus were first defined [5.1 and 5.5], a number of other approaches to the design of a relational data sublanguage have been investigated. In this chapter and the next we shall examine two of the most highly developed of these, namely, SEQUEL and Query By Example. Both of these languages are *more* than relationally complete; both have been at least partially implemented; and both have strong claims to being easier to use than the algebra and the calculus.

The original version of SEQUEL (Structured English Query Language) was based on an earlier language called SQUARE [7.1 and 7.2]. The two languages were essentially the same, in fact, but SQUARE used a rather mathematical notation whereas SEQUEL was much more English-like. A prototype implementation of this version of SEQUEL was built at the IBM San Jose Research Laboratory [7.3 and 7.4]. In addition, controlled experiments were carried out on the language's usability, employing college students as subjects [7.5]. On the basis of this work a number of language improvements were made, and the revised version of SEQUEL is currently being implemented as one of the interfaces to System R, a full-scale relational system under development at the IBM San Jose Research Laboratory [7.6]. In System R SEQUEL may be used both from an on-line terminal as an interactive, stand-alone language and from a host language such as PL/I (via subroutine calls) as a batch data sublanguage.

It should be stressed, incidentally, that SEQUEL is much more than just a query language (the "query" in its name notwithstanding): It provides a full range of storage operations—INSERT, DELETE, UPDATE—as well as many other facilities that will be discussed in later chapters.

7.2 RETRIEVAL OPERATIONS

The fundamental operation in SEQUEL is the *mapping*, represented syntactically as a SELECT-FROM-WHERE block. For example, the query "Get supplier numbers and status for suppliers in Paris" may be expressed in SEQUEL as follows.

```
SELECT S#,STATUS
FROM   S
WHERE  CITY='PARIS'
```

From this example it can be seen that the "mapping" operation is effectively a horizontal subsetting (find all rows where CITY = 'PARIS') followed by a vertical subsetting (extract S# and STATUS from these rows). In algebraic terms it may be considered as a SELECT followed by a PROJECT, except that, as we shall see, the horizontal subsetting operation may be considerably more sophisticated than the simple algebraic SELECT of Chapter 6. (Do not confuse the algebraic SELECT with the SEQUEL SELECT.)

It is possible to define a table-name and column-names for the result of a query by means of the *assignment* operation. For example,

```
RESULT (SNO, CODE)←SELECT S#,STATUS
                   FROM   S
                   WHERE  CITY='PARIS'
```

Note that column ordering within a table is significant in SEQUEL (otherwise we would not know whether SNO corresponded to S# or to STATUS). Incidentally, SEQUEL generally uses the terms table, column, and row in preference to relation, attribute, and tuple.

7.2.1 Simple retrieval. Get part numbers for all parts supplied. (Example 5.3.1)

```
SELECT UNIQUE P#
FROM   SP
```

We suggested above that a mapping may be thought of as a horizontal subsetting followed by a projection. In this example the horizontal subset is the entire table (no WHERE specified). As for the projection, SE-QUEL adopts a slightly "impure" approach and does not eliminate duplicates from a query result unless the user explicitly requests it via the keyword UNIQUE. The justification is that (a) duplicate elimination may be a costly operation, and (b) users will frequently not be bothered by the presence of duplicates in their output. (A similar philosophy is applied in QUEL [5.8].) However, if duplicate elimination is logically necessary in an *intermediate* result, SEQUEL will perform it automatically.

7.2.2 Simple retrieval.   Get full details of all suppliers. (Example 5.3.2)

```
SELECT *
FROM    S
```

The asterisk is a shorthand for an ordered list of all column-names in the FROM table.

7.2.3 Qualified retrieval.   Get supplier numbers for suppliers in Paris with status > 20. (Example 5.3.3)

```
SELECT S#
FROM    S
WHERE   CITY='PARIS'
AND     STATUS>20
```

The predicate following WHERE may include the comparison operators $=$, $\neg =$, $>$, $\geq$, $<$, $\leq$, the Boolean operators AND, OR, and NOT, and parentheses to enforce a desired order of evaluation.

7.2.4 Retrieval with ordering.   Get supplier numbers and status for suppliers in Paris, in descending order of status. (Example 5.3.4)

```
SELECT S#, STATUS
FROM    S
WHERE   CITY='PARIS'
ORDER   BY STATUS DESC
```

Ordering may be specified as

```
column-name ASC/DESC, column-name ASC/DESC,...
```

where ASC/DESC represent ascending/descending sequence respectively, and the left-to-right order of naming columns signifies major-to-minor sorting in the usual way.

SEQUEL has no counterpart to the DSL ALPHA "quota" (Examples 5.3.5 and 5.3.6).

7.2.5 Retrieval using a nested mapping. Get supplier names for suppliers who supply part P2. (Example 5.3.8)

To find supplier *numbers* for these suppliers, we can write (cf. Example 5.3.7):

```
SELECT S#
FROM   SP
WHERE  P#='P2'
```

The required supplier *names* are those for which the corresponding supplier number is in the set resulting from this query. Thus the overall query can be expressed as

```
SELECT SNAME
FROM   S
WHERE  S# IS IN
       (SELECT S#
       FROM  SP
       WHERE P#='P2')
```

Here IS IN is the SEQUEL representation of the set membership operator $\in$. SEQUEL also provides the operators IS NOT IN, CONTAINS, and DOES NOT CONTAIN; the meaning of A CONTAINS *b* is the same as that of *b* IS IN A (similarly for DOES NOT CONTAIN and IS NOT IN). IS IN may be abbreviated to simply IN or to = (the latter may seem more natural if the inner SELECT-FROM-WHERE block returns a single value). IS NOT IN may be abbreviated to NOT IN.

We remark that this query required an existential quantifier in DSL ALPHA. SEQUEL does not include either the existential or the universal quantifier, nor does it explicitly include the special relational algebra operations (projection, etc.), though as we shall see it does include UNION, INTERSECT, and MINUS.

7.2.6 Retrieval using a nested mapping. Get supplier numbers for suppliers who supply at least one red part. (Example 5.3.11)

```
SELECT UNIQUE S#
FROM   SP
WHERE  P# IN
       SELECT P#
       FROM   P
       WHERE  COLOR='RED'
```

Parentheses may be omitted from an inner block if no ambiguity results.

7.2.7   Retrieval using several levels of nesting.   Get supplier names for suppliers who supply at least one red part. (Example 5.3.12)

```
SELECT SNAME
FROM   S
WHERE  S# IN
          SELECT S#
          FROM   SP
          WHERE  P# IN
                    SELECT P#
                    FROM   P
                    WHERE  COLOR='RED'
```

7.2.8   Retrieval using a nested mapping, with interblock reference.   Get supplier names for suppliers who do not supply part P1. (Example 5.3.16)

```
SELECT SNAME
FROM   S
WHERE  'P1' NOT IN
          SELECT P#
          FROM   SP
          WHERE  S#=S.S#
```

In the last line here the unqualified reference to $S\#$ is implicitly qualified by table-name SP. To refer to an $S\#$ from the outer block within the inner block, an explicit qualifier (S) is needed.

7.2.9   Retrieval using a nested mapping, with same table involved in both blocks.   Get supplier numbers for suppliers who supply at least one part supplied by supplier S2.

```
SELECT UNIQUE S#
FROM   SP
WHERE  P# IN
          SELECT P#
          FROM   SP
          WHERE  S#='S2'
```

Again the unqualified reference to $S\#$ in the last line is implicitly qualified by table-name SP. In fact, the reference is entirely local to the inner block: It does not have the same meaning as a reference to $S\#$ (or $SP.S\#$) in the outer block (first line). The question arises, how then *can* we reference the outer $S\#$ in the inner block, since the same table is involved in both blocks? The answer is that we introduce a synonym for SP in the outer block and use that as a qualifier, as Example 7.2.10 illustrates.

7.2.10 Retrieval using a synonym. Get part numbers for all parts supplied by more than one supplier. (A simpler solution to this problem is given later as Example 7.4.7.)

```
SELECT UNIQUE P#
FROM    SP SPX
WHERE   P# IN
            SELECT P#
            FROM   SP
            WHERE  S#¬=SPX.S#
```

SPX is an arbitrary label used to link the reference SPX.S# in the inner block to the table of the outer block. The operation of the query may be explained as follows: "For each row in turn, say SPX, of table SP, extract the P# value if that P# value is in the set of P# values whose corresponding S# value is *not* that in row SPX—i.e., if that part is supplied by some supplier distinct from that identified by row SPX."

7.2.11 Retrieval from more than one table. For each part supplied, get part number and names of all cities supplying the part. (Example 5.3.14)

```
SELECT UNIQUE P#,CITY
FROM    SP,S
WHERE   SP.S#=S.S#
```

This example illustrates the SEQUEL analogue of a join operation. The user may name several tables in the FROM clause, and may use the table-names as qualifiers in the SELECT and WHERE clauses to resolve ambiguities (if necessary). If the same table appears more than once in the list, the user may invent labels (as in Example 7.2.10) to distinguish between the different appearances, and use these labels as qualifiers where necessary.

7.2.12 Retrieval involving set comparison. Get supplier names for suppliers who supply all parts. (Example 5.3.17)

```
SELECT SNAME
FROM    S
WHERE  (SELECT P#
            FROM   SP
            WHERE  S#=S.S#)
        =
       (SELECT P#
            FROM   P)
```

We are requesting supplier names such that the set of parts they supply (the result of the first inner mapping) is equal to the set of all parts (the result of the second inner mapping). The operator = here is the set equality operator. SEQUEL also permits the operators ¬ = (set inequality), IN and NOT IN for set inclusion and noninclusion, and CONTAINS and DOES NOT CONTAIN for set containment and noncontainment. The predicate A IN B, where A and B are sets, is true if and only if every element *a* of A is also in B; the other operators have analogous definitions. Example 7.2.13 illustrates the CONTAINS operator.

We observe that this query involved a universal quantifier in DSL ALPHA.

7.2.13   Retrieval involving set comparison.   Get supplier numbers for suppliers who supply at least all those parts supplied by supplier S2. (Example 5.3.19)

```
SELECT UNIQUE S#
FROM   SP SPX
WHERE (SELECT P#
          FROM   SP
          WHERE  S#=SPX.S#)
       CONTAINS
       (SELECT P#
          FROM   SP
          WHERE  S#='S2')
```

7.2.14   Retrieval involving GROUP BY, HAVING, and SET.   Get supplier numbers for suppliers who supply at least all those parts supplied by supplier S2 (the same as Example 7.2.13).

```
SELECT S#
FROM   SP
GROUP  BY S#
HAVING SET(P#) CONTAINS
          (SELECT P#
             FROM   SP
             WHERE  S#='S2')
```

Whenever a WHERE clause involves reference to the set of all values from one column corresponding to a given value in another column—as in the first inner mapping in Example 7.2.13—we can simplify the query by means of the GROUP BY operator, the HAVING clause, and the special library function SET. First, the effect of GROUP BY is to partition the table concerned into groups, such that within any one group all rows have the same value within the indicated column(s). Second, the HAVING clause is in effect a special form of WHERE clause applying to groups rather than to individual rows: The predicate in a HAVING clause always refers (via special library functions such as SET) to properties of groups rather than rows, and entire groups are selected or discarded on the basis of this predicate. Third, the value of a SET function reference is the set of values occurring in the specified column(s) within a given group. Thus, in the example under consideration, the query is evaluated as follows. First, table SP is partitioned into groups, such that each group consists of all rows having a particular S# value. Then, for each group in turn, the set of all P# values in the group is compared with the set of all P# values corresponding to supplier S2. When the first of these two sets contains the second as a subset (including, of course, the special case when the two sets are equal), the corresponding S# value is extracted. Note that the need for the label SPX has disappeared, and that UNIQUE is no longer necessary.

7.2.15   Retrieval involving MINUS.   Get supplier numbers for suppliers not currently supplying any parts.

```
(SELECT S#
  FROM    S)
  MINUS
(SELECT S#
  FROM    SP)
```

MINUS is the set difference operator (see Chapter 6). SEQUEL also provides UNION and INTERSECT. Duplicates are automatically eliminated from both operands before these operators are applied; hence there is no need for UNIQUE in the second mapping of this query.

7.2.16   Retrieval involving a set of constants.   Get supplier numbers for suppliers who supply both part P1 and part P2.

```
SELECT UNIQUE S#
FROM    SP
GROUP   BY S#
HAVING SET(P#) CONTAINS ('P1','P2')
```

The reader should be able to provide at least two more solutions to this problem, using the operators already introduced (one solution will involve AND, the other INTERSECT).

7.2.17 Retrieval involving an enumerated tuple. Get supplier numbers for suppliers having the same status and city as supplier S1.

```
SELECT S#
FROM   S
WHERE  <STATUS,CITY> IN
       SELECT STATUS,CITY
       FROM   S
       WHERE  S#='S1'
```

7.3 STORAGE OPERATIONS

7.3.1 Simple update. Change the color of part P2 to yellow. (Example 5.4.1)

```
UPDATE P
SET    COLOR='YELLOW'
WHERE  P#='P2'
```

Unlike DSL ALPHA, SEQUEL does not provide a <u>HOLD</u> statement; rather, the selection and replacement functions are combined into a single operation, UPDATE. Neither does SEQUEL have any special prohibition against updating the primary key (cf. Example 5.4.6). However, SEQUEL does resemble DSL ALPHA in that all three storage operations (UPDATE, INSERT, DELETE) are restricted to operating on a single table at a time.

7.3.2 Multiple-table update. Suppose that table P includes an extra column QOH (quantity on hand). Supplier S1 is now supplying 10 more of part P1 than before; add 10 to the quantity on hand for P1 and to the quantity of P1 supplied by S1. (Example 5.4.2)

```
UPDATE P
SET    QOH=QOH+10
WHERE  P#='P1'

UPDATE SP
SET    QTY=QTY+10
WHERE  S#='S1' AND P#='P1'
```

7.3.3 Insertion. Add part P7 (name 'WASHER', color 'GREY', weight 2, city 'ATHENS') to table P. (Example 5.4.3)

```
INSERT INTO P:
       <'P7','WASHER','GREY',2,'ATHENS'>
```

INSERT may be used to insert a single row, as here; or a set of any number of rows specified as a list of tuples enclosed in parentheses; or, more generally, a set of rows resulting from an inner query, as in Example 7.3.4.

7.3.4 Insertion.   Table W contains a set of rows concerning parts (in the same format as the rows of table P). Copy all rows for red parts into table P.

```
INSERT  INTO P:
        SELECT   *
        FROM     W
        WHERE    COLOR='RED'
```

7.3.5 Deletion.   Delete supplier S1. (Example 5.4.5)

```
DELETE S
WHERE   S#='S1'
```

7.3.6 Unqualified deletion.   Delete all parts. (Example 5.4.7)

```
DELETE P
```

Table P still exists but is now empty.

7.4 LIBRARY FUNCTIONS

Like DSL ALPHA, SEQUEL includes an open-ended list of library functions. Those currently defined are COUNT, SUM (the SEQUEL analogue of the ALPHA function TOTAL), AVG (average), MAX, MIN, and SET; of these, SET (see Examples 7.2.14 and 7.2.16) may only be used in a predicate, while the others may be used both in predicates and also in SELECT clauses, as the examples below illustrate.

7.4.1 Function in the SELECT clause.   Get the total number of suppliers. (Example 5.5.1)

```
SELECT COUNT(S#)
FROM    S
```

or

```
SELECT COUNT(*)
FROM    S
```

7.4.2   Function in the SELECT clause.   Get the total number of suppliers currently supplying parts. (Example 5.5.2)

```
SELECT COUNT(UNIQUE S#)
FROM   SP
```

7.4.3   Function in the SELECT clause, with a predicate.   Get the number of suppliers who supply part P2. (Example 5.5.4)

```
SELECT COUNT(S#)
FROM   SP
WHERE  P#='P2'
```

7.4.4   Function in the SELECT clause, with a predicate.   Get the total quantity of part P2 supplied. (Example 5.5.5)

```
SELECT SUM(QTY)
FROM   SP
WHERE  P#='P2'
```

Duplicate QTY values are not automatically eliminated before SUM is applied (contrast Example 7.4.2).

7.4.5   Function in the predicate.   Get the supplier numbers of all suppliers such that no other supplier has a higher status. (Example 5.5.6)

```
SELECT S#
FROM   S
WHERE  STATUS=
           SELECT MAX(STATUS)
           FROM   S
```

7.4.6   Function in the SELECT clause, with GROUP BY.   For each part supplied, get the part number and a count of the number of suppliers who supply that part. (Example 5.5.7)

```
SELECT P#,COUNT(S#)
FROM   SP
GROUP  BY P#
```

Here the GROUP BY operator partitions table SP by $P\#$, and the SELECT then retrieves the unique $P\#$ value and a count of all corresponding $S\#$ values for each partition in turn. In general, when GROUP

BY is used, each item in the SELECT clause must be a unique property of a whole group rather than of an individual row. Note that the use of GROUP BY enables us to use the same library functions as both "simple" and "image" functions, to use DSL ALPHA terminology.

7.4.7 Function in the predicate, with GROUP BY. Get part numbers for all parts supplied by more than one supplier (the same as Example 7.2.10).

```
SELECT P#
FROM   SP
GROUP  BY P#
HAVING COUNT(S#)>1
```

7.5 SUMMARY

We have surveyed the retrieval and storage operations of SEQUEL. A more complete treatment of these and other aspects of the language will be found in [7.2 and 7.6]. We shall return to SEQUEL later in this book to examine some of these additional aspects when we discuss such topics as security, integrity, and the external model. In the meantime the reader may care to review the list of advantages claimed for the calculus and algebra at the end of Chapters 5 and 6 and to decide how SEQUEL measures up to the two earlier languages in these respects.

EXERCISES

7.1 SEQUEL is a relationally complete language. Try to convince yourself that this is so by giving a SEQUEL equivalent of each of the algebraic operators introduced in Chapter 6. (Such a demonstration will not constitute a proof, since Chapter 6 did not deal with all the operators in their most general form, but it will give an idea of what such a proof would be like.)

7.2 Give SEQUEL solutions to the exercises in Chapter 5. (The third question cannot be handled in SEQUEL as there is no analogue of DSL ALPHA's "quota." Also, ignore question 31: A row-at-a-time language is more suitable than SEQUEL for such a problem. Note, however, that the SEQUEL interface to System R does include a set of row-at-a-time operations; see [7.6] and [7.7] for details.)

REFERENCES AND BIBLIOGRAPHY

7.1 R. F. Boyce, D. D. Chamberlin, W. F. King III, and M. M. Hammer. "Specifying Queries as Relational Expressions: SQUARE." Versions of this paper have appeared in *Proc. ACM SIGPLAN/SIGIR Interface Meeting on Programming Languages and Information Retrieval* (November 1973), available from ACM; *Proc. IFIP TC-2 Working Conference on Data Base Management Systems* (eds., Klimbie and Koffeman) (North-Holland, 1974); and *CACM* **18,** No. 11 (November 1975).

7.2 D. D. Chamberlin and R. F. Boyce. "SEQUEL: A Structured English Query Language." *Proc. 1974 ACM SIGMOD Workshop on Data Description, Access and Control.* Available from ACM.

7.3 M. M. Astrahan and R. A. Lorie. "SEQUEL-XRM, a Relational System." *Proc. ACM Pacific Conference, San Francisco* (April 1975). Available from Mail Room, Boole and Babbage Inc., 850 Stewart Drive, Sunnyvale CA 94086.

7.4 M. M. Astrahan and D. D. Chamberlin. "Implementation of a Structured English Query Language." *CACM* **18,** No. 10 (October 1975).

7.5 P. Reisner, R. F. Boyce, and D. D. Chamberlin. "Human Factors Evaluation of Two Data Base Query Languages—SQUARE and SEQUEL." *Proc. NCC* **44** (May 1975).

7.6 M. M. Astrahan, M. W. Blasgen, D. D. Chamberlin, K. P. Eswaran, J. N. Gray, P. P. Griffiths, W. F. King, R. A. Lorie, P. R. McJones, J. W. Mehl, G. R. Putzolu, I. L. Traiger, B. W. Wade, and V. Watson. "System R: A Relational Approach to Data Base Management." *ACM Transactions on Database Systems* **1,** No. 2 (June 1976).

7.7 D. D. Chamberlin, M. M. Astrahan, K. P. Eswaran, P. P. Griffiths, R. A. Lorie, J. W. Mehl, P. Reisner, and B. W. Wade. "SEQUEL 2: A Unified Approach to Data Definition, Manipulation, and Control." *IBM J. R&D* **20,** No. 6 (November 1976).

8

Query
By Example

8.1 INTRODUCTION

In this chapter we examine yet another relational language, namely, Query By Example (developed by M. M. Zloof at the IBM Yorktown Heights Research Laboratory). Query By Example resembles SEQUEL in that in its original form it provided query facilities only, whereas in later versions storage operations and many other features have been included [8.1 and 8.2]. The general level of the language resembles that of SEQUEL, although as we shall see in Section 8.3 there are certain query operations available in Query By Example that have no counterpart in SEQUEL, or indeed in any other language (so far as the author is aware). A more immediately obvious difference between SEQUEL and Query By Example is that the latter has been primarily designed for use with a visual display terminal. Each operation in Query By Example is specified using one or more tables; each such table is built up on the display screen, with some parts being supplied by the system and others by the user. (We shall examine this process in slightly more detail in Section 8.2.) Since operations are specified in tabular form, we say that Query By Example has a two-dimensional syntax. Most traditional computer languages, by contrast, have a linear syntax.[1]

Like SEQUEL, Query By Example has undergone a certain amount of usability testing, with very encouraging results [8.5].

---

[1] A linear version of Query By Example has also been defined [8.4], but the linear syntax is not nearly so appealing as the two-dimensional form.

8.2   RETRIEVAL OPERATIONS

The really significant feature of Query By Example is its use of *examples* in the specification of queries (and also in all other operations, although for the time being we concentrate on retrieval). The basic idea is that the user formulates the query by entering an example of a possible answer in the appropriate place in an empty table. For example, consider the query "Get supplier numbers for suppliers in Paris." Initially the system will display a totally blank table to the user. The user, knowing that the answer to the query is in table S, will enter S as the table-name; the system will then respond by filling in the corresponding column-names. Now the user can express the query by making entries in two positions in this table, as follows.

S	S#	SNAME	STATUS	CITY
	P.S7			PARIS

The "P." stands for "print"; it indicates the target of the query, i.e., the values that are to appear in the result. S7 is an "example element," i.e., an example of a possible answer to the query; example elements are indicated by underlining. PARIS (not underlined) is a "constant element." The query may be paraphrased: "Print all S# values such as S7 (say) where the corresponding city is Paris." Note that S7 need not actually appear in the resulting set, or even in the original set; the example element is completely arbitrary, and we could have equally well used PIG, 7, or X without changing the meaning of the query.

Later we shall see that example elements are used to establish connections between rows in more complicated queries. If no connections are necessary, as in the simple query above, it is possible to omit example elements entirely (so that "P.S7" would reduce to just "P."), but for clarity we shall generally include them.

8.2.1   Simple retrieval.   Get part numbers for all parts supplied. (Example 7.2.1)

SP	S#	P#	QTY
		P.PX	

The user may specify ascending or descending ordering for the result, if desired; for details see [8.6]. Redundant duplicate values are always eliminated.

8.2.2   Simple retrieval.   Get full details of all suppliers. (Example 7.2.2)

S	S#	SNAME	STATUS	CITY
	P.SX	P.SN	P.ST	P.SC

The following is a shorthand representation of the same query.

S	S#	SNAME	STATUS	CITY
P.				

Here the print operator is applied to the entire row.

8.2.3 Qualified retrieval. Get supplier numbers for suppliers in Paris with status > 20. (Example 7.2.3)

S	S#	SNAME	STATUS	CITY
	P.SX		> 20	PARIS

Observe how the condition "status > 20" is specified. In general, any of the comparison operators =, ≠, <, ≤, >, ≥ can be used in this way (except that = is normally omitted, as in the CITY column above).

8.2.4 Qualified retrieval. Get supplier numbers for suppliers who are located in Paris or have status > 20 (or both).

S	S#	SNAME	STATUS	CITY
	P.SX			PARIS
	P.SY		> 20	

Conditions specified within a single row are considered to be "ANDed" together. To "OR" two conditions, therefore, it is necessary to specify them in separate rows. The query above is effectively asking for the *union* of all supplier numbers SX for suppliers in Paris and all supplier numbers SY with status > 20. Two different example elements are needed, because if we had used the same one twice it would have meant that the *same* supplier had to be in Paris and to have status > 20.

When a query involves more than one row, as in the present example, they may be entered in any order.

8.2.5 Qualified retrieval. Get supplier numbers for suppliers who supply both part P1 and part P2. (Example 7.2.16)

SP	S#	P#	QTY
	P.SX	P1	
	SX	P2	

Here the same example element *must* be used twice; we need two rows to express the query because we need to "AND" together two conditions on the same column.

8.2.6 Retrieval using a link. Get supplier names for suppliers who supply part P2. (Example 7.2.5)

S	S#	SNAME	STATUS	CITY
	SX	P.SN		

SP	S#	P#	QTY
	SX	P2	

The example element SX is used as a link between S and SP. Generally speaking, such links are used in Query By Example where SEQUEL would require a nested mapping, DSL ALPHA an existential quantifier, and the algebra a JOIN. (As a matter of fact, SX in the previous example was also acting as a link, but the rows being linked were in the same table.)

8.2.7 Retrieval using links. Get supplier names for suppliers who supply at least one red part. (Example 7.2.7)

S	S#	SNAME	STATUS	CITY
	SX	P.SN		

SP	S#	P#	QTY
	SX	PX	

P	P#	PNAME	COLOR	WEIGHT	CITY
	PX		RED		

8.2.8 Retrieval using negation. Get supplier names for suppliers who do not supply part P2. (Example 7.2.8)

S	S#	SNAME	STATUS	CITY
	SX	P.SN		

SP	S#	P#	QTY
¬	SX	P2	

Notice the NOT operator (¬) against the query row in table SP. The query may be paraphrased: "Print supplier names for suppliers SX such that it is not the case that SX supplies part P2."

8.2.9 Retrieval using a link within a single table. Get supplier numbers for suppliers who supply at least one part supplied by supplier S2. (Example 7.2.9; compare also Example 8.2.5)

SP	S#	P#	QTY
	P.SX	PX	
	S2	PX	

8.2.10   Retrieval using a link within a single table. Get part numbers for all parts supplied by more than one supplier. (Example 7.2.10)

SP	S#	P#	QTY
	SX	P.PX	
	≠ SX	PX	

This query may be paraphrased: "Print part numbers PX such that PX is supplied by some supplier SX and also by some supplier distinct from SX." The ≠ symbol may alternatively be written as ¬ = or simply as ¬.

8.2.11   Retrieval from more than one table. For each part supplied, get part number and names of all cities supplying the part. (Example 7.2.11)

The result of this query is not a projection of an existing table; rather, it is a projection of a join of two existing tables. In order to formulate such a query in Query By Example, the user must first create a skeleton table the same shape as the expected result (i.e., with the appropriate number of columns). This table and its columns may be given any names that the user desires—they may even be left blank. The user can then express the query using the "result" table and the two existing tables, as follows.

S	S#	SNAME	STATUS	CITY
	SX			SC

SP	S#	P#	QTY
	SX	PX	

RESULT	P#	CITY
	P.PX	P.SC

8.2.12   Retrieval involving ALL. Get supplier numbers for suppliers who supply all parts. (Example 5.3.18)

SP	S#	P#	QTY
	P.SX	ALL.PX	

P	P#	PNAME	COLOR	WEIGHT	CITY
	ALL.PX				

The expression ALL.PX in table P refers to the set of all part numbers present in this table. The expression ALL.PX in table SP refers to the set of all part numbers supplied by the supplier SX. Since the two expressions are identical, SX must be a supplier who supplies all parts.

Incidentally, if a column is too narrow for the expression—say, ALL.PX—that the user wants to enter, the system allows the user to increase the column width first. In this way each row of the query may genuinely be contained within a single line on the screen.

8.2.13 Retrieval involving ALL. Get supplier numbers for suppliers who supply at least all those parts supplied by supplier S2. (Example 7.2.13)

SP	S#	P#	QTY
	P.$\underline{SX}$	$\begin{bmatrix} \text{ALL.}\underline{PX} \\ \cdot \end{bmatrix}$	
	S2	ALL.$\underline{PX}$	

The expression ALL.$\underline{PX}$ in the second row of this query represents the set of all part numbers supplied by supplier S2. The first row means that we are looking for suppliers such as $\underline{SX}$ who supply ALL.$\underline{PX}$ and possibly more. (The dot indicates that $\underline{SX}$ may additionally supply some part not in the set ALL.$\underline{PX}$.) The square brackets serve merely to group the dot with ALL.$\underline{PX}$ in the first row.

8.2.14 Retrieval using a condition box. As Example 8.2.13, but eliminate supplier number S2 from the result.

SP	S#	P#	QTY
	P.$\underline{SX}$	$\begin{bmatrix} \text{ALL.}\underline{PX} \\ \cdot \end{bmatrix}$	
	S2	ALL.$\underline{PX}$	

Condition box
$\underline{SX} \neq S2$

Occasionally it is difficult to express some desired condition within the framework of the query table(s). In such a situation, Query By Example allows the user to enter the condition in a separate "condition box," as the foregoing example illustrates. In this particular case, however, the required result could be achieved *without* the use of a condition box by simply replacing P.$\underline{SX}$ in the original query (Example 8.2.13) by P.¬S2 (no underline).

8.2.15 Retrieval using negation. Get the supplier numbers of all suppliers such that no other supplier has a higher status. (Example 7.4.5)

S	S#	SNAME	STATUS	CITY
	P.$\underline{SX}$		$\underline{ST}$	
¬			$> \underline{ST}$	

The second row of this query may be read: "There does not exist a row in the table S with status $> \underline{ST}$."

8.3 RETRIEVAL OPERATIONS ON TREE-STRUCTURED RELATIONS

Consider the relation RS (reporting structure) shown in Fig. 8.1. This relation has two attributes, EMP# and MGR#, both drawn from an underlying domain of employee numbers. The meaning of a given tuple of RS is that the indicated employee (EMP#) works for the indicated manager (MGR#).

RS

MGR#	EMP#
E 1	E 6
E 1	E 7
E 1	E 8
E 6	E 18
E 8	E 15
E 8	E 16
E 15	E 20
E 15	E 24
E 24	E 32

Fig. 8.1 The reporting structure relation RS

We assume that the reporting structure represented by relation RS satisfies the following constraints (at all times).

1. No employee is his or her own manager.
2. No employee has more than one immediate manager.
3. If EX (for example) is the immediate manager of EY, then EY cannot be the manager at any level of EX.

The reader will observe that the sample tabulation of Fig. 8.1 does satisfy these constraints. Because of this fact we may represent the relation as a tree structure, as Fig. 8.2 illustrates.

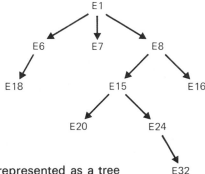

Fig. 8.2 Relation RS represented as a tree

We shall refer to a relation possessing two attributes defined on a common domain and satisfying constraints analogous to those above as a *tree-structured relation.* In Query By Example the user is able to formulate certain queries on a tree-structured relation that less powerful languages such as the relational algebra are unable to express. Let us consider some examples.

8.3.1   Retrieval going down one level.   Get employee numbers for employees reporting to employee E8 at the first level.

RS	MGR#	EMP#
	E8	P.EX

By "at the first level" we mean that E8 is the immediate manager of the employees we want. The answer to the query is employees E15 and E16. This example is straightforward and does not illustrate any new points.

8.3.2   Retrieval going down two levels.   Get employee numbers for employees reporting to employee E8 at the second level.

RS	MGR#	EMP#
	E8	EY
	EY	P.EX

Again the solution is straightforward—but observe that we have had to introduce a link, EY, and have had to enter the link into the table twice. In general, if we wanted to go down n levels in the tree, we would have to enter each of $n - 1$ links twice, a rather tedious process. Accordingly, Query By Example provides a convenient shorthand, which is illustrated in the following alternative formulation of the above query.

RS	MGR#	EMP#
	E8	P.EX(2L)

The "(2L)" stands for "second level." In general, a level entry may consist of any integer followed by the letter L, the whole enclosed in parentheses. Whenever a level entry is used, Query By Example includes relative levels in the tabulated result, for example, as follows.

EMP#
E20(2L)
E24(2L)

8.3.3 Retrieval going up two levels. Get the employee number of the manager two levels above employee E20.

RS	MGR#	EMP#
	P.MX(2L)	E20

Here the level entry appears in the MGR# column. In general, the direction of search (up or down the tree) is indicated by the column in which the level entry appears. In certain situations this rule could lead to an ambiguity, however [8.3]; to avoid this problem, Query By Example imposes the restriction that not more than two entries may appear in any given row in the formulation of a query involving levels.

8.3.4 Retrieval going down to all levels. Get employee numbers for employees reporting to employee E8 at *any* level.

RS	MGR#	EMP#
	E8	P.EX(6L)

Result:

EMP#
E15(1L)
E20(2L)
E24(2L)
E32(3L)
E16(1L)

This is an example of a query that cannot be expressed in the relational algebra or languages of equivalent power. Notice the underline in the level entry.

8.3.5 Retrieval going down to lowest level. Get employee numbers for employees reporting to employee E8 at the *lowest* level.

RS	MGR#	EMP#
	E8	P.EX(MAX.6L)

MAX is a library function (see Section 8.5). The meaning of this query is: "Get employee numbers for employees whose relative level below E8 is greatest." The result is the single employee E32(3L).

8.3.6 Retrieval going down to terminal levels. Get employee numbers for employees reporting to employee E8 who do not have anyone reporting to them.

RS	MGR#	EMP#
	E8	P.<u>EX</u>(LAST.L)

We are looking for employees at terminal nodes of the tree below E8. Since these employees will be at different relative levels, in general, we cannot enter either a constant integer or an example integer (a constant would mean a fixed level, while an example would mean all levels); therefore, Query By Example provides the special library function LAST.

8.3.7 Retrieval of level. At what level is employee E20 below employee E1?

RS	MGR#	EMP#
	E1	P.E20(<u>7</u>L)

Result:

EMP#
E20(3L)

8.4 STORAGE OPERATIONS

8.4.1 Simple update. Change the color of all red parts to yellow.

P	P#	PNAME	COLOR	WEIGHT	CITY
	<u>P2</u>		RED		
UPDATE.	<u>P2</u>		YELLOW		

To update a row or set of rows, the user enters an expression representing the old data and a corresponding expression representing the new data (in general). The word UPDATE indicates which of the two is the "new" one. In the example above, therefore, the first line indicates that any row, say that for part <u>P2</u>, having the value red for COLOR is to be changed to have the value yellow instead. Note that both old and new rows must have an entry in the primary key position. Primary key values may not be changed.

Some updates can be specified by means of a single expression (row). For example, to set the color of part P2 to yellow, regardless of its previous value (Example 7.3.1), the user need enter just the "new" row of the two above (*without* the underline on P2).

8.4.2 Multiple-table update. Suppose that table P includes an extra column QOH (quantity on hand). Supplier S1 is now supplying 10 more of part P1 than before; add 10 to the quantity on hand for P1 and to the quantity of P1 supplied by S1. (Example 7.3.2)

P	P#	PNAME	COLOR	WEIGHT	CITY	QOH
	P1					$\underline{N}$
UPDATE.	P1					$\underline{N}$ + 10

SP	S#	P#	QTY
	S1	P1	$\underline{Q}$
UPDATE.	S1	P1	$\underline{Q}$ + 10

8.4.3 Insertion. Add part P7 (name 'WASHER', color 'GREY', weight 2, city 'ATHENS') to table P. (Example 7.3.3)

P	P#	PNAME	COLOR	WEIGHT	CITY
INSERT.	P7	WASHER	GREY	2	ATHENS

8.4.4 Insertion. Table W contains a set of rows concerning parts (in the same format as the rows of table P). Copy all rows for red parts into table P. (Example 7.3.4)

W	P#	PNAME	COLOR	WEIGHT	CITY
	$\underline{PX}$	$\underline{PN}$	RED	$\underline{PW}$	$\underline{PC}$

P	P#	PNAME	COLOR	WEIGHT	CITY
INSERT.	$\underline{PX}$	$\underline{PN}$	RED	$\underline{PW}$	$\underline{PC}$

All entries except $\underline{PX}$ could be omitted from the INSERT row if desired.

8.4.5 Deletion. Delete supplier S1. (Example 7.3.5)

S	S#	SNAME	STATUS	CITY
DELETE.	S1			

8.4.6 Unqualified deletion. Delete all parts. (Example 5.4.7).

P	P#	PNAME	COLOR	WEIGHT	CITY
DELETE.	PX				

As with UPDATE, the user must always specify at least a primary key value for rows to be deleted.

8.5 LIBRARY FUNCTIONS

8.5.1 Simple retrieval using a function. Get the total number of suppliers. (Example 7.4.1)

S	S#	SNAME	STATUS	CITY
	P.COUNT.ALL. SX			

8.5.2 Simple retrieval using a function. Get the total number of suppliers currently supplying parts. (Example 7.4.2)

SP	S#	P#	QTY
	P.COUNT.U.ALL.SX		

"U." stands for "unique" (ALL does not automatically eliminate redundant duplicates).

8.5.3 Qualified retrieval using a function. Get the total number of suppliers who supply part P2. (Example 7.4.3)

SP	S#	P#	QTY
	P.COUNT.ALL.SX	P2	

8.5.4 Qualified retrieval using a function. Get the total quantity of part P2 supplied. (Example 7.4.4)

SP	S#	P#	QTY
		P2	P.SUM.ALL.Q

8.5.5   Retrieval with grouping.   For each part supplied, get the part number and a count of the number of suppliers who supply that part. (Example 7.4.6)

SP	S#	P#	QTY
	P.COUNT.ALL.<u>SX</u>	P.<u>PX</u>	

Note that an explicit grouping operator is not required—the ALL operator automatically gives the desired effect, since in this query (for instance) the expression ALL.SX means the set of all supplier numbers matching <u>PX</u> (see Example 8.2.12).

8.5.6   Qualified retrieval using a function and a condition box.   Get part numbers for all parts supplied by more than one supplier (the same as Example 8.2.10).

SP	S#	P#	QTY		Condition box
	ALL.<u>SX</u>	P.<u>PX</u>			COUNT.ALL.<u>SX</u> > 1

8.6   RETRIEVAL OPERATIONS ON THE DICTIONARY

Recall from Chapter 1 that the dictionary is a special database containing "data about data"—that is, *descriptions* of other entities in the system (sometimes called "metadata"). In a relational system the entities to be described are of course relations, domains, and so forth. If these descriptions themselves are presented to the user in the form of relations—in other words, if the user views the dictionary itself as a collection of relations—then the same data sublanguage may be used for manipulating the dictionary as is used for dealing with any other database, a very convenient simplification.

    To illustrate this point we first consider the System R implementation of SEQUEL [7.6]. The System R dictionary *is* represented to the user as a collection of relations; we mention only two of these relations here, namely, CATALOG and COLUMNS. CATALOG contains a row for each relation defined to the system, giving TNAME (table-name—this is the key), CREATOR (identification of the creator of this table), NCOLS (number of columns in this table), and other information. COLUMNS contains a row for every column of every relation defined to the system, giving TNAME and CNAME (table-name and column-name—this combination is the key), TYPE (data type for this column, e.g., character or numeric), LENGTH (number of characters or digits), and other information.

The user of System R, then, can use SEQUEL to interrogate these dictionary relations. For example, the query

```
SELECT TNAME
FROM    COLUMNS
WHERE   CNAME='S#'
```

will result in a list of table-names for all tables having a column called S#. Similarly, the query

```
SELECT CNAME
FROM    COLUMNS
WHERE   TNAME='S'
```

will give a list of all column-names for table S. Hence a user who wishes to retrieve information concerning suppliers but who initially knows only that suppliers are identified by an attribute called S# could use the two queries above as preliminaries to some final "genuine" query, say,

```
SELECT S#, STATUS, CITY
FROM    S
```

Now we return to Query By Example. In Query By Example the foregoing ideas have been taken a little further, in that the notion of querying the dictionary has actually been built into the language. The first SEQUEL query above, for instance, would be represented in Query By Example as follows.

8.6.1   Retrieval of table-name given a column-name.   Get names of all tables having a column called S#.

P.	S#		

The user formulates this query by calling for a blank table and entering the "P." in the table-name position and the constant element (S#) in a column-name position.

Result:

In general, a query such as the one above could request names of tables having any number of specified column-names (and the order in which the column-names are specified is entirely immaterial).

The second SEQUEL example above was "Get all column-names for a specified table." We have tacitly been using the Query By Example counterpart to this operation throughout this chapter; as explained in Section 8.2, as soon as the user enters a table-name into a blank table the system responds by filling in the corresponding column-names.

Our final Query By Example illustration does not have a SEQUEL equivalent.

8.6.2   Retrieval of table- and column-names given a column value.   Get names of all tables, with relevant column-names, in which the value "London" appears.

P.	P.		
	LONDON		

Result:

S	CITY		P	CITY

8.7   SUMMARY

Query By Example possesses a number of features that distinguish it from the other relational languages discussed in detail in this book. Among these features we may cite the use of examples in the specification of queries (and other operations), the availability of special operators for tree-structured relations and for interrogating the dictionary, the use of a simple two-dimensional syntax, and the orientation toward the use of display terminals. We will discuss certain additional aspects of Query By Example in later parts of the book.

We conclude this chapter by making special mention of the amount of *freedom* the Query By Example user enjoys—freedom, that is, to construct the query in whatever manner seems most natural. Specifically, the query may be built up in any *order* the user likes: The order of rows within a query table is entirely immaterial, and moreover the order in which the user fills in all the entries constituting these rows is also completely arbitrary. Take Example 8.2.7, for instance ("Get supplier names for suppliers supplying red parts"). The user may think about this query as follows: "Pick out red parts, then pick out numbers of suppliers supplying these parts, then pick out the corresponding names"—in which case he or she will probably complete the query tables in the order P, SP, S. Alternatively, the user may think about it as: "Pick out supplier names such that the corresponding suppliers supply a part that is red"—in which case he or she will probably fill in the tables in the order S, SP, P. Either way the final query is the same. In other words, Query By Example is a highly nonprocedural language that is capable of supporting several different ways of thinking about a problem; it does not force the user's thought processes into a possibly unnatural mold.

EXERCISES

Give Query By Example solutions to the exercises in Chapter 5.

REFERENCES AND BIBLIOGRAPHY

[8.1] introduces retrieval operations. [8.2] covers storage operations, retrieval operations on the dictionary, and the definition of tables and integrity constraints; we shall discuss the last of these topics in Part 5 of this book. [8.3] describes the special retrieval operations for tree-structured relations. [8.4] introduces a form of Query By Example for use on a hierarchical data model, and also describes a possible linear syntax.

8.1 M. M. Zloof. "Query By Example." *Proc. NCC* **44** (May 1975).

8.2 M. M. Zloof. "Query By Example: The Invocation and Definition of Tables and Forms." *Proc. International Conference on Very Large Data Bases* (September 1975). Available from ACM.

8.3 M. M. Zloof. "Query By Example: Operations on the Transitive Closure." IBM Research Report RC 5526 (July 1975).

8.4 M. M. Zloof. "Query By Example: Operations on Hierarchical Data Bases." IBM Research Report RC 5491 (June 1975).

8.5 J. C. Thomas and J. D. Gould. "A Psychological Study of Query By Example." *Proc. NCC* **44** (May 1975).

8.6 M. M. Zloof. "Query By Example: A Data Base Management Language." IBM Research Report (forthcoming).

9
Further
Normalization

9.1 INTRODUCTION

For reasons dealt with in Section 4.4 we permit only normalized relations
in the relational model. A normalized relation is one for which each of
the underlying domains contains atomic (nondecomposable) values only,
so that every value in the relation is in turn atomic. In Section 4.4 we
showed by example how an unnormalized relation may be reduced to an
equivalent normalized form. In this chapter we shall investigate the
concept of normalization in more detail; in particular, we shall show that
a given relation, even if it is normalized, may still possess certain
undesirable properties, and we shall indicate how to reduce such a
relation to a more desirable form.

  Codd, in [9.1], originally defined three *levels* of normalization, which
he called first, second, and third normal form, respectively. Briefly, all
normalized relations are in first normal form (1NF); some 1NF relations
are also in second normal form (2NF); and some 2NF relations are also in
third normal form (3NF). Subsequently, Fagin [9.17] defined a fourth
normal form (4NF), with the property that some 3NF relations are also in
4NF. See Fig. 9.1. The "more desirable form" mentioned in the previous
paragraph is *fourth* normal form; thus the objectives of this chapter are to
demonstrate the advantages of 4NF and to show how to convert a
non-4NF relation into an equivalent collection of 4NF relations. The
reader is warned that we shall make little attempt at rigor in our
arguments and definitions; rather, we shall rely to a considerable extent
on plain intuition. Indeed, part of the argument is that fourth normal
form, despite its somewhat esoteric name, is essentially a very simple and

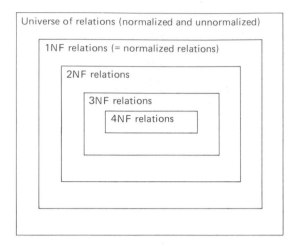

Fig. 9.1   Levels of normalization

common-sense idea. Many of the references treat the material in a more rigorous manner.

9.2   FUNCTIONAL DEPENDENCE

We begin by introducing the notion of functional dependence (within a relation)—a concept of absolutely paramount importance, most especially for the DBA in his work of data model design. Given a relation R, we say that attribute Y of R is functionally dependent on attribute X of R if and only if each X-value in R has associated with it precisely one Y-value in R (at any one time). Note that the same X-value may appear in many different tuples of R; if Y is functionally dependent on X, the definition tells us that every one of these tuples must contain the same Y-value. In the relation S of our suppliers-and-parts data model, for example, attributes SNAME, STATUS, and CITY are each functionally dependent on attribute S#: Given a particular S# value, there exists precisely one corresponding value for each of SNAME, STATUS, and CITY. We may represent these functional dependencies diagrammatically, as shown in Fig. 9.2.

Recognizing the functional dependencies is an essential part of understanding the meaning or semantics of the data. The fact that CITY is functionally dependent on S#, for example, means that each supplier is located in precisely one city. In other words, we have a constraint in the real world that the database represents, namely, that each supplier is

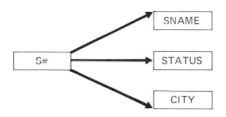

Fig. 9.2 Functional dependencies in the relation S

located in precisely one city. Since it is part of the semantics of the situation, this constraint must somehow be observed in the data model; the way to ensure that it is so observed is to specify the constraint in the data model definition (i.e., the conceptual schema), so that the DBMS can enforce it; and the way to specify it in the conceptual schema is to declare the functional dependency. Later we shall see that the concepts of further normalization lead to a simple means of declaring such functional dependencies.

The notion of functional dependence can be extended to cover the case where X or Y or both are *composite* attributes. For example, in the relation SP of our suppliers-and-parts data model, the attribute QTY is functionally dependent on the composite attribute (S#,P#): Given a particular combination of S# and P# values, there exists precisely one corresponding QTY value (assuming that the particular S#–P# combination occurs within SP). We may represent this situation as shown in Fig. 9.3.

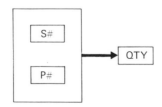

Fig. 9.3 Functional dependency in the relation SP

We also introduce the concept of *full* functional dependence. Attribute Y is fully functionally dependent on attribute X if it is functionally dependent on X and *not* functionally dependent on any subset of the attributes of X (X must be composite). For example, in the relation S, the attribute CITY is functionally dependent on the composite attribute

(S#,STATUS); however, it is not *fully* functionally dependent on this composite attribute because, of course, it is also functionally dependent on S# alone. Throughout this book we shall take "functional dependence" to mean full functional dependence unless explicitly stated otherwise.

All examples so far (in relations S and SP) have been of attributes functionally dependent on a primary key. The functional dependencies in relation P are also of this nature. This is not always so, however; the next section gives several counterexamples. [A relation in which this *is* so must be in at least third normal form, though not necessarily in fourth. (Relations S, P, and SP are in fact in fourth normal form.) But not all third normal form relations conform to this simple pattern, as we shall see.]

9.3   FIRST, SECOND, AND THIRD NORMAL FORMS

We are now in a position to describe the four normal forms. For reasons that will become clear later, we choose to deal only with the first three in the present section, leaving fourth normal form to Section 9.5. However, we present an initial, *very* intuitive, definition of fourth normal form here in order to give some idea of our ultimate objective. We then consider (in this section and the next two) the process of reducing an arbitrary relation to an equivalent collection of fourth normal form relations, giving somewhat more precise definitions of the four forms as we go.

- A relation R is said to be in fourth normal form (4NF) if and only if, for all time, each tuple of R consists of a primary key value that identifies some entity, together with a set of mutually independent attribute values that describe that entity in some way.[1]

For example, relation S is in 4NF: Each S tuple consists of an S# value, identifying some particular supplier, together with three pieces of descriptive information concerning that supplier—name, status, and location. Moreover, each of the three descriptive items is independent of the other two (two attributes are *mutually independent* if neither is functionally dependent on the other; again we allow the attributes to be composite). Relations P and SP are also in 4NF; the entities in these cases are parts and supplier-part shipments, respectively. In general, the entities

---

[1] For simplicity we assume throughout this section that each relation has a single candidate key. This assumption is reflected in our definitions, which (we repeat) are not totally rigorous. The case of a relation having two or more candidate keys will be discussed in Section 9.4.

identified by the primary key values are the fundamental entities about which data is recorded in the database (Section 1.1).

Now we turn to the reduction process. First we give a definition of first normal form.

■   A relation R is in *first normal form* (1NF) if and only if all underlying domains contain atomic values only.

This definition merely states that *any* normalized relation is in 1NF, which is of course correct. A relation that is only in first normal form (i.e., a 1NF relation that is not also in 2NF, and therefore not in 3NF or 4NF either) has a structure that is undesirable for a number of reasons. To illustrate the point, let us suppose that information concerning suppliers and shipments, rather than being split into two separate relations (S and SP), is lumped together into a single relation FIRST(S#,STATUS,CITY,P#,QTY). The attributes here have their usual meanings; however, for the sake of the example, we introduce an additional constraint, namely, that STATUS is functionally dependent on CITY. (The meaning of this constraint is that a supplier's status is determined by the corresponding location; e.g., all London suppliers *must* have a status of 20.) Also we ignore the attribute SNAME for simplicity. The primary key of FIRST is the combination (S#,P#). Figure 9.4 is the dependency diagram for this relation; note that the diagram is "more complex" than a 4NF diagram.

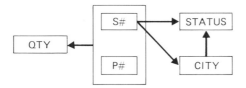

Fig. 9.4 Functional dependencies in the relation FIRST

We see from Fig. 9.4 that (a) STATUS and CITY are not fully functionally dependent on the primary key, and (b) STATUS and CITY are not mutually independent. It is these two conditions that make the diagram more complex than a 4NF diagram; and each of the two leads to problems. To illustrate some of the difficulties, we consider a sample tabulation of FIRST (Fig. 9.5). The data values shown are basically those of Fig. 4.7, except that the status of supplier S3 has been changed from 30 to 10 to be consistent with the new constraint that STATUS is dependent on CITY.

FIRST	S#	STATUS	CITY	P#	QTY
	S1	20	London	P1	300
	S1	20	London	P2	200
	S1	20	London	P3	400
	S1	20	London	P4	200
	S1	20	London	P5	100
	S1	20	London	P6	100
	S2	10	Paris	P1	300
	S2	10	Paris	P2	400
	S3	10	Paris	P2	200
	S4	20	London	P2	200
	S4	20	London	P4	300
	S4	20	London	P5	400

Fig. 9.5   Sample tabulation of FIRST

The relation FIRST suffers from anomalies with respect to storage operations that are very similar to those encountered in certain hierarchies (as described in Section 3.3). To fix our ideas we concentrate on the association between suppliers and cities—that is, on the functional dependency of CITY on S#. Problems occur with each of the three basic storage operations.

Inserting.   We cannot enter the fact that a particular supplier is located in a particular city until that supplier supplies at least one part. Indeed, the tabulation in Fig. 9.5 does not show that supplier S5 is located in Athens. The reason is that, until S5 supplies some part, we have no appropriate primary key value. (Remember from Section 4.3 that no component of a primary key value may be null; in relation FIRST, primary key values consist of a supplier number and a part number.)

Deleting.   If we delete the only FIRST tuple for a particular supplier, we destroy not only the shipment connecting that supplier to some part but also the information that the supplier is located in a particular city. For example, if we delete the FIRST tuple with S# value S3 and P# value P2, we lose the information that S3 is located in Paris. (As in Section 3.3, the insertion and deletion problems are really two sides of the same coin.)

Updating.   The city value for a given supplier appears in FIRST many times, in general. This redundancy causes update problems. For example, if supplier S1 moves from London to Amsterdam, we are faced with *either*

Fig. 9.6 Functional dependencies in the relations SECOND and SP

the problem of searching the FIRST relation to find every tuple connecting S1 and London (and changing it) *or* the possibility of producing an inconsistent result (the city for S1 may be given as Amsterdam in one place and London in another).

The solution to these problems is to replace the relation FIRST by the two relations SECOND(S#,STATUS,CITY) and SP(S#,P#,QTY). Figure 9.6 shows the dependency diagrams for these two relations; Fig. 9.7 shows sample tabulations corresponding to the data values of Fig. 9.5, except that information for supplier S5 has now been incorporated into relation SECOND (but not SP). Relation SP is now in fact exactly as given in Fig. 4.7.

It should be clear that this revised structure overcomes all the problems that we had with storage operations involving the S#–CITY association.

SECOND

S#	STATUS	CITY
S1	20	London
S2	10	Paris
S3	10	Paris
S4	20	London
S5	30	Athens

SP

S#	P#	QTY
S1	P1	300
S1	P2	200
S1	P3	400
S1	P4	200
S1	P5	100
S1	P6	100
S2	P1	300
S2	P2	400
S3	P2	200
S4	P2	200
S4	P4	300
S4	P5	400

Fig. 9.7 Sample tabulations of SECOND and SP

Inserting.   We can enter the information that S5 is located in Athens, even though S5 does not currently supply any parts, by simply inserting the appropriate tuple into SECOND (as in Fig. 9.7).

Deleting.   We can delete the shipment connecting S3 and P2 by deleting the appropriate tuple from SP; we do not lose the information that S3 is located in Paris.

Updating.   In the revised structure, the city for a given supplier appears once, not many times (the redundancy has been eliminated). Thus we can change the city for S1 from London to Amsterdam by changing it once and for all in the relevant SECOND tuple.

Comparing Figs. 9.6 and 9.4, we see that the effect of our structural revision has been to eliminate the *nonfull* functional dependencies, and it is this elimination that has resolved the difficulties. Intuitively we may say that in relation FIRST the attributes STATUS and CITY did not describe the entity identified by the primary key, namely, a supplier-part shipment; instead they described the supplier alone. Mixing the two types of information in the same relation was what caused the problems.

We now give a definition of second normal form.[2]

■   A relation R is in *second normal form* (2NF) if it is in 1NF and every nonkey attribute is fully dependent on the primary key.

(An attribute is *nonkey* if it does not participate in the primary key.)[3] Relations SECOND and SP are both 2NF [the primary keys are S# and the combination (S#,P#), respectively]. Relation FIRST is not 2NF. A relation that is in first normal form and not in second can always be reduced to an equivalent collection of 2NF relations [9.1]. The reduction consists of replacing the relations by suitable *projections;* the collection of these projections is equivalent to the original relation, in the sense that the original relation can always be recovered by taking an appropriate *join* of these projections, so no information is lost in the process (which is highly important, of course). In other words, the process is reversible. In our example, SECOND and SP are projections of FIRST, and FIRST is the join of SECOND and SP over S# (with one of the two identical S# columns eliminated from the result).

Notice, incidentally, that a 1NF relation that is not also 2NF must have a composite primary key.

Since no information is lost in the reduction process, any information that can be derived from the original structure can also be derived from

---

[2] See footnote 1 on p. 156.
[3] See footnote 1 on p. 156.

the new structure. The converse is not true, however: The new structure may contain information (such as the fact that S5 is located in Athens) that could not be represented in the original. In this sense, the new structure is a slightly more faithful reflection of the real world. (The new structure also introduces a minor consistency problem not present in the original, namely, that any S# value occurring in SP must also occur in SECOND. Questions of consistency are discussed in Chapter 24.)

The SECOND/SP structure still causes problems, however. Relation SP is satisfactory; as a matter of fact, relation SP is now in fourth normal form, and we shall ignore it for the remainder of this section. Relation SECOND, on the other hand, still suffers from a lack of mutual independence among its nonkey attributes. The dependency diagram for SECOND is still "more complex" than a 4NF diagram. To be specific, the dependency of STATUS on S#, though it *is* functional, is *transitive* (via CITY): Each S# value determines a CITY value, and this in turn determines the STATUS value. This transitivity leads, once again, to difficulties over storage operations. (We now concentrate on the association between cities and status values—i.e., on the functional dependency of STATUS on CITY.)

Inserting.   We cannot enter the fact that a particular city has a particular status value—for example, we cannot state that any supplier in Rome must have a status of 50—until we have some supplier located in that city. The reason is, again, that until such a supplier exists we have no appropriate primary key value.

Deleting.   If we delete the only SECOND tuple for a particular city, we destroy not only the information for the supplier concerned but also the information that that city has that particular status value. For example, if we delete the SECOND tuple for S5, we lose the information that the status for Athens is 30. (Once again, the insertion and deletion problems are two sides of the same coin.)

Updating.   The status value for a given city appears in SECOND many times, in general (the relation still contains some redundancy). Thus, if we need to change the status value for London from 20 to 30, we are faced with *either* the problem of searching the SECOND relation to find every tuple for London *or* the possibility of producing an inconsistent result (the status for London may be given as 20 in one place and 30 in another).

Again the solution to the problems is to replace the original relation (SECOND) by two projections, in this case SC(S#,CITY) and CS(CITY,STATUS). Figure 9.8 shows the corresponding dependency diagram and Fig. 9.9 the tabulation corresponding to the data values of

Fig. 9.8 Functional dependencies in the relations SC and CS

SC

S=	CITY
S1	London
S2	Paris
S3	Paris
S4	London
S5	Athens

CS

CITY	STATUS
Athens	30
London	20
Paris	10

Fig. 9.9 Sample tabulations of SC and CS

the original SECOND (Fig. 9.7). [The process is reversible, once again: SECOND is the join of SC and CS over CITY (with one of the identical CITY columns removed).]

It should be clear that this new structure overcomes all the problems over storage operations concerning the CITY-STATUS association. Detailed consideration of these problems is left to the reader. Comparing Figs. 9.8 and 9.6, we see that the effect of the further restructuring has been to eliminate the transitive dependence of STATUS on S#.

We now give a definition of third normal form.[4]

■ A relation R is in *third normal form* (3NF) if it is in 2NF and every nonkey attribute is nontransitively dependent on the primary key.

Relations SC and CS are both 3NF; relation SECOND is not. (The primary keys for SC and CS are S# and CITY, respectively.) A relation that is in second normal form and not in third can always be reduced to an equivalent collection of 3NF relations [9.1]. We have already indicated that the process is reversible, and hence that no information is lost in the reduction; however, the 3NF collection may contain information, such as the fact that the status for Rome is 50, that could not be represented in the original 2NF relation. Just as the SECOND/SP structure was a slightly better representation of the real world than the 1NF relation FIRST, so the SC/CS structure is a slightly better representation than the 2NF relation SECOND. Again, however, a minor consistency problem has been introduced. (What is it?)

---

[4] See footnote 1 on p. 156.

We conclude this section by stressing the fact that the level of normalization of a given relation is a matter of *semantics*, not a matter of the data values that happen to appear in that relation at some particular time. It is not possible just to look at the tabulation (snapshot) of a given relation at a given time and to say whether or not that relation is 3NF (for example)—it is necessary to know the meaning of the data, i.e., the dependencies involved, before such a judgment can be made. In particular, the DBMS cannot ensure that a relation is maintained in "the most desirable form" (4NF) without being informed of all relevant dependencies. For a relation in 3NF (or 4NF), however, all that is needed to inform the DBMS of these dependencies is an indication of the attribute(s) constituting the primary key. The DBMS will then know that all other attributes are functionally dependent on this attribute or attribute combination, and will be able to enforce this constraint.[5] For a relation that is not in 3NF, additional specifications would be necessary.

9.4   RELATIONS WITH MORE THAN ONE CANDIDATE KEY

It should perhaps be emphasized that 1NF and 2NF are not really very important in themselves—they are really just intermediate points on the way to 3NF and 4NF. Indeed, it is possible to give a definition of third normal form that makes no reference to first or second normal form as such, nor to the concepts of full and transitive dependence. Let us agree to call an attribute (possibly composite) on which some other attribute is (fully) functionally dependent a *determinant*. Then we can define 3NF as follows.

■   A normalized relation R is in *third normal form* (3NF) if every determinant is a candidate key.

Observe that we are now talking in terms of *candidate* keys, not just the primary key. A definition in approximately this form was first given by Heath [9.3]. A subsequent, equivalent definition, due to Boyce and Codd but based on a proposal by Kent [9.7], was given in [9.8]; for this reason a relation fitting the definition is sometimes said to be in Boyce/Codd normal form (BCNF) rather than 3NF, but we shall not make this distinction. From here on, we shall generally take the term "third normal form" to refer to the revised definition. However, the reader should be aware that the revised definition is not quite equivalent to the original definition as given in [9.1]; the original definition did not satisfactorily handle the case of a relation possessing two overlapping

---

[5] See footnote 1 on p. 156.

candidate keys (see below). It is still true, however, that any relation not in 3NF can be decomposed into an equivalent collection of 3NF relations [9.17].

Before considering examples involving more than one candidate key, let us convince ourselves that relations FIRST and SECOND, which were not 3NF under the old definition, are still not 3NF under the new; and also that relations SP, SC, and CS, which *were* 3NF under the old definition, are still 3NF under the new. Relation FIRST contains three determinants: S#, CITY, and the combination (S#,P#). Of these, only (S#,P#) is a candidate key; hence FIRST is not 3NF. Similarly, SECOND is not 3NF, because the determinant CITY is not a candidate key. Relations SP, SC, and CS, on the other hand, are each 3NF, because in each case the primary key is the only determinant in the relation.

We now look at an example involving two disjoint (nonoverlapping) candidate keys. Let us consider relation S(S#,SNAME,STATUS,CITY) once again. We now assume, as earlier in the book, that STATUS and CITY are mutually independent, but for the sake of the example we assume that supplier *names*, as well as supplier numbers, are unique (for all time)—in other words, we assume that SNAME is a candidate key. Figure 9.10 is the dependency diagram.

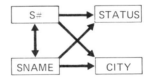

Fig. 9.10 Functional dependencies in relation S if SNAME is a candidate key

The revised S relation is 3NF. However, it is desirable to specify *both* keys in the definition of the relation: (a) to inform the DBMS, so that it may enforce the constraints implied by the two-way dependency between the two keys—namely, that corresponding to each supplier number there exists a unique supplier name, and conversely; and (b) to inform the users, since of course the uniqueness of the two attributes is an aspect of the semantics of the relation and is therefore of interest to people using it. The KEY entry within a relation definition is sufficient to specify the *primary* key; some other entry, say UNIQUE (attribute-name-combination), will be required for each additional *candidate* key. Thus, for example, relation S might be defined as follows.

```
RELATION S(S#,SNAME,STATUS,CITY)
         KEY(S#)
         UNIQUE(SNAME)
```

Now we present some examples in which the candidate keys overlap. Two candidate keys overlap if they involve two or more attributes each and have an attribute in common. For our first example, we suppose again that supplier names are unique, and we consider the relation SSP(S#,SNAME,P#,QTY). The keys are (S#,P#) and (SNAME,P#). Is this relation 3NF? The answer is no, because we have two determinants, S# and SNAME, which are not keys for the relation (S# determines SNAME, and conversely). As a matter of fact, this relation *was* 3NF under the original definition [9.1]; the original definition did not require an attribute to be fully dependent on the primary key if it was itself a component of some other key in the relation, and so the fact that SNAME is not fully dependent on (S#,P#)—assuming the latter to be the primary key—was ignored. However, this fact gives rise to redundancy, and hence to update problems, in the relation SSP. For instance, updating the name of supplier S1 from Smith to Robinson leads (once again) either to search problems or to possibly inconsistent results. The solution to the problems, as usual, is to decompose the relation SSP into two 3NF projections, in this case SS(S#,SNAME) and SP(S#,P#,QTY) [or SP(SNAME,P#,QTY)].

As a second example, we consider the relation SJT with attributes S (student), J (subject), and T (teacher). The meaning of an SJT tuple is that the specified student is taught the specified subject by the specified teacher. The semantic rules follow.

- For each subject, each student of that subject is taught by only one teacher.

- Each teacher teaches only one subject.

- Each subject is taught by several teachers.

Figure 9.11 shows a sample tabulation of this relation.

What are the functional dependencies in this relation? From the first semantic rule we have a functional dependency of T on the composite attribute (S, J). From the second semantic rule we have a functional dependency of J on T. The third semantic rule tells us that there is *not* a functional dependency of T on J. Hence we have the situation shown in Fig. 9.12.

SJT	S	J	T
	Smith	Math	Prof. White
	Smith	Physics	Prof. Green
	Jones	Math	Prof. White
	Jones	Physics	Prof. Brown

Fig. 9.11 Sample tabulation of the relation SJT

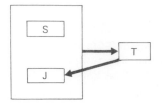

Fig. 9.12 Functional dependencies in the relation SJT

Again we have two overlapping candidate keys: the combination (S, J) and the combination (S, T). Once again the relation is 3NF according to the definition of [9.1] but not according to the revised definition of this section; and once again the relation suffers from certain anomalies in connection with storage operations. For example, if we wish to delete the information that Jones is studying physics, we cannot do so without at the same time losing the information that Professor Brown teaches physics. The difficulties are caused by the fact that T is a determinant but not a candidate key (and so SJT is not 3NF by the revised definition). Again we can get over the problem by replacing the original relation by two 3NF projections, in this case ST(S, T) and TJ(T, J). It is left as an exercise for the reader to give tabulations of these two relations corresponding to the data of Fig. 9.11, to draw a corresponding dependency diagram, to ensure that the two projections are indeed 3NF (what are the keys?),[6] and to convince himself that this solution does indeed avoid the problems. (But see reference [9.20].)

Our third and final example of overlapping keys concerns a relation EXAM with attributes S (student), J (subject), and P (position). The meaning of an EXAM tuple is that the specified student was examined in the specified subject and achieved the specified position in the class list. For the purposes of the example, we suppose that the following semantic rule holds.

■   There are no ties; that is, no two students obtained the same position in the same subject.

Then the functional dependencies are as illustrated in Fig. 9.13.

Again we have two candidate keys, (S, J) and (J, P). The relation is 3NF, despite the fact that the keys overlap, because the keys are the only determinants. The reader should convince himself that difficulties over

---

[6] As a matter of fact *any* binary relation must be in 3NF. (Why?)

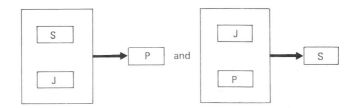

Fig. 9.13   Functional dependencies in the relation EXAM

storage operations such as those discussed earlier in this chapter do not occur with this relation. A possible declaration is:

$$\underline{\text{RELATION}} \text{ EXAM(S,J,P)}$$
$$\underline{\text{KEY}}\text{(S,J)}$$
$$\underline{\text{UNIQUE}}\text{(J,P)}$$

We see, therefore, that the revised definition of 3NF eliminates certain problem cases that could occur under the old definition. Moreover, the new definition is conceptually simpler than the old, in that it involves no reference to the concepts of primary key, transitive dependence, and full dependence. The reference to candidate keys can also be replaced by a reference to the more fundamental notion of functional dependence (the definition given in [9.8] actually makes this replacement). On the other hand, the original definition (suitably adjusted to avoid the aforementioned problems) may be more useful in practice, since it indicates the actual step-by-step process that the designer must go through in order to reduce an arbitrary relation to an equivalent collection of 3NF relations. We summarize this process in Section 9.6.

9.5   FOURTH NORMAL FORM

A relation may be in third normal form and may yet possess certain undesirable features. As an example, we consider the relation CTX(COURSE,TEACHER,TEXT), with meaning as follows: A tuple $\langle c, t, x \rangle$ appears in CTX if and only if course c is capable of being taught by teacher t and uses text x as a reference. We suppose that, for a given course, there may exist any number of corresponding teachers and any number of corresponding texts; moreover, we assume that teachers and texts are quite independent of each other. Figure 9.14 shows a sample tabulation for CTX involving just one course (physics), which can be taught by either Professor Green or Professor Brown and which uses as texts *Basic Mechanics* and *Principles of Optics*.

CTX	COURSE	TEACHER	TEXT
	Physics	Prof. Green	Basic Mechanics
	Physics	Prof. Green	Principles of Optics
	Physics	Prof. Brown	Basic Mechanics
	Physics	Prof. Brown	Principles of Optics

Fig. 9.14   The relation CTX

It is apparent that relation CTX contains some redundancy, leading as usual to problems over storage operations. For example, to add the information that the physics course uses a new text called *Advanced Mechanics*, it is necessary to create *two* new tuples, one for each of the two teachers. Nevertheless, CTX *is* in third normal form (in fact, it is "all key"); it may be thought of as the result of applying the normalization process sketched in Chapter 4 (Section 4.2) to an unnormalized relation involving two independent nonsimple attributes, or more intuitively to a set of records containing two distinct "repeating" fields (each such record would consist of a course, a set of teachers, and a set of texts).

The existence of such "problem" 3NF relations has been recognized for some time; see, for example, Schmid and Swenson [9.9]. So far as relation CTX is concerned, it is intuitively clear that the difficulties are caused by the mutual independence of teachers and texts; moreover, it is easy to see that matters would be improved if CTX were replaced by its two projections CT(COURSE,TEACHER) and CX(COURSE,TEXT). However, it was not until 1976 that these notions were formalized by Fagin [9.17] and also (independently) by Zaniolo [9.18]. We make no attempt to present the formal treatment here, but we will discuss the basic ideas in the context of the CTX example.

First of all, attribute COURSE of the CTX relation is said to "multidetermine" attribute TEACHER. Equivalently, we say that there is a "multivalued dependence" of TEACHER on COURSE. The meaning of these statements is basically that, although a given course does not have a *single* corresponding teacher (i.e., TEACHER is not *functionally* dependent on COURSE), nevertheless each course does have a well-defined *set* of corresponding teachers. More precisely, we may say that the set of TEACHER values matching a given COURSE and TEXT value pair depends only on the particular COURSE value specified—the TEXT value specified is irrelevant. (As a counterexample, consider the familiar relation SP(S#,P#,QTY). Here QTY is *not* "multidependent" on S#, because the set of QTY values—actually a single value—matching a given S# and P# value pair certainly does not depend on the S# value alone.) We note that attribute TEXT of CTX is also multidependent on COURSE; multivalued dependencies generally appear together in pairs in this way.

Functional dependence, as defined in Section 9.2, is a special case of multivalued dependence. The problem with 3NF relations such as CTX is that they involve multivalued dependencies that are not also functional dependencies. The two projections CT(COURSE,TEACHER) and CX(COURSE,TEXT) do not involve any such dependencies, which is why they represent an improvement over the original relation. We would therefore like to replace CTX by the combination of CT and CX. It can be shown that such a replacement is always valid [9.17]: That is, a relation R(A, B, C) in which B and C are each multidependent on A is always equal to a join on A of the two projections R1(A, B) and R2(A, C).

Given the validity of this decomposition process, we can now reduce any relation to an equivalent collection of relations in *fourth normal form*. Fourth normal form (4NF) may be defined as follows [9.17].

■   A normalized relation R is said to be in *fourth normal form* (4NF) if and only if, whenever there exists a multivalued dependency in R, say of attribute B on attribute A, then all attributes of R are also functionally dependent on A.

We can see that relation CTX is not in 4NF (take A as COURSE, B as TEACHER). Thus a 3NF relation is not necessarily in 4NF; however, any 4NF relation *is* in 3NF (in other words, referring back to Fig. 9.1, 4NF relations belong at the very heart of the diagram). The two projections CT and CX are each in 4NF. The example thus illustrates how reduction to fourth normal form can eliminate one final form of undesirable structure.

9.6   SUMMARY

In this chapter we have presented arguments for basing a relational data model on relations in fourth normal form. The examples of Sections 9.3 and 9.5 give some insight into the method of reducing an arbitrary 1NF relation to an equivalent collection of 4NF relations. The reduction process may be informally described as follows.

a)   Take projections of the original 1NF relation to eliminate any nonfull functional dependencies. This will produce a collection of 2NF relations.

b)   Take projections of these 2NF relations to eliminate any transitive dependencies. This will produce a collection of 3NF relations.

c)   Take projections of these 3NF relations to eliminate any multivalued dependencies that are not also functional dependencies. This will produce a collection of 4NF relations. (In practice, it is usually easiest to eliminate such dependencies *before* applying the other two normalization steps.)

The general objective of this process is to reduce redundancy, and hence to avoid certain problems with storage operations, as we discussed in Sections 9.2 and 9.5. Indeed, we can sum up the concept of 4NF, very loosely, as "one fact in one place." But the reader should realize that, in general, the collection of 4NF relations corresponding to a given 1NF relation may not be unique. In particular, this is so if the original 1NF relation includes more than one candidate key. This point is discussed by Rissanen and Delobel [9.4]. Codd [9.1] also touches on it when he warns against "over-projection," which we may define as the replacement of a relation that is already in 4NF by two or more of its (4NF) projections. See the discussion of "optimal third normal form" in [9.1].

In conclusion, we observe that the topic of this chapter is different in kind from that of the last few chapters. The notions of functional dependence and fourth normal form are concerned with the *meaning* of data. By contrast, data sublanguages such as the relational calculus and relational algebra are concerned only with actual data values: Any interpretation placed on these values is imposed from outside, and plays no part in the languages per se. In particular, such languages have no requirement that the relations they operate on be in any normal form other than 1NF. Fourth normal form may be viewed primarily as a *discipline*—a discipline by which the database designer (the DBA) can build a data model that captures part, albeit a small part, of the semantics of the real world.

EXERCISES

9.1 Figure 9.15 represents a hierarchical structure (see Chapter 3) that contains information about departments of a company. For each department the database contains a department number (unique), a budget value, and the department manager's employee number (unique). For each department the database also contains information about all employees working in the department, all projects assigned to the department, and all offices occupied by the department. The employee information consists of employee number (unique), the number of the project on which he or she is working, and his or her office number and phone number; the project information consists of project number (unique) and a budget value; and the office information consists of an office number (unique) and the area of that office (in square feet). Also, for each employee the database contains the title of each job the employee has held, together with date and salary for each

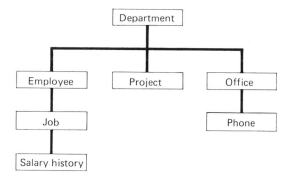

Fig. 9.15 A company database (hierarchical structure)

distinct salary received in that job; and for each office it contains the numbers (unique) of all phones in that office.

Convert this hierarchical structure to an appropriate collection of 4NF relations. Make any assumptions you deem reasonable about the functional dependencies involved.

9.2 A database used in an order-entry system is to contain information about *customers*, *items*, and *orders*. The following information is to be included.

- For each *customer*
  Customer number (unique)
  Valid "ship-to" addresses (several per customer)
  Balance
  Credit limit
  Discount

- For each *order*
  Heading information: customer number, "ship-to" address, date of order
  Detail lines (several per order), each giving item number, quantity ordered

- For each *item*
  Item number (unique)
  Manufacturing plants
  Quantity on hand at each plant
  Stock danger level for each plant
  Item description

For internal processing reasons a "quantity outstanding" value is associated with each detail line of each order. [This value is initially set equal to the quantity of the item ordered and is (progressively) reduced to zero as (partial) shipments are made.]

Design a data model for this data based on 4NF relations. As in the previous question, make any semantic assumptions that seem necessary.

9.3 Suppose that in Exercise 9.2 only a very small number of customers, say one percent, actually have more than one ship-to address. (This is typical of real-life situations, in which frequently just a very few exceptions—usually rather important ones—fail to conform to a general pattern.) Can you see any drawbacks to your solution to Exercise 9.2? Can you think of any improvements?

9.4 A relation TIMETABLE is defined with the following attributes.

D   Day of the week (1–5)
P   Period within day (1–8)
C   Classroom number
T   Teacher name
S   Student name
L   Lesson identifier

A tuple $\langle d, p, c, t, s, l \rangle$ is an element of this relation if at time $\langle d, p \rangle$ student s is taught lesson l by teacher t in classroom c. You may assume that lessons are one period in duration and that every lesson has an identifier that is unique among all lessons taught in the week. Reduce TIMETABLE to an equivalent set of 4NF relations.

REFERENCES AND BIBLIOGRAPHY

9.1 E. F. Codd. "Further Normalization of the Data Base Relational Model." In *Data Base Systems*, Courant Computer Science Symposia Series, Vol. 6. Englewood Cliffs, N.J.: Prentice-Hall (1972).

> Codd's original paper on the subject. It provides a comparatively formal treatment of the material covered somewhat informally in Sections 9.1–9.3. It also addresses the question of growth in the database (see Chapter 10).

9.2 E. F. Codd. "Normalized Data Base Structure: A Brief Tutorial." *Proc. 1971 ACM SIGFIDET Workshop on Data Description, Access and Control.* Available from ACM.

> This paper is probably the best starting point for reading on the relational approach. It contains a simple explanation of the relational model, considers its advantages with respect to the hierarchical and network models, and provides an introduction to the topic of further normalization.

9.3 I. J. Heath. "Unacceptable File Operations in a Relational Database." *Proc. 1971 ACM SIGFIDET Workshop on Data Description, Access and Control.* Available from ACM.

> This paper essentially formalizes the "storage anomaly" arguments of the present chapter. A storage operation is defined to be *violative* if it actually or potentially violates the internal consistency of the file (relation) concerned. For example, considering relation SPC of Fig. 9.8, updating the first tuple to $\langle$'S1','P1',300,'ROME'$\rangle$ actually violates; updating the ninth tuple to $\langle$'S3','P2',200,'ROME'$\rangle$ potentially violates. The problems caused by violative operations for both the DBMS and the user are discussed, and it is shown that for a relation in 3NF the *only* violative operation is the addition of a new tuple.

9.4 J. Rissanen and C. Delobel. "Decomposition of Files, a Basis for Data Storage and Retrieval." IBM Research Report RJ 1220 (May 1973).

The process of successive reduction of a 1NF relation to a more desirable form, referred to as further normalization in the present chapter and in Codd [9.1], is here called relational decomposition. The paper presents a rigorous and systematic development of a theory of relational decomposition, with the objective of providing a sound theoretical framework to assist with the problem of choosing that particular decomposition which is optimal with respect to some given performance criterion. A formal method for generating all decompositions of a given relation is explained, and the paper concludes with some remarks on the storage structure required to support a particular decomposition.

9.5 R. G. Casey and C. Delobel. "Decomposition of a Data Base and the Theory of Boolean Switching Functions." *IBM J. R & D* **17,** No. 5 (September 1973).

This paper is also concerned with the problem of relational decomposition (see [9.4]). The authors show that for any given 1NF relation the set of functional dependencies (called functional relations in this paper) may be represented by a Boolean function, and moreover that this function is unique in the following sense: The original dependencies may be specified in many (superficially) different ways, each one in general giving rise to a (superficially) different Boolean function—but all such functions may be reduced by the laws of Boolean algebra to the same canonical form. The problem of decomposing the 1NF relation is then shown to be logically equivalent to the well-understood Boolean algebra problem of finding a covering set of prime implicants for the Boolean function corresponding to the original relation together with its functional dependencies. Hence the original problem can be transformed into a problem in Boolean algebra, which has several potential advantages. For example, it should be possible to use analytic modeling techniques to evaluate alternative decompositions.

9.6 P. H. Prowse. "The Relational Model as a Systems Analysis Tool." Presented at BCS Symposium on Relational Database Concepts, London (5 April 1973).

The presentation consisted primarily of an actual case history, in which relational concepts in general and third normal form in particular were used to analyze existing data structures and to integrate these structures into a single design. Much emphasis was placed on the difficulty of doing such an analysis without such a tool. 3NF proved to be an invaluable tool for the job, even though other constraints meant that the resulting design had to be implemented on a nonrelational system.

9.7 W. Kent. "A Primer of Normal Forms." IBM Technical Report TR 02.600 (December 1973).

A comprehensive tutorial on first, second, and third normal forms. The paper includes a systematic explanation of the concepts underlying normalization and suggests improvements to some of the original definitions. The general organization of the paper resembles that of [9.1], so that the two papers can usefully be read in parallel.

9.8 E. F. Codd. "Recent Investigations into Relational Data Base Systems." *Proc. IFIP Congress 1974.* Also in *Proc. ACM Pacific Conference, San Francisco* (April 1975): Available from Mail Room, Boole and Babbage Inc., 850 Stewart Drive, Sunnyvale CA 94086.

Includes an improved definition of 3NF (see Section 9.5). The other topics discussed are data sublanguages, superimposition of multiple views (see Chapter 10), data exchange, and needed investigations. The most urgent "needed investigations" are said to be:

1. development of concurrency control techniques;

2. ascertaining the performance attainable on really large databases with concurrent access and modification;

3. development of superimposition theory;

4. development of storage, access, and modification theory; and

5. demonstration of viability of RENDEZVOUS-like subsystems [5.14].

9.9 H. A. Schmid and J. R. Swenson. "On the Semantics of the Relational Data Model." *Proc. 1975 ACM SIGMOD International Conference on the Management of Data.* Available from ACM.

As indicated in Section 9.6, the concepts of normalization may be seen as the beginnings of a theory of data semantics. The work reported in this paper carries the ideas further. Starting with the premise that the real world may be modelled as "complex independent objects" (entities) and associations between them, the authors are able to construct an insertion/deletion theory for the relational model. In terms of the suppliers-and-parts example, the theory formalizes such constraints as: (a) An SP tuple may be created only if the indicated supplier and part already exist, and (b) an S or P tuple may be deleted only if the indicated supplier or part does not participate in any SP association. The authors emphasize the distinction between "associations" (such as SP) and "characteristics." A characteristic may be represented by a simple attribute—for example, STATUS is a simple characteristic of suppliers—or by a subordinate relation—for example, in a personnel database, we may have the relations:

```
EMP (EMP#,DESCRIPTION)
EC  (EMP#,CAR#)
CAR (CAR#,DESCRIPTION)
```

Here employees are the "complex independent objects" (we are assuming for the sake of the example that the system has no interest in cars other than as employee possessions); each employee is represented by one EMP tuple, n EC tuples, and n CAR tuples. Cars are "complex characteristics" of employees. Using these ideas, the authors categorize 3NF relations into five different types, and suggest that this categorization should be reflected in the conceptual schema.

9.10 P. A. Bernstein, J. R. Swenson, and D. C. Tsichritzis. "A Unified Approach to Functional Dependencies and Relations." *Proc. 1975 ACM SIGMOD International Conference on the Management of Data.* Available from ACM.

The process of normalization discussed in the present chapter is essentially a process of *decomposition:* Given a 1NF relation and a set of functional dependencies among its attributes, we break the relation down into an equivalent set of 3NF relations. The authors of this paper propose a converse approach: Given a set of attributes and a set of functional dependencies over them, it should be possible to *synthesize* a corresponding set of 3NF relations. (This work was done before Fagin's work on 4NF.) Algorithms are presented for performing this task. However, since attributes (and hence functional dependencies) have no meaning outside the framework of a relation that contains them, it would be more accurate to regard the primitive construct not as a functional dependency but as a binary relation. The synthesis process is thus one of constructing n-ary relations from binary relations, with the constraint that all constructed relations be in third normal form. A more serious objection (recognized by the authors) is that the manipulations performed by the synthesis algorithm are purely syntactic in nature and take no account of semantics. For instance, given the functional dependencies (FDs)

$$R.A \rightarrow R.B \qquad \text{(meaning: in the binary relation } R(A, B),$$
$$B \text{ is functionally dependent on } A)$$

$$S.B \rightarrow S.C$$

$$T.A \rightarrow T.C$$

the third may or may not be redundant (deducible from the first and second), depending on the meaning of R, S, T. As an example of where it is not, take A as employee number, B as office number, C as department number; take R as "office of employee," S as "department owning office," T as "department of employee"; and consider the case of an employee working in an office belonging to a department not his own. The synthesis algorithm effectively assumes that S.C and T.C are one and the same; it relies on the existence of some external mechanism (i.e., human intervention) for avoiding semantically invalid manipulations. In the case at hand, it would be the responsibility of the person defining the original FDs to use distinct attribute names (C and D, say) in place of S.C and T.C. (In fact, relation names such as S and T are not recognized by the algorithm at all.)

9.11 R. Fadous and J. Forsyth. "Finding Candidate Keys for Relational Data Bases." *Proc. 1975 ACM SIGMOD International Conference on the Management of Data.* Available from ACM.

Presents an algorithm for finding all candidate keys in a 1NF relation, given the set of all functional dependencies in that relation.

9.12 W. W. Armstrong. "Dependency Structures of Data Base Relationships." *Proc. IFIP Congress 1974.*

Presents a theory of functional dependencies. The theory provides a set of axioms that characterize precisely all possible dependency structures within a relation. It also gives a complete characterization of candidate keys. The investigations reported in [9.10] and [9.11] draw on this theory.

9.13 C. P. Wang and H. H. Wedekind. "Segment Synthesis in Logical Data Base Design." *IBM J. R & D.* **19,** No. 1 (January 1975).

This paper is concerned with the problem of choosing the *optimal* relational representation for a given collection of data. It discusses some performance criteria that could influence the design so that, for example, some relations were in first rather than third normal form (so that some redundancy would be deliberately introduced). However, it is at least debatable whether the data model (as opposed to the storage structure) is the right place to introduce such considerations.

9.14 P. Hall, J. Owlett, and S. Todd. "Relations and Entities." *Proc. IFIP TC-2 Working Conference on Modelling in Data Base Management Systems* (January 1976). North-Holland (1976).

Argues that the conceptual model should be essentially relational but should distinguish between entities and associations. Entities are given system identifiers or "surrogates"; information about an entity, including its primary key (if it possesses one other than the surrogate), is represented by one or more tuples linking the surrogate to other values; associations between entities are represented by relations linking the surrogates. Surrogates cannot be updated. The advantage of this approach is that certain problems arising from key update operations are avoided. It is also suggested that all conceptual relations should be *irreducible*—i.e., it should not be possible to replace such a relation by two or more projections in such a way that the original relation may be recovered via suitable joins. [In practice, this means that many—but not all—conceptual relations would be binary. More precisely, each conceptual relation would consist of a candidate key (one or more attributes) plus at most one nonkey attribute.]

9.15 G. C. H. Sharman. "A Constructive Definition of Third Normal Form." *Proc. 1976 ACM SIGMOD International Conference on the Management of Data.* Available from ACM.

Presents an abstract syntax for a relational data definition language. Domains and relations are viewed as user-defined data types (composite in the case of relations); the syntax consists of a set of production rules for defining such types. It also caters for the definition of inter-relation dependencies and for a special kind of relation called a discriminated union. In some respects, however, the proposal departs from the strict relational framework—for example, it apparently permits pointers to be used in place of foreign keys.

9.16 R. Fagin. "Dependency in a Relational Database and Propositional Logic." IBM Research Report RJ 1776 (April 1976).

Armstrong's axioms [9.12] may be stated in the following form.

1. $A_1 A_2 \cdots A_m \to A_i$, for $i = 1, 2, \ldots, m$.

2. $A_1A_2 \cdots A_m \rightarrow B_1B_2 \cdots B_r$
    if and only if
    $A_1A_2 \cdots A_m \rightarrow B_i$, for each i in $1, 2, \ldots, r$.

3. If $A_1A_2 \cdots A_m \rightarrow B_1B_2 \cdots B_r$
    and $B_1B_2 \cdots B_r \rightarrow C_1C_2 \cdots C_p$,
    then $A_1A_2 \cdots A_m \rightarrow C_1C_2 \cdots C_p$.

(The A's, B's, and C's are attributes; the symbol $\rightarrow$ represents functional dependence.) The present paper [9.16] proves that this set of axioms is complete, in the sense that given a set S of dependency statements for a relation R, all dependency statements holding for R (for all time) and compatible with S may be derived from S by using the axioms. The paper also shows that this formal system is strictly equivalent to the system of implicational statements in propositional logic: That is, a given dependency statement is a consequence of a given set of dependency statements if and only if the corresponding implicational statement is a consequence of the corresponding set of implicational statements.

9.17 R. Fagin. "Multivalued Dependencies and a New Normal Form for Relational Databases." IBM Research Report RJ 1812 (July 1976).

9.18 C. A. Zaniolo. "Analysis and Design of Relational Schemata for Database Systems." Doctoral dissertation, Computer Science Department, University of California, Los Angeles (1976).

9.19 J.-M. Cadiou. "On Semantic Issues in the Relational Model of Data." Proc. International Symposium on Mathematical Foundations of Computer Science, Gdansk, Poland (September 1975). New York: Springer-Verlag, Lecture Notes in Computer Science.

9.20 J. Rissanen. "Independent Components of Relations." IBM Research Report (forthcoming).

Defines a precise notion of independence for relations and develops a corresponding theory. We illustrate the concept as follows. Consider relation SECOND (see Fig. 9.6). Projections SC(S#,CITY) and CS(CITY,STATUS) of this relation (Fig. 9.8) are independent, because at any given time their natural join over CITY represents a possible value (collection of tuples) for SECOND; that is, such a join cannot possibly violate the functional dependency constraints defined for SECOND. (The natural join [4.1] is essentially an equi-join with one of the two duplicate result columns projected out.) This statement is true regardless of any changes that may be made to either SC or CS. By contrast, projections SC(S#,CITY) and SS(S#,STATUS) are not independent—changes to either one must be monitored to ensure that the dependency of STATUS on CITY is not being violated.

It is clear in this example that the combination SC,CS is a more desirable reduction than the combination SC,SS. Thus the notion of independence leads to additional guidelines as to how best to perform the normalization process. The present paper formalizes and generalizes these ideas. In particular, it shows that projections R_1 and R_2 of a relation R are independent if and only if their common attributes form a candidate key for at least one of the pair *and* every time-independent functional dependency in R can be deduced from those in R_1 and R_2 by application of Armstrong's axioms [9.12]. This theorem makes checking for independence a very simple operation. The paper also extends the concept of independence to a *family* of projections [for example, projections SP(S#,P#,QTY), SC(S#,CITY), and CS(CITY,STATUS) form an independent family of projections of relation FIRST of Fig. 9.4].

A relation that cannot be decomposed into independent components is said to be *atomic*. Rissanen examines the implications of reducing all relations to their atomic components, and claims that such a reduction is useful in achieving a balanced database design. ("Balanced" here means that, of the three performance factors (a) retrieval speed, (b) update speed, and (c) space utilization, none is really bad, and some are near-optimal.) We observe, incidentally, that an atomic relation is not necessarily irreducible in the sense of [9.14]. Relation SJT (Fig. 9.11) is a case in point: The projections ST and TJ of this relation are not independent, because the dependency of T on the combination S,J cannot be deduced from the dependencies in these projections. In fact SJT is atomic, and reduction to the combination ST and TJ, while it solves some problems, introduces others.

9.21 P. A. Bernstein. "Synthesizing Third Normal Form Relations from Functional Dependencies." *ACM Transactions on Database Systems* **1,** No. 4 (December 1976).

A fuller and more formal treatment of the material introduced in reference [9.10].

10
The External
Model

10.1 INTRODUCTION

An external model is an individual user's view of the database. It may be thought of as a restriction of the conceptual model—the total community user view—to just that portion that is of interest to that particular user. Up to this point, however, we have ignored the external level and have assumed that users operate directly at the conceptual level, or, perhaps more accurately, we have assumed that the external model in question is identical to the conceptual model. In this chapter we turn our attention to the external level, and in particular, we examine the differences between the external and conceptual levels.

The reader is referred to Fig. 1.3 for a diagram showing the place of the external model (and corresponding external schema) in the overall architecture. For the present, we are concerned with the external level in a *relational* system—that is, a system in which the conceptual model is relational; the external model may also be relational, or it may take some other form, such as a network. (External models in hierarchical and network systems will be discussed in Parts 3 and 4 of this book.) For the most part, we shall assume that the external model is relational too. The reader will appreciate that the system we shall describe is hypothetical, in the sense that no complete implementations exist at the time of writing.

We begin by repeating some general remarks from Chapter 1.

In the first place, the external model must be defined by means of an external schema, written by the DBA and/or the user in an appropriate data definition language. The external schema defines the user's view of the database; in particular, if the user's view is relational, it defines the database as a collection of relations, with tuples of those relations forming the "external records" (see Chapter 1).

Second, there is a mapping, the external/conceptual mapping, between the external and conceptual schemas. This mapping specifies the rules for extracting the external model from the conceptual model. In practice the mapping will normally be defined in conjunction with the external schema—the data definition language mentioned above will include the necessary facilities for writing both—but of course the two are logically distinct.

Third, the reader is reminded that any number of external models may be defined on a given conceptual model; any number of users may share a given external model; and different external models may overlap.

We shall use the term "external data definition language" (or external DDL) to refer to the language for defining external schemas and external/conceptual mappings.

10.2   EXTERNAL RELATIONS

In general, an external relation—that is, a relation defined in an external schema—should be allowed to be any relation derivable from those in the conceptual model. "Derivable" here has exactly the meaning that it had in Section 5.3; in other words, the external relation may be any relation derivable by means of a predicate of the relational calculus, or by an equivalent expression in a language of comparable power, such as the relational algebra. Thus, the external DDL should permit the specification of such predicates or expressions.

Consider the suppliers-and-parts data model once again. Suppose that we wish to operate on the binary relation consisting of all partname/city-name pairs (where a particular pair occurs in the relation if a part with that name is supplied by a supplier in that city). One way of doing this, of course, is to retrieve this relation by means of an appropriate DSL ALPHA GET statement.

```
RANGE SP SPX
GET W (P.PNAME,S.CITY) : ∃SPX(SPX.P#=P.P#∧SPX.S#=S.S#)
```

We may now operate on the relation in the workspace W.[1]

Alternatively, we may define this relation as part of our external model, as shown in Fig. 10.1, for example.

---

[1] Note, however, that we have tacitly assumed here that relations S, P, and SP are all included in the *external* model. Thus these would all have to be defined as external relations, anyway.

```
RELATION PARTLOC (PNAME,CITY)
              .
              .
              .
     MAPPING RANGE P PX
             RANGE S SX
             RANGE SP SPX
             ∃PX∃SPX∃SX(PARTLOC.PNAME=PX.PNAME
                       ∧PX.P#=SPX.P#
                       ∧SPX.S#=SX.S#
                       ∧SX.CITY=PARTLOC.CITY)
```

Fig. 10.1 Definition and mapping for external relation PARTLOC

Figure 10.1 shows part of the external schema and associated mapping definition. The first line is the relation definition. It states that relation PARTLOC (a name local to users of this schema) is defined over domains PNAME and CITY. The remaining lines define the mapping between PARTLOC and the conceptual model, in a (hypothetical) mapping definition language based on relational calculus.

Once the external schema (with the mapping definition) has been created and entered into the system, it can be referenced by any (authorized) user at any time. To answer the query "Get the names of all parts available from London," for example, such a user may issue the following GET statement.

```
GET W (PARTLOC.PNAME) : PARTLOC.CITY='LONDON'
```

A *programmer* may extract the schema from the data dictionary and incorporate it into a program by means of some form of INCLUDE statement. An *on-line user* may simply quote the schema name. (This could be done implicitly as part of the logging-on procedure.)

As another example, suppose that the relation PARTLOC is extended to include a P# attribute.

```
RELATION PARTLOC (P#,PNAME,CITY)
```

The mapping definition of Fig. 10.1 will also have to be extended appropriately. The significant point about this example is that PARTLOC is now not 4NF. (Was it before? Which form is it in now?) In general, even if the underlying data model is composed entirely of 4NF relations, an external relation can be in any of the four normal forms. In fact, as indicated in Section 10.1, the external model need not be relational at all.

```
HIERARCHY PART(PNAME)
          OVER LOC(CITY)
            .
            .
            .
          MAPPING RANGE P  PX
                  RANGE S  SX
                  RANGE SP SPX

                  ∃PX∃SX∃SPX(PART.PNAME=PX.PNAME
                          ∧PX.P#=SPX.P#
                          ∧SPX.S#=SX.S#
                          ∧SX.CITY=LOC.CITY)
```

Fig. 10.2 Definition and mapping for external PART/LOC hierarchy

Suppose that the user wants to see the same information as in the PARTLOC example, but in the form of a hierarchy rather than a relation. The hierarchy is to consist of a record-type PART(PNAME) as the root, plus a record-type LOC(CITY) as the single dependent of this root. Figure 10.2 shows how we might extract such a hierarchy from the underlying (relational) conceptual model, once again using a hypothetical external DDL.

We conclude this section by giving a SEQUEL analogue of the definition and mapping of Fig. 10.1. SEQUEL has probably gone further than any other currently implemented language in the amount of variation permitted between the external and conceptual levels of the system. The SEQUEL term for an external relation is a *view*. Recognizing that any derivable relation is a valid view, SEQUEL uses exactly the same language constructs for defining the derivation (or mapping) as it uses for ordinary retrieval. See Fig. 10.3.

The example illustrates two further points. First, we can define new names, not only for the external relation itself, but also for attributes within the relation, if we so desire. If no local names are specified, then

```
DEFINE VIEW PARTLOC (PART,TOWN) AS
       SELECT PNAME,CITY
       FROM   P,SP,S
       WHERE  P.P#=SP.P#
       AND    SP.S#=S.S#
       ORDER  BY PNAME ASC, CITY DESC
```

Fig. 10.3 SEQUEL definition and mapping for PARTLOC

names are inherited from the conceptual schema in the obvious way. Second, a specific ordering can be imposed, if required, on the external relation by means of an appropriate ASC/DESC specification.

10.3 EXTERNAL DOMAINS

In general, an external schema will include definitions not only of the external relations but also of the domains on which those relations are defined. It follows that external domains may differ from the corresponding conceptual domains over such matters as data type (indeed, there may not even exist a corresponding conceptual domain; see the discussion of virtual domains below). We give some examples of the differences that may exist between an external domain and the corresponding conceptual domain (if any).[2]

- The data types may differ.

By "data type" here we mean the representation chosen for the domain values, e.g., as character strings (in some particular character code and of some particular length) or as numbers (with some particular base, scale, mode, and precision). For instance, in the conceptual schema we may have

DOMAIN WEIGHT NUMERIC (4)

whereas the corresponding domain in an external schema to be used in a PL/I application may be defined as

DOMAIN WEIGHT FIXED BINARY (14)

We assume here that the specification NUMERIC (4) defines a four-digit decimal integer.

- The units may differ (for numeric values).

For example, the conceptual domain WEIGHT may contain part weights measured in grams, whereas a given user may wish to handle the values in ounces. In such a situation we may associate with the definition of the external domain the name of a procedure to perform the necessary conversion.

DOMAIN WEIGHT FIXED BINARY (9)
FOR RETRIEVAL CALL GTOZ

Here GTOZ is the name of a procedure (to be supplied by the DBA) that

---

[2] Compare the list of aspects of the storage structure subject to variation in Section 1.3.

will convert grams to ounces and that is to be invoked every time a WEIGHT value is to be retrieved. Similarly, we may write <u>FOR STORAGE</u> <u>CALL</u> ZTOG (say) to specify a procedure to perform the opposite conversion required for <u>PUT</u> and <u>UPDATE</u> operations.

■   The conceptual domain may be coded.

Consider, for example, the domain COLOR. The DBA may decide that in the conceptual model COLOR values are to be represented as decimal integers, interpreted according to the table 1 = 'RED', 2 = 'BLUE', and so on. Thus in the conceptual schema we may have

```
DOMAIN COLOR NUMERIC  (1)
        CODED CHARACTER (6)
            (1='RED', 2='BLUE',...)
```

For a given external schema we may now decide to view the COLOR domain either as a set of decimal integers,

```
DOMAIN COLOR NUMERIC (1)
```

or as a set of character strings,

```
DOMAIN COLOR CODED CHARACTER (6)
```

■   The external domain may be virtual.

Just as a conceptual domain may be virtual with respect to the domains actually stored, so an external domain may be virtual with respect to the domains defined in the conceptual schema. An external domain is said to be virtual if its values are computed according to some algorithm from a set of several conceptual domain values. For example, consider the following external schema and mapping.

```
RELATION PN (P#,N)
        .
        .
        .
        MAPPING RANGE SP SPX
            ∃SPX(PN.P#=SPX.P#
            ∧PN.N=ICOUNT(SPX,P#,S#))
```

The relation PN consists of all pairs $\langle p, n \rangle$ such that n is the count of the number of suppliers who supply part number p (cf. Example 5.5.7).

10.4 DATA SUBLANGUAGE OPERATIONS

The effect of any given DSL operation is defined in terms of the external model. It is clear, however, that to support such an operation it is necessary, in effect, to convert it into an equivalent operation against the underlying conceptual model. For example, the statement

        <u>GET</u> W (PARTLOC.PNAME) : PARTLOC.CITY='LONDON'

(see Section 10.2) has to be interpreted as

        <u>GET</u> W (P.NAME) : ∃SPX∃SX(PX.P#=SPX.P#
                            ∧SPX.S#=SX.S#
                            ∧SX.CITY='LONDON')

(with appropriate <u>RANGE</u> declarations, of course). The conversion is performed by reference to the external/conceptual mapping. For retrieval operations, such a conversion is always possible, regardless of the complexity of this mapping; to put it another way, the statement that an external relation may be any derivable relation (Section 10.2) is certainly true so far as retrieval is concerned. For storage operations, however, the external relation must effectively be identical to the corresponding conceptual relation, except that

a) individual tuples can be omitted, and

b) nonkey attributes can be omitted.

This restriction is essentially a restatement of the restriction on the storage operations that they may operate on only one (conceptual) relation at a time: see Section 5.4. The restriction is a consequence of the following two rules [10.2]: (1) For a given storage operation on an external relation, there must exist a unique operation at the conceptual level that results in *exactly* the specified changes at the external level; and (2) this operation must affect *only* data that is visible in that external relation. For example, consider the external relation PARTLOC. It should be clear that each of the following external-level operations fails on at least one of these two counts: an attempt to update the tuple ⟨'NUT', 'LONDON'⟩ to ⟨'NUT', 'ROME'⟩; an attempt to insert the tuple ⟨'WASHER', 'ATHENS'⟩; an attempt to delete the tuple ⟨'NUT', 'LONDON'⟩.

   Points (a) and (b) above both raise questions in connection with <u>PUT</u> operations. From point (a) it appears that we may insert a new tuple with a primary key value that is not a duplicate so far as the external relation is concerned but is a duplicate so far as the underlying conceptual relation is concerned. This clearly cannot be allowed; such a <u>PUT</u> would have to be rejected, just as if it had been applied directly to the underlying conceptual relation.

Second, from point (b) it is possible to insert a tuple into a conceptual relation, via an external relation, in which one or more nonkey attribute values are unspecified. For example, suppose that the external relation PART, with attributes (P#, PNAME, COLOR, CITY), corresponds to the conceptual relation P—in other words, the nonkey attribute WEIGHT has been omitted from the external relation—and consider the effect of

```
W.P#='P7'
W.PNAME='WASHER'
W.COLOR='GREY'
W.CITY='ATHENS'
PUT W (PART)
```

The DBMS must append the appropriate null value for the missing attribute before inserting the new tuple into relation P. (The appropriate null value for each attribute must be defined by the DBA in the conceptual schema. A suitable null value for P.WEIGHT could be zero or any negative value.) Subsequently another user may <u>UPDATE</u> this tuple to replace the null value by a genuine weight.

Turning now to the question of DSL operations and allowable differences in *domains* between the external and conceptual levels (see Section 10.3), we find again that there are no restrictions so far as retrieval is concerned. For storage operations, however, it seems reasonable to forbid the use of virtual domains.

10.5 CHANGES TO THE CONCEPTUAL SCHEMA

As the database grows—i.e., as new types of information are added to it—so the conceptual schema must change to reflect this growth. The two possible types of change occasioned by such growth are

1. the extension of an existing relation to include a new attribute (corresponding to the addition of new information about an existing type of entity); and

2. the inclusion of a new relation (corresponding to the addition of a new type of entity).

Both these changes will be completely invisible to all current users of the database, because none of the new attributes and/or relations will appear in any current external schema. Forcing the user to view the data via an external schema, in fact, is the means by which that user is made

```
(before) : RELATION SECOND(S#,STATUS,CITY)

(after)  : RELATION SC (S#,CITY)
                   CS (CITY,STATUS)
```

Fig. 10.4 An example of attribute migration (conceptual schema)

independent of growth in the database—a simple but extremely important aspect of data independence.

However, these are not the only types of change that may occur in the conceptual schema. Another important type occurs when a relation is replaced by two or more of its projections (such that the original relation may be recovered via an appropriate join of these projections). We have already seen several examples of this in Chapter 9. To reduce the 2NF relation SECOND of Fig. 9.6 to an equivalent collection of 4NF relations, for example, we replaced it by two of its projections, namely, those over (S#,CITY) and (CITY,STATUS), respectively. Thus, if the 2NF relation SECOND was at one time part of the data model, it may be replaced at some later time by these two 4NF projections, causing a corresponding amendment to the conceptual schema (see Fig. 10.4).

Following Codd, we call this type of change "attribute migration." What effect will it have on the user? The answer so far as retrieval is concerned is *none*. The relation SECOND will be defined in the user's external schema. If the DBA amends the associated mapping definition to define the *old* relation SECOND in terms of the *new* ones SC and CS, then any existing GET operation on SECOND will work exactly as before (although it will require additional interpretation and additional overhead). The necessary amendment is illustrated in Fig. 10.5.

```
    RELATION SECOND (S#,STATUS,CITY)

(before) MAPPING RANGE SECOND X
                  ∃X(SECOND.S#=X.S#
                   ∧ SECOND.STATUS=X.STATUS
                   ∧ SECOND.CITY=X.CITY)

(after)  MAPPING RANGE SC SCX
                 RANGE CS CSX
                 ∃SCX∃CSX(SECOND.S#=SCX.S#
                         ∧ SECOND.CITY=SCX.CITY
                         ∧ SCX.CITY=CSX.CITY
                         ∧ SECOND.STATUS=CSX.STATUS)
```

Fig. 10.5 Remapping the external relation SPC

However, as explained in Section 10.4, any storage operations on the external relation SECOND will fail after the migration has occurred. Any program performing such operations will have to be rewritten (in general). In other words, such a program is not immune to this type of change.

The foregoing remarks on attribute migration may be interpreted as yet another argument for basing the original conceptual model on relations in 4NF. Certainly this will tend to minimize the amount of attribute migration that is likely to occur—clearly a desirable objective. It will not necessarily eliminate such changes altogether, however. It may still be necessary to replace a (4NF) relation by two or more of its (4NF) projections, e.g., to simplify authorization control. For example, the supplier relation S could be replaced by the following two projections.

```
S' (S#,SNAME,CITY)
S" (S#,STATUS)
```

Consider the effect on existing users of the relation S. As usual, retrieval is not affected. What about storage operations? This seems to be a situation in which the restrictions on such operations may be relaxed, since the effect of all possible storage operations on S is clearly defined in terms of S' and S". (You should convince yourself of the truth of this observation.)

10.6 SUMMARY

In sum, then, the separation of the individual user's view of the data (defined by the external schema) from the community view (defined by the conceptual schema) provides a number of important advantages. Most of the following points are applicable to any database system that includes this separation, not just to one based on the relational approach.

- Users are immune to growth in the database.
- Users may be immune to attribute migration.

This is certainly true for retrieval. For storage operations it may be true in certain special cases (see the last part of Section 10.5).

- The user's view is simplified.

It is obvious that the external schema focuses the user's attention on just those relations and domains that are of concern to that user. What is perhaps not so obvious is that, for retrieval at least, the external schema provides a powerful mechanism for considerably simplifying the DSL operations that the user must issue. Because the user may be provided with external relations obtained by joining together all appropriate con-

ceptual relations, the need for quantifiers in the user's retrieval statements
can be greatly reduced. (As a simple example, contrast the GET statement on relation PARTLOC shown in Section 10.2 with the GET
statement required to answer the same query from the underlying conceptual model.)

- The same data may be viewed by different users in different ways.

The implication here is that the users of the database may operate in
a multitude of different languages. Each such user is provided with an
external schema which defines the data in a format compatible with the
language to be used. This consideration is extremely important in a
real-life environment, where many different categories of user are all
interacting with a single integrated database.

- The external schema provides a degree of preconditioning.

In one sense the external schema is redundant, inasmuch as the user
could theoretically obtain any result desired by operating directly at the
conceptual level. However, one way of looking at the external schema is
to view it as a statement of how the user intends to process the conceptual
model. Thus it specifies to the DBMS just what relations and domains are
to be processed; it specifies various conversion operations that will be
required; it may also specify tuple orderings, and so on. All this information may be used by the DBMS to optimize its response to the user's
requests. For example, as soon as the external schema is extracted for
use from the data dictionary, the DBMS may ensure that all requested
orderings are supported by an appropriate index, building indexes
dynamically if necessary. This view of the external schema, in fact,
suggests one or two other candidates for inclusion: for example, a
statement against each relation as to the proposed method of use (any
meaningful combination of GET/UPDATE/PUT/DELETE), or an indication of the number of tuples expected or desired (compare the quota in
Example 5.3.5).

- Pre-database applications may still run.

This objective will be achieved, if it is possible at all, by providing the
pre-database application with an external schema that defines its data
structures (files, records, fields) in terms of the data model chosen for the
new database.

- Automatic security is provided for hidden data.

"Hidden data" refers to relations and attributes not defined in the
external schema. It is clear that such data is automatically secure from all
access by a user of this particular schema. Thus, forcing users to access

the data by means of an external schema is a simple but effective mechanism for authorization control, at least at one level. Additional levels of security will also be required, however (see Part 5 of this book).

EXERCISES

10.1 Define relation SP (Fig. 4.8) as an external relation derived from relation SPJ (see exercises in Chapter 5).

10.2 Consider how the data structures of a language with which you are familiar could be defined in terms of a relational data model. (That is, what facilities would be required in the external data definition language?)

10.3 So far as storage operations are concerned, external relations are generally required to be essentially the same as the corresponding conceptual relation. Interpret this constraint for the case of a *hierarchical* external model (defined, again, in terms of a relational conceptual model).

REFERENCES AND BIBLIOGRAPHY

Reference [9.8] includes a brief discussion of the support of insert and delete operations on derived relations. Reference [7.6] includes information over and above that in [10.2 and 10.3] on the handling of views in SEQUEL and the support of nonrelational models within a relational system.

10.1 C. J. Date and P. Hopewell. "File Definition and Logical Data Independence." *Proc. 1971 ACM SIGFIDET Workshop on Data Description, Access and Control.* Available from ACM.

This paper presents a number of ideas similar to those in this chapter in a somewhat different form.

10.2 D. D. Chamberlin, J. N. Gray, and I. L. Traiger. "Views, Authorization and Locking in a Relational Data Base System." *Proc. NCC* **44** (May 1975).

10.3 R. F. Boyce and D. D. Chamberlin. "Using a Structured English Query Language as a Data Definition Facility." IBM Research Report RJ 1318 (December 1973).

11
Some
Relational
Systems

11.1 INTRODUCTION

Relational ideas have had, and continue to have, a major impact on many areas of database technology. They form the basis for continuing investigations into such diverse fields as normalization and data semantics (see Chapter 9), support of natural language [5.14] and more formal casual user interfaces [5.12, 7.2, and 8.1], deductive inference [11.3 and 11.5], security, integrity, and concurrency control (see Part 5 of this book), database performance [5.6, 5.7, 6.1, 6.4, 6.5, and 11.24], high-level hardware database support [11.6, 11.8, and 11.9], and others. In this chapter we survey briefly some of the systems in which these investigations have been or are being carried out, and we identify some related reference material (over and above that already listed in Chapters 1–10). The reader is warned that we make no claim for completeness in either of these areas.

Until about 1974 the only implemented relational systems were to some degree experimental, and were not available commercially (although a few commercial systems, for example ADABAS [11.36], did provide certain relational features). All the systems discussed in this chapter fall into this category. More recently, however, commercial systems with more truly relational properties have begun to appear on the scene—see, for example, references [3.14] and [3.15].

11.2 EARLY SYSTEMS

A number of systems implemented prior to 1969 incorporated features that may fairly be described as relational. With one exception, however, these systems all handled *binary* relations only. The exception is STDS [11.4], which did support relations of arbitrary degree; in STDS, however, the emphasis was on general set-handling rather than on relations as such. The other systems were LEAP [11.1], TRAMP [11.2], and the Relational Data File [11.3].

The emphasis on binary relations is probably explained by the type of application for which these systems were developed. They were not really concerned with supporting large formatted databases of the sort required in industrial or similar enterprises; rather, they were intended primarily to provide an environment in which a user could ask an unanticipated question, make deductions based on the answer to that question, ask further questions on the basis of those deductions, and so on (in other words, the user could browse through the data). We observe that binary relations are logically sufficient, even for large formatted databases, since any relation of higher degree can be decomposed into a semantically equivalent set of binary relations. The supplier relation S, for example, could be replaced by the collection of three relations SN(S#,SNAME), SS(S#,STATUS), SC(S#,CITY). The shipment relation SP, which possesses a composite primary key, can be handled by first introducing a new, atomic key (say shipment number, SHIP#) and then splitting the relation into the collection SH(SHIP#,S#), PH(SHIP#,P#), QH(SHIP#,QTY). (In both of these examples, it would be necessary to impose the additional constraint that precisely the same set of key values appeared in each of the three binary relations.)[1]

Turning now to the data sublanguage, LEAP and TRAMP both provide languages that are essentially tuple-at-a-time. The STDS and Relational Data File languages, by contrast, provide the traditional set-handling operations (union, intersection, etc.), but not the special relational operations such as join. Both permit the use of quantifiers in the definition or construction of a set.

The reader's attention is also drawn to [11.12], which describes a language that may be seen as an interesting precursor of the relational algebra [5.5].

Further remarks on LEAP, TRAMP, and the Relational Data File will be found in the form of annotation to the references at the end of the chapter.

---

[1] Some authorities continue to advocate the use of binary relations [11.10 and 11.11]. However, as the examples illustrate, such an approach requires the introduction of many additional names (an n-ary relation involves $n+1$ names if expressed directly, $2n-1$ names if expressed as a collection of binary relations). The additional names are a burden to the user and complicate the expression of queries.

11.3 RECENT SYSTEMS

The publication of Codd's original paper on the relational approach [4.2] in 1969, and (more significantly) of the revised version [4.1] in 1970, gave a great impetus to the development of relational systems and associated research activities. We have already discussed in some detail a number of systems developed since that time: DAMAS [5.6 and 5.7], INGRES/QUEL/CUPID [5.8–5.13], RENDEZVOUS [5.14], SQUIRAL [6.4], SQUARE/SEQUEL/System R [7.1–7.6], and Query By Example [8.1–8.5]. In the present section we describe in outline a few more of the post-1969 systems.

MacAIMS

MacAIMS [11.13 and 11.14] appears to have been the earliest example of a system providing both an n-ary relational data model and a set-oriented data sublanguage. The language is algebraic. Some of the most interesting features of MacAIMS are described in the following paragraphs.

- The storage structure may vary from relation to relation (thus allowing each relation to be stored in the form most suited to it). For each structure a "relational strategy module" maintains the relations appropriately and permits the user to view them in the simple tabular form.

- Domains are stored as "data element sets." Each data element (domain value) is assigned a unique fixed-length reference number, and all reference to the data element within a relation is via the reference number. The algorithm for assigning reference numbers is such that, if A and B belong to the same data element set, the reference number for A will be greater than that for B if and only if A is greater than B. As a result, any comparison operation between two data elements (from the same data element set) can be made directly on the corresponding reference numbers; moreover, the actual comparison itself will probably be more efficient, because reference numbers are fixed-length whereas data elements may be variable-length. This fact is particularly significant in view of the claim that such comparisons are the operations most frequently performed in the system.

The system RDMS [11.15], which is currently in use within the administrative departments at M.I.T., is apparently an upgraded form of MacAIMS.

IS/1

IS/1 was developed at the IBM UK Scientific Centre in Peterlee, England [11.16]. It too supports n-ary relations and an algebraic language. Moreover, it also supports a limited form of external/conceptual mapping. An external relation (the IS/1 term is "implied relationship") is defined by means of a set of statements in the IS/1 data sublanguage which specify how other relations are to be joined, projected, and otherwise manipulated to produce the required result. Once written, the definition is compiled and stored in the system. The first time the user refers to this relation, the definition is invoked and the required relation is generated. Subsequent operations are performed directly on the generated relation.

- An interesting aspect of the IS/1 external level is that the "base" relations on which an external relation is defined may themselves be "implied relationships"; and this may apply to any number of levels. Hence the definition of an external relation may often be considerably simpler than it would otherwise be.

- It is apparent that, as more and more external relations are referenced, the storage space assigned to the database will eventually become full. When insufficient space is available for the generation of a new external relation, IS/1 invokes a procedure to free the space allocated to some other external relation and then uses that. The external relation to be erased in this way is chosen by means of a suitable algorithm. For example, it may be that relation least recently used or the one with the lowest number of references. (Observe that the erased relation may still be accessed, since its definition remains in the system.) This technique is called "logical paging."

- A generated external relation is automatically erased if a storage operation is performed on any of the underlying base relations. This means that the next reference to the external relation will cause that relation to be freshly generated, thus automatically incorporating the appropriate changes. On the other hand, a storage operation on an external relation is *not* reflected in any corresponding changes to the base relations, at least in the system as currently implemented. (Such an operation hence has no permanent effect, since the external relation may be erased and regenerated at any time.)

One other facility of IS/1 that should be mentioned is "function extensibility." This feature allows the user to extend the system to include an arbitrary set of library functions. This in turn implies that the user's language may be quite remote from the basic algebraic language, since it may reduce to a set of calls to library functions of any degree of sophistication. It is planned eventually to provide full "syntax extensibility," too, so that the user's language can be tailored to any possible set of requirements (corresponding to any possible category of user).

A revised version of IS/1, known as the Peterlee Relational Test Vehicle (PRTV [11.17]), has also been implemented. Both IS/1 and PRTV have been used in actual applications [11.18 and 11.19].

RDMS

This system, not to be confused with the M.I.T. system mentioned above, was implemented at General Motors Research [11.20 and 11.21]. In RDMS the primary means of communication between system and user is via CRT terminals (although the result of any operation may also be obtained in printed form if desired). Each relation is implemented as an (unordered) array in virtual storage. Paging the data in and out of main storage is handled by the underlying operating system, not by RDMS. Nonetheless, the system provides fast response to complex queries with high-volume (multiscreen) output. The data sublanguage is algebraic. Other commands available to the user include operations to control the output display (e.g., to "roll" forward or backward in the result relation), library functions such as counting and totaling, and a "command trace" facility which displays the last eight commands that the system has executed.

ZETA

ZETA is a multilevel system under implementation at the University of Toronto [11.22 and 11.23]. The lowest level (MINIZ) provides a set of tuple-at-a-time operations and the ability to "mark" those tuples in a relation that satisfy a simple Boolean predicate. Marks are implemented as unary relations containing tuple identifiers, and may themselves be marked. The next (intermediate) level of ZETA supports derived relations and multiple-relation retrievals, using MINIZ as a primitive access method. The highest level of the system provides three user interfaces: (1) a set of SEQUEL-like operators that may be invoked from a PL/I program; (2) a query language development facility, which allows the construction of individual on-line query languages tailored to specific user requirements; and (3) an intelligent natural language interface called TORUS.

GAMMA-0

GAMMA-0 [11.25] is a hypothetical low-level interface to a relational database (intended for use in the implementation of a higher-level interface such as the relational calculus). A list of some of the available operations will give the flavor of the interface.

create relation

drop relation

insert tuple

delete tuple

move tuple

update subtuple

get ID of next tuple

get subtuple given tuple ID

Additional operations provide for the creation and destruction of system-maintained indexes ("inversions") and the selection of subtuples one at a time according to preset "scan control conditions."

Although GAMMA-0 was not implemented, many of its ideas were incorporated into the Relational Storage Interface (RSI), the access method level of System R. Details of the RSI are given in [7.6]. The reader's attention is also called to XRM [11.26] (and its forerunner RAM [11.27]), which was used as the access method in the original SEQUEL prototype [7.3 and 7.4].

CASSM

CASSM (Context-Addressed Segment-Sequential Memory) represents a proposal for direct *hardware* support of relations and high-level relational operators [11.6]. The data structure and operations supported are very close to those provided at the external level of the system; thus, several levels of mapping can be eliminated. Reference [11.7] shows how a SEQUEL-like language called SLICK could be implemented on such a device.

Other hardware proposals are presented in [11.8] and [11.9].

REFERENCES AND BIBLIOGRAPHY

11.1 J. A. Feldman and P. D. Rovner. "An Algol-Based Associative Language." *CACM* **12,** No. 8 (August 1969).

This paper describes the LEAP language and its implementation. LEAP is essentially an extension of Algol 60 that provides set-manipulation operations (not only union, intersection, etc., but also a powerful loop operation, which allows the user to manipulate the individual set elements one by one). The set elements may be either simple items or "associations," i.e., triples of the form ⟨attribute, object, value⟩. A set of "associations" corresponds to a binary relation in which "attribute" is the relation name (all triples in one such set have the same "attribute" component) and within each triple, "object" and "value" are the two items that are associated. Association sets are implemented via a complex hashing scheme that, by means of data redundancy, enables any "associative operation" to be handled in a reasonably efficient manner.

11.2 W. Ash and E. H. Sibley. "TRAMP: An Interpretive Associative Processor with Deductive Capabilities." *Proc. ACM 23rd Nat. Conf.* (1968).

TRAMP is a system that, like LEAP [11.1], is designed for associative processing. Like LEAP, it works in terms of ⟨attribute, object, value⟩ triples; i.e., it stores binary relations. The storage structure is again based on hashing; however, there is no data redundancy—instead, a complex system of pointers is used to provide the required flexibility. The really significant difference between TRAMP and LEAP, however, is that TRAMP permits the user to state the definition of a (binary or unary) relation in terms of stored (binary) relations, using the "converse" and "composition" operators; for example, the relation "parent of" can be defined as the converse of "child of." Requests in terms of such a defined relation are then dynamically interpreted in terms of the relations actually stored.

11.3 R. E. Levein and M. E. Maron. "A Computer System for Inference Execution and Data Retrieval." *CACM* **10,** No. 11 (November 1967).

This paper describes the "Relational Data File" and a language for retrieving data from it. The Relational Data File is essentially a collection of binary relations, stored with a high degree of data redundancy to provide efficient response to retrieval operations. As in TRAMP [11.2], the user can define rules for deriving further relations from the ones actually stored.

11.4 D. L. Childs. "Description of a Set-Theoretic Data Structure." *Proc. FJCC* **33** (1968).

11.5 J. Minker. "Performing Inferences Over Relational Data Bases." *Proc. 1975 ACM SIGMOD International Conference on the Management of Data.* Available from ACM.

11.6 G. P. Copeland, G. J. Lipovski, and S. Y. W. Su. "The Architecture of CASSM: A Cellular System for Nonnumeric Processing." *Proc. 1st Annual Symposium on Computer Architecture, Gainesville, Florida* (December 1973).

11.7 G. P. Copeland and S. Y. W. Su. "A High Level Data Sublanguage for a Context-Addressed Segment-Sequential Memory." *Proc. 1974 ACM SIGMOD Workshop on Data Description, Access and Control.* Available from ACM.

11.8 E. A. Ozkarahan, S. A. Schuster, and K. C. Smith. "RAP: An Associative Processor for Data Base Management." *Proc. NCC* **44** (May 1975).

11.9 C. S. Lin, D. C. P. Smith, and J. M. Smith. "The Design of a Rotating Associative Memory for a Relational Database Management Application." *ACM Transactions on Database Systems* **1,** No. 1 (March 1976).

11.10 G. Bracchi, A. Fedeli, and P. Paolini. "A Multilevel Relational Model for Data Base Management Systems." *Proc. IFIP TC-2 Working Conference on Data Base Management Systems* (April 1974) (eds., Klimbie and Koffeman). North-Holland, 1974.

11.11 M. E. Senko. "DIAM as a Detailed Example of the ANSI/SPARC Architecture." *Proc. IFIP TC-2 Working Conference on Modelling in Data Base Management Systems* (January 1976). North-Holland (1976).

11.12 CODASYL Development Committee. "An Information Algebra." *CACM* **5,** No. 4 (April 1962).

11.13 R. C. Goldstein and A. J. Strnad. "The MacAIMS Data Management System." *Proc. 1970 ACM SICFIDET Workshop on Data Description and Access.* Available from ACM.

A very readable paper describing the overall structure of the MacAIMS system.

11.14 A. J. Strnad. "The Relational Approach to the Management of Data Bases." *Proc. IFIP Congress 1971.*

An introduction to the MacAIMS data sublanguage.

11.15 J. Stewart and J. Goldman. "The Relational Data Management System: A Perspective." *Proc. 1974 ACM SIGMOD Workshop on Data Description, Access and Control.* Available from ACM.

11.16 M. G. Notley. "The Peterlee IS/1 System." IBM (UK) Scientific Centre Report UKSC-0018 (March 1972), IBM (UK) Scientific Centre, Neville Rd., Peterlee, Co. Durham, England HA2 7HH.

11.17 S. J. P. Todd. "The Peterlee Relational Test Vehicle—A System Overview." *IBM Sys. J.* **15,** No. 4 (1976).

11.18 K. Soop, P. Svensson, and L. Wiktorin. "An Experiment with a Relational Data Base System in Environmental Research." *Information Systems: COINS IV* (ed., J. T. Tou). New York: Plenum Press (1974).

11.19 E. F. Codd (ed.). "Implementation of Relational Data Base Management Systems." Proceedings of panel discussion, NCC (May 1975). IBM Research Laboratory, San Jose CA 95193. Also in *FDT (bulletin of ACM SIGMOD)* **7,** Nos. 3–4 (1975).

11.20 V. K. M. Whitney. "A Relational Data Management System (RDMS)." *Information Systems: COINS IV* (ed., J. T. Tou). New York: Plenum Press (1974).

11.21 V. K. M. Whitney. "Relational Data Management Implementation Techniques." *Proc. 1974 ACM SIGMOD Workshop on Data Description, Access and Control.* Available from ACM.

11.22 B. Czarnik, S. A. Schuster, and D. Tsichritzis. "ZETA: A Relational Data Base Management System." *Proc. ACM Pacific Conference, San Francisco* (April 1975). Available from Mail Room, Boole and Babbage Inc., 850 Stewart Drive, Sunnyvale CA 94086.

11.23 J. Mylopoulos, S. A. Schuster, and D. Tsichritzis. "A Multilevel Relational System." *Proc. NCC* **44** (May 1975).

11.24 J. H. G. Farley and S. A. Schuster. "Query Execution and Index Selection for Relational Data Bases." University of Toronto, Computer Systems Research Group Technical Report CSRG-53 (March 1975).

11.25 D. Bjørner, E. F. Codd, K. L. Deckert, and I. L. Traiger. "The GAMMA-0 *n*-ary Relational Data Base Interface: Specifications of Objects and Operations." IBM Research Report RJ 1200 (April 1973).

11.26 R. A. Lorie. "XRM—An Extended (*n*-ary) Relational Memory." IBM Technical Report G320-2096 (January 1974).

11.27 M. F. Crick and A. J. Symonds. "A Software Associative Memory for Complex Data Structures." IBM Technical Report G320-2060.

11.28 G. Bracchi, A. Fedeli, and P. Paolini. "A Relational Data Base Management System." Internal Report No. 72-5, Laboratorio di Calcolatori, Istituto di Elettrotecnica ed Elettronica, Politechnico di Milano, Italy (February 1972).

11.29 D. J. McLeod and M. J. Meldman. "RISS: A Generalized Minicomputer Relational Data Base Management System." *Proc. NCC* **44** (May 1975).

11.30 P. J. Titman. "An Experimental Data Base System Using Binary Relations." *Proc. IFIP TC-2 Working Conference on Data Base Management Systems* (April 1974) (eds., Klimbie and Koffeman). North-Holland, 1974.

The major objective of the prototype described in this paper was to evaluate a particular storage structure and an associated access strategy; thus the emphasis was on those aspects of a database system that lie below the user interface. The "binary relations" of the title would more accurately be described as ordered binary *arrays*: Each value pair in the "relation" could be addressed via (a coded form of) its position in the sequence. Thus each value pair had an implicit identifier. Domains were represented by "value sets," i.e., ordered unary arrays in which, again, each element had an implicit identifier, namely, its position. The data values in a given pair within any one of the binary arrays were identifiers, either of elements in value sets or of other pairs. Thus, for example, the triple $\langle$'S1', 'P1', 300$\rangle$ of relation SP might be represented as the value pair $\langle a, b \rangle$, where b is the identifier of the value 300 in the QTY value set and a is the identifier of the pair $\langle c, d \rangle$ in the S#–P# binary array, and c and d are in turn identifiers of S1 and P1, respectively, in the S# and P# value sets. Both value sets and binary arrays employed some simple yet effective compression techniques—a space reduction of about 70 percent was achieved in the benchmark application (a bill of materials structure). Differential file techniques [2.24] were also used. To access the database, the system provided a collection of set operations, principally "collate," which may be considered as a join followed by a projection. Access times seemed to be reasonably acceptable. The paper concludes with some interesting observations on the reliability, security, and integrity aspects of such a system.

11.31 E. H. Beitz. "A Set-Theoretic View of Data-Base Representation." *Proc. 1974 ACM SIGMOD Workshop on Data Description, Access and Control.* Available from ACM.

11.32 E. H. Beitz. "Sets as a Model for Data Base Representation: Much Ado About Something." *Proc. ACM Pacific Conference, San Francisco* (April 1975). Available from Mail Room, Boole and Babbage Inc., 850 Stewart Drive, Sunnyvale CA 94086.

> These two papers [11.31 and 11.32], like [11.30], are not really concerned with the user's view of a database but rather with the conceptual and internal levels of the system. However, the conceptual model proposed could well prove suitable for supporting relational views. Every entity and every "property" (such as WEIGHT = 17) is given a unique system identifier; the conceptual model then consists of (a) the set of all entity identifiers, (b) the set of all property identifiers, and (c) a binary relation defined over (a) and (b). At the stored level this binary relation is represented twice, once in each direction, giving symmetry of access and incidentally an automatic backup copy. Each of the two representations actually consists of an index into the appropriate one of (a) or (b). Many advantages are claimed for such an approach.

11.33 D. E. Jordan. "Implementing Production Systems with Relational Data Bases." *Proc. ACM Pacific Conference, San Francisco* (April 1975). Available from Mail Room, Boole and Babbage Inc., 850 Stewart Drive Sunnyvale CA 94086.

> A brief but interesting introduction to the MAGNUM system [3.14].

11.34 L. S. Schneider. "A Relational View of the Data Independent Accessing Model." *Proc. 1976 ACM SIGMOD International Conference on the Management of Data.* Available from ACM.

> This paper is an interesting attempt to apply the ideas of the Data Independent Accessing Model, DIAM [2.22], to a relational system. The highest level of abstraction in DIAM, the entity set level, is replaced by a relational level, i.e., a level in which the primary objects of interest are relations. At the next level—the level specifying which associations or "strings" are to be represented in storage—the atomic, entity, and link strings of DIAM are shown to be suitable, more or less, as access paths to support the relational operations of projection, restriction, and join, respectively, and are accordingly renamed as P-, R-, and J-strings. The other two levels, which specify how and where each string is represented, are much as originally proposed in DIAM.

11.35 C. R. Carlson and R. S. Kaplan. "A Generalized Access Path Model and Its Application to a Relational Data Base System." *Proc. 1976 ACM SIGMOD International Conference on the Management of Data.* Available from ACM.

> Describes a relational system in which the user is able to express queries without having to specify all the linking "join terms." For example, the query "Find supplier names for suppliers who supply a red part" might be

expressed as SELECT SNAME WHERE COLOR = 'RED'. The system assumes responsibility for determining the necessary inter-relation links. Problems of ambiguity are discussed and several approaches to their solution briefly considered.

11.36 Software AG. ADABAS Introductory Manual. Obtainable from Software AG, Hilberstrasse 20, 61 Darmstadt, W. Germany, or from Software AG North America Inc., 11800 Sunrise Valley Drive, Reston, Virginia 22091.

11.37 F. Antonacci, P. Dell'Orco, and V. N. Spadavecchia. "AQL: An APL-Based System for Accessing and Manipulating Data in a Relational Database System." *Proc. APL 76 Conference, Ottawa* (September 1976). Available from ACM.

Describes a SEQUEL-like query language implemented as an extension to APL.

11.38 M. Stonebraker and E. Neuhold. "A Distributed Data Base Version of INGRES." Berkeley: University of California, Electronics Research Laboratory Memorandum ERL-M612 (September 1976).

A distributed database is a database that is not stored in its entirety in a single physical location, but rather is spread across a network of dispersed (but interconnected) computers. In principle, such a system could allow data to be physically stored close to the point where it is most frequently used—with obvious efficiency advantages—while at the same time permitting that same data to be shared by other, geographically remote users. However, there are numerous technical problems to be solved in implementing such a system. This paper discusses the approach being taken to these problems in the relational system INGRES [5.19].

Part 3
The Hierarchical Approach

Many present-day database systems are based on the hierarchical approach. In Part 3 we examine one such system, IMS, in considerable detail. Chapter 12 describes the overall structure of an IMS system. Chapters 13, 14, and 15 present the major features of the IMS data model, external model, and data sublanguage, respectively, introducing in each case the appropriate IMS terminology. Chapter 16 is concerned with those parts of an IMS system that lie below the user interface, i.e., the storage structure and the mapping between the data model and storage. Finally, Chapters 17 and 18 provide introductions to two special IMS features, namely, "logical databases" (Chapter 17) and secondary indexing (Chapter 18). Although not really part of the hierarchical approach as such, being very definitely special features of IMS, these topics have been included as interesting examples of how the hierarchical approach may be extended and also of its limitations.

The reader should note that in the later chapters (especially Chapter 16) we are discussing what are effectively the details of a database system *implementation*—the only place in the book where this is done in any real depth. The intention is to give some idea as to what must go on "under the covers" (i.e., below the user interface) of a working system. The fact that IMS has been chosen as the vehicle for such a discussion should not be construed as a criticism or otherwise either of IMS or of any other system.

Many other hierarchical systems are described in references [1.1, 1.2, 1.5, and 1.12].

12

The Architecture
of an
IMS System

12.1 BACKGROUND

The name IMS is an acronym for "Information Management System."
IMS is an IBM program product that is designed to support both batch
and on-line application programs. During its evolution several distinct
versions of IMS and related products have been made available by IBM;
the principal ones are IMS/360 Version 1, IMS/360 Version 2, and the
version current at the time of writing, IMS/VS (Information Management
System/Virtual Storage), Version 1, which runs under the IBM operating
system OS/VS (Operating System/Virtual Storage). We shall generally be
discussing only this most recent version; IBM manuals invariably refer to
this version as IMS/VS, but we shall use the abbreviated form "IMS"
throughout this book. We choose IMS as our main example of the
hierarchical approach since at the time of this writing it is one of the most
widely used of all database systems, hierarchical or otherwise.

In its basic form an IMS system provides facilities for the running of
batch applications only. It is possible to extend such a system, via the data
communications feature, to permit the development of on-line applications (that is, applications that support access to the database from a
remote terminal); however, such an application will use the same facilities
as a batch application for actually accessing the database—the data
communications feature provides the facilities required to access the
terminal, not the database.[1] For the most part, therefore, we shall ignore

---

[1] An example of such an application is IQF—Interactive Query Facility [12.2]—
another IBM program product, which permits on-line retrieval (only) from an
IMS database, using a query language that may be tailored to be as close as
desired to the user's natural language.

the on-line aspects of IMS, since they do not form part of an IMS *database* system as such.

12.2 ARCHITECTURE

The architecture of an IMS system is illustrated in Fig. 12.1. Note first of all that the stored data consists of several databases, not just one. An IMS database is a stored representation of a "physical database," and a physical database, to use relational terminology, is simply an unnor-

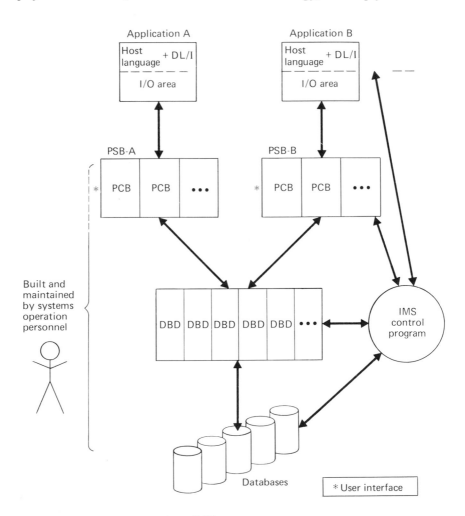

Fig. 12.1 Architecture of an IMS system

malized relation (more or less). It is therefore unlikely that the operational data of the enterprise would be contained entirely within one such database, in general.

The data model (not an IMS term) consists then of a collection of physical databases. The term "physical" is somewhat misleading in this context, since the user does *not* see such a database exactly as it is stored; indeed, IMS provides a fairly high degree of insulation of the user from the storage structure (and hence a fairly high degree of data independence), as we shall see in Chapter 16. Each physical database is defined by a *database description* (DBD). The mapping of the physical database to storage is also specified (at least in part; see Chapter 16) in the DBD. Hence the set of all DBDs corresponds to the conceptual schema plus (part of) the associated conceptual/internal mapping definition.

As in the general architecture of Chapter 1, the user does not operate directly on the data model but on an external model (not an IMS term). A particular user's external model consists of a collection of "logical databases," where each logical database is a subset (in a sense to be explained) of the corresponding physical database.[2] Each logical database is defined, together with its mapping to the corresponding physical database, by means of a *program communication block* (PCB). The set of all PCBs for one user, corresponding to the external schema plus the associated mapping definition, is called a *program specification block* (PSB).

Finally, as explained in Section 12.1, the users are ordinary application programmers, using a host language (PL/I, COBOL, or System/360 Assembler Language) from which the IMS data sublanguage DL/I— "Data Language/I"—may be invoked by subroutine call. ("Data sublanguage" is not an IMS term.) The "workspace" used for the transfer of the data between the program and a logical database is simply an input/output area (as commonly understood).

Figure 12.1 also shows the IMS terms for DBA and DBMS. "User interface" is not an IMS term.

---

[2] The term "logical database" actually has two distinct meanings in IMS. The meaning presented here is probably the less important of the two. The second meaning is introduced in Chapter 17. It must be emphasized that logical databases in this second sense are not really considered at all prior to Chapter 17; this has the effect of simplifying the presentation of much of the material in Chapters 12–16. Several of the topics introduced in these chapters are given an extended interpretation in Chapter 17.

Secondary indexing also has a significant effect on the external model. For tutorial reasons, again, we shall substantially ignore all aspects of this topic until we reach Chapter 18.

REFERENCES AND BIBLIOGRAPHY

12.1 IBM Corporation. Information Management System/Virtual Storage General Information Manual. IBM Form No. GH20-1260.

12.2 IBM Corporation. Interactive Query Facility (IQF) for IMS Version 2. IBM Form No. GH20-1074.

12.3 D. C. Tsichritzis and F. H. Lochovsky. "Hierarchical Data Base Management: A Survey." *ACM Computing Surveys* **8,** No. 1 (March 1976).

   Includes a brief tutorial not only on IMS but also on System 2000.

12.4 W. C. McGee. "The IMS/VS System." *IBM Sys. J.* (forthcoming).

13

The IMS
Data Model

13.1 PHYSICAL DATABASES

In the previous chapter the IMS data model was defined as a collection of *physical databases* (PDBs). A physical database is an ordered set, the elements of which consist of all occurrences of one type of *physical database record* (PDBR). A PDBR occurrence in turn consists of a hierarchical arrangement of fixed-length *segment* occurrences;[1] and a segment occurrence consists of a set of associated fixed-length *field* occurrences. The unit of access (the smallest amount of data that may be transferred by one DL/I operation) is the segment occurrence.

As an example we consider a PDB that contains information about the internal education system of a large industrial company. The hierarchical structure of this PDB—that is, the PDBR *type*—is illustrated in Fig. 13.1.

In this example we are assuming that the company maintains an education department whose function is to run a number of training courses. Each course is offered at a number of different locations within the company. The PDB contains details both of offerings already given and of offerings scheduled to be given in the future. The details follow.

- For each course: course number (unique), course title, course description, details of prerequisite courses (if any), and details of all offerings (past and planned)

- For each prerequisite course for a given course: course number and title

---

[1] Variable-length segments are also permitted, but the details are beyond the scope of this text.

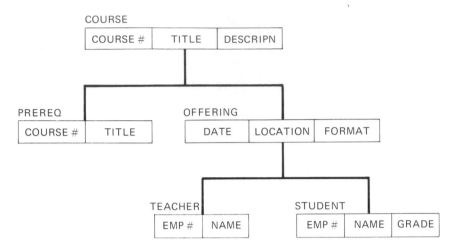

Fig. 13.1   PDBR type for the education database

- For each offering of a given course: date, location, format (e.g., duration, full-time or half-time), details of all teachers, and details of all students
- For each teacher of a given offering: employee number and name
- For each student of a given offering: employee number, name, and grade

As Fig. 13.1 shows, we have here five types of segment: COURSE, PREREQ, OFFERING, TEACHER, and STUDENT, each one consisting of the field types indicated. COURSE is the *root* segment type; the others are dependent segment types. Each dependent (segment type) has a *parent* (segment type)—the parent of TEACHER (and STUDENT) is OFFERING, for example.[2] Similarly, each parent (segment type) has at least one *child* (segment type); COURSE, for example, has two.

It is important to understand that for one occurrence of any given segment type there may be any number of occurrences (possibly zero) of each of its child segment types. Figure 13.2 illustrates this point.

---

[2] Occasionally we might also consider a segment type higher up in the hierarchical path as a parent; for example, COURSE might also be considered as a parent of TEACHER (and STUDENT). In general, given a particular position in the hierarchical structure, any type of segment in the path from that point back to the root may be considered as a parent. However, in this book the term should be taken to refer to the *immediate* parent, unless we explicitly state otherwise.

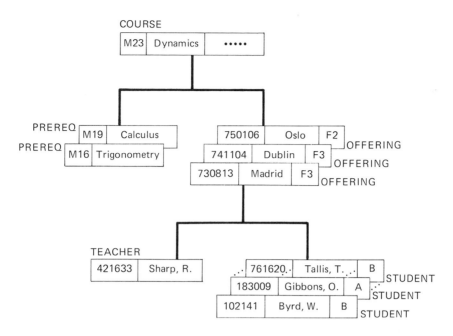

Fig. 13.2   Sample PDBR occurrence for the education database

Here we have one occurrence of the root (COURSE), and hence, by definition, one occurrence of the education PDBR type. The complete PDB will contain many PDBR occurrences, representing information about many courses. In the particular PDBR occurrence shown in Fig. 13.2, we have dependent on the COURSE occurrence two occurrences of PREREQ and three of OFFERING. The first OFFERING occurrence in turn has one TEACHER occurrence and several STUDENT occurrences (only three shown) dependent on it. The other OFFERINGs have no teachers or students assigned to them as yet.

The parent-child nomenclature, introduced earlier for segment types, applies also to segment occurrences. Thus each dependent segment occurrence has a parent (segment occurrence)—the parent of the TEACHER occurrence (and the STUDENT occurrences) is the first OFFERING occurrence, for example.[3] Conversely, the TEACHER and STUDENT occurrences are considered as children (child segment occur-

----

[3] The root may also be considered as a parent for these occurrences; compare the situation with respect to segment types.

rences) of this OFFERING occurrence. In addition, all occurrences of a particular type of child segment that share a common parent occurrence are said to be *twins*. Thus the OFFERING occurrences in Fig. 13.2, for example, are twins, even though there are three of them.

To sum up, then:

- A PDBR type contains a single type of root segment.
- The root may have any number of child segment types.
- Each child of the root may also have any number of child segment types, and so on (up to a maximum of 15 segment types in any one hierarchical path and a maximum of 255 segment types in the complete PDBR type).[4]
- For one occurrence of any given segment type there may be any number of occurrences (possibly zero) of each of its children.
- No child segment occurrence can exist without its parent.

The last point is essentially a restatement of the hierarchical philosophy. It means, for example, that if a given segment occurrence is deleted, so are all its children (as explained in Chapter 3).

From this point on we shall drop the terms "type" and "occurrence" if there is no possibility of confusion; indeed, we have already started to do so, as the reader may have noticed.

13.2   THE DATABASE DESCRIPTION

Each physical database is defined, together with its mapping to storage, by a database description (DBD). In its source form the DBD consists of a set of System/360 Assembler Language macro statements. Once written, the DBD is assembled and the object form is stored away in a system library, from which it may be extracted when required by the IMS control program.

We shall ignore for now that part of the DBD concerned with the mapping to storage. We shall also ignore a few statements concerned purely with housekeeping details (such as error message generation). The remainder—what we may call the "conceptual schema part"—for the education database example is shown in Fig. 13.3. The statements have been numbered as reference points for the explanations that follow.

---

[4] These are of course characteristics of IMS, not a fundamental part of the hierarchical approach.

```
 1  DBD            NAME=EDUCPDBD
 2  SEGM           NAME=COURSE,BYTES=256
 3  FIELD          NAME=(COURSE#,SEQ),BYTES=3,START=1
 4  FIELD          NAME=TITLE,BYTES=33,START=4
 5  FIELD          NAME=DESCRIPN,BYTES=220,START=37
 6  SEGM           NAME=PREREQ,PARENT=COURSE,BYTES=36
 7  FIELD          NAME=(COURSE#,SEQ),BYTES=3,START=1
 8  FIELD          NAME=TITLE,BYTES=33,START=4
 9  SEGM           NAME=OFFERING,PARENT=COURSE,BYTES=20
10  FIELD          NAME=(DATE,SEQ,M),BYTES=6,START=1
11  FIELD          NAME=LOCATION,BYTES=12,START=7
12  FIELD          NAME=FORMAT,BYTES=2,START=19
13  SEGM           NAME=TEACHER,PARENT=OFFERING,BYTES=24
14  FIELD          NAME=(EMP#,SEQ),BYTES=6,START=1
15  FIELD          NAME=NAME,BYTES=18,START=7
16  SEGM           NAME=STUDENT,PARENT=OFFERING,BYTES=25
17  FIELD          NAME=(EMP#,SEQ),BYTES=6,START=1
18  FIELD          NAME=NAME,BYTES=18,START=7
19  FIELD          NAME=GRADE,BYTES=1,START=25
```

Fig. 13.3   DBD (conceptual schema part) for the education PDB

Explanations

Statement 1 merely assigns the name EDUCPDBD ("education physical database description") to the DBD. Incidentally, all names in IMS are limited to a maximum length of eight characters.

Statement 2 defines the root segment type as having the name COURSE and as being 256 bytes in length.

Statements 3–5 define the field types that go to make up COURSE. Each is given a name, a length in bytes, and a start position within the segment. The first field, COURSE#, is defined as the sequence field for the segment. This means that within the education PDB, PDBR occurrences will be sequenced in ascending course number order.

Statement 6 defines PREREQ as a 36-byte segment dependent on COURSE.

Statements 7–8 define the fields of PREREQ. The first field, COURSE# (again), is defined as the sequence field for PREREQ. This means that for each occurrence of the parent (COURSE), occurrences of this child (PREREQ) will be sequenced in ascending course number order—in other words, it specifies twin sequence (this is generally true, even for the root, if we agree to consider all root occurrences as twins of each other).

Statement 9 defines OFFERING as a child of COURSE.

Statements 10–12 define the fields of OFFERING. DATE is defined as the sequence field for OFFERING. The specification M (multiple) means that twin OFFERING occurrences may contain the *same* date value (implying in this case that two offerings of the same course are being taught concurrently).

Statements 13–15 define the TEACHER segment (a child of OF-FERING) and its fields.

Statements 16–19 define the STUDENT segment (a child of OF-FERING) and its fields.

The sequence of statements in the DBD is very important. Specifically, SEGM statements must appear in the sequence that reflects the hierarchical structure (top to bottom, left to right);[5] also, each SEGM statement must be immediately followed by the appropriate FIELD statements. As we shall see, the first of these points has a very definite effect on the user. It means that the sequence, not only of segment occurrences but also of segment *types*, is built into the data model, so that, for example, the user can issue a DL/I "get next" operation to step from a TEACHER occurrence to a STUDENT occurrence.

A few additional points:

- Specification of a sequence field is optional, except as noted below.

- The sequence field, if specified, is taken to be *unique* unless M (multiple) is specified. By "unique" here we mean that no two occurrences of the given segment type under a common parent occurrence—or, in the case of the root, no two occurrences of the given segment type in the database—may have the same value for the sequence field.

- A unique sequence field is required for the root segment in HISAM and HIDAM (see Chapter 16).

- The simple rule given earlier for twin sequence (ascending values of the sequence field) does not specify what happens if the sequence field is omitted or is nonunique. In such a case additional specifica-

---

[5] Internally IMS identifies each type of segment by its position in the hierarchical structure. Thus, in the education PDB, COURSE has type code 1, PREREQ has type code 2, OFFERING 3, TEACHER 4, and STUDENT 5.

tions are needed in the DBD, and additional programming may be required on the part of the user when a new segment is to be inserted. In certain situations, moreover, the lack of a unique sequence field can lead to serious logical difficulties [16.1]; the details are beyond the scope of this book, but for reasons such as these we shall generally restrict ourselves to unique sequence fields throughout this book.

■ The FIELD statement for the sequence field, if there is one, must be the first such statement for the segment.

■ Overlapping fields may be defined; for example, the COURSE segment may be defined to contain a field COURSE#N (BYTES = 2, START = 2), representing the second and third (numeric) characters of the COURSE# field. [Note that this permits the combination of several (contiguous) fields to be defined as the sequence field.]

■ It is actually necessary to define only those fields that will be used as search arguments in a DL/I operation. For example, the field DESCRIPN in the COURSE segment need not be defined if no user will ever search for a COURSE occurrence satisfying some condition on the value of DESCRIPN. However, for documentation purposes, at least, it is probably best to define them all.

13.3 HIERARCHICAL SEQUENCE

The concept of hierarchical sequence within a database is a very important one in IMS. We may formally define it as follows.

■ For each segment occurrence, we define the "hierarchical sequence key value" to consist of the sequence field value for that segment, prefixed with the type code for that segment (see footnote 5), prefixed with the hierarchical sequence key value of its parent, if any. For example, the hierarchical sequence key value for the STUDENT occurrence for "Byrd, W." (see Fig. 13.2) is

$$1M233730813510214 1$$

Then the hierarchical sequence for an IMS database is that sequence of segment occurrences defined by ascending values of the hierarchical sequence key.[6]

---

[6] We do not consider the case where sequence fields are omitted or are nonunique.

The reason for the importance of this notion is that IMS databases are stored in hierarchical sequence,[7] in general; hence certain DL/I operations—essentially those concerned with sequential retrieval and with loading the database—are defined in terms of this sequence. (Actually this is not quite true for HDAM; see Chapter 16.)

13.4 SOME REMARKS ON THE EDUCATION DATABASE

Before we leave the subject of the IMS data model, there are a few additional points to be made in connection with the education example. They arise from the various redundancies deliberately introduced into that example.

Consider students, first of all. For every course offering attended by a particular student, the PDB will contain that student's employee number *and* his or her name. Hence the association between a particular number and the corresponding name will appear many times, in general. This in turn introduces the possibility that a given employee number may have different names associated with it at different points, i.e., that the PDB may be inconsistent.

Similar remarks apply to teachers, where again the redundancy concerns employee numbers and names, and to prerequisite courses. For the latter, the redundancy concerns the relationship between a course number and a title; not only will a given instance of this association appear every time the particular course is a prerequisite for some other course, but it will also appear in the root for the PDBR occurrence for the particular course itself.

However, it may actually be desirable to provide the user with a data model containing redundancies such as these. The "logical database" feature of IMS allows redundancy to be built into the data model *without* necessarily entailing a corresponding redundancy in the data as stored, and hence *without* the possibility of inconsistency. ("Logical database" is being used here in the sense of Chapter 17.) To see why redundancy may be desirable in the data model, let us consider what would happen if it were removed in the example.

To remove the employee name redundancy, we can eliminate the employee name field from the TEACHER and STUDENT segments and introduce another PDB containing a single type of segment—EMP, say—with fields EMP# and NAME. This PDB represents the required association between employee numbers and names. Similarly, we can

---

[7] This statement should not be taken to mean that the data is *physically* stored in this sequence. Several techniques—chaining, indexing, and so on—are actually used to represent the hierarchical sequence. See Chapter 16 for details.

eliminate the course title field from the PREREQ segment; the association between course numbers and titles is already represented in the education PDB (in the COURSE segment). However, the effect of removing the redundancies in this way is to make more work for the user, as the following paragraphs explain.

Observe first that the data model—the user's view of the data—is made more complicated, in that it now contains two (interconnected) PDBs instead of one. Second, the nature of DL/I is such that within one operation the user can process only one database. Hence the programming required in many cases will be more complex than before. Consider, for example, the query "Find the names of all students on a specified offering of a specified course." With the original data model this task is comparatively straightforward, involving only a simple scan of all STUDENT occurrences subordinate to the specified OFFERING of the specified COURSE. With the revised data model the user must still scan the same set of STUDENT occurrences; in addition, however, the user must extract the EMP# value from each such STUDENT and use it to retrieve an EMP occurrence from the second database.

As another example, take the query "Find the titles of all prerequisites of a specified course." With the original data model, this query requires only a simple scan of all PREREQ occurrences subordinate to the specified COURSE. With the revised data model, it requires such a scan, followed by the extraction of prerequisite COURSE# values and additional retrieval operations (on the same database)—with further complications arising from the IMS notion of current position (to be explained in Chapter 15).

For reasons such as these, it is quite usual to choose a data model in IMS that does involve a certain amount of redundancy. As mentioned above, this does not necessarily imply redundancy in the data as stored.

EXERCISE

13.1 Figure 13.4 represents the hierarchical structure of a physical database that contains information about publications in a number of selected subject areas.

For the purposes of this database, we assume that publications are of two types: articles and monographs. An article is a paper appearing in a journal or magazine that will also, in general, contain other articles (by different authors). A monograph is a publication devoted entirely to the work of one author or one team of authors. Note that a publication may appear in several different places; for example, the same article may be published in both *Communications of the ACM* and the *BCS Computer Bulletin* (reference [1.3] is an example).

The segments contain the following fields.

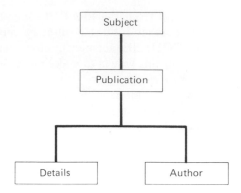

Fig. 13.4   PDBR type for the publications database

- Subject: subject classification number (unique), name of subject
- Publication: type flag (A = article, M = monograph), title
- Details: date of publication, publishing house (if a monograph), journal name plus volume number and issue number (if an article)
- Author: author name and address

  Write (the conceptual schema part of) an appropriate DBD.

REFERENCES AND BIBLIOGRAPHY

13.1 IBM Corporation. Information Management System/Virtual Storage Utilities Reference Manual. IBM Form No. SH20–9029.

This manual includes full details of DBD specification (also PSB specification; see Chapter 14).

14
The IMS
External
Model

14.1 LOGICAL DATABASES

In Chapter 12 a particular user's external model was defined as a collection of logical databases, and a logical database, in turn, was defined as a subset of the (unique) corresponding physical database. We can now amplify these ideas. A logical database (LDB) is an ordered set, the elements of which consist of all occurrences of one type of logical database record (LDBR). An LDBR type is a hierarchical arrangement of segment types; this hierarchy is a subhierarchy of some particular PDBR type, the only difference between the two being that any PDBR segment type, *together with all its children,* may be omitted in the LDBR. Observe the implication that the LDBR root must be the same as the PDBR root. (Example: There are ten distinct LDBs that may be derived from the education PDB of Fig. 13.1. One is illustrated in Fig. 14.1. What are the others?)

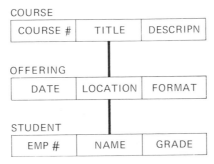

COURSE

COURSE #	TITLE	DESCRIPN

OFFERING

DATE	LOCATION	FORMAT

STUDENT

EMP #	NAME	GRADE

Fig. 14.1 Sample LDBR type for the education database

Those PDBR segments included in the LDBR—e.g., segments COURSE, OFFERING, and STUDENT in Fig. 14.1—are said to be "sensitive." A user of this LDB will not be aware of the existence of any other segments; for example, the DL/I "get next" operation, which in general is used for sequential retrieval, will simply skip over any segments not sensitive for that user. The only exception is that if the user deletes a sensitive segment (occurrence), all children of that segment will be deleted, too, regardless of whether they are sensitive or not. In practice, a user should presumably not be given the authority to delete a segment if it permits the deletion of other hidden segments as well (see the discussion of PROCOPT in Section 14.2).

The sensitive-segment concept protects the user from certain types of growth in the PDB (not all types, however). Specifically, a new type of segment may be added (as the child of an existing segment) at any point, provided only that it does not affect any existing parent-child relationship in any way.[1] The new segment will simply not be sensitive for any existing user. In the case of the education PDB, a new segment may be added at any of the following points.

1. Subordinate to PREREQ
2. Subordinate to TEACHER
3. Subordinate to STUDENT
4. Subordinate to COURSE (at the same level as PREREQ and OFFERING)
5. Subordinate to OFFERING (at the same level as TEACHER and STUDENT)

However, introducing a new segment between COURSE and OFFERING would definitely affect current users of that particular hierarchical path. (Similarly, adding a new field to an existing segment would normally mean that changes would have to be made to programs using that segment.)

The sensitive-segment concept also provides a degree of control over data security, inasmuch as users can be prevented from accessing particular segment types by the omission of those segments from the LDB (except as noted above for deletions).

---

[1] Of course, a new DBD will have to be created, and in most cases the PDB will have to be unloaded and reloaded according to the new DBD. (Reloading is unnecessary if the new segment appears after all existing segments in the top-to-bottom, left-to-right sequence.)

14.2 THE PROGRAM COMMUNICATION BLOCK

Each logical database is defined by a program communication block (PCB). The PCB includes a specification of the mapping between the LDB and the corresponding PDB (which is of course very simple). Like the DBD, the PCB in its source form consists of a set of System/360 Assembler Language macro statements. The set of all PCBs for a given user forms that user's program specification block (PSB); the object form of the PSB is stored in a system library, from which it may be extracted when required by the IMS control program.

Figure 14.2 shows the PCB for the LDB of Fig. 14.1. The statements are again numbered as reference points for the explanations that follow.

```
1 PCB          TYPE=DB,DBDNAME=EDUCPDBD,KEYLEN=15
2 SENSEG       NAME=COURSE,PROCOPT=G
3 SENSEG       NAME=OFFERING,PARENT=COURSE,PROCOPT=G
4 SENSEG       NAME=STUDENT,PARENT=OFFERING,PROCOPT=G
```

Fig. 14.2 PCB for the LDB of Fig. 14.1

Explanations

Statement 1 specifies (a) that this is a database PCB as opposed to a terminal PCB;[2] (b) that the DBD for the underlying physical database is called EDUCPDBD; and (c) that the length of the key feedback area is 15 bytes. The last point requires some explanation. When the user accesses an LDB, the corresponding PCB is held in storage and acts as a communication area between the user's program and IMS. One of the fields in the PCB is the key feedback area. When the user retrieves a segment from the LDB (via a DL/I "get" operation), IMS not only fetches the requested segment but also places a "fully concatenated key" into the key feedback area. The fully concatenated key consists of the concatenation of the sequence field values of all segments in the hierarchical path from the root down to the retrieved segment. For example, if the user retrieves the STUDENT occurrence for "Byrd, W." (see Fig. 13.2), IMS will place the value

$$M23730813102141$$

in the key feedback area. In order for IMS to be able to reserve a

---

[2] Terminal PCBs are used in connection with the data communications feature.

sufficiently large key feedback area within the PCB, the maximum length
for a fully concatenated key (considering all hierarchical paths in the
LDBR type) must be calculated and quoted in the KEYLEN entry of the
PCB statement. In our example the value is 15 (3 for COURSE# plus 6
for DATE plus 6 for EMP#).

Note that the fully concatenated key of a segment is not quite the
same as the "hierarchical sequence key" of Section 13.3—it does not
include the segment type code information.

Statement 2 specifies the first sensitive segment (the root) in the
LDB. Note that the name of a sensitive segment must be the same as the
name assigned to the segment in the DBD. The PROCOPT ("processing
options") entry specifies the types of operation that the user will be
permitted to perform on this segment. In the example the entry is G
("get"), indicating retrieval only. Other possible values are I ("insert"), R
("replace"), and D ("delete"); any or all of G, I, R, and D may be
specified, in any order. Some other entries are explained in reference
[13.1].

Statement 3 defines the next sensitive segment in the LDB. As in the
DBD, the segments must be specified in the correct hierarchical sequence
(top to bottom, left to right). The PARENT entry specifies the appropriate parent segment (which must be as defined in the DBD). Again
PROCOPT has been quoted as G.

Statement 4 defines the last sensitive segment. In our example
statements 3 and 4 are very similar. In the PCB of Fig. 14.1 the
PROCOPT entry is the same for each of the three sensitive segments. In
such a situation we may specify PROCOPT in the PCB statement instead
of in each SENSEG statement. If PROCOPT is specified in both the PCB
statement and in a SENSEG statement, the SENSEG entry overrides the
PCB entry, in general. However, there is one entry, L ("load"—i.e.,
create the initial version of the database), which may be specified only in
the PCB statement and which cannot be overridden. Also, there is one
entry, K, which may be specified only in the SENSEG statement. K ("key
sensitivity") is used when the designer of the PCB is forced by the
hierarchical structure of the underlying physical database to include a
segment that the user of the PCB does not really require (or perhaps is
not allowed to access). Suppose, for example, that a particular application
is interested only in courses and students, not in offerings. The PCB for
this user must include the OFFERING segment, because it forms part of
the hierarchical path from COURSE to STUDENT. However, if
PROCOPT = K is specified in the SENSEG statement for OFFERING,
the user may largely ignore the presence of OFFERINGs in the hierarchy. For most purposes, in other words, the user may think of the logical

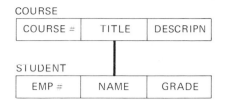

Fig. 14.3   Effect of specifying PROCOPT=K for OFFERING

database as if it had the structure shown in Fig. 14.3; the main difference is that when a STUDENT occurrence is retrieved, the fully concatenated key in the key feedback area will include the date value from the parent OFFERING. To be more precise, the user may issue DL/I retrieval requests exactly as if key-sensitive segments were *not* absent—in the case at hand, in particular, the user may refer to the OFFERING segment and to fields within it in the usual way—and IMS will handle such requests in exactly the normal manner,[3] right up to the point at which the retrieved data (if any) is due to be delivered to the program. At that point, delivery will be suppressed for any segment for which key sensitivity was specified (although the segment's sequence field value will be placed in the key feedback area). A key-sensitive segment may not be the direct target of a DL/I storage operation (insert, delete, or replace), although of course it is possible to delete such a segment by deleting its parent.

EXERCISE

14.1 Write a PCB (all segments sensitive) for the publications PDB (see Exercise 13.1). This PCB is to be used for retrieval operations only.

REFERENCES AND BIBLIOGRAPHY

See [13.1].

---

[3] An exception to this statement is that retrieval requests without SSAs—see Examples 15.3.6 and 15.3.9 in the following chapter—will skip over key-sensitive segments.

15

The IMS Data
Sublanguage

15.1 DEFINING THE PROGRAM COMMUNICATION BLOCK (PCB)

The IMS data sublanguage (DL/I) is invoked from the host language
(PL/I, COBOL, or System/360 Assembler Language) by means of ordinary subroutine calls. As mentioned in Section 14.2, when an application
program is operating on a particular logical database (LDB), the PCB for
that LDB is kept in storage to serve as a communication area between the
program and IMS; in fact, when the program calls DL/I, it has to quote
the storage address of the appropriate PCB to identify to DL/I which
LDB it is to operate on (remember that one program may be accessing
many LDBs, in general).

How, then, does the program know the PCB address? The answer is
that it is supplied to the program by IMS when the program is first
entered. What actually happens is this. When a database application is to
be run, IMS is loaded and given control first. IMS determines which PSB
and DBD(s) are required, fetches them from their respective libraries,
and loads them into storage (note that the DBD(s) are specified in the
PSB and the PSB is specified by means of a Job Control Language
statement [16.3]). IMS then fetches and loads the application program
and gives it control, passing it the PCB addresses as parameters.

In order for the application program to be able to access the
information in the PCB for a particular LDB, it must contain a definition
of that PCB. The definition will not reserve any storage space but will act
as a mask to fit over the real PCB (which will not physically reside within
the application's own storage area). A reference to a field within the PCB
definition will be interpreted as a reference to the corresponding field in
the real PCB.

```
DLITPLI: PROCEDURE(COSPCB_ADDR) OPTIONS(MAIN);
          .
          .
          .
        DECLARE 1 COSPCB      BASED(COSPCB_ADDR),
                2 DBDNAME     CHARACTER(8),
                2 SEGLEVEL    CHARACTER(2),
                2 STATUS      CHARACTER(2),
                2 PROCOPT     CHARACTER(4),
                2 RESERVED    FIXED BINARY(31),
                2 SEGNAME     CHARACTER(8),
                2 KEYFBLEN    FIXED BINARY(31),
                2 #SENSEGS    FIXED BINARY(31),
                2 KEYFBAREA CHARACTER(15);
```

Fig. 15.1   Example of program entry and PCB definition (PL/I)

For example, suppose that we have a PL/I application that operates on the course-offering-student LDB of Fig. 14.1, and suppose also that this is the only LDB used in this application. Then part of the program might look like Fig. 15.1.

Explanations

The PROCEDURE statement (labeled DLITPLI) is the program entry point. The name DLITPLI is mandatory (for PL/I); all other names shown (COSPCB, DBDNAME, SEGLEVEL, etc.) are arbitrary. The expression in parentheses following the keyword PROCEDURE represents the parameters to be passed to the program by IMS; in general, it will consist of a list of pointers, one for each PCB in the PSB, where the first pointer gives the address of the first PCB, and so on. In the example there is only one PCB and hence only one pointer in the list.

The rest of Fig. 15.1 consists of a DECLARE statement that defines a structure (named COSPCB) to represent the single PCB used in this application. This structure is based on the pointer COSPCB _ ADDR. The fields of the structure serve the following purposes.

The field DBDNAME contains the name of the underlying DBD (in our example, EDUCPDBD) throughout execution of the program.

The SEGLEVEL field is set after a DL/I operation to contain the segment level number of the segment just accessed (where the root segment is considered to be level 1, its children level 2, and so on).

The STATUS field is easily the most important in the PCB so far as the user is concerned. After each and every DL/I call, a two-character value is placed in this field to indicate the success or otherwise of the requested operation. A blank value indicates that the operation was completed satisfactorily; any other value represents an exceptional or error condition (for example, a value of GE means "segment not found").

The PROCOPT field contains the PROCOPT value as specified in the PCB statement when the PCB was originally defined.

RESERVED is a field reserved for IMS's own use.

The SEGNAME field contains the name of the segment last accessed.

The KEYFBLEN field contains the current significant length of the fully concatenated key in the key feedback area (see KEYFBAREA below).

The #SENSEGS field contains a count of the number of sensitive segments. In our example the value would be 3 throughout execution.

The field KEYFBAREA is the key feedback area; as explained in Section 14.2, it contains the fully concatenated key (left-justified) of the segment last accessed.

The reader will appreciate that these programming details have very little to do with the hierarchical approach as such. However, it is necessary to have a general understanding of this material in order to appreciate the operations of the IMS data sublanguage properly. These operations *can* reasonably be regarded as typical of the hierarchical approach although, again, they will of course involve a certain amount of IMS-specific detail.

15.2 THE DL/I OPERATIONS

Figure 15.2 summarizes the DL/I operations. As explained before, the application invokes a DL/I operation by means of a subroutine call, one of the parameters of which consists of the address of the appropriate PCB. The other parameters include the operation required (e.g., GU), the address of the input/output area, and (in some cases) one or more qualification conditions, referred to as "segment search arguments"

GET UNIQUE (GU)	Direct retrieval
GET NEXT (GN)	Sequential retrieval
GET NEXT WITHIN PARENT (GNP)	Sequential retrieval under current parent
GET HOLD (GHU, GHN, GHNP)	As above but allow subsequent DLET/REPL
INSERT (ISRT)	Add new segment
DELETE (DLET)	Delete existing segment
REPLACE (REPL)	Replace existing segment

Fig. 15.2 DL/I operations (summary)

```
GU COURSE    (TITLE='DYNAMICS')
   OFFERING  (FORMAT='F1'∨FORMAT='F3')
   STUDENT   (GRADE='A')
```

Fig. 15.3 Example of simplified DL/I syntax

(SSAs). The name of the subroutine is fixed by IMS; for a PL/I application it is PLITDLI. To simplify the examples we shall not normally use genuine DL/I syntax in this book, but rather the hypothetical syntax illustrated by the example in Fig. 15.3. (However, one "genuine" example is given in Section 15.4.)

If we assume that the data is as shown in Fig. 13.2 (ignoring PREREQ and TEACHER segments since they are not sensitive), the result of this DL/I operation is to retrieve the STUDENT segment for "Gibbons, O." The explanation is as follows. "Get unique" (GU) always causes a sequential scan forward from the start of the database[1] (at least conceptually, although beneath the user interface indexing or hashing is normally used; see Chapter 16). The segment retrieved will be the first encountered that satisfies the three SSAs. SSAs are considered in more detail below; in this example the three SSAs specify the hierarchical path to the desired segment—that is, they specify the segment type at each level from the root down, together with an occurrence-identifying condition for each type. The effect of these SSAs is to cause IMS to search in a forward direction for the first COURSE occurrence containing a TITLE value of 'DYNAMICS', then to scan that COURSE's subordinate OFFERING occurrences for the first containing a FORMAT value of 'F1' or 'F3', then to scan that OFFERING's subordinate STUDENT occurrences for the first containing a GRADE value of 'A'. If no such STUDENT exists for that OFFERING, the STUDENTs of the next F1 or F3 format OFFERING of this COURSE will be scanned, and so on. If no further F1 or F3 format OFFERINGs of this COURSE exist, IMS will search for the next COURSE occurrence containing a TITLE value of 'DYNAMICS' and repeat the process (of course, there may not be another such, in which case the retrieval operation will fail and a nonblank status value will be returned to the user).

Note that only the segment at the bottom of the hierarchical path is retrieved. Note, too, that in our simplified syntax we have completely omitted the specification of the input/output area and of the PCB (the course-offering-student logical database was tacitly assumed to be the relevant LDB).

---

[1] This is true provided an SSA has been specified for the root. See [15.1] for details of what happens if this is not the case.

In general, an SSA consists of a segment name, optionally followed by a condition. If the condition is omitted, any occurrence of the indicated segment will satisfy this SSA (provided that it forms part of a hierarchical path as defined by any associated SSAs). If the condition is included, it must consist of a set of comparison expressions connected by means of the Boolean operators "and" and "or"; each comparison expression consists of a ⟨field, comparison operator, value⟩ triple, where the field must belong to the specified segment and the comparison operator may be any one of the usual set ($=$, $\neq$, $<$, $\leq$, $>$, $\geq$). All comparison operations are performed by IMS bit by bit from left to right (i.e., no particular data representation is assumed for the values concerned).

To simplify the IMS rules somewhat, we may say that "get unique" and "insert" operations require SSAs specifying the entire hierarchical path, from the root down; "get next" and "get next within parent" operations may or may not involve SSAs, and if they do, the SSAs must again specify a hierarchical path, but one that may start at any hierarchical level, not just at the root; and "delete" and "replace" operations do not involve SSAs at all. We now give examples of all these possibilities. For these examples we shall assume that the LDB is identical to the PDB of Chapter 13 (i.e., all segments are sensitive).

15.3   DL/I EXAMPLES

For convenience, the structure of the sample database is shown again here as Fig. 15.4.

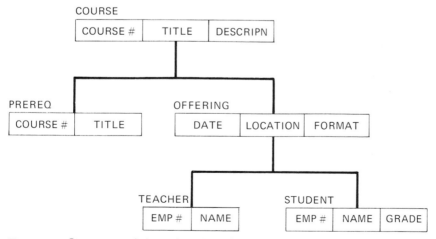

Fig. 15.4   Structure of the education database

15.3.1 Direct retrieval.   Get the first OFFERING occurrence where the location is Stockholm.

```
GU COURSE
   OFFERING (LOCATION='STOCKHOLM')
```

This illustrates (a) the use of an SSA without a condition and (b) a hierarchical path stopping short of a lowest-level segment. Incidentally, this "get unique," like all other DL/I operations, should in practice be followed by an appropriate test on the status value returned; we shall generally ignore this step in our examples. Note that "get unique" is something of a misnomer—the operation is really "get first."

15.3.2 Sequential retrieval with an SSA.   Get all STUDENT occurrences in the LDB, starting with the first student for the offering found in Example 15.3.1.

```
   GU COURSE
      OFFERING (LOCATION='STOCKHOLM')
      STUDENT
NS GN STUDENT
   go to NS
```

The "get unique" retrieves the first student for the first offering in Stockholm. This establishes a current position within the database. The first time "get next" is executed, it retrieves the first student following this position (in a forward direction), and establishes a new current position; the second time it is executed, it retrieves the next one following *this* position, and so on. All other segment types will be ignored. Eventually a status value indicating "segment not found" will be returned.

   In general, the operation of "get next" is defined in terms of the current position, and the current position is defined as the segment last accessed via a "get" operation (of any type) or an "insert" operation.

15.3.3 Sequential retrieval with a conditional SSA.   Like Example 15.3.2, except that only STUDENT occurrences with a grade of A are to be retrieved.

```
    GU COURSE
       OFFERING (LOCATION='STOCKHOLM')
       STUDENT   (GRADE='A')
NSA GN STUDENT   (GRADE='A')
    go to NSA
```

15.3.4 Sequential retrieval with an SSA. Like Example 15.3.3, except that the search is to start at the beginning of the database.

```
        GU COURSE
     NX GN STUDENT (GRADE='A')
        go to NX
```

The "get unique" is used here merely to establish the first segment in the database (the first occurrence of the root) as the initial position. Note that it also retrieves that segment, which is not really required.

15.3.5 Sequential retrieval with multiple conditional SSAs. Like Example 15.3.3, except that only STUDENT occurrences with a grade of A for Stockholm offerings are to be retrieved.

```
        GU COURSE
           OFFERING (LOCATION='STOCKHOLM')
           STUDENT  (GRADE='A')
     NY GN OFFERING (LOCATION='STOCKHOLM')
           STUDENT  (GRADE='A')
        go to NY
```

15.3.6 Sequential retrieval without SSAs. Get all segments.

```
        GU COURSE
     NZ GN
        go to NZ
```

The user can determine the type of each segment after it is retrieved by inspecting the PCB.

15.3.7 Sequential retrieval with an SSA within a parent. Get all students for the offering on 13 August 1973 of course M23. (See Fig. 13.2. We assume that there is only one offering of this course on this date.)

```
        GU  COURSE   (COURSE#='M23')
            OFFERING (DATE='730813')
     NP GNP STUDENT
        go to NP
```

The operation of "get next within parent" is the same as that of "get next," except that when all segments satisfying the SSAs have been retrieved for the current parent, the next attempt to execute the GNP will return a status value indicating this fact. The current parent is the segment last accessed by means of "get unique" or "get next" (*not* "get next within parent").

15.3.8 Sequential retrieval with a conditional SSA within a parent. Get all students who achieved a grade of A on (any offering of) course M23.

```
         GU  COURSE   (COURSE#='M23')
     NQ GNP STUDENT   (GRADE='A')
        go to NQ
```

In this case the "parent" for the GNP operation is not the immediate parent of the segment to be retrieved; see the footnotes on this point in Section 13.1.

15.3.9 Sequential retrieval without SSAs within a parent. Get all subordinate segments (of all types) for course M23.

```
         GU  COURSE   (COURSE#='M23')
     NN GNP
        go to NN
```

As in Example 15.3.6, the user can determine the type of each segment after it is retrieved by inspecting the PCB.

15.3.10 Segment insertion. Add a new STUDENT occurrence for the offering on 13 August 1973 of course M23. (Again we assume that there is only one offering of this course on this date.)

```
        build new segment in I/O area
        ISRT   COURSE   (COURSE#='M23')
               OFFERING (DATE='730813')
               STUDENT
```

When a segment occurrence is to be inserted, the parent occurrence must already exist in the database. The "insert" operation specifies the complete hierarchical path to this parent (note the conditions in the COURSE and OFFERING SSAs in the example) and also the type of the segment to be inserted. IMS will enter the new occurrence at the correct position, as defined by the value of its sequence field (in this case EMP#).

It is in fact possible to omit the specification of the hierarchical path and to quote just the type of the new segment. In this case IMS will use the current position—i.e., the segment last accessed via a "get" or "insert" operation—to determine where to insert the new segment.

Consider, for example, the "insert" operation:

```
ISRT STUDENT
```

If the current segment is an OFFERING, the new STUDENT will be inserted beneath it; if it is a TEACHER or a STUDENT, it will be inserted beneath the OFFERING above that TEACHER or STUDENT. In all cases the sequence field value will be used to determine the position of the new segment with respect to any existing twins.

    "Insert" is also used to perform the initial loading of the database. Since segment occurrences to be loaded must be presented in hierarchical sequence,[2] specifying just the segment type in the ISRT is the normal method of operation in this case. (Basically each new segment has to be loaded immediately following the current segment.)

15.3.11   **Segment deletion.**   Delete the offering of course M23 on 13 August 1973.

```
GHU  COURSE   (COURSE#='M23')
     OFFERING (DATE='730813')
DLET
```

The segment to be deleted must first be retrieved via one of the "get hold" operations—"get hold unique" (GHU), "get hold next" (GHN), or "get hold next within parent" (GHNP). The "delete" operation may then be issued (unless the user decides not to delete the segment after all, in which case he or she may simply continue processing as usual, e.g., issue another "get hold"). Note that the "delete" operation has no SSAs; however, it does specify the I/O area (not shown in our simplified syntax), and the retrieved segment remains in the I/O area after the deletion has been performed. Remember that a successful "delete" operation deletes the specified segment occurrence and also all its children.

15.3.12   **Segment replacement.**   Change the location of the 13 August 1973 offering of course M23 to Helsinki.

```
GHU  COURSE   (COURSE#='M23')
     OFFERING (DATE='730813')
change location to 'HELSINKI' in I/O area
REPL
```

---

[2] Not quite true for HDAM; see Chapter 16.

As with "delete," the segment to be replaced must first be retrieved via one of the "get hold" calls. It is then modified in the I/O area, and the "replace" operation is issued. The sequence field cannot be modified, however; its value must remain unchanged in the I/O area (incidentally, this applies to "delete" as well). Again, if the user decides not to replace the segment after all, he or she may simply continue processing in the usual way; and again there are no SSAs involved.

15.4   CONSTRUCTING THE SEGMENT SEARCH ARGUMENT (SSA)

The process of constructing a segment search argument is a detail of IMS, not a part of the hierarchical approach as such. However, a little should be said about the subject here in order to avoid leaving the reader with a false impression. The simple syntax we have been using has concealed the fact that an SSA is actually a character string, forming one of the parameters of a subroutine call. A typical value for this character string might be

'STUDENTb(GRADEbbb=bA)'

(We now show genuine IMS syntax, in which blank padding characters—shown as b above—must be used to make each portion of the SSA a predefined fixed length, and the comparison value is not enclosed in quotation marks.) The point about this example is that the comparison value is a constant, whereas in practice it is far more likely that the value of a variable would be required. Consequently, before issuing the DL/I subroutine call, the programmer must dynamically *construct* the SSA character string by actually moving the value of the comparison variable into the appropriate position. (In general, of course, the programmer may dynamically vary any portion of the SSA in this way.) As an illustration, we show in Fig. 15.5 part of a PL/I program that is using genuine IMS syntax. The code shown corresponds to the first DL/I call (GU) of Example 15.3.3.

15.5   SSA COMMAND CODES

An SSA may optionally include one or more "command codes." Each command code is represented by a single character (e.g., F, for "first"); command codes are specified by writing an asterisk followed by the appropriate character(s) immediately after the segment name in the SSA. We give examples of the use of command codes D (probably the most useful of the set), F, and V. Note in the case of command code D that

```
DLITPLI: PROC(EDPCB_ADDR) OPTIONS(MAIN);
  DCL 1 EDPCB BASED(EDPCB_ADDR),...;
  DCL STUDENT_AREA CHAR(25);  /* input area */
  DCL CSSA      CHAR(9),
      CSEGNAME CHAR(8) INITIAL('COURSEbb')
                       DEFINED(CSSA) POSITION(1),
      CSSAEND  CHAR(1) INITIAL('b')
                       DEFINED(CSSA) POSITION(9);
  DCL OSSA      CHAR(32),
      OSEGNAME CHAR(8) INITIAL('OFFERING')
                       DEFINED(OSSA) POSITION(1),
      OLPAREN  CHAR(1) INITIAL('(')
                       DEFINED(OSSA) POSITION(9),
      OFLDNAME CHAR(8) INITIAL('LOCATION')
                       DEFINED(OSSA) POSITION(10),
      OCOMPOP  CHAR(2) INITIAL('=b')
                       DEFINED(OSSA) POSITION(18),
      OFLDVAL  CHAR(12)
                       DEFINED(OSSA) POSITION(20),
      ORPAREN  CHAR(1) INITIAL(')')
                       DEFINED(OSSA) POSITION(32);
  DCL SSSA      CHAR(21),
      SSEGNAME CHAR(8) INITIAL('STUDENTb')
                       DEFINED(SSSA) POSITION(1),
      SLPAREN  CHAR(1) INITIAL('(')
                       DEFINED(SSSA) POSITION(9),
      SFLDNAME CHAR(8) INITIAL('GRADEbbb')
                       DEFINED(SSSA) POSITION(10),
      SCOMPOP  CHAR(2) INITIAL('=b')
                       DEFINED(SSSA) POSITION(18),
      SFLDVAL  CHAR(1)
                       DEFINED(SSSA) POSITION(20),
      SRPAREN  CHAR(1) INITIAL(')')
                       DEFINED(SSSA) POSITION(21);
  DCL GU CHAR(4) INITIAL('GUbb');
  DCL SIX FIXED BIN(31) INITIAL(6);
    ........
  OFLDVAL='STOCKHOLMbbb';  /* would be variables in practice, */
  SFLDVAL='A';              /* not constants              */
  CALL PLITDLI (SIX, GU, EDPCB , STUDENT_AREA, /* call DL/I   */
              CSSA, OSSA, SSSA);
  IF EDPCB.STATUS='GE' THEN.../* segment not found */
    ........
END DLITPLI;
```

Fig. 15.5   Example of IMS syntax

PROCOPT in the PCB must include the entry P [13.1]. We shall discuss command code Q in Chapter 24. For details of the remaining codes (C, L, P, U, N, −), see reference [15.1].

15.5.1 Path retrieval. Get the first OFFERING occurrence where the location is Stockholm, together with its parent COURSE occurrence (cf. Example 15.3.1).

```
GU  COURSE*D
    OFFERING  (LOCATION='STOCKHOLM')
```

The "D" stands for data. The effect of this "get unique" is to locate the first Stockholm offering (as in Example 15.3.1), and then to retrieve the entire hierarchical path of segments to that point—in this case, two segments. In general, command code D may be specified at some levels and not at others; the effect is to retrieve just the indicated segments from the hierarchical path and to concatenate them in the I/O area. Note that it is not necessary to specify *D at the lowest level in the path, since this segment is retrieved anyway.

It is interesting to observe that this facility is really a step toward providing the user with a normalized view of the data instead of a hierarchical one.

The reader should consider how this example could be handled without the path retrieval facility. (One possibility: Retrieve the OFFER-ING occurrence as in Example 15.3.1; extract the number of the COURSE from the key feedback area in the PCB; using this value, construct an SSA and hence retrieve the COURSE directly, via another "get unique.")

If the "get hold" preceding a "delete" or "replace" operation is a path retrieval, the DLET/REPL operation is normally taken to apply to the entire path. However, it is possible to be more selective than this; for details see reference [15.1].

15.5.2 Path insertion. Insert a new course (M40), together with an offering at Brussels on 4 January 1976, for which the teacher is employee number 876225.

```
build three segments concatenated in I/O area
ISRT COURSE*D
       OFFERING
       TEACHER
```

Note that *D is required only for the first segment in the path. This segment is inserted (in this example it is a root, so it has no parent); the second segment in the path may now be inserted, since its parent exists; and similarly for the third.

15.5.3   Use of command code F.   Get the teacher (we assume that there is only one) of the first offering (of any course) attended by student 183009.

```
        GU    COURSE
   NO   GN    OFFERING
        GNP   STUDENT   (EMP#='183009')
        if not found go to NO
        GNP   TEACHER*F
```

The "get unique" positions us to the start of the database. The "get next" establishes an offering as the current parent, and the "get next within parent" for STUDENT searches to see whether the specified student has attended this offering. These two operations are repeated until an offering attended by this student has been found. We now wish to retrieve the corresponding teacher. However, "get next within parent" (without the *F) will return "segment not found," since it will search in a forward direction, and teachers precede students in the hierarchical sequence. Similarly, "get next" (not within parent) will retrieve a teacher, but it will be the teacher of some subsequent offering. What we require is a means of stepping *backward* under the current parent, and this is what the *F does; it causes IMS to start the search at the first occurrence of the specified segment type under the current parent. In this example, since the TEACHER SSA is unconditional, the first occurrence is in fact the one that satisfies the search, and is hence the one retrieved.

15.5.4   Use of command code V.   Get all students for the offering on 13 August 1973 of course M23 (the same as Example 15.3.7).

```
        GU COURSE    (COURSE#='M23')
           OFFERING  (DATE='730813')
   NP   GN OFFERING * V
           STUDENT
        go to NP
```

This sequence of operations produces exactly the same result as that in Example 15.3.7. Before explaining it in detail, it is necessary to amplify slightly the concept of "current position." Basically, current position is defined as the segment last accessed via a "get" or "insert" operation. In addition, however, each *ancestor* of the current segment—that is, each segment in the path from the current segment to the root—is considered as the current of the relevant segment type. For example, if the segment last retrieved is a STUDENT, then that STUDENT is the current segment; also, that STUDENT's parent is the current OFFERING, and that OFFERING's parent is the current COURSE. This OFFERING and this COURSE are the current segments of their respective types, but they are not *the* current segment.

An SSA with a V command code directs IMS not to move away from the current segment (of the type named in the SSA) in searching for a segment to satisfy the request. Returning now to the example, let X be the OFFERING occurrence located by the GU. The GN operation may then be paraphrased as "Get the next STUDENT under X" (because of the *V in the OFFERING SSA). In other words, it is equivalent to a "get next within parent" for STUDENTs under X. It follows that the code above has the same effect as that in Example 15.3.7.

This example does not illustrate the true value of *V. The advantage in using *V in preference to GNP is that the "parent" referenced by *V need not be the "current parent" as defined under Example 15.3.7—rather, it can be any ancestor of the current segment. The following example demonstrates this point.

15.5.5 Use of command code V. Get the teacher of the first offering attended by student 183009 (the same as Example 15.5.3).

```
GU   STUDENT   (EMP#='183009')
GN   OFFERING*V
     TEACHER*F
```

The GU retrieves the first STUDENT occurrence in the database for employee 183009. This retrieval has the effect (among other things) of making the parent of this STUDENT the current OFFERING. The GN then retrieves the first TEACHER under this OFFERING (note that the *F on TEACHER is still necessary).

Comparing this example with Example 15.5.3, we see (a) that we now do not need a special GU to position us at the start of the database, (b) nor do we need to retrieve OFFERINGs—we had to do this before simply to establish a "current parent"—and finally (c) we have eliminated a loop, since we are able to go directly to the desired STUDENT occurrence.

The V command code may not be used at the lowest level in a sequence of SSAs, nor may it be used in an SSA that includes qualification conditions on the fields of the segment. However, since it provides almost all the function of GNP and more besides, it might be desirable always to use it in preference to GNP wherever possible.

EXERCISES

The following exercises are based on the publications database (see Exercise 13.1). You may assume that all segments are sensitive. Ignore status value testing as far as possible.

15.1 Get all authors of publications on the subject of "information retrieval" (you may assume that this subject name is unique).

15.2 Get the names of all publications for which Grace or Hobbs is (one of) the author(s).

15.3 Get the names of all subjects on which Bradbury has published a monograph.

15.4 Get the name of the article and date of first publication for all articles published by Owen.

15.5 Get the names of all authors who have had a monograph published by the Cider Press since 1 January 1970.

15.6 A monograph on the subject of science fiction, entitled "Computers in SF," has just been published (1 January 1973) by the Galactic Publishing Corporation. The author's name is Hal. Add this information to the database. (You may assume that the subject "science fiction" is already represented.)

15.7 For all publications currently available from more than one source, delete all details segments except the most recent. (You may ignore the possibility that two segments may include the same date and hence both be "most recent.")

15.8 Change the title of the publications segment inserted in Exercise 15.6 to "Computers and SF."

15.9 For each of the foregoing questions (where applicable), determine whether the use of *V instead of GNP offers any advantages.

REFERENCES AND BIBLIOGRAPHY

15.1 IBM Corporation. Information Management System/Virtual Storage Application Programming Reference Manual. IBM Form No. SH20–9026.

16
IMS Storage
Structures

16.1 INTRODUCTION

Continuing our study of IMS as an example of the hierarchical approach, we now take a look below the user interface and consider the IMS storage structure. IMS actually provides four different storage structures, known as HSAM, HISAM, HDAM, and HIDAM,[1] and a stored database (i.e., the stored representation of a physical database) may be in any one of the four.

In Chapter 2 we drew a distinction between the DBMS on the one hand and the access method it used on the other. The function of the access method was to present a "stored record interface" to the DBMS. Such an interface does in fact exist within an IMS system, although the picture is rather more complicated than the one given in Chapter 2. See Fig. 16.1.

The first point is that IMS actually uses several access methods below the stored record interface, not just one. They are as follows:

- The OS/VS Sequential Access Methods (QSAM and BSAM, collectively known as SAM)

- The OS/VS Indexed Sequential Access Method (ISAM)

- The OS/VS Virtual Storage Access Method (VSAM)

- A special IMS access method called the Overflow Sequential Access Method (OSAM)

---

[1] We follow the standard IMS usage here, although strictly speaking it would be more accurate to reserve these names for the corresponding sets of routines within the IMS control program; see the subsequent explanation of the acronyms.

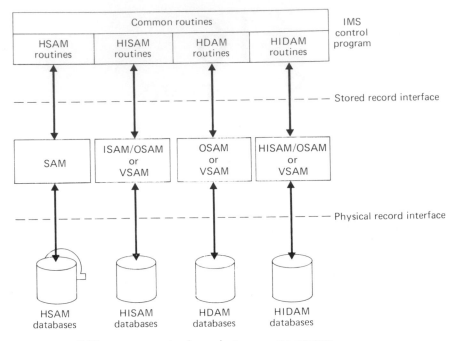

Fig. 16.1 IMS access methods and storage structures

For example, the HISAM routines—those routines within the IMS control program that process HISAM databases—use either VSAM or a combination of ISAM and OSAM, and the function of these access methods is to enable the HISAM routines to consider the underlying data as being in the HISAM structure. The HISAM routines are thus not involved in any details of (for example) the indexing required to support this particular structure. It is not our purpose here to describe the access methods below the stored record interface in any detail; such descriptions can be found in [16.2] (for SAM and ISAM), [16.4] (for VSAM), and [16.1] (for OSAM).

The term "access method" is also used for the routines within the IMS control program that process the four different structures. These "access methods" are as follows.[2]

---

[2] In addition to these four, IMS also provides an access method known as GSAM (Generalized Sequential Access Method) which allows a very restricted set of DL/I operators to be used on ordinary OS/VS sequential (SAM or VSAM) data sets. Using GSAM could mean that the program is not involved in conventional input/output at all—all such operations could be handled via DL/I. However, GSAM is not really a *database* access method as such, and we shall ignore it from this point on.

- The Hierarchical Sequential Access Method (HSAM)
- The Hierarchical Indexed Sequential Access Method (HISAM)
- The Hierarchical Direct Access Method (HDAM)
- The Hierarchical Indexed Direct Access Method (HIDAM)

The situation is complicated slightly by the fact that the HISAM routines also appear below the stored record interface as one of the access methods used for HIDAM. This does not really affect the overall picture, however. In what follows we shall generally restrict ourselves to discussion at the level of the stored record interface.

As we have said, each physical database (PDB) is represented as a stored database in one of the four structures. Within the stored database each PDB segment occurrence is represented by means of a *stored* segment occurrence, which contains the data—exactly as the user sees it[3]—together with a *prefix* that the user does not see.[4] The prefix contains control information for the segment: deletion flags, segment type code, pointers, and so on. PDB segments as such, then, are represented in essentially the same way in each of the four structures. Where the four structures differ is in the means used (a) to tie PDB segment occurrences together to form PDBR occurrences, and (b) to tie PDBR occurrences together to form the PDB. In other words, the difference lies in the manner in which the hierarchical sequence of the PDB is represented.

We now proceed to investigate each of the four structures in some detail.

16.2   HSAM

The adjective that best describes HSAM is *tape-like*. Indeed, as can be seen from Fig. 16.1, an HSAM database may actually be on tape. The hierarchical sequence is represented entirely by physical contiguity. For an example, see Fig. 16.2 (where we assume that course M27 is the next in sequence after course M23 in the education database—there is no M24, M25, or M26).

An HSAM database, then, is represented by means of a single SAM *data set* [16.2] containing fixed-length stored records.[5] Each stored record may contain any number of stored segments; however, each stored segment must be contained entirely within one stored record (i.e., stored

---

[3] For HDAM and HIDAM, a PDB segment consisting of an odd number of bytes is extended to an even number by the addition of a single pad byte, which the user does not see.

[4] Segments in "simple HSAM" and "simple HISAM" do not have a prefix. See Section 16.8.

[5] The OS/VS term for stored record is "logical record."

COURSE	PREREQ	PREREQ	OFFERING	TEACHER	STUDENT	STUDENT	
M23	M16	M19	730813	421633	102141	183009	...

STUDENT	OFFERING	OFFERING	COURSE	PREREQ	OFFERING	TEACHER	TEACHER	
761620	741104	750106	M27	L02	740602	421633	502417	...

Fig. 16.2   Part of the education database (HSAM)

segments may not "span" stored records), which means that bytes at the end of a stored record may be left unused—depending on the stored record length chosen by the DBA. (In fact, none of the four structures permits segments to span stored records.) Apart from the occasional gaps this may cause, however, each stored segment is immediately followed by its successor in hierarchical sequence.

An HSAM database is created by means of a series of "insert" operations; note that the segments to be loaded must be presented in hierarchical sequence. Once created, the database may be used only for input; that is, only the "get" operations are valid (GU, GN, and GNP, not the "get hold" operations). It follows that the most common use of HSAM involves the "old master/new master" technique familiar from sequential file processing. In other words, transactions are applied to an existing version of the database to generate a new (physically separate) version. The DL/I operations "delete" and "replace" may not be used. Instead, the user can delete an existing segment by not inserting it into the new database, and can replace an existing segment by modifying it before inserting it into the new database.

16.3   HISAM

We may sum up HISAM, a little inaccurately, by saying that it provides indexed access to the root segments, sequential access to the subordinate segments. (The index is on the root segment sequence field.) At least, this statement is true of a HISAM database just after it has been loaded; as we shall see, however, the picture may become somewhat distorted after insertions and deletions have occurred. The picture is also slightly different if secondary data set groups are used; we defer discussion of this case to Section 16.7.

As we indicated in Section 16.1, HISAM uses either VSAM or a combination of ISAM and OSAM as its supporting access method. We consider first the ISAM/OSAM case, then describe the differences for VSAM.

HISAM using ISAM/OSAM

A HISAM database under ISAM/OSAM consists of two data sets, an ISAM data set and an OSAM data set. Each is divided up into fixed-length stored records. In both data sets, stored records are created sequentially and may be retrieved either sequentially or directly—for ISAM via the ISAM index (generally nondense, incidentally; see Section 2.3) and for OSAM via the relative address of the record within the data set (compare the SRA of Section 2.1). Figure 16.3 shows the structure of one of these stored records.

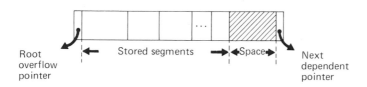

Root |←— Stored segments —→|←Space→| Next
overflow   dependent
pointer   pointer

Fig. 16.3 Structure of a stored record in HISAM (using ISAM/OSAM)

When the database is initially loaded (remember that loading must be done in hierarchical sequence), each root segment presented causes a new ISAM stored record to be created; the root segment is placed at the front of this record, and as many dependent segments as will fit are placed after the root. If the ISAM record is filled before all dependents of the current root have been loaded, then a new OSAM record is created and the next dependent is placed at the front of that; also the relative address of the OSAM record is placed in the "next dependent pointer" position in the ISAM record.[6] Subsequent dependents follow this one in the OSAM record. If the OSAM record is in turn filled, another is created (and its address is placed in the previous one), and so on. Thus each physical database record occurrence is represented as a chain containing one ISAM record together with zero or more OSAM records; any free space at the end of a record in the chain is considered as belonging to the PDBR occurrence concerned (it may assist with subsequent "insert" operations).

Figure 16.4 shows part of the education database as it might appear in HISAM just after loading.

Deletion of a segment in HISAM is accomplished by setting a flag in the segment prefix. Dependents of the deleted segment are automatically

---

[6] In practice, the last stored segment in the record is followed by a byte of zeros (effectively a zero segment type code), and the "next dependent" pointer immediately follows this byte. Figure 16.3 and others show the pointer at the far end of the stored record, for reasons of clarity.

ISAM data set   OSAM data set

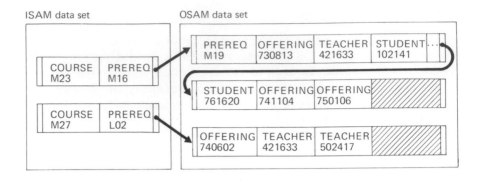

Fig. 16.4 Part of the education database (HISAM, using ISAM/OSAM)

considered as deleted; it is not normally necessary to set their deletion flags, since any attempt to access them must be via the deleted segment anyway. (This is *not* necessarily true for an HDAM or HIDAM database; see Chapter 17.) The deleted segment continues to occupy space in the database; this space is not available for reuse.

As for insertion, the method of operation depends on whether the new segment is a root or a subordinate. If it is a root, a new OSAM record is automatically created and the new segment is placed at the front of it. Let Y be the sequence field value for the new root, and let X and Z be the sequence field values of the roots that immediately precede and immediately follow the new root, respectively, in the hierarchical sequence.[7] Suppose that the X and Z roots are in (consecutive stored records in) the ISAM data set; i.e., this is the first insertion that has occurred at this position. Then, as explained above, the Y root is placed in a new OSAM record; also, a pointer to this OSAM record is placed in the "root overflow pointer" position in the ISAM record containing the Z root. If now a new root is inserted, with sequence field value Y', such that $X < Y' < Z$, then again a new OSAM record will be created. If $Y < Y'$, then a pointer to the new OSAM record will be set in the Y record; but if $Y' < Y$, then the pointer in the ISAM record will be changed to point to the Y' record, and in turn a pointer in the Y' record will be set to point to the Y record. In general, the Z record may point to a chain of any

---

[7] The Z segment always exists, because IMS automatically places a dummy root in the database at the end of the loading process with a sequence field value greater than any possible real value. The X segment may not exist, but this does not really matter, as the subsequent explanation makes clear.

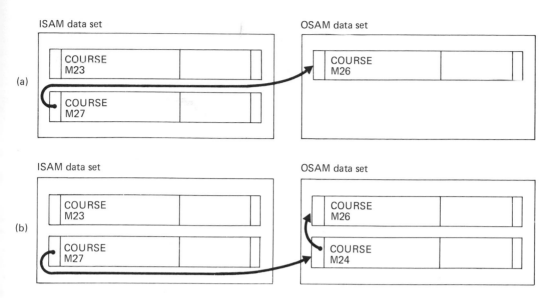

Fig. 16.5 Root segment insertion examples (HISAM, using ISAM/OSAM)

number of OSAM records, each containing one inserted root segment, and this chain will be maintained in ascending root sequence. Figure 16.5 shows the situation after (a) root M26 and then (b) root M24, in that order, have been inserted into the HISAM database of Fig. 16.4 (only the root segments are shown). Note, incidentally, that as a result of the technique used for root insertion, no new key is ever entered into the ISAM index once the database has been loaded.

Dependent segments are inserted at the correct point in hierarchical sequence. This involves scanning the chain of stored records representing the relevant PDBR occurrence to find the record containing the predecessor of the new segment. Segments following this predecessor (if any) are then shifted right within the stored record to make room for the new segment.[8] Provided that there is sufficient free space to accommodate both the new segment and the shifted segments, no further processing is necessary. However, it will frequently be the case that one or more segments will no longer fit into the record; indeed, there may not even be room for the new segment itself (this situation will arise if the length exceeds the number of bytes between the predecessor and the end

---

[8] Deleted segments are treated just like other segments in this process.

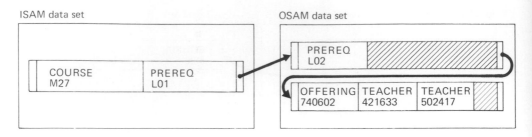

Fig. 16.6   Dependent segment insertion example (HISAM, using ISAM/OSAM)

of the record). All such overflow segments are placed into the OSAM data set, occupying one or possibly two OSAM records. The "next dependent" pointer chain is adjusted appropriately to maintain the required sequence. Figure 16.6 illustrates the situation after the insertion of a PREREQ segment (L01) subordinate to root M27 (only relevant stored records are shown).

HISAM using VSAM

We summarize below the most important ways in which HISAM using VSAM differs from HISAM using ISAM/OSAM.

■   The ISAM and OSAM data sets are replaced by a VSAM key-sequenced and a VSAM entry-sequenced data set, respectively.

■   All root segments reside in the key-sequenced data set, even insertions. When a new root is inserted, it is placed in its proper position in this data set and the VSAM index is updated if necessary. The root overflow pointer shown in Fig. 16.3 for ISAM/OSAM does not exist for VSAM. (As a matter of fact, the "next dependent" pointer appears in place of it, i.e., at the front of the record, instead of after all stored segments in the record as with ISAM/OSAM.)

■   Under certain circumstances—see [16.1] for details—deleting a root segment will free the storage space for the record containing it (in the key-sequenced data set) for later reuse.

To conclude our discussion of HISAM, we amplify the remarks made at the beginning of the section. Access to the root segments in a HISAM database is by means of an (ISAM or VSAM) index on the root segment sequence field. However, the indexing is generally only partial for the following reasons.

- The index is nondense, so that in general there will be many roots for each index entry—basically N per entry, where N is the number of ISAM records per track or VSAM records per control interval.[9]

- In addition, some roots (insertions) may exist in the OSAM data sct rather than the ISAM data set if the ISAM/OSAM combination is being used.

Access to dependent segments is sequential, inasmuch as to access the Nth dependent (in hierarchical sequence) of a particular root, it is necessary to traverse all the $(N-1)$ dependents that precede it. This may involve traversing deleted segments. It may also involve traversing chains from one stored record to another.

16.4 HD STRUCTURES: POINTERS

The two hierarchical direct structures, HDAM and HIDAM, both involve the use of pointers to link segments together. If VSAM is the underlying access method, all data in the database is stored in one or more VSAM entry-sequenced data sets; otherwise it is stored in one or more OSAM data sets. In either case the pointers just mentioned consist of byte offsets within the relevant data set. Physically they are stored as part of the segment prefix. They are used (a) to represent the hierarchical sequence of segments within a PDBR occurrence, and (b) to represent the sequence of PDBR occurrences—at least to some extent. We shall consider these pointers in some detail before moving on to discuss HDAM and HIDAM as such.

Let us consider first the hierarchical sequence of segments within a PDBR occurrence. Basically this may be represented in two ways, either by means of "hierarchical" pointers or by means of "child/twin" pointers. Figure 16.7 shows a PDBR occurrence in which hierarchical pointers are used.

Observe that within the stored PDBR occurrence, each segment includes a pointer to the next in hierarchical sequence. (However, the last segment does *not* contain a pointer to the next root.) As an option, the hierarchical pointers can be made two-way; that is, each segment can additionally include a pointer to its predecessor (again, within one PDBR occurrence).

Figure 16.8 shows how the same PDBR occurrence would appear if child/twin pointers were used instead. Here each parent segment occurrence includes a pointer to the first occurrence of each of its child segment

---

[9] However, the DBA may arrange that $N = 1$.

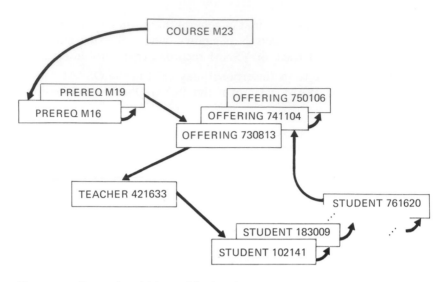

Fig. 16.7 Example of hierarchical pointers

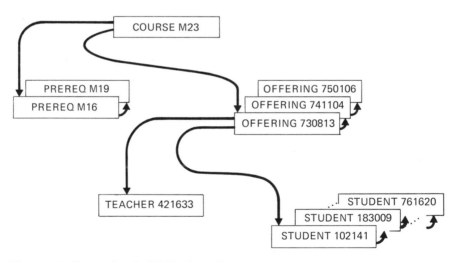

Fig. 16.8 Example of child/twin pointers

types, and each child segment occurrence includes a pointer to the next occurrence—if there is one—of that child under the current parent (i.e., to the next twin). Like the hierarchical pointers, these twin pointers may optionally be made two-way. In addition, each parent may include a pointer to the last (as well as the first) occurrence of any or all of its child segment types.

Now let us consider the sequence of PDBR occurrences within the database, which may also be represented, in whole or in part, by means of pointers. The pointers concerned are actually the twin pointer(s) in the root prefix. The possibilities are as follows.

- In HDAM all roots that collide at a position K (see Section 16.5) are kept on a chain (one-way or two-way) that starts at record K and is maintained in ascending root sequence. (This is only a partial representation of the sequence of PDBR occurrences, as Section 16.5 explains.)

- In HIDAM, if the one-way option is selected, all roots within one stored record are chained, but in reverse chronological sequence, not in proper root sequence; i.e., the most recently inserted root will be at the start of the chain. In this case it is the HIDAM index that defines the sequence of PDBR occurrences (see Section 16.6); the chain is provided for IMS's own use and is in no way directly accessible to the user.

- In HIDAM, if the two-way option is selected, all roots in the database are maintained in proper root sequence on the two-way chain, thus permitting sequential retrieval of the roots without reference to the index (see Section 16.6).

Each of the chains mentioned here uses the root segment twin pointer(s). This is true regardless of whether hierarchical or child/twin pointers are specified (in the mapping portion of the DBD; see Section 16.8).

Finally, we observe that it is possible to mix the two types of pointer within one PDBR type; that is, hierarchical pointers may be specified for some segments in the hierarchy, child/twin pointers for others. It is beyond the scope of this book to describe in detail all the relative performance advantages and disadvantages that influence the choice of a particular arrangement of pointers. However, since access to subordinate segments must obviously be sequential with hierarchical pointers, whereas it is (relatively) direct with child/twin pointers, we may say that, as a general rule, hierarchical pointers would be chosen if most processing were sequential in nature, and child/twin pointers would be chosen otherwise. Note, however, that child/twin pointers will normally occupy more space than hierarchical pointers.

16.5 HDAM

HDAM provides direct access (by sequence field value) to the root segments, via a hashing and chaining technique, together with pointer access to the subordinate segments (as we have seen). In its simplest form, an HDAM database consists of a single OSAM data set or a single

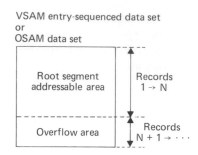

VSAM entry-sequenced data set
or
OSAM data set

| Root segment addressable area | Records 1 → N |
| Overflow area | Records N + 1 → ... |

Fig. 16.9   Structure of an HDAM database

VSAM entry-sequenced data set, divided up into fixed-length stored records. The stored records are numbered from 1; records 1 to N form the "root segment addressable area," and the remaining records form an overflow area. (The value of N is specified in the DBD; see Section 16.8.) Figure 16.9 shows the structure of an HDAM database.

HDAM differs from the other three structures in that the initial loading of the database need not be performed in sequence. More accurately, *root* segments may be presented for loading in any order; however, all dependents of a given root must be presented in strict hierarchical sequence before the next root is loaded. When a root segment is presented for loading, the value of its sequence field is passed to a DBA-supplied hashing routine, which hashes the value and generates the address, K, of a record within the root segment addressable area (hence $1 \le K \le N$). The new root will be placed in record K, provided that record K contains sufficient space for it. If it does not, the new root will be placed in the nearest record in the root segment addressable area that does contain sufficient space. If no space exists anywhere in the root segment addressable area, the new root will be placed in the next available position in the overflow area. (This description is somewhat simplified; see reference [16.1] for more details.)

The procedure just described is followed in exactly the same way when new roots are presented for insertion into an existing database.

Two root segments whose sequence field values hash to the same value K are said to *collide* at K (not IMS terminology). All such K-collisions are maintained in ascending root sequence on a chain that starts at an "anchor point" within record K (actually, this is the twin chain; see Section 16.4). Note that, in general, some of these K-collisions will actually be in record K, some will be in other records within the root segment addressable area, and some will be in overflow records. Note, too, that each of the N collision chains is entirely separate from all the rest—they are not linked to one another in any way. (Thus in HDAM—depending on the hashing routine supplied by the DBA—the logical sequence of root segment occurrences may not be completely represented, inasmuch as two roots that are consecutive in hierarchical sequence will probably be on different collision chains. Underneath any one root, however, the hierarchical sequence of subordinate segment occurrences is always represented completely by means of the appropriate pointers.)

As an example, suppose that $N = 100$ and the hashing algorithm is "Divide the root sequence field value by N, and let $K =$ remainder plus 1." Suppose that the following sequence of events occurs.

- Root 322 is presented for insertion.
  $K = 23$; record 23 has space available.

- Root 522 is presented for insertion.
  $K = 23$; record 23 has space available.

- Root 222 is presented for insertion.
  $K = 23$; record 23 is full; nearest record with space is record 25.

- Root 422 is presented for insertion.
  $K = 23$; root segment addressable area is full; next available position in overflow area is in record 144.

Then the collision chain will appear as shown in Fig. 16.10.

We can see that access to the root segments in HDAM will be very fast, provided that the collision chains do not get too long. Indeed, this is

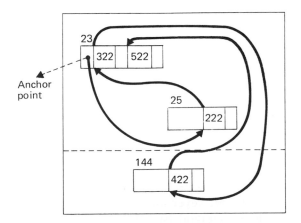

Fig. 16.10 Example of a collision chain (HDAM)

one of the major objectives of the HDAM structure. As for the subordinate segments, an attempt is made to provide fast access to these, too, by placing them physically near the corresponding root (thus minimizing the amount of seeking involved with a moving-head device). Suppose that the root resides in record K. When the first dependent is inserted (either during loading or subsequently), it will be placed as close as possible to the root, possibly even in record K; the method used to search for space is exactly the same as that used for a root that hashes to K. If the next DL/I operation is the insertion of another dependent of this root, that dependent will also be placed as close as possible to the root. The process continues until either (a) the series of insertions under the current root comes to an end—i.e., some other DL/I operation is performed, perhaps an insertion involving another PDBR occurrence; or (b) placing another dependent in the root segment addressable area would mean that more than M bytes of this area had been assigned to this PDBR occurrence during this series of insertions, in which case all further dependents inserted in this series will be placed in the overflow area. (The value M, which is specified in the DBD, acts as a safety limit to prevent an unusually large PDBR occurrence from swamping the root segment addressable area during loading.) The whole process is repeated the next time a series of insertions involving this PDBR occurrence is performed.

Note that inserting a new segment does not cause any existing segments to be moved in HDAM—a significant performance advantage over HISAM. This is made possible by the pointers, of course, which allow the space allocation routines to place an inserted segment at any convenient position while still maintaining both the hierarchical sequence and the ability to access the segment directly. The deletion of segments is also performed differently in the two structures. In HISAM, deletions were indicated merely by setting a flag in the segment prefix. In HDAM, however, the space occupied by the deleted segment is made available for reuse, so that a subsequent insertion may cause the segment to be physically overwritten.

16.6   HIDAM

HIDAM provides indexed access to the root segments, pointer access to the subordinate segments. As in HISAM, the indexing is on the root segment sequence field. However, in HIDAM the index is controlled by IMS, not by the access method (see the remarks on DBMS-controlled indexing in Chapter 2). A HIDAM database actually consists of *two* databases: a "data" database, which contains the actual data, and an associated INDEX database, which provides the (dense) index.

The "data" database consists in its simplest form of a single OSAM data set or a single VSAM entry-sequenced data set, divided up into fixed-length stored records. The initial loading of the database must be performed in hierarchical sequence. As each segment is presented, it is placed in the data set at the next available position in sequence, exactly as if this were an HSAM database. In addition, of course, the appropriate pointer values are placed in relevant prefixes. Subsequent deletions are handled exactly as in HDAM; that is, the space is freed and may be used for segments added later. The subsequent insertion of a root segment will cause the new root to be placed as near as possible to the root that precedes it in hierarchical sequence. Subsequent insertion of a dependent segment will cause the new segment to be placed as near as possible to its immediate predecessor in hierarchical sequence. (As in HDAM, segments never move once they have been stored.) For further details of the method used to search for space, see reference [16.1].

The INDEX database is actually a special form of HISAM database—that is, either an ISAM-OSAM data set pair or a single VSAM key-sequenced data set (no entry-sequenced data set is needed). It contains just one type of segment, the index segment.[10] There is one occurrence of the index segment for each root occurrence in the "data" database; it contains the root sequence field value, together with a pointer to that root. This pointer forms part of the index segment prefix (it is in fact a logical child pointer; see Chapter 17).

Figure 16.11 shows how the example of Fig. 16.5(a) would appear in HIDAM, using HISAM/OSAM. Using VSAM the "data" database would consist of a VSAM entry-sequenced data set; the INDEX database would consist of a VSAM key-sequenced data set (only), and all index segments would be contained in it, including the one for M26. (The pointer from the M27 index segment to this index segment would not exist.)

16.7 SECONDARY DATA SET GROUPS

So far we have assumed that each stored database consists of a single "data set group" (DSG). However, a HISAM, HDAM, or HIDAM database—not an INDEX or HSAM database—may be split into one *primary* data set group and from one to nine *secondary* data set groups. Each DSG consists of an ISAM-OSAM data set pair (for HISAM),[11] or a

---

[10] The INDEX database is thus "root segment only," which is why no entry-sequenced data set is necessary in the VSAM case.
[11] Secondary DSGs may not be used in HISAM if VSAM is the supporting access method.

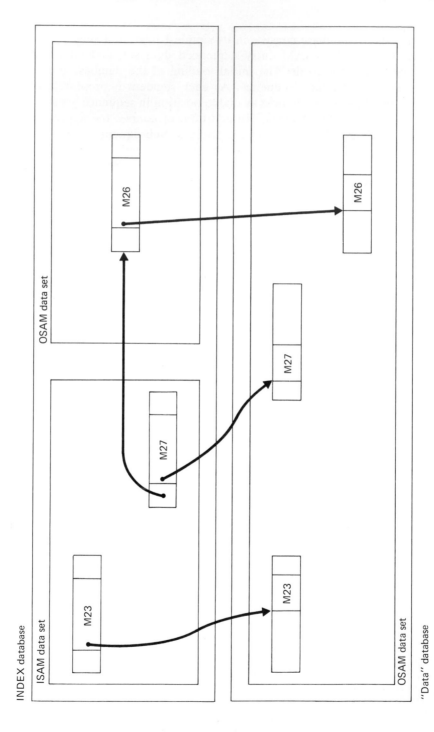

INDEX database

ISAM data set

OSAM data set

"Data" database

OSAM data set

M23

M27

M26

M27

M26

M23

Fig. 16.11 Root segment insertion example (HIDAM, using HISAM/OSAM)

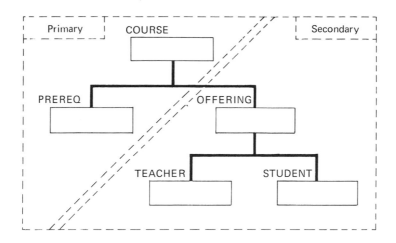

Fig. 16.12   Splitting the education database into two DSGs (HISAM)

single OSAM data set or single VSAM entry-sequenced data set (for HDAM and HIDAM). In each case all occurrences of any one type of segment are contained entirely within one DSG (on the other hand, several different segment types may all be contained in the same DSG). The primary DSG is the one containing the roots.

In HISAM the basic advantage (not the only one) of splitting a database into a number of DSGs is that each secondary DSG will provide indexed access, via the ISAM index in that DSG, to certain dependent segments. This will have the effect of improving the response time for some direct-access operations (e.g., a "get unique" for a segment near the bottom righthand corner of the hierarchy need not involve traversing all segments that precede it in the hierarchy). Other advantages may accrue from the fact that the database may be spread across several devices, thus allowing (for example) the concentration of highly active portions of the database into comparatively small areas, and the possibility of greater concurrency in access to different portions. On the other hand, response time for some operations may be increased, owing (for example) to the additional space required for the extra indexes.

Figure 16.12 shows how the education database of Fig. 13.1 might be split into two DSGs, the primary one containing COURSE and PREREQ segments and the (single) secondary one containing OFFERING, TEACHER, and STUDENT segments. Figure 16.13 shows part of this database as it might appear just after loading (cf. Fig. 16.4).

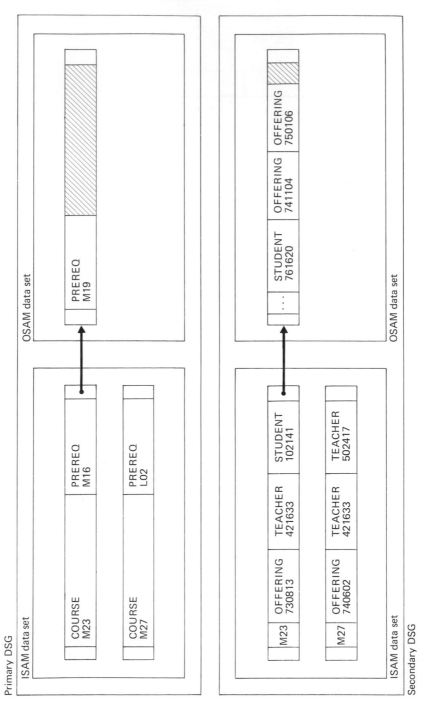

Fig. 16.13 Part of the education database (HISAM, two DSGs)

In general, the split into multiple DSGs is performed under HISAM as follows.

1. Choose a second-level segment type (i.e., an immediate child of the root).
2. Assign that segment and all segments following it in the hierarchical structure to a secondary DSG.
3. Remove these segments from the hierarchy and repeat steps 1–3 on the hierarchy that remains (if desired).

Note that each secondary DSG starts off with a second-level segment. What happens when the database is loaded is this. Segments in the primary DSG (COURSEs and PREREQs in the example) are loaded exactly as if they were the only segments in a single-DSG situation. Segments in a secondary DSG (OFFERINGs, TEACHERs, and STUDENTs in the example) are loaded into their DSG in exactly the same way, except that the segments belonging to a single PDBR occurrence are preceded in their DSG by a copy of the sequence field from the corresponding root occurrence. This effectively acts as the "root" for the secondary DSG (see Fig. 16.13). The ISAM index in the secondary DSG is an index on this "root."

For HDAM and HIDAM there is another reason for splitting a database into several DSGs (in addition to the advantages already mentioned that derive from spreading the data across several devices): It may help to reduce the amount of storage fragmentation. As a somewhat simplified example, suppose that an HD database contains two types of segment, A (100 bytes) and B (60 bytes), and suppose also that the database consists of a single DSG. Suppose that an A segment is deleted, thus making a space of 100 bytes available for subsequent insertions. Suppose now that a B segment is inserted and is stored in this space. This insertion will leave 40 bytes that cannot be used at all, i.e., 40 bytes totally wasted. If, on the other hand, A segments and B segments are assigned to different DSGs, this problem cannot arise: Only an A segment will be allowed to use the space freed by the deletion of an A segment, and B segments will always be inserted in the other DSG.

There is no restriction in HDAM/HIDAM on the assignment of segment types to DSGs (contrast the situation with HISAM). For example, if the education database were stored in HDAM or HIDAM, COURSEs could be assigned to one DSG (the primary one), OFFERINGs could be assigned to another (a secondary DSG), and PREREQs, TEACHERs, and STUDENTs to a third (another secondary DSG). In the case of HDAM, only the primary DSG contains a root segment addressable area; all others consist entirely of overflow area. One restriction that does exist is that segments in different DSGs cannot be connected by hierarchical pointers; child pointers *must* be used in this case.

Insertions and deletions in a secondary DSG are handled in essentially the same way as for the primary DSG. For further details see reference [16.1].

16.8   THE MAPPING DEFINITION

As mentioned in Section 13.2, the mapping of a PDB into storage is defined as part of the DBD. We can now investigate this in more detail. The mapping definition involves additional entries in the DBD and SEGM statements and two additional statements (the LCHILD and DATASET statements).

The additional entries in the DBD statement follow.

■   ACCESS=HSAM/HISAM/HDAM/HIDAM/INDEX

This entry specifies the relevant structure. Note that INDEX is one of the possibilities; for HIDAM *two* DBDs are required, one for the "data" database (for which ACCESS = HIDAM must be specified) and one for the INDEX database. The two DBDs will be referred to as the HIDAM DBD and the INDEX DBD, respectively. These two DBDs are cross-referenced. (Note, however, that the user need not be aware of the existence of the INDEX database; the INDEX DBD is not part of the "data model definition"—it is part of the mapping definition solely.)

Other parameters in the ACCESS entry, not shown above, specify the underlying access method (e.g., OSAM or VSAM). In addition, a variation of HSAM, known as "simple HSAM" (SHSAM), may be specified; a simple HSAM database is an HSAM database containing only one type of segment, and does not contain any stored prefixes. HISAM has an analogous "simple" form known as SHISAM (available only with VSAM, not with ISAM/OSAM).

■   RMNAME=

This entry is required only if ACCESS = HDAM. It specifies the name of the DBA-supplied hashing routine (which must exist in a system library available to IMS). It also specifies the values N and M, which are, respectively, the number of stored records in the root segment addressable area and the maximum number of bytes within the root segment addressable area that may be assigned to one PDBR occurrence during one series of insertions (see Section 16.5).

The additional entries in the SEGM statement are concerned with the pointer options available in HDAM and HIDAM; they do not apply

to HSAM, HISAM, or INDEX databases. The first and more important
of the additional entries is the POINTER operand.

■ POINTER=HIER/HIERBWD/TWIN/TWINBWD

HIER specifies that each occurrence of this segment is to contain a
pointer to the next segment occurrence (of any type) in hierarchical
sequence, except that the last dependent segment occurrence under a
given root does *not* contain a pointer to the next root. In addition, if the
segment being defined is the root, each occurrence will also include a
pointer to the next[12] root occurrence. HIERBWD is the same as HIER,
except that the pointers are two-way. TWIN specifies that each occurrence of this segment is to contain a pointer to the next occurrence (if
there is one) of the same type of segment under the same parent
occurrence *and* a pointer to the first occurrence of each type of child
under this occurrence. If the segment being defined is the root, each
occurrence's twin pointer will actually point to the next[12] root occurrence.
TWINBWD is the same as TWIN, except that the twin pointers are
two-way.

The second new entry in the SEGM statement consists of a new
parameter in the PARENT operand. It is required only if child/twin
pointers are being used (POINTER = TWIN/TWINBWD for the parent)
and a pointer from each occurrence of the parent to the last (as well as
the first) occurrence of this particular type of child under that parent
occurrence is desired. The entry is specified for the particular child
segment concerned, and it is written as follows (the double parentheses
are required):

■ PARENT=((parent,DBLE))

The LCHILD statement is primarily used in connection with logical
databases (to be discussed in Chapter 17). However, it is also used in
HIDAM to link the index segment in the INDEX database with the
segment being indexed in the corresponding "data" database; the data
segment is considered as a "logical child" of the INDEX segment. The
INDEX DBD will contain one SEGM statement and one FIELD statement. For example, part of the INDEX DBD for the database of Fig.
16.11 might look as follows:

```
SEGM   NAME=XSEG,BYTES=3
FIELD  NAME=(COURSE#,SEQ),BYTES=3,START=1
```

---

[12] See Section 16.4 for details of what "next" means in this context.

(Incidentally, the field name need not be the same as the field name specified in the HIDAM DBD, although it is in this example.) In addition to these two statements, the INDEX DBD must include an LCHILD statement (either before or after the FIELD statement) to specify the data segment and the field within it on which the indexing is to be performed (which must be the sequence field). For example,

```
LCHILD  NAME=(COURSE,EDUCPDBD),INDEX=COURSE#
```

An LCHILD statement must also be included in the HIDAM DBD, preceding or following the FIELD statements for the HIDAM root. In our example it might be

```
LCHILD  NAME=(XSEG,XDBD),POINTER=INDX
```

where XDBD is the name of the INDEX DBD. The "POINTER = INDX" entry is required.

The other additional statement is the DATASET statement. DATASET statements are used for two main purposes. First, they specify, by their positioning with respect to the SEGM statements in the DBD, which segments are to be assigned to which data set groups. Second, they specify the names of the OS/VS Job Control Language statements that will be required when an application is scheduled to operate on the database. We shall consider each of these functions in turn.

For HISAM, one DATASET statement must be supplied for each data set group. Each must immediately precede the SEGM statements for the segments in that DSG. Figure 16.14 shows the sequence of statements required to define the database of Fig. 16.12 (only the relevant statements and entries are shown).

```
DBD        NAME=EDUCPDBD,ACCESS=HISAM
DATASET    ...
SEGM       NAME=COURSE,...
SEGM       NAME=PREREQ,...
DATASET    ...
SEGM       NAME=OFFERING,...
SEGM       NAME=TEACHER,...
SEGM       NAME=STUDENT,...
```

Fig. 16.14 Example of DATASET statement positioning (HISAM)

For HDAM and HIDAM, more than one DATASET statement may be required for a given DSG, because segments do not have to be adjacent to each other in the hierarchical structure (which is defined by the sequence of SEGM statements) in order to be placed in the same DSG. In such a situation *labeled* DATASET statements are used. As with HISAM, each segment is assigned to the DSG identified by the nearest preceding DATASET statement; however, two (or more) DATASET statements with the same label are considered as referring to the same DSG. Figure 16.15 shows the statements required to define an HDAM structure for the education database consisting of three DSGs, one containing COURSEs, one containing OFFERINGs, and one containing PREREQs, TEACHERs, and STUDENTs. PRIME, SECONDA, and SECONDB are labels.

```
          DBD       NAME=EDUCPDBD,ACCESS=HDAM,...
PRIME     DATASET   ...
          SEGM      NAME=COURSE,...
SECONDA   DATASET   ...
          SEGM      NAME=PREREQ,...
SECONDB   DATASET   ...
          SEGM      NAME=OFFERING,...
SECONDA   DATASET   (blank)
          SEGM      NAME=TEACHER,...
          SEGM      NAME=STUDENT,...
```

Fig. 16.15   Example of DATASET statement positioning (HD)

A DATASET statement containing a label that is the same as that in a preceding DATASET statement may not contain any other entries.

The second function performed by the DATASET statement is the specification of the appropriate Job Control Language "ddnames." When an application is to be run against the database, OS/VS requires "DD statements," identified by ddnames, for each data set in each DSG. A DD statement defines the final details of the mapping of a data set into physical storage. For example, it may specify the device on which the storage volume containing the data set is mounted (which can in general vary from run to run). Broadly speaking, these details form (at least part of) the definition of the mapping from the stored to the physical record interface, and we shall not concern ourselves with them any further here. The interested reader is referred to [16.3]. We content ourselves with pointing out that, when an IMS application is to be run, either the user or the DBA must supply all appropriate DD statements, with ddnames as specified in the DATASET statements. The relevant DATASET entries are as follows.

- `DD1=ddname`

For HSAM this is the ddname for the input data set (SAM) which forms an existing ("old master") database. For a HISAM DSG or an INDEX database it is the ddname for the ISAM data set or VSAM key-sequenced data set. For an HDAM or HIDAM DSG it is the ddname for the OSAM data set or VSAM entry-sequenced data set.

- `DD2=ddname`

For HSAM (the only case in which the entry is needed), this is the ddname for the output data set (SAM) which forms a new ("new master") database.

- `OVFLW=ddname`

For a HISAM DSG or INDEX database using ISAM/OSAM (the only cases in which the entry is used) this is the ddname for the OSAM data set.

The DATASET statement also contains a few other entries concerned with such details as stored record length, blocking factors, and so on. See reference [16.1].

16.9 REORGANIZATION

From Sections 16.3–16.6 it is apparent that, as time progresses and more and more insertions and deletions are performed on a database, the organization of that database in storage will become more and more untidy. For example, with HISAM, more and more space may be taken up by unwanted (deleted) segments. (Of course, IMS is not alone in this respect; similar problems arise in every database system.) As the stored database organization degenerates, so also will the overall performance of the system, in terms of both space utilization and response time. Eventually a point will be reached where it is necessary to reorganize the database in order to prevent performance—particularly space utilization—from degenerating to an unacceptable level. Reorganization is the process of unloading the database and reloading it. More accurately, it involves retrieving all (nondeleted) segments from the existing database and loading them into a new database. (In practice, because of limitations on the number of available devices, it is usual to unload the old database to tape—probably in the form of an HSAM database—and then to reload it from there, overwriting the old database with the new one. This technique has the additional advantage of providing a back-up copy of the database.)

In practice an IMS utility program is normally used to perform the reorganization. For explanatory purposes, however, let us assume that the user actually has to write such a program. In general, all that is required is a series of unqualified "get next" operations on the old database and a corresponding series of "insert" operations on the new database. This will retrieve all existing segments in hierarchical sequence (not quite true for HDAM, where the sequence will be hierarchical only within each PDBR occurrence) and load them in the same sequence into the new database.

For HISAM, this process will recover the space occupied by deleted segments, since the deletions will not be written to the new database. Under ISAM/OSAM, it will also move any root segments in the OSAM data set (insertions) into their correct position within the ISAM data set of the new database.

For HDAM, reorganization will normally have the effect of moving root segments from the overflow area into the root segment addressable area. It will also recover space lost through fragmentation.

For HIDAM, reorganization will arrange all segments into a physical sequence that reflects the hierarchical sequence. Again, space lost through fragmentation will be recovered.

As a general rule it should not be necessary to reorganize an HDAM or HIDAM database as often as a HISAM database, because of the differences in the techniques employed in the two cases for insertion and deletion.

16.10 DATA INDEPENDENCE

In the previous section we tacitly assumed that when reorganization is performed, the DBD for the new database is essentially the same as the DBD for the old one. In practice many differences between the two are possible; i.e., the storage structure for the new database may differ considerably from that of the old one. In other words, IMS does provide a fair degree of data independence. Below are some of the possible variations.

- New segment types may be added at certain points in the hierarchy (see Section 14.1).
- Stored record size may be changed.

- Different pointer options may be chosen in HDAM or HIDAM.
- The division of a database into data set groups may be changed.
- For HDAM the values of N (number of stored records in the root segment addressable area) and M (maximum number of bytes in the root segment addressable area to be allocated to a single PDBR occurrence in one series of insertions) may be changed.
- The HDAM hashing routine may be changed.
- The underlying access method may be changed (e.g., in HDAM, OSAM may be replaced by VSAM).

In addition, it is possible to convert a database from one of the four basic structures to another—from HISAM to HIDAM, say—subject to certain restrictions. The possibilities are summarized in Fig. 16.16.

From \ To	HSAM	HISAM	HDAM	HIDAM
HSAM		OK	Note 3	OK
HISAM	Note 1		Note 3	OK
HDAM	Note 1 Note 2	Note 2		Note 2
HIDAM	Note 1	OK	Note 3	

Fig. 16.16   Stored database transformations in IMS

Notes

1. These transformations are extremely unlikely in practice, since HSAM will not permit "delete," "replace," or "insert" operations (except for initial loading).

2. The new database must be loaded in hierarchical sequence. This requirement may cause difficulties if the root segment "twin" sequence— i.e., the sequence defined by ascending values of the root segment sequence field—is not properly represented in the old (HDAM) database. See Section 16.5.

3. The new (HDAM) database will probably contain no representation of the root segment "twin" sequence (see note 2). Hence "get next" operations at the root level will not in general function in terms of this sequence. (Details of how they do function are beyond the scope of this book.)

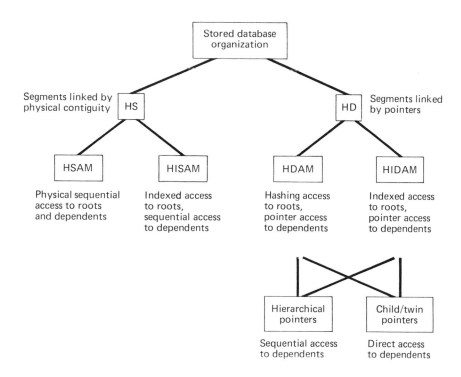

Fig. 16.17   The four basic storage structures

16.11 SUMMARY

Figure 16.17 constitutes an attempt to summarize Sections 16.2–16.6, which form the major part of the present chapter. Note that pointers are used in HISAM as well as HDAM and HIDAM, but that in HISAM they are used to link stored records, not segments. Section 16.7 explained an extension of the basic storage structures, namely, the concept of the secondary data set group (not applicable to HSAM). Section 16.8 showed how the storage structure for a given PDB is defined (via the DBD). Sections 16.9 and 16.10 discussed the concept of reorganization and the types of change that may be made when a database is reorganized. Finally, the advantages and disadvantages of the various possible structures have been mentioned at several points throughout the chapter.

EXERCISES

16.1 Suppose that the education PDB is to be stored as an HDAM database, with pointer options as indicated below.

```
DBD   NAME=EDUCPDBD,ACCESS=HDAM,...
SEGM  NAME=COURSE,POINTER=TWIN,BYTES=256,...
SEGM  NAME=PREREQ,POINTER=HIER,BYTES=36,...
SEGM  NAME=OFFERING,POINTER=TWINBWD,BYTES=20,...
SEGM  NAME=TEACHER,POINTER=TWIN,BYTES=24,...
SEGM  NAME=STUDENT,POINTER=HIER,BYTES=25,...
```

Draw a diagram showing all pointers involved in the PDBR occurrence of Fig. 13.2.

16.2 Each prefix in HDAM/HIDAM consists of a 1-byte type code, a delete byte, a 4-byte counter, and a number of pointers (4 bytes each). On the basis of the DBD in Exercise 16.1, work out the relative amounts of storage space required for prefixes and for data. You may assume that on average there are two PREREQs and eight OFFERINGs for any given course, and 1.5 TEACHERs and 16 STUDENTs for each OFFERING.

16.3 Again on the basis of the DBD in Exercise 16.1, would it be possible to divide the database into data set groups as follows?

- a) COURSE, PREREQ (primary); OFFERING, TEACHER, STUDENT (secondary).
- b) COURSE, OFFERING, STUDENT (primary); PREREQ, TEACHER (secondary).
- c) COURSE,TEACHER (primary); PREREQ,OFFERING (secondary); STUDENT (another secondary).

For those cases where it is possible, show the DATASET statements required to effect the division. Which of these divisions would be permissible if HISAM were used instead?

REFERENCES AND BIBLIOGRAPHY

See also [13.1].

16.1 IBM Corporation. Information Management System/Virtual Storage System/Application Design Guide. IBM Form No. SH20-9025.

16.2 IBM Corporation. Operating System/Virtual Storage Access Method Services. IBM Form No. GC26-3836.

16.3 IBM Corporation. Operating System/Virtual Storage Job Control Language Reference Manual. IBM Form No. GC28-0618.

16.4 IBM Corporation. Operating System/Virtual Storage VSAM Programmers' Guide. IBM Form No. GC26-3838.

17
IMS Logical Databases

17.1 LOGICAL DATABASES (LDBs)

We have already mentioned several times that the term "logical database" has two distinct meanings in IMS. The first meaning was dealt with in Chapter 14. The present chapter is concerned with the second, and perhaps more important, of the two. However, it is an introduction only; more details will be found in references [13.1] and [16.1].

A logical database (LDB), then—second meaning—is an ordered set of logical database record (LDBR) occurrences. Like a PDBR, an LDBR is a hierarchical arrangement of fixed-length segments.[1] Like a PDB, an LDB is part of the data model in an IMS system. However, an LDB differs from a PDB in that it has no existence in its own right; instead, it is defined in terms of one or more existing PDBs. Specifically, each LDBR occurrence consists of segments from several distinct PDBR occurrences (from one PDB or several). Thus the LDB imposes a (hierarchical) structure on the data that is different from the (hierarchical) structure represented by the underlying PDB(s); in other words, it provides the user with an alternative view of the data.

We can see that logical databases are to some extent the IMS equivalent of the general "external relations" of Section 10.2, and indeed, the overall objectives are similar for the two constructs. However, in IMS the LDB is really part of the conceptual model rather than the external model. The storage structure, in fact, does represent the LDB directly, inasmuch as it contains additional pointers linking stored seg-

---

[1] See footnote 1, Chapter 13, p. 209.

ments together into the desired structure (over and above the pointers already discussed in the previous chapter). Thus it is not entirely true to say that the LDB as such does not exist (but the point is that the *data* really belongs to one or more PDBs rather than to the LDB). Since it is part of the data model, an LDB should ideally look exactly like a PDB to the user, and so it does, at least so far as retrieval is concerned. The situation with respect to storage operations is not quite so straightforward. however, for reasons that will be discussed in Sections 17.5 and 17.6.

17.2   AN EXAMPLE

The ornithological section of a nature conservation institute is conducting a survey of the bird life of a particular region. The region is divided up into areas, and for each area, observations are to be recorded in a survey database. The information recorded for an area is to consist of area number (a unique identifier), area name and description, and, for each type of bird observed in the area, the common name, date of observation, observer's remarks, and also the bird's scientific name and a set of descriptive information. Thus the database record, as seen by the user, is to appear (approximately) as shown in Fig. 17.1.

The institute already maintains a PDB of bird information, however. This PDB is a "root segment only" database with a record structure as shown in Fig. 17.2. Here BNAME (common name) is the sequence field.

Therefore, if a new PDB were built with the structure shown in Fig. 17.1, much of the data it contained would be a repetition of the data in this bird database. Also, the new PDB would have a high degree of

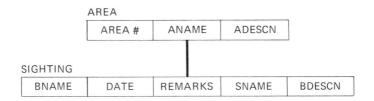

Fig. 17.1   Required record structure for the survey database

BIRD

BNAME	SNAME	BDESCN

Fig. 17.2   Record structure of the bird database

AREA PDB

BIRD PDB

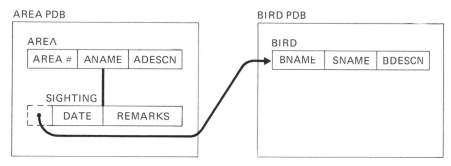

Fig. 17.3 AREA and BIRD PDBs

internal redundancy, in that many PDBR occurrences would contain identical information—specifically, the scientific name and description would be recorded once for each sighting of a particular type of bird, instead of once only.

These inefficiencies can be avoided by means of a logical database, as follows. First, a *physical* database is defined with a structure similar to that shown in Fig. 17.1. However, the SIGHTING segment contains only the fields DATE and REMARKS, together with a *pointer* to the appropriate BIRD segment in the bird PDB. (This pointer is part of the segment prefix[2] and is not seen by the user.) Thus we have the situation illustrated in Fig. 17.3.

Second, a *logical* database can now be defined with the structure shown in Fig. 17.4, which shows what the user does see (contrast Fig. 17.1). The user can now process this LDB as if it were a PDB—within certain limits (to be discussed).

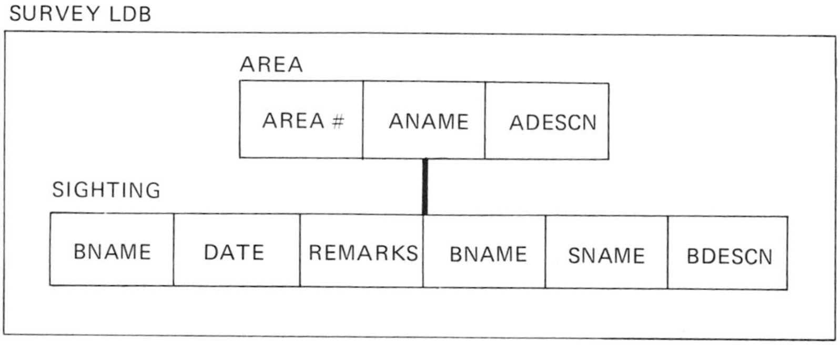

SURVEY LDB

Fig. 17.4 The SURVEY LDB

---

[2] This assumes "direct pointing." See Section 17.4.

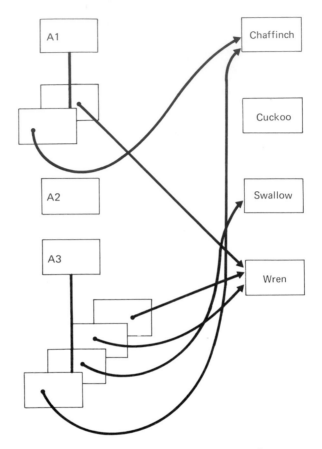

Fig. 17.5 Sample PDBs (AREA and BIRD)

For example, suppose that Fig. 17.5 represents the actual data in the PDBs at some particular time.

Then the LDB seen by the user is as shown in Fig. 17.6. (Only the sequence fields are shown, but the reader should understand that each dependent segment occurrence includes all the fields given in SIGHTING in Fig. 17.4. Note that there are *two* SIGHTINGs for 'WREN' under area A3.)

(Actually the foregoing explanation is slightly oversimplified. In order that an LDB may be defined in terms of one or more existing PDBs, those PDBs must be appropriately defined; that is, their DBDs must specify that they are involved in the LDB concerned. In other words, the DBA must be aware that the PDBs are to be involved in an

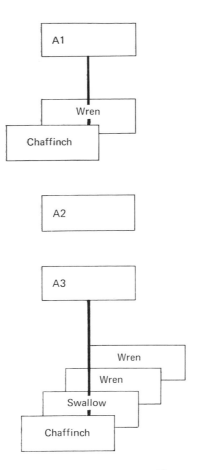

Fig. 17.6   Corresponding LDB (SURVEY)

LDB at the time that their DBDs are written. Thus, in the example, either it must have been foreseen that the BIRD PDB was eventually to participate in the SURVEY LDB, or else it will be necessary to unload the BIRD PDB and then to reload it in accordance with a revised DBD. The latter tends to be the method most often used in practice. See Section 17.4.)

17.3   TERMINOLOGY

The "pointer segment" SIGHTING of Fig. 17.3 is of course a child of the AREA segment. It is also considered a child of the BIRD segment (the segment it points to). Thus SIGHTING has two parent segments. To distinguish between the two, we refer to AREA as the *physical* parent, BIRD as the *logical* parent; also, we refer to SIGHTING both as the physical child of AREA and as the logical child of BIRD. The pointer is a "logical parent" pointer.

The terminology of logical-parent/logical-child, like that of physical-parent/physical-child, applies to both types and occurrences. Thus the BIRD segment 'CHAFFINCH', for example, is the logical parent of two SIGHTING segments, whose physical parents are, respectively, the 'A1' AREA segment and the 'A3' AREA segment. Moreover, these two SIGHTINGs are considered as "logical twins"; by analogy with physical twins, all occurrences of one type of logical child with a common logical parent occurrence are known as logical twins.

As the example of the previous section illustrates, it is permitted—though not required—for the "pointer segment" to contain data fields in addition to the pointer. These fields contain "intersection data"—that is, data that describes the physical-parent/logical-parent *combination*. The intersection data would normally be functionally dependent on the combination of physical parent sequence field and logical parent sequence field (see Chapter 9), but this is not mandatory.

We are now in a position to explain Fig. 17.4. The SIGHTING segment in that diagram is a concatenation of the following three items.

1. The fully concatenated key of the logical parent

2. The intersection data

3. The logical parent (including the logical parent sequence field value)

This is in general how a logical child always appears to the user. (Actually, it is possible to omit *either* the first two of these *or* the third, but we shall never do so in our examples. What is *not* possible is to see the intersection data without the fully concatenated key of the logical parent.)

17.4 THE DATABASE DESCRIPTIONS (DBDs)

A logical database, like a physical database, is defined by means of a database description (DBD). This DBD is said to be a "logical" DBD, as opposed to a "physical" DBD, which is a DBD for a physical database. Each logical DBD is defined in terms of one or more underlying physical DBDs, which must already exist. Thus in our example we shall require (a) a physical DBD for the BIRD PDB, (b) a physical DBD for the AREA PDB, and (c) a logical DBD for the SURVEY LDB. We consider each of these in turn.

Figure 17.7 illustrates in outline the DBD for the BIRD PDB. The only thing to note here is that the SEGM statement for the BIRD

```
DBD     NAME=BIRDPDBD,...
SEGM    NAME=BIRD,POINTER=TWIN,...
LCHILD  NAME=(SIGHTING,AREAPDBD)
(FIELD  statements for BIRD)
```

Fig. 17.7   DBD for the BIRD PDB (outline)

segment is followed by an LCHILD statement specifying the SIGHTING segment—defined in the DBD for the AREA PDB (Fig. 17.8)—as a logical child of BIRD.

Figure 17.8, which illustrates in outline a possible DBD for the AREA PDB, requires rather more explanation. Consider first the POINTER entry for the SIGHTING segment, which specifies that the SIGHTING prefix is to contain the following pointers.

■   A logical parent pointer (as explained in Section 17.2)

This of course provides the basic linkage necessary to construct the LDB. However, LPARNT may be specified only if the logical parent resides in HDAM or HIDAM; if instead it resides in HISAM (HSAM cannot be used) then symbolic pointers must be used (see below).

■   A physical twin pointer (explained in Chapter 16)

TWIN (or TWINBWD or HIER or HIERBWD) may be specified, provided that the SIGHTING segment resides in HDAM or HIDAM; if instead it resides in HISAM, then of course physical twin sequence will be represented by physical position. But what is the physical twin sequence? Clearly BNAME is the field we would like as the sequence field for SIGHTING (see Fig. 17.6).[3] However, this raises additional problems,

```
DBD     NAME=AREAPDBD,...
SEGM    NAME=AREA,POINTER=TWIN,...
(FIELD  statements for AREA)
SEGM    NAME=SIGHTING,POINTER=(LPARNT,TWIN),
        PARENT=((AREA),(BIRD,VIRTUAL,BIRDPDBD)),...
FIELD   NAME=BNAME,...
FIELD   NAME=DATE,...
FIELD   NAME=REMARKS,...
```

Fig. 17.8   DBD for the AREA PDB (outline)

---

[3] We will have to specify NAME = (BNAME,SEQ,M) to allow for multiple sightings of one type of bird within one area (see Section 13.2). Alternatively, if (say) no more than one sighting per day of each type of bird within each area is to be recorded in the database, the combination of BNAME and DATE could be defined as the sequence field (and values would then be unique).

since BNAME is physically part of the BIRD segment, not the SIGHT-ING segment. We shall return to this point in a moment.

Consider next the PARENT entry, which specifies (a) that the physical parent of this segment is AREA, and (b) that the logical parent of this segment is BIRD, which is defined in the DBD for the BIRD PDB. VIRTUAL specifies that the fully concatenated key of the logical parent is a virtual field—field BNAME—so far as this segment is concerned; i.e., it is not physically stored as part of the segment. Note, however, that a FIELD statement for BNAME *is* provided.

The alternative to VIRTUAL is PHYSICAL, which means that a copy of the BNAME field is to be physically stored as part of the SIGHTING segment. If PHYSICAL is specified, then (and only then) BNAME may be specified (in the FIELD statement) as the sequence field for this segment. Thus, if this sequencing is required, PHYSICAL *must* be specified in the PARENT entry. (The fully concatenated key returned in the PCB when a SIGHTING is retrieved will then consist of an AREA# value followed by a BNAME value.)

But if PHYSICAL is specified, the logical parent pointer in the prefix is conceptually redundant. If the logical parent resides in HDAM or HIDAM, this pointer may still be included for performance reasons, although it is perfectly valid to omit it; however, if the logical parent resides in HISAM, the pointer *must* be omitted (and PHYSICAL must be specified). (It is never possible to use pointers to point to segments in HISAM, since in HISAM the insertion of a new segment may cause existing segments to be moved.)

In general, therefore, we have two distinct ways of representing the link from a logical child to its logical parent (except when the logical parent resides in HISAM): either via a "direct" pointer (i.e., including a logical parent pointer in the logical child prefix) or via a "symbolic" pointer (i.e., physically recording the logical parent fully concatenated key as the first field of the logical child). The relative advantages of the two are essentially as discussed in Section 2.4: Direct pointers provide faster access; symbolic pointers need no adjustment if the database they point to is reorganized. Some other considerations affecting the choice are discussed in reference [16.1]. (It is also possible to use both techniques in combination.) However, the choice of method in no way affects the contents of the logical child segment as seen by the user. For simplicity, we shall assume for the rest of this chapter that all physical databases are in HDAM or HIDAM, and that symbolic pointers are not being used (unless it is explicitly stated otherwise). We are now in a position to examine the logical DBD (Fig. 17.9).

Observe first that ACCESS = LOGICAL must be specified in the

```
DBD      NAME=SVEYLDBD,ACCESS=LOGICAL
DATASET  LOGICAL
SEGM     NAME=AREA,SOURCE=((AREA,,AREAPDBD))
SEGM     NAME=SIGHTING,PARENT=AREA,
         SOURCE=((SIGHTING,,AREAPDBD),(BIRD,,BIRDPDBD))
```

Fig. 17.9 DBD for the SURVEY LDB

DBD statement, and that LOGICAL must also be specified in the
DATASET statement. The remaining statements define the segments of
the LDB; note that FIELD statements may not be included. The first
SEGM statement states that the root segment of the LDB, AREA, is in
fact the AREA segment defined in the DBD for the AREA PDB (the
segment could be given a different name within the LDB if desired). The
double comma indicates an omitted operand; see reference [13.1] for
details. The second SEGM statement states that within this LDB,
SIGHTING is dependent on AREA, and it consists of the concatenation
of the SIGHTING segment defined in the DBD for the AREA PDB
together with the BIRD segment defined in the DBD for the BIRD PDB.
(As seen by the user, of course, the segment also includes as its first field
the BIRD fully concatenated key.)

17.5 LOADING THE LOGICAL DATABASE

The process of loading a logical database consists essentially of loading
the underlying physical database(s) and setting up the required pointers.
For a number of reasons, this operation is performed directly on the
underlying PDB(s), not on the LDB as such. To see why this is necessary,
suppose for a moment that the SURVEY LDB were to be loaded via an
appropriate series of ISRT operations issued directly against that LDB.
Several problems would arise. For example, the insertion of a SIGHT-
ING occurrence would sometimes have to cause the creation of a BIRD
occurrence, sometimes not, depending on whether the BIRD occurrence
already existed in the BIRD PDB. Also, what about a BIRD for which
there are no SIGHTINGs (e.g., 'CUCKOO' in Fig. 17.5)? How would it
get loaded? What about the restriction that PDBs must be loaded in
hierarchical sequence (at least in HISAM and HIDAM)? And again
considering the data in Fig. 17.5, what if the BDESCN value for 'CHAF-
FINCH' (say) were given differently for the A1 and A3 SIGHTINGs?
 For reasons such as these, the procedure actually followed is to load
the LDB by inserting segments directly into the underlying PDB(s), i.e.,

by loading each of the underlying PDBs as a separate operation. Let us assume, therefore, that the BIRD PDB has already been loaded (in the form shown in Fig. 17.5), and let us consider what is involved in loading the AREA PDB.

AREA A1 is loaded (inserted) in the usual way. A SIGHTING segment, containing fields BNAME (with value 'CHAFFINCH'), DATE, and REMARKS may then be loaded, followed by a similar SIGHTING segment for 'WREN'. Then follow AREA A2, AREA A3, a SIGHTING for 'CHAFFINCH' under A3, and similar SIGHTINGs for 'SWALLOW' and 'WREN'. Note, however, that at this stage the SIGHTING segments do not contain the logical parent pointers. These are inserted subsequently by a special utility program, which must be executed before the loading process can be considered complete. Moreover, the logical parent prefixes must also be adjusted; this is also handled by a special utility program, which operates on the BIRD PDB.

For further details of the loading process see reference [13.1].

17.6 PROCESSING THE LOGICAL DATABASE

Once the LDB has been loaded, the user can process it exactly as if it were a PDB, at least so far as retrieval operations are concerned.[4] Storage operations are more complicated, however. In general, the effect of a storage operation on a segment that participates in a logical relationship—that is, a logical child, a logical parent, or a physical parent of a segment that also has a logical parent—is defined by the *rule* specified by the DBA for that operation and that segment. The DBA is required to specify, in the SEGM statement in the appropriate *physical* DBD, an insert rule, a delete rule, and a replace rule for each such segment. Each of these rules, in general, may be specified as "physical," "logical," or "virtual." It is not our intention here to go into full details of these rules (see [13.1]), but we shall consider their significance with respect to the SURVEY LDB. Note that the specified rules govern *all* storage operations on the segment; the operation in question may actually be issued either (a) directly against the relevant PDB or (b) "indirectly" against some LDB built on top of the PDB.

Consider ISRT operations first. It is always possible to insert an AREA, and the effect is simply to insert that AREA into the AREA PDB. What about SIGHTINGs? The problem here, as mentioned in the

---

[4] A PCB is required for the LDB, just as if it were a PDB. See Chapter 14.

previous section, is that the BIRD to which the SIGHTING refers may or may not already exist in the BIRD PDB. If it does, the ISRT is accepted (that is, the SIGHTING is inserted into the AREA PDB); moreover, if the insert rule for BIRD is "virtual," the SNAME and BDESCN values from the SIGHTING segment as presented by the user actually replace the previous values in the corresponding BIRD segment. If, on the other hand, the BIRD does not currently exist in the BIRD PDB, the ISRT will be (a) rejected if the insert rule for BIRD is "physical"; (b) accepted otherwise, in which case the effect will be not only to insert the SIGHT-ING into the AREA PDB but also to insert the BIRD into the BIRD PDB (again, remember that the SIGHTING as presented by the user includes SNAME and BDESCN).

(Of course, it is always possible to insert new BIRDs into the BIRD PDB, independently of the SURVEY LDB.)

Now consider DLET operations. Deletion of an AREA will remove that AREA and its subordinate SIGHTINGs from the AREA PDB. Deletion of a SIGHTING (either directly or via deletion of its parent AREA) will remove that SIGHTING from the AREA PDB, and if this is the last SIGHTING for the BIRD concerned and BIRD has a delete rule of "virtual," it will also remove the BIRD from the BIRD PDB.

As for an attempt to delete a BIRD directly from the BIRD PDB, the effect depends on the delete rule for BIRD. "Physical" will permit the deletion of a BIRD only if no SIGHTINGs refer to it. "Logical" and "virtual" will permit the deletion of a BIRD from the BIRD PDB while at the same time keeping it available via the SURVEY LDB so long as any SIGHTING refers to it (this effect is achieved via appropriate flags in the BIRD prefix). Such a BIRD will be removed entirely when the last SIGHTING referring to it is deleted.

Finally, consider REPL operations. Replacement of an AREA sim-ply causes the corresponding replacement to occur in the AREA PDB. Replacement of the insersection data (DATE and REMARKS) in a SIGHTING also simply causes the corresponding replacement to occur in the AREA PDB. Replacement of the logical parent data (SNAME and BDESCN) in a SIGHTING is permitted only if the replace rule for BIRD is "virtual"; the effect in this case is to replace the BIRD segment, which in turn causes the logical parent data to change accordingly in all other SIGHTINGs for that BIRD. (Of course, a BIRD may always be replaced directly by means of a REPL operation on the BIRD PDB.)

To sum up, therefore, the SURVEY LDB may be made to look more or less like a PDB, provided that the DBA specifies rules as shown in Fig. 17.10 (P, L, and V stand for "physical," "logical," and "virtual").

Rule \ Segment	AREA	SIGHTING	BIRD
Insert	P, L, or V	V (Note 1)	L or V (Note 3)
Delete	V (Note 2)	P, L, or V	P or L (Note 4)
Replace	P, L, or V	P, L, or V	V (Note 3)

Fig. 17.10   Rules for AREA and BIRD PDBs

Notes

1. The insert rule for a logical child segment is always given as V.[5]

2. The delete rule for a physical parent segment is always given as V.[5]

3. Observe that the structure of the SURVEY LDB makes it appear that (for example) to change the BDESCN value for an existing BIRD, it would be necessary to make the change in every SIGHTING for that BIRD, whereas, in fact, this is not required; that is, the LDB structure permits redundancy in the user's view of the data without requiring a corresponding redundancy in what is actually stored.

4. The delete rule for BIRD could be V without affecting the behavior of the LDB as such, but this would allow operations on the LDB (or the AREA PDB) to have possibly undesirable side effects on the BIRD PDB. For example, deletion of an AREA might cause deletion of a BIRD (if there are now no SIGHTINGs for that BIRD).

We can see that it is only the BIRD segment for which the rules are critical (in this example). However, bear in mind that so far we have discussed only the simplest possible type of LDB, that is, one involving a "unidirectional relationship," with one physical parent, one logical parent, and one logical child. The effect of the rules in more complicated situations is beyond the scope of this book.

17.7   BIDIRECTIONAL LOGICAL RELATIONSHIPS

The SURVEY LDB, being hierarchical, represents the association between AREAs and BIRDs as if it were a one-to-many correspondence. In fact, of course, the correspondence is really many-to-many: Not only are there many BIRDs for a given AREA, there are also many AREAs for a given BIRD. Thus (as was pointed out in Chapter 3) an operation

---

[5] Actually IMS will always assume V in these cases, regardless of what is specified, in order to prevent certain inconsistencies in the data that might otherwise be allowed to occur.

such as "Find all areas in which a particular bird has been sighted" is comparatively difficult with the SURVEY LDB. We may overcome this difficulty by means of another LDB—BASURVEY, say—in which AREA is viewed as subordinate to BIRD. (For consistency, let us rename the original LDB, in which BIRD is subordinate to AREA, as ABSURVEY.) Thus we have a "bidirectional logical relationship" between AREAs and BIRDs.

Bidirectional logical relationships may be implemented in IMS in two ways, known respectively as physical and virtual pairing.

Physical Pairing

Physical pairing involves the introduction of a new type of segment—BASIGHT, say—as a physical child of BIRD and a logical child of AREA. (Again for consistency, let us rename the original SIGHTING segment as ABSIGHT.) See Fig. 17.11.

The purpose of the BASIGHT segment is exactly analogous to that of the ABSIGHT segment; that is, it contains a pointer (in its prefix) to its logical parent (AREA), together with intersection data (DATE and REMARKS, as in ABSIGHT). This enables us to define the BASURVEY LDB (as well as the ABSURVEY LDB). A BASIGHT occurrence as seen by the user will consist of the concatenation of the logical parent fully concatenated key (an AREA# value), the intersection data, and the logical parent data (including the AREA# value again). ABSIGHT and BASIGHT are "paired segments" and are declared as such to IMS in the DBDs for the AREA and BIRD PDBs; see Figs. 17.12 and 17.13.

Figure 17.12 shows (in the lines with asterisks) the changes involved in the DBD for the AREA PDB (compare Fig. 17.8). The SEGM

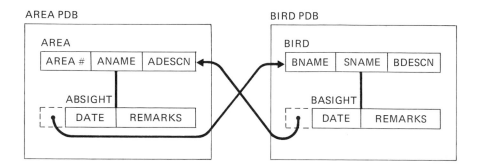

Fig. 17.11 AREA and BIRD PDBs (with physical pairing)

```
     DBD       NAME=AREAPDBD,...
     SEGM      NAME=AREA,POINTER=TWIN,...
*    LCHILD    NAME=(BASIGHT,BIRDPDBD),PAIR=ABSIGHT
     (FIELD    statements for AREA)
*    SEGM      NAME=ABSIGHT,POINTER=(LPARNT,TWIN,PAIRED),
*              PARENT=((AREA),
*                   (BIRD,PHYSICAL,BIRDPDBD)),...
     FIELD     NAME=(BNAME,SEQ,M),...
     FIELD     NAME=DATE,...
     FIELD     NAME=REMARKS,...
```

Fig. 17.12   DBD for the AREA PDB (outline)—physical pairing

```
     DBD       NAME=BIRDPDBD,...
     SEGM      NAME=BIRD,POINTER=TWIN,...
*    LCHILD    NAME=(ABSIGHT,AREAPDBD),PAIR=BASIGHT
     (FIELD    statements for BIRD)
*    SEGM      NAME=BASIGHT,POINTER=(LPARNT,TWIN,PAIRED),
*              PARENT=((BIRD),
*                   (AREA,PHYSICAL,AREAPDBD)),...
*    FIELD     NAME=(AREA#,SEQ,M),...
*    FIELD     NAME=DATE,...
*    FIELD     NAME=REMARKS,...
```

Fig. 17.13   DBD for the BIRD PDB (outline)—physical pairing

statement for the AREA segment is followed by an LCHILD statement specifying the BASIGHT segment—defined in the DBD for the BIRD PDB (Fig. 17.13)—as a logical child of AREA. The LCHILD statement also specifies that the logical child (BASIGHT) is paired with the AB-SIGHT segment, defined subsequently in the current DBD. The other change to this DBD is in the POINTER entry for ABSIGHT, which specifies PAIRED (among other things); this specification is required.

Note, incidentally, that BNAME has been physically included in the ABSIGHT segment. This permits the sightings within one area to be sequenced on bird name.

Figure 17.13 shows the changes involved in the DBD for the BIRD PDB (compare Fig. 17.7).

The BIRD DBD is essentially similar to the DBD for AREA. Note again that the logical parent fully concatenated key field—AREA#—has been physically included in the logical child segment (BASIGHT), to permit the sightings of one bird to be sequenced on area number.

The DBD for the ABSURVEY LDB is the same as before (Fig. 17.9). The DBD for the BASURVEY LDB is essentially similar.

Note that physical pairing involves redundant storage of the intersection data; that is, every item of intersection data will be physically recorded twice, once in an ABSIGHT occurrence and once in the paired BASIGHT occurrence. (For example, the ABSIGIIT occurrence that links area A1 to 'CHAFFINCH' for a particular date will contain precisely the same intersection data as the BASIGHT occurrence that links 'CHAFFINCH' to area A1 for that date.) However, since the segments are paired, when the user inserts an occurrence of either one, IMS will automatically create the corresponding occurrence of the other (except during loading, when it is the user's responsibility to create both). Similarly, if the user deletes or replaces an occurrence of one of the pair, IMS will automatically make the appropriate change to the other.

Virtual Pairing

Virtual pairing is a means of avoiding the redundancy above. The idea is that one of the two paired segment types may be eliminated; for example, the BASIGHT segment need not physically exist, since its data may be found from the ABSIGHT segment. The directed relationship from BIRD to AREA is then represented, not via a logical parent pointer from BASIGHT to AREA but via a logical child pointer from BIRD to ABSIGHT *plus* a physical parent pointer[6] from ABSIGHT to AREA. (Logical twin pointers are also required; see below.) Figure 17.14 illustrates this organization.

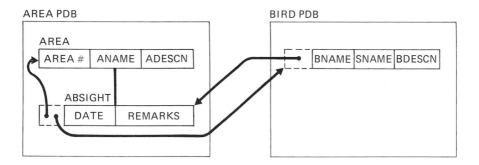

AREA PDB   BIRD PDB

Fig. 17.14 AREA and BIRD PDBs (with virtual pairing)

---

[6] This is not the only situation in which physical parent pointers are required. They are also necessary if a logical child points via a direct pointer to a logical parent that is not a root. In such a situation each segment in the physical hierarchical path to the logical parent will include a physical parent pointer, to allow the construction of the logical parent fully concatenated key.

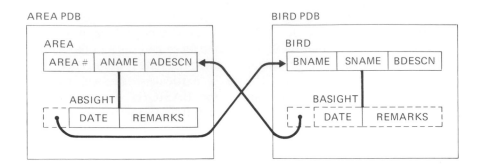

Fig. 17.15   AREA and BIRD PDBs (with virtual pairing)—conventional representation

The first point to be made is that virtual pairing looks exactly like physical pairing to the user. In the example, although the segment BASIGHT no longer exists, IMS makes it look as if it did; for this reason BASIGHT is said to be a virtual segment. (Actually, there is one very minor difference between a virtual segment and a real one as seen by the user: A virtual segment cannot be "loaded" as part of the process of loading the PDB that contains it; instead it is "created" when the real segment is loaded.) The conventional representation of a virtual pairing situation is shown in Fig. 17.15 (but bear in mind that Fig. 17.14 represents the true picture).

A second general point is that the real member of the pair (ABSIGHT in the example) must reside in HDAM or HIDAM, since the logical parent segment prefix contains a direct pointer to it, namely, the logical child pointer. (Logical parent pointers are the only ones that may be symbolic.)

Now consider the sequencing involved in this example. The sightings within one area are sequenced on bird name; this is done by physically including the BNAME field in the ABSIGHT segment and specifying POINTER = TWIN (which links all ABSIGHTs for one AREA on a physical twin chain). What about the sequence of sightings of one bird? That is represented by another chain, the logical twin chain, which links all ABSIGHTs that point to the same BIRD in physical parent fully concatenated key sequence. Hence the sightings of one bird are sequenced on area number, as required.

Conceptually, however, this second sequencing is achieved by making AREA# the SEQ field for the (virtual) segment BASIGHT, and this is what is specified in the DBD. See Figs. 17.16 and 17.17.

```
      DBD   NAME=AREAPDBD,...
      SEGM  NAME=AREA,POINTER=TWIN,...
*     (LCHILD statement for BASIGHT must not be included)
      (FIELD statements for AREA)
*     SEGM  NAME=ABSIGHT,POINTER=(LPARNT,TWIN,LTWIN),
*           PARENT=((AREA),
*                  (BIRD,PHYSICAL,BIRDPDBD)),...
      FIELD NAME=(BNAME,SEQ,M),...
      FIELD NAME=DATE,...
      FIELD NAME=REMARKS,...
```

Fig. 17.16   DBD for the AREA PDB (outline)—virtual pairing

```
      DBD   NAME=BIRDPDBD,...
      SEGM  NAME=BIRD,POINTER=TWIN,...
*     LCHILD NAME=(ABSIGHT,AREAPDBD),PAIR=BASIGHT,
*            POINTER=SNGL
      (FIELD statements for BIRD)
*     SEGM  NAME=BASIGHT,POINTER=PAIRED,
*            PARENT=BIRD,
*            SOURCE=((ABSIGHT,,AREAPDBD))
      FIELD NAME=(AREA#,SEQ,M),...
      FIELD NAME=DATE,...
      FIELD NAME=REMARKS,...
```

Fig. 17.17   DBD for the BIRD PDB (outline)—virtual pairing

Figure 17.16 shows (see asterisks) the changes involved in the DBD for the AREA PDB (compare Fig. 17.12). An LCHILD statement for the virtual segment BASIGHT is *not* supplied. Also, the POINTER entry for ABSIGHT no longer specifies PAIRED but instead requests a logical twin pointer to be included in the prefix. The sequencing for this logical twin chain is specified in the *other* DBD; see below. (It is also possible to request a two-way logical twin chain by specifying LTWINBWD.) Note that there is no mention here of the physical parent pointer, which IMS provides automatically.

Figure 17.17 shows the changes involved in the DBD for the BIRD PDB (compare Fig. 17.13). The LCHILD statement includes the additional entry POINTER = SNGL, which is a request for each occurrence of BIRD to include a logical child pointer in its prefix to the first ABSIGHT occurrence on the logical twin chain corresponding to this BIRD occurrence. (It is also possible to request each BIRD to point to both the first and the last of its logical children, by specifying POINTER = DBLE.) The SEGM statement for the virtual segment BASIGHT specifies (a) POINTER = PAIRED, (b) the physical parent (only), (c) a new entry—SOURCE—which refers to the corresponding real segment; this statement contains no other entries (not even BYTES). Lastly, there is *no* change in the FIELD statements for BASIGHT; in particular, the first defines "BASIGHT sequence," i.e., logical twin sequence for ABSIGHT.

The logical DBDs are the same as before.

17.8   A NOTE ON THE STORAGE STRUCTURE

From the foregoing sections we can see that, although the user sees an LDB as a hierarchical structure—at least so far as retrieval is concerned—the underlying stored representation is somewhat more complex. It is in fact a *network*, inasmuch as certain segments, namely, the logical parents, may be pointed at by any number of (logical parent) pointers and hence may participate in any number of LDBR occurrences. However, since IMS does not support "n-directional logical relationships" for any value of $n > 2$, such networks are not completely general. Instead, they are essentially limited (at their most complex) to what we may call "two-entity nets." In the networks of Section 17.7, for example, the two types of entity are of course AREA and BIRD.[7] The supplier-part-project problem (see the exercises in Chapter 5) is an example of a situation in which a "three-entity net" would be required, and thus one that would have to be handled in a somewhat indirect fashion in IMS.

To ensure that he or she understands these points, the reader is strongly urged to tackle Exercises 17.2 and 17.7.

17.9   LOGICAL DATABASES INVOLVING A
SINGLE PHYSICAL DATABASE

In the introduction to the present chapter we stated that the segments constituting an LDBR occurrence are drawn from several distinct PDBR occurrences, and that the PDBR occurrences, in turn, may belong to one or more distinct PDBs. As an example involving only one PDB, consider the hierarchical structure illustrated in Fig. 13.1 (the education database), in which the root segment COURSE (fields COURSE#, TITLE, DE-SCRIPN) has a dependent segment PREREQ (fields COURSE#, TITLE). Clearly, we can avoid the redundancy that this PDB structure

_____

[7] But see Exercise 20.5.

EDUC PDB

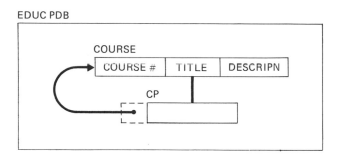

Fig. 17.18   The EDUC PDB

EDCP LDB

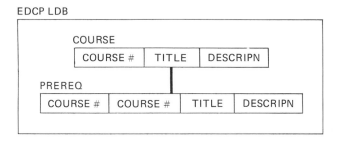

Fig. 17.19   The EDCP LDB

entails by replacing PREREQ by a "pointer segment," so that each
COURSE occurrence has a set of dependent pointer segment occurrences
that point to the appropriate COURSEs. Figures 17.18 and 17.19 show,
respectively, the conventional way of representing such a situation on
paper and the hierarchical structure seen by the user[8] (for simplicity we
ignore the OFFERING, TEACHER, and STUDENT segments, as well
as any intersection data that may exist).

The segment CP is both a physical child and a logical child of
COURSE. Conversely, COURSE is both the physical parent and the
logical parent of CP. We must stress, however that no CP *occurrence* will

---

[8] On the basis of the same PDB, it would also be possible to define an LDB of
three levels, consisting of COURSE (root), PREREQ1 (first dependent level),
and PREREQ2 (second dependent level); PREREQ1 would represent the immediate prerequisites of COURSE, and PREREQ2 would represent the immediate prerequisites of PREREQ1. Similarly, LDBs of four, five, ... levels may
be defined (up to a maximum of 15 levels). In practice this is an extremely useful
facility, but for simplicity we shall stick to two levels in our examples.

have the same COURSE *occurrence* as both physical and logical parent (Fig. 17.18 notwithstanding). The DBD for the education PDB will include an LCHILD statement for CP (following the SEGM statement for COURSE), and in addition the SEGM statement for CP will specify COURSE as both physical and logical parent.

The education PDB of Fig. 17.18 involves a unidirectional logical relationship (from CP to COURSE) which, as we have just seen, enables us to find all PREREQs for a given COURSE. It is also possible to add a logical relationship in the other direction (thus converting it into a bidirectional relationship), so that, in addition, we can find all COURSEs that have a given PREREQ. This is done by including a second type of pointer segment—PC, say—physically dependent on COURSE, such that each COURSE occurrence has a set of PC occurrences that point to occurrences of COURSEs for which the original course is actually a PREREQ. PC and CP will be paired segments. If we assume that virtual pairing is used (and that PC is the virtual member of the pair), Figs. 17.20, 17.21, and 17.22 show, respectively, the conventional way of representing such a situation, the structures that actually exist, and the two LDBs that can be seen by the user.

Once again, let it be emphasized that no child *occurrence* will have the same segment *occurrence* as both physical parent and logical parent. The two pointers in Fig. 17.21 from CP to COURSE are, respectively, a logical parent and a physical parent pointer; for one CP occurrence they will point to *different* COURSE occurrences. Referring now to Fig. 17.22, the user will employ the EDCP LDB to find PREREQs for a given COURSE, the EDPC LDB to find COURSEs for a given PREREQ.

EDUC PDB

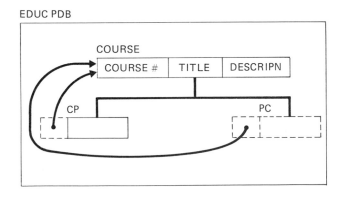

Fig. 17.20 The EDUC PDB (with virtual pairing)— conventional representation

EDUC PDB

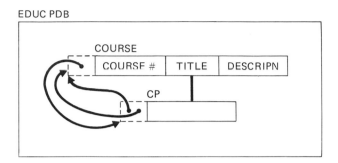

Fig. 17.21   The EDUC PDB (with virtual pairing)

EDCP LDB

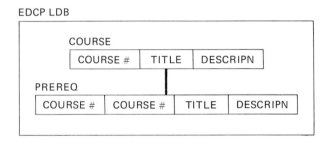

EDPC LDB

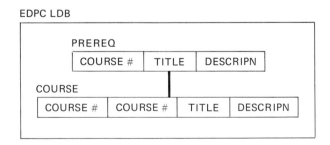

Fig. 17.22   The EDCP and EDPC LDBs

(The segment names in these LDBs are of course arbitrary; the significant point is that EDCP must be defined in terms of the CP logical child, and EDPC must be defined in terms of the PC logical child.)

See Exercises 17.3, 17.4, and 17.5.

17.10   SOME RULES AND RESTRICTIONS

The definition of an LDB is subject to a number of rules and restrictions, documented in some detail in [16.1]. In this section we shall examine some of these rules, probably the most important ones from a practical point of view. Development of suitable diagrams to illustrate these points has been left as an exercise for the reader.

1. The root of an LDB must also be a root of a PDB.

2. A logical child segment must have one physical parent and one logical parent. It follows that (a) a root cannot be a logical child; (b) IMS cannot support "n-directional relationships" for $n > 2$.

3. A physical child of a logical child may appear as a dependent of the concatenated (logical-child/logical-parent) segment in the LDB. For example, consider the databases of Section 17.2. Suppose that in the AREA PDB (Fig. 17.3) REMARKS actually consists of a character string that varies in length between (say) 100 and 1000 characters. Instead of including REMARKS as a field within the SIGHTING segment, it might be preferable in such a situation to have a REMARKS segment physically dependent on the SIGHTING segment (if the REMARKS segment is 100 bytes long, there would be from 1 to 10 occurrences of it for each SIGHTING occurrence). The SURVEY LDB (Fig. 17.4) could then consist of three levels, with AREA at the root level, the concatenated SIGHTING segment at the second level, and REMARKS at the third level. This is an example of how "variable intersection data" is handled in IMS ("variable" here meaning "variable-length"). Incidentally, the RE-MARKS segment would probably not include a sequence field (see the end of Section 13.2).

4. A physical child of a logical parent may appear as a dependent of the concatenated (logical-child/logical-parent) segment in the LDB, provided that the logical parent is the first such encountered in the definition of the LDB hierarchical path.[9] To continue with the example of Section 17.2, suppose that BDESCN is represented as a segment physically dependent on BIRD (like REMARKS, it may actually consist of a character string that is highly variable in length). Then BDESCN may appear as a child of the concatenated SIGHTING segment in the SURVEY LDB. (Also, if BDESCN has a physical child called SUBDESCN, say, then SUBDESCN may appear as a child of BDESCN in the SURVEY LDB.) However, if BIRD also has a physical child—X, say—that in turn has a logical parent,

---

[9] This restriction is relaxed for an LDB defined in terms of a single PDB, as described in footnote 8.

Y, so that X is a logical child as well as a physical child, then although the concatenation of X and Y *could* be included in SURVEY (as a child of the SIGHTING segment), no physical child of Y could be so included.

5. A physical parent of a logical parent may appear as a dependent of the concatenated (logical-child/logical-parent) segment in the LDB. Suppose that BIRD has a physical parent segment GENUS. Then GENUS may be seen as a *child* of the concatenated SIGHTING segment in the SURVEY LDB. Moreover, if GENUS in turn has a physical parent segment FAMILY, then FAMILY may be seen as a child of GENUS in the SURVEY LDB; and so on, up to 15 levels (always the overall limit in IMS). In other words, it is possible to invert the hierarchical structure of the PDB, at least to a certain extent. For further details the reader is referred to [16.1].

6. If X and Y are two segments in an LDB hierarchical path, all segments traversed in the path between X and Y in the underlying PDB(s) must also be included (in the same relative positions) in that LDB hierarchical path.

Some further rules and restrictions are described in [16.1].

17.11 SUMMARY

The logical database facility of IMS makes it possible to overcome some of the "retrieval complexity" problems mentioned in the section on hierarchies (Section 3.3) in Chapter 3. It provides a method of reducing redundancy in the data as stored, while at the same time permitting redundancy in the data model where this is considered desirable. More important, perhaps, it provides a means of allowing users to view the data in many different ways (although each individual user view is still hierarchical). These objectives are achieved by means of an extended storage structure which is in effect a (limited) network, although once again we must emphasize that the user does not actually *see* a network structure. In conclusion, however, we should perhaps point out that logical databases provide an essentially *static* restructuring of the data. There is no means of *dynamically* creating a structure not previously known to the system, as was done in many examples in Parts 1 and 2 of this book—see Example 3.5.4, for instance.

EXERCISES

17.1 Restructure the publications database of Exercise 13.1 as two PDBs, so that LDBs can be defined that are specifically suited to responding to both of the following requests.

Find the authors of a given publication.

Find all publications for a given author.

What LDBs may the user see with your design? Write all relevant DBDs (in outline); for simplicity you may assume that both PDBs use hierarchical direct organization.

17.2 Assuming the sample data of Fig. 17.5, draw a diagram of the storage structure (showing all relevant pointers) corresponding to the following.

a) The SURVEY LDB (Figs. 17.7, 17.8, and 17.9)

b) The ABSURVEY and BASURVEY LDBs with physical pairing (Figs. 17.12 and 17.13)

c) The ABSURVEY and BASURVEY LDBs with virtual pairing (Figs. 17.16 and 17.17)

17.3 Sketch all segment occurrences together with their logical parent pointers for the EDUC PDB (Fig. 17.18), assuming the sample data in Fig. 17.23.

COURSE #	PREREQ COURSE #s
L02	—
M16	—
M19	—
M23	M16, M19
M27	L02
M30	L02, M23, M27

Fig. 17.23   Sample data for the EDUC PDB

17.4 Sketch all segment occurrences together with their logical parent, logical child, and physical parent pointers for the EDUC PDB (Fig. 17.21), assuming the same sample data as in the previous exercise.

17.5 Define in reasonable detail DBDs for the EDUC PDB of Fig. 17.21 and the LDBs of Fig. 17.22.

17.6 What is involved in loading the EDUC PDB of Fig. 17.21?

17.7 How would you handle the supplier-part-project problem (see the exercises in Chapter 5) in IMS?

17.8 The bidirectional logical relationship of Section 17.7 can be implemented in three ways: via physical pairing, via virtual pairing with ABSIGHT virtual, or via virtual pairing with BASIGHT virtual. To what extent can the DBA switch between these three techniques without affecting existing users?

REFERENCES AND BIBLIOGRAPHY

See [13.1] and [16.1].

18
IMS
Secondary
Indexing

18.1   INTRODUCTION

As explained in Chapter 16, the root sequencing in a HISAM or HIDAM database is supported by means of an *index* on the root segment sequence field. For HISAM the indexing is provided by a standard OS/VS access method (either ISAM or VSAM); for HIDAM the index is actually an IMS database in its own right, with either VSAM or a combination of ISAM and OSAM as the underlying access method. Since these indexes are on the root segment sequence field, we may refer to them as *primary* indexes (the root segment sequence field, which must take unique values in HISAM and HIDAM, may be thought of as the primary key for the physical database record); and the corresponding root ordering, namely, by ascending values of the sequence field, may be referred to as the primary processing sequence. In this chapter we present an introduction to IMS *secondary* indexing and the associated notion of secondary processing sequence.

In Chapter 2 we defined a secondary index as an index on a field other than the primary key. At that point, however, we were tacitly assuming that the file to be indexed was no more complex than a traditional sequential file. In IMS, of course, the file (database) to be indexed is hierarchical in structure, and the concept of secondary indexing needs to be extended accordingly. In fact, a secondary index in IMS can be used:

- to index a given segment, root or dependent, on the basis of any field of that segment;

- to index a given segment, root or dependent, on the basis of any field in a dependent (not necessarily an immediate child) of that segment.[1]

In all cases the "field" on which the index is based may actually be a concatenation of up to five fields, not necessarily contiguous, taken in any order. The index is implemented as an INDEX database, rather like the primary index in HIDAM, except that the underlying access method for this INDEX database *must* be VSAM, not ISAM/OSAM. The database to be indexed must be in HISAM, HDAM, or HIDAM, not in HSAM (nor may it be an INDEX itself). It is also possible to index a logical database, but details of this case are beyond the scope of this book.

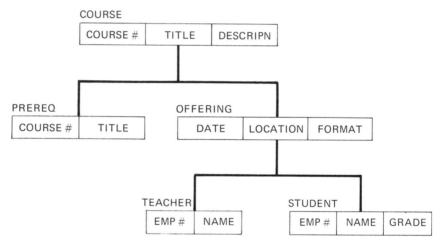

Fig. 18.1   Structure of the education database

To illustrate the possibilities, we consider once again the education database of Fig. 13.1 (shown again here as Fig. 18.1). The following list outlines some of the many possible indexes that could be constructed for this database.

- An index to COURSEs on the TITLE field
- An index to COURSEs on the LOCATION field from the OFFER-ING segment
- An index to OFFERINGs on the LOCATION field
- An index to OFFERINGs on the EMP# field from the TEACHER segment

We now proceed to consider each of these examples in detail.

---

[1] By "dependent of that segment" here we mean a dependent of the segment in its *physical* database.

18.2 INDEXING THE ROOT ON A FIELD NOT THE SEQUENCE FIELD

As our first example, we consider an index on COURSEs based on values of the TITLE field. We shall assume initially that TITLE values are unique. In order to establish *any* secondary index we need a DBD for that index—much like the DBD for the INDEX database in HIDAM—together with entries in the DBD for the database being indexed to indicate the field(s) the index is to be based on and other details. The index will then automatically be constructed by IMS as the database is loaded, and it will automatically be maintained as the database is subsequently updated. In the case at hand we need the following two additional statements in the DBD for the education database:

```
LCHILD  NAME=(TPTR,TXDBD),POINTER=INDX
XDFLD   NAME=XTITLE,SRCH=TITLE
```

These two statements must appear together as shown. They may appear anywhere after the SEGM statement for COURSE (and before the next SEGM statement), except that they may not precede the FIELD statement for the sequence field (COURSE#), and if the education database is HIDAM then they may not precede the LCHILD statement connecting COURSE to the primary index (see Section 16.8).

The LCHILD statement defines the COURSE segment to be a logical child of the segment TPTR in the database defined in the DBD called TXDBD. As we show below, TXDBD is the DBD that defines the secondary index database, and TPTR is the "index segment"—i.e., it is the (single) segment type in the index database. The "POINTER = INDX" entry specifies that the link between COURSE and TPTR is really an index connection rather than a logical-child/logical-parent connection. The XDFLD ("indexed field") statement specifies the field on which the secondary index is to be built. In the example this field is TITLE—see the SRCH entry. However, an SSA that includes a condition on the field-name TITLE—e.g., TITLE = 'DYNAMICS'—will *not* cause IMS to use the index in searching for the required segment occurrence. Rather, the user must *force* use of the index (when required) by using the field-name XTITLE, specified in the NAME entry of the XDFLD statement. To force IMS to use the secondary index in searching for the COURSE with TITLE 'DYNAMICS', for example, the user could write

```
GU COURSE (XTITLE='DYNAMICS')
```

This GU will cause IMS to fetch the 'DYNAMICS' index segment and then to fetch the COURSE segment this index segment points to. Note that the retrieved segment (in the I/O area) is exactly as usual—specifically, it does not include an extra field corresponding to XTITLE.

We turn now to the DBD for the secondary index.

```
DBD      NAME=TXDBD,ACCESS=INDEX
SEGM     NAME=TPTR,BYTES=33
FIELD    NAME=(TITLE,SEQ),BYTES=33,START=1
LCHILD   NAME=(COURSE,EDUCPDBD),INDEX=XTITLE
```

As mentioned earlier, the DBD for a secondary index is very similar to that for a primary index in HIDAM (see Section 16.8 for details). The only significant difference in the example above is that the INDEX entry in the LCHILD statement refers to XTITLE rather than to TITLE, i.e., to the "XD field" rather than to the actual field. Some other possible differences are discussed later in this section.

The secondary index on COURSEs just defined will contain one index segment occurrence for each COURSE occurrence. Each index segment will contain a TITLE value and a pointer to the corresponding COURSE. Given this index, the user can now choose to see the education database in a *secondary processing sequence*, namely, by ascending values of the course title field. (The *primary* processing sequence is by ascending values of the course number field.) To specify that this secondary sequence is required, the user simply includes the entry

```
PROCSEQ=TXDBD
```

in the PCB statement of the PCB (see Section 14.2). "Get unique" and "get next" operations using this PCB will now operate in terms of this sequence; note, however, that if such operations include an SSA involving a condition on the title field, the condition should be expressed in terms of XTITLE rather than TITLE.

If the PCB does not include a PROCSEQ entry, the *primary* processing sequence is used by default. In this case SSAs may still include references to "XD fields" such as XTITLE, but normally they should not, for reasons of efficiency. For example, the operation

```
GU COURSE (XTITLE='DYNAMICS')
```

will be implemented as follows if the primary processing sequence is used:

```
      get to start of primary sequence
loop: get next COURSE in primary sequence
      get index segment for DYNAMICS
      if index segment points to current COURSE, go to exit
      go to loop
```

The reason is that the "get unique" (which is really a "get first") must locate that COURSE which is the first to satisfy the SSA according to the *primary* sequence. IMS therefore scans COURSEs in this sequence, testing each in turn against the SSA; and since the SSA involves an XD field, each such test causes an access to the secondary index. Using TITLE rather than XTITLE would mean that each such test could be performed directly on the data in the COURSE segment and would not involve any index access at all.

Remarks similar to those above apply to the use of an XD field in an SSA in conjunction with a *secondary* processing sequence, if that secondary sequence is not the one associated with that XD field. For instance, the "get unique" in the example above (using XTITLE) would result in similarly poor performance if the processing sequence were based on values of the DESCRIPN field. It follows that a single SSA should usually not include references to two distinct XD fields, since at least one of them must fail to match the processing sequence. There *are* some situations when it could be advantageous to use a secondary index in conjunction with a processing sequence not based on that index, but the details are beyond the scope of this text; for further information see reference [16.1]. From this point on we shall restrict our attention to the case where the processing sequence is the one associated with the XD field concerned.

We list below some additional points the user must be aware of when using a secondary processing sequence.

- Values of the indexed field need not be unique. In our illustration, for example, courses need not have unique titles. If they do not, the FIELD statement in the DBD for the index (TXDBD in the example) must include the specification M (multiple) in the NAME entry:

```
FIELD  NAME=(TITLE,SEQ,M),...
```

  If *n* COURSEs all have the same title there will be *n* index segments for that title in the INDEX database; i.e., each COURSE occurrence will have an index entry pointing to it. See [16.1] for details of how "duplicates" are ordered with respect to the secondary processing sequence.

- The fully concatenated key returned in the key feedback area (in the PCB) will contain a TITLE value in place of a COURSE# value. In effect the indexed field is being treated as the sequence field for COURSE segments.

- Notwithstanding the previous point, the user is allowed to update TITLE fields (using REPL) and is not allowed to update COURSE# fields. In other words, the rules for REPL are unaffected by the use of a secondary index. Note that updating the TITLE field for a particular COURSE may cause that COURSE to change position in the secondary sequence; for example, changing the title of course M19 from 'CALCULUS' to 'INTEGRAL CALCULUS' will move it from before 'DYNAMICS' to after 'DYNAMICS'. (IMS automatically maintains all secondary indexes to reflect such updates, by deleting the old index segment and creating a new one.) A subsequent "get next" operation may therefore retrieve the same COURSE again.

■ The "index target segment" (i.e., the segment pointed to by the index—COURSE in our example) may not be the object of ISRT or DLET operations when processing is via the secondary sequence. If the index target is a dependent rather than the root, this restriction applies not only to it but also to all its ancestors (see Sections 18.4 and 18.5).

■ If the database to be indexed resides in HISAM rather than in HDAM or HIDAM, the pointers in the index must be symbolic rather than direct (cf. the situation with logical parent pointers when the logical parent is in HISAM, as described in Chapter 17). In this case, the "POINTER = INDX" entry in the LCHILD statement for the database to be indexed must be replaced by "POINTER = SYMB" *and* "POINTER = SYMB" must also be specified in the LCHILD statement for the INDEX database itself.

■ A secondary index cannot be defined over a HISAM database that includes any secondary data set groups.

The foregoing points, suitably modified where appropriate, apply whenever a secondary processing sequence is being used, not merely to the particular case considered in this section.

18.3   INDEXING THE ROOT ON A FIELD IN A DEPENDENT

Suppose we wish to find course numbers for all COURSEs that have an OFFERING in Stockholm. The following code (using a path call) represents a possible solution to the problem.

```
NC  GN    COURSE*D
          OFFERING (LOCATION='STOCKHOLM')
      if not found, go to exit
      add COURSE# to result list
      go to NC
```

(We assume that we are initially positioned at the start of the database. Also we ignore the question of eliminating duplicate course numbers from the result.) This code is not particularly efficient, however, since it consists essentially of a sequential scan of the entire database (though some segments may be skipped over if the stored database contains child/twin pointers). Also, the user is forced to retrieve OFFERING segments although they are not really wanted.

A more efficient solution to the problem can be achieved using a secondary index, indexing COURSE segments on the basis of LOCATION values—i.e., indexing the root on a field in a dependent. The necessary DBDs are basically as in Section 18.2, except that: (a) for the COURSE segment, the XDFLD statement is

```
XDFLD  NAME=XLOC,SRCH=LOCATION,SEGMENT=OFFERING
```

(specifying that the XD field XLOC is derived from the LOCATION field in the OFFERING segment); and (b) in the INDEX database DBD, the LCHILD statement is

```
LCHILD  NAME=(COURSE,EDUCPDBD),INDEX=XLOC
```

Incidentally we could have given the XD field the name LOCATION without risk of ambiguity, but for clarity we choose the distinct name XLOC.

The secondary index will contain one index segment for each OFFERING occurrence in the education database. Each such index segment will point to the corresponding COURSE occurrence (the parent of the OFFERING concerned). If the education database contains m COURSEs and an average of n OFFERINGs per COURSE, the index will contain mn index segments, with an average of n index segments pointing at any given COURSE. The secondary processing sequence for the education database is defined by the sequence of these index segments, i.e., by ascending values of LOCATION (again, see [16.1] for details of ordering within duplicates). Note that, on average, each individual COURSE (together with all its dependents) will appear n times in this sequence, and that all occurrences of a given COURSE will *not* appear together, in general. In other words, when seen via the secondary index, the database appears to contain n times as many database records—though these records are not all independent of each other: For example, changing the title in a given COURSE occurrence will cause the same change in all other COURSE occurrences for the course concerned.

Assuming that the PCB specifies the secondary processing sequence (PROCSEQ = index-DBD-name), we can now write

```
NC  GN   COURSE (XLOC='STOCKHOLM')
         if not found, go to exit
         add COURSE# to result list
         go to NC
```

(Note that the syntax makes it look as if XLOC is a field within the COURSE segment.) Each iteration of this code causes IMS to fetch the next index segment for 'STOCKHOLM' and then to fetch the COURSE segment that this index segment points to. It is thus more efficient than the code given earlier, since basically it involves only $2N$ database accesses (where N is the number of Stockholm offerings) instead of a scan of the entire database. Again, however, we have ignored the problem of eliminating duplicate course numbers.

Note that the fully concatenated key returned in the key feedback area when this secondary sequence is used will contain a LOCATION value in place of a COURSE# value (true for all segment types in the hierarchy).

The Independent AND

When a segment is indexed on the basis of a field in some dependent of that segment, it is possible to write an SSA for that segment involving two or more distinct conditions on the XD field, separated by the special operator # ("independent AND")—for example,

        GU   COURSE (XLOC='STOCKHOLM'#XLOC='OSLO')

To understand what this means, the reader must realize first of all that for a given occurrence of the indexed segment (COURSE in the example), there is really a *set* of values of the XD field (XLOC in the example). An SSA such as the one above is considered as satisfied if, for each of the distinct conditions separated by # operators, there exists at least one value in the set for which the condition is true. In the example, therefore, the GU will retrieve the first COURSE that has both a Stockholm offering and an Oslo offering—first, that is, according to the specified processing sequence.

Note that if the # were replaced by the ordinary ("dependent") AND operator, the SSA would be requesting a COURSE with some *single* offering in both Stockholm and Oslo. IMS would not recognize any contradiction in the request but would search the database and eventually return a "not found" status code.

As another example, suppose that COURSEs were indexed on the basis of DATE values from the OFFERING segment, and consider the following operation:

        GU   COURSE (XDATE>'691231'#XDATE<'710101')

(where XDATE is the XD field name). As written, this operation will retrieve the first course with an offering later than 1969 and an offering—

not necessarily the same one—earlier than 1971. If the independent AND were replaced by the dependent AND, the operation would retrieve the first course with an offering in 1970.

18.4 INDEXING A DEPENDENT ON A FIELD IN THAT DEPENDENT

As indicated in Section 18.1, the index target segment—the segment pointed to by the index—does not have to be the root. However, if it is not, the effect is to restructure the hierarchy so that it *becomes* the root in the structure seen by the user.[2] As an example we consider the case of indexing OFFERINGs on the basis of LOCATION field values.

The DBDs are again essentially the same as in Section 18.2. The education DBD will include appropriate LCHILD and XDFLD statements for OFFERING; the index DBD will refer to the appropriate XD field name (XLOC, say; we *cannot* use the name LOCATION this time, because the genuine field and the XD field must be uniquely named with respect to all fields of OFFERING). Note once again that, syntactically, XD fields are always considered as fields of the target segment. The index will contain one index segment for each OFFERING occurrence in the education database; in fact, it is exactly the same as the index in Section 18.3, except that the index segments point to OFFERINGs instead of COURSEs.

Figure 18.2 shows the *secondary data structure* that results when the user specifies this secondary processing sequence in the PCB. Figure 18.3 shows the corresponding PCB (relevant details only; LXDBD is the name of the DBD for the LOCATION index).

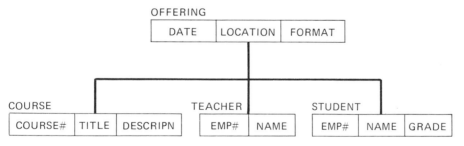

Fig. 18.2 Indexing OFFERINGs on LOCATION: Secondary data structure

---

[2] We are assuming, as usual, that the secondary processing sequence is used. As indicated earlier, there may be situations in which a secondary index can profitably be used with the primary processing sequence; in such a situation the restructuring of the hierarchy does not occur.

```
PCB     TYPE=DB,...,KEYLEN=12,PROCSEQ=LXDBD
SENSEG NAME=OFFERING
SENSEG NAME=COURSE,PARENT=OFFERING
SENSEG NAME=TEACHER,PARENT=OFFERING
SENSEG NAME=STUDENT,PARENT=OFFERING
```

Fig. 18.3   PCB for secondary data structure (Fig. 18.2)

The rules for defining a secondary data structure are as follows.

- The index target segment becomes the root.

- Ancestors of the index target segment become the leftmost dependents of this root, in reverse order. (If COURSE had had a parent
  CATEGORY in the education database, CATEGORY would be a
  dependent of COURSE in the secondary structure.)

- Dependents of the index target segment appear exactly as in the
  original database, except that they are to the right of the dependent
  segment(s) introduced as explained in the previous paragraph.

- No other segments are included. (In the example, the secondary
  structure does not include PREREQs.)

The PCB of Fig. 18.3 defines a structure in accordance with these rules.

There are some similarities between a secondary data structure such
as that of Fig. 18.2 and a logical database; in particular, the reader is
invited to compare the foregoing rules with the notes in Section 17.10.
"Get unique" and "get next" operations function in terms of the secondary structure (and secondary sequence). Fully concatenated keys (for the
structure of Fig. 18.2) consist of a LOCATION value followed, if
appropriate, by a COURSE# or EMP# value. ISRT/DLET operations
may be used for TEACHER and STUDENT but not for OFFERING or
COURSE.

As an illustration of a possible use for such a structure, we extend
our Stockholm courses example as follows. Suppose we wish to find, not
only course numbers, but also corresponding teacher employee numbers,
for all courses with an offering in Stockholm. To keep matters simple we
assume that each offering has exactly one teacher. In other words, we
wish to produce a report containing one line for each Stockholm offering,
giving course number and teacher number (possibly other information
too, such as the offering date). The index of Section 18.3 is not particularly helpful here: It will enable us to find a qualifying course, but we
have no immediate way of knowing which of the several dependent

teachers is the one we want. With the structure of Fig. 18.2, however, we can write

```
NC  GN    OFFERING (XLOC='STOCKHOLM')
          COURSE
      if not found, go to exit
      GN  TEACHER
      print COURSE# and teacher EMP#
      go to NC
```

The point is that once we have found a Stockholm offering, we know that there must be exactly one corresponding course and one corresponding teacher, and these are the ones we want.

It is interesting to observe, incidentally, how a slight variation in the problem statement (find teacher numbers too) leads to a major change in the solution (a restructured hierarchy becomes desirable, with the consequence that the accessing procedure needs revision also). In other words, a small perturbation in the query leads to a large perturbation in the solution. This perturbation effect may be attributed to the fact that secondary indexes represent an attempt to provide symmetry of access (access to the database via an indexed field should be similar to access via the "primary key," i.e., the root sequence field), whereas a hierarchy is a fundamentally asymmetric structure (providing access via an indexed field therefore requires a restructuring so that the indexed field *becomes* the root sequence field).

18.5 INDEXING A DEPENDENT ON A FIELD IN A LOWER-LEVEL DEPENDENT

This, the last of the four possible combinations, does not really illustrate any new points, but we include it for completeness. As our example we consider the case of indexing OFFERINGs on the basis of TEACHER employee numbers.

Once again the DBDs are essentially the same as before. The education DBD will include appropriate LCHILD and XDFLD statements for OFFERING; the XDFLD statement must include the entry "SEGMENT = TEACHER" (since the XD field is derived from a field of the TEACHER segment, not the OFFERING segment). The index DBD will refer to the XD field name (XEMP#, say). The index will contain one index segment for each TEACHER occurrence, and each such index segment will point to the corresponding OFFERING. The user will see the same secondary structure as in Fig. 18.2; however, OFFERINGs may now be accessed via the XD field XEMP#, and sequencing and fully concatenated keys will be defined in terms of XEMP#. We present a single coding example. The problem is: "Find the date of all offerings taught by employee number 876225 in Stockholm."

```
NO  GN    OFFERING (LOCATION='STOCKHOLM'∧XEMP#='876225')
          if not found, go to exit
          print DATE
          go to NO
```

18.6 ADDITIONAL FEATURES

The secondary indexing feature of IMS includes a number of facilities in addition to those discussed so far. We outline two of these additional facilities below. For information on the remainder—user data in the index, the use of subsequence fields, shared index databases, and the use of "system-related fields"—the reader is referred to [16.1].

■ Sparse indexing

It is possible to suppress the creation of index segments for particular values of the XD field (see the discussion of selective indexing in Chapter 2). It is assumed that suppressed values are of no interest so far as that index is concerned; an attempt to find a segment via an SSA specifying a suppressed value for the XD field will simply cause a "not found" condition, even if a qualifying segment exists. In other words, nonindexed segments simply do not appear in the secondary processing sequence.

■ Duplicate data

A secondary index is a database in its own right and may be processed independently of the database it indexes. To enhance the usefulness of this feature, the database administrator may specify that certain fields from the index source segment (the segment from which values of the XD field are derived) are to be duplicated in the corresponding segment in the index. IMS will automatically maintain these duplicate fields when an update is made to the source segment. An application for which high performance is a necessity and which requires only data that has been duplicated in the index may then actually use the index in place of the original database.

18.7 SUMMARY

We may summarize the major points introduced in this chapter as follows.

- In general, a secondary index in IMS can be used to index a given segment on the basis of any field in that segment or in any physical dependent of that segment. (There are some exceptions to this statement: Certain types of segment, for example, logical child segments, cannot be indexed; for details, see [16.1].) The field on which the index is built is represented by an "XD field" which is made to look like an additional field of the index target segment. SSAs must be expressed in terms of this XD field if IMS is to make use of the index in responding to a DL/I request.

- Given the existence of a secondary index, the user may choose to process the corresponding database in the secondary sequence defined by that index. If the index target segment is not the physical root, selecting the secondary sequence will cause a restructuring of the hierarchy as explained in Section 18.4; in particular, the index target segment will become the root in this restructuring. In the secondary sequence, the indexed field acts as the root segment sequence field: The user sees exactly as many database records as there are occurrences of the indexed field in the physical database, and these records are sequenced on ascending values of that field. Values of the indexed field are returned as the root portion of the fully concatenated key in the key feedback area. Secondary sequence and secondary structure (if applicable) are specified in the PCB; note that here we have a situation in which the view defined in the PCB is not just a simple subset of the view defined in the underlying DBD.

- The reader is also reminded of the independent AND, which can be useful if the XD field corresponds to a field in a physical dependent of the target segment.

In conclusion, let us attempt to relate the concepts of secondary indexing as implemented in IMS to the ANSI/SPARC architecture presented in Chapter 1. At the *external* level the user is no longer restricted to the primary processing sequence, nor to the primary hierarchical structure (where "primary" refers to what is defined at the *conceptual* level). However, secondary sequence and secondary structure are supported at the external level—i.e., an appropriate external schema and mapping to the conceptual schema can be defined—only if an appropriate index exists, so that the index must be considered as part of the conceptual level, not just the storage (internal) level. To be more explicit, the user at the external level must effectively be aware of the existence of the secondary index—use of the index is not automatic but must be *forced* by reference to the XD field. In other words, the decision as to whether or not to use the index is in the hands of the application programmer, instead of being under the control of the system. This is unfortunate, since not only do programs that use a secondary index therefore lose some measure of data independence, but also, as we have seen, system performance may be critically dependent on a judicious choice of when and when not to use a particular index.

EXERCISES

The following exercises are based on the publications database (see Exercise 13.1). The segment and field names are those defined in the answer to Exercise 13.1.

18.1 A secondary index is to be built for this database. What structure does the user see:

  a) if segment SUB is indexed on the field AUTHNAME (in segment AUTHOR);

  b) if segment PUB is indexed on this field;

  c) if segment AUTHOR is indexed on this field?

18.2 For case (b) above, show the DBD for the index and the additions needed in PUBDBD (the publications database DBD). You may assume that the publications database is HDAM or HIDAM, not HISAM. Show also a corresponding PCB.

18.3 Using the secondary structure of case (b) above, get names of all publications for a given author (Adams, say).

18.4 For the same structure, show the form of the fully concatenated key returned on retrieval for each of the segment types involved.

18.5 What restrictions apply to the use of the DL/I operators against this structure?

18.6 If the publications database contains:

  100 SUB segments

  average of 100 PUB segments per SUB

  average of 1.5 DETAILS segments per PUB

  average of 1.2 AUTHOR segments per PUB

how many segments of each type are seen in the secondary structure of case (b) in Exercise 18.1?

18.7 Can you think of a situation in which it could be useful to build a secondary index on the root segment *primary* sequence field?

18.8 Referring back to Exercise 18.3 above, compare and contrast the use of a logical database (see Exercise 17.1) to obtain the same result.

REFERENCES AND BIBLIOGRAPHY

See [16.1].

Part 4
The Network
Approach

A great deal of attention has been focused on the network approach since the publication in April 1971 of the DBTG final report [19.1]. In Part 4 we take a detailed look at the DBTG proposal. As in Part 3, therefore, much of the detail here is specific to a particular system, in this case DBTG, but the underlying concepts may be regarded as typical of any network-based system. In any case, DBTG is easily the most important single example of this approach. Chapter 19, then, describes the overall structure of a DBTG system, and Chapters 20, 21, and 22 present the major features of the DBTG data model, external model, and data sublanguage, respectively. No chapter is included on storage structures, because it is tacitly assumed throughout the DBTG proposal that the storage structure is very close to the data model as seen by the user.

A number of other network systems are described in references [1.1, 1.2, 1.5, and 1.12].

19

The
Architecture
of a
DBTG System

19.1 BACKGROUND

The acronym DBTG refers to the Data Base Task Group of the CODASYL Programming Language Committee (PLC). The PLC is the body responsible for development of the COBOL language; its activities are documented in the *COBOL Journal of Development*, which is published every two or three years and which serves as the COBOL language specification. The Data Base Task Group, though a task group of the PLC, did not confine its attention to COBOL alone, however. In fact, the DBTG final report [19.1], which appeared in April 1971, contained proposals for three distinct languages: the schema data description language (schema DDL), a sub-schema data description language (sub-schema DDL), and a data manipulation language (DML). The second and third of these did consist basically of extensions to COBOL, but the first was definitely a distinct and self-contained language, albeit one possessing a certain COBOL flavor.

The purpose of these three languages is as follows. The schema DDL is a language for defining a network-structured data model (or conceptual model); however, it also includes features concerned more with the storage or internal level of a database system, so that the DBTG "schema" must be considered as an amalgam of the conceptual and internal schemas, in ANSI/SPARC terms. It is intended that the schema DDL should be able to meet the requirements of many distinct programming languages, not just COBOL—as with IMS, the user in a DBTG system is considered to be an ordinary application programmer—and the language therefore should not be biased toward any single specific programming language. A sub-schema DDL, on the other hand, is a language for defining an external model (the DBTG "sub-schema" corresponds to the ANSI/SPARC external schema), and therefore it must have a syntax compatible with that of some particular programming language, as explained in Chapter 1. Similarly, a data manipulation language—the DBTG term for data sublanguage—must have a syntax compatible with that of some particular host language. The DML and sub-schema DDL defined in [19.1] were intended for use with COBOL; it was the hope of the Task Group that other responsible bodies would define DMLs and sub-schema DDLs for use with other programming languages such as PL/I.

Toward the end of 1971 a new CODASYL committee was established, the Data Description Language Committee (DDLC). The DDLC was formed to serve the same function with respect to the schema DDL as the PLC does with respect to COBOL; in other words, it is responsible for the continued development of the schema DDL and for producing a corresponding *Journal of Development* documenting the current status of that language. The first version of this journal appeared in 1973 [19.9]. However, the language defined in [19.9] differs only marginally from that of [19.1]—the DDLC took as their first task "clarification of, rather than extension to, the base document." A number of more significant changes have been debated and resolved since that time, and these are reflected in the current working version of the *Journal* [19.10].

The COBOL portions of the original DBTG proposal (COBOL DML, COBOL sub-schema DDL) underwent some minor syntactic revisions and were eventually incorporated into the 1976 version of the *COBOL Journal of Development* [19.8] as "The COBOL Data Base Facility." It should perhaps be emphasized at this point that, as yet, neither the *COBOL* nor the *DDL Journal of Development* represents any form of official standard. Standardization in the United States is the responsibility of the American National Standards Institute, not CODASYL. The only link between ANSI and CODASYL is that COBOL specifications produced by the PLC are automatically considered as a *candidate* for standardization by the ANSI COBOL committee (X3J4)—actual standardization of such specifications is certainly *not* automatic. It is appropriate to mention this fact since the DBTG proposals have been, and continue to be, the subject of much controversy in the data processing community. We shall return to this topic in Part 6 of this book.

Though somewhat controversial, as we just indicated, the DBTG proposals are clearly extremely important, and the Data Base Task Group deserves widespread recognition for the great deal of effort that went into its report. The proposals have already formed the basis of several commercial systems, and further implementations are rumored to be in hand at the time of writing. We therefore take DBTG as our example of the network approach. (We continue to use "DBTG" as a convenient label, although all language details in the next few chapters will be based on the revised definitions given in the two *Journals of Development* [19.8 and 19.10], rather than on the original report [19.1]. Where a particular construct is known by distinct names in the two journals we shall give both, for purposes of reference.)

Henceforth we shall use "DDL" to mean the schema DDL, unless otherwise qualified, and "COBOL" to mean the version of COBOL documented in [19.8], which includes the Data Base Facility.

19.2   ARCHITECTURE

The architecture of a DBTG system is illustrated in Fig. 19.1.

The data model (not a DBTG term) is defined by the *schema*. The schema consists essentially of definitions of the various types of *record* in the data model, the *data-items* they contain, and the *sets* into which they are grouped. (The DBTG set concept is explained in detail in the next chapter. Broadly speaking, it is the means by which relationships are represented in a DBTG system.) However, as mentioned in Section 19.1, the schema also includes part of the definition of the mapping to storage. Indeed, in some respects the user interface, as represented by the DBTG data model, is very close to the stored record interface (as defined in Chapter 2). Those aspects of the mapping to storage *not* specified in the schema are relegated in the DBTG report to an undefined "device/media control language" (DMCL), which appears to be of a level similar to that of OS/VS Job Control Language [16.3]. For example, indexing, if required, may be specified in the schema, rather than via the DMCL (although the presence or absence of such an index has no effect on users' programs except in terms of performance).

An external model (not a DBTG term) is defined by a *sub-schema*, which must be "a consistent and logical subset of the schema from which it is drawn" [19.1]. A sub-schema thus consists essentially of a specification of which schema record types the user is interested in, which schema data-items he or she wishes to see in those records, and which schema relationships (sets) linking those records he or she wishes to consider. By default, all other types of record, data-item, and set are excluded. It is not possible, at least in the sub-schema DDL as currently specified, to define any structuring in the sub-schema—e.g., a new type of relationship (set) or a record that spans two or more schema records—that does not explicitly exist in the schema.

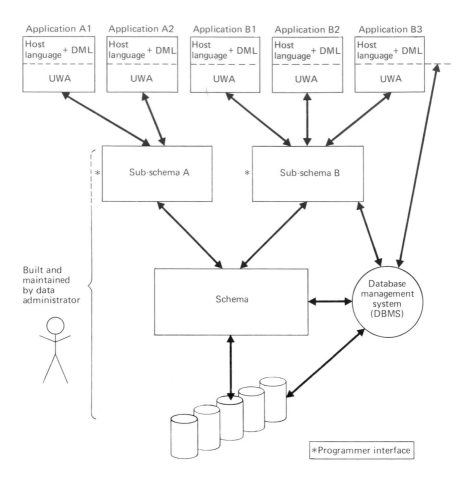

Fig. 19.1 Architecture of a DBTG system

Finally, as explained in Section 19.1, the users are application programmers, writing in an ordinary programming language, such as COBOL, which has been extended to include the DBTG data manipulation language. Each application program "invokes" the corresponding sub-schema; using the COBOL Data Base Facility, for example, the programmer simply specifies the name of the required sub-schema in the Data Division of the program. This invocation provides the definition of the "user work area" (UWA) for that program. The UWA is the DBTG equivalent of the "workspace" introduced in Chapter 1; it actually contains a distinct location for each type of record (and hence for each type of data-item) defined in the sub-schema. The program may refer to these data-item and record locations by the names defined in the sub-schema. (The term "user work area" is not used in COBOL; instead, each record-type has a distinct "record area." The concept is the same, however.)

The DBTG terms for "DBA" and "user interface" are "data administrator" and "programmer interface," respectively. "DBMS" is a DDL term in its own right; the corresponding COBOL term is "DBCS" (Data Base Control System).

REFERENCES AND BIBLIOGRAPHY

Some implemented systems are described in [3.7, 3.8, 3.9, and 3.12].

19.1 Data Base Task Group of CODASYL Programming Language Committee. *Report* (April 1971). Available from ACM, BCS, and IAG.

19.2 Data Base Task Group of CODASYL Programming Language Committee. *Report* (October 1969). Available from ACM, BCS, and IAG.

An early version of [19.1].

19.3 British Computer Society. Collected notes and papers from conference on [19.2] (October 1970). Available from BCS.

19.4 British Computer Society. Collected notes and papers from conference on [19.1] (October 1971). Available from BCS.

The GUIDE/SHARE requirements report [1.4] and the IBM position paper [19.5] are included as appendixes to this document.

19.5 R. W. Engles. "An Analysis of the April 1971 DBTG Report—A Position Paper Presented to the Programming Language Committee by the IBM Representative to the Data Base Task Group." Appendix B of [19.4]. Also published in somewhat revised form in *Proc. 1971 ACM SIGFIDET Workshop on Data Description, Access and Control.* Available from ACM.

Engles was the IBM representative on the Data Base Task Group at the time the final report [19.1] was produced. This paper—the so-called "IBM position paper"—documents a number of major objections to the proposals of [19.1].

19.6 R. G. Canning. "The Debate on Data Base Management." *EDP Analyzer* **10,** No. 3 (March 1972).

An independent assessment of the DBTG proposals, the IBM objections, and the GUIDE/SHARE requirements.

19.7 T. W. Olle. "An Assessment of How the CODASYL DBTG Proposal Meets the GUIDE/SHARE Requirements." Norwegian Computing Centre, Forskningsveien 1B, Oslo, Norway.

An early and much abridged version of this paper also appears in [19.4].

19.8 CODASYL Programming Language Committee. *COBOL Journal of Development* (1976).

19.9 CODASYL Data Description Language Committee. *DDL Journal of Development* (1973).

> In addition to the DDL language specifications, this document includes an interesting historical survey of the entire DBTG project.

19.10 CODASYL Data Description Language Committee. *DDL Journal of Development, Current Working Version* (1976).

> The reader is cautioned that this is a *working* document, and its contents are subject to change—though it is reasonable to expect such changes to consist primarily of additions rather than alterations. Accordingly, however, the reader should realize that information given in this book that is based on this version of the *DDL Journal of Development* is also subject to change. Those portions most likely to be affected are Sections 20.6, 20.9, and 20.11.

19.11 F. A. Manola. "The CODASYL Data Description Language: Status and Activities, April 1976." To appear in *Proc. 2nd SHARE Working Conference on Data Base Management Systems* (Montreal, May 1976). North-Holland (forthcoming). Also available as Report No. NRL 8038, Naval Research Laboratory, Washington D.C. (November 1976).

> Includes a description of the changes made to the DDL in the period from 1973 to 1976.

19.12 G. G. Dodd. "APL—A Language for Associative Data Handling in PL/I." *Proc. FJCC.* Montvale, N.J.: AFIPS Press (1966).

> Dodd's Associative Programming Language was one of the two major original influences on DBTG (the other was IDS [3.13]).

19.13 R. W. Taylor and R. L. Frank. "CODASYL Data Base Management Systems." *ACM Computing Surveys* **8,** No. 1 (March 1976).

19.14 R. H. Canaday, R. D. Harrison, E. L. Ivie, J. L. Ryder, and L. A. Wehr. "A Back-end Computer for Data Base Management." *CACM* **17,** No. 10 (October 1974).

> Discusses the advantages and disadvantages of using a dedicated "back-end" computer for database management, and describes an experimental implementation (XDMS) based on DBTG.

20
The DBTG
Data Model

20.1 INTRODUCTION

The plan of this chapter is as follows. Sections 20.2, 20.3, and 20.4 are concerned with the DBTG *set* concept, which is the most important single aspect of the DBTG data model. Specifically, Section 20.2 shows how sets can be used to construct hierarchical data models; Section 20.3 performs the same function for network data models; and Section 20.4 deals with a special type of construct known as a singular set. Section 20.5 introduces the concept of the *area*, also a feature of the DBTG data model, though somewhat different in kind from the set. Section 20.6 discusses *database-keys*. Section 20.7 then presents a complete schema for a DBTG version of the suppliers-and-parts database of earlier chapters.

Section 20.8 is concerned with the problem of "membership class." Since membership class is specified in the schema, an explanation of it has been included in this chapter. However, the reader will probably find it necessary to refer back to this section after reading in Chapter 22 the descriptions of those DML statements that membership class affects. Sections 20.9 and 20.10 discuss two further DDL features, LOCATION MODE and SET SELECTION. Again the reader may find that he or she wishes to review these sections after working through Chapter 22, since both features depend to some extent on certain aspects of the DML.

Finally, Section 20.11 gives examples of some comparatively minor features of the schema, and Section 20.12 summarizes the differences in terminology between the schema DDL and COBOL.

20.2   THE SET CONSTRUCT: HIERARCHICAL EXAMPLES

20.2.1   Hierarchy with one dependent level.   Figure 20.1 illustrates the data model for a database that contains information about departments and employees.

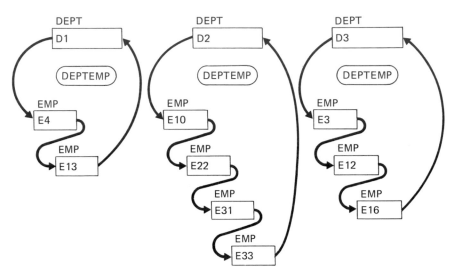

Fig. 20.1   The data model for Example 20.2.1

The data model contains two types of record: DEPT (department) and EMP (employee). In general, each of these records would include several data-items, although in the diagram only one has been shown in each, namely, DNO (department number) for DEPT and ENO (employee number) for EMP. There are three occurrences of DEPT and nine of EMP. These record occurrences are grouped into three occurrences of a *set* called DEPTEMP. The set is the major construct of the DBTG data model. A set *type* is defined in the schema to have a certain type of record as its *owner* and some other type of record as its *member;* in the example, set type DEPTEMP would be declared in the schema with DEPT as its owner and EMP as its member.[1] Each *occurrence* of DEPTEMP consists of precisely one occurrence of its owner together with zero or more occurrences of its member. (The zero case would arise if some department currently had no employees. In such a situation the set occurrence still exists—it consists of an owner occurrence only—but is

---

[1] We ignore the possibility of sets that contain more than one type of member. See [19.10].

said to be empty.) No EMP occurrence may participate in more than one occurrence of the set DEPTEMP at any one time, although it may of course participate in different occurrences at different times.

Each occurrence of a set represents a hierarchical relationship between the owner occurrence and the corresponding member occurrences; this is the justification for the restriction that no member occurrence may belong to more than one occurrence of the set at any one time. In the example, of course, the relationship is the normal one of departments to employees. The means by which each owner occurrence is connected to the corresponding member occurrences is irrelevant so far as the user is concerned. One way of making these connections (not the only way) is via a chain of pointers that originates at the owner occurrence, runs through all the member occurrences, and finally returns to the owner occurrence (as shown in Fig. 20.1). For simplicity this method will be assumed throughout this part of the book; if some other method is adopted in practice, it must be functionally equivalent to the pointer chain method, so this simplification is a reasonable one. (The point is that the user may always think of the pointer chains as physically existing, even if they are not actually represented as pointers in storage. See Chapter 3.)

Drawing set occurrences as chains of pointers, as in Fig. 20.1, has come to be an accepted convention. An equally widely accepted convention for the representation of set *types* is the "data structure diagram" technique of Bachman [20.1]; for an illustration see Fig. 20.2, where the structure of DEPTEMP has been shown rather as if it were an IMS structure. The differences between Bachman's symbolism and that used in IMS are that (a) the link between the owner and the member is *labeled* with the set name, whereas such links are anonymous in IMS, and (b) the link is *directed* to indicate which is the owner and which the member. (Specifying the direction of the link becomes necessary in more complex situations, where it is not always possible to show the owner as being

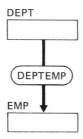

Fig. 20.2 Structure of the set DEPTEMP

"above" the member.) It is usually clearer to sketch some sample set occurrences rather than simply to show the set type, however, and we shall generally do this in our examples.

The reader will have realized by now that the DBTG "set" is rather different from a set as the term is commonly understood in mathematics. The DBTG terminology is somewhat unfortunate, since one often needs to refer (for example) to the set of member records—normal meaning—belonging to a particular set—DBTG meaning. To avoid such confusions, some writers employ special terminology to refer to the DBTG construct; among the terms that have been used are "DBTG set," "CODASYL set," "database set," "data structure set," "owner-coupled set," and "fan set." In this book we shall continue to use the unqualified term "set" for the most part, except where this usage may lead to ambiguity.

20.2.2 Hierarchy with more than one dependent level.   Figure 20.3 illustrates (part of) the data model for a database that contains information about divisions, departments, and employees.

This example illustrates the fact that a particular type of record (DEPT in the example) can be declared in the schema to be a member of one type of set (DIVDEPT) and the owner of another (DEPTEMP). Two occurrences of DIVDEPT and three of DEPTEMP are shown in Fig.

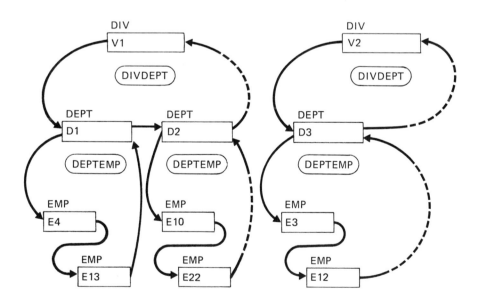

Fig. 20.3 (Part of) the data model for Example 20.2.2

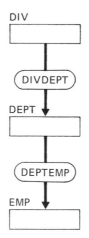

Fig. 20.4 Structure of the sets DIVDEPT and DEPTEMP

20.3. (It is *always* true, by definition, that the number of occurrences of a set is precisely the same as the number of occurrences of the owner.) Hence we have a hierarchical structure with two dependent levels (see Fig. 20.4). In general, of course, we can build up a hierarchy in this way with any number of dependent levels.

20.2.3 Hierarchy with more than one type of record at a dependent level.   Figure 20.5 illustrates (part of) the data model for a database that contains information about employees, their job history, and their education history.

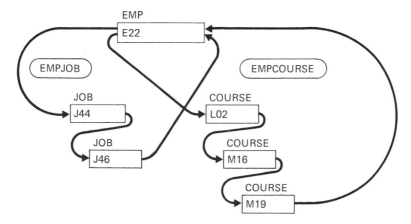

Fig. 20.5 (Part of) the data model for Example 20.2.3

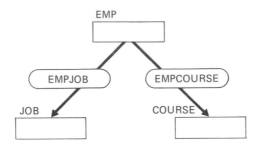

Fig. 20.6   Structure of the sets EMPJOB and EMPCOURSE

Here each EMP occurrence is the owner of two set occurrences: an occurrence of EMPJOB, in which the members represent jobs the employee has held, and an occurrence of EMPCOURSE, in which the members represent courses the employee has attended. In general, a given type of record (EMP in the example) can be declared in the schema to be the owner of any number of types of set. Hence we can build hierarchical structures that not only may have any number of levels but also may have any number of types of record at each dependent level. See Fig. 20.6.

Incidentally, there is a significant difference between the DBTG structure of Fig. 20.6 and the corresponding IMS structure. In DBTG the two branches of the structure could be interchanged without in any way affecting the data model, whereas in IMS such a change would affect the hierarchical sequence (in which the user sees JOBs as preceding COURSEs, for example, if the JOB branch is to the left of the COURSE branch).

20.2.4 Hierarchy with the same type of record at more than one level.   Figure 20.7 illustrates (part of) the data model for a database that contains information about the managerial structure of a company.

It is not permitted for the same type of record to be both owner and member of the same type of set. To represent a hierarchical relationship between different occurrences of the same type of record, therefore, it is necessary to introduce a level of indirection, as Fig. 20.7 illustrates. Here the relationship to be represented is the normal one of manager to employees (where a manager is also considered as an employee and in turn has a manager, and so on). We introduce a second record type (LINK), and define two types of set: EL (owner EMP, member LINK) and LE (owner LINK, member EMP). Each EMP occurrence representing a manager is the owner of an EL occurrence containing precisely one LINK; this LINK in turn is the owner of an LE occurrence whose members are the EMP occurrences representing the manager's immediate

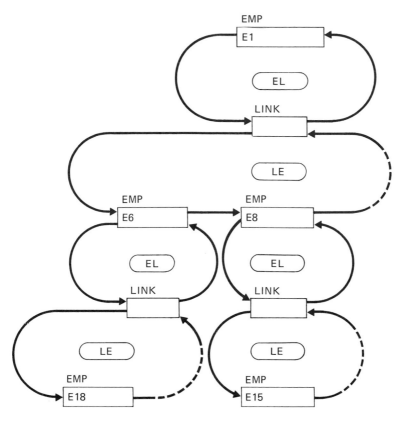

Fig. 20.7 (Part of) the data model for Example 20.2.4

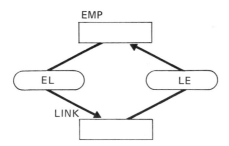

Fig. 20.8 Structure of the sets EL and LE

subordinates. Thus, for example, employee E1 is the manager of employees E6, E8, ... ; E6 is the manager of E18, ... ; and so on. Figure 20.8 illustrates the structure of this data model. Note that there is no requirement for the LINK record to contain any data-items at all.

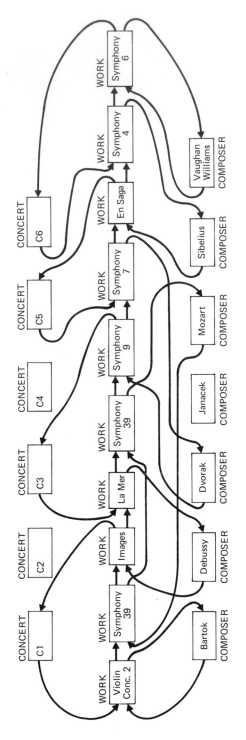

Fig. 20.9 The data model for Example 20.3.1

20.3   THE SET CONSTRUCT: NETWORK EXAMPLES

20.3.1   Network involving two types of entity.   Figure 20.9 illustrates the data model for a database that contains the current plans for a series of orchestral concerts.

We have here a typical network situation since, in general, each concert will include works by several composers and each composer will have works in several concerts. We can represent this situation in DBTG by introducing a "connection" record type (WORK), whose function is to connect the two basic types of entity (represented by the record types CONCERT and COMPOSER, respectively). Each WORK occurrence represents a connection between one concert and one composer. We also introduce two types of set: CONCW (owner CONCERT, member WORK) and COMPW (owner COMPOSER, member WORK).[2] To establish a connection between a particular concert and a particular composer, we must ensure that the appropriate WORK occurrence is entered into the CONCW set occurrence for the concert and the COMPW set occurrence for the composer. For example, there is a connection between the concert C1 and the composer Bartok (see Fig. 20.9). In general, then, the CONCW set occurrence for a given concert contains WORK occurrences for all the works in that concert, and the COMPW set occurrence for a given composer contains WORK occurrences for all the works by that composer to be performed in any concert.

Figure 20.9 shows six occurrences of the set CONCW (two are empty, representing concerts whose programs have not been planned yet) and seven of the set COMPW (one is empty, representing a composer who is intended for inclusion in some concert when program plans are completed). For reasons of space the set names are not shown. Note that each WORK occurrence contains data describing the connection it represents, i.e., the name of the appropriate work. This is the DBTG equivalent of the IMS "intersection data" concept (see Chapter 17).

Figure 20.10 illustrates the structure of this data model.

20.3.2   Networks involving more than two types of entity.   The previous example illustrates the general method of constructing a network data model in DBTG. Specifically, if n types of entity (represented by n record types) are to be connected, we introduce a connection record type and n set types; each of the n "entity" record types is made the owner of one of the set types, and the connection record type is made the member of all of them; and each connection record occurrence is made a member of

---

[2] Do not be misled by Fig. 20.9 into thinking that WORK is the *owner* of COMPW.

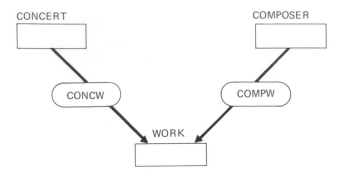

Fig. 20.10   Structure of the sets CONCW and COMPW

exactly one occurrence of each of the *n* types of set and thus represents the connection between the corresponding *n* entities.

Example 20.3.1 can be extended in many ways to illustrate this technique. A few outline examples follow.

■   A new type of entity, SOLOIST, is introduced. A soloist may play at several concerts, and some concerts may have several soloists.

■   A new type of entity, CONDUCTOR, is introduced. Each conductor may conduct several concerts. (This by itself is a hierarchical relationship, but if more than one conductor may appear at the same concert, as sometimes occurs, we have a network situation.)

■   A new type of entity, ORCHESTRA, is introduced.

■   A new type of entity, WORK-CATEGORY, is introduced (possible work categories are symphony, overture, tone poem, violin concerto, and so on). Each concert includes works in several categories, and each category is represented at many concerts. Furthermore, each composer produces works in several categories, and each category includes works by many composers.

The reader is urged to invent some sample data and to sketch the corresponding data model for some of these examples.

20.3.3   Network involving only one type of entity.   Figure 20.11 represents the data model for a database containing information about parts and components (where a component is itself a part and may have further components, and so on).

Here we have a network involving only one type of entity, parts. However, each part, in general, is playing two roles: It is the *assembly* of certain immediate components, and it is also a *component* of certain immediate assemblies. Hence this is merely a special case of the "two-entity" situation in which the two types of entity are in fact one and the

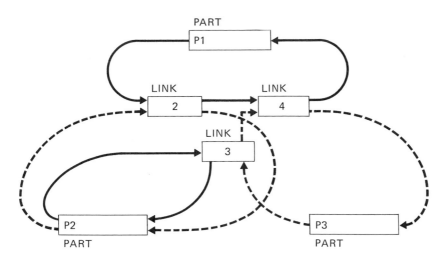

Fig. 20.11   The data model for Example 20.3.3

same, and we tackle it in the same way. First we introduce a connection record, LINK. Then we define two types of set: BM (bill of materials) and WU (where used), both with PART as owner, LINK as member.[3] In Fig. 20.11 BM set occurrences are indicated by solid arrows, WU set occurrences by broken arrows. The BM set occurrence for a given part contains a link for each part that is an immediate component of that part; the WU set occurrence for a given part contains a link for each part that contains that part as an immediate component. Thus, in Fig. 20.11 we see that P1 contains P2 and P3 as immediate components, and P2 in turn also contains P3 as an immediate component; conversely, P3 is an immediate component of P1 and P2, and P2 in turn is also an immediate component of P1. The numbers within the LINK occurrences represent the corresponding quantities (e.g., each "P1" part includes as components two "P2" parts and four "P3" parts).

The reader is urged to take the data of relation COMPONENT (Fig. 4.4) and to sketch an equivalent DBTG data model. (Incidentally, what is the relational representation of the data in Fig. 20.11?) Note that we have here an example of two distinct types of set having the same owner and the same member (the two set types represent two different hierarchical relationships, of course). The structure diagram is shown in Fig. 20.12.

---

[3] Remember that a given type of set may not have the same type of record as both owner and member. Thus declaring the set BM (say) to have owner PART and member PART would not be an allowable approach in this example.

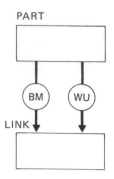

PART

BM   WU

LINK

Fig. 20.12   Structure of the sets BM and WU

20.4   SINGULAR SETS

The set construct introduced in the previous two sections provides a way of grouping member records such that the records in any one group are logically related in some way. For instance, consider the departments-and-employees example once again (Fig. 20.1). In that example, each group represents the collection of all employees in some given department. A "find next within group" operator in the data manipulation language (more accurately, a format 4 FIND statement—see Section 22.9.4) will allow a group to be used as an *access path* to the corresponding records; considering Fig. 20.1 again, each occurrence of the set DEPTEMP provides an access path from a DEPT occurrence to the related EMP occurrences, and user programs will exploit these access paths.

With the data model of Fig. 20.1 as it stands, however, there is no access path connecting *all* EMP record occurrences together; nor is there one connecting all DEPT record occurrences together. Let us restrict our attention to departments only, for the moment. If some program needs an access path linking all DEPT occurrences, then of course such a path can be added. Using the set construct as described so far for this purpose turns out to be rather clumsy, however. We would have to introduce another record type, DEPTS-OWNER say, and make it the owner of a set type, DEPTSET say, with DEPT as member. There would exist exactly one occurrence of DEPTS-OWNER—possibly with no data-items in it—and one occurrence of DEPTSET, and every DEPT record occurrence would be a member of this single DEPTSET occurrence.

Singular sets provide a more convenient solution to the problem. A singular set may be thought of as a set having exactly one occurrence and having no owner record (in the schema, the set owner is actually declared as SYSTEM instead of as some named record type). In the example, therefore, we could gather all DEPT occurrences together into a singular set DEPTSET, and thus avoid having to introduce the DEPTS-OWNER record type. Similarly, we could gather all EMP occurrences together into another singular set called EMPSET. Including two such singular sets in the data model would be exactly like having a sequential file of employees and another of departments, to use traditional terminology, and would enable the user to access all employees in ascending employee number sequence (for example).

20.5 AREAS

The total storage space of a DBTG database is divided into a number of (named) *areas*. For each type of record the schema specifies the area or areas into which occurrences of that record are to be placed when they are entered into the database. (If more than one area is specified for a given type of record, the final decision as to which area a particular occurrence is to be placed in is made at the time the occurrence is created. Depending on specifications in the schema, this decision may be made by the DBMS, by a special DBA-supplied procedure, or by the application program concerned. For details, see [19.10].

It is up to the implementation to define exactly what an area is in physical terms. For example, it may be a disk pack, a cylinder, an extent, or simply a stored file (as defined in Chapter 1). The major reason for introducing such a concept is to give the DBA a basis on which to define procedures for allocating portions of the database to storage volumes and devices, for dumping and restoring the database, for reorganizing the database, and so on. However, the application programmer must also know about areas, in general, because (for example) it may be the responsibility of the program that creates a given record to assign that record to the correct area, as already mentioned. For instance, consider a personnel application that creates employee records. Suppose each employee has a (fixed) status of either "exempt" or "nonexempt." The DBA may decide for a variety of reasons that instead of representing status as a data-item in the employee record type, the classification is to be made by storing employee records in two distinct areas, EXEMPT and NONEX-EMPT, and that the allocation of records to these areas is to be handled by the application.

It follows from the foregoing that a given set type—possibly even a given set occurrence—may span any number of areas (consider a singular set EMPSET linking all employee record occurrences, for example).

For simplicity we shall generally ignore the possibility of a particular record type being associated with more than one area—i.e., we shall assume that all occurrences of a given type of record are to go into a single area.

Areas are called *realms* in COBOL. Programs are responsible for *opening* areas before using them and for *closing* them when they no longer need them. The COBOL terms for OPEN and CLOSE are READY and FINISH, respectively.

20.6 DATABASE-KEYS

In principle the concept of the *database-key* is a simple one. When a record occurrence is first created and stored in the database, it is automatically assigned a database-key—that is, a unique value that identifies that record occurrence and distinguishes it from all other record occurrence by quoting that database-key—the intention being that this address—though not necessarily the *physical* address—of the record concerned. (Compare the "stored record address" introduced in Chapter 2.) At execution time a program can discover the database-key of a given record occurrence, and can subsequently obtain direct access to that occurrence by quoting that database-key—the intention being that this form of access should be fast and efficient.

The original DBTG proposal [19.1] and the versions of COBOL and the DDL documented in [19.8] and [19.9] took the concept further, however. For example, a program creating a record occurrence was allowed under certain circumstances to specify that the new occurrence should be stored near some existing occurrence, to optimize subsequent access; and "near" was defined to mean that the difference between the database-keys of the two occurrences concerned was small. It was also possible to access all records in an area in ascending or descending database-key sequence. Moreover, a programmer could discover the database-key of a record and save it, perhaps by storing it in the database itself, and then use it to access the record occurrence again, possibly years later—by which time that database-key could have been reassigned to some quite different record.

The "extended" notion of the database-key implied by properties such as those just outlined has come in for a good deal of criticism; see, for example, Engles [19.5]. As a result the subject is currently undergoing a reevaluation, both by the PLC and the DDLC. What seems likely to emerge is a simpler feature, possibly under a new name, somewhat along the following lines.[4]

- Each record occurrence has a unique database-key, which may be thought of as the address of that occurrence.

- The database-key of a given occurrence is guaranteed not to change while the area that contains that occurrence is available to a run-unit, but is *not* guaranteed to remain constant from one run-unit to a subsequent one. ("Run-unit" is a term meaning the execution of a program.)

- The database-key of a given occurrence may be supplied by the DBMS to a given run-unit and may be used subsequently by that same run-unit to obtain fast reaccess to that occurrence. However, the run-unit will not be allowed to store database-keys in the database, to perform arithmetic on them, or indeed to use them in any way at all *except* for the "fast reaccess" function. When the run-unit closes an area, the DBMS will invalidate (set to null) all program data-items containing database-keys for that area. (These data-items must clearly be known to the DBMS.)

From this point on we shall assume that the database-key facility has indeed been revised along the lines just indicated. However, the reader is cautioned that the suggested revision represents the author's speculations only and does not have any basis in official CODASYL documentation; the final form of the database-key facility may be totally different.

20.7 A SAMPLE SCHEMA

In this section we present a possible schema for the suppliers-and-parts database of Chapter 4. We return to that example in order to facilitate a direct comparison between the relational approach and the network approach. Figure 20.13 shows the sample data (cf. Fig. 4.7), redrawn to

---

[4] The revised DDL of [19.10] includes no mention of database-keys whatsoever. It is not possible to dispense with the concept entirely, however, since it is axiomatic that individual record occurrences must be mutually distinguishable, and DBTG does not *require* any form of distinction between two records other than that they have distinct database-keys. In other words, the only way to distinguish between two occurrences of the same record type that have identical values, data-item for data-item, is by the fact that they occupy distinct locations, i.e., have distinct database-keys. Note that DBTG does not require each record-type to have a primary key (nor would it be reasonable to do so, given the existence of the set construct).

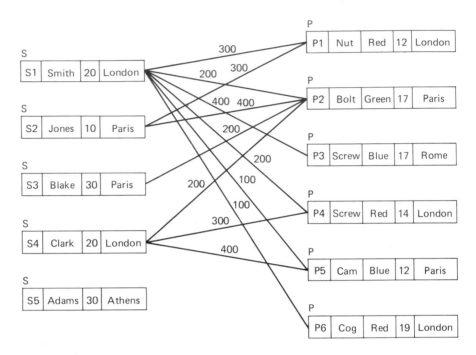

Fig. 20.13 Sample data (suppliers and parts)

emphasize the network structure. The lines represent supplier-part connections (SP tuples in relational terminology), and the numbers alongside
them are the appropriate quantities.

We choose a network data model to represent this information,
introducing a connection record, SP (data-items SNO, PNO, and QTY),
and two sets: S-SP (owner S, member SP) and P-SP (owner P, member
SP).[5] The structure of this data model is shown in Fig. 20.14.

Part of the data model corresponding to the sample data is shown in
Fig. 20.15.

Rather than attempt to draw the entire data model in the style of Fig.
20.15, we shall take Fig. 20.13 as a simplified representation of it from
this point on. The lines in that diagram must therefore be considered as
SP record occurrences. Note that each SP record occurrence explicitly
includes the appropriate SNO and PNO values; that is, the data model
includes a degree of redundancy (the SNO value for a given SP occur-

---

[5] We use SNO, PNO rather than S#, P# because # is not a valid character in the
schema DDL.

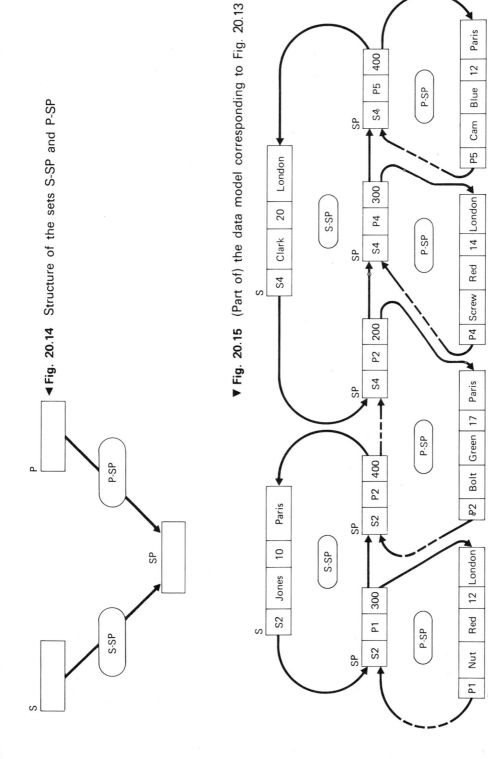

◀Fig. 20.14   Structure of the sets S-SP and P-SP

▼ Fig. 20.15   (Part of) the data model corresponding to Fig. 20.13

rence could always be found from the owner of the S-SP set occurrence in which that SP occurrence appears, and similarly for the PNO value). This redundancy has been introduced deliberately, to allow us to order the SP occurrences on PNO within each S-SP occurrence and on SNO within each P-SP occurrence. It does *not* follow that a corresponding redundancy exists in storage; see Section 20.11.1.

The schema is shown in Fig. 20.16.

Explanations

Statement 1 assigns a name to the schema.

Statements 3–4 name the areas constituting the database. Purely for the sake of the example, we have divided the database into two areas: BASIC-DATA-AREA, which is to contain all S and P occurrences, and LINK-DATA-AREA, which is to contain all SP occurrences.

Statement 6 defines the existence of a record type S.

Statement 7 defines a LOCATION MODE for record type S. Detailed explanation of this clause is deferred to Section 20.9. A partial explanation is as follows. CALC HASH-SNO USING SNO IN S means that the programmer may supply a value for the data-item SNO IN S (by moving the value into the data-item location with this name in the User Work Area) and then issue (an appropriate form of) the DML FIND statement. This will cause the DBMS to apply the procedure HASH-SNO to the SNO value supplied to discover the location of the corresponding S record occurrence within the database. For example, the sequence

```
MOVE 'S1' TO SNO IN S
FIND ANY S
```

will locate the S occurrence for supplier S1. (This is not the only way of locating record occurrences.) The procedure HASH-SNO, then, is a randomizing procedure, which must be supplied by the DBA and which will hash a supplier number (the "CALC-key") to generate a record address.[6]

Statement 8 specifies the relevant area for the S record type.

Statement 9 indicates that no two S occurrences may contain the same SNO value. IDENTIFIER is the DBTG term for candidate key. A given record type can have any number of identifiers, including zero.

---

[6] Although CALC is normally taken to imply hashing, the concept is actually much more general. The only requirement is that the CALC procedure accept a CALC-key as input and produce an appropriate address as output. For example, the procedure might perform an index search rather than a hash. However, in this book we shall usually assume that CALC means hashing.

```
 1  SCHEMA NAME IS SUPPLIERS-AND-PARTS.
 2
 3  AREA NAME IS BASIC-DATA-AREA.
 4  AREA NAME IS LINK-DATA-AREA.
 5
 6  RECORD NAME IS S;
 7      LOCATION MODE IS CALC HASH-SNO USING SNO IN S;
 8      WITHIN BASIC-DATA-AREA;
 9      IDENTIFIER IS SNO IN S.
10      02 SNO   ;  TYPE IS CHARACTER 5.
11      02 SNAME ;  TYPE IS CHARACTER 20.
12      02 STATUS;  TYPE IS FIXED DECIMAL 3.
13      02 CITY  ;  TYPE IS CHARACTER 15.
14
15  RECORD NAME IS P;
16      LOCATION MODE IS CALC HASH-PNO USING PNO IN P;
17      WITHIN BASIC-DATA-AREA;
18      IDENTIFIER IS PNO IN P.
19      02 PNO   ;  TYPE IS CHARACTER 6.
20      02 PNAME ;  TYPE IS CHARACTER 20.
21      02 COLOR ;  TYPE IS CHARACTER 6.
22      02 WEIGHT;  TYPE IS FIXED DECIMAL 4.
23      02 CITY  ;  TYPE IS CHARACTER 15.
24
25  RECORD NAME IS SP;
26      LOCATION MODE IS SYSTEM-DEFAULT;
27      WITHIN LINK-DATA-AREA;
28      IDENTIFIER IS SNO IN SP, PNO IN SP.
29      02 SNO   ;  TYPE IS CHARACTER 5.
30      02 PNO   ;  TYPE IS CHARACTER 6.
31      02 QTY   ;  TYPE IS FIXED DECIMAL 5.
32
33  SET NAME IS S-SP;
34      OWNER IS S;
35      ORDER IS PERMANENT SORTED BY DEFINED KEYS.
36      MEMBER IS SP;
37          INSERTION IS AUTOMATIC
38          RETENTION IS MANDATORY;
39          KEY IS ASCENDING PNO IN SP
40              DUPLICATES ARE NOT ALLOWED
41              NULL IS NOT ALLOWED;
42          SET SELECTION IS THRU S-SP OWNER
43              IDENTIFIED BY IDENTIFIER SNO IN S.
44                                              (continued)
```

Fig. 20.16 The schema SUPPLIERS-AND-PARTS

```
45  SET NAME IS P-SP;
46       OWNER IS P;
47       ORDER IS PERMANENT SORTED BY DEFINED KEYS.
48       MEMBER IS SP;
49            INSERTION IS AUTOMATIC
50            RETENTION IS MANDATORY;
51            KEY IS ASCENDING SNO IN SP
52                 DUPLICATES ARE NOT ALLOWED
53                 NULL IS NOT ALLOWED;
54            SET SELECTION IS THRU P-SP OWNER
55                 IDENTIFIED BY IDENTIFIER PNO IN P.
```

Fig. 20.16   (continued)

Statements 10–13 define the types of data-item constituting S. The 02 in front of each data-item name is a level number.

Statements 15–23 define record type P similarly.

Statements 24–28 define record type SP similarly, except for the fact that LOCATION MODE has been specified as SYSTEM-DEFAULT. *One* of the implications of this specification is that the programmer will never be able to use the "hashing" format FIND statement

```
                    FIND ANY SP
```

to locate a particular SP occurrence. (The programmer may still locate SP occurrences using some other format of the FIND statement, however. For example, a "sequential scanning" format FIND statement will allow an SP occurrence to be located by searching through an occurrence of set S-SP or set P-SP.) It would have been perfectly possible to declare some other LOCATION MODE for SP, however; in particular, if the LOCATION MODE were specified as CALC, the CALC-key would probably be the combination SNO IN SP, PNO IN SP.

Statement 33 defines the existence of a set type S-SP.

Statement 34 specifies the owner record type for S-SP, namely, S.

Statement 35 defines the sequence of SP occurrences within each S-SP set occurrence to be SORTED BY DEFINED KEYS. The sort control data-item, or "sort-key," is defined by the KEY clause— statement 39—to be ASCENDING PNO IN SP. In other words, for each S record occurrence the SP record occurrences in the corresponding S-SP set occurrence are in ascending part number sequence. The DBMS is responsible for maintaining this sequence throughout the life of the database. (Several other forms of ordering are permitted; for details see [19.10]. The specification PERMANENT is required if ORDER IS SORTED.)

Statement 36 specifies the member record type for S-SP, namely, SP.

Statements 37–38 specify the class of membership for SP within S-SP. An explanation of membership class is deferred to Section 20.8.

Statement 39 has already been explained. In general, the KEY clause may specify ASCENDING or DESCENDING, and the "key" concerned may be the combination of any number of data-items in the record; a mixture of ascending and descending keys may be specified by a sequence of ASCENDING/DESCENDING entries within the KEY clause. The left-to-right order of specifying data-items (within one ASCENDING/ DESCENDING entry or across several) signifies major-to-minor sorting in the usual way.

Statement 40 specifies that no two SP occurrences within a given S-SP occurrence may contain the same PNO value. A DUPLICATES clause (specifying either that duplicates are not allowed or that they *are* allowed and are to be handled in a particular manner) is required if ORDER IS SORTED and a DUPLICATES clause is *not* included in the ORDER specification; see [19.10].

Statement 41 specifies that no SP occurrence within a given S-SP occurrence may contain a null value for PNO. This clause or its converse (NULL IS ALLOWED) is required if KEY is specified.

Statements 42–43 concern SET SELECTION, an explanation of which is deferred to Section 20.10.

Statements 45–55 define set type P-SP similarly.

20.8   MEMBERSHIP CLASS

Each MEMBER clause in the schema must include a specification of the *membership class* for the record type concerned in the set type concerned. Membership class is specified by means of the INSERTION/RETENTION entry. It may be thought of as a combination of a *storage* class (specified by INSERTION) and a *removal* class (specified by RETENTION).[7] The storage class is AUTOMATIC or MANUAL. The removal class is FIXED, MANDATORY, or OPTIONAL. A given record type may have any combination of storage class and removal class with respect to a given set type; moreover, it may have different combinations—that is, different classes of membership—in different set types. Broadly speaking, the membership class of a record in a set affects programs concerned with the maintenance of that set—that is, programs that create, modify, or delete instances of the hierarchical relationship which that set represents. Specifically, the interpretation of

---

[7] Storage class and removal class are COBOL terms. The DDL does not appear to have its own terms for the two concepts.

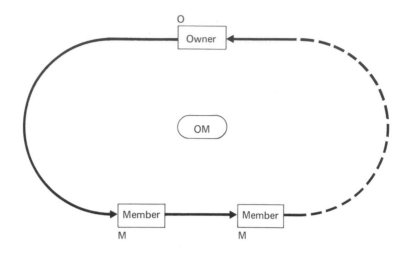

Fig. 20.17 Typical set occurrence

the DML statements INSERT, REMOVE, MODIFY USING, STORE, and DELETE is affected. (The DDL assumes the existence of such functions in the DML, and the schema may include references to them by these names. The COBOL names for the same functions will be introduced later.)

To fix our ideas, let us consider a typical set OM (owner O, member M). Figure 20.17 shows a sample occurrence of this set.

- Removal class (FIXED/MANDATORY/OPTIONAL)

If the membership of M in OM is FIXED, then once an occurrence of M (*m*, say) has been entered into an occurrence of OM, it can never have any existence in the database *not* as a member of that occurrence of OM. Specifically, it can never be taken out of the OM occurrence by means of a REMOVE operation, nor may it be transferred from one OM occurrence to another by means of a MODIFY USING operation. The only way to destroy the association between *m* and OM is by erasing *m* entirely from the database by means of a DELETE operation. Note the implication here that if an occurrence of O is deleted, all corresponding occurrences of M must also be deleted.

If the membership of M in OM is MANDATORY, then once an occurrence of M (*m*, say) has been entered into an occurrence of OM, it can never have any existence in the database not as a member of *some* occurrence of OM. Specifically, it can never be taken out of the OM occurrence by means of a REMOVE operation, but it may be transferred from one OM occurrence to another by means of a MODIFY USING operation. In other respects, MANDATORY is the same as FIXED.

Finally, if the membership of M in OM is OPTIONAL, an occurrence of M *can* be removed from an occurrence of OM (e.g., by means of a REMOVE operation) without being entirely erased from the database.

As an example, consider the singular set EMPSET, the set of all employees of Section 20.4. Since, by definition, we should never have an employee in the database *not* a member of this set, it seems reasonable to make the membership FIXED (or MANDATORY—the two are equivalent in the case of a singular set). On the other hand, consider the set CONCW (owner CONCERT, member WORK) of Example 20.3.1. An occurrence of this set represents the planned program for a particular concert. If the program for that concert changes, a WORK occurrence may have to be taken out of that CONCW occurrence and not entered into any other (i.e., if the work is now not scheduled to be played at all). However, it may still be desirable to retain the WORK occurrence in the database, on the grounds that it may be entered into another CONCW occurrence at a later time. It therefore seems reasonable in this case to make the membership OPTIONAL.

- Storage class (AUTOMATIC/MANUAL)

If the membership of M in OM is AUTOMATIC, then when an occurrence of M (*m*, say) is first created and placed in the database (by means of a STORE operation), the DBMS will automatically insert it into the appropriate occurrence of OM. (It is in general up to the program that stores *m* to specify the OM occurrence concerned; see Section 20.9.) On the other hand, if the membership of M in OM is MANUAL, storing an occurrence *m* does not cause this automatic insertion; to insert *m* into an OM occurrence, the program must issue an explicit INSERT operation.

As an example, consider again the singular set EMPSET of Section 20.4. Since, as stated before, we should never have an employee in the database *not* a member of this set, it seems reasonable to make the membership AUTOMATIC. On the other hand, consider again the set CONCW (owner CONCERT, member WORK) of Example 20.3.1. Here it may well be a requirement to be able to store a particular WORK occurrence in the database without immediately connecting it to some CONCERT occurrence, and to be able later to insert it into a CONCW set occurrence when the work is added to the program for that concert. Hence it seems reasonable in this case to make the membership MANUAL.

	AUTOMATIC		MANUAL	
FIXED	INSERT	X	INSERT	√
	REMOVE	X	REMOVE	X
	MODIFY USING	X	MODIFY USING	X
MANDATORY	INSERT	X	INSERT	√
	REMOVE	X	REMOVE	X
	MODIFY USING	√	MODIFY USING	√
OPTIONAL	INSERT	√	INSERT	√
	REMOVE	√	REMOVE	√
	MODIFY USING	√	MODIFY USING	√

Fig. 20.18 Effect of membership class on INSERT, REMOVE, and MODIFY USING

Figure 20.18 represents a partial summary of the foregoing. The apparent anomaly in this table—that INSERT is valid when the membership is OPTIONAL AUTOMATIC—is explained by the fact that, even though automatic insertion will occur when the STORE is executed, the record occurrence may later be REMOVEd and subsequently reINSERTed (possibly into a different occurrence of the set). The point is that, whereas removal class (FIXED/MANDATORY/OPTIONAL) is a time-independent property, storage class (AUTOMATIC/MANUAL) has meaning only when the record occurrence concerned is actually being created (i.e., at STORE time); it is irrelevant thereafter.

20.9 LOCATION MODE

Every record type has a LOCATION MODE specified for it in the schema. The primary purpose of the LOCATION MODE clause is to control the placement of new occurrences of the record type when they are first stored in the database. As already mentioned in Section 20.7, however, one particular form of LOCATION MODE, namely, CALC, has a very important secondary purpose, in that it permits an occurrence of the record type to be located via the "hashing" (format 2) FIND statement

```
FIND ANY record.
```

This is the only LOCATION MODE that affects in any way the FIND formats that the programmer is allowed to use, and format 2 is the only FIND format that depends in any way on LOCATION MODE.

The three formats of LOCATION MODE, and their effect on record placement, are summarized below.

■   LOCATION MODE IS SYSTEM-DEFAULT

With this format, placement of new occurrences is entirely under the control of the DBMS; the program creating a new occurrence is not involved in placement details at all.

■   LOCATION MODE IS CALC procedure
                        USING data-item, data-item, . . .

In this case, the CALC-key must be initialized before an occurrence of the record can be stored; however, since the CALC-key must be part of the record, the initializing will already have been done, in fact, as part of the process of constructing the new occurrence in the UWA. The specified procedure is responsible for taking the CALC-key and using it to decide where to place the record in the database.

■   LOCATION MODE IS VIA set SET

In this case, the record type concerned must be defined as a member in the indicated set. The DBMS will select an occurrence of this set and will then place the new record occurrence "as close as possible to the actual or logical insert point in the selected set occurrence" (from [19.1]—reference [19.10] is much less specific). To enable the DBMS to select the required set occurrence, the programmer must presumably initialize all appropriate SET SELECTION data-items (see Section 20.10) before storing the new record, though again [19.10] is very unspecific on this point. Note that the placement procedure just outlined occurs regardless of whether the record type is AUTOMATIC or MANUAL with respect to the designated set type.

20.10 SET SELECTION

There are certain situations in which the DBMS needs to be able to select a particular occurrence of a set automatically. One such situation has already been mentioned (Section 20.9): A new record occurrence is to be stored in the database, and the LOCATION MODE for that record is VIA SET. The other three situations are as follows.

■   A format 7 FIND statement, without the CURRENT option, is to be executed: see Section 22.9.7. The function of this FIND format is to locate a record occurrence by first selecting a set occurrence and then scanning the members of that set for the required record.

- A MODIFY USING (in COBOL, MODIFY INCLUDING or MODIFY ONLY) statement is to be executed: see Section 22.4.2. The function of this MODIFY format is to remove a record occurrence from one occurrence of a set, to select another occurrence of that set, and to insert that same record into that second set occurrence.

- A STORE statement is to be executed and the record type concerned is an AUTOMATIC member of one or more sets: see Section 22.8. For each such set the DBMS must select the appropriate occurrence and insert the new record into that set occurrence.

To permit the DBMS to perform this automatic selection of a set occurrence when necessary, the DBA must define a SET SELECTION clause within the (MEMBER subentry of the) set declaration in the schema. The SET SELECTION clause may be thought of as defining an *access strategy* for the set. The present section consists of a somewhat simplified explanation of this clause. To fix our ideas, let us restrict our attention to the set S-SP (see Section 20.7), and let us consider the situation where it is required to store the new SP occurrence 'S5/P6/700'. (SP is declared in the schema—Fig. 20.16—to be an AUTOMATIC member of S-SP; of course, it is also an AUTOMATIC member of P-SP, but we shall ignore this set for simplicity.)

In the simplest case the SET SELECTION clause for set S-SP (member SP) is

```
SET SELECTION IS THRU S-SP OWNER
    IDENTIFIED BY APPLICATION
```

This simply means that the application program is responsible for procedurally selecting the correct occurrence of S-SP before storing the new SP occurrence. It will normally do this by FINDing the correct occurrence of the owner (record type S), but this step may not be necessary if the current S-SP occurrence is already the one required. In other words, the DBMS will simply assume that the current occurrence of S-SP is the correct one. To store the SP occurrence 'S5/P6/700', therefore, a possible code sequence is as follows.

```
build SP occurrence 'S5/P6/700' in UWA
MOVE 'S5' TO SNO IN S.
FIND ANY S.
STORE SP.
```

The code above is valid provided that SNO IN S has been declared as a CALC-key for record S. Of course, this is only one of many possible ways of preselecting the correct S-SP occurrence; another way is to locate the S occurrence for S5 directly by quoting its database-key (using a "format 1" FIND).

The second case is the one illustrated in the schema of Fig. 20.16:

```
SET SELECTION IS THRU S-SP OWNER
     IDENTIFIED BY IDENTIFIER SNO IN S
```

This means that when the DBMS is to select an S-SP occurrence, it is to do so by locating the corresponding occurrence of its owner (S), using the identifier SNO IN S (the specified data-item [combination] must have been defined as an identifier in the record declaration for the owner). This in turn means that the programmer must correctly initialize this data-item before storing the new SP occurrence, e.g., as follows:

```
build SP occurrence 'S5/P6/700' in UWA
MOVE 'S5' TO SNO IN S.
STORE SP.
```

The third form of SET SELECTION is a variation on the previous case. In the example at hand we could have specified

```
SET SELECTION IS THRU S-SP OWNER
     IDENTIFIED BY IDENTIFIER SNO IN S EQUAL TO SNO IN SP
```

This would mean, again, that the DBMS is to select an SP occurrence using a value for the specified identifier in the owner (SNO IN S), but this time the specified value is in the UWA data-item SNO IN SP instead of in the UWA data-item corresponding to the owner identifier. Since the data-item SNO IN SP is part of the SP record, the code to store the SP occurrence 'S5/P6/700' now reduces to

```
build SP occurrence 'S5/P6/700'
STORE SP.
```

To illustrate the fourth form of SET SELECTION we change our example, as follows. Suppose that (a) supplier numbers are not unique across all suppliers but only within a given city; (b) the database includes a record type C representing city information, with data-item CITY as an identifier; and (c) a set type C-S, with owner C and member S, is added to the database. See Fig. 20.19.

For simplicity we continue to ignore record type P and set type P-SP. Note that the S record type no longer contains a CITY data-item; this information is now carried by the set C-S (i.e., to discover the city for a given supplier, it is necessary to look at that supplier's owner record in set C-S). It is now possible to specify that an occurrence of set S-SP is to be selected by first selecting an occurrence of set C-S and then scanning the

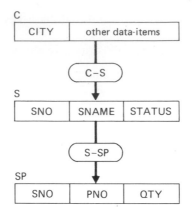

Fig. 20.19 The sets C-S (new) and S-SP (revised)

members of that C-S occurrence for the desired S-SP owner (S) occurrence:

```
SET SELECTION IS THRU C-S OWNER
       IDENTIFIED BY IDENTIFIER CITY IN C
       THEN THRU S-SP WHERE OWNER
       IDENTIFIED BY SNO IN S
```

(Observe that this SET SELECTION clause is still part of the declaration
of set S-SP, not set C-S.) The code to create the SP occurrence
'S5/P6/700' is now

```
build SP occurrence 'S5/P6/700' in UWA
MOVE 'ATHENS' TO CITY IN C.
MOVE 'S5' TO SNO IN S.
STORE SP.
```

The data-item CITY IN C must be an identifier for C. The data-item
SNO IN S must have DUPLICATES ARE NOT ALLOWED specified
in the MEMBER subentry of the C-S set declaration, meaning that SNO
IN S takes unique values within any one occurrence of this set; note that
SNO IN S is now *not* an identifier for S. (For example, there could be
another supplier S5 located in London.)

   An EQUAL TO option could have been specified for either or both
of the "owner-identifying" data-items CITY IN C and SNO IN S.

   In general, the form of SET SELECTION just illustrated could
specify an access strategy involving any number of sets, not just two. At
the top level a set occurrence is selected without reference to any other

sets (e.g., via a specified value for an owner identifier); at each lower level an occurrence is selected by locating the owner among the members of the occurrence just selected at the immediately higher level. Each level except possibly the highest will require appropriate UWA data-items to be initialized by the programmer.

The last form of SET SELECTION to be discussed here is

```
SET SELECTION IS THRU set SYSTEM
```

This form must be used if and only if the set concerned is singular. In effect, it states that the single occurrence of the set is always the current occurrence. ("Set" is the name of the set concerned.)

The process of SET SELECTION has no effect on the currency status indicators for the run-unit. For more details on SET SELECTION—in particular, for information on additional SET SELECTION formats—the reader is referred to [19.10].

20.11 SOURCE AND RESULT DATA-ITEMS

In this section we present a brief description of two further aspects of the DBTG data model. There are still many other features that are not touched on at all in this part of the book. Some will be discussed in Part 5; the rest tend to be somewhat peripheral to the main ideas of the proposal (e.g., the ability to specify indexing, which, though defined in the schema, makes no real difference to the user's view of the data), and will not be further discussed.

We observe that the features described in this section could more accurately be considered part of the mapping of the data model to storage than of the data model itself.

20.11.1 ACTUAL/VIRTUAL SOURCE

Consider the data-item SNO IN SP (Fig. 20.16). As we pointed out earlier in this chapter, this data-item is actually redundant, in that its value within any SP occurrence must be identical to the value of the SNO data-item in the S occurrence owning the corresponding occurrence of the set S-SP. (Similar remarks apply to the data-item PNO IN SP.) However, this redundancy need not be reflected in the storage structure. For example, SNO IN SP could be defined as follows:

```
02 SNO; IS VIRTUAL
      SOURCE IS SNO OF OWNER OF S-SP.
```

This declaration specifies (a) that this data-item is "virtual"—that is, it does not physically exist in the stored form of the SP record, although it is to appear to the programmer as if it did; (b) that the DBMS is responsible for ensuring that the value of this data-item, as seen by the programmer, is identical to the value of the SNO data-item in the appropriate S occurrence (or null, if the SP occurrence concerned is not currently a member of any S-SP occurrence).

Alternatively, a SOURCE data-item may be declared as ACTUAL, instead of VIRTUAL, meaning that the data-item concerned does physically exist in the record (of course, this reintroduces redundancy into the storage structure, but such redundancy may be desirable for performance reasons). In other respects an ACTUAL SOURCE data-item is the same as a VIRTUAL SOURCE data-item.

There are a number of problems in connection with ACTUAL/ VIRTUAL SOURCE—specifically, with the precise significance of the guarantee that the DBMS will ensure that the value of the SOURCE data-item is correct. (Consider, for example, the implications of an attempt to execute a DML MODIFY statement to change the value of some occurrence of SNO IN SP.) Such problems will not be considered in detail here.

20.11.2 ACTUAL/VIRTUAL RESULT

Again we shall not attempt to define this feature in detail but shall content ourselves with a simple example of its use. Suppose that the record P includes an additional data-item TOTQTY, representing the total quantity of this part supplied (by all suppliers who supply it). Then this data-item could be defined as follows:

```
02 TOTQTY ; TYPE IS FIXED DECIMAL 7;
           IS VIRTUAL
           RESULT OF procedure ON MEMBERS OF P-SP.
```

This definition specifies (a) that the data-item is virtual and (b) that the value of the data-item in any given P occurrence is the result of applying the procedure to the members of the corresponding P-SP occurrence; in this case, of course, the procedure would have to sum the individual QTY values in the relevant SP occurrences. For more details of such procedures see [19.10].

A RESULT data-item, like a SOURCE data-item, may alternatively be declared as ACTUAL instead of VIRTUAL. Regardless of whether it is ACTUAL or VIRTUAL, such a data-item cannot be the object of a DML MODIFY statement.

20.12   DDL/COBOL TERMINOLOGY

We conclude this chapter by showing the COBOL terms (Fig. 20.20) for some of the many DDL concepts introduced in this chapter.

DDL term	COBOL term
AREA	REALM
OPEN	READY
CLOSE	FINISH
FIXED	concept does not exist
MANDATORY	PERMANENT
OPTIONAL	TRANSIENT
AUTOMATIC	AUTOMATIC
MANUAL	MANUAL
INSERT	CONNECT
REMOVE	DISCONNECT
MODIFY (USING)	MODIFY (INCLUDING or ONLY)
STORE	STORE
DELETE	ERASE

Fig. 20.20   DDL/COBOL equivalences

EXERCISES

20.1 Define a schema for a DBTG version of the publications database of Exercise 13.1. (Retain the hierarchical structure; i.e., do not attempt to convert it to a network.)

20.2 Define a schema (in outline) for the "managerial structure" database of Example 20.2.4.

20.3 Define a schema for a DBTG version of the supplier-part-project database (see the exercises in Chapter 5). *Note:* Several of the exercises in Chapter 22 will be based on this schema.

20.4 Define a schema (in outline) for the parts-and-components database of Example 20.3.3.

20.5 Consider the areas-and-birds database of Section 17.7. Define a schema for a DBTG version (a) as a "two-entity net," involving AREAs and BIRDs; (b) as a "three-entity net" involving AREAs, BIRDs, and DATEs. (Observe that the situation is fundamentally a "three-entity" one, since a given AREA-BIRD combination may recur on many DATEs. You may assume that no more than one sighting per day of each type of bird within each area is to appear within the database.)

20.6 Design a DBTG database to represent a transportation network. You may base your design on any network with which you are familiar—for example, the New York subway system.

REFERENCES AND BIBILOGRAPHY

See also [19.1], [19.9], and [19.10].

20.1 C. W. Bachman. "Data Structure Diagrams." *Data Base* (journal of ACM SIGBDP) **1,** No. 2 (summer 1969). Available from ACM.

20.2 C. W. Bachman. "Implementation Techniques for Data Structure Sets." In reference [1.10].

> This paper describes a number of possible techniques for mapping the DBTG set construct into storage. Comparative performance characteristics are included.

20.3 B. C. M. Douqué and G. M. Nijssen (eds.). "Data Base Description." *Proc. IFIP TC-2 Special Working Conference on Data Base Description* (January 1975). North-Holland (1975).

> Contains a number of interesting and thought-provoking papers; in particular, the reader's attention is called to the paper by Waghorn [20.4]. The major objective of the conference was to perform a critical evaluation of the CODASYL schema DDL. At the end of the conference, the participants formulated a set of recommendations for improving the DDL. These recommendations are summarized below.
>
> - Allow a given set type to have the same record type as both owner and member.
>
> - Eliminate repeating groups.
>
> - Allow the specification of any number of identifiers for a given record type. (This feature has since been incorporated into the DDL.)
>
> - Allow the specification of a SEARCH KEY for a given record type, to allow optimization of access to record occurrences on the basis of specified data-item values.
>
> - Allow access (from the DML) to record occurrences on the basis of specified data-item values. (This point and the previous one go together.)
>
> - Allow SET SELECTION to be based on identifiers other than CALC-keys. (This feature has since been incorporated into the DDL.)
>
> - Allow only one member record type per set type.
>
> - Consolidate SEARCH KEY and SORTED INDEXED.
>
> - Improve the selective power of SET SELECTION—in particular, support existential quantification.
>
> - Allow cardinality constraints (number of member occurrences per owner occurrence) to be specified in the set declaration.

20.4 W. J. Waghorn. "The DDL as an Industry Standard?" In [20.3].

> A long but very worthwhile paper; highly recommended. Waghorn analyzes the DDL with respect to its support for common ownership of data, data independence, multiple physical file organizations, and concurrent use of

data. In each of these areas he identifies serious shortcomings in the DDL as proposed and suggests possible improvements. As he points out in his conclusions, these improvements, though generally simple in nature, are also fairly fundamental and likely to have a major impact on implementations. They therefore deserve to be considered with some urgency.

20.5 H. Schenk. "Implementational Aspects of the CODASYL DBTG Proposal." In "Data Base Management" (eds., Klimbie and Koffeman), *Proc. IFIP TC-2 Working Conference on Data Base Management Systems* (April 1974). North-Holland (1974).

Includes a description of how records and sets are implemented in a DBTG system called PHOLAS. Also discusses the handling of the UWA, system buffers, and the object forms of the schema and sub-schema.

20.6 R. Gerritsen. "A Preliminary System for the Design of DBTG Data Structures." *CACM* **18,** No. 10 (October 1975).

Describes an automatic method (already implemented in the form of a program called the Designer) of generating a DBTG database design given a set of anticipated queries. This technique is referred to as the functional approach to database design, and is contrasted with the "existential" approach of modelling the enterprise in a manner that is independent of the uses to be made of the information. As a simple example, the query "list all suppliers who supply part P1" will cause the Designer to generate the assertion "ABOVE (SUPPLIER PART)"—meaning that supplier records should probably be hierarchically above part records in the resulting structure.

20.7 R. W. Taylor. "Observations on the Attributes of Database Sets." In [20.3].

Examines, and proposes major changes to, the concepts of membership class and "dynamic sets" (the latter are not discussed in this book).

20.8 D. C. Tsichritzis. "A Network Framework for Relation Implementation." In [20.3].

20.9 T. W. Olle. "An Analysis of the Flaws in the Schema DDL and Proposed Improvements." In [20.3].

21

The DBTG
External
Model

21.1 INTRODUCTION

As explained in Chapter 19, an external model in DBTG is defined by means of a *sub-schema*. In this chapter we examine the COBOL sub-schema DDL as defined in [19.8]. Broadly speaking, a sub-schema is a simple subset of the corresponding schema; precise details of differences that may exist between a given sub-schema and the corresponding schema are given in Section 21.2.

Any number of sub-schemas can be defined on a given schema; any number of programs may share a given sub-schema; different sub-schemas can overlap. Remember that it is the "invocation" of the sub-schema by a program which provides that program with the definition of its User Work Area (UWA). An example of such an invocation is

```
DB SUPPLIERS WITHIN SUPPLIERS-AND-PARTS.
```

This statement (which appears in the Data Division of the COBOL program) invokes the sub-schema called SUPPLIERS, which is derived from the schema called SUPPLIERS-AND-PARTS. We show a possible definition of SUPPLIERS in Section 21.3.

21.2 DIFFERENCES BETWEEN THE SUB-SCHEMA AND SCHEMA

First let us make precise the statement that a sub-schema is a subset of the schema. Specifically, any of the following schema entries may be omitted in a given sub-schema.

349

- The declaration of one or more areas
- The declaration of one or more sets
- The declaration of one or more records[1]
- The declaration of one or more data-items

Of course, the sub-schema must be self-consistent. For example, a record declaration cannot be omitted if a set declaration referring to it is included.

It follows from the foregoing that, as with IMS, users are protected from certain types of growth in the schema (certainly not all types, but rather more in some respects than with IMS). For example, a new type of data-item can be added to an existing type of record. Similarly, new record types and new areas can be added. (The area assigned to a particular type of record cannot be changed, however.) New types of set can be added under certain circumstances (see Exercise 21.1).

It also follows that the sub-schema automatically provides a level of data security, inasmuch as a program cannot possibly access any data not defined in the corresponding sub-schema.

Other important differences that may exist between the sub-schema and the schema follow.

- Private names ("aliases") may be defined for areas, sets, records, and data-items.
- Data-items may be given different data types.
- The relative order of data-items within their containing record may be changed.
- Sets may be given different SET SELECTION clauses.

Of these, only the last one seems to require any explanation. The idea is that the SET SELECTION clause in the schema can be overridden by one in the sub-schema. For example, the schema could specify APPLI-CATION, implying that set occurrence selection is to be completely procedural, whereas an individual sub-schema could specify one of the IDENTIFIER forms, so that for programs invoking that particular sub-schema, the operation could be somewhat less procedural.

---

[1] If the occurrences of a particular type of record are scattered across several areas, it is also possible to include those in certain areas and to exclude the rest—that is, selected record *occurrences* can be omitted from the external model in this case. For simplicity, however, we shall continue to assume that all occurrences of any given type of record are in a single area.

21.3   A SAMPLE SUB-SCHEMA

Figure 21.1 consists of a simple example of a COBOL sub-schema based on the schema of Fig. 20.16. We remind the reader that areas are called *realms* in COBOL.

From this point on—in Chapter 22 in particular—we shall generally assume that the sub-schema is identical in all major respects to the corresponding schema.

```
TITLE DIVISION.

SS SUPPLIERS WITHIN SUPPLIERS-AND-PARTS.

MAPPING DIVISION.

ALIAS SECTION.
AD S-SP SET-NAME BECOMES SUPPLIES.

STRUCTURE DIVISION.

REALM SECTION.
RD BASIC-DATA-AREA.
RD LINK-DATA-AREA.

SET SECTION
SD SUPPLIES.

RECORD SECTION.
01 S.
    02 SNO  ; PICTURE IS X(5).
    02 CITY ; PICTURE IS X(24).
01 SP.
    02 PNO  ; PICTURE IS X(6).
    02 SNO  ; PICTURE IS X(5).
    02 QTY  ; PICTURE IS S9(5).
```

Fig. 21.1   A sample sub-schema (COBOL)

EXERCISE

21.1 Suppose that a new type of set OM (owner O, member M) is added to the schema. To what extent can existing programs remain unaffected by this addition? You should consider each of the following cases.

a) O and M both new types of record (additions)

b) O and M both old (existing) types of record

c) O old and M new

d) O new and M old

(*Note:* Membership class is important here; so also may be SET SELECTION and LOCATION MODE. You may prefer to postpone detailed consideration of this exercise until after you have read Chapter 22 and reviewed Sections 20.8–20.10.)

REFERENCES AND BIBLIOGRAPHY

See [19.8] and [19.10].

21.1 M. H. Kay. "An Assessment of the CODASYL DDL for Use with a Relational Subschema." In "Data Base Description" (eds., Douqué and Nijssen), *Proc. IFIP TC-2 Working Conference on Data Base Description* (February 1975). North-Holland (1975).

> Presents some ideas on the support of a relational sub-schema on top of a DBTG schema. In general, such a sub-schema would be more than just a "simple subset of the schema." The paper identifies some problems that arise and criticizes the schema DDL in the light of these problems.

22
The DBTG Data Sublanguage

22.1 INTRODUCTION

As with the sub-schema DDL, we shall base our explanation of the DBTG data sublanguage on the DML defined for COBOL in [19.8]. The general plan of the chapter is as follows. Section 22.2 deals with the concept of currency, an understanding of which is prerequisite to an understanding of any of the DML statements. Sections 22.3–22.9 deal with all the major statements of the language; the FIND statement in particular is dealt with last, in Section 22.9, because, although it is easily the most important single statement in the DML, it is also the most complex. Section 22.10 gives a brief description of some of the remaining statements.

All examples will be based on the data of Fig. 20.13 and the schema of Fig. 20.16 (suppliers and parts). As noted before, we shall be assuming that the sub-schema is essentially the same as the schema; the sub-schema is actually invoked as indicated in Section 21.1. For convenience the sample data is shown again as Fig. 22.1.

22.2 CURRENCY

Before we examine the statements of the DML in any detail, it is essential to discuss the fundamental concept of currency. The basic idea is that, for each program operating under its control, the DBMS maintains a table of "currency status indicators." These indicators are actually database-key values; they specify the record occurrence most recently accessed[1] by the program for each of the following.

---

[1] "Most recently accessed" is not strictly accurate here; see Section 22.9.8.

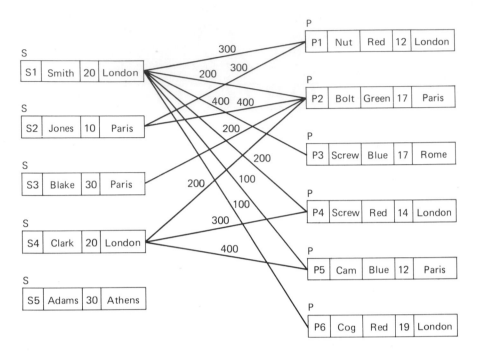

Fig. 22.1 Sample data (suppliers and parts)

- Each realm

    For a realm R the most recently accessed record occurrence within R is referred to as the "current of R" or "current of realm R."

- Each type of record

    For a record type T the most recently accessed T occurrence is referred to as the "current of T" or (more clearly) the "current T occurrence."

- Each type of set

    For a set type S the most recently accessed record occurrence that participates in S may be an occurrence of either the owner or a member. Whichever it is, it is referred to as the "current of S" or "current of set S." Note that the "current of S" refers to a *record* occurrence, but that it also uniquely identifies a *set* occurrence, namely, the unique S occurrence containing it; this set occurrence is referred to as the "current S occurrence."

■   Any type of record

The most recently accessed record occurrence, no matter what its type is (and no matter what realm it belongs to and what sets it participates in), is referred to as the "current of run-unit." This is the most important currency of all, as will shortly be made clear.

For example, consider the following sequence of DML statements.

```
MOVE 'S4' TO SNO IN S.
FIND ANY S.
FIND FIRST SP WITHIN S-SP.
FIND OWNER WITHIN P-SP.
```

The effect of these statements is as follows. The MOVE initializes the CALC-key for record S, data-item SNO IN S (in the UWA). The first FIND then locates the corresponding S record occurrence, namely, that for supplier S4. The next FIND locates the first SP occurrence within the S-SP set occurrence owned by supplier S4, namely, the SP occurrence 'S4/P2/200'; and the last FIND then locates the owner of this SP occurrence within the set P-SP, namely, the P occurrence for part P2. At the end of the sequence, therefore, this P occurrence is the current of run-unit. Now complete the following table.

Current of run-unit	P 'P2'
Current S occurrence	
Current P occurrence	
Current SP occurrence	
Current of set S-SP	
Current of set P-SP	
Current S-SP occurrence	
Current P-SP occurrence	
Current of BASIC-DATA-AREA	
Current of LINK-DATA-AREA	

(The complete table is given in the answer section at the back of the book.)

The following summary of the major DML statements shows why currency—and in particular "current of run-unit"—are such important notions.

■   FIND   locates an existing record occurrence and establishes it as the current of run-unit (also updating other currencies as appropriate).

- GET   retrieves the current of run-unit.
- MODIFY   updates the current of run-unit.
- CONNECT   inserts the current of run-unit into one or more set occurrences.
- DISCONNECT   removes the current of run-unit from one or more set occurrences.
- ERASE   deletes the current of run-unit.
- STORE   creates a new record occurrence and establishes it as the current of run-unit (also updating other currencies as appropriate).

The importance of the FIND statement is apparent from this summary: It is logically required before each of the other statements, except STORE. However, as mentioned in the introduction, we shall defer treatment of FIND until after the other statements have been dealt with, restricting ourselves to formats of the FIND statement already illustrated when a FIND of some sort is necessary.

We now present a number of examples illustrating the major features of the DML.

22.3 GET

22.3.1 Get full details of supplier S4.

```
MOVE 'S4' TO SNO IN S.
FIND ANY S.
GET S.
```

The effect of this code is to bring the S record occurrence for supplier S4 into the S location within the UWA. Note that the FIND statement itself does *not* retrieve any data. Incidentally, since GET (like most other statements) operates on the current of run-unit, it would be perfectly valid to write simply

```
GET.
```

This would bring the current of run-unit, whatever its type, into the appropriate UWA location. However, by specifying a record name (S in the example), the programmer is effectively enabling the DBMS to check that the current of run-unit is actually an occurrence of the appropriate type (and in any case such explicit specification is clearer). In the example, if for some reason the current of run-unit were not an S occurrence, the GET would fail and a nonzero value (actually 0803300) would be placed in the special register DB-STATUS. (Part of the effect of every DML statement is to place a value into DB-STATUS. A zero value indicates normal completion of the statement; a nonzero value indicates some exceptional or error situation. The program must provide a USE FOR DB-EXCEPTION procedure to be invoked whenever DB-STATUS is set to a nonzero value; see [19.8] for details. We shall usually ignore DB-STATUS in our examples.)

Most of the DML statements allow the specification of the record name to be omitted in the same way that GET does. However, the practice is not recommended, and we shall not adopt it in our examples.

22.3.2 Get supplier name and city for supplier S4.

```
FIND S occurrence for S4 as in Example 22.3.1.
GET SNAME IN S, CITY IN S.
```

In this example only the name and city for supplier S4 are brought into the UWA; other UWA data-items remain unchanged.

22.4 MODIFY

22.4.1 Add 10 to the status value for supplier S4.

```
FIND S occurrence for S4 as in Example 22.3.1.
GET S.
ADD 10 TO STATUS IN S.
MODIFY S.
```

The MODIFY statement replaces (portions of) the current of run-unit with values taken from the UWA. Thus, to add 10 to S4's status value, the user must retrieve it, increase it in the UWA, and then put it back. If the MODIFY specifies a record name, the entire record is replaced. If it specifies a list of data-items, just those items are replaced. In the example, therefore, the desired effect could equally well have been achieved by specifying STATUS IN S (instead of simply S) in both the GET and the MODIFY.

22.4.2 The quantity (200) of part P2 supplied by supplier S4 should actually be supplied by supplier S3 instead. Make the appropriate adjustments to the database.

The "appropriate adjustments" consist of removing the SP occurrence 'S4/P2/200' from the S-SP occurrence owned by supplier S4 and inserting it into the S-SP occurrence owned by S3, while at the same time changing the value of the data-item SNO IN SP from S4 to S3. For simplicity we assume that there does not already exist an SP occurrence connecting S3 and P2.

A procedure to perform these adjustments can be written using a sequence of DISCONNECT, MODIFY, and CONNECT statements (or GET, ERASE, and STORE statements if the membership class is such as to prohibit the DISCONNECT—see Section 20.8). Alternatively (another format of) the MODIFY statement can be made to perform *both* the function of changing the value of SNO IN SP to S3 *and* the function of removing the corresponding SP record occurrence from one S-SP occurrence and inserting it into another. In this case the S-SP occurrence to which the SP occurrence is to be moved is chosen by the DBMS on the basis of the SET SELECTION clause for S-SP. In Fig. 20.16 that clause is THRU S-SP OWNER IDENTIFIED BY IDENTIFIER SNO IN S. Consequently, before executing the MODIFY statement, the programmer must correctly initialize the UWA data-item SNO IN S. A possible procedure is

```
MOVE 'S4' TO SNO IN S.
FIND ANY S.
FIND FIRST SP WITHIN S-SP.
MOVE 'S3' TO SNO IN S.
MOVE 'S3' TO SNO IN SP.
MODIFY SP INCLUDING S-SP MEMBERSHIP.
```

The first two statements here locate the S occurrence for S4 in the usual way. The third statement locates the SP occurrence 'S4/P2/200'. In general, this would *not* be the appropriate FIND format to use at this point—a sequential scanning FIND would actually be required—but as previously explained, we are restricting ourselves for the time being to FIND formats that have already been encountered. With the sample data of Fig. 22.1, the FIND FIRST does in fact locate the required SP occurrence. The fourth statement initializes the UWA data-item SNO IN S, ready for the process of SET SELECTION. The fifth statement sets the UWA data-item SNO IN SP to the value that is to replace the corresponding item in the database when the MODIFY is executed. Finally, the sixth statement performs the desired replacement (because of the portion of the statement MODIFY SP) and moves the SP occurrence out of the old S-SP occurrence and into the new one (SET SELECTION being performed because of the clause INCLUDING S-SP MEMBERSHIP).

After the MODIFY, the SP occurrence (value now 'S3/P2/200') is the current of set S-SP (even if it was not so before; see Section 22.9.8).

An alternative form of MODIFY, namely, MODIFY record ONLY set MEMBERSHIP, may be used to move a record from one set occurrence to another (within the same set type) without changing any data-items in the record.

22.5 CONNECT

22.5.1 Suppose that record type S is declared in the schema to be a member of an additional type of set, SETX (owner X). Insert the S occurrence for supplier S4 into the SETX occurrence owned by the X occurrence *x*.

The insertion process consists essentially of (1) locating the required occurrence of SETX, (2) locating the required occurrence of S, and (3) executing a CONNECT statement to insert the latter into the former. The procedure for step 1 can be any procedure that makes the required occurrence of SETX the *current* occurrence of SETX: typically, a procedure to FIND the appropriate occurrence (*x*) of its owner X.

1. `FIND ... x.`
2. `FIND S occurrence for S4 as in Example 22.3.1.`
3. `CONNECT S TO SETX.`

The CONNECT statement inserts the current of run-unit into the current occurrence(s) of the specified set(s). Note in the example that the class of membership of S in SETX must not be AUTOMATIC unless it is also OPTIONAL[2] (and the S occurrence for S4 must not currently be a member of any occurrence of SETX). Note, too, that step 1 *must* be performed before step 2. (Why?) After the CONNECT, the S occurrence for S4 is the current of set SETX.

22.6 DISCONNECT

22.6.1 Remove the S occurrence for S4 from the SETX occurrence that contains it. (See Example 22.5.1.)

```
FIND S occurrence for S4 as in Example 22.3.1.
DISCONNECT S FROM SETX.
```

The DISCONNECT statement removes the current of run-unit from the occurrence(s) of the specified set(s) containing it; the record occurrence still exists in the database but no longer participates in (any of) the specified set(s). However, it is still considered to be the current of (each of) the specified set(s), provided that it was so before. Note in the example that S must be an OPTIONAL member of SETX; note, too, that the S occurrence for S4 must currently be a member of some SETX occurrence.

---

[2] The COBOL term for OPTIONAL is TRANSIENT.

22.7 ERASE

22.7.1 Delete the S occurrence for supplier S4.

The problem here, of course, is that this S occurrence is the owner of a nonempty set occurrence. The effect of attempting to delete any particular record occurrence depends, in general, on the format of the ERASE statement; there are four possible formats, as the following code illustrates.

```
FIND S occurrence for S4 as in Example 22.3.1.
                    ⎡ PERMANENT ⎤
      ERASE S       │ SELECTIVE │.
                    ⎣ ALL       ⎦
```

The meaning of each of the formats follows.

■ No qualification

The current of run-unit is deleted only if it is not the owner of any nonempty set occurrence.

■ PERMANENT

The current of run-unit is deleted, together with MANDATORY—and presumably FIXED—member occurrences of any set occurrence of which it is the owner (OPTIONAL member occurrences being merely removed, not deleted entirely).

■ SELECTIVE

The effect is the same as for ONLY, except that OPTIONAL member occurrences not participating as members in any other set occurrence are deleted, not just removed.

■ ALL

The current of run-unit is deleted, together with all member occurrences of any set occurrence of which it is the owner (regardless of their membership class).

In each case, if any deleted member occurrence is itself the owner of another set occurrence, then the effect is as if the original ERASE (with the appropriate qualification) had been applied directly to that occurrence. The current of run-unit becomes null, but no other currency indicators are affected.

In the example, therefore, the unqualified ERASE would fail (DB-STATUS would be nonzero); each of the qualified forms would delete the S occurrence and all SP occurrences for S4. Incidentally, all sets and records affected by an ERASE statement must be included in the corresponding sub-schema—at least according to [19.1], though [19.8] and [19.10] are not specific on this point. For example, the sub-schema should include the declaration of set P-SP for the foregoing qualified ERASEs to be accepted, since SP occurrences are to be removed from an occurrence of this set.

22.8 STORE

22.8.1 Create the SP occurrence 'S5/P6/700'.

1. MOVE 'S5' TO SNO IN SP
   MOVE 'P6' TO PNO IN SP
   MOVE 700 TO QTY IN SP.

2. MOVE 'S5' TO SNO IN S
   MOVE 'P6' TO PNO IN P.

3. STORE SP.

Step 1 consists of statements—three MOVEs—to construct the new SP occurrence in the UWA. It can now be stored in the database (step 3). However, SP is declared in the schema of Fig. 20.16 to be an AUTOMA-TIC member of both S-SP and P-SP; hence, when an SP occurrence is stored, the DBMS must automatically insert it into the appropriate occurrences of these two sets—in the example, the S-SP occurrence owned by S5 and the P-SP occurrence owned by P6. In general, the occurrences of S-SP and P-SP into which the new SP occurrence is to be inserted are chosen by the DBMS on the basis of the SET SELECTION clauses given in the schema for these two sets. A full explanation of this clause is given in Section 20.10; it is sufficient here to note that, in order for the process of SET SELECTION to pick the correct occurrences of the sets in this example, the programmer must first initialize—step 2—the UWA data-items SNO IN S and PNO IN P with the correct values.

For details of other UWA data-items that may require initialization before STORE, see the description of LOCATION MODE in Section 20.9.

After the STORE in the example, the new SP occurrence is the current of run-unit, the current SP occurrence, the current of realm LINK-DATA-AREA, and the current of both S-SP and P-SP. (In general, a newly stored record occurrence becomes the current of all sets for which it is the owner or an AUTOMATIC member, except as explained subsequently in Section 22.9.8.)

22.9 FIND

Seven basic formats of the FIND statement are defined in [19.8]. Moreover, most of the seven have several permitted variations. It is not our intention here to illustrate every possible variation; however, all variations will at least be mentioned, and examples will be presented of the most important formats.[3] In general, the function of the FIND statement is to locate a record occurrence in the database and to make it the current of run-unit—also the current of the appropriate realm, the current of the appropriate record type, and the current of all sets in which it participates (but see Section 22.9.8).

22.9.1   Format 1—the "fast access" format.   The data-item SKEY (a data-item local to the run-unit, not part of the database) contains the database-key of an S record occurrence. Find this S occurrence.

```
FIND S DB-KEY IS SKEY.
```

SKEY must have been defined with a USAGE IS DB-KEY clause.

22.9.2   Format 2—the "hashing" format.   The basic format 2 FIND has been illustrated many times already in this part of the book. It is the format that can be used if (and only if) the LOCATION MODE for the record concerned is CALC. There is an important variation on the basic format, however, which is needed when the CALC-key is not an identifier, i.e., when values of the CALC-key are not necessarily unique. For the sake of the example, therefore, suppose that a LOCATION MODE has been declared for record SP as CALC on values of the data-item SNO IN SP:

```
RECORD NAME IS SP;
    LOCATION MODE IS CALC HASH-SP-SNO
                 USING SNO IN SP;
                        . . . . .
```

It is required to find all SP occurrences for supplier S4 via format 2 (hashing) FINDs.

```
         MOVE 'S4' TO SNO IN SP.
    NXT. FIND DUPLICATE SP.
         IF NOTFOUND='YES' GO TO QUIT.
         (GET SP and process it)
         GO TO NXT.
```

The effect of the FIND statement illustrated here is as follows. If the value of the UWA data-item SNO IN SP is the same as the value of the

---

[3] In particular, formats 1, 4, and 5 permit the omission of the record name (cf. GET, MODIFY, etc.), but this option will not be illustrated.

same data-item in the current of run-unit (assuming the current of run-unit to be an SP occurrence), the FIND statement will select the next SP occurrence found by the DBMS with the same value for this data-item; otherwise, it will select the first SP occurrence found by the DBMS with a value for this data-item equal to the value of the UWA data-item (i.e., it will operate as if ANY had been specified instead of DUPLI-CATE). If no further SP occurrence with SNO equal to S4 can be found, the DBMS will place a nonzero value—actually 0502400—into DB-STATUS and will invoke the programmer-supplied exception routine. We have assumed that this routine moves the value 'YES' to the data-item NOTFOUND. Thus the effect of the procedure shown is to find, one by one, all SP occurrences containing the SNO value S4.

As a matter of speculation, we observe that the dependency of the format 2 FIND on a LOCATION MODE of CALC could very well be eliminated. A similar dependency has already been eliminated from the schema DDL—SET SELECTION as defined in [19.10] effectively per-mits records to be found on the basis of an *identifier* value, whereas in the original version of the language [19.1] the search item usually had to be a CALC-key.

We remind the reader that CALC does not necessarily imply hashing.

22.9.3 Format 3—a "sequential scanning" format.

Suppose that the current of set P-SP is the SP record occurrence 'S3/P2/200', and we wish to find another supplier (i.e., not S3) who supplies the indicated part (P2) in the same quantity (200).

```
FIND DUPLICATE WITHIN P-SP USING QTY IN SP.
IF ENDSET='YES' GO TO QUIT.
GET SP.
(print SNO IN SP)
```

The format 3 FIND in this example scans the current occurrence of set P-SP, looking for the next SP occurrence that contains the same QTY value as the current of P-SP, i.e., 200. "Next" here means relative to the current of P-SP, according to the ordering defined for P-SP in the schema. With the sample data of Fig. 22.1 the FIND will locate the SP occurrence 'S4/P2/200' and the value S4 will be printed. If we were to loop back and execute the FIND again, an "end of set" condition would occur (DB-STATUS will be 0502100—we have assumed that the pro-grammer's exception routine will set the data-item ENDSET to 'YES' in this situation).

See also Section 22.9.7.

22.9.4   Format 4—another "sequential scanning" format.   Find PNO values for parts supplied by supplier S4.

```
        MOVE 'S4' TO SNO IN S.
        FIND ANY S.
        IF S-SP EMPTY GO TO NONE-SUPPLIED.
NXT.    FIND NEXT SP WITHIN S-SP.
        IF ENDSET='YES' GO TO ALL-FOUND.
        GET SP.
        (add PNO IN SP to result list)
        GO TO NXT.
```

The IF statement preceding the loop will pass control to the statement labeled NONE-SUPPLIED if the current occurrence of S-SP is empty. [This test could alternatively have been made by examining NOTFOUND as well as ENDSET after the format 4 FIND (where NOTFOUND and ENDSET are as in Sections 22.9.2 and 22.9.3, respectively; note that the two conditions are distinct and result in distinct DB-STATUS values). However, this would have involved the inefficiency of performing the test on every iteration of the loop.] With the sample data of Fig. 22.1, this test fails, and so the loop is entered. The statement NXT locates the next SP occurrence within the current occurrence of the set S-SP, relative to the current of S-SP; the first time statement NXT is executed, the current of S-SP is the owner occurrence for S4, and so the SP occurrence located is actually the first one.

The word NEXT in a format 4 FIND can be replaced by PRIOR, FIRST, LAST, an integer n, or the name of a data-item having an integer value. In the last two cases a positive integer represents the number of the desired record occurrence counting in the NEXT direction from the beginning of the set occurrence (1 = FIRST), and a negative integer represents the number of the desired record occurrence counting in the PRIOR direction from the end of the set occurrence (−1 = LAST). Also, the set name can be replaced by a realm name, in which case NEXT, PRIOR, etc., are interpreted in terms of positions within the realm.

22.9.5   Format 5—the "current" format.   Establish the current of set S-SP as the current of run-unit (note that the current of set S-SP is not necessarily the current of run-unit already). We assume that the current of S-SP is an SP occurrence.

```
        FIND CURRENT SP WITHIN S-SP.
```

The format 5 FIND is somewhat different from the others, in that its *only* function is to update the table of currencies; the record to be found must already be one of the current records, and so must already have been found (or stored) within the run-unit (in other words, no access to the database is necessary). The WITHIN option may refer to a realm instead of a set, in which case the record to be found is the current of that realm; or it may be omitted, in which case the record to be found is the current of the indicated record type. If both the record name and the WITHIN option are omitted, the record to be found is the current of run-unit.

22.9.6 Format 6—the "owner" format.   At a particular point in the execution of a program, the current of P-SP is a particular SP occurrence. Find the corresponding P occurrence.

```
FIND OWNER WITHIN P-SP.
```

22.9.7 Format 7—another "sequential scanning" format.   Find the quantity of part P5 supplied by supplier S4.

```
MOVE 'S4' TO SNO IN S.
FIND ANY S.
IF S-SP EMPTY GO TO NOT-SUPPLIED.
MOVE 'P5' TO PNO IN SP.
FIND SP WITHIN S-SP CURRENT USING PNO IN SP.
IF ENDSET='YES' GO TO NOT-SUPPLIED.
GET SP.
(print QTY IN SP)
```

The first thing to notice here is that we have a strategy problem. Do we start at supplier S4 and scan the S-SP set occurrence, or do we start at part P5 and scan the P-SP set occurrence?[4] The code above assumes that we start at supplier S4. The FIND SP scans the current S-SP occurrence (the one owned by S4) for the first SP occurrence with a PNO value equal to the value of the UWA data-item PNO IN SP (established by the previous statement).

If CURRENT is omitted from this FIND format, then SET SELEC-TION is performed for the specified set. In the foregoing procedure, for example, the statement FIND ANY S could have been omitted, provided the CURRENT option was also omitted from the format 7 FIND. Thus there are not two but four possible procedures that can be used to answer the original question in this example (starting with S4 or P5, including or omitting CURRENT). As an exercise, the reader is advised to consider the effect on currency of each of the four (each one, of course, results in

---

[4] Matters would be simpler if the data model included a singular set linking all SP occurrences.

the same current of run-unit, namely, the SP occurrence 'S4/P5/400', but other resultant currencies are *not* the same in every case).

As another example illustrating both format 7 and format 3, consider the problem of finding SNO values for all suppliers who supply part P2 in quantity 200.

```
        MOVE 'P2' TO PNO IN P.
        FIND ANY P.
        IF P-SP EMPTY GO TO NOT-SUPPLIED.
        MOVE 200 TO QTY IN SP.
        FIND SP WITHIN P-SP CURRENT USING QTY IN SP.
   NXT. IF ENDSET='YES' GO TO QUIT.
        GET SP.
        (print SNO IN SP)
        FIND DUPLICATE WITHIN P-SP USING QTY IN SP.
        GO TO NXT.
```

The first five statements here locate the first SP occurrence (if there is one) for part P2 that contains a QTY value of 200 (the procedure is essentially the same as in the previous example and makes use of a format 7 FIND). With the sample data of Fig. 22.1, the SP occurrence found is 'S1/P2/200' (and thus DB-STATUS is zero). The format 3 FIND (FIND DUPLICATE . . .) then scans the current S-SP occurrence in the NEXT direction, starting from the current of S-SP and looking for the next SP occurrence that contains the same QTY value. Note that the format 7 FIND cannot be used at this point, since it would simply locate 'S1/P2/200' again; we need a statement to scan forward from the current position, as the format 3 FIND does. The loop is repeated until an "end of set" condition occurs.

It is important to understand that the effect of the clause 'USING QTY IN SP' in the format 3 FIND is to cause the DBMS to search for the next SP occurrence with the same QTY value as the current of the set—not the same value as the UWA data-item QTY IN SP. (Contrast the semantics of the same clause in the format 7 FIND.) In the example above, the two values are in fact the same, but the statement "GET SP" could be replaced by the statement, say,

```
        MOVE 400 TO QTY IN SP
```

without having the least effect on which SP occurrence is found by the format 3 FIND.

The USING clause in both format 3 and format 7 FIND statements can take the form "USING data-item, data-item, . . . ," in which case the search is for an occurrence containing the desired values for all specified data-items.

22.9.8 The RETAINING clause. For each supplier who supplies part P4, find another part supplied by the same supplier, and print supplier number, supplier name, and part number. For simplicity assume that part P4 is supplied by at least one supplier, and that at least one other part exists for each such supplier.

In principle, the required procedure is as follows. Starting at part P4, we inspect each SP occurrence for that part. For each such SP occurrence, we extract SNO and SNAME from the corresponding S occurrence, and then search the SP occurrences for that supplier, looking for one linking the supplier to a part that is *not* P4. As soon as we find such an SP occurrence, we extract the relevant PNO. Thus, given the sample data of Fig. 22.1, a possible result from such a procedure would be

SNO	SNAME	PNO
S1	Smith	P1
S4	Clark	P2

```
        MOVE 'P4' TO PNO IN P.
        FIND ANY P.
NS.     FIND NEXT SP WITHIN P-SP.
        IF ENDSET='YES' GO TO EXIT.
        FIND OWNER WITHIN S-SP.
        GET S.
NP.     FIND NEXT SP WITHIN S-SP.
        GET SP.
        IF PNO IN SP='P4' GO TO NP.
        (print SNO IN S, SNAME IN S, PNO IN SP)
        GO TO NS.
```

This code is not correct, however; it contains a logical error. Try finding the error before reading the explanation below; it is probably a good idea to "execute" the procedure on the sample data of Fig. 22.1. The result is

SNO	SNAME	PNO
S1	Smith	P1
S2	Jones	P1

It is interesting to observe that the procedure does not terminate abnormally in any way. It simply gives an answer that looks right but is in fact wrong.

The error is as follows. When statement NP is executed, it establishes an SP occurrence as the current of run-unit. This occurrence, being the

SP occurrence most recently accessed, also becomes the current of set for all sets in which it participates—including, in particular, the set P-SP. This in turn makes the current P-SP occurrence the one containing this SP occurrence. Thus, when control goes back to NS (in an attempt to find the next supplier of P4), the P-SP occurrence referenced in that statement will no longer be the one owned by P4 (in general). To avoid this situation, the statement NP must be extended to include an appropriate RETAINING clause:

```
NP.  FIND NEXT SP WITHIN S-SP
          RETAINING CURRENCY FOR P-SP.
```

The effect of this clause is to prevent the updating of the currency status indicator for set P-SP. In general, currency updating may be suppressed for the realm involved, for the record type involved, for any or all set types involved, or for any combination of these; see [19.8] for details of syntax in each case. The only currency indicator for which updating can never be suppressed is that for "current of run-unit."

A RETAINING clause may be specified in any FIND or STORE statement.

22.10 MISCELLANEOUS STATEMENTS

We conclude this chapter with examples of some of the remaining DML statements (READY, FINISH, ORDER, ACCEPT).

22.10.1 READY

As an example of READY, consider the statement

```
READY BASIC-DATA-AREA, LINK-DATA-AREA USAGE-MODE IS UPDATE.
```

The run-unit must ready all realms it intends to use, specifying a USAGE-MODE of UPDATE or RETRIEVAL, as appropriate. (RE-TRIEVAL and UPDATE may both be further qualified, as either PRO-TECTED or EXCLUSIVE; see Part 5 of this book.) The precise meaning of "use" here is somewhat complicated; see [19.10] for details. For example, a record occurrence containing an ACTUAL RESULT data-item must be automatically modified if a record occurrence containing one of the parameters to the RESULT procedure is stored; if the two occurrences are in different realms then both realms are "used" at the time of the STORE.

22.10.2 FINISH

The run-unit must release realms when it has finished with them, for example,

```
FINISH BASIC-DATA-AREA, LINK-DATA-AREA.
```

22.10.3

The ORDER statement permits the run-unit to impose a new ordering on the member records of the current occurrence of a specified set. If ORDER IS SORTED has been specified in the schema—the only case we shall consider—the relevant realm(s) must have a usage-mode of exclusive retrieval or protected retrieval, and the new ordering is temporary, in that the set occurrence reverts to its original ordering when the realm is FINISHed. As an example, the statement

```
ORDER P-SP LOCALLY ON DESCENDING KEY QTY IN SP
```

sequences the SP occurrences (temporarily) within the current P-SP occurrence by descending QTY value.

22.10.4 ACCEPT (CURRENCY STATUS)

A special form of ACCEPT statement is provided to enable a run-unit to discover the value (a database-key) of any of the currency status indicators. For example, suppose that the run-unit creates and stores a new P occurrence and wishes to note the database-key that has been assigned to it. The sequence

```
STORE P.
ACCEPT PK FROM CURRENCY.
```

will place a copy of this database-key in the data-item PK (which must have been declared with a USAGE IS DB-KEY clause). The word CURRENCY may optionally be preceded by a realm name, record name, or set name, to extract the database-key of the current of the specified realm, record, or set, respectively.

EXERCISES

Using your answer to Exercise 20.3 (schema for the supplier-part-project database) as a basis, give DBTG solutions to some of the exercises of Chapter 5. For convenience ten of those exercises are repeated here as Exercises 22.1–22.10.

22.1 (Exercise 5.4) Get SNO values for suppliers who supply project J1.

22.2 (Exercise 5.5) Get SNO values for suppliers who supply project J1 with part P1.

22.3 (Exercise 5.9) Get SNO values for suppliers who supply project J1 with a red part.

22.4 (Exercise 5.23) Get PNO values for parts supplied to all projects in London.

22.5 (Exercise 5.15) Get JNO values for projects not supplied with any red part by any London supplier.

22.6 (Exercise 5.24) Get JNO values for projects supplied with at least all parts supplied by supplier S1.

22.7 (Exercise 5.18) Get all pairs of CITY values such that a supplier in the first city supplies a project in the second city.

22.8 (Exercise 5.30) Change the color of all red parts to orange.

22.9 (Exercise 5.31) The quantity of P1 supplied to J1 by S1 is now to be supplied by S2 instead. Make all the necessary changes.

22.10 (Exercise 5.33) Delete all red parts and the corresponding SPJ occurrences.

22.11 Suppose that the SPJ record in the supplier-part-project schema contains only the data-item QTY; i.e., the redundant recording of SNO, PNO, and JNO has been eliminated. It is still possible—procedurally—to maintain the desired ordering of SPJ occurrences within any given set occurrence, e.g., to maintain all SPJ occurrences for a given supplier in project number order within part number order. (Note, however, that this change will have considerable repercussions on the programs concerned with maintaining these sets.)

Suppose, therefore, that the redundancy has been eliminated but that the ordering within the sets has been maintained. What effect will this have on your solutions to Exercises 22.1, 22.2, and 22.9? (*Note:* You will need to refer to [19.10] for the last of these to find out how to maintain ordering within a set when ORDER IS SORTED has not been specified.)

22.12 Suppose that the membership class of SPJ in each of S-SPJ, P-SPJ, and J-SPJ is changed from OPTIONAL to MANDATORY. What effect will this have on your solution to Exercise 22.9?

22.13 Consider the "managerial structure" schema of Exercise 20.2. Write statements to create an EMP occurrence for employee E15 and to place it at the appropriate point within the hierarchy. You may assume that EMP occurrences for employees E1 and E8 (see Fig. 20.7) already exist and that a LINK occurrence connecting them also exists; do not, however, assume that a LINK occurrence already exists subordinate to E8. State the assumptions you make with respect to membership class.

22.14 Consider the "parts and components" schema of Exercise 20.4. Write statements to print for each part its part number, the numbers of its immediate components, and the numbers of parts for which it is an immediate component. You will probably find it helpful to add a singular set (member PART) to the schema to enable you to process the parts one by one.

22.15 Consider the "areas and birds" database of Exercise 20.5. Write statements to find all types of bird that have been observed in area A1 on 1 January 1973 (a) using the "two-entity" schema; (b) using the "three-entity" schema.

REFERENCES AND BIBLIOGRAPHY

See [19.8] and [19.10].

22.1 G. M. Stacey. "A FORTRAN Interface to the CODASYL Data Base Task Group Specifications." *Comp. J.* **17,** No. 2 (May 1974).

> This paper addresses the question of extending FORTRAN to operate on a DBTG-style database. So far as the DML functions are concerned, it argues that host languages—in particular, FORTRAN—should *not* be extended but should use a CALL interface to a common set of DML functions, namely, the set proposed by the Data Base Task Group for COBOL. Given this approach, there is no need to define database objects such as the "DBTG set" within the host language either, so it is proposed that the sub-schema DDL be divided into two parts: one which extracts the required subset of the schema in a manner that is independent of the host language, and one which maps this subset into host language constructs. These two portions correspond, respectively, to the external/conceptual map and the external schema, in ANSI/SPARC terms—but the external schema becomes almost trivial, consisting as it does merely of redefinitions of database record types as FORTRAN working areas (i.e., the UWA). (Specifically, it does not contain any reference to sets.) Of course, the COBOL sub-schema language [19.8] does not really permit the *definition* of such constructs either, despite the fact that the COBOL DML is considered part of the host language.
>
> It is pertinent here to mention two additional CODASYL groups, the Sub-Schema Task Group (SSTG) and the FORTRAN Data Manipulation Language Committee (FORTRAN DMLC). The SSTG is a task group of the DDLC and is considering the "language-independent" aspects of the sub-schema (i.e., the "subset extraction" portion suggested by Stacey, in effect). It is also considering the definition of relational and hierarchical sub-schemas. The FORTRAN DMLC is a committee at the same organizational level as the PLC and the DDLC; it is investigating the design of a DBTG-like DML for FORTRAN. At the time of writing neither of these groups has produced a final report.

22.2 C. W. Bachman. "The Programmer as Navigator." *CACM* **16,** No. 11 (November 1973).

> Contains the lecture Bachman gave on the occasion of his receiving the 1973 Turing Award. Bachman contrasts the earlier view of data processing, in

which the computer was central and data was considered as flowing through the machine as it was processed, with the more modern view, in which the database is the major resource and the computer is merely a tool for accessing it. The term "navigation" is used to describe the process of travelling through the database, following explicit paths from one record to the next in the search for some required piece of data.

Part 5
Security and Integrity

This part of the book consists of a discussion of the twin problems of security and integrity in a database system. Chapter 23 deals with security and Chapter 24 with integrity. In each case the problem is considered in general terms first, and the relevant features of various systems—in particular, IMS and DBTG—are then presented in the light of this general discussion.

23
Security

23.1 INTRODUCTION

We use the term "security" to mean the protection of the data in the database against unauthorized disclosure, alteration, or destruction. The reader will be aware of the current high degree of interest in this area. It is not our intention here to review the ethical or social aspects of the problem. Many excellent discussions of these have already appeared (see, for example, *The Computerized Society* by Martin and Norman [23.7], particularly Chapters 14, 15, and 24–27). Instead we shall consider some of the technical safeguards and countermeasures that can be used to assist with security enforcement; in particular, we shall describe the security features of IMS and DBTG.

We start with an example (based on an example in a paper by Conway, Maxwell, and Morgan [23.2]) that illustrates to some extent the nature of the problem. Suppose that the database (which for simplicity we assume to be relational in structure) includes a relation EMPLOYEE, with attributes EMP# (employee number), NAME, ADDRESS, DEPT# (department number), SALARY, DATE (date of last salary increase), and ASSESSMENT (manager's evaluation of employee's performance). Then each of the following statements indicates a level of access to this relation that might reasonably be granted to some particular category of user.[1]

---

[1] By "user" here we mean either an application programmer or a user at a terminal (as in Chapter 1)—that is, someone who is trying to access the database *via the system* (the DBMS). The case of a "user" who attempts to bypass the system is considered separately later.

1. The user has unconstrained access to the entire relation for all types of operation.
2. The user has no access to any part of the relation for any type of operation.
3. The user may see any part of the relation, but may not change its contents.
4. The user may see exactly one tuple in the relation (that user's "own" tuple), but may not change it.
5. The user may see exactly one tuple in the relation (the user's own), and alter some but not all of the values therein.
6. The user may see only the EMP#, NAME, ADDRESS, and DEPT# attributes, and within any one tuple may alter only the NAME and ADDRESS values.
7. The user may see the EMP# and SALARY attributes, and within any one tuple may alter the SALARY value, but only between the hours of 9 A.M. and 5 P.M. and only from a terminal located in the payroll office.
8. The user may see the EMP# and SALARY attributes, and within any one tuple may alter the SALARY value, if and only if the current SALARY value is less than 5000 dollars.
9. The user may apply statistical operators to the SALARY attribute (e.g., to obtain average salary per department), but may not see or alter individual values.
10. The user may see the EMP# and ASSESSMENT attributes, and within any one tuple may alter the ASSESSMENT value, if and only if that user is the manager of the department identified by the DEPT# value.

The foregoing list, which is by no means exhaustive, should begin to give some idea of the range and flexibility required of a general-purpose security enforcement scheme. In the next two sections we consider in some detail the features such a scheme should possess. None of these features is beyond the bounds of current technology; however, the cost of implementing all of them would at present be prohibitively high (both financially and in terms of performance degradation), which is one reason why no existing system actually does provide them all. However, it seems reasonable to assume that new legislation, public demand, decreasing costs, and other factors will force future systems toward the provision of a complete protection scheme along the lines suggested in the next two sections.

23.2 IDENTIFICATION AND AUTHENTICATION

From the definition of security given at the start of the chapter, it follows that the DBMS must not allow any operation to be performed on the database unless the user is *authorized* for the operation concerned. Authorization is in general the responsibility of the DBA; that is, the DBA—or someone delegated by the DBA—must (a) define to the system the operations each user is allowed to perform,[2] and (b) provide a means for users to identify themselves to the system. Before accessing the database, then, users will have to *identify* themselves (i.e., say who they are—for example, by entering an operator number at a terminal). Ideally, they should also *authenticate* this identification (i.e., prove they are who they say they are—for example, by supplying a password supposedly known only to the system and to legitimate users of the specified operator number). In general, these two steps (identification and authentication) could be repeated as many times as desired. In the case of an on-line user, for example, they will typically form part of the user's sign-on procedure, and thus be performed once per terminal session; but they could be required as frequently as once per individual operation if the database contains particularly sensitive information.

The process of *identification* may involve supplying an operator number, as in the example above, or using machine-readable identity cards or badges. Many terminals now available have special features to assist in this process, such as the ability to suppress the display of data being entered to preserve its secrecy, the ability to read specially designed cards or badges, and the ability to furnish a unique terminal identification to the computer (this would help by informing the system *where*, as well as who, the user is). Remote terminals of the future might allow identification by voiceprint or fingerprints (in which case authentication as a separate step would not be necessary).

The process of *authentication* involves supplying information known only to the person the user has claimed to be (in the identification procedure). This may be done by quoting a password, as in the example above, or by answering some question from the system. It is possible to devise quite simple authentication procedures that are almost impossible to crack. One such procedure, due to Earnest, is described by Hoffman [23.5] somewhat as follows. First the system supplies the user with a

---

[2] As explained in the next section, however, it will not generally be practicable for the DBA to specify *all* the operations permitted for any given user. Specifically, many "access constraints" are more logically associated with the *data* than with any given user, and these will have to be specified as part of the data definition rather than as part of a user definition.

pseudorandom number x. The user then performs some simple mental transformation T on x and sends the result $y = T(x)$ back to the system. The system then performs the same transformation on x and verifies that the result is indeed y. Any would-be infiltrator will see at most the values x and y, from which it is almost impossible to work out exactly what the transformation is—even for a fairly simple T, such as the following:

$$T(x) = (\text{Sum of 1st, 3rd, 5th, } \ldots \text{ digits of } x)^2 + (\text{Hour of the day}).$$

Petersen and Turn [23.9] discuss a number of other authentication techniques, including "one-time-use" passwords and "hang-up and call-back" procedures. Some others are discussed by Hoffman [23.5].

23.3 ACCESS CONTROL

For each user the system will maintain a *user profile*, generated from the user definition supplied by the DBA and giving details of the appropriate identification and authentication procedures and of the operations this user is allowed to perform. In all but the simplest cases, however, the user profile alone will not be sufficient to determine whether the user should be allowed to perform a given operation; for many operations it will be necessary for the system to check a password supplied with the request (for example) or to interrogate some other part of the database to see whether access should be granted. For example, a request to see an employee's assessment may be granted only if the database includes the information that the requestor is the employee's manager.

In general, then, the DBMS must check each DSL operation as it is issued to see whether it violates any security restrictions, and must suppress it if so.[3] In this section we consider the nature of the checks that must be performed. For convenience we assume that the underlying system is relational; most of the following discussion is based on a paper by Codd [23.1], in which he describes the principles of access control in a relational database system.

Since, as we have seen, user profiles (as specified by the DBA) are not enough by themselves, we assume that each relation in the database has a set of *access constraints* associated with it. These are supplied initially by the person responsible for creating the relation concerned;

---

[3] In particularly sensitive situations the system may react to an attempted breach of security by canceling the program or locking the terminal. Failing this, the system should at least send some form of error signal back to the user. In addition, it may be desirable to record the attempted security violation in a special log file ("threat monitoring"). This will permit subsequent analysis of such attempts and may in itself act as a deterrent against illegal infiltration.

they are held in the data dictionary (they may be thought of as part of the conceptual schema). They may specify, for example, a password that must be supplied to modify tuples in the relation, a password that must be supplied to retrieve certain attribute combinations from the relation, a condition that the user must satisfy in order to access the relation at all, and so on. (Incidentally, predicate calculus may once again be a suitable basis for a language in which to define such constraints. For example, the constraint that an employee's assessment may be seen only by the employee's department manager might be written as follows:

```
    RELATION DEPARTMENT (DEPT#, MGR#,...)
                      .
                      .
                      .
    RELATION EMPLOYEE (EMP#,...DEPT#,...ASSESSMENT)
                      .
                      .
                      .
          CONSTRAINT FOR GET (EMP#,ASSESSMENT)
                     RANGE DEPARTMENT D
                     ∃D(D.MGR#=user.EMP#
                       ∧D.DEPT#=EMPLOYEE.DEPT#)
```

Here "user.EMP#" refers to the employee number given in the appropriate user profile.)

In general, an access constraint may refer to any data whatsoever in the entire database. We assume, therefore, that there exists a highly privileged and protected program called the *arbiter* (part of the DBMS), whose function is to check each user request for access and to grant or deny permission, as appropriate, and which has unconstrained access to the entire database. On the basis of the combination (X, say) of user identification and operation requested,[4] the arbiter will go through a series of tests to determine whether to grant or deny access. Codd [23.1] has identified 14 distinct tests that may be necessary in the general case; they are arranged in a sequence of increasing complexity, so that the arbiter may reach its final decision as quickly as possible (the sequence may differ between installations). A possible sequence (based on [23.1]) is shown in Fig. 23.1. Note that each test after the first is performed only if the preceding test gives the result NO; the arbiter's final decision is reached as soon as a test gives a result of YES. Note, too, that some tests will involve the user profile, others (perhaps the majority) the access constraints associated with the relation concerned.

---

[4] The operation requested may include the application of statistical functions, such as AVERAGE.

Test number	Action if Yes
1. Are all *relations* mentioned in the request unconditionally accessible to X?	Grant
2. Is there a *relation* mentioned in the request unconditionally prohibited to X?	Deny
3. Are all *generations* mentioned in the request unconditionally accessible to X?	Grant
4. Is there a *generation* mentioned in the request unconditionally prohibited to X?	Deny
5. Are all attributes mentioned in the request unconditionally accessible to X?	Grant
6. Is there an *attribute* mentioned in the request unconditionally prohibited to X?	Deny
7. Are all *attribute combinations* mentioned in the request unconditionally accessible to X?	Grant
8. Is there an *attribute combination* mentioned in the request unconditionally prohibited to X?	Deny
9. For each sensitive attribute combination mentioned in the request, is there a *qualification subexpression* which constrains values of the participating attributes to lie within ranges accessible to X?	Grant
10. Is there a sensitive attribute combination mentioned in the request which has a subcombination whose values are permitted by the *qualification expression* to lie inside the range prohibited to X?	Deny

Fig. 23.1 Security interrogation sequence

The remaining tests are tests on X extended by "indirect attributes of the requestor" [23.1], that is, by information about the user over and above the simple combination of user identification and operation requested (Fig. 23.2). Such "indirect attributes" may consist of a password supplied by the user with the request for access, the result (true or false) of evaluating an access constraint specified in the form of a condition the user must satisfy, or any other information available about the user anywhere in the database.

If all 14 tests give the answer NO, the arbiter should generate an exception code to inform the user that the request is denied because of lack of information in the system (as opposed to being explicitly forbidden).

Test number	Action if Yes
11. Is test 7 satisfied with X extended by indirect attributes of the requestor?	Grant
12. Is test 8 satisfied with X extended by indirect attributes of the requestor?	Deny
13. Is test 9 satisfied with X extended by indirect attributes of the requestor?	Grant
14. Is test 10 satisfied with X extended by indirect attributes of the requestor?	Deny

Fig. 23.2 Security interrogation sequence continued

It is worth noting four simple "security axioms" [23.1] which define some restrictions on the access constraints that can sensibly be specified, and which also indicate some economies that could be made within these specifications as they appear in the dictionary. The axioms follow.

- If attribute combination A is accessible to X subject to condition C, then every subcombination of A is conditionally accessible to X, and so far as X is concerned, no condition for any subcombination can be stronger than C.

- If attribute combination A is prohibited to X under condition C, then every attribute combination containing A as a subcombination is conditionally prohibited to X, and so far as X is concerned, no condition for any supercombination can be weaker than C.

- If user U is allowed to HOLD attribute combination A subject to condition C, then U is conditionally allowed to GET A, and the condition concerned cannot be stronger than C.

- If user U is unconditionally forbidden to GET attribute combination A, then U is unconditionally forbidden to HOLD A.

As an illustration of this general discussion of access control principles, we draw the reader's attention to a paper by Owens [23.8], which describes the security features of MacAIMS [11.13 and 11.14]. In this system four levels of access are provided: null (prohibits all access), manipulate (permits the application of relational algebra operations, e.g., join, union), statistical (permits the application of statistical functions, such as AVERAGE), and print (permits retrieval). The creator of a relation—or anyone else authorized to do so—may specify access constraints for that relation for each level of access. The constraints may require that a password be supplied, they may specify sensitive attribute combinations or sensitive attribute values, and they may involve attributes of the requestor. Thus we have here a system in which several of the ideas discussed in this section have been (independently) developed and implemented.

We conclude this section by describing briefly the security aspects of three relational systems: Query By Example, System R, and INGRES.

Query By Example

As mentioned in Chapter 8, *all* operations in Query By Example are specified by making entries in skeleton tables. "Operations" here includes not only ordinary retrieval and storage operations, but also the specification of security constraints (and integrity constraints too, as explained in the next chapter). We showed in Section 8.6 how the ordinary query facilities of Query By Example could be used to retrieve information from the dictionary. In the same fashion, the ordinary insert facilities may be used to specify security and integrity constraints, since such specifications really involve the insertion of new information into the dictionary. The basic operator used in such specifications is thus "INSERT." (abbreviated "I."). In the case of security constraints the keyword "AUTR" (authorize) is used to indicate the nature of the information to be inserted. We show in Fig. 23.3 specifications corresponding to some of the examples from the list in Section 23.1. For more information the reader is referred to [8.6].

System R

The System R authorization mechanism is based on the concept of the *view*. Recall from Chapter 10 that SEQUEL (the principal language for interacting with System R) includes a comprehensive view definition facility; in fact, a view can be any relation derivable from the base relations by means of a SEQUEL query. As pointed out in Section 10.6, we can easily protect secure data from a user not authorized to access it by simply ensuring that that data does not appear in that user's view. Considering the EMPLOYEE relation of Section 23.1 once again, for example, we might define views as follows.

a) For a user allowed access to the EMPLOYEE relation but not to the SALARY, DATE, and ASSESSMENT attributes:

```
DEFINE VIEW BASICINFO AS
        SELECT EMP#, NAME, ADDRESS, DEPT#
        FROM    EMPLOYEE
```

EMPLOYEE		EMP#	NAME	ADDRESS	DEPT#	SALARY	DATE	ASSESSMENT	Comments
I.AUTR.X	I.	EX	NX	ADDRX	DX	SX	TX	ASMTX	User X has unconstrained access to entire table for all operations
I.AUTR(P.).Y	I.	EY	NY	ADDRY	DY				User Y can see (PRINT) only EMP#, NAME, ADDRESS, DEPT#
I.AUTR(U.).Y	I.		NY	ADDRY					User Y can change (UPDATE) NAME and ADDRESS
I.AUTR(P.).Z	I.	Z	NZ	ADDRZ	DZ	SZ	TZ	ASMTZ	Users can see only their own tuples
I.AUTR(U.).W	I.					SW < 5000			User W can change SALARY only if currently < 5000

Fig. 23.3 Sample security constraints in Query By Example

b) For a user allowed access only to EMPLOYEE tuples for employees belonging to the department for which the user is the manager:

```
DEFINE VIEW MYEMPS AS
        SELECT *
        FROM    EMPLOYEE
        WHERE   DEPT#=
                SELECT DEPT#
                FROM    DEPARTMENT
                WHERE   MGR#=USER
```

USER is a special SEQUEL keyword referring to the identification number in the user profile.

c) For a user allowed access only to average salary by department, not to individual salaries:

```
DEFINE VIEW AVGSALS AS
        SELECT DEPT#, AVG(SALARY)
        FROM    EMPLOYEE
        GROUP   BY DEPT#
```

As these examples illustrate, a given user may easily be restricted to a vertical subset, a horizontal subset, or a statistical summary of a given relation. In fact, however, the System R security scheme is considerably more sophisticated than this. Basically what happens is the following. When a given user creates a new base relation, he or she has full access rights to that relation—including the right to define views on it—and no one else has any rights to it at all. If this user wishes to share the new relation, or some view of it, with other users, then he or she must explicitly grant appropriate access rights to those other users, using the SEQUEL GRANT operation. The syntax of GRANT is

$$
\text{GRANT} \left\{ \begin{array}{l} \text{ALL RIGHTS} \\ \text{rights} \\ \text{ALL BUT rights} \end{array} \right\} \text{ON table TO users}
$$

where "rights" includes READ, INSERT, DELETE, and UPDATE; "table" may be a base relation or a view; and "users" is a list of one or more users, or the special keyword PUBLIC (meaning all users). Thus it is possible to grant, not just the right to see certain data, but more specifically the right to perform certain designated operations on that data.

It is also possible to REVOKE rights previously granted. For more information on REVOKE and on other aspects of the System R authorization mechanism—in particular, for details of other possible access rights—see [23.17], [7.6], and [7.7].

INGRES

INGRES, like System R, also provides a comprehensive view definition facility; however, it does not employ views as such to deal with authorization. Instead it enforces security by dynamically modifying the user's access requests, appending an access constraint predicate to the request before attempting to satisfy it [23.13]. This process may be thought of as a very dynamic method of defining views for access control purposes. We give a single example to illustrate the procedure.

Suppose that some particular user is allowed to access only those EMPLOYEE tuples for employees in department D8. The user profile for this user, then, will include the following access constraint (expressed in QUEL [5.8–5.11], the INGRES data sublanguage).

```
RANGE OF EX IS EMPLOYEE
RETRIEVE ... (EX) WHERE EX.DEPT#='D8'
```

Now suppose the user issues the following QUEL request (which is an attempt to retrieve salaries for all employees earning more than two thousand dollars a month).

```
RANGE OF EY IS EMPLOYEE
RETRIEVE INTO W (EY.EMP#, EY.SALARY)
              WHERE EY.SALARY>2000
```

INGRES will convert the request into the following form.

```
RANGE OF EY IS EMPLOYEE
RETRIEVE INTO W (EY.EMP#, EY.SALARY)
              WHERE EY.SALARY>2000
              AND    EY.DEPT# ='D8'
```

The result of executing this RETRIEVE will be to return the information the user wants, but only for employees in department D8.

23.4 SECURITY IN IMS

As explained in Chapter 14, all access from a program to an IMS database is via the appropriate program communication block (PCB). This immediately provides two levels of protection: First, the program cannot access "nonsensitive" segments at all (except that deleting a parent will cause deletion of all corresponding children, regardless of whether they are sensitive or not); second, the program is constrained to those operations defined by the PROCOPT entries in the PCB. (In fact, of course, the PCB is the IMS analogue of the System R view definition.)

Further security control is provided if the data communications feature is installed. First, it is possible to specify that certain (application) programs may be invoked and certain (system) commands issued from designated terminals only; second, it is possible to specify that a password must be supplied to invoke certain programs or to issue certain commands.

23.5 SECURITY IN DBTG

In a DBTG system all access from a program to the database is via the sub-schema, which, like the PCB in IMS, immediately provides automatic security for "hidden data." (In DBTG, incidentally, unlike IMS, this applies to delete operations as well.) A significant difference between the PCB and the sub-schema is that there is no "PROCOPT" information in the sub-schema; thus it is not possible to detect security violations until execution time (in theory, IMS could detect some violations at translation time, although at present it does not).

In addition to the protection afforded by the sub-schema, DBTG provides a comprehensive set of facilities based on ACCESS CONTROL LOCKs and ACCESS CONTROL KEYs (originally called PRIVACY LOCKs and PRIVACY KEYs). Figure 23.4 is a simple example of the way in which these facilities can be used.

In this example a character-string literal has been declared in the schema as the access control lock on deletion for record type S. A program that wishes to perform such an operation must supply a matching access control key, by moving the appropriate value into the special register DB-ACCESS-CONTROL-KEY. Initialization of DB-ACCESS-CONTROL-KEY must be done in a USE FOR ACCESS CONTROL procedure, which will be invoked when the relevant realm is readied. After the procedure has been executed the DBMS will compare the lock and the key. If they are equal, the program will be allowed to perform the operation concerned. If they are not equal, an attempt to perform this operation will result in an "access control exception" code being placed in DB-STATUS.

In general, an access control lock may be defined as a literal (as in Fig. 23.4), as a data-item (i.e., a variable), or as a procedure. In the case of a data-item, the data-item concerned is considered to be implicitly declared as a "lock item" with a format defined by the implementation; the lock itself is the value of this data-item at the time the realm is readied, and it is this value that is compared with the key.[5] In the case of a procedure, it is the result of invoking the procedure with the key as an argument that determines whether the operation is to be allowed; the procedure may

---

[5] It is not clear from [19.10] how a value can be assigned to the lock item.

```
Schema:    RECORD NAME IS S;
               .
               .
               .
           ACCESS CONTROL LOCK FOR DELETE IS 'NJAL'...
Program:   PROCEDURE DIVISION.
           DECLARATIVES.
           USE FOR ACCESS CONTROL ON ERASE FOR S.
               MOVE 'NJAL' TO DB-ACCESS-CONTROL-KEY.
               .
               .
               .
           END DECLARATIVES.
               .
               .
               .
           ERASE S.
```

Fig. 23.4 ACCESS CONTROL LOCKs and KEYs (example)

return a "yes" or a "no," or it may take any other action desired by the implementation.

An access control lock may also be specified as a sequence of literals and/or lock items and/or procedures, connected by ORs. Such a lock is considered to be satisfied as soon as one member of the sequence is satisfied (the testing is performed in left-to-right order). Also, one AC-CESS CONTROL LOCK clause may specify several distinct operations (e.g., INSERT, REMOVE, DELETE,...), all to be protected by the same lock. Access control keys may also be defined to cover a number of separate operations. Figure 23.5 is a summary of the protection provided by access control locks and keys.

For the *schema*, the functions that may be controlled are ALTER (make alterations to the schema itself), DISPLAY (display the schema), LOCKS (display the access control locks in the schema), and COPY

Schema	Sub-schema	Area	Record	Set
ALTER	ALTER	RETRIEVAL	DELETE	FIND
DISPLAY	DISPLAY	-PROTECTED	FIND	INSERT
LOCKS	LOCKS	-EXCLUSIVE	GET	ORDER
COPY	COMPILE	UPDATE	INSERT	REMOVE
		-PROTECTED	MODIFY	
		-EXCLUSIVE	REMOVE	
		support	STORE	
		functions		

Fig. 23.5 Functions subject to DBTG access control

(define a sub-schema on the basis of the schema); here the corresponding access control key must be specified within the relevant utility program (for ALTER/DISPLAY/LOCKS) or in the relevant sub-schema (for COPY). Similarly, the *sub-schema* may include locks against ALTER, DIS-PLAY, LOCKS (display the access control locks in the sub-schema—see below), or COMPILE (invoke the sub-schema from an application pro-gram); here the corresponding access control key must again be specified in the relevant utility (for ALTER/DISPLAY/LOCKS) or in the relevant application program (for COMPILE).

For *areas* (or realms), locks may be provided for each of the six possible USAGE-MODEs (RETRIEVAL/UPDATE, PROTECTED RE-TRIEVAL/UPDATE, EXCLUSIVE RETRIEVAL/UPDATE). Locks may also be provided for implementation-defined "support func-tions" (such as area reorganization, for example, which might be per-formed by a support utility).

For *records*, locks may be provided for each of the DML statements that take a record occurrence as their operand, except KEEP, FREE, and REMONITOR (see Chapter 24). In addition, individual data-items[6] may be locked against GET, MODIFY, and STORE operations. (There seems to be a slight anomaly here, since it is not possible to STORE an individual data-item.) Finally, for *sets*, locks may be provided for each of the DML statements that include a set-name as one of their arguments.

For all the cases above, except that of area "support functions," access control keys are specified in the application program, and access control locks in the schema or alternatively in the sub-schema. If a given operation has a lock specified in both the schema and the sub-schema, the schema lock is ignored (although in such a situation it would seem preferable to ignore the sub-schema lock instead).

23.6   BYPASSING THE SYSTEM

The techniques outlined so far in this chapter are not sufficient to protect the database against an infiltrator who attempts to bypass the system. The most obvious example of bypassing the system involves a user—for convenience we retain this term although it is somewhat inappropriate for a would-be infiltrator—who physically removes part of the database, e.g., by stealing a disk pack. Apart from normal security measures to prevent unauthorized personnel from entering the computer center, the most effective safeguard against this threat is the use of scrambling techniques

---

[6] Or data-aggregates. A data-aggregate is a named collection of data-items within a record. Two types of data-aggregate may be specified in the schema DDL, vectors and repeating groups; see [19.10].

(also referred to as "encryption" and "privacy transformations" [23.19]). If sensitive data is recorded in the database in a scrambled form, a user who succeeds in accessing the data other than via the system is faced with the problem of unscrambling it; ideally, the scrambling technique employed (see below) should be such that the "work factor" involved in unscrambling far outweighs the potential advantage to be gained [23.5].

Several scrambling techniques exist. One of the simplest (and least secure) merely involves shuffling the characters of each tuple (or record or message...) into a different order. A more sophisticated technique involves the replacement of each character (or group of characters) by a different character (or group of characters), from the same alphabet or a different one. Probably the most generally satisfactory are the so-called additive techniques, in which groups of characters are algebraically combined in some way with a special group of characters (the privacy key) supplied by the owner of the data. The accepted ultimate objective for the design of such a method is that the inventor of the method, holding matching scrambled and unscrambled texts, should be unable to determine the privacy key (and consequently unable to unscramble another piece of scrambled text).

In a system including remote terminals, *wiretapping* in various forms constitutes another threat. As Petersen and Turn [23.9] point out, the communication lines are actually the most vulnerable part of the system. Using only comparatively inexpensive equipment, an infiltrator could monitor all communication between a genuine user and the database, discover passwords (for example), and thus be able to masquerade as that user to the system on a subsequent occasion. By tapping a special terminal into a communication line, an infiltrator could (a) cancel a genuine user's sign-off signals in order to continue operating in the user's name; (b) perform "between lines" entry to the system while a genuine user is holding the line but is inactive; (c) perform "piggy-back" entry to the system by selectively intercepting communications between a genuine user and the system and then releasing them with modifications. The single countermeasure against all these possibilities again involves scrambling, this time of data transmitted down the communication line. The scrambling and unscrambling functions must now of course be performed at the remote terminal, perhaps by special software if the terminal is programmable, otherwise by hardware.

EXERCISE

23.1 Design a DBTG system that will allow a user at the operator's console to display an employee's salary if and only if the user is either the employee concerned or that employee's immediate manager. You should write the schema and the enquiry program (at least in outline), incorporating whatever security checking you think necessary. You may assume that the user's own employee number (ascertained during the identification/authentication procedure) is given in the data-item location USERNO. You may ignore the sub-schema. (*Note:* Base your answer on the "managerial structure" schema of Exercise 20.2.)

REFERENCES AND BIBLIOGRAPHY

See also [1.1], [1.2], [12.1] (for IMS), and [19.8 and 19.9] (for DBTG).

23.1 E. F. Codd. "Access Control Principles for Security and Privacy in Integrated Data Banks." IBM internal memo (July 1970). Presented in somewhat revised form as part of "Access Control for Relational Data Base Systems" at BCS Symposium on Relational Database Concepts, London (5 April 1973).

23.2 R. W. Conway, W. L. Maxwell, and H. L. Morgan. "On the Implementation of Security Measures in Information Systems." *CACM* **15,** No. 4 (April 1972).

> This paper starts with a general discussion of the problem of security, introducing the concept of the "security matrix." The columns of this matrix represent data structures (files, records, fields, field combinations, etc.) in the system; the rows represent potential users of the system. The element $D[i, j]$ of the matrix specifies the level of access permitted for user i to data structure j. A functional model of a security system based on this matrix is then presented, and several implemented systems are described in terms of this model, in particular a system called ASAP which was implemented by the authors. Much emphasis is placed on the possibility of making access control decisions at translation time rather than at execution time (since many such decisions are based on the *names* of data structures, not their values); however, the distinction would seem to be a useful one only in a batch environment, not in an on-line situation.

23.3 R. C. Daley and P. G. Neumann. "A General Purpose File System for Secondary Storage." *Proc. FJCC* **27** (1965).

> A description of the Multics file system, including detailed consideration of the access control facilities. The database is viewed as a file hierarchy, in which the terminal nodes are data files and all other nodes are directory files. Access control is handled by associating a list with each node that specifies all permitted users of the file at that node and each user's permitted "modes" (write, read only, etc.). (In other words, the system employs "file profiles" rather than "user profiles.") The hierarchical structure presumably allows factoring to be applied to the access control lists (that is, an entry common to all nodes subordinate to some given node may be factored out and placed at the given node).

23.4 A. L. Dean, Jr. "Data Privacy and Integrity Requirements for Online Data Management Systems." *Proc. 1971 ACM SIGFIDET Workshop on Data Description, Access and Control.* Available from ACM.

This paper consists of a detailed statement of the requirements that should be met by a generalized on-line database management system in the areas of both security and integrity. It examines the hardware, operating system, and application programs within such a system and indicates in each case the security and integrity features which that component of the system should provide.

23.5 L. J. Hoffman. "Computers and Privacy: A Survey." *Computing Surveys* **1,** No. 2 (June 1969).

The four sections of this paper are (a) "The privacy problem," a discussion of the potential dangers inherent in "the databank society"; (b) "Legal and administrative safeguards," a review of the legal position; (c) "Technical methods proposed to date" (the longest section), a discussion much along the lines of the present chapter; and (d) "Promising research problems." A useful annotated bibliography is included.

23.6 D. K. Hsiao. "Access Control in an On-Line File System." In *File Organization*, IAG Occasional Publication No. 3 (Selected Papers from File 68: an IAG conference). Swets and Zietlinger N.V., Amsterdam (1969).

This paper describes the file management component of the Problem Solving Facility of the Moore School of Electrical Engineering (University of Pennsylvania). In this system the problem of identification/authentication is handled by allowing the owner of any given file to supply a log-in program that is to be invoked whenever any user attempts to open the file. In addition, the system maintains an "authority item" (user profile) for each user. The authority item gives details of all files that the user concerned is allowed to access, together with the permitted mode of use (read only, read and write, etc.) for each. Moreover, for each file listed as accessible in a given authority item, further conditions may also be stated in the authority item restricting the records from that file that the user concerned may access (e.g., all those with a value in a specified field less than some limit). Thus this is an example (the first?) of a working system in which access control is applied below the file level. The conditions that may be stated appear to be limited to comparison expressions (with the usual Boolean and comparison operators) involving fields of the file and constants; i.e., they cannot involve "attributes of the requestor." A disadvantage of the system seems to be that the same access control information may appear in many distinct authority items.

23.7 J. Martin and A. R. D. Norman. *The Computerized Society.* Englewood Cliffs, N.J.: Prentice-Hall (1970); Pelican Books (1973).

A thorough and comprehensive survey of the effect computers are likely to have on society in the next fifteen years. The book is divided into three parts: "Euphoria," in which the many advantages are imaginatively described; "Alarm," in which the nature of the threat to privacy (among other problems) is spelled out in detail; and "Protective action," in which possible safeguards (technical and legislative) are examined and various recommendations made. The chapters on privacy are particularly good. Strongly recommended.

23.8 R. C. Owens, Jr. "Evaluation of Access Authorization Characteristics of Derived Data Sets." *Proc. 1971 ACM SIGFIDET Workshop on Data Description, Access and Control.* Available from ACM.

23.9 H. E. Petersen and R. Turn. "System Implications of Information Privacy." *Proc. SJCC* **30** (1967).

> An outstanding survey. Much of the material in the present chapter is taken from this paper.

23.10 J. H. Saltzer and M. D. Schroeder. "A Hardware Architecture for Implementing Protection Rings." *CACM* **15,** No. 3 (March 1972).

> A description of the security mechanism employed in the Multics segmented virtual memory system and a method of implementing this mechanism in hardware. An extremely interesting paper, but not specifically about file security as such. See also the related paper [23.3].

23.11 Younger Committee (the Committee on Privacy). *Report* (July 1972), Cmmd.5012. Her Majesty's Stationery Office, London.

> The Committee on Privacy (chairman, the Rt. Hon. Kenneth Younger) was set up in May 1970 "to consider whether legislation is needed to give further protection to the individual citizen and to commercial and industrial interests against intrusions into privacy by private persons and organizations or by companies, and to make recommendations." Note that the terms of reference did not include threats to privacy from government bodies. The committee was unable to agree on a definition of privacy and thus could not recommend the establishment of legislation to ensure a general right to privacy; however, it did lay down a set of ten principles, which should be of assistance in preventing possible abuses.
>
> 1. Information should be regarded as held for a specific purpose and not be used, without appropriate authorization, for other purposes.
> 2. Access to information should be confined to those authorized to have it for the purpose for which it was supplied.
> 3. The amount of information collected and held should be the minimum necessary for the achievement of the specified purpose.
> 4. In computerized systems handling information for statistical purposes, adequate provision should be made in their design and programs for separating identities from the rest of the data.
> 5. There should be arrangements whereby the subject could be told about the information held concerning him.
> 6. The level of security to be achieved by a system should be specified in advance by the user and should include precautions against the deliberate abuse or misuse of information.
> 7. A monitoring system should be provided to facilitate the detection of any violation of the security system.
> 8. In the design of information systems, periods should be specified beyond which the information should not be retained.

9. Data held should be accurate. There should be machinery for the correction of inaccuracy and the updating of information.

10. Care should be taken in coding value judgments.

23.12 J. Martin. *Security, Accuracy, and Privacy in Computer Systems.* Englewood Cliffs, N.J.: Prentice-Hall (1973).

A thorough and exhaustive survey of all aspects of the problem.

23.13 M. Stonebraker and E. Wong. "Access Control in a Relational Data Base Management System by Query Modification." *Proc. ACM National Conference 1974.*

23.14 D. E. Avison and T. Crowe. "Computers and Privacy." *Comp. Bull. Series* **2,** No. 7 (March 1976).

A useful brief summary of legislation and related activities.

23.15 I. S. Herschberg. "Case Studies in Breaking the Security of Time-Sharing Systems." In *Proc. IBM Data Security Symposium* (April 1973). IBM Form No. G520–2838.

An entertaining description of how security was deliberately breached in a number of (unspecified!) systems. In all cases it proved possible to breach the system while acting as a legitimate user, using only publicly available information, and leaving absolutely no trace of the intrusion. The writer concludes that suppliers' claims with respect to the security of their systems should not be taken at face value, but that a community of sophisticated users intent on finding possible breaches and informing suppliers of them may eventually be a major force behind the provision of truly secure systems.

23.16 J. G. Bergart, M. Denicoff, and D. K. Hsiao. "An Annotated and Cross-Referenced Bibliography on Computer Security and Access Control in Computer Systems." Technical Report OSU-CISRC-TR-72-12, Computer and Information Science Research Center, Ohio State University, Columbus, Ohio 43210 (November 1972).

An excellent survey of published material in the field prior to 1973.

23.17 P. P. Griffiths and B. W. Wade. "An Authorization Mechanism for a Relational Data Base System." *ACM Transactions on Database Systems* **1,** No. 3 (September 1976).

See also [10.2], [7.6], and [7.7].

23.18 E. B. Fernandez, R. C. Summers, and C. D. Coleman. "Access Control in a Shared Data Base." IBM Technical Report G320-2666 (December 1974). IBM Los Angeles Scientific Center, 1930 Century Park West, Los Angeles, CA 90067. A somewhat revised version of this paper, under the title "An Authorization Model for a Shared Data Base," is available in *Proc. 1975 ACM SIGMOD International Conference on the Management of Data.*

Presents a very general scheme for dealing with access control. The scheme makes use of an access matrix, which may be seen as a generalization of the security matrix of [23.2]. The "users" may be specified application programs or individual users using these programs (and the system guarantees consistency between entries for an application and entries for users of that application); also the "level of access" specified in the matrix may contain simple predicates to control access still further. Emphasis is on access from a high-level language and hence on compile-time checking. Algorithms are presented for propagating access rights through different levels of data aggregation. The paper includes a number of examples illustrating ways in which the proposed scheme could be used.

23.19 R. Turn. "Privacy Transformations for Databank Systems." *Proc. NCC* (1973).

24
Integrity

24.1 INTRODUCTION

The problem of integrity is the problem of ensuring—insofar as it can be ensured—that the data in the database is accurate at all times. There is a limit on the extent to which this objective can be achieved. In particular, the system cannot check the correctness of every individual value entered into the database (although it clearly can check each such value for *plausibility*). For example, there may be no way of detecting the fact that an input value of 35 (for hours worked, say) should really be 33; on the other hand, a value of 350 would obviously be in error, and the system should reject it. Apart from limitations of this nature, however, it should be possible—and it is certainly desirable—to maintain a high degree of integrity in the database. In this chapter we examine this topic in some detail. As in the previous chapter, our basic approach is to consider the problem in general terms first, taking a relational system as the basis for our discussions; we then describe the relevant features of IMS and DBTG.

Maintaining the integrity of the database can be viewed as protecting the data against invalid (as opposed to illegal) alteration or destruction. Integrity is thus distinct from security, although the two topics are closely allied, and indeed the same mechanism may be used to achieve the preservation of both, at least to some extent. For example, a DBTG ACCESS CONTROL LOCK procedure could be used to ensure not only that a given operation is authorized but also that it is not violating any integrity constraint. In general, each relation in the database will have a set of integrity constraints associated with it; like security constraints, integrity constraints will be held in the data dictionary as part of the conceptual schema. Typical constraints will specify, for example, that values of a particular attribute in some relation are to lie within certain bounds, or that within each tuple of some relation the value of one attribute may not exceed that of another (e.g., consider attributes QTYOUT and QTYORD in the solution to Exercise 9.2). We discuss such constraints in more detail in Section 24.2.

Maintaining integrity in accordance with constraints such as those above is a difficult enough problem (and one with which there is not really very much experience) in a "single-user" system—i.e., one in which no more than one user may be operating on the database at any one time. In a "multiple-user" system—i.e., one in which many users may access the database concurrently—an additional complication arises, namely, the problem of control over data sharing. Several difficulties can occur. For example, if two users are allowed to <u>HOLD</u> the same tuple concurrently, the first of the two subsequent <u>UPDATE</u> operations will be nullified by the second, since the effect of the second will be to overwrite the result of the first (in other words, the first user's update will be lost). Such problems are discussed in more detail in Section 24.3.

In general, loss of integrity may be caused by any of the following: hardware failure at any point in the system (e.g., at a central processor, on a data channel, or at an input/output device); human error on the part of the computer operator or a terminal user; programming errors within the DBMS or the underlying operating system; programming errors in one of the database applications. It follows that situations of lost integrity may occur even in the best-regulated of systems, since one or another of these errors is bound to occur from time to time, no matter how thorough the controls are. It is important, therefore, to be able to detect such situations when they arise and to be able to recover from them. This will require a comprehensive set of support routines, probably somewhat separate from the main body of the DBMS. These routines are discussed briefly in Section 24.4.

24.2 INTEGRITY CONSTRAINTS

As mentioned in the previous section, each relation will have a set of integrity constraints associated with it. These constraints may in theory be of arbitrary complexity, although in practice many of them will be fairly simple. Once again, predicate calculus notation, or some other notation of equivalent expressive power (e.g., SEQUEL), could serve as a basis for the definition of such constraints; however, for the simpler cases some simpler method of definition would probably prove more suitable. These simpler methods may be viewed as a shorthand for the corresponding predicates.

In this section we present some examples of the types of constraint it may be necessary to specify in various situations, and we consider briefly the implications for the DBMS. We assume, incidentally, that an authorized user may define a new integrity constraint at any time. On receipt of a new constraint, the DBMS should check to see if it is satisfied by the current contents of the database: If not, it should reject the constraint; otherwise it should enter it into the dictionary and enforce it from that point on.

1. By definition the primary key of any relation possesses the property of uniqueness: No two tuples in the relation may have the same value for this attribute or attribute combination. It is also usual to insist that no component of a primary key value may be null (see [24.1] for a detailed discussion of null data values). The KEY entry in the definition of the relation is sufficient to specify both these constraints. To enforce them, the DBMS must reject any attempt (via a PUT or UPDATE operation)[1] to generate a tuple whose key value is null or partly null, or is a duplicate of one that already exists.

2. If a relation contains any further candidate keys in addition to the primary key, an entry such as UNIQUE(A)—where A is the attribute or attribute combination concerned—may be used to specify that fact. Examples of UNIQUE have already been given in Section 9.4. The first of the examples in that section, in which the entry UNIQUE(SNAME) is used to define SNAME as a candidate key for relation S, could equivalently be expressed in a predicate calculus notation as follows.

```
RELATION S (S#,SNAME,STATUS,CITY)
         KEY (S#)
           .
           .
           .
         CONSTRAINT
           RANGE S SX
           RANGE S SY
           ∀SX∀SY(SX.SNAME=SY.SNAME
                ⇒SX.S#=SY.S#)
```

3. Functional dependencies represent another form of integrity constraint. If the relation concerned is in third (or preferably fourth) normal

---

[1] We assume here that UPDATE is allowed for the primary key.

form, the KEY and UNIQUE entries are sufficient between them to specify all such dependencies: By definition, every attribute not participating in a given candidate key in such a relation is functionally dependent on that key. If the relation involves any additional dependencies—i.e., if it is not in third normal form—then some further entry, say a DEPENDS entry, will be required to specify such dependencies. For example, the definition of relation FIRST (see Fig. 9.4 in Chapter 9) would have to include the entry CITY DEPENDS S#.

To enforce constraints such as those of the last two examples, the DBMS will again have to monitor PUT and UPDATE operations. The same is true of the next four cases, except that these are somewhat simpler to handle: Each one involves no more than a check against the single tuple concerned, whereas the first three cases above involve checking an entire *set* of tuples. To distinguish the two types of constraint we will refer to tuple constraints and set constraints, as appropriate.

4. Functional dependencies are not the only dependencies that may exist among the attributes of a given relation. For example, within each tuple of the relation ORDLINE (see the solution to Exercise 9.2), the QTYOUT value must not exceed the QTYORD value. Such a constraint may be specified by means of an appropriate comparison expression (i.e., a simple predicate).

5. Values occurring in a particular attribute may be required to lie within certain bounds (e.g., values of SP.QTY must be greater than zero; values of EMPLOYEE.AGE must be greater than 15 and less than 66). Such constraints may be specified by a BOUNDS entry in which a lower limit or an upper limit (or both) may be defined. Disjoint pairs of bounds could be specified in a single BOUNDS entry. For example, BOUNDS $(0:9, 20:29)$ could specify that for each value ν of the relevant attribute, $0 \le \nu \le 9$ *or* $20 \le \nu \le 29$.

6. There may be a very small set of permitted values for some particular attribute or attribute combination. For example, permitted values for P.COLOR are 'RED', 'BLUE', 'GREEN', and so on. In such a case the permitted values could simply be listed in a VALUES entry for the relevant attribute or attribute combination. (VALUES is really a degenerate case of BOUNDS.)

As a variation on BOUNDS and VALUES, it might be desirable to list values or ranges of values that are *not* permissible for the attribute(s) concerned.

7. Values of a particular attribute may have to conform to a particular format. For example, the first character of a supplier number must be the

letter S, say. Such a constraint may be specified in a FORMAT entry for the relevant attribute.

8. The set of values of a particular attribute of a particular relation may have to satisfy some "statistical" constraint. For example, no employee may earn a salary that is more than twice the average salary for the department (another example of a set constraint, incidentally). The predicate defining this constraint will clearly involve the library function AVERAGE. To enforce it the DBMS will have to monitor all storage operations against the employee relation (not just PUT and UPDATE, but DELETE as well).

9. The set of values appearing in a particular column within one relation may be required to be the same as, or a subset of, the set of values appearing in some other column, in the same relation or in a different one. (The two columns concerned should be defined on the same underlying domain.) For example, any value appearing in SP.S# should also appear in S.S#, to reflect the obvious real-world constraint that only a supplier who actually exists should be allowed to supply parts.

Once again this is an example of a set constraint, this time involving two distinct relations. The DBMS will have to monitor both PUT and UPDATE operations on SP and DELETE and UPDATE operations on S. It follows that the specification of such a constraint should not be tied too closely to the definition of any individual relation.

10. All the examples given so far are of *static* constraints; that is, they specify conditions that must hold for every given state of the database. Another important type of constraint involves *transitions* from one state to another. For example, when an employee's salary is updated, the new value must be greater than the old value (a tuple constraint); or the new average salary must not exceed the old average salary by more than five percent (a set constraint). To specify such constraints we will need a means of referring to the old and new values (in SEQUEL, for example, the keywords OLD and NEW are reserved for this purpose).

11. A special case of transition is that from nonexistence to existence (i.e., PUT of a new tuple) or from existence to nonexistence (i.e., DELETE of an existing tuple). An example of a constraint applying to such a transition might be as follows: When an account tuple is deleted, the balance value must be zero. Keywords such as OLD and NEW are inadequate to specify constraints such as this one; rather, we need to be able to specify *when* the constraint is to be applied, i.e., the particular operations that should cause the check to be made (in the example, the operation is deletion of an account tuple).

In general it may always be desirable, even if it is not strictly necessary, to specify the operations causing a particular constraint to be applied, for documentation purposes and for reasons of efficiency if for nothing else.

12. Our last example illustrates the concept of the *deferred* constraint. First we introduce the important notion of "transaction." A transaction is a unit of work that is *atomic* from the point of view of the enterprise. For example, in a banking system, a typical transaction might be "transfer amount X from account A to account B." The user of this system—the bank clerk—would view this as a single operation; typically, to cause the operation to take place, all such a user would have to do would be to enter a command such as

TRANSFER X=100 A=462351 B=901554

at the terminal. However, this transaction (like most others, apart from pure queries) requires several changes to be made to the underlying database; specifically, it involves updating the balance value in two distinct account tuples. Although the database is in a state of integrity before and after this sequence of changes, it is clear that it may *not* be throughout the entire transaction; that is, some of the intermediate states (or transitions) may violate one or more integrity constraints.

It follows that there is a need to be able to specify that certain constraints should not be checked until the end of a transaction. We call such constraints *deferred*. By contrast, constraints that are enforced continuously, including during the intermediate steps of a transaction, are called *immediate*.

It also follows from the foregoing that the data sublanguage must include some means of signalling the end of a transaction, in order to cause the DBMS to apply the deferred checks. (Of course, the signal could simply be termination of the program.)

This completes our list of examples. We have introduced the ideas of tuple and set constraints, static and transition constraints, and deferred and immediate constraints. (All possible combinations are valid.) We have also indicated that it may be desirable for constraint definitions to include a list of operations which are to cause that constraint to be checked. To conclude this section, we consider briefly the integrity constraint features of three relational systems: Query By Example, System R, and INGRES.

Query By Example

We mentioned in Chapter 23 that integrity constraints in Query By Example are specified by means of skeleton table entries, together with the normal INSERT operation ("I."). Query By Example provides analogues of every one of Examples 1–12 above; however, it makes no explicit distinction between immediate and deferred constraints, as the following explanation shows. Operations are initiated in Query By Example by the user hitting the "enter" key on the display terminal, which causes an entire screen load of information to be transmitted to the system. Constraints are applied after the operations specified in that screen load have been performed. Note that it is possible to specify several operations within a single screen load; the highly nonprocedural syntax of Query By Example allows the user to formulate a fairly complicated transaction, involving several discrete operations, on the display screen before hitting "enter." The system may therefore execute one or several operations before applying integrity checks, and thus the same constraint may be "immediate" on one occasion and "deferred" on another. We show in Fig. 24.1 some possible constraints for tables S and SP. For more information the reader is referred to [8.6].

System R

The SEQUEL language permits the System R user to define integrity constraints by means of *assertions*, which may be specified at any time (i.e., not just at table definition time). Almost all the constraints given in our list of twelve examples may be handled. The basic form of a SEQUEL assertion is as follows [7.7].

```
ASSERT assertion-name [ON table-name]:predicate
```

We give below SEQUEL assertions corresponding to most of our twelve examples.

1. SEQUEL does not explicitly support the concepts of primary and candidate key; consequently, it does not provide any shorthand predicate to express the fact that a given attribute is such a key. In order to specify that S# is the primary key for S, therefore, it is necessary to assert that the number of distinct values of S.S# is the same as the number of S tuples, and moreover that S.S# is never null.

```
ASSERT A1 ON S:(SELECT COUNT(S#) FROM S)
              =
              (SELECT COUNT(*)  FROM S)
              AND
              S# ¬= NULL
```

2. See previous paragraph.

3. Like Query By Example, SEQUEL has no direct counterpart to

S		S#	SNAME	STATUS	CITY	Comments
I. TYPE.	I.	CHAR	CHAR	FIXED	CHAR	
I. LENGTH.	I.	5	20	3	15	
I. KEY.	I.	K	NK	NK	NK	S# is primary key
I. CONSTR.	I.	ALL.<u>SX</u>	<u>SN</u>			SNAME unique (functionally dependent on S#: see Condition box)
I. CONSTR (I., U.).	I.	ALL.<u>SX</u>	<u>SN</u>			Same as previous, but checks done only on INSERT, UPDATE
I. CONSTR.	I.				LONDON PARIS ATHENS ROME	Permitted values of S.CITY
I. CONSTR (U.).	I.	<u>SX</u>		> <u>ST</u>		When STATUS is updated, new value must be > old value
	I.	<u>SX</u>		<u>ST</u>		
		ALL.<u>SY</u>				See table SP

SP		S#	P#	QTY	
I. CONSTR (I., U.).	I.			≥ 0	SP.QTY must be ≥ 0
I. CONSTR (D.).	I.			= 0	Can DELETE SP tuple only if QTY = 0
I. CONSTR (I.)	I.	ALL.<u>SY</u>			Can INSERT SP tuple only if S# exists in S table

Condition box
COUNT.ALL.<u>SX</u> = 1

See 4th, 5th rows of table S

Fig. 24.1 Sample integrity constraints in Query By Example

<u>DEPENDS</u>. To specify that FIRST.CITY is functionally dependent on FIRST.S#, therefore, we must assert that the number of distinct CITY values corresponding to a given S# value is one. Notice the use of a label (FX) in this assertion.

```
ASSERT A3 ON FIRST FX : (SELECT COUNT(UNIQUE CITY)
                         FROM    FIRST
                         WHERE   S#=FX.S#)=1
```

Of course, assertions such as this one will be unnecessary if all relations are in third or fourth normal form.

4. ASSERT A4 ON ORDLINE : QTYOUT ¬> QTYORD

5. ASSERT A5 ON EMPLOYEE : AGE BETWEEN 15 AND 66

6. ASSERT A6 ON P : COLOR IN ('RED','BLUE','GREEN',...)

7. The only SEQUEL analogue of <u>FORMAT</u> is the column data type, which is specified when the column is initially defined. The only data types supported are character strings (fixed- or variable-length), large and small binary integers, fixed-point decimal numbers, and floating-point numbers.

8. ASSERT A8 ON EMP E : SAL≤2*(SELECT AVG(SAL)
                            FROM   EMP
                            WHERE   DEPT#=E.DEPT#)

9. ASSERT A9 : (SELECT S# FROM SP)
           IS IN
           (SELECT S# FROM S)

   Note here that the assertion is not tied to one particular table.

10. ASSERT A10 ON UPDATE OF EMP(SAL) : NEW SAL>OLD SAL

    Note here that we have specified not only the table concerned but also the operation (UPDATE) and the column (SAL).

11. ASSERT A11 ON DELETION OF ACCOUNT : BALANCE=0

12. In SEQUEL, all integrity constraints are deferred unless the keyword IMMEDIATE is specified after the assertion name.

INGRES

Integrity constraints are specified in INGRES using the language QUEL [24.4 and 24.5]. As an illustration we give below the QUEL equivalent of the SEQUEL assertion A5.

> RANGE OF EX IS EMP
> INTEGRITY EX.AGE>15 AND EX.AGE<66

INGRES does not support transition constraints or deferred constraints, nor does it allow a given constraint to be associated with a specific list of operations. There is no counterpart to <u>FORMAT</u>, except for the column data type—integer, floating, or character—specified when the relation is originally defined; but all other constraints in our original twelve examples—namely, numbers 1–6, 8, and 9—can be specified in QUEL, one way or another.

The interesting aspect of integrity constraints in INGRES, however, is the technique used to implement them. Basically the technique is the same as that used to implement security constraints (see Chapter 23); in other words, the user's request is modified before execution so that it cannot possibly violate any integrity constraints. We give a single example to illustrate the procedure. (The reader is cautioned that this technique cannot be used for constraints involving library functions such as COUNT. For more details see [24.4 and 24.5].)

Required: Add one to the age of employee 427610.

Original QUEL statements:

```
RANGE OF EY IS EMP
REPLACE EY (AGE=AGE+1) WHERE EY.EMP#='427610'
```

After modification:

```
RANGE OF EY IS EMP
REPLACE EY (AGE=AGE+1) WHERE EY.EMP#='427610'
                       AND
                       (EY.AGE+1>15
                       AND
                       EY.AGE+1<66)
```

Hence the age of employee 427610 will be increased only if the new value is still less than 66. In general, if the user attempts to update a set of tuples in a single operation, some tuples will actually be updated and some will not (because updating them would violate an integrity constraint). The user can ask for copies of the latter tuples to be returned to a workspace, FAILURES say, by appending a phrase such as

```
ERRORS TO FAILURES
```

to the original REPLACE statement. In the example above this phrase would cause INGRES to generate the statement

```
RETRIEVE INTO FAILURES (EY.ALL) WHERE EY.EMP#='427610'
                        AND NOT
                        (EY.AGE+1>15
                        AND
                        EY.AGE+1<66)
```

as part of the expansion of the original QUEL statements.

24.3 DATA SHARING

Several problems can arise in connection with the sharing of access to the database. First of all, there is the "lost update" problem mentioned in Section 24.1: If two users are allowed to <u>HOLD</u> the same tuple concurrently, the first of the two subsequent <u>UPDATE</u> operations will have no lasting effect.[2] The usual solution to this problem is to grant the user issuing the first <u>HOLD</u> an "exclusive lock" on the data held. No other user will be allowed to access the data while it is locked to the first user; thus the user issuing the second <u>HOLD</u> will have to wait until the first user releases the lock. (The second user will in turn be granted an exclusive lock on the data. The effect of the second <u>HOLD</u> will be to retrieve the data as updated by the first user.) For a discussion of when locks are released see later in this section.

However, the exclusive locking technique leads in turn to another problem, known variously as deadlock, interlock, or the deadly embrace (a term due to Dijkstra). The following is a simple example of a sequence of events that will give rise to a deadlock situation.

- User A <u>HOLD</u>s tuple T_1.
- User B <u>HOLD</u>s tuple T_2.
- User A attempts to <u>HOLD</u> tuple T_2 (and so has to wait).
- User B attempts to <u>HOLD</u> tuple T_1 (and so has to wait).

Neither user is now able to proceed, and thus we have a deadlock situation. It is evident that deadlocks involving two, three, four, ... users may also arise, in general. There are several techniques for avoiding such situations [24.7]; one of the most common is to insist that no user be allowed to obtain a new lock if that user already holds a lock on some other data. (In other words, the user must request all the locks needed in a single operation—such a request will then be granted only if *all* the data asked for is available.) Unfortunately such techniques are generally not appropriate in the environment of a shared database [24.8]. For example, a user needing to lock two tuples may be unable to identify the second tuple, and hence unable to request a lock for it, until the first tuple has been locked and examined (the identity of the second tuple may be determined by a data value in the first). It follows that a system supporting locking should include a means of detecting and resolving deadlocks (see below).

---

[2] Allowing several users to update the same data concurrently is definitely a requirement in some systems. Consider a theater ticket system, for example, in which agents at several remote locations may be handling bookings and updating the database to record the seats they have sold. It is obviously important not to sell the same seat twice.

In Section 24.2 we introduced the concept of the *transaction*. A transaction is a unit of work with the property that the database (a) is in a consistent state—i.e., a state of integrity—both before it and after it but (b) is possibly *not* in such a state between these two times. In general, then, any changes made to the database during a transaction should not be visible to concurrent transactions until *all* such changes have been made, in order to prevent these concurrent transactions from seeing the database in an inconsistent state. Moreover, if the transaction has to be backed out (see below), any changes it has made will actually be undone—the effect is as if they were never made. Therefore, it becomes even more important that such changes be screened from concurrent transactions until a point is reached, namely, the successful completion of the transaction, at which it can be guaranteed that all updates have been done and will not be undone. From this discussion it follows that any data changed by a given transaction—including data created or destroyed by that transaction—should remain locked until that transaction terminates. This discipline must be enforced by the DBMS.

A transaction will be *backed out* if on completion it is found that the database is not in a state of integrity (i.e., one or more deferred integrity constraints are not satisfied). A transaction may also be backed out if the system detects a deadlock: A general strategy for such a situation is to choose one of the deadlocked transactions, say the one most recently started or the one that has made the fewest changes, and to remove it from the system, thus freeing its locked resources for use by other transactions. (We observe that a transaction may have locked other system resources in addition to data in the database; deadlock is a system-wide problem, not just a database problem.) The process of backout involves undoing all changes that the transaction has made, releasing all resources locked by the transaction, and (if appropriate) scheduling the transaction for re-execution. If the transaction is serving a user at a remote terminal, this process ideally should be completely transparent to that user (except that response time may deteriorate).

So far we have discussed only exclusive locks. In practice a second type of lock, the shared lock, is also provided in many systems. The function of a shared lock is to prevent concurrent users from changing the locked data, while *not* preventing them from merely seeing it. (An exclusive lock prevents *all* shared access to the data, and thus results in a lower degree of concurrency in the system.) A user will request a shared lock on a piece of data if he or she does not want to change that data in any way but does wish to ensure that it will not be changed by anyone else. As an example, consider a user who wishes to compute the total of a set of account balances. Once a particular balance has been added into the total it should obviously not be allowed to change until the totaling operation is complete (in particular, consider what would happen if a concurrent user were allowed to transfer an amount from a balance not yet processed to one that has been). As each new account is selected, therefore, the user should place a shared lock on it; the locks can be released after the computation is complete.

We conclude this section by describing in outline the data sharing facilities of System R [7.6].

System R

System R supports three distinct *levels of consistency*. When the user initiates a transaction, using the BEGIN_TRANS operator, he or she is responsible for specifying the level at which the transaction is to execute. Broadly speaking, the levels differ in the amount of automatic protection they give the user against sharing problems and in the amount of overhead they incur (Level 3 gives the most protection and the least concurrency). At all three levels the system sets locks automatically in order to guarantee the functions of the level concerned, although at levels 1 and 2 the user may employ an explicit HOLD operator (and corresponding RELEASE operator) if desired.

All three levels guarantee that any data changed by the transaction will not be changed by any other before the given transaction completes. Thus it is always possible to back a transaction out in the sure knowledge that the changes that are about to be undone are solely those made by the transaction concerned.

At Level 1 a transaction is allowed to see "uncommitted" changes. (An uncommitted change is a change made by a transaction that is still in progress; the change becomes "committed" when the transaction reaches a successful conclusion.) In other words, the transaction may see the database in an inconsistent state; it may even see a state that "never really existed," if the other transaction is subsequently backed out. It is clear that a Level 1 transaction should operate with a certain amount of circumspection—specifically, it should beware of making changes to the database or commitments to the outside world on the basis of possibly inaccurate data. However, Level 1 may be perfectly adequate for a transaction that (for example) is merely gathering statistical information from the database and is not interested in 100-percent accuracy. Also, of course, a Level 1 transaction can explicitly employ the HOLD operator, if it wishes, to protect itself against seeing uncommitted changes and also against losing updates.

At Level 2 a transaction is protected from seeing uncommitted changes. However, this protection is not a guarantee that the transaction will see the same value for a given piece of data every time it accesses it ("read reproducibility" is not guaranteed): It is quite possible for a concurrent transaction to come in, change the item, and commit the change in the interval between the two accesses. Again the HOLD operator may be used to guard against such an event, if desired; and again HOLD will be required for any data the transaction wishes to change, to protect against losing updates. The discussions earlier in the present section were effectively assuming Level 2 consistency.

At Level 3 a transaction may behave with impunity as if it were the only transaction in the system. Explicit HOLDs are not required; moreover, all reads are guaranteed to be reproducible (except for changes made by the transaction itself, of course). For example, a request for all suppliers in London will select the same tuples every time it is executed; concurrent transactions will be prevented, not only from updating or deleting an existing London supplier, but also from creating new ones and from changing the city of some existing supplier to London. This statement is true even in the special case where there are *no* London suppliers. At Level 3, then, the transaction is guaranteed that the data it sees is consistent at all times (again, except for changes made by the transaction itself). The lost update problem can be ignored.

As indicated, System R sets locks automatically to support the three levels of consistency. These locks may be applied at various "granularities" [24.11 and 24.12]. For example, individual tuple locks are suitable for transactions that access comparatively few tuples, because they allow a high degree of concurrency. On the other hand, such a fine granularity becomes very expensive (both in time and space) for a transaction accessing many tuples, and a coarser granularity, say at the level of whole relations, is more appropriate in such a case. (Locking an entire relation may be thought of as a shorthand for locking every tuple in that relation; the advantage is, of course, that it involves a single lock instead of many, thus reducing the size of the system's lock tables and the time spent in searching them.)

24.4 SUPPORT ROUTINES

As explained in Section 24.1, several support routines will be required to assist in maintaining the integrity of the database. They include the following.

- Journaling routines

Every operation on the database should be recorded in the *system journal* (usually a tape). For each operation the journal will typically include the following information: an identification of the transaction concerned, a time stamp, an identification of the terminal and user concerned, the full text of the input message, and, in the case of an operation involving change to the database, the type of change and the address of the data changed, together with its before and after values. In general, entries should be made in the journal for *all* operations on the database, including system-generated operations such as updates to an index.

In some systems the system journal is known as the *system log* or the *audit trail.*

- Dump routines

Dump routines are used to take back-up copies of (selected portions of) the database, also usually on tape. It is normal practice to dump the database regularly—say, once a week. [If the database is very large, it may be more practicable to dump one seventh of it every day (say).] Each time a dump is taken, a new system journal may be started and the previous one erased (or archived). Note, incidentally, that the dump routines will probably require at least a shared lock on the data they are dumping.

- Recovery routines

Recovery routines are used to restore the database, or some portion of the database, to an earlier state after a system failure (hardware or software) has caused the contents of the database or (more commonly) of buffers in main storage to be lost. They take as input a back-up copy of the database (produced by the dump routines) together with the system journal (which contains details of operations that have occurred since the dump was taken), and produce as output a new copy of the data as it was before the failure occurred. Note that any transactions that were in progress at the time of the failure will probably have to be restarted (see below).

- Backout routines

The need for backout routines has already been explained. Their function is to remove the effects of a specified transaction from the database, using the information in the system journal to undo all changes caused by that transaction. Backout, if needed, is normally initiated automatically by the DBMS before the transaction has committed its changes (see Section 24.3).

We observe that backout is a particularly simple process if a differential file technique [2.24] is employed for recording changes. Such a technique is employed in System R, incidentally.

- Checkpoint/restart routines

Backing out and rerunning a long transaction in its entirety can be a time-consuming process. Accordingly, some systems permit transactions to take *checkpoints* at suitable points in their execution; if backout subsequently becomes necessary, it may then be possible to go back to the last checkpoint instead of all the way to the start of the transaction. The checkpoint routines will cause all changes made since the last checkpoint to be committed (in effect the checkpoint facility allows a long transaction to be divided up into a sequence of short ones); they may also record values of specified program variables in a checkpoint entry in the system journal. The corresponding restart routines will then use this checkpoint entry to restore the transaction to the state it was in at the time that the relevant checkpoint was taken, so that it may continue processing. A transaction that can be restarted at an intermediate point in this way may have to include special code to handle conditions arising from the restart.

- Detection routines

The existence of integrity constraints implies the existence of routines to search for any violations of such constraints. Such routines will be invoked after each change (for immediate constraints), or at the time that changes are committed (for deferred constraints). If any violations are detected, the routines may simply back the transaction out of the system (*without* rescheduling it), or they may pass information back so that the transaction itself can attempt to do something about the error. The information passed back should include such things as a list of the constraints that have been violated, together with a list of the offending tuples. The transaction may then modify its original change request and try again, or it may simply decide to print an error message and then itself ask to be backed out (using an appropriate data sublanguage operator).

24.5 INTEGRITY IN IMS

Integrity Constraints

There are two features of IMS that can be viewed as mechanisms for handling integrity constraints. The first concerns uniqueness of sequence field values. If a segment is declared in the DBD to have a sequence field, and if M ("multiple-valued") is *not* specified, IMS will guarantee that no two occurrences of the segment under a given parent will contain the same value in this field. In other words, it will reject any ISRT operation that attempts to introduce a duplicate. The second feature concerns the fundamental hierarchical structure of an IMS database, which in effect forces certain integrity constraints to be built into the data structure itself. Suppose, for example, that the suppliers-and-parts database is represented (as in Fig. 3.3) by a hierarchy in which parts are superior to suppliers. Then it is not possible for the database to contain a shipment showing that a supplier is supplying a nonexistent part, because of the nature of the hierarchy (every supplier segment must be subordinate to some existing part segment). On the other hand, of course, the database can contain a shipment showing a part being supplied by a nonexistent supplier. (Here we are assuming a physical database; if instead it is a logical database, defined in terms of distinct "supplier" and "part" physical databases, then a judicious choice of insert and delete rules—see Section 17.6—can prevent such an inconsistency.)

Data Sharing

The data communications feature of IMS provides a comprehensive set of data sharing facilities. First of all, IMS will load and initiate a requested application program only if the PROCOPT entries in the relevant PCB do not conflict with those in any PCB for an application program that is already executing. Two PROCOPT entries for the same segment type conflict if either one specifies 'E' (exclusive, meaning that an exclusive lock is to be applied to the entire set of occurrences of that segment type for the program concerned).

Second, a program that retrieves a segment occurrence by means of a "get hold" operation is automatically granted a (form of) *shared* lock on that occurrence. Concurrent users will be allowed to retrieve the same occurrence but not with a "get hold" operation. If this user updates the occurrence then the lock is automatically raised to the *exclusive* level, meaning that concurrent users will now not be able to access the occurrence at all (except as noted below for "express read"). Similarly, concurrent users will not be allowed to access any occurrence newly created by this user (again, except for "express read").

The shared lock granted in response to a "get hold" is normally released as soon as the segment concerned ceases to be current, i.e., as soon as the program moves on to select some other segment (unless the lock has been upgraded to the exclusive level). However, the program may acquire a shared lock on a segment and retain it for as long as it likes by means of the Q command code. For example, the DL/I operation

```
GN  STUDENT*QB (GRADE='A')
```

will apply a shared lock to the STUDENT occurrence retrieved. The 'B' following the *Q is the lock *class*. The STUDENT occurrence may subsequently be released by the DL/I "dequeue" operation

DEQ B

which will release all segments (in all databases) locked in class B, except for any that have been updated and hence are now locked exclusive. Thus the *Q facility may be used to ensure that no other user can change any of a given set of segments until this user has finished with them. (However, there is a limit—specified in the PSB—on the number of segments the user can have locked under *Q at any one time.)

Segments that are "locked exclusive" are released when the transaction reaches a *synchronization point*. Transaction completion is one form of synchronization point; another is the execution of a DL/I CHKP (checkpoint) operation. Any segments that are "locked shared" at the synchronization point are also released at this time. If it becomes necessary to back the transaction out it will be backed out to the last synchronization point, and subsequently restarted from this point. (Another DL/I operation, ROLL—short for "roll back"—is provided to allow the transaction itself to request backout to the last synchronization point.)

Finally, IMS provides a feature known as "express read" which resembles the System R notion of Level 1 consistency. Express read is specified by a PROCOPT of GO or GOP in the PCB statement (*not* in a SENSEG statement). A transaction using such a PCB will be allowed to retrieve segments (but not with "get hold" or *Q) even if they represent uncommitted changes on the part of some concurrent transaction.

Support Routines

IMS provides a fairly sophisticated set of support routines, including routines for maintaining the IMS log (a system journal), for dumping and restoring individual data sets of a given database, for editing the log to accumulate all changes to a given database (to assist with a subsequent restore operation), and for backing out changes made to a given database by a given program. Checkpoint/restart routines are also provided, as indicated earlier in this section.

24.6 INTEGRITY IN DBTG

The DBTG proposals—more accurately, the DDL of [19.10] and the DML of [19.8]—include a number of integrity features, both for specifying integrity constraints (in the form of declarations in the schema) and for dealing with data sharing problems (in the form of manipulative statements in the program). Again we shall examine each of these areas in turn. (There are no explicit DBTG proposals for support routines, although the need for them is recognized.)

Integrity Constraints

The possibility of using ACCESS CONTROL LOCK procedures for integrity checking has already been mentioned. However, the schema DDL also includes the means for introducing additional procedures— "CALL procedures," so called because they are specified by means of CALL clauses—which seem to be specifically intended for performing integrity checks. For example, in the suppliers-and-parts schema of Fig. 20.16, the declaration of record SP could include the clause CALL CHECK-SNO-PNO BEFORE STORE. The procedure CHECK-SNO-PNO will then be automatically invoked whenever a new SP occurrence is about to be stored. It can then perform any processing it likes; for example, it may check that the SNO and PNO values match those in the relevant S and P occurrences.

     CALL clauses may be specified for the schema itself and for areas, records, data-items,[3] and sets. The DML operations that may be specified in each case are the same as those for which an ACCESS CONTROL LOCK clause may be supplied (see Fig. 23.5), except that (a) "support functions" may not be specified for areas, and (b) FIND may not be specified for sets. In each case the clause may specify that the procedure is to be invoked BEFORE, AFTER, or ON ERROR DURING the relevant operation. The working copy of the *DDL Journal of Development* [19.10] does not mention the question of passing parameters to a CALL procedure, but presumably the procedure will need to know (for example) details of the operation concerned and details of the corresponding operands (object type and name, possibly values too).

     In the case of data-items (only),[4] further constraints may be defined by means of a CHECK clause, which may specify any or all of the following. (The checking specified is performed after the execution of a STORE or MODIFY involving the data-item, in general.)

-    VALUE [NOT] m1 [THRU n1], m2 [THRU n2],...

---

[3] For "data-item" here, read "data-item or data-aggregate" (see footnote 6, Chapter 23, on p. 388).
[4] CHECK may also be applied to a data-aggregate so long as it is a vector, not a repeating group.

This corresponds to the <u>BOUNDS</u> and <u>VALUES</u> entries of Section 24.2. The values m1, n1, m2, n2, . . . are literals.

- NONNULL

This is effectively a special case of VALUE. If NONNULL is *not* stated, a null value is automatically considered to pass all validity checks for this data-item.

- PICTURE

This corresponds to the <u>FORMAT</u> entry of Section 24.2. It specifies that the characteristics of any value supplied for this data-item must exactly match the characteristics declared for the data-item in the schema (via a TYPE clause—see Chapter 20 for examples—or a PICTURE clause—see [19.10] for details).

- Procedure

The specified procedure is invoked at the appropriate time to perform any checking desired. (Again [19.10] does not mention the question of parameters.)

Another integrity constraint that may be defined is *uniqueness*, specified in DBTG by the IDENTIFIER clause and by the DUPLI-CATES ARE NOT ALLOWED clause. The first of these corresponds to the <u>UNIQUE</u> entry of Section 24.2; i.e., it defines a data-item or data-item combination as a candidate key. The second is used to specify uniqueness of a data-item or data-item combination *within a set occurrence*, i.e., among all member occurrences under a given owner occurrence. (It may be specified as part of the ORDER clause, part of the KEY clause, as a separate clause in its own right, or as part of the SEARCH clause; the last two of these cases are not discussed in this book—for details, see [19.10]. In the case of the KEY clause the schema also specifies whether or not null values are allowed for the sort-key.)

Finally, as in IMS, certain integrity constraints are actually built into the data structure itself, since the set construct is really a hierarchy. The situation is complicated, however, by the concept of membership class: Each possible combination of storage class and removal class represents a particular integrity constraint affecting the set of operations that may validly be performed. (IMS provides a similar set of constraints through its insert and delete rules for logical databases, but these rules are not so directly visible to the user. The only "membership class" directly visible in IMS is AUTOMATIC FIXED.) For more details see Section 20.8.

Data Sharing

The proposals of [19.8] for handling the data sharing problem may be summarized as follows.

1. The user must READY each realm (area) before using it, specifying the intended USAGE-MODE, which may be any one of the following.

```
RETRIEVAL
UPDATE
PROTECTED RETRIEVAL
PROTECTED UPDATE
EXCLUSIVE RETRIEVAL
EXCLUSIVE UPDATE
```

EXCLUSIVE means "Prevent other users from readying this realm"; PROTECTED means "Prevent other users from readying this realm except for RETRIEVAL." (More accurately, PROTECTED RETRIEVAL will allow a concurrent run-unit to ready the realm for RETRIEVAL or PROTECTED RETRIEVAL; PROTECTED UPDATE will allow a concurrent run-unit to ready the realm for RETRIEVAL only.) An attempt to ready a realm will be accepted by the system, provided that it does not conflict with a USAGE-MODE already established for that realm. If it does conflict, the READY operation will fail (the value 1309400 will be placed in DB-STATUS, and the name of the realm concerned will be placed in DB-REALM-NAME).

2. A user who has RETRIEVAL or UPDATE rights to a realm (not PROTECTED or EXCLUSIVE) must be aware of the fact that a concurrent user may be updating records in that realm. (In the case of RETRIEVAL, the concurrent user may have specified either UPDATE or PROTECTED UPDATE. In the case of UPDATE, the concurrent user must have specified UPDATE also.) In these circumstances DBTG does *not* provide a locking protocol to deal with the problems of interference between users; instead it provides what may be called a "notify" protocol. The basic idea is that when a user requests a change to be made to a record—e.g., via MODIFY—the request will be rejected if some concurrent user has changed that record since the first user initially selected it, and the first user will be notified of this fact. The mechanism for handling this protocol involves the three statements KEEP, FREE, and REMONITOR.[5]

Executing a KEEP statement places the current of run-unit into "extended monitored mode" for the run-unit; this status is retained until a FREE statement is executed on the same record. In addition, the current of run-unit is always considered to be in "monitored mode" (not extended) anyway; however, unless KEEP is applied to it, the record will no longer be in monitored mode when it ceases to be current.

---

[5] Actually KEEP seems to be redundant: Its function could always be performed by REMONITOR.

An attempt to change a record in either form of monitored mode will fail (with a nonzero DB-STATUS value) if that record has been changed by a concurrent run-unit since it entered that mode. "Change" here refers to the successful execution of any of the following: MODIFY, CONNECT, DISCONNECT, ERASE. If such a failure occurs, the run-unit will then normally issue a REMONITOR statement for the record concerned; this will clear the error condition on the record and will reestablish extended monitored mode for it. The run-unit can then do what it likes. (Assuming that it still intends to change the record itself, it should clearly decide what has happened before attempting to make any further change; however, it is under no obligation to do any such thing.)

Monitored mode has come in for a great deal of criticism [19.5 and 24.13]. The basic problem is that a record in monitored mode is not locked. The meaning of monitored mode, extended or otherwise, is merely that the run-unit wishes to be informed if any concurrent run-unit changes the record concerned in the interval between the time it enters that mode and the time the run-unit itself tries to change it. Should this situation arise, moreover, there is no way of forcing the run-unit to handle it correctly. The following example (based on Example 22.4.1) illustrates this point.

```
FIND S occurrence for supplier S4.
KEEP.
GET S.
ADD 10 TO STATUS IN S.
MODIFY S.
IF DB-STATUS='1101100' REMONITOR
                       go to label.
```

Here we are attempting to add 10 to the status value for supplier S4. A DB-STATUS value of 1101100 after the MODIFY means that some other run-unit has executed a MODIFY, CONNECT, DISCONNECT, or ERASE statement on the S occurrence for S4 since it entered monitored mode for this run-unit. (Incidentally, the KEEP statement is not necessary in this example, since the record concerned remains the current of run-unit throughout.) If this DB-STATUS value occurs, the run-unit must issue an appropriate REMONITOR and then branch to some point to continue processing. In the example the appropriate branch would probably be back to the GET statement; but there is nothing to stop the run-unit from, for example, branching directly back to the MODIFY statement. If there is a possibility that the S record has been *deleted*, the appropriate branch would be back to the FIND statement (and a corresponding test on DB-STATUS should follow the FIND; otherwise the wrong S occurrence might be modified). Similar remarks apply if the record might have been the object of a CONNECT or DISCONNECT operation (not possible in this particular example). We can see that, in general, the "correct" procedure for recovery may be quite complex.

However, as Engles [24.13] points out, a far more fundamental problem with monitored mode is that it does not provide any protection against seeing uncommitted changes, nor does it provide any way of preventing concurrent users from changing data that this user is currently working on (see the account totaling problem of Section 24.3, for example). In addition, it does not solve a highly DBTG-specific problem that Engles calls *currency confusion*. (As an example, run-unit A may happen to transfer run-unit B's current of run-unit from one occurrence to another of a given set, with the result that B may—without realizing it at all—find itself traversing the wrong set occurrence.)

The shortcomings of monitored mode are widely known, and it seems safe to assume that a locking scheme will eventually replace it. We conclude this section with a brief summary of a proposal for such a scheme, taken from a working paper [24.14] submitted by UNIVAC to the CODASYL Programming Language Committee. (Some similar ideas were proposed earlier in [24.20].) It is significant, incidentally, that UNIVAC's DBTG-based system DMS 1100 supports locking rather than the notify protocol.

Selecting a record (by means of a FIND statement) causes that record to enter "selection locked mode." Executing a LOCK statement will cause the record (the current of run-unit) to enter "extended selection locked mode." The difference between the two is that the extended mode continues to apply when the record ceases to be the current of run-unit. The user is guaranteed that no concurrent run-unit may make any changes to a record that is in selection locked mode, extended or otherwise. If this run-unit itself makes any change to such a record (note that a record to be changed must be the current of run-unit and hence in one of the selection locked modes), then that record enters "update locked mode"; no concurrent run-unit may access such a record in any way at all.

The LOCK statement may include a name under which the record is to be extended-selection-locked. A subsequent UNLOCK statement referring to the same name will release all records selection-locked under that name, except for any that have since become update-locked. Update locks (and any outstanding selection locks) are released by the execution of a FREE statement, which is the statement used to "establish a consistency point," i.e., to commit all changes made to the database.

As an exercise, the reader is urged to draw up a detailed comparison between the foregoing proposal and the locking features of IMS and System R.

REFERENCES AND BIBLIOGRAPHY

Descriptions of the integrity features of the following systems will be found in the references indicated: Query By Example [8.6]; System R [7.6 and 7.7]; IMS [15.1 and 16.1] (for data sharing aspects) and [13.1] (for support utilities); DBTG [19.10] (for integrity constraints) and [19.8] (for "monitored mode"). The reader's attention is also drawn to [23.4] and [23.12], both of which include general discussions of integrity, though neither dwells on the problems introduced by concurrency.

24.1 E. F. Codd. "Understanding Relations." Installment No. 6 (*ACM SIG-MOD Bulletin FDT* **7,** No. 1, 1975); Installment No. 7 (*ACM SIGMOD Bulletin FDT* **7,** Nos. 3–4, 1975). Available from ACM.

24.2 K. P. Eswaran and D. D. Chamberlin. "Functional Specifications of a Subsystem for Data Base Integrity." *Proc. International Conference on Very Large Data Bases* (September 1975). Available from ACM.

> This paper is concerned primarily with integrity constraints, not with concurrency problems. Constraints are categorized into tuple versus set constraints, state versus transition constraints, immediate versus delayed constraints, and "hard" versus "soft" constraints. (The classification of constraints in Section 24.2 owes a lot to this paper.) The paper also considers the role of domains in maintaining integrity (see [24.3]), gives an interesting discussion of the treatment of null values (see [24.1]), and suggests that an authorized user should be able to use the normal query language—e.g., SEQUEL—to make inquiries such as "What constraints pertain to employee salaries?" and "What relations are affected by constraint C?"

24.3 D. J. McLeod. "High Level Domain Definition in a Relational Data Base." *Proc. ACM SIGPLAN/SIGMOD Conference on Data: Abstraction, Definition and Structure* (March 1976). Joint Issue: *ACM SIGPLAN Notices* **11** (Special Issue)/*ACM SIGMOD Bulletin FDT* **8,** No. 2 (1976).

> The underlying domains in a relational database, and the association of individual attributes with an appropriate domain, represent between them a very fundamental and important aspect of the semantics of the database. For example, it is generally only meaningful to compare values of two attributes, or to assign one attribute value to another, if those two attributes are defined on the same domain. Moreover, comparisons other than for equality or inequality are only meaningful if an ordering rule is known for the elements of the domain concerned. Domain definitions may thus be regarded as a particular form of integrity constraint. This paper presents a language for defining domains; for each domain the definition gives a name, a specification of the values constituting that domain (e.g., by enumeration or by means of a predicate), an ordering rule (e.g., lexicographic order, numeric order, no order), and a specification of the action to be taken on an attempt to introduce an attribute value that is not a value from the underlying domain (a common error, according to the author's experience with the system RISS [11.29]).

24.4 M. Stonebraker. "High Level Integrity Assurance in Relational Data Base Management Systems." Memorandum No. ERL-M473, University of California, Berkeley (August 1974).

24.5 M. Stonebraker. "Implementation of Integrity Constraints and Views by Query Modification." *Proc. 1975 ACM SIGMOD International Conference on the Management of Data* (May 1975). Available from ACM.

24.6 G. C. Everest. "Concurrent Update Control and Database Integrity." *Proc. IFIP TC-2 Working Conference on Data Base Management Systems,* April 1974 (eds., Klimbie and Koffeman). North-Holland (1974).

24.7 E. G. Coffman, Jr., M. J. Elphick, and A. Shoshani. "System Deadlocks." *Computing Surveys* **3,** No. 2 (June 1971).

24.8 R. S. S. Wee. "Problems of the Dynamic Sharing of Data in a Relational Data Base Environment." IBM UK Scientific Centre Report UKSC 0067 (June 1975).

24.9 D. D. Chamberlin, R. F. Boyce, and I. L. Traiger. "A Deadlock-Free Scheme for Resource Locking in a Data Base Environment." Proc. IFIP Congress 1974.

> As pointed out in Section 24.3, it is generally not practicable in a database environment to require transactions to specify all their lock requests in a single operation. This paper proposes a generalization of this protocol that is somewhat more reasonable. Transactions are required to specify all their lock requests in a "seize block" before doing any processing on the database. A seize block contains a *sequence* of lock requests, each of which may be dependent on values of data "seized" by an earlier request in the seize block. Thus, for example, the first request could be for employee tuples in which the job title is "programmer," and the second could be for department tuples corresponding to these employee tuples. Seize blocks contain lock requests only. Given this protocol, together with the rule that a transaction must release all its seized data at the same time, the paper gives an algorithm that enables the system to recover safely from deadlock and to guarantee that the database will appear consistent to each individual user. The algorithm is based on "preemption"; that is, the system may interrupt a user during the process of locking a set of data and preempt some of the locked data on behalf of another user. In addition, it includes a means of avoiding the possibility that some particular user may be blocked indefinitely.

24.10 K. P. Eswaran, J. N. Gray, R. A. Lorie, and I. L. Traiger. "The Notions of Consistency and Predicate Locks in a Data Base System." *CACM* **19,** No. 11 (November 1976). Also available as IBM Research Report RJ 1487 (December 1974).

> This paper is in two major parts. In the first part, "General Properties of Locking," it is shown that consistency implies that every transaction must consist of a growing phase followed by a shrinking phase; that is, in order for every transaction to see the database in a consistent state, each one must obey the protocol that it cannot request any new locks once it has released a

lock. The second part, "Predicate Locks," considers the special problems of locking in a database environment. The question of "phantoms" is discussed. Suppose a given transaction locks the set of London suppliers, and suppose a concurrent transaction then creates a new supplier tuple with city value "London." The new tuple is a *phantom* so far as the first transaction is concerned; it is not clear whether it should be made available to that transaction or not. The paper proposes as a theoretical solution to this problem that transactions should lock by predicate—that is, lock that set of tuples satisfying some given predicate P. (In the example, both transactions would have to specify the predicate CITY = 'LONDON', and the conflict would be clear.) In general, however, it is impossible to tell whether two predicates conflict; the paper therefore suggests as a practical solution that predicates be restricted to a particular simple (but still useful) form.

24.11 J. N. Gray, R. A. Lorie, and G. R. Putzolu. "Granularity of Locks in a Large Shared Data Base." *Proc. International Conference on Very Large Data Bases* (September 1975). Available from ACM.

Presents the case for supporting multiple lock granularities within a single system. Lockable resources are assumed to form a directed acyclic graph, such as the one shown below.

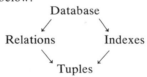

The graph is a graph of node *types:* It is understood that for each occurrence of a given node there will be many occurrences of each of its dependent nodes. Applying an exclusive or shared lock to a given node occurrence implicitly applies an exclusive or shared lock, as appropriate, to all dependents of that node. (The authors note that this approach amounts to an implementation of a very restricted form of predicate locking [24.10].) The paper introduces an additional mode of locking, namely, *intention* locking, which is applied to a given node to prevent concurrent users from obtaining an exclusive or shared (but not an intention) lock on that node. A user holding an intention lock (intention-exclusive or intention-shared) on *all* ancestors of a given node may then apply an explicit lock (exclusive or shared, as appropriate) to that node.

The paper gives a protocol for requesting locks which we repeat here in somewhat simplified form.

- Before requesting a shared or intention-shared lock on a node, a transaction should obtain an intention-shared (or stronger) lock on at least one immediate parent of that node.

- Before requesting an exclusive or intention-exclusive lock on a node, a transaction should obtain an intention-exclusive (or stronger) lock on all immediate parents of that node.

- Locks should be released in leaf-to-root sequence.

The paper includes a discussion of implementation issues (scheduling, granting, and converting lock requests).

24.12 J. N. Gray, R. A. Lorie, G. R. Putzolu, and I. L. Traiger. "Granularity of Locks and Degrees of Consistency in a Shared Data Base." *Proc. IFIP TC-2 Working Conference on Modelling in Data Base Management Systems* (January 1976). North-Holland (1976).

Contains a discussion of granularity, essentially as in [24.11] but excluding the implementation issues, a thorough description of the concept of consistency levels (see the discussion of System R in Section 24.3), and a comparison of both sets of ideas with the locking features of IMS and DMS 1100.

24.13 R. W. Engles. "Currency and Concurrency in the COBOL Data Base Facility." *Proc. IFIP TC-2 Working Conference on Modelling in Data Base Management Systems* (January 1976). North-Holland (1976).

The primary purpose of this paper is to show that significant changes are needed to the COBOL Data Base Facility [19.8]. The areas of concern are database-keys, currency indicators, and concurrency; for each of these areas the paper presents a detailed analysis of the proposals of [19.8] and gives reasons why these proposals are unsatisfactory. In particular, it shows that the "monitored mode" mechanism, while it *may* be used to solve the lost update problem, does not provide any solution for three other problems of concurrency, namely, inconsistent analysis, dependence on uncommitted changes, and "currency confusion" (a problem bound up with the DBTG notion of implicit currency indicators). A unified solution to all these problems (concurrency and others) is proposed, based on locking and the concept of the *cursor*. (For a discussion of cursors, see Chapter 25.)

24.14 Proposal UNI-76001.01 to the CODASYL Programming Language Committee (12 April 1976).

24.15 C. T. Davies, Jr. "Recovery Semantics for a DB/DC System." Proc. ACM Annual Conference 1973.

24.16 L. A. Bjork. "Recovery Scenario for a DB/DC System." Proc. ACM Annual Conference 1973.

24.17 N. J. Giordano and M. S. Schwartz. "Data Base Recovery at CMIC." *Proc. 1976 ACM International Conference on the Management of Data* (June 1976). Available from ACM.

24.18 P. P. Macri. "Deadlock Detection and Resolution in a CODASYL-Based Data Management System." *Proc. 1976 ACM SIGMOD International Conference on the Management of Data* (June 1976). Available from ACM.

Describes a set of algorithms that were developed as an alternative to the standard deadlock detection/resolution algorithms in DMS 1100. The author claims that the new algorithms resulted in approximately double the throughput rate on a given set of benchmarks.

24.19 B. Fossum. "Data Base Integrity as Provided for by a Particular Data Base Management System." *Proc. IFIP TC-2 Working Conference on Data Base*

Management Systems, April 1974 (eds., Klimbie and Koffeman). North-Holland (1974).

Describes the recovery features of DMS 1100.

24.20 D. A. Hawley, J. S. Knowles, and E. E. Tozer. "Database Consistency and the CODASYL DBTG Proposals." *Comp. J.* **18,** No. 3 (August 1975).

24.21 R. Bayer. "Integrity, Concurrency, and Recovery in Databases." In *Proc. ECI Conference 1976: Lecture Notes in Computer Science*, Vol. 44 (eds., Goos and Hartmanis). Springer-Verlag (1976).

A good survey and discussion of the problems and some proposed solutions.

24.22 P. F. King and A. J. Collmeyer. "Database Sharing—An Efficient Mechanism for Supporting Concurrent Processes." *Proc. NCC* (1973).

Part 6
Review, Analysis,
and Comparisons

The purpose of this, the final part of the book, is to draw together some of the themes introduced in the preceding chapters, to analyze certain aspects of the three approaches in somewhat greater depth than before, and to offer some opinions as to the suitability of specific approaches for specific functions within the overall system. However, we do not claim that our treatment of the material is in any way exhaustive.

25
The Three
Approaches
Revisited

25.1 THE ANSI/SPARC ARCHITECTURE

We begin by briefly reviewing, and commenting on, the ANSI/SPARC architecture introduced in Chapter 1. The three levels of this architecture are the external, conceptual, and internal levels. (In this chapter we shall employ the ANSI/SPARC terminology almost exclusively.)

The heart of the system is the conceptual level. The conceptual *model* is a representation, more or less abstract, of the operational data of the enterprise; to put it another way, the conceptual *schema*, which describes the conceptual model, is a description of the various types of entity—for example, parts, suppliers, courses, students, departments, employees, and so on—that are of interest to the enterprise. (As usual, we consider "entities" as including associations.) As we have seen, the conceptual schema will include appropriate authorization and integrity constraints: Such constraints are just as much a property of the operational data as are the data attributes associated with each type of entity.

It is highly important that the conceptual schema be *stable*. By this we mean that a given entry, say the description of a particular type of entity, should never have to change once it has been incorporated into the conceptual schema, *unless* a change occurs in the portion of the real world that that particular entry describes. It should be obvious that, if the conceptual schema is not stable in this sense, applications and external schemas are likely to be unstable too, leading to user confusion, an increased need for reprogramming, and an increased chance of error. To repeat: The conceptual schema should not have to be changed unless some adjustment in the real world requires some definition to be adjusted too, so that it may continue to reflect reality. Of course, one particular type of adjustment that is frequently necessary is the *extension* of the conceptual schema to reflect a larger portion of reality; see the discussion of growth in the conceptual schema, Section 10.5. Such an extension does not conflict with the basic objective of stability, however. (As an example of a change in the real world that would require alteration to, rather than merely extension of, the conceptual schema, consider the following change in the rule associating employees and departments: Under the old rule each employee had to belong to exactly one department; under the new rule an employee may belong to any number of departments simultaneously.)

Designing the conceptual schema is without any doubt the most important single step in the installation of a database system. Ideally it should be the *first* such step. In any case it should certainly not be unduly influenced by considerations of how the data is to be physically stored and accessed, on the one hand, or how it is going to be used in specific applications, on the other. In other words, the design of the conceptual schema should be undertaken quite independently of the design of the associated internal schema and external schemas—for if it is not, there is a danger that the design will not be stable but will continually be undergoing revisions, with consequent impacts on other components of the system. (Alternatively, if such revisions are not made, the installation will find itself locked into a conceptual schema that becomes increasingly unsuitable as more and more applications are brought into the system.)

Given the database management systems of today, however, the notion of designing the conceptual schema independently of the internal and external schemas is something of an ideal. Most systems currently available severely constrain the set of possibilities available to the designer at the conceptual level. Indeed, as we indicated in Chapter 1, most existing installations do not really have a conceptual schema at all; today's designers simply provide an internal schema and a set of external schemas, and the "conceptual schema" is then effectively nothing more than the union of all the external schemas. (Moreover, the amount of significant variation possible between the external and internal levels is usually quite limited.) But the fact that this is the way design has traditionally been done does not mean it is the right way. Experience has shown that the problems mentioned earlier (instability, unsuitability for new applications) do tend to arise after installations have been running for a while [1.10].

It is strongly to be hoped, therefore, that database management systems of the future will support conceptual schemas of an adequate level of abstraction, thus permitting the independent design technique advocated above. At the same time, of course, the system should be able to support a wide variety of external schemas, and should do so, moreover, with an efficiency at least comparable to that of today's systems. For the remainder of this chapter we shall assume that such a system can and will eventually exist.

In this book we have restricted ourselves to the three best-known approaches to the design of the conceptual schema, namely, the relational, hierarchical, and network approaches. Many other approaches have been advocated at one time or another, but most of these can be regarded as variations (albeit important ones, in some cases) on one of the three just mentioned.[1] In Section 25.3 we shall examine, in a little more depth than hitherto, the relative merits of each of the three as a basis for building conceptual schemas.

We turn now to the external level of the system. An external *model* is a model of that portion of the operational data that is of interest to some particular user or group of users. An external *schema* is the description of such a model. In general, many distinct external schemas will coexist within a given installation; moreover, it may well be possible for relational, hierarchical, and network external schemas all to be supported within the same installation, regardless of the form of the underlying conceptual schema. Indeed, one of the objectives of System R is to examine the feasibility of providing exactly this "multiple view type" support [7.6].

For the most part in this book we have concentrated on users of a certain fairly sophisticated kind—namely, users whose interactions with the computer are expressed in some form of programming language, either a general-purpose language such as COBOL or a specially designed language (probably of a higher level but still requiring some programming skill) such as SEQUEL or Query By Example. Such a user may quite naturally perceive the database as a network or as a collection of hierarchies or as a collection of relations. However, what about a user such as the bank clerk of Section 24.3, whose interactions with the system

---

[1] Perhaps the most important variation is that based on generalized graph structures (not to be confused with the network structures of DBTG). A generalized graph consists of a set of nodes and a set of edges; each node represents an elementary data value, and each edge represents an association between two nodes. Such graphs are used in the work of Abrial [25.24], for instance. It can readily be seen, however, that such a structure is basically a collection of binary relations, although viewing it as a graph may be useful from the standpoint of intuition.

For a discussion of the differences between generalized graphs and DBTG networks, see [1.11].

simply involve the invocation of certain prespecified transactions? (Recall, for example, that the bank clerk was able to invoke a transaction that would transfer an amount of money from one account to another, simply by entering the transaction name, the amount, and the relevant account numbers.) The bank clerk is an example of what is frequently known as a *parametric* user—i.e., one whose only inputs to the system are simple parameters. What constitutes the external model for a parametric user?

The answer to this question is clearly not the same as for a programming user. The bank clerk, for example, presumably perceives the database as a collection of bank accounts; details of how these accounts are represented at the programming level, e.g., as tuples in a relation, are irrelevant. The user simply knows that they can be manipulated in certain ways, e.g., by means of the transfer operation already discussed. The "external model" for such a user, then, is essentially that view of the database presented by the transactions that may be invoked; in other words, it is defined *operationally*—the "external schema" is not made explicit but is embedded in the logic of the transactions concerned. For the purposes of this chapter we shall not concern ourselves any further with the parametric user, and we shall consider only external schemas that *are* represented in some explicit form. (For further discussion of how the database might be perceived and manipulated by parametric users, the reader is referred to [25.23].)

For a programming user (at either the COBOL level or the SEQUEL level), the external schema may be regarded as the declarative portion of the program. (It represents the declarations of all the *database* objects the program intends to manipulate. Of course there may be additional declarations for non-database objects.) Here we are using "program" in a somewhat abstract sense; we do not mean to imply that the external schema must physically appear as part of the original program source code. In the case of a COBOL program, for example, the programmer will almost certainly not be responsible for writing the external schema; instead, the program will include a COPY statement to copy the source form of the external schema into the program from the dictionary, or some control statement outside the program will direct the compiler to refer to the object form of the external schema during the compilation process. At any rate, a source form of the schema should appear as part of the program listing, for documentation purposes. In the case of a SEQUEL "programmer" operating from a terminal, the SEQUEL statements may be seen as completing a skeleton program that is built into the system and that already includes the appropriate external schema.

In Section 25.2 we describe in outline a language for writing external schemas and for manipulating the objects defined by such a schema. The language is intended as a basis for extending the existing procedural languages (COBOL, PL/I, . . .) to support database operations. One of its most significant features is that it supports all three views of data (relations, hierarchies, networks), all within the framework of a single integrated language. By considering the three approaches in a uniform manner in this way, we shall be able to emphasize more clearly than hitherto the similarities and differences between them.

Finally we consider (very briefly) the internal level. The internal *model* is a representation of the database at a very low level of abstraction. (Note, however, that it *is* still an abstraction—there are certain aspects of the physical representation that are considered as lying beneath the internal level. In the terminology of Chapter 2, the internal model corresponds to the stored record interface rather than to the physical record interface.) The internal *schema* is a definition of the internal model (the storage structure definition). As such, it specifies how the data is stored and how it can be accessed; that is, it includes definitions of all *access paths* to the data (an index on a specified field is an example of an access path).

We have tended to deemphasize the internal level in this book, and the present chapter is no exception to this pattern. The underemphasis is deliberate: We do not wish to suggest that the internal level is not important, but in many ways it is the most familiar and best understood of the three, and it has already received a great deal of attention elsewhere. We do wish to suggest that the other levels of the system are at least as important as the internal level.

25.2 THE EXTERNAL LEVEL

As indicated in the previous section, our approach to this topic will be to introduce a language that handles all three views of data in a consistent and unified fashion, and then to use this language as the basis for some further discussions. The language is based on some proposals of [25.8]; it is not intended as a self-contained set of facilities, but rather is offered as a candidate for incorporation (in some suitable syntactic form) into any of the existing procedural languages, such as COBOL. We shall use a PL/I-like syntax in our examples.

The language not only supports all three views of data, it also provides both record-at-a-time and set-at-a-time functions for each of them. (The set-at-a-time operations are desirable for reasons of simplic-

View of data / Level of access	Relational	Hierarchical	Network
Record	√	√	√
Set	√	√	√

Fig. 25.1 Language support of views of data

ity, usability, and productivity;[2] the record-at-a-time operations are necessary in order to provide a bridge to existing language functions.) We may summarize these features of the language as shown in Fig. 25.1.

We start with a key observation.

- A relation may be considered as a special case of a hierarchy—namely, one that is "root only." Likewise, a hierarchy may be considered as a special case of a network—namely, one in which each child record has exactly one parent record.

It is by recognizing this pattern among the three data structures that the language is able to handle them in a unified fashion. Of course, the "key observation" is much too vague to be useful other than as a general statement of direction. We may make it a little more precise as follows.

1. We define a *record set* as a set of ordered pairs $\langle R_i, P_i \rangle$, such that all the records R_i in a given set are of the same type, and no two records have the same position (address) P_i.

2. The particular record set involving *all* records of a given type (in a given database[3]) is the *base set* for that record type.

3. A *database* is a collection of one or more base sets, together with zero or more fan sets (see number 7 below).[4]

4. A *relation* is a record set for which $i \neq j$ (see number 1 above) implies $R_i \neq R_j$.

5. A *relational database* is a collection of one or more base sets, each of which is a relation.

---

[2] A striking example in support of this contention will be found in the appendix to [25.3].

[3] Throughout the present section we shall use "database" to mean the user's view, i.e., the external model (or part of the external model, if the user is operating on several distinct databases at the same time).

[4] It may also include "window sets," which correspond to DBTG's singular sets, but we choose not to discuss these for reasons of space.

6. A *fan* on base sets P and C, in that order, is an ordered pair ⟨parent, children⟩, such that "parent" is a record of P and "children" is a subset (possibly empty) of the records of C.

7. A *fan set F* on base sets P and C, in that order, is a set of fans on P and C, in that order. Each record of P is the parent for exactly one fan of F (see number 6), and no other records are parents in F; each record of C is a child in at most one fan of F, and no other records are children in F. (Fan sets correspond to DBTG's set types. The DBTG terms for parent and child are owner and member, respectively.)

8. A *network database* is simply a database as defined in number 3 above.

9. A *hierarchical database* is a network database satisfying the following constraints: (a) If it includes a fan set F on base sets P and C, in that order, then each record of C is a child in exactly—not "at most"—one fan of F; (b) every base set except one—the "root"—is the child set for exactly one fan set; (c) there exists a path from the root to each nonroot—where a path from base set A to base set B is a sequence of fan sets $F_1, F_2, \ldots, F_n$ such that A is the parent set for F_1, the child set for F_1 is the parent set for $F_2, \ldots$, and the child set for F_n is B.

The reader is cautioned that the foregoing definitions are still very imprecise. Moreover, they do not cater for IMS's "hierarchical sequence," which is a total ordering of all records in the database, nor for those DBTG set types that have more than one type of member (child). These features are considered to be of rather minor importance. (It is true that hierarchical sequence is of more than minor importance in IMS today, but this is largely due to the way DL/I is defined. In most cases equivalent function could be provided without relying on this sequence, and indeed it is not hard to find situations where the concept is a positive hindrance.) If these restrictions are accepted, it can be seen from the definitions that, as stated earlier, a relation is a special case of a hierarchy, and a hierarchy is a special case of a network. These facts are reflected in the structure of the language we are describing. To be specific:

■ the language features required to declare a relational database are a subset of those required to declare a hierarchical database, and these in turn are a subset of those required to declare a network database;

■ the language operators required to manipulate a relational database are a subset of those required to manipulate a hierarchical database, and these in turn are a subset of those required to manipulate a network database;

■   (for a given operator, as applicable) the language operands required for a relational database are a subset of those required for a hierarchical database, and these in turn are a subset of those required for a network database.

The language thus has an "onion-layer" structure, as illustrated in Fig. 25.2.

We now give some examples in support of the foregoing claims. All examples are based on a variation of the education database of Chapter

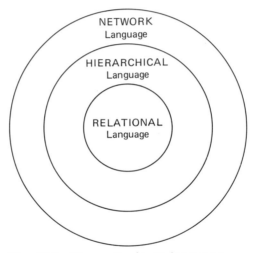

Fig. 25.2 The onion-layer language

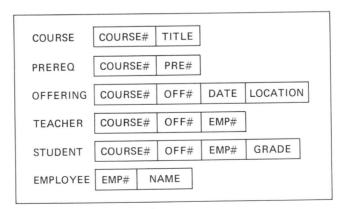

Fig. 25.3 Relational view of the education database

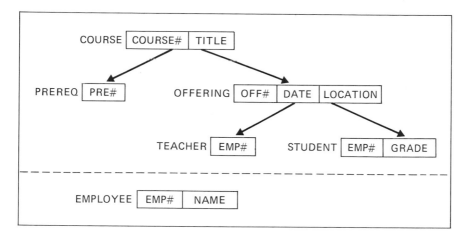

Fig. 25.4 Hierarchical view of the education database

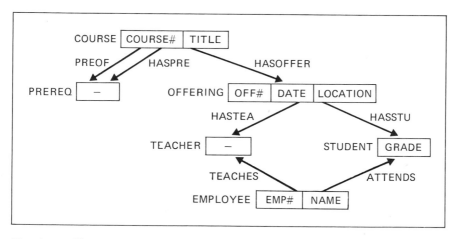

Fig. 25.5 Network view of the education database

13. Figures 25.3, 25.4, and 25.5 show, respectively, a relational, hierarchical, and network view of the data. Note that two hierarchies, one of
them root only, are required in Fig. 25.4 in order to avoid redundancy.

   In the declaration for this database (i.e., the external schema), we
first define the six record types as six *structures*, each "based" on a *cursor*.
A cursor is conceptually similar to a pointer (i.e., a pointer *variable*),
except that it points at records in the database instead of at records in

program-local storage. Cursor S, for example, will be used to point to—and thus make accessible to the executing program—individual STUDENT records.

```
DCL 1 COURSE    BASED(C),
      2 COURSE#  CHAR(3),
      2 TITLE    CHAR(33);

   DCL 1 PREREQ   BASED(P),
**    2 COURSE#  CHAR(3),
*     2 PRE#     CHAR(3);

   DCL 1 OFFERING BASED(O),
**    2 COURSE#  CHAR(3),
      2 OFF#     CHAR(3),
      2 DATE     CHAR(6),
      2 LOCATION CHAR(12);

   DCL 1 TEACHER  BASED(T),
**    2 COURSE#  CHAR(3),
**    2 OFF#     CHAR(3),
*     2 EMP#     CHAR(6);

   DCL 1 STUDENT  BASED(S),
**    2 COURSE#  CHAR(3),
**    2 OFF#     CHAR(3),
*     2 EMP#     CHAR(6),
      2 GRADE    CHAR(1);

   DCL 1 EMPLOYEE BASED(E),
      2 EMP#     CHAR(6),
      2 NAME     CHAR(18);
```

Lines marked with a single asterisk would be omitted for the network of Fig. 25.5; lines marked with a double asterisk would be omitted both for the network of Fig. 25.5 and for the hierarchy of Fig. 25.4. (Note that the PREREQ and TEACHER records will contain no data at all in the network case.) These omissions are possible because the relevant information is carried by the fan set structuring, instead of by a correspondence between a foreign key and a primary key as in the relational structure. It would be possible to include the foreign keys—for example, to include the COURSE# field in the OFFERING record—but the fan sets would then become "inessential," i.e., they would be redundant from an information-bearing point of view. We shall discuss the notion of essentiality in more detail in the next section; here we simply note that we shall concern ourselves in the present section with essential fan sets only, for reasons of space.

We now give (in Figs. 25.6, 25.7, and 25.8) declarations of the database corresponding to the three cases. For simplicity we have not shown all aspects of the declarations; for example, ordering is assumed to be system-defined (default) throughout. UNIQUE in a base set entry specifies a field or field combination that has a unique value for each record in the base set (i.e., a candidate key). UNIQUE in a fan set entry specifies a field or field combination that has a unique value for each record in any given fan of the fan set. (Omitting the field names from a UNIQUE entry is equivalent to specifying the combination of all fields in the record concerned.) We have left the fan sets unnamed in the hierarchical case and have named them in the network case; however, the only cases where names are *required* are the fan sets PREOF and HASPRE in Fig. 25.8 (if these were unnamed, we would be unable to distinguish between them). In *all* other cases names may be supplied or omitted at will.

```
DCL EDUCATION DATABASE
    BASESET (RECORD(COURSE)    UNIQUE(COURSE#),
             RECORD(PREREQ)    UNIQUE,
             RECORD(OFFERING)  UNIQUE((COURSE#,OFF#)),
             RECORD(TEACHER)   UNIQUE,
             RECORD(STUDENT)   UNIQUE((COURSE#,EMP#)),
             RECORD(EMPLOYEE)  UNIQUE(EMP#));
```

Fig. 25.6   Relational database declaration

```
DCL EDUCATION DATABASE
    BASESET (RECORD(COURSE)    UNIQUE(COURSE#),
             RECORD(PREREQ),
             RECORD(OFFERING),
             RECORD(TEACHER),
             RECORD(STUDENT),
             RECORD(EMPLOYEE)  UNIQUE(EMP#))
    FANSET  (RECORD(PREREQ)    UNDER(COURSE)    UNIQUE,
             RECORD(OFFERING)  UNDER(COURSE)    UNIQUE(OFF#),
             RECORD(TEACHER)   UNDER(OFFERING)  UNIQUE,
             RECORD(STUDENT)   UNDER(OFFERING)  UNIQUE(EMP#));
```

Fig. 25.7   Hierarchical database declaration

```
DCL EDUCATION DATABASE
    BASESET (RECORD(COURSE)              UNIQUE(COURSE#))
            RECORD(PREREQ),
            RECORD(OFFERING),
            RECORD(TEACHER),
            RECORD(STUDENT),
            RECORD(EMPLOYEE)             UNIQUE(EMP#))
    FANSET  (PREOF     RECORD(PREREQ)    UNDER(COURSE)
                                         UNIQUE(COURSE#   OVER PREREQ
                                                          VIA HASPRE),

             HASPRE    RECORD(PREREQ)    UNDER(COURSE)
                                         UNIQUE(COURSE#   OVER PREREQ
                                                          VIA PREOF),

             HASOFFER  RECORD(OFFERING)  UNDER(COURSE)
                                         UNIQUE(OFF#),
             HASTEA    RECORD(TEACHER)   UNDER(OFFERING)
                                         UNIQUE(EMP# OVER TEACHER),
             HASSTU    RECORD(STUDENT)   UNDER(OFFERING)
                                         UNIQUE(EMP# OVER STUDENT),
             TEACHES   RECORD(TEACHER)   UNDER(EMPLOYEE)
                                         UNIQUE((COURSE# OVER TEACHER,
                                                  OFF#    OVER TEACHER)),
             ATTENDS   RECORD(STUDENT)   UNDER(EMPLOYEE)
                                         UNIQUE(COURSE# OVER STUDENT));
```

Fig. 25.8 Network database declaration

Now we turn to some manipulative examples. Consider the following problem. Suppose that the structure GIVEN—declaration

```
DCL 1 GIVEN,
      2 COURSE# CHAR(3),
      2 OFF#    CHAR(3),
      2 EMP#    CHAR(6);
```

contains a set of input values, representing an employee's application to enroll himself in a particular offering of a particular course. We wish to check that the employee has attended all appropriate prerequisite courses—if so, we will accept the application; otherwise we will reject it. We present relational, hierarchical, and network procedures for this problem, first using the record-at-a-time language and then the set-at-a-time language.

```
DO PREREQ WHERE PREREQ.COURSE# = GIVEN.COURSE#;
   FIND UNIQUE(STUDENT WHERE STUDENT.EMP#    = GIVEN.EMP#
                         & STUDENT.COURSE# = PREREQ.PRE#);
   ELSE reject application and RETURN;
END;
CREATE STUDENT FROM (GIVEN, 'b');
```

Fig. 25.9 Record-at-a-time relational procedure

Figure 25.9 shows the relational record-at-a-time solution. The logic of this procedure is as follows. For each PREREQ record with a COURSE# value equal to the given course number, we attempt to find a STUDENT record indicating that the given employee has attended (some offering of) the corresponding prerequisite course. If the attempt fails for any such PREREQ, we reject the application. If it succeeds for all such PREREQs, we enroll the employee in the specified offering by creating an appropriate STUDENT record (with a blank grade, represented by the symbol 'b').

A few aspects of the code in Fig. 25.9 require some further explanation. First, the expression PREREQ WHERE ... refers to a *set* of PREREQ records; the DO—END loop is executed once for each record in this set (assuming that the employee concerned has actually attended all prerequisite courses). On the ith iteration, cursor P (the cursor associated with PREREQs in the declaration of the PREREQ record type) is set to point to the ith PREREQ in the set. (Successful execution of a DO or FIND statement causes a cursor to be set to point to a record. The cursor to be set is specified by means of the phrase "SET (cursor-name)"; if this phrase is omitted, as in Fig. 25.9, the cursor named in the declaration of the record type concerned is used by default.)

Second, we can refer to the ith PREREQ (on the ith iteration) by means of the *cursor-qualified reference* P → PREREQ. Cursor qualification is analogous to pointer qualification in PL/I today; the expression P → PREREQ is a reference to the individual PREREQ record identified by the current value of the cursor P. (It would be an error if P were not pointing at a PREREQ.) Similarly, the expression P → PREREQ.PRE# is a reference to the PRE# value within the PREREQ identified by P. The cursor-qualification portion "cursor-name → " may be omitted from such expressions, in which case (again) the cursor named in the declaration of the record type concerned is used by default; again we have made use of this default rule in the example (in the expression PREREQ.PRE# in the third line).

Third, the expression STUDENT WHERE ... is also a reference to a *set* of records. However, the database would be in error if this set contained more than one record. UNIQUE is an operator that selects the single record in a single-record set. Assuming that the database is not in error, then, the expression STUDENT WHERE ... will evaluate either to a single-record set or to the empty set; in the former case the FIND will locate the single record (and will set cursor S to point to it), in the latter case the ELSE portion will be executed.

Note, incidentally, that setting a cursor to point to a record gives the programmer addressability to that record directly ("direct reference")—it is not necessary to execute any form of GET or READ to bring a copy of the record into some program-local area. In other words, the database appears to the programmer as if it were all in main storage. For arguments in support of this approach see [25.8].

Now we turn to a hierarchical solution (Fig. 25.10). The logic is essentially the same as before; however, for reasons of efficiency, we start by setting cursor C (default) to point to the appropriate COURSE. (This step is not required—we could replace each of the subsequent references to this COURSE record by the entire expression to select it, if desired.) Also, a CONNECT option is necessary in the CREATE statement to identify the OFFERING under which the new STUDENT is to be placed.

It can be seen that, compared with the relational procedure, the hierarchical procedure requires the following additional constructs: (a) UNDER, (b) OVER, and (c) CONNECT.

Figure 25.11 shows the corresponding network procedure. The additional constructs here, over and above those of Fig. 25.10, are (a) VIA, and (b) multiple UNDERs in the CONNECT option.

```
FIND UNIQUE(COURSE WHERE COURSE.COURSE# = GIVEN.COURSE#);
DO PREREQ UNDER COURSE;
    FIND UNIQUE(STUDENT WHERE STUDENT.EMP# = GIVEN.EMP#
                        & (COURSE.COURSE# OVER STUDENT)
                                    = PREREQ.PRE#);
    ELSE reject application and RETURN;
END;
CREATE STUDENT FROM (GIVEN.EMP#, 'b')
        CONNECT (UNDER UNIQUE(OFFERING UNDER COURSE
                        WHERE OFFERING.OFF# = GIVEN.OFF#));
```

Fig. 25.10 Record-at-a-time hierarchical procedure

```
FIND UNIQUE(COURSE WHERE COURSE.COURSE# = GIVEN.COURSE#);
DO PREREQ UNDER COURSE VIA HASPRE;
   FIND UNIQUE(STUDENT WHERE (EMPLOYEE.EMP# OVER STUDENT)
                                    = GIVEN.EMP#
                           & (COURSE.COURSE# OVER STUDENT)
                                    = (COURSE.COURSE#
                                           OVER PREREQ VIA PREOF));
   ELSE reject application and RETURN;
END;
CREATE STUDENT FROM ('b')
      CONNECT (UNDER UNIQUE(OFFERING UNDER COURSE
                            WHERE OFFERING.OFF# = GIVEN.OFF#),
              UNDER UNIQUE(EMPLOYEE WHERE EMPLOYEE.EMP# = GIVEN.EMP#));
```

Fig. 25.11   Record-at-a-time network procedure

For interest we show a DBTG procedure for the same problem (Fig. 25.12). We ignore the declarative portion of the program (part of which is not in the "external schema" anyway but in the "conceptual schema" instead; see Chapter 21). However, we do show the exception-handling routines (USE procedures). We have assumed that SET SELECTION for ATTENDS and HASSTU is BY APPLICATION, and that COURSENO and EMPNO are CALC-keys for COURSE and EMPLOYEE respectively.

Some comparisons are of interest (Fig. 25.13).

We also offer the following comment on the relative performance of the three procedures (Figs. 25.9, 25.10, and 25.11). If we assume that the employee concerned actually has attended all necessary prerequisite courses, and if there are p such prerequisites for the given course, the number of database operations in the loop in each case is $2p$ (a FIND for PREREQ implied by the DO, and an explicit FIND for STUDENT). However, the individual operations themselves become progressively more complex as we move from relations to hierarchies to networks. If the average number of offerings per course is x, and the average number of students per offering is y, and if we make some reasonable assumptions[5] about search strategies, it is quite easy to show that the average

---

[5] The basic assumption is that base sets possessing a primary key are indexed on that key. Also, of course, fan sets provide access paths in the hierarchical and network cases. Note, however, that the expressions quoted on p. 440 do not include any term for *index* records accessed.

```
PROCEDURE DIVISION.
DECLARATIVES.
NOTFOUND SECTION.
   USE  FOR DB-EXCEPTION
        ON '0502100' MOVE 'YES' TO ENDSET.
FAILURE SECTION.
   USE  FOR DB-EXCEPTION
        ON OTHER ...
   .....
END DECLARATIVES.

        MOVE COURSENO OF GIVEN TO COURSENO IN COURSE.
        FIND ANY COURSE.
        MOVE 'NO' TO ENDSET.
NXTPRE. FIND NEXT PREREQ WITHIN HASPRE.
        IF ENDSET = 'YES' GO TO ENROL.
        FIND OWNER WITHIN PREOF RETAINING CURRENCY FOR HASPRE.
NXTOFF.    FIND NEXT OFFERING WITHIN HASOFFER.
           IF  ENDSET = 'YES' reject application and STOP RUN.
NXTSTU.       FIND NEXT STUDENT WITHIN HASSTU.
              IF ENDSET = 'YES' MOVE 'NO' TO ENDSET
                                GO TO NXTOFF.
              FIND OWNER WITHIN ATTENDS.
              GET EMPLOYEE.
              IF EMPNO OF EMPLOYEE = EMPNO OF GIVEN GO TO NXTPRE.
              GO TO NXTSTU.

ENROL.  FIND ANY EMPLOYEE.
        MOVE OFFNO OF GIVEN TO OFFNO OF OFFERING.
        FIND OFFERING WITHIN HASOFFER USING OFFNO.
        MOVE 'b' TO GRADE OF STUDENT.
        STORE STUDENT.
```

Fig. 25.12 DBTG procedure

number of *external* records examined during the execution of the loop is:

- for the relational procedure $\qquad 2p$
- for the hierarchical procedure $\qquad (\frac{1}{2}xy + 2)p$
- for the network procedure $\qquad (xy + \frac{1}{2}x + 2)p$

If $p = 3$, $x = 8$, and $y = 16$, these expressions evaluate to 6, 198, and 402, respectively. (The DBTG figure is the same as for the network procedure; for DBTG, however, the number of *individual* calls to the database management system is also equal to this figure, and hence the interface-crossing overhead may well be higher.) Thus, *if* the internal model is very

	Relational	Hierarchical	Network	DBTG
Database as seen by user	6 base sets	6 base sets + 4 fan sets	6 base sets + 7 fan sets (2 names nec.)	6 record types + 7 (named) "sets"
Number of tokens in procedure (Note 1)	40	65	81	157
Manipulative language constructs (Note 2)	FIND WHERE	FIND WHERE FIND UNDER FIND OVER	FIND WHERE FIND UNDER [VIA] FIND OVER [VIA]	FIND ANY − LOCATION MODE FIND NEXT WITHIN FIND OWNER WITHIN FIND WITHIN USING − LOCATION MODE − SET SELECTION GET RETAIN CURRENCY
	CREATE	CREATE [CONNECT]	CREATE [CONNECT [VIA]]	STORE − LOCATION MODE − SET SELECTION

Note 1. A token is an indivisible unit in the source program; e.g., the line "MOVE 'NO' TO ENDSET" contains four tokens. (All figures are based on COBOL versions of the examples in order to be fair to the DBTG-COBOL of Fig. 25.12.)

Note 2. DO is equivalent to a sequence of FIND WHERE operators.

Fig. 25.13 Some comparisons

similar to the external model in each case, the relational solution can easily outperform the other two solutions. The point of these remarks is to refute the frequently-heard claim that a relational system must necessarily perform badly. But of course we cannot draw any *general* conclusions from this single example.

We make one final point concerning the enrollment example. In practice in such a situation, the program should verify that the given course number, offering number, and employee number are genuine, by looking for corresponding records in the database. We omitted this verification step in our solutions for reasons of simplicity. It is important to note, however, that including such a step would not make any significant difference to the comparisons of Fig. 25.13 or to the performance argument above.

We now present set-at-a-time procedures for the enrollment problem (Figs. 25.14, 25.15, and 25.16). The basic logic in each case is as follows: If the set of prerequisite course numbers for the given course is a subset of the set of course numbers for courses attended by the given employee,

```
IF (PREREQ.PRE# WHERE PREREQ.COURSE# = GIVEN.COURSE#)
   SUBSETOF
   (STUDENT.COURSE# WHERE STUDENT.EMP# = GIVEN.EMP#)
THEN CREATE STUDENT FROM (GIVEN, 'b');
ELSE reject application;
```

Fig. 25.14 Set-at-a-time relational procedure

```
FIND UNIQUE(COURSE WHERE COURSE.COURSE# = GIVEN.COURSE#);
IF (PREREQ.PRE# UNDER COURSE)
   SUBSETOF
   (COURSE.COURSE# OVER (STUDENT WHERE STUDENT.EMP# = GIVEN.EMP#))
THEN CREATE STUDENT FROM (GIVEN.EMP#, 'b')
             CONNECT (UNDER UNIQUE(OFFERING UNDER COURSE
                                   WHERE OFFERING.OFF# = GIVEN.OFF#));
ELSE reject application;
```

Fig. 25.15 Set-at-a-time hierarchical procedure

```
FIND UNIQUE(COURSE WHERE COURSE.COURSE# = GIVEN.COURSE#);
IF (COURSE.COURSE# OVER (PREREQ UNDER COURSE VIA HASPRE) VIA PREOF)
   SUBSETOF
   (COURSE.COURSE# OVER (STUDENT WHERE STUDENT.EMP# = GIVEN.EMP#))
THEN CREATE STUDENT FROM ('b')
             CONNECT (UNDER UNIQUE(OFFERING UNDER COURSE
                                   WHERE OFFERING.OFF# = GIVEN.OFF#),
                 UNDER UNIQUE(EMPLOYEE WHERE EMPLOYEE.EMP# = GIVEN.EMP#));
ELSE reject application;
```

Fig. 25.16 Set-at-a-time network procedure

the application is accepted; otherwise it is rejected. We observe once again that the relational language features are a subset of the hierarchical features, and these in turn are a subset of the network features.

It is not our purpose here to describe the unified language in full. We will conclude our description of it with a brief survey of the remaining manipulative statements. (The only ones mentioned so far have been FIND, DO, and CREATE.) As pointed out earlier, *retrieval*, in the sense of bringing a copy of a record into some program-local area, is not usually necessary; however, a record, or a field within a record, can be "retrieved" using an ordinary assignment statement (for example, ASSIGN

S → STUDENT TO S_AREA). Similarly, a record, or a field within a record, may be updated by means of an assignment statement (for example, ASSIGN S_AREA.GRADE TO S → STUDENT.GRADE). The CREATE statement is used to insert a record or set of records into a base set. The DESTROY statement is used to delete a record or set of records. The language also provides CONNECT, DISCONNECT, and RECONNECT statements for manipulating fan sets; CONNECT connects one or more child records to a specified fan, DISCONNECT disconnects one or more child records from a specified fan, and RECONNECT moves one or more child records from one fan to another. We remark that CONNECT and DISCONNECT apply to networks only, while RECONNECT applies to both hierarchies and networks. Finally, the language includes a full range of locking facilities and an extensive repertoire of built-in functions and exception-handling features.

The reader will appreciate that we have done little more than scratch the surface of the language in this short description. However, sufficient examples have been given to illustrate the onion-layer structure and to demonstrate that both the declarative and the manipulative portions of the language necessarily become more complex as the database structure becomes more complex. We have also drawn a comparison between the proposed language and DBTG (which is of course a record-at-a-time network system), and we have made some remarks concerning the relative performance of the three approaches. We conclude with the following observation: Although the relational approach seems the best candidate as a basis for a general-purpose database language in the long term, there is no question that networks and hierarchies will continue to be around for some time yet, for the very good reason that there is already a lot of investment in such systems. In other words, all three approaches will be used at the *external* level for some time to come. (We emphasize that in this section we are considering the external level only.) Given this fact, the idea of using a single, well-structured language as a common programming interface to a variety of distinct systems seems a very attractive one; it could greatly simplify problems of communication between users of different systems, it could ease education problems, and it could assist with the migration of programs and programmers from one system to another (including, in particular, migration from a current system to some future system, say a relational system).

25.3 THE CONCEPTUAL LEVEL

The importance of *stability* at the conceptual level was stressed in Section 25.1. It cannot be overemphasized. The conceptual schema is intended to provide a solid and enduring foundation for the total operation of the enterprise; indeed, it may even have to survive the replacement of one underlying database management system by another. In the light of such requirements it should be clear that the conceptual schema must not be dependent on the quirks of any individual system.

We have already suggested that few systems today support a truly "conceptual" level; they may provide a community view of the database, but this is frequently little more than a simple union of all external views, and these in turn are generally rather system-dependent and even data-dependent. We would like to suggest now that, notwithstanding this state of affairs, it is still important to construct a conceptual schema, at a suitable level of abstraction, even if the database management system available is such that this schema will exist only in manuscript or type-script form. If the system does not support a true conceptual level, the schema designer—presumably the DBA—will then have to perform a manual mapping of the conceptual design into a form that the system does support. If the system does support the design directly, of course, so much the better. Either way, the enterprise will find itself immeasurably better off for having a self-contained, succinct description of its opera-tional data, expressed ideally in terms that—albeit precise—are human-oriented rather than machine-oriented. (It is becoming increasingly recog-nized that the biggest obstacle of all to progress in the use of computers is the difficulty of *communication* among all the many people involved—end-users, enterprise management, programming specialists, the database administrator, and so on [22.2]. The role of the conceptual schema in overcoming such problems is obvious.)

The conceptual schema, then, should not depend on the peculiarities of a specific system. However, it must be based on *some* view of data. In this section we discuss the relative suitability of n-ary relations and DBTG-like networks for performing this function (we do not deal explicitly with hierarchies, treating them for the purposes of this discussion as merely a restricted form of network).[6] We begin by describing some properties that the conceptual view of data should possess; we then examine relations and networks in turn to see to what extent they possess these desirable properties. We conclude by raising (but not answering) some rather important questions.

---

[6] We concentrate on relations and networks because at the time of writing they are the two major candidates for the role. However, we most certainly do not wish to suggest that there will never be any other serious contenders. As already stated, we are interested here in the *relative* merits of these two approaches, not necessarily in their *absolute* merits.

The two most important properties that the conceptual view of data should possess are the following.

1. It should be as simple as is practically possible.
2. It should have a sound theoretical base.

We consider each of these in turn.

Simplicity

When we say that the conceptual view should be simple, we really mean that it should be easy to understand and easy to manipulate. We do not necessarily mean that it should be minimal in any sense. (An analogy from arithmetic may help to clarify the distinction. When we represent a number in the familiar positional notation, we generally use decimal as the base, not binary, even though binary is logically sufficient. Binary is minimal, but decimal is simpler [more usable] from the user's point of view.)

The requirement that the view be easy to understand should not require any justification. Comprehensibility is obviously crucial if the communication problem mentioned earlier is to be addressed. Of course there are many aspects to comprehensibility; we list some of them below.

- The number of basic constructs should be small.

The conceptual schema will be built out of a set of basic building blocks. It is obviously desirable that the number of distinct building blocks be kept to a manageable and convenient size. (As already indicated, however, we certainly do not want to sacrifice *conciseness* in the interests of this objective. The key word here is "convenient.")

- Distinct concepts should be cleanly separated.

An individual construct (building block) should not "bundle together" two or more distinct concepts; for if it does, it becomes difficult to tell exactly what purpose that construct is serving in a given situation (and it may be used for a purpose for which it was not intended). Separation of concepts also yields cleaner and sharper control of the database.

- Symmetry should be preserved.

It should not be necessary to represent a naturally symmetric structure in an asymmetric manner. Symmetry is important in aiding understanding. To quote Polya (writing in a different context): "Try to treat symmetrically what is symmetrical, and do not destroy wantonly any natural symmetry" [25.22].

- Redundancy should be carefully controlled.

Redundancy in the sense of the same fact appearing in two places should probably not be allowed at all. (By "fact" we mean the association between a given entity and some property of that entity—e.g., the association between an item and its price.) However, there are other types of redundancy [4.1] that cannot be eliminated, in general. In such cases the conceptual schema should include a statement of exactly what the redundancy is. (We note in passing that we currently do not seem to have a good definition of redundancy; we have only a somewhat vague idea that it is bad in some situations and good in others.)

Likewise, the requirement that the conceptual model be easy to manipulate should also require little justification. Although the user may not actually operate directly at the conceptual level, he or she must understand what operations are possible at that level, since these operations will be used to model the transactions of the enterprise. In an implementation in which the user's view is the same as or close to the conceptual view, of course, it becomes even more imperative that these operations be easy to understand. To paraphrase [25.3]: "The reader is cautioned to avoid comparing different data models solely on the basis of differences in the data constructs they support. An adequate appreciation of the differences must entail consideration of the operator types also."

We list some aspects that will help to make the model easy to manipulate. No additional comment is necessary in the first case.

- The number of operator types should be small.
- Very high-level (i.e., powerful) operators should be available.

It goes without saying that the operators must be precisely defined. However, it is also desirable that operators should exist at a level close to the imprecise, but very high-level, "operators" used in natural language (e.g., the operator "increase" in the transaction "Increase all programmers' salaries by ten percent"). Ideally each transaction would be expressible at the conceptual level in one and only one way. The burden of irrelevant decisions (concerning access strategies, for example) should be removed from the user.

- Symmetry should be preserved.

Transactions that have a naturally symmetric formulation should be expressible symmetrically in the manipulative language. For example, the queries "List all employees working for department D3" and "List all employees earning a salary of 30,000 dollars" should have symmetric representations.

Theoretical Base

Given the importance of the conceptual level, it is absolutely essential that it be founded on a solid base of theory [25.20]. The model *must* behave in a totally predictable fashion—surprises, especially unpleasant ones, simply cannot be tolerated. Whatever formal system we choose as a basis for the conceptual level, we *must* be fully aware of exactly what is and is not possible in that system. Specifically, we should be familiar with all potential pitfalls and problem areas, and we should be certain that ambiguity and paradox cannot occur. In short, we should know exactly what we are doing.

The Relational Approach

Let us now see how the relational approach measures up to these requirements. First, there can be little doubt that relations are easy to understand. The number of basic data constructs is *one*, namely, the relation (or table) itself; all information in the database is represented using just this one construct, and moreover this one construct is both simple and highly familiar—people have been using tables for centuries. (We remind the user that the schema itself, and all other information in the dictionary, can also be held in relational form, as mentioned in Chapter 8.) As for keeping distinct concepts separate, there seem to be few, if any, instances of "bundling" in the relational model.[7] Indeed, it is significant that most of the research since 1970 into such areas as concurrency, locking, security, integrity, view definition, and so on, has taken the relational model as a starting point precisely *because* it provides a clean conceptual base. And as for symmetry and nonredundancy, the relational model again seems to meet the requirements. [In the latter case the normalization discipline (fourth normal form) guarantees that the same "fact" will not appear in two places.]

    Relations are also easy to manipulate; numerous examples from this book and elsewhere can be cited in support of this statement. Moreover, the statement is true at both the tuple-at-a-time and set-at-a-time levels; in other words, very high-level operators are available, as well as the more familiar low-level operators. (The very high-level operators are those of the relational algebra and equivalent languages.) The number of

---

[7] Some writers would argue that *n*-ary relations do bundle together several distinct *facts*, and that the purposes of the conceptual level are better served by an equivalent collection of binary relations (or "irreducible" relations [9.14]). There is some merit in this position. However, we consider the distinction between the *n*-ary and irreducible relational views as being far less significant than that between relational views of any kind and the DBTG-like network view.

distinct operators in any given language is small because there is only one type of data construct to deal with; essentially we need just one operator for each of the four basic functions retrieve, insert, delete, update. If we also consider—as we must—the operators needed for authorization and integrity purposes (e.g., the SEQUEL GRANT and ASSERT operators), we again find that a single set of operators is all that is necessary, and for the same reason. Last, relational languages generally provide what Codd [4.1] calls "symmetric exploitation": the ability to access a relation by specifying known values for any combination of its attributes, seeking the (unknown) values for its other attributes. Symmetric exploitation is possible because all information is represented in the same uniform way.

As for the question of an underlying theory, the relational approach is not only soundly based on certain aspects of mathematical set theory, it also possesses a considerable body of theory in its own right aimed specifically at its application to database problems. The normalization theory discussed in Chapter 9 provides a rigorous set of guidelines for the design of a relational schema. The theory of relational completeness provides a valuable tool for measuring the selective power of a language and for comparing different candidate languages (indeed, now that the concept has been defined, it is incumbent on the designer of any such language either to make that language complete in this sense or else to justify each and every departure from such an objective). Under the heading of theory we may also mention *closure* (discussed in Chapter 6): The result of any operation of the relational algebra, or equivalent language, is itself a relation, which allows us to write nested expressions.[8] The closure property is particularly important in the provision of support for the nonprogramming user [25.3].

The Network Approach

Before discussing DBTG networks in any detail, we first introduce the important notion of essentiality [25.3]. The declaration D of some data construct in a schema S is *essential* if there exists an instantaneous database B conforming to S such that removal from B of the construct defined by D would cause a loss of information from B. By saying that a loss of information would occur, we mean, precisely, that some relation would no longer be derivable.

We present some examples to illustrate this idea, using a simplified form of the syntax of Section 25.2.

---

[8] Incidentally, binary (or irreducible) relations do not possess this same closure property. For example, the join of two binary relations is not a binary relation.

1. Schema S1:

       BASESET COURSE(COURSE#,TITLE)
       BASESET OFFERING(COURSE#,OFF#,DATE,LOCATION)

   Both declarations are essential in S1. (Also, both base sets are relations.)

2. Schema S2:

       BASESET COURSE(COURSE#,TITLE)
       BASESET OFFERING(OFF#,DATE,LOCATION)
       FANSET OFFERING UNDER COURSE

   All three declarations are essential in S2. (The first base set is a relation; the second is not.)

3. Schema S3:

       BASESET COURSE(COURSE#, TITLE)
       BASESET OFFERING(COURSE#,OFF#,DATE,LOCATION)
       FANSET OFFERING UNDER COURSE
               USING COMMON VALUE FOR COURSE#

   The two base set declarations are essential in S3, the fan set declaration is not; there is no information that can be derived from this database that cannot also be derived from the two base sets alone. (Again, the two base sets are relations.)

Given this notion of essentiality, we can now state an absolutely crucial distinction between the relational and network approaches. In a relational schema the entire information content of the database is represented by means of a single data construct, namely, the n-ary relation.[9] In a network schema, by contrast, there exists at least one fan set bearing information essentially; for if there did not, the schema would degenerate into a relational schema with certain explicit access paths.[10] In other words, there are at least two essential data constructs in the

---

[9] Sometimes we permit relations to be ordered, but such ordering is always inessential. For example, the supplier relation may be ordered by ascending supplier number; however, the ordering is merely a convenience—we could still find (say) the supplier with the third supplier number in this sequence, even if the relation was in totally random order.

[10] The suppliers-and-parts schema of Fig. 20.16 does not contain any essential fan sets, and is thus not a network schema by this definition. Our reasons for making the fan sets inessential in that example were given in the text; basically the problem was that maintaining the proper child sequence is difficult in an essential fan set under DBTG. But this is really a criticism of DBTG—it is not a state of affairs that is intrinsic to networks per se.

network approach, the base set and the fan set. In DBTG, in particular, there are *six* data constructs, any or all of which may be used to bear information essentially:

- record type (corresponds to base set);
- DBTG set (corresponds to fan set);
- singular set;
- ordering;
- area;
- repeating group.

Now we consider how the network approach measures up to the criteria specified earlier for the conceptual level of the system. The first criterion was ease of understanding. A comparison of Figs. 25.17 (a repeat of Fig. 4.4) and 25.18 (a network version of the same data) suggests that, in terms of occurrences at least, networks are somewhat less easy to understand than relations. A comparison of Figs. 25.3 and 25.5 (see the previous section) suggests that the same is true for the schemas. A possible reason for the increase in complexity is the increase in the number of basic constructs the user has to understand and deal with.

A more severe criticism of networks is that the fan set construct bundles together at least three distinct concepts.

1. It *carries information* (either essentially or inessentially), namely, the association between the two record types involved.
2. It provides an *access path* (actually several such paths: parent to first and last child, child to next and previous child, child to parent).
3. It represents certain *integrity constraints* (primarily the constraint that the association between parents and children is one-to-many, though the concept of membership class provides for a number of variations on this basic theme).

In addition, fan sets may be used to establish a scope for authorization purposes; also the ordering of children within a given fan may be used to carry information (again, either essentially or inessentially). A result of this bundling is that, for example, programs may come to rely on an access path that is really a side-effect of the way the designer chose to represent a certain integrity constraint. If that integrity constraint changes, the schema has to be restructured, with a strong likelihood of consequent impact on the corresponding program—even if that program was completely uninterested in the integrity constraint as such. As an example, the reader is invited to consider the effect on a program that

COMPONENT	MAJOR.P#	MINOR.P#	QUANTITY
	P1	P2	2
	P1	P4	4
	P5	P3	1
	P3	P6	3
	P6	P1	9
	P5	P6	8
	P2	P4	3

Fig. 25.17 A parts-and-components structure: Relational view

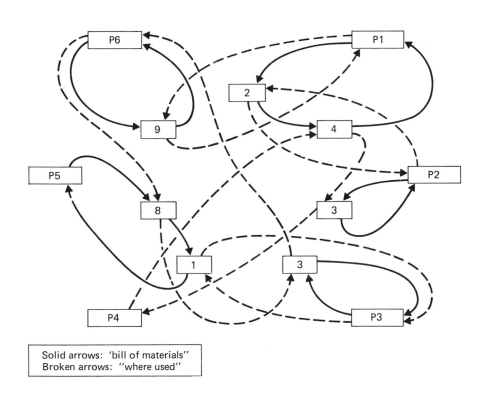

Solid arrows: 'bill of materials''
Broken arrows: ''where used''

Fig. 25.18 A parts-and-components structure: Network view

lists employee numbers by department number (a) using a relation ED(EMP#,DEPT#) and (b) using a fan set DEPTEMP (parent DEPT, child EMP), if the department-to-employee correspondence changes from one-to-many to many-to-many. (In the relational case, the worst that can occur is a trivial change to the external/conceptual mapping—ED may have to be derived as a projection of a department/employee "linking" relation instead of as a projection of the employee relation. In the network case, the changes required at the conceptual level are rather more extensive, and either the program or the external/conceptual mapping will require significantly more rewriting. If the rewriting is contained within the mapping, incidentally, we will then have the situation that the program is using an access path, namely, DEPTEMP, which is no longer directly supported. See number 2 below.)

Let us examine each of the three "bundled" concepts in a little more detail.

1. Fan sets represent certain associations between entities. However, not all such associations will be represented as fan sets, in general; in all likelihood, not even all one-to-many associations will be so represented. As an example of one that is not, consider the association between cities and suppliers. Of course, there is no record type corresponding to cities; but if such a record type were added to the schema, would a fan set also be added with cities as parents, suppliers as children? If the answer is yes, the fan set will be inessential, unless the city field type is removed from the supplier record type. This removal is unlikely, for the following reasons: (a) Suppliers would have to be MANUAL members of the fan set (to allow for the fact that the supplier records exist *before* the city records are created); therefore (b) a new program will be needed to connect suppliers to cities; and (c) this program will need to obtain the city value for a given supplier from *somewhere*—presumably from the city field. We conclude that the addition of essential fan sets with existing records as members is a nontrivial operation, which raises questions about the usefulness of the construct.

2. Fan sets represent certain access paths. However, not all such paths are represented by fan sets; for example, the system may provide various forms of indexing under the covers. User programs are not dependent on the existence of such "invisible" access paths, but they very definitely are dependent on the existence of the visible paths that are represented by fan sets. (This observation suggests that fan sets cannot be viewed as purely logical constructs—they must be supported fairly directly at the physical level, for otherwise there is little justification for representing just these particular associations in this rather privileged manner. See

number 1 above.) The question arises: Why is this particular form of access path made visible, when others are not?[11]

3. Fan sets represent certain integrity constraints. However, not all such constraints are represented by fan sets; indeed, most constraints are specified separately from the data structure (see Chapter 24). An example of the problems caused by bundling such constraints with the data structure has already been given. The question arises: Why are these particular constraints given this special treatment?

A more general question arising from these three paragraphs is the following: How does the schema designer decide which associations/paths/constraints to express as fan sets and which to represent in some other way?

Returning to our "ease of understanding" criteria, the last two in the list were *symmetry* and *nonredundancy*. A network schema involving essential fan sets has less symmetry of representation than an equivalent relational schema, since some information is represented as records and some as links between records; it follows that such a network cannot totally support "symmetric exploitation." Second, a network schema can certainly be just as nonredundant as an equivalent relational schema (but no more so), but only if it does not involve any inessential fan sets; an inessential fan set does contain some redundancy, in that the association between parent and child is represented both by field values and by links.

We turn now to *ease of manipulation*. We observe first that each information-bearing construct needs its own set of operators to manipulate it, in general. Thus, even if we restrict our attention to just record types and fan sets, we see that networks necessarily require more operators than relations. The unified language of Section 25.2 has already demonstrated the truth of this statement. For example, in DBTG we have STORE to create a record and CONNECT to create a link, ERASE to destroy a record and DISCONNECT to destroy a link, and so on. (Actually DBTG does not provide individual operators for each of the

---

[11] As Waghorn [20.4] points out, fan sets are actually a very general and widely applicable structure, considered purely as an access mechanism and not as a logical construct. They are thus a strong candidate for implementation at the *internal* or storage structure level (as opposed to the conceptual level). Indeed, System R, which of course uses relations at the conceptual level, relies heavily on fan sets at the internal level (as well as on indexing and on other access paths). It is likely, however, that "internal" fan sets would not use FIXED, MANDATORY, or AUTOMATIC membership—everything would be MANUAL and OPTIONAL. The work of Kay [21.1] supports these remarks.

four basic functions for each information-bearing construct. However, this does not mean that such operators are not needed—it simply means that in such cases the user has to program the function for himself. For example, there is no direct way to modify information that is represented by essential ordering; to achieve the desired effect, the user has to DISCONNECT the record and then CONNECT it into another point in the sequence.) The foregoing remarks are applicable regardless of operator level; thus we can certainly provide very high-level (set-at-a-time) network operators, but there will necessarily be more of them than there will for relations.

We also need more authorization and integrity operators. Moreover, authorization and integrity controls can be quite complicated to apply. Suppose, for example, that within the department-employee fan set, employees are ordered by ascending values of the salary field, and suppose we have a user who needs to see employees by department—perhaps as an access path—but who is not allowed any access to salary information. It is not sufficient simply to omit the salary field from the user's view; the user can still discover that Smith earns more than Jones, for example, by observing that Smith follows Jones in the sequence. (Inessential information-carriers do still carry information, and corresponding controls are still necessary.

Last, we consider the question of a supporting theory. This writer knows of no theory to assist with the design of a network schema that is as complete as the normalization theory is for relations. It is true that normalization theory can be applied to the *records* of the network, but only *after* the decision has been made as to which information is to be represented by records and which by other means—and of course this first decision is critical. The consequences of a wrong choice are likely to be instability in the schema. As an example, consider a network schema representing a subway network in which each subway line is represented by a singular set, and the order of the stations on the line is represented by the order of the records in the set (a realistic example of essential ordering). Suppose that at a later time it is required to incorporate the distance between adjacent stations into this schema. This distance is a property, not of a station per se, but rather of a pair of adjacent stations; however, adjacency is represented by ordering, not by records, which makes it difficult to introduce a distance field. If we introduce a new "pair-of-adjacent-stations" record type we can obviously use it to hold the distance field; however, the existing schema then becomes totally redundant. (The new record type would have to include a field identifying the relevant subway line.) If we place the distance field in the existing station record type (more precisely, if we incorporate a "distance to next station" field into the station record type, thus relying once again on the ordering), we introduce an unpleasant asymmetry into the schema. For example, the algorithm for computing the distance between two stations X and Y on a given line will vary significantly according to whether X precedes or follows Y on the line. The problems are entirely due to the use of ordering as an essential construct.

Another important theoretical question is the following: Is it possible to support a relational external schema on a conceptual schema that involves essential fan sets? It is generally accepted that nonprogramming users, at least, will require a relational view of the database. Again, this writer knows of no completely general method of supporting such a view if the conceptual schema involves essential fan sets.[12] It is not hard to produce examples that suggest that such a general mapping would be rather complex. (The information represented by the essential fan set will be represented by a foreign key in the child record in the relational view. Difficulties arise if the relational user updates this foreign key and sets it to a value not matching any existing parent record. In some situations this operation must be allowed; in others it must not.)

Some Questions

We can summarize this rather lengthy discussion of the conceptual level by turning the problem around and asking a number of questions (see [25.3]). Suppose that we start with relations as the sole data construct available at the conceptual level. What is the effect of introducing new constructs (e.g., fan sets) that bear information essentially?

- So far as the *system* is concerned, do not more operators become necessary? Do not concurrency, authorization, and similar controls become more complex? Hence, does not the implementation become more complex and less reliable?

- So far as the *user* is concerned, is there not an increased burden in choosing which operators to use? Is there not an increased variety of possible errors to cope with, and a correspondingly increased variety of remedial actions to consider?

- So far as the *database administrator* is concerned, are there not too many structural choices available? *Are there dependable guidelines for making these choices?* (This is one of the most critical questions of

---

[12] We note in passing that the closure properties of relations do not apply to essential fan sets. For example, a "union" of two fans of a given fan set that retains all linkage information is not itself another fan.

all.) Are not the mappings to the internal level significantly more complicated to define and maintain? Are not authorization and integrity constraints more complicated to specify?

If it turns out that fan sets have to be *inessential* (for example, to support a relational external view), then their role at the conceptual level must again be questioned. It is interesting to note, incidentally, that Bachman himself in his Turing Award lecture [22.2] suggests that fan sets are fundamentally inessential and are intended primarily for improving performance: "... The field named 'department code' appears in both the employee record and the department record ... The use of the same data value as a primary key for one record and as a secondary key for a set of records is the basic concept upon which data structure sets are declared and maintained ... With database sets, all redundant data can be eliminated, reducing the storage space required ... Performance is enhanced ... where the owner and some or most of the members of a set are physically stored and accessed together on the same block or page." And later: "The joint usage of the department code by both [employee and department] records and the declaration of a set based upon this data key provide the basis for the creation and maintenance of the set relationship between a department record and all the records representing the employees of that department. [A benefit of this construct is] the significant improvement in performance that accrues from using the database sets in lieu of both primary and secondary indices to gain access to all the records with a particular data key value."

25.4   CONCLUSION

Many papers have appeared over the last few years on the relative merits of different models of data and different ways of manipulating them [25.2–25.20]. In this chapter we have attempted to extract and present some of the most significant themes from these papers; at the conceptual level, in particular, we have tried to show the advantages of n-ary relations over DBTG-like networks, but the reader who remains unconvinced is strongly urged to study the original papers themselves. The problem is too important to be dismissed lightly.

We may summarize the chapter as follows.

At the *external* level it seems likely that relational, hierarchical, and network views will coexist for some years to come. In Section 25.2 we presented a language that supports all three views in a unified fashion. (The "onion-layer" structure of this language may itself be seen as a powerful argument for basing external views on relations wherever possible.) We also mentioned some advantages of using such a language as a common interface to a variety of distinct systems, namely, that it would help to ease communication, education, and migration problems.

At the *conceptual* level we stressed the importance of stability. We also claimed that the conceptual schema should be simple and should have a firm base in theory. We presented many arguments for basing this level on *n*-ary relations rather than on DBTG-like networks (we suggested, however, that the DBTG set would be a very valuable construct at the *internal* level). We concluded with a number of questions that deserve serious attention from anyone involved in deciding on a suitable basis for the conceptual schema, most especially from anyone concerned in standardizing such a basis.

It seems appropriate to conclude with Codd's statement of objectives for the relational approach [9.8]. They are as follows:

1. To provide a high degree of data independence;

2. To provide a community view of the data of spartan simplicity, so that a wide variety of users in an enterprise (ranging from the most computer-naive to the most computer-sophisticated) can interact with a *common* model (while not prohibiting superimposed user views for specialized purposes);

3. To simplify the potentially formidable job of the database administrator;

4. To introduce a theoretical foundation (albeit modest) into database management (a field sadly lacking in solid principles and guidelines);

5. To merge the fact retrieval and file management fields in preparation for the addition at a later time of inferential services in the commercial world;

6. To lift database application programming to a new level—a level in which sets (and more specifically relations) are treated as operands instead of being processed element by element.

No one would claim that all these objectives have now been attained; much more work remains to be done. However, a strong foundation has been established, and there seems good reason to be optimistic about the eventual outcome.

REFERENCES AND BIBLIOGRAPHY

25.1 R. Rustin (ed.). "Data Models: Data Structure Set versus Relational." *Proc. 1974 ACM SIGMOD Workshop on Data Description, Access and Control, Vol. II* (May 1974). Available from ACM.

The proceedings of a debate held at the 1974 SIGMOD conference. Includes references [25.2–25.5], additional comments by D. C. Tsichritzis and J. R. Lucking, and the transcript of an unusually interesting panel-and-audience discussion.

25.2 C. W. Bachman. "The Data Structure Set Model." In [25.1].

Presents Bachman's arguments that the two approaches are fundamentally compatible.

25.3 E. F. Codd and C. J. Date. "Interactive Support for Non-Programmers: The Relational and Network Approaches." In [25.1].

Section 25.3 of the present chapter draws heavily from this paper.

25.4 E. H. Sibley. "On the Equivalence of Data Based Systems." In [25.1].

25.5 C. J. Date and E. F. Codd. "The Relational and Network Approaches: Comparison of the Application Programming Interfaces." In [25.1].

A companion paper to [25.3]. Somewhat unfair, in that it contrasts a relational set-at-a-time language (DSL ALPHA) with a network record-at-a-time language (the DML of DBTG).

25.6 A. E. Bandurski and D. K. Jefferson. "Data Description for Computer-Aided Design." *Proc. ACM SIGMOD International Conference on Management of Data* (May 1975). Available from ACM.

Includes some very interesting criticisms of both relations and networks.

25.7 A. P. G. Brown. "Modelling a Real World System and Designing a Schema to Represent It." In [20.3].

Suggests an informal set of guidelines for designing a DBTG schema.

25.8 C. J. Date. "An Architecture for High-Level Language Database Extensions." *Proc. 1976 ACM SIGMOD International Conference on the Management of Data* (June 1976); available from ACM. Also in *Proc. ECI Conference 1976: Lecture Notes in Computer Science*, Vol. 44 (eds., Goos and Hartmanis). New York: Springer-Verlag (1976).

25.9 C. P. Earnest. "A Comparison of the Network and Relational Data Structure Models." Available from Computer Sciences Corporation, 650 N. Sepulveda Blvd., El Segundo, California 90245.

Earnest's major conclusions are: "(1) The two models are in practice not very different; (2) the relational structures are somewhat simpler than networks; but (3) the price for this is that the network model has more structural power and *more*, not less, data independence than the relational, and is therefore likely to be a better basis for a standard." These conclusions are clearly somewhat at variance with those of the present chapter; the reader is urged to study both documents and to make up his or her own mind.

25.10 M. Stonebraker and G. Held. "Networks, Hierarchies, and Relations in Data Base Management Systems." *Proc. 1975 ACM PACIFIC Conference, San*

Francisco (April 1975). Available from Mail Room, Boole and Babbage Inc., 850 Stewart Drive, Sunnyvale, California 94086.

> Suggests that language level (set-at-a-time or record-at-a-time) is a more important factor than the underlying view of data. However, most of the arguments of the present chapter—e.g., the claim that relations provide a kernel set of facilities and networks add complexity but not function—are not addressed.

25.11 M. H. H. Huits. "Requirements for Languages in Data Base Systems." In [20.3].

> Includes some good examples of problems for which record-at-a-time languages are more appropriate than set-at-a-time languages.

25.12 W. C. McGee. "A Contribution to the Study of Data Equivalence." *Proc. IFIP TC-2 Working Conference on Data Base Management Systems* (eds., Klimbie and Koffeman), April 1974. North-Holland (1974).

25.13 W. C. McGee. "File-Level Operations on Network Data Structures." *Proc. 1975 ACM SIGMOD International Conference on the Management of Data* (May 1975). Available from ACM.

> Presents a possible set-at-a-time network language.

25.14 W. C. McGee. "On the Evaluation of Data Models." *ACM Transactions on Database Systems* **1,** No. 4 (December 1976).

> Defines a set of criteria for choosing a particular view of data. The criteria are as follows: simplicity, elegance, logicalness, picturability, modelling directness, modelling uniqueness, provision of structure "schemas," overlap with coresident models, partitionability, consistent terminology, proximity to implementation base, and applicability of safe implementation techniques. Of course, some of these criteria clash with others.

25.15 A. Metaxides. "Information-Bearing and Non-Information-Bearing Sets." In [20.3].

> The terms "information-bearing" and "non-information-bearing" in the title of this paper are unfortunately sometimes used in place of "essential" and "inessential." As Metaxides quite rightly observes, the terms are misleading since essential and inessential constructs both bear information. The paper claims that eliminating essential sets (a) provides no data independence benefits, (b) provides no integrity benefits, (c) does not really increase simplicity (simplification in the schema is achieved only at the expense of complication in programs), (d) reduces flexibility, and (e) leads to design and update problems.
>
> Metaxides was the DBTG chairman at the time the final report [19.1] was produced.

25.16 A. S. Michaels, B. Mittman, and C. R. Carlson. "A Comparison of the Relational and CODASYL Approaches to Data Base Management." *ACM Computing Surveys* **8,** No. 1 (March 1976).

> Discusses the two approaches under the headings of data definition, data

manipulation (language level, complexity), data protection, data independence, and performance. The major conclusion is that no single approach to database management is desirable (sic) and no single approach is likely to emerge as dominant in the near future.

25.17 G. M. Nijssen. "Data Structuring in DDL and the Relational Data Model." *Proc. IFIP TC-2 Working Conference on Data Base Management Systems* (eds., Klimbie and Koffeman), April 1974. North-Holland (1974).

Compares and contrasts the network and relational models, and proposes a discipline for network users. The "DDL" of the title is the CODASYL Data Description Language. It is interesting to compare the discipline suggested with another such discipline proposed in [25.3].

25.18 G. M. Nijssen. "Set and CODASYL Set or Coset." In [20.3].

Considers the CODASYL DDL as a language for defining conceptual schemas, and suggests a number of improvements to the language with this aim in mind. The changes proposed include the following.

- All record types should include a primary key.
- All set types should be inessential.
- All ordering should be inessential.
- A set type should be allowed to have the same record type as both owner and member.
- A set type should not be allowed to have more than one type of member.
- The concept of membership class should be replaced by a statement of whether the functional dependence of owners on members is total or partial, together with certain additional integrity constraints.

The paper includes some good illustrations of why sets should not be essential. However, the author does not discuss the question (see Section 25.3) "If sets must be inessential, what purpose are they really serving in the conceptual schema?"

25.19 K. A. Robinson. "An Analysis of the Uses of the CODASYL Set Concept." In [20.3].

Supports the contention of Section 25.3 that DBTG sets should not appear at the conceptual level but may be very useful at the internal level.

25.20 T. B. Steel, Jr. "Data Base Standardization: A Status Report." In [20.3].

An outline description of the ANSI/SPARC architecture, with emphasis on the conceptual schema. The author argues strongly for his own conviction that the only acceptable formalism for the conceptual level is that of modern symbolic logic.

25.21 E. F. Codd. "Understanding Relations, Instalment No. 4." *SIGMOD bulletin FDT* **6,** No. 4 (1974).

Includes a very clear description of the differences among the following concepts: (1) the domain concept; (2) comparability of attributes; (3) the association between a foreign key and a primary key; and (4) the DBTG set or fan set. (The differences are important; the claim is frequently made that fan sets are the DBTG equivalent of one or other of the first three, and this is not the case.)

25.22 G. Polya. "How To Solve It." Princeton University Press: Princeton Paperback (Second ed., 1971).

25.23 End User Facility Task Group of CODASYL Systems Committee. Progress Report (June 1975). In *FDT (Bulletin of ACM Special Interest Group on Management of Data)* **8,** No. 1 (1976).

25.24 J. R. Abrial. "Data Semantics." In *Data Base Management: Proc. IFIP TC-2 Working Conference on Data Base Management Systems* (eds., Klimbie and Koffeman). North-Holland (1974).

25.25 W. Kent. "The Limitations of Record-Oriented Data Models" (tentative title). Forthcoming.

Continuing his thesis that the structure of information in the real world tends to be highly complex [1.11], Kent here argues strongly that *any* formalism involving "records" (and this category includes both *n*-ary relations and DBTG-like networks) is probably inadequate as a basis for the conceptual schema. It is implied, though certainly not stated, that a scheme based on surrogates and irreducible relations [9.14] is perhaps more satisfactory.

Answers to Selected Exercises

CHAPTER 2: STORAGE STRUCTURES

2.4

Values recorded in index	Expanded form
0-2-AB	AB
1-3-CKE	ACKE
3-1-R	ACKR
1-7-DAMS,Tb	ADAMS,Tb
7-1-R	ADAMS,TR
5-1-O	ADAMSO
1-1-L	AL
1-1-Y	AY
0-7-BAILEY,	BAILEY,
6-1-M	BAILEYM

Notes

1. The two figures preceding each recorded value represent, respectively, the number of leading characters that are the same as those in the preceding value, and the number of characters actually recorded.

2. The expanded form of each value shows what can be deduced from (a sequential scan of) the index alone, i.e., without looking at the data.

3. It is assumed that the next value of the indexed field does not have BAILEYM as its first seven characters.

If we take the 8-bit byte as the unit of storage space and assume (a) that the two counts are accommodated in a single byte, and (b) that each recorded character also requires a single byte, the percentage saving in storage space is

$$\frac{150-35}{150} \cdot 100 = 76.67\%.$$

The index search algorithm is as follows.

Let V be the specified value (padded with blanks if necessary to make it 15 characters long).

1. Form next expanded index entry; let N = corresponding length $(1 \leqslant N \leqslant 15)$.

2. Compare expanded index entry with leftmost N characters of V.

3. If equal, go to step 6.

4. If index entry is high, no stored record occurrence for V exists; go to exit.

5. Go to step 1.

6. Retrieve corresponding stored record occurrence, and check V against value stored therein.

If no "next" entry exists (step 1), no stored record occurrence for V exists.

For ACKROYD,S we get a match on the third iteration; we retrieve the stored record occurrence and find that it is indeed the one we want.

For ADAMS,V we get "index entry high" on the sixth iteration, so no appropriate stored record occurrence exists.

For ALLINGHAM,M we get a match on the seventh iteration; however, the stored record occurrence retrieved is for ALLEN,S, so it is permissible to insert a new one for ALLINGHAM,M. (We are assuming here that the indexed field is the primary key, so that values should be unique.) This involves the following steps.

1. Finding space and storing the new occurrence

2. Adjusting the index entry for ALLEN,S to read

    `1-3-LLE`

3. Inserting an index entry between those for ALLEN,S and AYRES,ST to read

    `3-1-I`

Note that the preceding entry in the index has to be changed. In general, making a new entry in the index may affect the preceding entry or the following entry, or possibly neither—but never both.

2.5 The number of *levels* in the index is the unique positive integer k such that $n^{k-1} < N \leqslant n^k$. Taking logs to base n, we have $k-1 < \log_n N \leqslant k$; hence

$$k = \text{ceil}(\log_n N),$$

where ceil (x) denotes the smallest integer greater than or equal to x.

Now let the number of *blocks* in the ith level of the index be B_i (where $i = 1$ corresponds to the lowest level). We show that

$$B_i = \text{ceil}\left(\frac{N}{n^i}\right),$$

and hence that the total number of blocks is

$$\sum_{i=1}^{i=k} \text{ceil}\left(\frac{N}{n^i}\right).$$

Consider the expression

$$\text{ceil}\left(\frac{\text{ceil}\left(\dfrac{N}{n^i}\right)}{n}\right) = x, \text{ say.}$$

Suppose $N = qn^i + r$ $(0 \leqslant r \leqslant n^i - 1)$. Then

a) If $r = 0$, $x = \text{ceil}\left(\dfrac{q}{n}\right)$

$$= \text{ceil}\left(\frac{qn^i}{n^{i+1}}\right)$$

$$= \text{ceil}\left(\frac{N}{n^{i+1}}\right).$$

b) If $r > 0$, $x = \text{ceil}\left(\dfrac{q+1}{n}\right)$.

Suppose $q = q'n + r'$ $(0 \leqslant r' \leqslant n - 1)$. Then $N = (q'n + r')n^i + r = q'n^{i+1} + (r'n^i + r)$; since $0 < r \leqslant n - 1$ and $0 \leqslant r' \leqslant n - 1$,

$$0 < (r'n^i + r) \leqslant n^{i+1} - (n^i - n + 1) < n^{i+1};$$

hence $\text{ceil}\left(\dfrac{N}{n^{i+1}}\right) = q' + 1$.

But

$$x = \text{ceil}\left(\frac{q'n + r' + 1}{n}\right)$$

$$= q' + 1$$

since $1 \leqslant r' + 1 \leqslant n$. Thus in both cases (a) and (b) we have that

$$\text{ceil}\left(\frac{\text{ceil}\left(\dfrac{N}{n^i}\right)}{n}\right) = \text{ceil}\left(\frac{N}{n^{i+1}}\right).$$

Now, it is immediate that $B_1 = \text{ceil}(N/n)$. It is also immediate that $B_{i+1} = \text{ceil}(B_i/n)$, $1 \leqslant i Q k$. Thus, if $B_i = \text{ceil}(N/n^i)$, then

$$B_{i+1} = \text{ceil}\left(\frac{\text{ceil}\left(\dfrac{N}{n^i}\right)}{n}\right) = \text{ceil}\left(\frac{N}{n^{i+1}}\right).$$

The rest follows by induction.

2.6 (a) 3. (b) 6. For example, if the four field names are A,B,C,D, and if we denote an index by the appropriate ordered combination of field names, the following indexes will suffice: ABCD, BCDA, CDAB, DABC, ACBD, BDAC. (c) In general the number of indexes required is

$$^N C_n$$

(the number of ways of selecting n elements from a set of N elements), where n is the smallest integer $\geq N/2$. For proof see Lum [2.8].

CHAPTER 3: DATA MODELS AND DATA SUBLANGUAGES

3.1

PERSON

PNAME	ADDR	———
Arthur	——	———
Bill	——	———
Charlie	——	———
Dave	——	———

SKILL

SNAME	COURSE	JOBCODE	———
Programming	——	——	———
Operating	——	——	———
Engineering	——	——	———

PERSKIL

PNAME	SNAME	DATE
Arthur	Programming	——
Bill	Operating	——
Bill	Programming	——
Charlie	Engineering	——
Charlie	Programming	——
Charlie	Operating	——
Dave	Operating	——
Dave	Engineering	——

3.2 The two possible hierarchical models consist of (a) four hierarchical occurrences, one for each person, with skills subordinate to persons; and (b) three hierarchical occurrences, one for each skill, with persons subordinate to skills.

3.3 The network model consists of four person record occurrences, three skill record occurrences, and eight "connector" record occurrences. Each connector record occurrence represents the connection between one person and one skill, and contains the date the person attended the corresponding course. Each connector is on one "person" chain and one "skill" chain.

3.4 (a) Find names of all persons having a specified skill (S, say). This is very similar to the queries Q1 and Q2 of Fig. 3.2. For the relational model of Answer

3.1, the required tuple-at-a-time procedure resembles the two relational procedures of Fig. 3.2; an algebraic procedure is:

```
SELECT PERSKIL WHERE SNAME=S GIVING TEMP.
PROJECT TEMP OVER PNAME GIVING RESULT.
```

For hierarchy (a) of Answer 3.2—persons superior to skills—the required procedure follows that shown for Q2 in Fig. 3.4; for hierarchy (b)—skills superior to persons—it follows that shown for Q1 in Fig. 3.4. For the network of Answer 3.3 the required procedure follows that for Q1 (or Q2) in Fig. 3.6.

(b) Find names of all persons having at least one skill in common with a specified person (P, say). This is much more difficult.

Relational model of Answer 3.1

Tuple-at-a-time solution

```
part1:
nexta:      get next PERSKIL tuple where PNAME = P
            tuple found? if not, go to part2
            add SNAME to working list
            go to nexta
part2:
            get to start of PERSKIL relation
nextb:      get next PERSKIL tuple
            tuple found? if not, go to exit
            does SNAME exist in working list? if not, go to nextb
            merge PNAME into result list (eliminating duplicates)
            go to nextb
exit:       print result list
```

Note that we require an "initialize" operator (used at the beginning of part2). Incidentally the procedure could be made more efficient, and the "eliminate duplicates" step would be unnecessary, if we could rely on PERSKIL being ordered in ascending (PNAME, SNAME) sequence—see Chapter 4.

Algebraic solution

```
SELECT PERSKIL WHERE PNAME=P GIVING TEMP1.
PROJECT TEMP1 OVER SNAME GIVING TEMP2.
JOIN TEMP2 AND PERSKIL OVER SNAME GIVING TEMP3.
PROJECT TEMP3 OVER PNAME GIVING RESULT.
```

Hierarchy (a) of Answer 3.2

```
part1:
            get [next] person where PNAME = P
```

```
nexta:      get next skill for this person
            skill found? if not, go to part2
            add SNAME to working list
            go to nexta
part2:
            get to start of database
nextb:      get next person
            person found? if not, go to exit
nextc:      get next skill for this person
            skill found? if not, go to nextb
            does SNAME exist in working list? if not, go to nextc
            add PNAME to result list
            go to nextb
exit:       print result list
```

Hierarchy (b) of Answer 3.2

```
part1:
nexta:      get next skill
            skill found? if not, go to part2
            get [next] person for this skill where PNAME = P
            person found? if not, go to nexta
            add SNAME to working list
            go to nexta
part2:
            get to start of working list
nextb:      set S = next SNAME in working list
            next SNAME found? if not, go to exit
            get to start of database
            get [next] skill where SNAME = S
nextc:      get next person for this skill
            person found? if not, go to nextb
            merge PNAME into result list (eliminating duplicates)
            go to nextc
exit:       print result list
```

If we are allowed an additional form of the "initialize" operator (see the fifth line below), an alternative strategy is:

```
nexta:      get next skill
            skill found? if not, go to exit
            get [next] person for this skill where PNAME = P
            person found? if not, go to nexta
            get to start of persons for this skill
nextb:      get next person for this skill
            person found? if not, go to nexta
```

                    merge PNAME into result list (eliminating duplicates)
                    go to nextb
exit: print result list

Network of Answer 3.3

part1:
                    get [next] person where PNAME = P
nexta: get next connector for this person
                    connector found? if not, go to part2
                    get superior skill for this connector
                    add SNAME to working list
                    go to nexta
part2:
                    get to start of working list
nextb: set S = next SNAME in working list
                    next SNAME found? if not, go to exit
                    get to start of database
                    get [next] skill where SNAME = S
nextc: get next connector for this skill
                    connector found? if not, go to nextb
                    get superior person for this connector
                    merge PNAME into result list (eliminating duplicates)
                    go to nextc
exit: print result list

CHAPTER 4: THE RELATIONAL DATA MODEL

4.2   <u>DOMAIN</u> PNAME   CHARACTER(15)
                   ADDR   CHARACTER(40)
                   SNAME   CHARACTER(15)
                   COURSE   CHARACTER(30)
                   JOBCODE   CHARACTER(2)
                   DATE   CHARACTER(6)
                   . . . . .
           <u>RELATION</u> PERSON   (PNAME,ADDR,...) <u>KEY</u>(PNAME)
                   SKILL   (SNAME,COURSE,JOBCODE,...) <u>KEY</u>(SNAME)
                   PERSKIL (PNAME,SNAME,DATE) <u>KEY</u>(PNAME,SNAME)

CHAPTER 5: A DATA SUBLANGUAGE BASED ON RELATIONAL CALCULUS

5.1   <u>GET</u> W (J)

5.2   <u>GET</u> W (J) : J.CITY='LONDON'

5.3   <u>GET</u> W (1) (P.P#) : <u>UP</u> P.WEIGHT

5.4   <u>GET</u> W (SPJ.S#) : SPJ.J#='J1'

5.5   <u>GET</u> W (SPJ.S#) : SPJ.P#='P1'∧SPJ.J#='J1'

5.6   <u>RANGE</u> SPJ SPJX
        <u>GET</u> W (J.JNAME) : ∃SPJX(SPJX.J#=J.J#
                                     ∧SPJX.S#='S1')

5.7   <u>RANGE</u> SPJ SPJX
        <u>GET</u> W (P.COLOR) : ∃SPJX(SPJX.P#=P.P#
                                     ∧SPJX.S#='S1')

5.8   <u>RANGE</u> SPJ SPJX
        <u>GET</u> W (S.S#) : ∃SPJX(SPJX.S#=S.S#∧SPJX.J#='J1')
                         ∧∃SPJX(SPJX.S#=S.S#∧SPJX.J#='J2')

5.9   <u>RANGE</u> P PX
        <u>GET</u> W (SPJ.S#) : ∃PX(PX.COLOR='RED'∧SPJ.P#=PX.P#
                                  ∧SPJ.J#='J1')

5.10   <u>RANGE</u> J JX
        <u>GET</u> W (SPJ.P#) : ∃JX(JX.CITY='LONDON'∧SPJ.J#=JX.J#)

5.11   <u>RANGE</u> P PX
        <u>RANGE</u> J JX
        <u>GET</u> W (SPJ.S#) : ∃PX∃JX(PX.COLOR='RED'
                            ∧(JX.CITY='LONDON'∨JX.CITY='PARIS')
                                  ∧SPJ.P#=PX.P#∧SPJ.J#=JX.J#)

5.12   <u>RANGE</u> S SX
        <u>RANGE</u> J JX
        <u>GET</u> W (SPJ.P#) : ∃SX∃JX(SX.CITY=JX.CITY
                            ∧SPJ.S#=SX.S#∧SPJ.J#=JX.J#)

5.13   <u>RANGE</u> S SX
        <u>RANGE</u> J JX
        <u>GET</u> W (SPJ.P#) : ∃SX∃JX(SX.CITY='LONDON'∧JX.CITY='LONDON'
                            ∧SPJ.S#=SX.S#∧SPJ.J#=JX.J#)

5.14   <u>RANGE</u> S SX
        <u>RANGE</u> J JX
        <u>GET</u> W (SPJ.J#) : ∃SX∃JX(SX.CITY≠JX.CITY
                                  ∧SPJ.S#=SX.S#
                                  ∧SPJ.J#=JX.J#)

5.15   <u>RANGE</u> S SX
        <u>RANGE</u> P PX
        <u>RANGE</u> SPJ SPJX
        <u>GET</u> W (J.J#) : ¬∃SPJX∃SX∃PX(SX.CITY='LONDON'
                                  ∧PX.COLOR='RED'
                                  ∧SPJX.S#=SX.S#∧SPJX.P#=PX.P#
                                  ∧SPJX.J#=J.J#)

5.16   RANGE P PX
       RANGE SPJ SPJY
       RANGE SPJ SPJZ
       GET W (SPJ.S#) : ∃SPJY(SPJY.P#=SPJ.P#
                          ∧∃SPJZ(SPJZ.S#=SPJY.S#
                                ∧∃PX(PX.P#=SPJZ.P#
                                    ∧PX.COLOR='RED')))

5.17   RANGE SPJ SPJZ
       GET W (SPJ.J#) : ∃SPJZ(SPJ.P#=SPJZ.P#
                      ∧SPJZ.S#='S1')

5.18   RANGE SPJ SPJX
       GET W (S.CITY,J.CITY) : ∃SPJX(SPJX.S#=S.S#∧SPJX.J#=J.J#)

The result of this <u>GET</u> is a binary relation in which the domain CITY appears twice. See the annotation to reference [5.8] for some comments on the naming problems arising in such a situation.

5.19   RANGE SPJ SPJX
       GET W (S.CITY,P.P#,J.CITY) : ∃SPJX(SPJX.S#=S.S#
                                 ∧SPJX.P#=P.P#
                                 ∧SPJX.J#=J.J#)

5.20   RANGE SPJ SPJX
       GET W (S.CITY,P.P#,J.CITY) : ∃SPJX(SPJX.S#=S.S#
                                 ∧SPJX.P#=P.P#
                                 ∧SPJX.J#=J.J#
                                 ∧S.CITY≠J.CITY)

5.21   RANGE P PX
       RANGE J JX
       RANGE SPJ SPJX
       GET W (S.S#) : ∃PX∀JX∃SPJX(SPJX.S#=S.S#∧
                              SPJX.P#=PX.P#∧
                              SPJX.J#=JX.J#)

5.22   RANGE SPJ SPJX
       GET W (J.J#) : ∀SPJX(SPJX.J#=J.J#⇒SPJX.S#='S1')

Note that this <u>GET</u> would retrieve J# values for projects that are not supplied at all. If we wanted to exclude such values, we could extend the predicate as follows:

$$...∧∃SPJX(SPJX.J\#=J.J\#)$$

Incidentally, it is perfectly allowable to use the same range variable SPJX again (though possibly a bit confusing).

5.23   RANGE J JX
RANGE SPJ SPJX
GET W (P.P#) : ∀JX(JX.CITY='LONDON'
⇒∃SPJX(SPJX.P#=P.P#∧SPJX.J#=JX.J#))

5.24   RANGE P PX
RANGE SPJ SPJY
RANGE SPJ SPJZ
GET W (J.J#) : ∀PX(∃SPJY(SPJY.S#='S1'∧SPJY.P#=PX.P#)
⇒ ∃SPJZ(SPJZ.J#=J.J#∧SPJZ.P#=PX.P#))

5.25   RANGE P PX
RANGE SPJ SPJY
RANGE SPJ SPJZ
GET W (J.J#) : ∀PX(∃SPJY(SPJY.P#=PX.P#∧SPJY.J#=J.J#)
⇒ ∃SPJZ(SPJZ.P#=PX.P#∧SPJZ.S#='S1'))

5.26   RANGE P PX
RANGE SPJ SPJY
RANGE SPJ SPJZ
GET W (J.J#) : ∀PX(∃SPJY(SPJY.S#='S1'∧SPJY.P#=PX.P#)
⇒∃SPJZ(SPJZ.S#='S1'∧SPJZ.P#=PX.P#
∧SPJZ.J#=J.J#))

5.27   RANGE P PX
RANGE SPJ SPJY
RANGE SPJ SPJZ
GET W (J.J#) : ∀PX(∃SPJY(SPJY.P#=PX.P#∧SPJY.J#=J.J#)
⇒∃SPJZ(SPJZ.P#=PX.P#∧SPJZ.J#=J.J#
∧SPJZ.S#='S1'))

5.28   RANGE S SX
RANGE P PX
RANGE SPJ SPJY
RANGE SPJ SPJZ
GET W (J.J#) : ∀SX(∃SPJY∃PX(PX.COLOR='RED'
∧PX.P#=SPJY.P#
∧SPJY.S#=SX.S#)
⇒∃SPJZ(SPJZ.S#=SX.S#
∧SPJZ.J#=J.J#))

5.29   HOLD W (J.J#,J.JNAME) : J.J#='J6'
W.JNAME='VIDEO'
UPDATE W

5.30   HOLD W (P.P#,P.COLOR) : P.COLOR='RED'
W.COLOR='ORANGE' (an array assignment)
UPDATE W

5.31 HOLD WX (SPJ) : SPJ.S#='S1'∧SPJ.P#='P1'∧SPJ.J#='J1'
<u>DELETE</u> WX
<u>HOLD</u> WY (SPJ) : SPJ.S#='S2'∧SPJ.P#='P1'∧SPJ.J#='J1'
IF WY EMPTY THEN BEGIN
                 WX.S#='S2'
                 <u>PUT</u> WX (SPJ)
           END
        ELSE BEGIN
                 WY.QTY=WY.QTY+WX.QTY
                 <u>UPDATE</u> WY
           END

5.32 We assume that workspace W is appropriately structured already.

W.P#(1)='P7'   W.P#(2)='P8'
W.PNAME(1)='WASHER'   W.PNAME(2)='SCREW'
W.COLOR(1)='GREY'   W.COLOR(2)='YELLOW'
W.WEIGHT(1)=1   W.WEIGHT(2)=2
            <u>PUT</u> W (P)

5.33 <u>RANGE</u> P PV
<u>HOLD</u> W (SPJ) : ∃PV(PV.COLOR='RED'∧PV.P#=SPJ.P#)
<u>DELETE</u> W
<u>HOLD</u> W (P) : P.COLOR='RED'
<u>DELETE</u> W

5.34 <u>GET</u> W (COUNT(SPJ.J#)) : SPJ.S#='S3'

5.35 <u>GET</u> W (ITOTAL(SPJ,(S#,P#),QTY)) : SPJ.S#='S1'
                                        ∧SPJ.P#='P1'

5.36 <u>GET</u> W (SPJ.P#,SPJ.J#,ITOTAL(SPJ,(P#,J#),QTY))

CHAPTER 6: A DATA SUBLANGUAGE BASED ON RELATIONAL ALGEBRA

In the following solutions we have shown algebraic *expressions* rather than statements (no GIVING clause is included). Questions have been assumed to be numbered 6.n, where n is the number of the original exercise in Chapter 5.

6.1 SELECT J

6.2 SELECT J WHERE CITY='LONDON'

6.3 Cannot be done with the available operations (in DSL ALPHA terms, we need to be able to specify an ordering and a quota).

6.4 PROJECT (SELECT SPJ WHERE J#='J1') OVER S#

6.5 PROJECT (SELECT SPJ WHERE J#='J1' AND P#='P1') OVER S#

6.6 PROJECT (JOIN J AND
                   (SELECT SPJ WHERE S#='S1')
                          OVER J#) OVER JNAME

6.7   PROJECT (JOIN P AND
                                (SELECT SPJ WHERE S#='S1')
                                                OVER P#) OVER COLOR

6.8   (PROJECT (SELECT SPJ WHERE J#='J1') OVER S#)
            INTERSECT
            (PROJECT (SELECT SPJ WHERE J#='J2') OVER S#)

6.9   PROJECT (JOIN (SELECT SPJ WHERE J#='J1')
                        AND
                        (SELECT P WHERE COLOR='RED')
                        OVER P#) OVER S#

6.10   PROJECT (JOIN SPJ AND
                                (SELECT J WHERE CITY='LONDON')
                                        OVER J#) OVER P#

6.11   PROJECT (JOIN (SELECT J WHERE CITY='LONDON' OR CITY='PARIS')
                            AND (JOIN SPJ AND (SELECT P WHERE COLOR='RED')
                                        OVER P#) OVER J#) OVER S#

6.12   DIVIDE (PROJECT SPJ OVER P#,S#,J#)
                BY (PROJECT (JOIN S AND J OVER CITY) OVER S#,J#)
                        OVER S#,J#

Here we are considering the dividend as a binary relation with attributes P# and
(S#, J#)—a composite attribute—and the divisor as a unary relation with the
same combination (S#, J#) as its single attribute. The syntax is somewhat
inadequate.

6.13   DIVIDE (PROJECT SPJ OVER P#,S#,J#)
                BY (PROJECT (JOIN (SELECT S WHERE CITY='LONDON')
                                AND (SELECT J WHERE CITY='LONDON')
                                OVER CITY) OVER S#,J#) OVER S#,J#

See 6.12.

6.14   PROJECT (JOIN (PROJECT (JOIN S AND J WHERE CITY≠CITY) OVER S#,J#)
                        AND (PROJECT SPJ OVER S#,J#) OVER S#,J#) OVER J#

Again we are treating the combination (S#, J#) as a single attribute. This
example illustrates the fact that, as with the calculus, we need to be able to specify
names for result attributes, in general—the operand of the outermost PROJECT
actually has two (identical) S# attributes and two (identical) J# attributes, so that
the final "OVER J#" is strictly ambiguous. For present purposes we shall ignore
this ambiguity, assuming from here on that in such a situation redundant duplicate
attributes are simply eliminated before the PROJECT is applied.

6.15   (PROJECT J OVER J#)
      MINUS
      (PROJECT (JOIN (SELECT S WHERE CITY='LONDON')
                 AND (JOIN (SELECT P WHERE COLOR='RED')
                             AND SPJ OVER P#) OVER S#) OVER J#)

6.16   PROJECT (JOIN SPJ AND
               (PROJECT (JOIN SPJ AND
                       (PROJECT (JOIN SPJ AND
                             (SELECT P WHERE COLOR='RED')
                             OVER P#)
                         OVER S#)
                       OVER S#)
                     OVER P#)
                 OVER P#)
             OVER S#

6.17   PROJECT (JOIN SPJ AND
               (PROJECT (SELECT SPJ WHERE S#='S1')
                         OVER P#) OVER P#) OVER J#

6.18   PROJECT (JOIN S AND
               (JOIN SPJ AND J OVER J#)
                   OVER S#) OVER S_CITY,J_CITY

Here we are forced to introduce a makeshift scheme for naming result attributes.

6.19   PROJECT (JOIN S AND
               (JOIN SPJ AND J OVER J#)
                   OVER S#) OVER S_CITY,P#,J_CITY

See 6.18.

6.20   SELECT (PROJECT (JOIN S AND
                    (JOIN SPJ AND J OVER J#)
                        OVER S#) OVER S_CITY,P#,J_CITY)
                    WHERE S_CITY≠J_CITY

See 6.18.

6.21   PROJECT (DIVIDE (PROJECT SPJ OVER S#,P#,J#)
                   BY (PROJECT J OVER J#) OVER J#) OVER S#

We are treating $(S\#, P\#)$ as a composite attribute.

6.22   (PROJECT (SELECT SPJ WHERE S#='S1') OVER J#)
      MINUS
      (PROJECT (SELECT SPJ WHERE S#≠'S1') OVER J#)

6.23   DIVIDE (PROJECT SPJ OVER P#,J#)
          BY (PROJECT (SELECT J WHERE CITY='LONDON') OVER J#) OVER J#

6.24   DIVIDE (PROJECT SPJ OVER J#,P#)
          BY (PROJECT (SELECT SPJ WHERE S#='S1') OVER P#) OVER P#

6.25   (PROJECT J OVER J#)
          MINUS
          (PROJECT (JOIN SPJ AND
                         ((PROJECT P OVER P#)
                         MINUS
                         (PROJECT (SELECT SPJ WHERE S#='S1') OVER P#))
                         OVER P#) OVER J#)

6.26   DIVIDE (PROJECT SPJ OVER J#,S#,P#)
          BY (PROJECT (SELECT SPJ WHERE S#='S1') OVER S#,P#)
             OVER S#,P#

We are treating (S#, P#) as a composite attribute.

6.27   (PROJECT J OVER J#)
          MINUS
          (PROJECT ((PROJECT SPJ OVER J#,P#)
                   MINUS
                   (PROJECT (SELECT SPJ WHERE S#='S1') OVER J#,P#))
                                                    OVER J#)

6.28   DIVIDE (PROJECT SPJ OVER J#,S#)
          BY (PROJECT (JOIN SPJ AND
                           (SELECT P WHERE COLOR='RED')
                           OVER P#) OVER S#) OVER S#

CHAPTER 7: THE DATA SUBLANGUAGE SEQUEL

7.1 Let A and B be any two members of the given set of named relations. Further (unnamed) relations may be derived by means of unnested algebraic expressions involving exactly one of the algebraic operators and one or both, as appropriate, of A and B. For each such unnested expression it is fairly straightforward to find a semantically equivalent SEQUEL expression, as indicated below. (Notation is intended to be self-explanatory.)

Algebra	SEQUEL
A UNION B	SELECT all-columns-of-A FROM A UNION SELECT all-columns-of-B FROM B
A INTERSECT B	SELECT all-columns-of-A FROM A INTERSECT SELECT all-columns-of-B FROM B

```
A MINUS B                      SELECT all-columns-of-A FROM A
                               MINUS
                               SELECT all-columns-of-B FROM B

A TIMES B                      SELECT all-columns-of-A,all-columns-of-B
                               FROM A,B

SELECT A WHERE p               SELECT all-columns-of-A FROM A
                               WHERE p

PROJECT A OVER x               SELECT x FROM A
                               (We shall ignore UNIQUE.)

JOIN A AND B WHERE p           SELECT all-columns-of-A,all-columns-of-B
                               FROM A,B
                               WHERE p

DIVIDE A BY B OVER Y AND Z     SELECT X
                               FROM A
                               GROUP BY X
                               HAVING SET (Y) CONTAINS
                                        SELECT Z
                                        FROM B
```

(For DIVIDE we assume that A is a binary relation with attributes X and Y, and that B is a unary relation with attribute Z.)

Given that SEQUEL also provides an assignment operator, allowing us to retain (and give a name to) the result of any query, a procedure along the lines of the foregoing is sufficient to demonstrate the completeness of the language in Codd's original sense [5.5]. However, we indicate below how one might show completeness in the more demanding sense that any relation derivable via a single algebraic expression be derivable via a single SEQUEL expression.

In outline the proof runs as follows.

Step 1. (Already done.) We show that, if A and B are any two members of the given set of named relations, any relation derivable via a single unnested algebraic expression involving exactly one of the algebraic operators and A and/or B may be derived via a single SEQUEL expression.

Step 2. Now let A and B be any two relations derivable from the given set of named relations via possibly nested algebraic expressions. Further (unnamed) relations may be derived from A and B by means of expressions involving exactly one of the algebraic operators applied to one or both, as appropriate, of A and B. We show that *if* there exist SEQUEL expressions representing A and B, *then* there exists a SEQUEL expression representing each such derived relation.

Step 3. From Steps 1 and 2 taken together it follows that any relation derivable by means of an arbitrarily complex single algebraic expression is also derivable by means of a suitable single SEQUEL expression.

Now for the details.

Step 1

(Already done.)

Step 2

The following identity allows us to ignore the DIVIDE operator. (A is a binary relation with attributes X and Y, B is a unary relation with attribute Z.)

```
DIVIDE A BY B OVER Y AND Z ≡ PROJECT (A MINUS ((PROJECT A OVER X)
                                             TIMES B) MINUS A)
                                        OVER X
```

The following identities allow us to ignore the cases where A (or B) is of the form C UNION D.

```
(C UNION D) UNION E        ≡  C UNION D UNION E

(C UNION D) INTERSECT E  ≡  (C INTERSECT E)
                            UNION
                            (D INTERSECT E)

(C UNION D) MINUS E       ≡  (C MINUS E)
                            UNION
                            (D MINUS E)

E MINUS (C UNION D)       ≡  (E MINUS C)
                            INTERSECT
                            (E MINUS D)

(C UNION D) TIMES E       ≡  (C TIMES E)
                            UNION
                            (D TIMES E)
                            (Similarly for E TIMES (C UNION D).)

SELECT (C UNION D) WHERE p
                          ≡  (SELECT C WHERE p)
                            UNION
                            (SELECT D WHERE p)

PROJECT (C UNION D) OVER x
                          ≡  (PROJECT C OVER x)
                            UNION
                            (PROJECT D OVER x)

JOIN (C UNION D) AND E OVER x
                          ≡  (JOIN C AND E OVER x)
                            UNION
                            (JOIN D AND E OVER x)

                            (Similarly for
                            JOIN E AND (C UNION D) OVER x.)
```

From these identities it follows that we need never consider an algebraic expression in which one of the operands is a union—such an expression can always be replaced by an expression consisting of the union (or in one case the intersection) of two subexpressions not involving a union. Without going into details we assert that it is also possible to ignore operands of the form C INTERSECT D and C MINUS D.

Now suppose that SEQUEL expressions giving rise to A and B are, respectively,

```
SELECT column-list-A  and  SELECT column-list-B
FROM    table-list-A        FROM    table-list-B
WHERE   predicate-A         WHERE   predicate-B
```

We refer to these two expressions as QA and QB. We shall consider later whether it is reasonable to suppose that QA and QB exist.

Algebra	SEQUEL
A UNION B	QA UNION QB
A INTERSECT B	QA INTERSECT QB
A MINUS B	QA MINUS QB
A TIMES B	SELECT column-list-A,column-list-B FROM table-list-A,table-list-B WHERE predicate-A AND predicate-B
SELECT A WHERE p	SELECT column-list-A FROM table-list-A WHERE predicate-A AND p
PROJECT A OVER x	SELECT x FROM table-list-A WHERE predicate-A
JOIN A AND B OVER x	SELECT column-list-A,column-list-B FROM table-list-A,table-list-B WHERE predicate-A AND predicate-B AND x

Step 3

From Steps 1 and 2 it follows that *if* there exists a SEQUEL expression corresponding to the application of a single algebraic operator, *then* there exists a SEQUEL expression corresponding to the application of two algebraic operators in sequence, and *therefore* there exists a SEQUEL expression for a sequence of 3, 4,..., any number of operators. In other words, we would have demonstrated SEQUEL's relational completeness.

The flaw is that there does *not* exist a SEQUEL expression of the assumed form (SELECT-FROM-WHERE) corresponding to the algebraic UNION operator. (We have not shown a SELECT-FROM-WHERE block for IN-TERSECT or MINUS either, but it is easy to see that single blocks do exist in these cases: e.g., for INTERSECT the block is SELECT all-columns-of-A FROM A WHERE ⟨all-columns-of-A⟩ IS IN B.) Thus in Step 2 our assumption should have been that QA and QB were SEQUEL expressions of the form

$$Q \text{ UNION } Q \text{ UNION } Q \cdot \cdot \cdot \cdot \cdot$$

where each Q was a SELECT-FROM-WHERE block. It is left as an exercise to the reader to reexamine the "equivalences" of Step 2 under this revised assumption and to satisfy himself that SEQUEL is indeed relationally complete in the more demanding sense of the term.

7.2 Many of the following answers are not unique.

7.2.1
```
SELECT *
FROM   J
```

7.2.2
```
SELECT *
FROM   J
WHERE  CITY='LONDON'
```

7.2.4
```
SELECT UNIQUE S#
FROM   SPJ
WHERE  J#='J1'
```

7.2.5
```
SELECT S#
FROM   SPJ
WHERE  P#='P1' AND J#='J1'
```

7.2.6
```
SELECT JNAME
FROM   J
WHERE  J# IN
          SELECT J#
          FROM   SPJ
          WHERE  S#='S1'
```

7.2.7
```
SELECT UNIQUE COLOR
FROM   P
WHERE  P# IN
          SELECT P#
          FROM   SPJ
          WHERE  S#='S1'
```

7.2.8
```
SELECT UNIQUE S#
FROM   SPJ X
WHERE  ('J1','J2') IN
          SELECT J#
          FROM   SPJ
          WHERE  S#=X.S#
```

or:

```
SELECT S#
FROM   SPJ
GROUP  BY S#
HAVING SET(J#) CONTAINS ('J1','J2')
```

7.2.9
```
SELECT UNIQUE S#
FROM   SPJ
WHERE  J#='J1'
AND    P# IN
       SELECT P#
       FROM   P
       WHERE  COLOR='RED'
```

7.2.10
```
SELECT UNIQUE P#
FROM   SPJ
WHERE  J# IN
       SELECT J#
       FROM   J
       WHERE  CITY='LONDON'
```

7.2.11
```
SELECT UNIQUE S#
FROM   SPJ
WHERE  J# IN
       (SELECT J#
       FROM   J
       WHERE  CITY='LONDON'
       OR     CITY='PARIS')
AND    P# IN
       (SELECT P#
       FROM   P
       WHERE  COLOR='RED')
```

Note that parentheses are required in this case to resolve a potential ambiguity.

7.2.12
```
SELECT UNIQUE P#
FROM   SPJ
WHERE  (SELECT CITY
       FROM   J
       WHERE  J#=SPJ.J#)
       =
       (SELECT CITY
       FROM   S
       WHERE  S#=SPJ.J#)
```

7.2.13 SELECT UNIQUE P#
        FROM   SPJ
        WHERE   J# IN
                (SELECT J#
                 FROM   J
                 WHERE   CITY='LONDON')
        AND   S# IN
                (SELECT S#
                 FROM   S
                 WHERE   CITY='LONDON')

7.2.14 SELECT UNIQUE J#
        FROM   SPJ
        WHERE   (SELECT CITY FROM J WHERE J#=SPJ.J#)
                    ¬=
                (SELECT CITY FROM S WHERE S#=SPJ.S#)

7.2.15 SELECT J#
        FROM   J
        WHERE   ('LONDON','RED') NOT IN
                (SELECT CITY,COLOR
                 FROM   S,P
                 WHERE   (S#,P#) IN
                        (SELECT S#,P#
                         FROM   SPJ
                         WHERE   J#=J.J#))

7.2.16 SELECT UNIQUE S#
        FROM   SPJ
        WHERE   P# IN
                SELECT P#
                FROM   SPJ
                WHERE   S# IN
                        SELECT S#
                        FROM   SPJ
                        WHERE   P# IN
                                SELECT P#
                                FROM   P
                                WHERE   COLOR='RED'

7.2.17 SELECT UNIQUE J#
        FROM   SPJ
        WHERE   P# IN
                SELECT P#
                FROM   SPJ
                WHERE   S#='S1'

7.2.18 SELECT UNIQUE S.CITY,J.CITY   *or:*   SELECT UNIQUE S.CITY,J.CITY
        FROM   S,J   FROM   S,SPJ,J
        WHERE   (S#,J#) IN   WHERE   S.S#=SPJ.S#
                (SELECT S#,J#   AND   J.J#=SPJ.J#
                 FROM   SPJ)

7.2.19 SELECT S.CITY,P#,J.CITY
FROM   S,SPJ,J
WHERE   S.S#=SPJ.S#
AND   J.J#=SPJ.J#

7.2.20 SELECT S.CITY,P#,J.CITY
FROM   S,SPJ,J
WHERE   S.S#=SPJ.S#
AND   J.J#=SPJ.J#
AND   S.CITY¬=J.CITY

7.2.21 SELECT UNIQUE S#   *or:*   SELECT UNIQUE S#
FROM   SPJ X   FROM   SPJ
WHERE (SELECT J#   GROUP BY S#,P#
        FROM   SPJ   HAVING SET(J#) =
        WHERE   S#=X.S# AND P#=X.P#)   (SELECT J#
        =   FROM   J)
       (SELECT J#
        FROM   J)

7.2.22 SELECT J#
FROM   SPJ
GROUP BY J#
HAVING SET(S#)=('S1')

7.2.23 SELECT UNIQUE P#
FROM   SPJ X
WHERE (SELECT J#
        FROM   SPJ
        WHERE   P#=X.P#)
       CONTAINS
       (SELECT J#
        FROM   J
        WHERE   CITY='LONDON')

7.2.24 SELECT UNIQUE J#
FROM   SPJ
GROUP BY J#
HAVING SET(P#) CONTAINS
        (SELECT P#
         FROM   SPJ
         WHERE   S#='S1')

7.2.25 SELECT J#
FROM   SPJ
GROUP BY J#
HAVING SET(P#) IN
        (SELECT P#
         FROM   SPJ
         WHERE   S#='S1')

7.2.26   SELECT UNIQUE J#
        FROM   SPJ X
        WHERE (SELECT P#
               FROM   SPJ
               WHERE J#=X.J# AND S#='S1')
               =
              (SELECT P#
               FROM   SPJ
               WHERE S#='S1')

7.2.27   SELECT J#
        FROM   SPJ X
        GROUP BY J#
        HAVING SET(P#) =
            (SELECT P#
             FROM   SPJ
             WHERE S#='S1'
             AND   J#=X.J#)

7.2.28   SELECT UNIQUE J#
        FROM   SPJ
        GROUP BY J#
        HAVING SET(S#) CONTAINS
            (SELECT S#
             FROM   SPJ
             WHERE P# IN
                  SELECT P#
                  FROM   P
                  WHERE COLOR='RED')

7.2.29   UPDATE J
        SET   JNAME='VIDEO'
        WHERE J#='J6'

7.2.30   UPDATE P
        SET   COLOR='ORANGE'
        WHERE COLOR='RED'

7.2.32   INSERT INTO P:
            (('P7','WASHER','GREY',1),
            ('P8','SCREW','YELLOW',2))

7.2.33   DELETE SPJ
        WHERE P# IN
            SELECT P#
            FROM   P
            WHERE COLOR='RED'
        DELETE P
        WHERE COLOR='RED'

7.2.34   SELECT COUNT(UNIQUE J#)
         FROM   SPJ
         WHERE S#='S3'

7.2.35   SELECT SUM(QTY)
         FROM   SPJ
         WHERE S#='S1'
         AND   P#='P1'

7.2.36   SELECT P#,J#,SUM(QTY)
         FROM   SPJ
         GROUP BY P#,J#

CHAPTER 8: QUERY BY EXAMPLE

Solutions are given below only for some of the less straightforward exercises.

8.2

J	J#	JNAME	CITY
P.			LONDON

8.3

P	P#	PNAME	COLOR	WEIGHT
¬	P.PX			$\begin{array}{c} W \\ < \underline{W} \end{array}$

It is not possible to obtain just *one* such part number; Query By Example does not provide a "quota."

8.11

P	P#	PNAME	COLOR	WEIGHT
	PX		RED	
	PY		RED	

J	J#	JNAME	CITY
	JX		LONDON
	JY		PARIS

SPJ	S#	P#	J#	QTY
	P.SX	PX	JX	
	P.SY	PY	JY	

Note that two distinct example part numbers are needed.

8.14

S	S#	SNAME	STATUS	CITY
	SX			C

J	J#	JNAME	CITY
	JX		¬C

SPJ	S#	P#	J#	QTY
	SX		P.JX	

8.15

S	S#	SNAME	STATUS	CITY
	SX			LONDON

P	P#	PNAME	COLOR	WEIGHT
	PX		RED	

SPJ	S#	P#	J#	QTY
¬	SX	PX	JX	
			P.JX	

8.16

SPJ	S#	P#	J#	QTY
	P.SX	PX		
	SY	PX		
	SY	PY		

P	P#	PNAME	COLOR	WEIGHT
	PY		RED	

8.17

SPJ	S#	P#	J#	QTY
	S1	PX		
		PX	P.JX	

8.18

S	S#	SNAME	STATUS	CITY
	SX			SC

J	J#	JNAME	CITY
	JX		JC

SPJ	S#	P#	J#	QTY
	SX		JX	

RESULT	SCITY	JCITY
	P.SC	P.JC

8.21

SPJ	S#	P#	J#	QTY
	P.<u>SX</u>	<u>PX</u>	ALL.<u>JX</u>	

J	J#	JNAME	CITY
	ALL.<u>JX</u>		

8.22

SPJ	S#	P#	J#	QTY
	S1		P.<u>JX</u>	
¬	¬S1		<u>JX</u>	

8.23

SPJ	S#	P#	J#	QTY
		P.<u>PX</u>	[ALL.<u>JX</u>]	

J	J#	JNAME	CITY
	ALL.<u>JX</u>		LONDON

8.24

SPJ	S#	P#	J#	QTY
		[ALL.<u>PX</u>]	P.<u>JX</u>	
	S1	ALL.<u>PX</u>		

8.25

SPJ	S#	P#	J#	QTY
		ALL.<u>PX</u>	P.<u>JX</u>	
	S1	ALL.<u>PX</u>		

8.26

SPJ	S#	P#	J#	QTY
	S1	ALL.<u>PX</u>	P.<u>JX</u>	
	S1	ALL.<u>PX</u>		

8.27

SPJ	S#	P#	J#	QTY
		ALL.<u>PX</u>	P.<u>JX</u>	
	S1	ALL.<u>PX</u>	<u>JX</u>	

8.28

SPJ	S#	P#	J#	QTY
	[ALL.<u>SX</u>]		P.<u>JX</u>	
	ALL.<u>SX</u>	<u>PX</u>		

P	P#	PNAME	COLOR	WEIGHT
	<u>PX</u>		RED	

8.31 If S2-P1-J1 row does not already exist:

SPJ	S#	P#	J#	QTY
	S1	P1	J1	<u>M</u>
UPDATE.	S2	P1	J1	<u>M</u>

Else:

SPJ	S#	P#	J#	QTY
DELETE.	S1	P1	J1	<u>M</u>
	S2	P1	J1	<u>N</u>
UPDATE.	S2	P1	J1	<u>M</u> + <u>N</u>

8.32

P	P#	PNAME	COLOR	WEIGHT
INSERT.	P7	WASHER	GREY	1
INSERT.	P8	SCREW	YELLOW	2

8.33

P	P#	PNAME	COLOR	WEIGHT
DELETE.	<u>PX</u>		RED	

SPJ	S#	P#	J#	QTY
DELETE.	<u>SX</u>	<u>PX</u>		

8.34

SPJ	S#	P#	J#	QTY
	S3		P.COUNT.U.ALL.<u>JX</u>	

8.35

SPJ	S#	P#	J#	QTY
	S1	P1		P.SUM.ALL.<u>Q</u>

8.36

SPJ	S#	P#	J#	QTY
		P.<u>PX</u>	P.<u>JX</u>	P.SUM.ALL.<u>Q</u>

CHAPTER 9: FURTHER NORMALIZATION

9.1 The diagram shows all direct functional dependencies involved, both those implied by the wording of the exercise and those corresponding to "reasonable assumptions" about the semantics (stated explicitly below). The attribute names are intended to be self-explanatory.

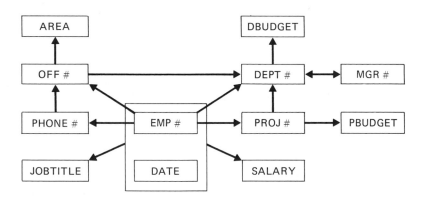

Semantic assumptions

- No employee is the manager of more than one department at a time.
- No employee works in more than one department at a time.
- No employee works on more than one project at a time.
- No employee has more than one office at a time.

- No employee has more than one phone at a time.
- No employee has more than one job at a time.
- No project is assigned to more than one department at a time.
- No office is assigned to more than one department at a time.

Step 0

First observe that the hierarchical structure may be considered as an unnormalized relation DEPT0 defined on domains DEPT# (the primary key), DBUDGET, MGR#, and three further domains whose elements are nonatomic: XEMP0, XPROJ0, and XOFFICE0, say. We may represent this unnormalized relation as

DEPT0(<u>DEPT#</u>,DBUDGET,MGR#,XEMP0,XPROJ0,XOFFICE0)

(the primary key is indicated by underlining). Now let us ignore employees and offices for a moment and concentrate on projects. Define the relation

PROJ0(<u>PROJ#</u>,PBUDGET)

to be the set of *all* PROJ#-PBUDGET pairs. Then the XPROJ0 value associated with any particular department is some subset of this set. Hence the domain XPROJ0 actually consists of the set of all subsets of PROJ0 (the so-called power set of PROJ0).

Similar remarks apply to XEMP0, XOFFICE0, and indeed to all domains in the example whose elements are nonatomic: In each case the domain is the power set of a relation defined as the set of all tuples of a particular type. We shall indicate each such power set by a prefix X. Then the complete collection of relations, normalized and unnormalized, is as follows.

DEPT0(<u>DEPT#</u>,DBUDGET,MGR#,XEMP0,XPROJ0,XOFFICE0)
EMP0(<u>EMP#</u>,PROJ#,OFF#,PHONE#,XJOB0)
JOB0(<u>JOBTITLE</u>,XSALHIST0)
SALHIST0(<u>DATE</u>,SALARY)
PROJ0(<u>PROJ#</u>,PBUDGET)
OFFICE0(<u>OFF#</u>,AREA,XPHONE0)
PHONE0(<u>PHONE#</u>)

Step 1

We now reduce this set to a collection of 1NF relations. This preliminary reduction process is explained by Codd [4.1] as follows. Starting with the relation at the top of the hierarchy, we take its primary key and expand each of the immediately subordinate relations by inserting this primary key. The primary key of each expanded relation is the combination of the primary key before expansion, together with the primary key copied down from the parent relation. Now we strike out from the parent relation all nonsimple attributes (i.e., those whose elements are nonatomic), remove the top node of the hierarchy, and repeat the same sequence of operations on each remaining subhierarchy. We obtain the following collection of 1NF relations. Note that we have lost the power sets. In fact, by considering each subhierarchy separately, we have immediately eliminated all multivalued dependencies that are not also functional dependencies (the final step of the reduction process of Section 9.6).

DEPT1(<u>DEPT#</u>,DBUDGET,MGR#)
EMP1(<u>DEPT#</u>,<u>EMP#</u>,PROJ#,OFF#,PHONE#)
JOB1(<u>DEPT#</u>,<u>EMP#</u>,JOBTITLE)
SALHIST1(<u>DEPT#</u>,<u>EMP#</u>,<u>JOBTITLE</u>,<u>DATE</u>,SALARY)
PROJ1(<u>DEPT#</u>,<u>PROJ#</u>,PBUDGET)
OFFICE1(<u>DEPT#</u>,<u>OFF#</u>,AREA)
PHONE1(<u>DEPT#</u>,<u>OFF#</u>,<u>PHONE#</u>)

Step 2

We may now reduce the 1NF relations to an equivalent 2NF collection by eliminating nonfull dependencies. We shall consider the 1NF relations one by one.

DEPT1:   This relation is already in 2NF.

EMP1:   First observe that DEPT# is actually redundant as a component of the primary key for this relation. We may take EMP# alone as the primary key, in which case the relation is in 2NF as it stands.

JOB1:   Again, observe that DEPT# is not required as a key component. Since DEPT# is functionally dependent on EMP#, we have a nonkey attribute (DEPT#) that is not fully functionally dependent on the primary key (the combination EMP#-JOBTITLE), and hence JOB1 is not 2NF. We can replace it by

JOB2(<u>EMP#</u>,<u>JOBTITLE</u>)

and

JOB2'(<u>EMP#</u>,DEPT#)

However, JOB2 is a projection of SALHIST2 (see below), and JOB2' is a projection of EMP1 (renamed as EMP2 below); hence both these relations may be discarded.

SALHIST1:   As with JOB1, we can project out DEPT# entirely. Moreover, JOBTITLE is not required as a key component; we may take the combination EMP#-DATE as the primary key, to obtain the 2NF relation

SALHIST2(<u>EMP#</u>,<u>DATE</u>,JOBTITLE,SALARY)

PROJ1:   As with EMP1, we may consider DEPT# as a nonkey attribute; the relation is then 2NF.

OFFICE1:   Similar remarks apply.

PHONE1:   We can project out DEPT# entirely, since the relation (DEPT#,OFF#) is a projection of OFFICE1 (renamed as OFFICE2 below). Also, OFF# is functionally dependent on PHONE#, so we may take PHONE# alone as the primary key, to obtain the 2NF relation

PHONE2 (<u>PHONE#</u> , OFF#)

Note that this is not necessarily a projection of EMP2 (phones or offices may exist without being assigned to employees), so that we cannot discard this relation.

Hence our collection of 2NF relations is

DEPT2 (<u>DEPT#</u> , DBUDGET , MGR#)
EMP2 (<u>EMP#</u> , DEPT# , PROJ# , OFF# , PHONE#)
SALHIST2 (<u>EMP#</u> , <u>DATE</u> , JOBTITLE , SALARY)
PROJ2 (<u>PROJ#</u> , DEPT# , PBUDGET)
OFFICE2 (<u>OFF#</u> , DEPT# , AREA)
PHONE2 (<u>PHONE#</u> , OFF#)

Step 3

Now we may reduce the 2NF relations to an equivalent 3NF set by eliminating transitive dependencies. The only 2NF relation that is not already 3NF is the relation EMP2, in which OFF# and DEPT# are both transitively dependent on the primary key EMP#: OFF# via PHONE#, and DEPT# via PROJ# *and* via OFF# (and hence PHONE#). The 3NF relations (projections) corresponding to EMP2 are

EMP3 (<u>EMP#</u> , PROJ# , PHONE#)
X (<u>PHONE#</u> , OFF#)
Y (<u>PROJ#</u> , DEPT#)
Z (<u>OFF#</u> , DEPT#)

However, X is PHONE2, Y is a projection of PROJ2, and Z is a projection of OFFICE2. Hence our collection of 3NF relations is

DEPT3 (<u>DEPT#</u> , DBUDGET , MGR#)
EMP3 (<u>EMP#</u> , PROJ# , PHONE#)
SALHIST3 (<u>EMP#</u> , <u>DATE</u> , JOBTITLE , SALARY)
PROJ3 (<u>PROJ#</u> , DEPT# , PBUDGET)
OFFICE3 (<u>OFF#</u> , DEPT# , AREA)
PHONE3 (<u>PHONE#</u> , OFF#)

Finally, each of these 3NF relations is already in 4NF (because of the way we performed the reduction to 1NF in Step 1). Note that in DEPT3 we have two candidate keys, DEPT# and MGR#.

We observe also that, given certain (reasonable) additional semantic constraints, this collection of relations is *strongly redundant* [4.1], in that the projection of relation PROJ3 over (PROJ#,DEPT#) is a projection of the join of EMP3 and PHONE3 and OFFICE3 (over PHONE# for EMP3 and PHONE3 and over OFF# for PHONE3 and OFFICE3).

Note finally that it is possible to "spot" the 4NF relations from the functional dependence diagram. (How?)

9.2 The diagram shows all direct functional dependencies involved.

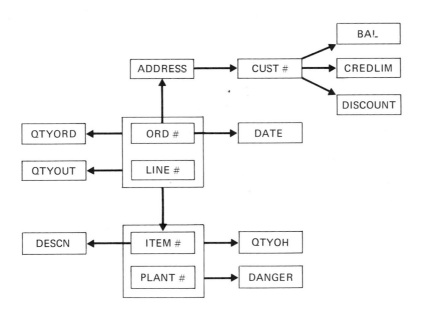

Semantic assumptions

■ No two customers have the same ship-to address.

■ Each order is identified by a unique order number.

■ Each detail line within an order is identified by a line number, unique within the order.

4NF relations

```
CUST(CUST#,BAL,CREDLIM,DISCOUNT)
SHIPTO(ADDRESS,CUST#)
ORDHEAD(ORD#,ADDRESS,DATE)
ORDLINE(ORD#,LINE#,ITEM#,QTYORD,QTYOUT)
ITEM(ITEM#,DESCN)
IP(ITEM#,PLANT#,QTYOH,DANGER)
```

9.3 Consider the processing that must be performed by a program handling orders. We assume that the input order specifies customer number, ship-to address, and details of the items ordered (item numbers and quantities).

```
GET W1 (CUST) : CUST.CUST#=input.CUST#
check balance, credit limit etc
GET W2 (SHIPTO) : SHIPTO.ADDR=input.ADDR
                 ∧SHIPTO.CUST#=input.CUST#
(this checks ship-to address)
if everything is OK go ahead and process the order
```

If 99 percent of customers actually have only one ship-to address, it would be rather inefficient to put that address in a relation other than CUST (considering only the 99 percent, ADDR is in fact functionally dependent on CUST#). We can improve matters as follows. For each customer we designate one valid ship-to address as that customer's *primary* address. For the 99 percent, of course, the primary address is the only address. Any remaining addresses we refer to as *secondary*. Relation CUST can then be redefined as

```
CUST(CUST#,ADDR,BAL,CREDLIM,DISCOUNT)
```

and relation SHIPTO can be replaced by

```
SECOND(ADDR,CUST#)
```

Here CUST.ADDR refers to the primary address, and SECOND contains all secondary addresses (and corresponding customer numbers). These relations are 4NF. The order-processing program now looks like this:

```
GET W1 (CUST) : CUST.CUST#=input.CUST#
check balance, credit limit etc
IF CUST.ADDR ≠ input.ADDR THEN
    GET W2 (SECOND) : SECOND.ADDR=input.ADDR
                     ∧,SECOND.CUST#=input.CUST#
    (this checks ship-to address)
if everything is OK go ahead and process the order
```

The advantages of this approach are as follows:

▪ Processing is simpler and marginally more efficient for 99 percent of customers.

▪ If the ship-to address is omitted from the input order, the primary address could be used by default.

▪ Suppose that the customer may have a different discount for each ship-to address. With the original approach (shown in the answer to Exercise 9.2), the DISCOUNT attribute would have to be moved to the SHIPTO relation, making processing still more complicated. With the revised approach, however, the primary discount (corresponding to the primary address) can be represented by an appearance of DISCOUNT in CUST, and secondary discounts by a corresponding appearance of DISCOUNT in SECOND. Both relations are still in 4NF, and the processing is again simpler for 99 percent of customers.

One disadvantage is that we now have an interrelation dependency, namely, that any CUST# value appearing in SECOND must also appear in CUST.

To sum up: Isolating exceptional cases is probably a valuable technique for obtaining the best of both worlds—i.e., combining the advantages of 4NF with the simplification in retrieval operations that may occur if the restrictions of 4NF are violated.

9.4 The diagrams illustrate the (most important) functional dependencies.

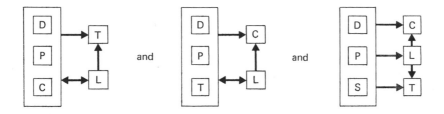

An optimal collection of 4NF relations is

```
        RELATION SCHED (L,T,C,D,P)
             KEY (L)
             UNIQUE (T,D,P)
             UNIQUE (C,D,P)

        RELATION STUDY (S,L)
             KEY (S,L)
```

This reduction is not unique.

CHAPTER 10: THE EXTERNAL MODEL

10.1 The problem here is, how should the attribute SP.QTY be defined? The sensible answer seems to be that, for given S# and P#, the SP.QTY value should be defined as the *total* of all SPJ.QTY values, taken over all J#'s for that S# and P#.

```
RELATION SP (S#,P#,QTY)
    .
    .
    .
MAPPING RANGE SPJ SPJX
           ∃SPJX(SP.S#=SPJX.S#
              ∧SP.P#=SPJX.P#
              ∧SP.QTY=ITOTAL(SPJX,(S#,P#),QTY))
```

Relation SP may be used for retrieval only.

10.3 For retrieval operations any derivable hierarchy is valid. For storage operations there are many constraints to be observed. We do not give a complete solution to the problem, but content ourselves with an illustrative example. Consider the following hierarchy (suppliers over parts over projects)

```
HIERARCHY SUPPLIER(S#,CITY)
         OVER (PART(P#)
                  OVER PROJECT(J#,QTY))
```

which we suppose to be derived in an obvious way from the suppliers-parts-projects relational model of Fig. 5.1. We observe that occurrences of the root record-type (SUPPLIER) in this hierarchy constitute a relation that is essentially the same as the underlying relation S, except that certain nonkey attributes have been omitted. It would also have been possible to omit individual tuples. We observe further that each record-type below the root (PART, PROJECT) consists of a primary key from another of the underlying relations together with zero or more nonkey attributes that are fully functionally dependent on the "fully concatenated key" (see Chapter 15) of that record-type. Given this structure, update, insert, and delete operations may be performed against each of the three record-types SUPPLIER, PART, PROJECT, and each such operation can be mapped into an equivalent operation on the underlying conceptual model, *except* for the following: (1) A PROJECT record occurrence may be deleted *only* as a side-effect of deleting a PART or SUPPLIER record occurrence; (2) a PART record occurrence may be inserted *only* if at least one subordinate PROJECT record occurrence is inserted simultaneously.

We remark in passing that this example illustrates some guidelines that could be useful in designing a hierarchical *conceptual* model. As in the case of the relational discipline (namely, fourth normal form), a guiding principle is "one fact in one place"—i.e., avoid redundancy. However, the guidelines are by no means as complete as the 4NF discipline is for relations. For example, they do not indicate whether the hierarchy should be suppliers over parts over projects, as above, or suppliers over projects over parts, or one of the other four possibilities. Nor do they indicate whether the hierarchy should contain only "SPJ information" or whether the root should contain nonkey attributes for the entity-type concerned. Finally, whichever hierarchy is selected, it will still have to be supplemented by two *relations* for the nonroot entity-types.

CHAPTER 13: THE IMS DATA MODEL

13.1
```
DBD     NAME=PUBDBD
SEGM    NAME=SUB,BYTES=45
FIELD   NAME=(SUB#,SEQ),BYTES=7,START=1
FIELD   NAME=SUBNAME,BYTES=38,START=8
SEGM    NAME=PUB,PARENT=SUB,BYTES=45
FIELD   NAME=(PUBNAME,SEQ,M),BYTES=44,START=1
FIELD   NAME=AMFLAG,BYTES=1,START=45
SEGM    NAME=DETAILS,PARENT=PUB,BYTES=25
FIELD   NAME=(DATE,SEQ,M),BYTES=6,START=1
FIELD   NAME=PUBHOUSE,BYTES=19,START=7
FIELD   NAME=JNVOLISS,BYTES=19,START=7
SEGM    NAME=AUTHOR,PARENT=PUB,BYTES=50
FIELD   NAME=(AUTHNAME,SEQ),BYTES=16,START=1
FIELD   NAME=AUTHADDR,BYTES=34,START=17
```

Note the M specifications for PUBNAME and DATE.

CHAPTER 14: THE IMS EXTERNAL MODEL

14.1
```
PCB     TYPE=DB,DBDNAME=PUBDBD,KEYLEN=67
SENSEG  NAME=SUB,PROCOPT=G
SENSEG  NAME=PUB,PARENT=SUB,PROCOPT=G
SENSEG  NAME=DETAILS,PARENT=PUB,PROCOPT=G
SENSEG  NAME=AUTHOR,PARENT=PUB,PROCOPT=G
```

CHAPTER 15: THE IMS DATA SUBLANGUAGE

15.1
```
    GU  SUB(SUBNAME='INFORMATION RETRIEVAL')
GNP GNP AUTHOR
    add author name to result list (eliminating duplicates)
    go to GNP
```

15.2
```
   GU  SUB
GN GN  PUB*D
       AUTHOR(AUTHNAME='GRACE'∨AUTHNAME='HOBBS')
       add publication name to result list
       go to GN
```

With this code a publication will appear twice in the list if Grace and Hobbs are both authors of that publication.

15.3   GU   SUB
```
GN  GN   SUB*D
             PUB(AMFLAG='M')
             AUTHOR(AUTHNAME='BRADBURY')
         add subject name to result list (eliminating duplicates)
         go to GN
```

Note that it might be more efficient to issue another 'GN SUB' before branching back. Note, too, that if we did not care whether the publication concerned was an article or a monograph, we could omit the second SSA; IMS would assume that an unconditional SSA on PUB was intended.

15.4   GU   SUB
```
GN  GN   PUB(AMFLAG='A')
         GNP AUTHOR(AUTHNAME='OWEN')
         if not found go to GN
         GNP DETAILS*F
         add publication name and date to result list
         go to GN
```

15.5   GU   SUB
```
GN  GN   PUB(AMFLAG='M')
         GNP DETAILS(PUBHOUSE='CIDER PRESS'∧DATE>'700101')
         if not found go to GN
GNP GNP AUTHOR
         if not found go to GN
         add author name to result list (eliminating duplicates)
         go to GNP
```

15.6   build PUB and DETAILS segments concatenated in I/O area
```
         ISRT SUB(SUBNAME='SCIENCE FICTION')
                 PUB*D
                 DETAILS
         build AUTHOR segment in I/O area
         ISRT AUTHOR
```

15.7   GU   SUB
```
GN  GN   PUB
         set counter = 0
GNP GNP  DETAILS
         if not found go to TST
         set counter = counter + 1
         go to GNP
TST if counter = 1 go to GN
         GHNP DETAILS*F
         DLET
         set counter = counter - 1
         go to TST
```

15.8
```
       GU    SUB(SUBNAME='SCIENCE FICTION')
       GHNP PUB*D(PUBNAME='COMPUTERS IN SF')
             AUTHOR(AUTHNAME='HAL')
       DLET
       change publication name in I/O area
       ISRT PUB*D
             AUTHOR
```
We must use "delete" and then "insert," rather than "replace," because the field concerned is the sequence field. Since the author segment will be deleted anyway, we may as well use it in the SSAs for the GHNP to ensure (as far as possible) that we are deleting the right publication (there may be two with the specified title). Note that part of the hierarchical path has not been specified for the ISRT, as in the answer to Exercise 15.6.

15.9 The use of *V instead of GNP has the effect of reducing the number of subroutine calls to IMS, and hence improving performance, in questions 15.4 and 15.5. In the foregoing solution to 15.4 we can replace the GN and first GNP by a single GN
```
              GN    PUB(AMFLAG='A')
                    AUTHOR(AUTHNAME='OWEN')
```
and the second GNP by
```
              GN    PUB*DV
                    DETAILS*F
```
(Note the use of two command codes within a single SSA.) The replacements in 15.5 are similar, except that the D and F command codes are not required.

CHAPTER 16: IMS STORAGE STRUCTURES

16.1

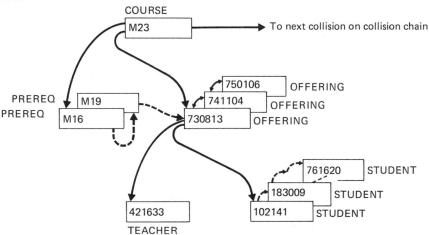

Broken arrows represent hierarchical pointers, solid arrows child/twin pointers.

16.2

Segment	Data	Pointers (number)	Prefix size	Occurrences per PDBR occurrence (average number)	Data bytes per PDBR occurrence (number)	Prefix bytes per PDBR occurrence (number)
COURSE	256	3	18	1	256	18
PREREQ	36	1	10	2	72	20
OFFERING	20	4	22	8	160	176
TEACHER	24	1	10	12	288	120
STUDENT	26	1	10	128	3328	1280
					4104	1614

(A pad byte has been added to the STUDENT segment.)

Ratio prefix bytes to data bytes = 1614/4104 = 39% approximately.

Ratio prefix bytes to total bytes = 1614/5718 = 28% approximately.

16.3 Cases (a) and (b) are impossible because hierarchical pointers are not allowed to cross the boundary between two DSGs. Case (c) may be specified as follows:

```
      DBD       ...
  P   DATASET ...
      SEGM      NAME=COURSE,...
  Q   DATASET ...
      SEGM      NAME=PREREQ,...
      SEGM      NAME=OFFERING,...
  P   DATASET
      SEGM      NAME=TEACHER,...
  R   DATASET ...
      SEGM      NAME=STUDENT,...
```

Case (a) is the only one possible if the storage structure is HISAM (and then only if the supporting access method is ISAM/OSAM).

CHAPTER 17: IMS LOGICAL DATABASES

17.1 The diagram shows a possible pair of PDBs. Observe that PALINK and APLINK are paired segments and that virtual pairing is being used. APLINK has been (arbitrarily) chosen to be the virtual member of the pair (in practice such a choice is made on the basis of performance criteria).

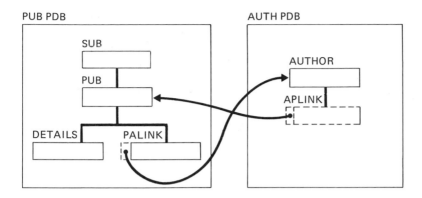

The following LDBs may be defined. (Intersection data and logical parent fully concatenated keys are not shown.)

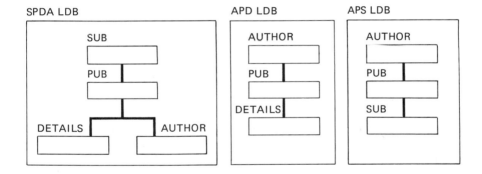

The PUB and AUTH physical DBDs are essentially similar to the AREA and BIRD physical DBDs of Figs. 17.16 and 17.17. The most significant difference is in the specification of the SEQ field for APLINK (the virtual member of the pair):

```
SEGM    NAME=APLINK,POINTER=PAIRED,
        PARENT=AUTHOR,SOURCE=((PALINK,,PUBPDBD))
FIELD   NAME=(FCKEY,SEQ),START=1,BYTES=51
FIELD   NAME=SUB#,START=1,BYTES=7
FIELD   NAME=PUBNAME,START=8,BYTES=44
```

The sequence field is the *fully concatenated* logical parent key, i.e., the combination of SUB# and PUBNAME.

The three logical DBDs are essentially similar to the logical DBD of Fig. 17.9.

17.5 For the EDUC PDB (Fig. 17.21):

```
DBD      NAME=EDUCPDBD,...
SEGM     NAME=COURSE,POINTER=TWIN,...
LCHILD   NAME=(CP,EDUCPDBD),PAIR=PC,POINTER=SNGL
FIELD    NAME=(COURSE#,SEQ),BYTES=3,START=1
FIELD    NAME=TITLE,...
FIELD    NAME=DESCRIPN,...
SEGM     NAME=CP,POINTER=(LPARNT,TWIN,LTWIN),
         PARENT=((COURSE),(COURSE,PHYSICAL,EDUCPDBD))
FIELD    NAME=(COURSE#,SEQ),...
SEGM     NAME=PC,POINTER=PAIRED,PARENT=COURSE,
         SOURCE=((CP,,EDUCPDBD))
FIELD    NAME=(COURSE#,SEQ),...
```

For the EDCP LDB (Fig. 17.22):

```
DBD      NAME=EDCPLDBD,ACCESS=LOGICAL
DATASET  LOGICAL
SEGM     NAME=COURSE,SOURCE=((COURSE,,EDUCPDBD))
SEGM     NAME=PREREQ,PARENT=COURSE,
         SOURCE=((CP,,EDUCPDBD),(COURSE,,EDUCPDBD))
```

For the EDPC LDB (Fig. 17.22):

```
DBD      NAME=EDPCLDBD,ACCESS=LOGICAL
DATASET  LOGICAL
SEGM     NAME=PREREQ,SOURCE=((COURSE,,EDUCPDBD))
SEGM     NAME=COURSE,PARENT=PREREQ,
         SOURCE=((PC,,EDUCPDBD),(COURSE,,EDUCPDBD))
```

17.6 If we assume that segments are presented for loading in (physical) hierarchical sequence, it will not in general be true that the logical parent will already exist when a logical child is submitted for insertion (although it *is* always so with the sample data of Exercise 17.3). Thus, after the data has been loaded into the database, it will be necessary to run a utility program against it to resolve all logical relationships. Alternatively, the "loading" process could involve COURSE segments only, and a subsequent updating program could then be run to insert all the dependent segments as a separate operation.

17.8 For retrieval-only applications there is no problem. The effect on applications that perform storage operations on any of the databases (PDBs or LDBs) will depend on the insert/delete/replace rules specified for the segments involved. See [16.1].

CHAPTER 18: IMS SECONDARY INDEXING

18.1 The user sees

(a)

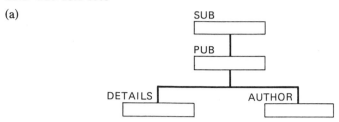

In this case the hierarchical structure is unchanged.

(b)

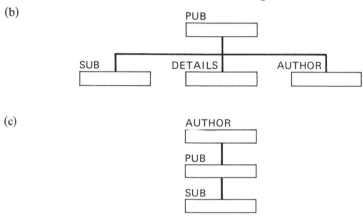

(c)

In all three cases (a), (b), and (c), the structure is seen in AUTHNAME sequence, with as many occurrences of the root as there are AUTHOR occurrences in the original database and, for each root occurrence, the corresponding number of occurrences of each of the dependents. See the answer to Exercise 18.6.

18.2 Index DBD:

```
DBD    NAME=AUTHXDBD,ACCESS=INDEX
SEGM   NAME=XSEG,BYTES=16
FIELD  NAME=(AUTHNAME,SEQ,M),BYTES=16,START=1
LCHILD NAME=(PUB,PUBDBD),INDEX=XAUTH
```

For PUBDBD the following two additional statements are needed for the PUB segment:

```
LCHILD NAME=(XSEG,AUTHXDBD),POINTER=INDX
XDFLD  NAME=XAUTH,SRCH=AUTHNAME,SEGMENT=AUTHOR
```

Corresponding PCB:

```
PCB     TYPE=DB,...,KEYLEN=32,PROCSEQ=AUTHXDBD
SENSEG  NAME=PUB
SENSEG  NAME=SUB,PARENT=PUB
SENSEG  NAME=DETAILS,PARENT=PUB
SENSEG  NAME=AUTHOR,PARENT=PUB
```

18.3   GU   PUB(XAUTH='ADAMS')
    TST if not found, exit
        print PUBNAME
        GN   PUB(XAUTH='ADAMS')
        go to TST

18.4   PUB   : AUTHNAME (i.e., XAUTH)
        SUB   : AUTHNAME followed by SUB#
        DETAILS: AUTHNAME followed by DATE
        AUTHOR : AUTHNAME followed by AUTHNAME
                  (the two names are not necessarily the same)

18.5   Get   : no restrictions
        Insert : not allowed for PUB or SUB
        Delete : not allowed for PUB or SUB
        Replace: not allowed for PUBNAME, SUB#, DATE, AUTHNAME

18.6   PUB   : 12000
        SUB   : 12000
        DETAILS: 18000
        AUTHOR : 14400

18.7 A possible method of supporting key-sequential access to root segments in HDAM.

CHAPTER 20: THE DBTG DATA MODEL

20.1 (To be compared with the answer to Exercise 13.1.)

SCHEMA NAME IS PUB-SCHEMA.

AREA NAME IS PUB-AREA.

RECORD NAME IS SUB;
    LOCATION MODE IS CALC RANDOMIZE-SUBNO
                USING SUBNO IN SUB;
    WITHIN PUB-AREA;
    IDENTIFIER IS SUBNO IN SUB.
    02 SUBNO   ; TYPE IS CHARACTER 7.
    02 SUBNAME   ; TYPE IS CHARACTER 38.

```
RECORD NAME IS PUB;
     LOCATION MODE IS CALC RANDOMIZE-PUBNAME
                    USING PUBNAME IN PUB;
     WITHIN PUB-AREA.
     02 PUBNAME      ; TYPE IS CHARACTER 44.
     02 AMFLAG       ; TYPE IS BIT       1.

RECORD NAME IS DETAILS;
     LOCATION MODE IS CALC RANDOMIZE-DATE
             USING DATE IN DETAILS, PHJV IN DETAILS;
     WITHIN PUB-AREA.
     02 DATE         ; TYPE IS CHARACTER 6.
     02 PHJV         ; TYPE IS CHARACTER 19.

RECORD NAME IS AUTHOR;
     LOCATION MODE IS CALC RANDOMIZE-AUTHNAME
                    USING AUTHNAME IN AUTHOR;
     WITHIN PUB-AREA.
     02 AUTHNAME     ; TYPE IS CHARACTER 16.
     02 AUTHADDR     ; TYPE IS CHARACTER 34.

SET NAME IS SUBJECTS;
    OWNER IS SYSTEM;
    ORDER IS PERMANENT SORTED BY DEFINED KEYS.
    MEMBER IS SUB;
        INSERTION IS AUTOMATIC
        RETENTION IS FIXED;
        KEY IS ASCENDING SUBNO IN SUB
            DUPLICATES ARE NOT ALLOWED
            NULL IS NOT ALLOWED;
        SET SELECTION IS THRU SUBJECTS SYSTEM.

SET NAME IS SUBPUB;
    OWNER IS SUB;
    ORDER IS PERMANENT SORTED BY DEFINED KEYS.
    MEMBER IS PUB;
        INSERTION IS AUTOMATIC
        RETENTION IS FIXED;
        KEY IS ASCENDING PUBNAME IN PUB
            DUPLICATES ARE SYSTEM-DEFAULT
            NULL IS NOT ALLOWED;
        SET SELECTION IS THRU SUBPUB OWNER
            IDENTIFIED BY APPLICATION.

SET NAME IS PUBDET;
    OWNER IS PUB;
    ORDER IS PERMANENT SORTED BY DEFINED KEYS.
    MEMBER IS DETAILS;
```

```
            INSERTION IS AUTOMATIC
            RETENTION IS FIXED;
            KEY IS DESCENDING DATE IN DETAILS
                 DUPLICATES ARE SYSTEM-DEFAULT
                 NULL IS NOT ALLOWED;
            SET SELECTION IS THRU PUBDET OWNER
                 IDENTIFIED BY APPLICATION.

SET NAME IS PUBAUTH;
    OWNER IS PUB;
    ORDER IS PERMANENT SORTED BY DEFINED KEYS.
    MEMBER IS AUTHOR
        INSERTION IS AUTOMATIC
        RETENTION IS FIXED;
        KEY IS ASCENDING AUTHNAME IN AUTHOR
             DUPLICATES ARE NOT ALLOWED
             NULL IS NOT ALLOWED;
        SET SELECTION IS THRU PUBAUTH OWNER
             IDENTIFIED BY APPLICATION.
```

Notes

1. AMFLAG has been declared as BIT 1 simply to show that BIT is a permissible data-type.

2. The ordering in set PUBDET has been specified as descending date sequence simply to show that this can be done. A like feature in IMS would have considerably simplified Exercise 15.7.

3. The singular set SUBJECTS has been introduced in order that SUB occurrences may be sequenced on SUBNO (as in the corresponding IMS database).

4. Membership class has been specified in all cases as AUTOMATIC FIXED. This is to make the DBTG structure reflect as closely as possible the corresponding IMS structure (in which no child segment can exist independently of its parent).

5. DUPLICATES ARE SYSTEM-DEFAULT means that duplicates are allowed (for example, two publications on the same subject may have the same title), and that the relative position of two member records with the same sort-key will be determined by the DBMS, not by the user. For information on other DUPLICATES options, see [19.10].

6. SET SELECTION for the three nonsingular sets has been specified as APPLICATION, to match most closely the situation in IMS.

7. Note that in one respect at least, the DBTG structure is more powerful than the IMS structure, inasmuch as the programmer has "hashing" access to any record occurrence, including those at a low hierarchical level.

20.2   SCHEMA NAME IS MANAGERIAL-STRUCTURE.

AREA NAME IS EMP-AREA.

RECORD NAME IS EMP;
     LOCATION MODE IS CALC HASH-ENO USING ENO IN EMP;
     WITHIN EMP-AREA;
     IDENTIFIER IS ENO IN EMP.
     02 ENO ...

RECORD NAME IS LINK;
     LOCATION MODE IS SYSTEM-DEFAULT;
     WITHIN EMP-AREA.

SET NAME IS EL;
     ...
     OWNER IS EMP;
     MEMBER IS LINK;
     ...

SET NAME IS LE;
     ...
     OWNER IS LINK;
     MEMBER IS EMP;
     ...

20.3   SCHEMA NAME IS S-P-J-SCHEMA.

AREA NAME IS S-AREA.
AREA NAME IS P-AREA.
AREA NAME IS J-AREA.
AREA NAME IS SPJ-AREA.

RECORD NAME IS S;
     LOCATION MODE IS CALC HASH-SNO USING SNO IN S;
     WITHIN S-AREA;
     IDENTIFIER IS SNO IN S.
     02 SNO   ; TYPE IS CHARACTER 5.
     02 SNAME ; TYPE IS CHARACTER 20.
     02 STATUS ; TYPE IS FIXED DECIMAL 3.
     02 CITY   ; TYPE IS CHARACTER 15.

RECORD NAME IS P;
     LOCATION MODE IS CALC HASH-PNO USING PNO IN P;
     WITHIN P-AREA;
     IDENTIFIER IS PNO IN P.
     02 PNO   ; TYPE IS CHARACTER 6.
     02 PNAME ; TYPE IS CHARACTER 20.
     02 COLOR ; TYPE IS CHARACTER 6.
     02 WEIGHT ; TYPE IS FIXED DECIMAL 4.

```
RECORD NAME IS J;
     LOCATION MODE IS CALC HASH-JNO USING JNO IN J;
     WITHIN J-AREA;
     IDENTIFIER IS JNO IN J.
     02 JNO    ; TYPE IS CHARACTER 4.
     02 JNAME  ; TYPE IS CHARACTER 20.
     02 CITY   ; TYPE IS CHARACTER 15.

RECORD NAME IS SPJ;
     LOCATION MODE IS SYSTEM-DEFAULT;
     WITHIN SPJ-AREA;
     IDENTIFIER IS SNO IN SPJ,
                   PNO IN SPJ,
                   JNO IN SPJ.
     02 SNO    ; TYPE IS CHARACTER 5.
     02 PNO    ; TYPE IS CHARACTER 6.
     02 JNO    ; TYPE IS CHARACTER 4.
     02 QTY    ; TYPE IS FIXED DECIMAL 5.

SET NAME IS S-SPJ;
    OWNER IS S;
    ORDER IS PERMANENT SORTED BY DEFINED KEYS.
    MEMBER IS SPJ
       INSERTION IS AUTOMATIC
       RETENTION IS MANDATORY;
       KEY IS ASCENDING PNO IN SPJ, JNO IN SPJ
          DUPLICATES ARE NOT ALLOWED
          NULL IS NOT ALLOWED;
       SET SELECTION IS THRU S-SPJ OWNER
          IDENTIFIED BY IDENTIFIER SNO IN S
                     EQUAL TO SNO IN SPJ.

SET NAME IS S-SET;
    OWNER IS SYSTEM;
    ORDER IS PERMANENT SORTED BY DEFINED KEYS.
    MEMBER IS S
       INSERTION IS AUTOMATIC
       RETENTION IS FIXED;
       KEY IS ASCENDING SNO IN S
          DUPLICATES ARE NOT ALLOWED
          NULL IS NOT ALLOWED;
       SET SELECTION IS THRU S-SET SYSTEM.

SET NAME IS P-SPJ;
    OWNER IS P;
    ORDER IS PERMANENT SORTED BY DEFINED KEYS.
    MEMBER IS SPJ
       INSERTION IS AUTOMATIC
```

```
        RETENTION IS MANDATORY;
        KEY IS ASCENDING JNO IN SPJ, SNO IN SPJ
            DUPLICATES ARE NOT ALLOWED
            NULL IS NOT ALLOWED;
        SET SELECTION IS THRU P-SPJ OWNER
            IDENTIFIED BY IDENTIFIER PNO IN P
                            EQUAL TO PNO IN SPJ.


SET NAME IS P-SET;
    OWNER IS SYSTEM;
    ORDER IS PERMANENT SORTED BY DEFINED KEYS.
    MEMBER IS P
        INSERTION IS AUTOMATIC
        RETENTION IS FIXED;
        KEY IS ASCENDING PNO IN P
            DUPLICATES ARE NOT ALLOWED
            NULL IS NOT ALLOWED;
        SET SELECTION IS THRU P-SET SYSTEM.


SET NAME IS J-SPJ;
    OWNER IS J;
    ORDER IS PERMANENT SORTED BY DEFINED KEYS.
    MEMBER IS SPJ
        INSERTION IS AUTOMATIC
        RETENTION IS MANDATORY;
        KEY IS ASCENDING SNO IN SPJ, PNO IN SPJ
            DUPLICATES ARE NOT ALLOWED
            NULL IS NOT ALLOWED;
        SET SELECTION IS THRU J-SPJ OWNER
            IDENTIFIED BY IDENTIFIER JNO IN J
                            EQUAL TO JNO IN SPJ.


SET NAME IS J-SET;
    OWNER IS SYSTEM;
    ORDER IS PERMANENT SORTED BY DEFINED KEYS.
    MEMBER IS J
        INSERTION IS AUTOMATIC
        RETENTION IS FIXED;
        KEY IS ASCENDING JNO IN J
            DUPLICATES ARE NOT ALLOWED
            NULL IS NOT ALLOWED;
        SET SELECTION IS THRU J-SET SYSTEM.
```

20.4   SCHEMA NAME IS PARTS-AND-COMPONENTS.

AREA NAME IS PART-AREA.

RECORD NAME IS PART;
      LOCATION MODE IS CALC HASH-PNO USING PNO IN PART;
      WITHIN PART-AREA;
      IDENTIFIER IS PNO IN PART.
      02 PNO ...

RECORD NAME IS LINK;
      LOCATION MODE IS SYSTEM-DEFAULT;
      WITHIN PART-AREA.
      02 QTY ...

SET NAME IS BM;
      ...
      OWNER IS PART;
      MEMBER IS LINK;
      ...

SET NAME IS WU;
      ...
      OWNER IS PART;
      MEMBER IS LINK;
      ...

20.5 AREA is one of many "reserved words" in the schema DDL (see [19.10]) and hence cannot be chosen as a data-name.

(a)   SCHEMA NAME IS AREA-BIRD-SURVEY.

AREA NAME IS SURVEY-FILE.

RECORD NAME IS AREA-REC;
      LOCATION MODE IS VIA AREA-SET SET;
      WITHIN SURVEY-FILE;
      IDENTIFIER IS ANO IN AREA-REC.
      02 ANO   ; TYPE IS CHARACTER 3.
      02 ANAME ; TYPE IS CHARACTER 24.
      02 ADESCN ; TYPE IS CHARACTER 473.

RECORD NAME IS BIRD-REC;
      LOCATION MODE IS VIA BIRD-SET SET;
      WITHIN SURVEY-FILE;
      IDENTIFIER IS BNAME IN BIRD-REC;
      IDENTIFIER IS SNAME IN BIRD-REC.
      02 BNAME ; TYPE IS CHARACTER 44.
      02 SNAME ; TYPE IS CHARACTER 44.
      02 BDESCN ; TYPE IS CHARACTER 412.

```
RECORD NAME IS SIGHTING;
        LOCATION MODE IS SYSTEM-DEFAULT.
        WITHIN SURVEY-FILE.
        02 DATE    ; TYPE IS CHARACTER 6.
        02 REMARKS; TYPE IS CHARACTER 494.

SET NAME IS AREA-SET;
        OWNER IS SYSTEM;
        ORDER IS PERMANENT SORTED BY DEFINED KEYS.
        MEMBER IS AREA-REC;
            INSERTION IS AUTOMATIC
            RETENTION IS FIXED;
            KEY IS ASCENDING ANO IN AREA-REC
                DUPLICATES ARE NOT ALLOWED
                NULL IS NOT ALLOWED;
            SET SELECTION IS THRU AREA-SET SYSTEM.

SET NAME IS BIRD-SET;
        OWNER IS SYSTEM;
        ORDER IS PERMANENT SORTED BY DEFINED KEYS.
        MEMBER IS BIRD-REC;
            INSERTION IS AUTOMATIC
            RETENTION IS FIXED;
            KEY IS ASCENDING SNAME IN BIRD-REC
                DUPLICATES ARE NOT ALLOWED
                NULL IS NOT ALLOWED;
            SET SELECTION IS THRU BIRD-SET SYSTEM.

SET NAME IS AREA-SIGHTINGS;
        OWNER IS AREA-REC;
        ORDER IS PERMANENT INSERTION IS NEXT.
        MEMBER IS SIGHTING;
            INSERTION IS AUTOMATIC
            RETENTION IS MANDATORY;
            SET SELECTION IS THRU AREA-SIGHTINGS OWNER
                IDENTIFIED BY APPLICATION.

SET NAME IS BIRD-SIGHTINGS;
        OWNER IS BIRD-REC;
        ORDER IS PERMANENT INSERTION IS NEXT.
        MEMBER IS SIGHTING;
            INSERTION IS AUTOMATIC
            RETENTION IS MANDATORY;
            SET SELECTION IS THRU BIRD-SIGHTINGS OWNER
                IDENTIFIED BY APPLICATION.
```

Since the SIGHTING record does not contain a data-item corresponding to ANO IN AREA-REC or a data-item corresponding to SNAME (or BNAME) in BIRD-REC, it is not possible to define a sort-key for SIGHTINGs with respect to the sets BIRD-SIGHTINGS and AREA-SIGHTINGS. It therefore becomes the responsibility of the programmer to maintain SIGHTING records in bird name sequence within area and area number sequence within bird, if these sequences are required. INSERTION IS NEXT (in the ORDER clause) means that the programmer must procedurally select the predecessor of the new record in the set before creating that new record.

(b) The following alterations should be made to schema (a).

- Eliminate DATE from the SIGHTING record.

- Introduce a new type of record:

```
RECORD NAME IS DATE-REC;
        LOCATION MODE IS CALC HASH-DATE
                          USING DATE IN DATE-REC;
        WITHIN SURVEY-FILE;
        IDENTIFIER IS DATE IN DATE-REC.
        02 DATE   ; TYPE IS CHARACTER 6.
```

- Introduce a new type of set:

```
SET NAME IS DATE-SIGHTINGS;
      OWNER IS DATE-REC;
      ORDER IS PERMANENT INSERTION IS NEXT.
      MEMBER IS SIGHTING
         INSERTION IS AUTOMATIC
         RETENTION IS MANDATORY;
         SET SELECTION IS THRU DATE-SIGHTINGS OWNER
             IDENTIFIED BY APPLICATION.
```

CHAPTER 21: THE DBTG EXTERNAL MODEL

21.1 A couple of observations may be helpful. If O is old, any program currently executing DELETE operations against O will *probably* have to be changed (together with the corresponding sub-schema). If M is old and membership class is AUTOMATIC, any program currently executing STORE operations against M will have to be changed (together with the corresponding sub-schema).

CHAPTER 22: THE DBTG DATA SUBLANGUAGE

The completion of the currency table in Section 22.2 follows.

Current of run-unit	P 'P2'
Current S occurrence	S 'S4'
Current P occurrence	P 'P2'
Current SP occurrence	SP 'S4/P2/200'

Current of set S-SP   SP 'S4/P2/200' (member)
Current of set P-SP   P 'P2' (owner)
Current S-SP occurrence   owned by S 'S4'
Current P-SP occurrence   owned by P 'P2'
Current of BASIC-DATA-AREA   P 'P2'
Current of LINK-DATA-AREA   SP 'S4/P2/200'

22.1
```
      MOVE 'J1' TO JNO IN J.
      FIND ANY J.
      IF J-SPJ EMPTY GO TO QUIT.
      MOVE BLANK TO TEMP-SNO.
NXT.  FIND NEXT SPJ WITHIN J-SPJ.
      IF end of set GO TO QUIT.
      GET SPJ.
      IF SNO IN SPJ = TEMP-SNO GO TO NXT.
      MOVE SNO IN SPJ TO TEMP-SNO.
      (add TEMP-SNO value to result list)
      GO TO NXT.
```

This code relies on the ordering declared for set J-SPJ.

22.2
```
       MOVE 'J1' TO JNO IN J.
       FIND ANY J.
       MOVE 'P1' TO PNO IN SPJ.
       FIND SPJ WITHIN J-SPJ CURRENT USING PNO IN SPJ.
TEST.  IF end of set GO TO QUIT.
       GET SPJ.
       (add SNO value to result list)
       FIND DUPLICATE WITHIN J-SPJ USING PNO IN SPJ.
       GO TO TEST.
```

22.3
```
      MOVE 'J1' TO JNO IN J.
      FIND ANY J.
      IF J-SPJ EMPTY GO TO QUIT.
      MOVE BLANK TO TEMP-SNO.
NXT.  FIND NEXT SPJ WITHIN J-SPJ.
      IF end of set GO TO QUIT.
      GET SPJ.
      IF SNO IN SPJ = TEMP-SNO GO TO NXT.
      MOVE SNO IN SPJ TO TEMP-SNO.
      FIND OWNER WITHIN P-SPJ.
      GET P.
      IF COLOR IN P = 'RED' add TEMP-SNO value to result list
      ELSE MOVE BLANK TO TEMP-SNO.
      GO TO NXT.
```

22.4 First we construct a table LONJNO containing JNO values (in ascending sequence) for projects in LONDON.

```
             MOVE 'LONDON' TO CITY IN J.
             FIND J WITHIN J-SET USING CITY IN J.
      TEST1. IF end of set GO TO NEXTP.
             GET J.
             (add JNO value to LONJNO table)
             FIND DUPLICATE WITHIN J-SET USING CITY IN J.
             GO TO TEST1.
```

Suppose that after this procedure the table LONJNO contains N JNO values ($N \geq 0$). We now scan P occurrences, looking for parts for which there exist SPJ occurrences linking the part to every one of these N projects. (Here, as elsewhere, we assume that the first execution of FIND NEXT (format 4) on a singular set is equivalent to executing FIND FIRST. We could avoid having to make this assumption by executing FIND NTH, say, where NTH is the name of an integer data-item whose value is 1 initially and is incremented by 1 on each iteration.)

```
      NEXTP.   FIND NEXT P WITHIN P-SET.
               IF end of set GO TO QUIT.
      GETP.    GET P.
               MOVE 1 TO I.
      NEXTJ.   IF I > N GO TO GOODP.
               MOVE LONJNO (I) TO JNO IN SPJ.
               FIND SPJ WITHIN P-SPJ CURRENT USING JNO IN SPJ.
               IF end of set GO TO NEXTP.
               ADD 1 TO I.
               GO TO NEXTJ.
      GOODP.   (add PNO value to result list)
               GO TO NEXTP.
```

22.5   NEXTJ.   FIND NEXT J WITHIN J-SET.

```
               IF end of set GO TO QUIT.
               GET J.
               IF J-SPJ EMPTY GO TO GOODJ.
      NEXTSPJ.           FIND NEXT SPJ WITHIN J-SPJ.
                         IF end of set GO TO GOODJ.
                         FIND OWNER WITHIN P-SPJ.
                         GET P.
                         IF COLOR IN P NOT EQUAL TO 'RED'
                                 GO TO NEXTSPJ.
                         FIND OWNER WITHIN S-SPJ.
                         GET S.
                         IF CITY IN S NOT EQUAL TO 'LONDON'
                                 GO TO NEXTSPJ.
                         GO TO NEXTJ.
      GOODJ.  (add JNO value to result list)
              GO TO NEXTJ.
```

22.6 First we construct a table S1PNO containing PNO values for parts supplied by supplier S1, using a procedure essentially the same as that used in Exercise 22.1. Suppose that after this procedure the table S1PNO contains N PNO values ($N \geq 0$).

```
NEXTJ.   FIND NEXT J WITHIN J-SET.
         IF end of set GO TO QUIT.
         GET J.
         MOVE 1 TO I.
NEXTP.   IF I>N GO TO GOODJ.
         MOVE S1PNO(I) TO PNO IN SPJ.
         FIND SPJ WITHIN J-SPJ CURRENT USING PNO IN SPJ.
         IF end of set GO TO NEXTJ.
         ADD 1 TO I.
         GO TO NEXTP.
GOODJ.   (add JNO value to result list)
         GO TO NEXTJ.
```

22.7 In order to be able to eliminate duplicate CITY value pairs, we construct a result list that is ordered on project city within supplier city. Note that once again we have a strategy problem; the problem would be simplified if the data model included a singular set linking all SPJ occurrences.

```
NEXTS.   FIND NEXT S WITHIN S-SET.
         IF end of set GO TO QUIT.
         IF S-SPJ EMPTY GO TO NEXTS.
         GET S.
NEXTSPJ. FIND NEXT SPJ WITHIN S-SPJ.
         IF end of set GO TO NEXTS.
             FIND OWNER WITHIN J-SPJ.
             GET J.
             (add CITY IN S, CITY IN J values to
                 result list unless already present)
             GO TO NEXTSPJ.
```

22.8
```
NEXTP.   MOVE 'RED' TO COLOR IN P.
         FIND P WITHIN P-SET CURRENT USING COLOR IN P.
         IF end of set GO TO QUIT.
         MOVE 'ORANGE' TO COLOR IN P.
         MODIFY P.
         GO TO NEXTP.
```

22.9 We assume that an SPJ occurrence for S1/P1/J1 exists; however, we do *not* assume that an SPJ occurrence for S2/P1/J1 does *not* already exist. The first step, therefore, is to FIND and GET the SPJ occurrence for S2/P1/J1 if it exists, so that the appropriate QTY value can be added to the QTY value for S1/P1/J1 to form the new QTY value for S2/P1/J1. If it does not exist, of course, nothing need be added to the QTY value for S1/P1/J1. We also delete the SPJ occurrence for S2/P1/J1 if it exists.

```
MOVE 'S2' TO SNO IN S.
FIND ANY S.
MOVE 'P1' TO PNO IN SPJ.
MOVE 'J1' TO JNO IN SPJ.
FIND SPJ WITHIN S-SPJ CURRENT USING PNO IN SPJ,
                                    JNO IN SPJ.
    IF end of set GO TO DOES-NOT-ALREADY-EXIST.
DOES-ALREADY-EXIST.
    GET QTY IN SPJ.
    MOVE QTY TO TEMPQTY.
    ERASE SPJ.
    GO TO FIND-S1-P1-J1.
DOES-NOT-ALREADY-EXIST.
    MOVE ZERO TO TEMPQTY.
```

We now proceed to FIND and MODIFY the SPJ occurrence for S1/P1/J1. The modification process consists of changing the SNO value from S1 to S2, increasing the QTY value by the value in TEMPQTY, and moving the SPJ occurrence from the S-SPJ occurrence owned by S1 to the S-SPJ occurrence owned by S2. There are two ways of doing this. One is to use the second format of MODIFY (see Example 22.4.2, in Chapter 22), as follows:

```
FIND-S1-P1-J1.
    MOVE 'S1' TO SNO IN S.
    FIND ANY S.
    FIND SPJ WITHIN S-SPJ CURRENT USING PNO IN SPJ,
                                        JNO IN SPJ.
    GET QTY IN SPJ.
    MOVE 'S2' TO SNO IN SPJ.
    ADD TEMPQTY TO QTY IN SPJ.
    MODIFY SPJ INCLUDING S-SPJ MEMBERSHIP.
```

It is interesting, however, to consider how the same result could be achieved without using this format of MODIFY. Note the problems of currency in the following procedure. (The first six statements are the same as before.) We are assuming that SPJ is an OPTIONAL member of S-SPJ.

```
FIND-S1-P1-J1.
    MOVE 'S1' TO SNO IN S.
    FIND ANY S.
    FIND SPJ WITHIN S-SPJ CURRENT USING PNO IN SPJ,
                                        JNO IN SPJ.
```

```
GET QTY IN SPJ.
MOVE 'S2' TO SNO IN SPJ.
ADD TEMPQTY TO QTY IN SPJ.
MODIFY SPJ.   (changes data values only)
MOVE 'S2' TO SNO IN S.
FIND ANY S.   (current S-SPJ occurrence is
                        one owned by S2)
FIND CURRENT SPJ RETAINING CURRENCY FOR S-SPJ.
DISCONNECT SPJ FROM S-SPJ. (occurrence owned by S1)
CONNECT SPJ TO S-SPJ. (occurrence owned by S2)
```

22.10
```
NEXTP.MOVE 'RED' TO COLOR IN P.
     FIND P WITHIN P-SET USING COLOR IN P.
     IF end of set GO TO QUIT.
     ERASE P ALL.
     GO TO NEXTP.
```

22.11 Statements that refer to SNO IN SPJ, PNO IN SPJ, or JNO IN SPJ will have to be replaced by statements that locate the S, P, or J occurrence corresponding to the SPJ occurrence concerned and refer to SNO IN S, PNO IN P, or JNO IN J, as appropriate.

In Exercise 22.1, the seventh, eighth, and ninth statements (GET, IF, MOVE) must be replaced by the following.

```
FIND OWNER WITHIN S-SPJ.
GET S.
IF SNO IN S = TEMP-SNO GO TO NXT.
MOVE SNO IN S TO TEMP-SNO.
```

In Exercise 22.2 all statements after the first two must be replaced by the following.

```
NXT.  FIND NEXT SPJ WITHIN J-SPJ.
      IF end of set GO TO QUIT.
      FIND OWNER WITHIN P-SPJ.
      GET P.
      IF PNO IN P NOT EQUAL TO 'P1' GO TO NXT.
      FIND OWNER WITHIN S-SPJ.
      GET S.
      (add SNO value to result list)
      GO TO NXT.
```

Exercise 22.9 depends on the ORDER specified in the schema for S-SPJ. If ORDER IS NEXT (see [19.10]) has been specified—the most likely case—then at the time the SPJ occurrence for S1/P1/J1 is to be inserted into the S-SPJ occurrence owned by S2, the current of S-SPJ must be the record occurrence that immediately precedes the new SPJ occurrence with respect to the desired sequencing (project number within part number). (In this example the current of S-SPJ must in fact be the S occurrence for S2.) In general, ORDER IS NEXT can cause considerable currency difficulties.

22.12 No effect if the format 2 MODIFY (with INCLUDING) is employed. If it is not, the procedure (from FIND-S1-P1-J1) is as follows (the first four statements are the same as before):

```
FIND-S1-P1-J1.
     MOVE 'S1' TO SNO IN S.
     FIND ANY S.
     FIND SPJ WITHIN S-SPJ CURRENT USING PNO IN SPJ,
                                         JNO IN SPJ.
     GET QTY IN SPJ.
     ERASE SPJ.
     MOVE 'S2' TO SNO IN SPJ.
     ADD TEMPQTY TO QTY IN SPJ.
     MOVE 'S2' TO SNO IN S.
     FIND ANY S.
     STORE SPJ.
     CONNECT SPJ TO S-SPJ.
```

We are assuming that SPJ is a MANUAL member of S-SPJ.

22.13 The membership class of LINK in EL would probably be (MANDATORY) AUTOMATIC, since it would be unreasonable for a LINK occurrence not to be connected to a superior (manager) EMP occurrence. Assuming that LINK's membership is AUTOMATIC, then, the membership class of EMP in LE must be (MANDATORY?) MANUAL, to allow at least one EMP occurrence (at the top of the tree) not to be subordinate to any others.

     We assume that SET SELECTION for EL is THRU EL OWNER IDENTIFIED BY ENO IN EMP.

```
     MOVE 'E8' TO ENO IN EMP.
     STORE LINK.   (no UWA data for this record)
     MOVE 'E15' TO ENO IN EMP.
     MOVE ...     (create E15 EMP occurrence in UWA)
     STORE EMP.
     CONNECT EMP TO LE.
```

22.14 We assume that PART-SET is a singular set containing as members all PART occurrences.

```
NP.  FIND NEXT PART WITHIN PART-SET.
     IF end of set GO TO QUIT.
     GET PART.
     (print PNO value)
     NC.  FIND NEXT LINK WITHIN BM.
          IF end of set GO TO CONTINUE.
          FIND OWNER WITHIN WU
                RETAINING CURRENCY FOR PART-SET, BM.
          GET PART.
          (print PNO value, i.e., component number)
          GO TO NC.
     CONTINUE.
          FIND CURRENT PART WITHIN PART-SET. (return to original part)
     NA.  FIND NEXT LINK WITHIN WU.
          IF end of set GO TO NP.
          FIND OWNER WITHIN BM
                RETAINING CURRENCY FOR PART-SET, WU.
          GET PART.
          (print PNO value, i.e., assembly number)
          GO TO NA.
```

22.15 (a) Using the two-entity schema:

```
          MOVE 'A1' TO ANO IN AREA-REC.
          FIND AREA-REC WITHIN AREA-SET USING ANO IN
                                           AREA-REC.
          MOVE '730101' TO DATE IN SIGHTING.
          FIND SIGHTING WITHIN AREA-SIGHTINGS CURRENT USING
                                           DATE IN SIGHTING.
     ET.  IF end of set GO TO QUIT.
          FIND OWNER WITHIN BIRD-SIGHTINGS.
          GET BIRD-REC.
          (add BNAME value to result list)
          FIND DUPLICATE WITHIN AREA-SIGHTINGS
                     USING DATE IN SIGHTING.
          GO TO ET.
```

(b) Using the three-entity schema, we have essentially two ways of tackling the problem. We can start from area A1 and look for corresponding sightings for 1 January 1973, or we can start from this date and look for corresponding sightings in A1. The following code starts at area A1.

```
          MOVE 'A1' TO ANO IN AREA-REC.
          FIND AREA-REC WITHIN AREA-SET USING ANO IN
                                           AREA-REC.
          IF AREA-SIGHTINGS EMPTY GO TO QUIT.
```

```
FN.  FIND NEXT SIGHTING WITHIN AREA-SIGHTINGS.
     IF end of set GO TO QUIT.
     FIND OWNER WITHIN DATE-SIGHTINGS.
     GET DATE-REC.
     IF DATE IN DATE-REC NOT EQUAL TO '730101' GO TO FN.
     FIND OWNER WITHIN BIRD-SIGHTINGS.
     GET BIRD-REC.
     (add BNAME value to result list)
     GO TO FN.
```

CHAPTER 23: SECURITY

23.1 The following solution assumes that an access control lock procedure can be written using the DML of [19.8]. Note that the procedure requires access to the UWA of the run-unit concerned. We assume that every DML statement causes the DBMS to inspect the appropriate entry in the "permission table."

Schema

```
        .
        .
        .

RECORD NAME IS EMP;
        .
        .
        .

     ACCESS CONTROL LOCK FOR FIND IS
                    PROCEDURE CHECK-USERNO.
```

Application program

```
USE FOR ACCESS CONTROL ON FIND FOR EMP.
    MOVE USERNO TO DB-ACCESS-CONTROL-KEY.
DISPLAY 'ENO FOR REQD EMP PLEASE'.
ACCEPT ENO IN EMP.
READY EMP-REALM.
FIND ANY EMP.
IF access control exception DISPLAY 'ILLEGAL REQUEST'
                ELSE GET EMP
                    DISPLAY SALARY IN EMP.
```

Procedure CHECK-USERNO

```
IF ENO IN EMP = USERNO place 'yes' in permission table.
MOVE 'N' TO FLAG.
FIND ANY EMP.
FIND OWNER WITHIN LE.
FIND OWNER WITHIN EL.
MOVE ENO IN EMP TO SAVE-ENO.
GET ENO IN EMP.
IF ENO IN EMP = USERNO MOVE 'Y' TO FLAG.
MOVE SAVE-ENO TO ENO IN EMP.
IF FLAG = 'Y' place 'yes' in permission table
        ELSE place 'no' in permission table.
```

ABOUT THE AUTHOR

Mr. Date is a Project Programmer with IBM UK Laboratories Ltd., Hursley, Hampshire, England. At present (1977) he is on a temporary assignment to IBM General Products Division, San Jose, California.

On graduating in mathematics from Cambridge University in 1962, Mr. Date joined Leo Computers Ltd., London, as a programmer and programming instructor. He moved to IBM in 1967 as an instructor to help develop and teach a comprehensive training program in computer system fundamentals, System/360 assembler language, and PL/I. Subsequently he helped to establish the IBM European Laboratories Integrated Professional Training Program (ELIPT), a cooperative education scheme intended for computer professionals in the IBM development laboratories in Austria, England, France, Germany, the Netherlands, and Sweden. This involved developing and teaching several new courses, covering such topics as system programming techniques and Operating System/360 (both externals and internals).

In 1970, Mr. Date worked on a database language project at Hursley. Since that time he has been more or less continuously active in the database field, both inside and outside IBM. In particular he has designed and has been teaching a highly successful course on database concepts in the IBM ELIPT program mentioned previously. The present book has benefited greatly from the author's experience in teaching this course. In addition Mr. Date has lectured widely on database topics—particularly on relational database—both in the United States and in many countries in Europe and South America. He is a member of ACM and the ACM Special Interest Group on Management of Data (SIGMOD). For some time he was actively involved in a British Computer Society working group on relational database. He is the author/coauthor of several technical papers.

Index

Entries marked with an asterisk (for example, *TDMS) are database management systems or software systems in some closely related field.

Abrial, J. R., 427, 461
abstract representation, 15
ACCEPT CURRENCY STATUS
  (DBTG), 369
access constraints (integrity), 396–404
  classification of, 397–400
  in DBTG, 413–414
  in IMS, 410–411
  in INGRES, 403–404
  in Query By Example, 400–401, 402
  in System R, 401–403
access constraints (security), 378
  in DBTG, 386–388
  in IMS, 385–386
  in INGRES, 385
  in Query By Example, 382, 383
  in System R, 382, 384
ACCESS CONTROL KEY (DBTG),
  386
ACCESS CONTROL LOCK (DBTG),
  386
access method, 27
access path, 326

access strategy, 9
  in DBTG, 340
ACTUAL/VIRTUAL RESULT
  (DBTG), 344
ACTUAL/VIRTUAL SOURCE
  (DBTG), 343
*ADABAS, 191
*ADAM, 22
ADL, see APL Data Language
ALL (Query By Example), 141
Altman, E. B., 48
American National Standards Institute,
  24
ANSI, see American National
  Standards Institute
ANSI/SPARC, 13
  architecture, 13–21, 425–429
  Study Group on DBMS, 13
ANSI/X3, 24
ANSI/X3/SPARC, see ANSI/SPARC
Antonacci, F., 201
APL (A Programming Language), 67,
  201

APL (Associative Programming
    Language), 314
APL Data Language (relational DSL),
    67, 107
APL Query Language (relational
    DSL), 201
AQL, *see* APL Query Language
arbiter (access control program), 379
area (DBTG), 327–328
Armstrong, W. W., 175
Armstrong's axioms, 176–177
*ASAP, 390
ASCENDING /DESCENDING KEY
    (DBTG), 334–335
Ash, W., 197
ASSERT (SEQUEL), 401
assertion (integrity), 401
assignment (SEQUEL), 124
association, *see* relationship
associative retrieval, 85
Astrahan, M. M., 48, 135
atomic relation, 178
attribute (of a relation), 53, 75
attribute migration, 187
audit trail, 409
authentication (security), 377–378
authorization, 8, 375ff.
AUTOMATIC membership class
    (DBTG), 337
AVERAGE (DSL ALPHA), 101
AVG (SEQUEL), 132
Avison, D. E., 393

Bachman, C. W., 69, 317, 346, 371,
    456, 458
Bachman diagram, *see* data structure
    diagram
backout (transaction), 406, 409
Bandurski, A. E., 458
base set (UDL), 430
Bayer, R., 422
BCNF, *see* Boyce/Codd Normal Form
Beitz, E. H., 200
Bergart, J. G., 393
Bernstein, P. A., 175, 178

bidirectional relationship (IMS),
    280–286
binary relation, 74, 192, 427, 447
Bjork, L. A., 421
Bjørner, D., 199
Blasgen, M. W., 122, 135
Bleier, R. E., 68
block (physical record), 37
BOTTOM (DSL ALPHA), 101
BOUNDS (integrity constraint), 398
Boyce, R. F., 134, 135, 163, 190, 419
Boyce/Codd Normal Form, 163
Bracchi, G., 198, 199
Brown, A. P. G., 458
Buchholz, W., 44

Cadiou, J.-M., 177
CALC location mode (DBTG), 332, 362
CALC-key (DBTG), 332, 362
CALL procedure (DBTG), 413
Canaday, R. H., 314
candidate key, 78, 175, 176
Canning, R. G., 22, 313
cardinality (of a relation), 74
Carlson, C. R., 200, 459
Cartesian product, 74
    relational algebra, 114
Casey, R. G., 173
CLASSM (storage device), 196
casual user, 110
CATALOG (System R), 149
chain (DBTG), 317
chain (network model), 60
chain (storage structure), 33
Chamberlin, D. D., 82, 134, 135, 190,
    418, 419
Chang, P. Y.-T., 121
CHECK (DBTG integrity constraint),
    413–414
checkpoint/restart, 410
Chiang, T. C., 47
child segment (IMS), 210
    logical, 274
    physical, 274
child/twin pointers (IMS), 249–251
Childs, D. L., 197

CLOSE (DBTG), 328
closure (relational languages), 118, 448
COBOL Data Base Facility, 310
COBOL:DDL terminology, 345
COBOL Journal of Development, 309
CODASYL Data Description
    Language Committee, 310, 314
CODASYL Development Committee,
    198
CODASYL Programming Language
    Committee, 309
CODASYL set, 318
CODASYL Systems Committee, 22
Codd, E. F., 81, 107, 110, 153, 163,
    170, 172, 174, 187, 198, 199, 379,
    390, 418, 448, 457, 458, 460
Codd's reduction algorithm, 107
Coffman, E. G., Jr., 419
Coleman, C. D., 393
collision (hash-addressing), 37
    in HDAM, 252
Collmeyer, A. J., 422
COLUMNS (System R), 149
combined index, 40–41, 49
command codes (IMS), 234
    D, 236
    F, 237
    Q, 411
    V, 237
committed change, 407
complete indexing, 44
completeness (of DSL), *see* relational
    completeness
composite attribute, 155
compression techniques, 41–42
conceptual level (ANSI/SPARC), 15,
    443–457
conceptual model, 16, 425
conceptual record, 16
conceptual schema, 17, 425
conceptual/internal mapping, 18
concurrency, 405–408
condition box (Query By Example),
    142
conformable representation, 45
CONNECT (DBTG), 359

connection trap, 6
consistency, 8, 81
consistency level (System R), 407–408
constant element (Query By Example),
    138
Conway, R. W., 390
Copeland, G. P., 197
coset, 460
COUNT (DSL ALPHA), 99
COUNT (Query By Example), 148
COUNT (SEQUEL), 132
Crick, M. F., 199
Crowe, T., 393
CUPID (casual user system), 66,
    110–111
currency (DBTG), 353–355, 356ff.
currency confusion, 417
current parent (IMS), 231
current position (IMS), 230, 237–238
    for get next, 230
    for insert, 232–233
cursor (UDL), 433
cursor-qualified reference (UDL), 437
*CZAR, 22
Czarnik, B., 198

Daley, R. C., 390
*DAMAS, 84, 108
data administrator (DBTG), 313
data base, *see* database
Data Base Control System (COBOL),
    313
data coding, 12, 184
data communications feature (IMS),
    205
data definition language, 19
Data Description Language
    Committee, 310
data description language (DBTG), 309
    schema, 309
    sub-schema, 309
data dictionary, 21, 25, 149, 379, 397
    in Query By Example, 150–151, 382
    in System R, 149–150
data independence, 9–13, 24

in DBTG, 351–352
in IMS, 265–266
Data Independent Accessing Model, 48, 198, 200
Data Language/I (IMS), 207, 255ff.
data manipulation language (DBTG), 310, 353ff.
data materialization, 12
data model, 16
  entity set, 48
  graph, 427
  hierarchical, 55
  network, 58
  relational, 52, 79
data set, 243
data set group (IMS), 255–260
data sharing, 405–408
  in DBTG, 414–417
  in IMS, 411–412
  in System R, 407–408
data structure diagram, 317
data structure set, 318
data sublanguage, 15
data submodel, 15
data-aggregate (DBTG), 388
data-item (DBTG), 316
database, 4, 18
  integrated, 2
  user's view of, 81, 430
database administrator, 7
  responsibilities of, 19
database description (IMS), 207, 212–215
  index, 260–262, 293ff.
  logical, 274ff.
  physical, 212–215, 260–264
database management system, 18
database set, 318
database system, 1, 2, 7
database-key (DBTG), 328–329
*dataBASIC, 22
Date, C. J., 45, 68, 190, 458
Davies, C. T., Jr., 421
DBA, see database administrator
DBCS, see Data Base Control System
DBD, see database description

DBMS, see database management system
*DBOMP, 22, 67
DBTG set, 318
DB-ACCESS-CONTROL-KEY (DBTG), 386
DB-REALM-NAME (DBTG), 415
DB-STATUS (DBTG), 357
DDL, see data definition language; data description language
DDL Journal of Development, 310
DDL:COBOL terminology, 345
DDLC, see Data Description Language Committee
De Maine, P. A. D., 46
deadlock, 405
deadly embrace, 405
Dean, A. L., Jr., 390
Deckert, K. L., 199
Dee, E., 112
degree (of a relation), 73
DELETE (DBTG), see ERASE
DELETE (Query By Example), 147
DELETE (SEQUEL), 132
DELETE (DSL ALPHA), 98
delete (IMS), 233
  HDAM, 254
  HIDAM, 255
  HISAM, 245–246, 248
  HSAM, 244
  logical database, 279
  secondary indexing, 298
Dell'Orco, P., 201
Delobel, C., 170, 173
Denicoff, M., 393
dense index, 33
dependency diagram, 154ff.
detection routines (integrity), 410
determinant (in a relation), 163
device/media control language (DBTG), 311
DIAM, see Data Independent Accessing Model
dictionary, see data dictionary
difference (relational algebra), 114
difference (SEQUEL), 130

differential file, 49
Dijkstra, E. W., 405
D'Imperio, M. E., 45
DISCONNECT (DBTG), 359
*Disk Forte, 22
distributed database, 201
DIVIDE (relational algebra), 116
division/remainder (hashing
    technique), 35
DLET, see delete (IMS)
DMCL, see device/media control
    language
DML, see data manipulation language
*DMS 1100, 23, 67, 421, 422
Dodd, G. G., 45, 314
Dodd, M., 46
domain, 53, 73, 418
    external, 183–184
Douqué, B. C. M., 346
DOWN (DSL ALPHA), 87
DSG, see data set group
DSL, see data sublanguage
dump routines, 409
duplicate elimination, see elimination
    of duplicates
DUPLICATES (DBTG), 335
    for member data-items, 414
    for sort-keys, 335
Dzubak, B. J., 45

Earnest, C. P., 458
Earnest, L., 377
*EDMS, 23
elimination of duplicates, 63, 65, 86
    in INGRES, 125
    in Query By Example, 138
    in SEQUEL, 125
Elphick, M. J., 419
empty set (DBTG), 317
encryption, see scrambling
End User Facility Task Group, 461
Engles, R. W., 4, 22, 313, 328, 417, 421
enterprise, 4
entity, 5ff.
entity set model, 48
equi-join, 116

ERASE (DBTG), 360–361
essentiality (in data declaration),
    448–449
Eswaran, K. P., 122, 135, 418, 419
EUFTG, see End User Facility Task
    Group
Everest, G. C., 23, 419
example element (Query By Example),
    138
EXCLUSIVE (DBTG), 415
exclusive lock, 405
express read (IMS), 412
external data definition language, 180
external DDL, see external data
    definition language
external level (ANSI/SPARC), 15,
    429–443
external model, 15, 179–190, 427
    in System R, 182
external record, 16
external schema, 16, 179, 427
external/conceptual mapping, 18,
    180ff.

Fadous, R., 175
Fagin, R., 153, 168, 176, 177
fan set, 318, 431, 449–453
Farley, J. H. G., 199
Fedeli, A., 198, 199
Fehder, P. L., 48
Feldman, J. A., 196
Fernandez, E. B., 393
field (IMS), 209
FIND (DBTG), 332, 361–368
    current format, 364–365
    fast access format, 362
    hashing format, 332, 362–363
    owner format, 365
    sequential scanning formats,
        362–364, 365–366
FIND (UDL), 437ff.
FINISH (DBTG), 328, 369
first normal form, 157
FIXED membership class (DBTG),
    336
foreign key, 78

FORMAT (integrity constraint), 399
Forsyth, R. J., 175
FORTRAN DMLC, 371
Fossum, B., 421
fourth normal form, 169
    informal definition of, 156
    reduction to, 169
Frank, R. L., 314
FREE (DBTG), 415
front compression, 42
Fry, J. P., 25, 46
full functional dependence, 155
fully concatenated key (IMS), 221, 227
    in a logical database, 276
    in secondary indexing, 297, 302
functional dependence, 154ff.
functional relation, 173
Furtado, A. L., 122

*GAMMA-O, 195
Generalized Sequential Access
        Method (IMS), 242
Gerritsen, R., 347
GET (DBTG), 356–357
GET (DSL ALPHA), 84ff.
get (IMS), 230ff.
    hold, 233
    next, 230
    next within parent, 231
    unique, 228, 230
GHN (IMS: get hold next), 233
GHNP (IMS: get hold next within
        parent), 233
GHU (IMS: get hold unique), 233
Giordano, N. J., 421
*GIS, 22
GN (IMS: get next), 230
GNP (IMS: get next within parent), 231
Goldman, J., 198
Goldstein, R. C., 198
Gotlieb, L. R., 121
Gould, J. D., 152
GRANT (SEQUEL), 384
granularity (locking), 408, 420, 421
graph structure, 427
Gray, J. N., 135, 190, 419, 420, 421

greater-than join, 116
Griffiths, P. P., 135, 393
GROUP BY (SEQUEL), 129, 133–134
grouping (Query By Example), 149
growth in the database, 13, 172,
        186–188
    in DBTG, 351, 452
    in IMS, 220
GSAM, see Generalized Sequential
        Access Method
GU (IMS: get unique), 228, 230
GUIDE/SHARE, 22, 313

Hall, P. A. V., 121, 176
Hammer, M. M., 134
Harary, F., 45
Harrison, R. D., 314
hash-addressing, 35
    in DBTG, 332, 362
    in IMS, 252–254
HAVING (SEQUEL), 129
Hawley, D. A., 422
HDAM, see Hierarchical Direct
        Access Method
Heath, I. J., 163, 172
Held, G. D., 48, 109, 112, 458
Herschberg, I. S., 393
HIDAM, see Hierarchical Indexed
        Direct Access Method
hidden data, 189, 220, 350, 360–361
hierarchical database, 431
Hierarchical Direct Access Method
        (IMS), 241, 243, 251–254, 504
Hierarchical Indexed Direct Access
        Method (IMS), 241, 243, 254–255
Hierarchical Indexed Sequential
        Access Method (IMS), 241, 243,
        244–249
hierarchical model, 55
hierarchical pointers (IMS), 249–251
hierarchical sequence (IMS), 215
Hierarchical Sequential Access
        Method (IMS), 241, 243–244
hierarchical storage structure, 34
Hilder, W., 112

HISAM, *see* Hierarchical Indexed
    Sequential Access Method
  using ISAM/OSAM, 245–248
  using VSAM, 248–249
Hoffman, L. J., 377, 378, 391
HOLD (DSL ALPHA), 96
Hopewell, P., 45, 190
host language, 15
HSAM, *see* Hierarchical Sequential
    Access Method
Hsiao, D. K., 45, 391, 393
Huits, M. H. H., 459

IAVERAGE (DSL ALPHA), 102
ICOUNT (DSL ALPHA), 101
identification (security), 377
IDENTIFIER (DBTG), 332
*IDMS, 67
*IDS, 22, 23, 67, 314
image function (DSL ALPHA), 101
IMAX (DSL ALPHA), 102
IMIN (DSL ALPHA), 102
implication (logical), 95
IN (SEQUEL), 126, 129
independent AND (IMS), 300–301
independent component (of a relation),
  177
index, 33
INDEX database (IMS), 254
  in HIDAM, 254–255
  in secondary indexing, 294–306
index segment (IMS), 255, 295
index target segment (IMS), 298
Indexed Sequential Access Method
  (OS/VS), 241
indirect attributes of requestor, 380
inference, 191, 197, 457
infological approach, 25
Information Algebra, 198
*INGRES, 84, 109, 112, 385, 403–404
INSERT (DBTG), *see* CONNECT
INSERT (Query By Example), 147
INSERT (SEQUEL), 131
insert (IMS), 232
  HDAM, 252–254
  HIDAM, 255

HISAM, 246–248
HSAM, 244
logical database, 278
secondary indexing, 298
integrity, 8, 395–422
integrity constraints, *see* access
  constraints
intention locking, 420
interlock, *see* deadlock
internal level (ANSI/SPARC), 13
internal model, 17, 429
internal record, 17
internal schema, 18, 429
INTERSECT (relational algebra), 114
INTERSECT (SEQUEL), 130
intersection data (IMS), 274
  variable-length, 290
inverted organization, 34
*IQF, 205
irreducible relation, 176
*IS/1, 120, 194–195
ISAM, *see* Indexed Sequential Access
  Method
*ISL-1, 22
ISRT, *see* insert (IMS)
ITOTAL (DSL ALPHA), 102
Ivie, E. L., 314

Jardine, D., 23
Jefferson, D. K., 458
JOIN (relational algebra), 64, 116
  equi-join, 116
  greater-than join, 116
  natural join, 121, 177
Jordan, E. E., 200
journaling, 21, 408–409

Kaplan, R. S., 200
Kay, M. H., 352, 453
KEEP (DBTG), 415
Kent, W., 23, 163, 173, 461
Kerschberg, L., 122
key (of a relation), 77ff.
  candidate, 78
  foreign, 78
  primary, 78

key feedback area (IMS), 227
key sensitivity (IMS), 222
King, P. F., 422
King, P. J. H., 112
King, W. F. III, 134, 135
Knowles, J. S., 422
Knuth, D. E., 47
Kreps, P., 112

Langefors, B., 25
LAST (Query By Example), 146
LCHILD, see logical child
LDB, see logical database
LDBR, see logical database record
*LEAP, 192, 196
Lefkovitz, D., 46
Levein, R. E., 197
Lewis, T. G., 47
library functions (DSL ALPHA),
    99–102
library functions (Query By Example),
    148–149
library functions (SEQUEL), 132–134
Lin, C. S., 197
link (hierarchies, networks), 56, 58,
    450–455
Lipovski, G. J., 197
loading the database, 21, 222
    HDAM, 252
    HIDAM, 255
    HISAM, 245, 259
    HSAM, 244
    IMS, 233
    logical database, 277–278
LOCATION MODE (DBTG), 332,
    334, 338–339, 361–362
    CALC, 332, 334, 339, 362
Lochovsky, F. H., 208
locking, 405ff.
    exclusive, 405
    granularity of, 408, 420, 421
    shared, 406
logical child (IMS), 274
    for INDEX/HIDAM, 260–262
    in secondary indexing, 295ff.
logical child pointer (IMS), 283

logical database (IMS), 207
    data model, 216, 269–292
    external model, 207, 219
logical database record (IMS), 219
logical inference, 191, 197, 457
logical parent (IMS), 274
logical parent pointer (IMS), 274
logical record, 11, 12, 16
    in OS/VS, 243
logical twin (IMS), 274
logical twin pointer (IMS), 284
Lohman, G. M., 49
Lorie, R. A., 135, 199, 419, 420, 421
lost updates, 396, 405
Lucking, J. R., 458
Lum, V. Y., 46

*MacAIMS, 66, 120, 193, 381
Macri, P. O., 421
*MAGNUM, 67, 200
MANDATORY membership class
    (DBTG), 336–337
Manola, F. A., 314
MANUAL membership class (DBTG),
    337
mapping (conceptual/internal), 18
    in DBTG, 311
    in IMS, 260–264
mapping (external/conceptual), 18,
    179ff.
    in DBTG, 349–352
    in IMS, 219–223, 274ff., 295ff.
    in System R, 182
mapping operation (SEQUEL), 124ff.
*MARK IV, 22, 66
Maron, M. E., 197
Marron, B. A., 46
*MARS III, 22
Martin, J., 47, 391, 392
Maurer, W. D., 47
MAX (DSL ALPHA), 101
MAX (Query By Example), 145
MAX (SEQUEL), 132
Maxwell, W. L., 390
McDonald, N., 109, 110
McGee, W. C., 23, 46, 208, 459

McJones, P. R., 135
McLeod, D. J., 199, 418
Mehl, J. W., 135
Meldman, M. J., 199
Meltzer, H. S., 6, 11, 23
member (DBTG), 316
membership class (DBTG), 335–338
metadata, 149
Metaxides, A., 459
Michaels, A. S., 459
MIN (DSL ALPHA), 101
MIN (SEQUEL), 132
Minker, J., 197
MINUS (relational algebra), 114
MINUS (SEQUEL), 130
Mittman, B., 459
MODIFY (DBTG), 357–358
    INCLUDING, 358
    ONLY, 358
monitored mode (DBTG), 415–417
Morgan, H. L., 390
Morris, R., 46
Mullin, J. K., 46
Multics, 390, 392
multidependence, see multivalued
    dependence
multilevel index, 38, 44
multilist organization, 33
multiple-relation target list, 92, 93
multivalued dependence, 168
Mylopoulos, J., 199

n-ary relation, see relation
n-entity net, 286, 323
n-tuple, see tuple
name inheritance, 85
    in DSL ALPHA, 85, 99, 471
    in QUEL, 110
    in relational algebra, 64, 474, 475
    in SEQUEL, 124
natural join, 121, 177
navigation, 372
network database, 431
network model, 58
Neuhold, E., 201
Neumann, P. G., 390

Nijssen, G. M., 346, 460
*NIPS/FFS, 22
*NOMAD, 67
nondense index, 38
nonkey attribute, 160
normal forms, 153ff.
    1NF, 157
    2NF, 160
    3NF, 162, 163
    4NF, 156, 169
normalization, 76, 153–178, 489–493
normalized relation, 76
Norman, A. R. D., 391
notify protocol, 415
Notley, M. G., 198
null, 76, 78, 158, 186
    in DBTG, 335, 414

objectives of relational approach, 457
Olle, T. W., 313, 347
onion-layer language, 432
OPEN (DBTG), 328
operational data, 4
optimal 3NF, 170
OPTIONAL membership class
    (DBTG), 337
ordering
    among attributes, 75
    among tuples, 74, 449
    essential, 454–455
    in DBTG DDL, 334–335
    in DBTG DML, 369
    in DSL ALPHA, 87, 97
    in Query By Example, 138
    in SEQUEL, 125
OSAM, see Overflow Sequential
    Access Method
Overflow Sequential Access Method
    (IMS), 241
Owens, R. C., Jr., 392
Owlett, J., 176
owner (DBTG), 316
owner-coupled set, 318
Ozkarahan, E. A., 197

pad byte (HDAM, HIDAM), 243
paired segment (IMS), 281

pairing (IMS), 281–286
  physical, 281–283
  virtual, 283–286
Palermo, F. P., 111, 121
Palmer, I. R., 24
Paolini, P., 198, 199
parametric user, 428
parent segment (IMS), 210
  current, 231
  logical, 274
  physical, 274
path call (IMS), 236–237
PCB, *see* program communication
  block
PDB, *see* physical database
PDBR, *see* physical database record
Pecherer, R. M., 121
Petersen, H. E., 378, 389, 392
Peterson, W. W., 46
phantom, 420
*PHOLAS, 347
physical child (IMS), 274
physical database (IMS), 207, 209
physical database record (IMS), 209
physical pairing (IMS), 281–283
physical parent (IMS), 274
physical parent pointer (IMS), 283
physical record, *see* block
physical record interface, 37
physical twin (IMS), 274
physical twin pointer (IMS), 249
piped mode (DSL ALPHA), 85
PLC, *see* Programming Language
  Committee
pointers
  in DBTG, 328
  direct, 42, 276
  in HDAM/HIDAM, 249–251
  in HISAM, 245–247
  in logical database, 274ff.
  in secondary indexing, 298
  symbolic, 42, 276
Polya, G., 445, 461
power set, 490
preconditioning, 189
predicate, 83

predicate locking, 420
preemption, 419
prefix, *see* segment prefix
prenex normal form, 91
primary data set group (IMS), 255–256
primary key, 78
primary processing sequence (IMS),
  296
PRIVACY KEY (DBTG), *see*
  ACCESS CONTROL KEY
privacy key (scrambling), 389
PRIVACY LOCK (DBTG), *see*
  ACCESS CONTROL LOCK
privacy transformation, *see* scrambling
processing options (IMS), 222, 236,
  411, 412
processing sequence (IMS), 296
PROCOPT, *see* processing options
program communication block (IMS),
  207
  defining within application, 225–227
  as external schema, 221
program specification block (IMS),
  207, 221
Programming Language Committee,
  309
PROJECT (relational algebra), 63, 115
PROTECTED (DBTG), 415
Prowse, P. H., 173
*PRTV, 120, 121, 195
PSB, *see* program specification block
PUT (DSL ALPHA), 97
Putzolu, G. R., 135, 420, 421

quantifier, 89
  existential, 89
  universal, 93
QUEL (relational DSL), 66, 109, 385,
  403–404
quota (DSL ALPHA), 87–88
quotient relation, 122

RANGE (DSL ALPHA), 88
range variable (DSL ALPHA), 88
RAP (storage device), 197
RARES (storage device), 197

*RDMS (system at GM Research), 195
*RDMS (system at MIT), 193
READY (DBTG), 328, 368, 415
realm (DBTG), 328
rear compression, 42
record area (DBTG), 313
recovery, 20, 21, 409
reduction to normalized form, *see*
    normalization
redundancy, 7, 81, 446
    in DBTG, 330–332, 453
    in IMS, 216, 271
    in relations, 158, 161, 168
    strong, 493
regular organization, 34
Reisner, P., 135
relation, 53, 73, 74, 430
    external, 180–183
relational algebra, 65, 107, 113ff.
relational calculus, 83ff., 107
relational completeness, 95, 107, 120
    SEQUEL 134, 476–480
*Relational Data File, 192, 197
relational database, 81, 430
relational decomposition, 173
relational model, 52, 79
relations and files, 80
relationship, 5ff.
RELEASE (DSL ALPHA), 96
REMONITOR (DBTG), 416
removal class (DBTG), 336–337
REMOVE (DBTG), *see*
    DISCONNECT
RENDEZVOUS (casual user system),
    110
reorganization, 21
    in IMS, 264–265
REPL, *see* replace (IMS)
replace (IMS), 233
    logical database, 279
    secondary indexing, 297
reserved words (schema DDL), 510
restriction (relational algebra), 113
RETAINING CURRENCY (DBTG),
    367–368
REVOKE (SEQUEL), 384

Richardson, J. S., 47
*RISS, 199, 418
Rissanen, J., 170, 173, 177
Robinson, K. A., 460
role, 76
role name, 76
root, 56
root segment (IMS), 210
    in logical database, 219, 290
    in secondary structure, 302
root segment addressable area
    (HDAM), 252
Rothnie, J. B., Jr., 108
Rovner, P. D., 196
RSI (System R), 196
rules
    for defining logical database, 290–291
    for defining secondary structure, 302
    for ISRT/DLET/REPLY, 278–280
    for updating views, 185
run-unit, 329
Rustin, R., 457
Ryder, J. C., 314

Saltzer, J. H., 392
SAM, *see* Sequential Access Methods
*SC-1, 22
schema (DBTG), 309, 311, 315–345
schema DDL (DBTG), 309
Schenk, H., 347
Schmid, H. A., 168, 174
Schneider, L. S., 200
Schroeder, M. D., 392
Schuster, S. A., 197, 198, 199
Schwartz, M. S., 421
scrambling, 388
second normal form, 160
secondary data set group (IMS),
    255–260
secondary data structure (IMS),
    301–302
secondary index, 33
    in IMS, 293–306
secondary processing sequence (IMS),
    296
secondary storage, 27

security, 8, 189, 375–394
security axioms, 381
security constraints, *see* access
    constraints
security matrix, 390
segment (IMS), 209
segment prefix (IMS), 243, 268
segment search argument (IMS),
    227–229, 234
segment type code (IMS), 214
SELECT (relational algebra), 63, 115
SELECT (SEQUEL), 124ff.
selective index, 41
    in IMS, 304
Senko, M. E., 48, 198
sensitive segment (IMS), 220
SEQUEL/2, 135
sequence field (IMS), 213–214
    nonunique (multiple), 214
Sequential Access Methods (OS/VS),
    241
*SERIES, 22
SET (SEQUEL), 129
set (DBTG), 316
    empty, 317
    member, 316
    occurrence, 316
    owner, 316
    singular, 326–327
    type, 316
SET SELECTION (DBTG), 339–343,
    361
Severance, D. G., 48, 49
shared lock, 406
Sharman, G. C. H., 176
SHISAM, *see* simple HISAM
Shneiderman, B., 25, 49
Shoshani, A., 419
SHSAM, *see* simple HSAM
Sibley, E. H., 25, 197, 458
simple domain, 77
simple HISAM, 243, 260
simple HSAM, 243, 260
singular set (DBTG), 326–327
SLICK (relational DSL), 196
Smith, D. C. P., 197

Smith, J. M., 121, 197
Smith, K. C., 197
Soop, K., 198
sort-key (DBTG), 334
Spadavecchia, V. N., 201
sparse indexing, 41
    in IMS, 304
SQUARE (relational DSL), 66, 123
*SQUIRAL, 121
SRA, *see* stored record address
SSA, *see* segment search argument
SSDLTG, *see* Storage Structure
        Definition Language Task Group
SSTG, *see* Sub-Schema Task Group
stability (of conceptual schema), 425,
    443
Stacey, G. M., 371
status field in PCB, 226
*STDS, 192
Steel, T. B., Jr., 460
Stewart, J., 198
Stonebraker, M. R., 24, 109, 110, 112,
    201, 393, 419, 458
storage class (DBTG), 337
storage fragmentation, 259
storage operation, 8
storage structure, 9, 27–49
storage structure definition, 18, 29
Storage Structure Definition Language
        Task Group, 46
STORE (DBTG), 361
stored database, 18
stored field, 10
    occurrence, 10
    type, 10
stored file, 11
stored record, 10
    occurrence, 10
    type, 11
stored record address, 29
stored record interface, 28
    in DBTG, 307
    in IMS, 241
strategy problems, 60–61
Strnad, A. J., 198
strong redundancy, 493

Su, S. Y. W., 197
sub-schema (DBTG), 310, 311, 349–352
    invocation, 312–313, 349
sub-schema DDL, 310
Sub-Schema Task Group, 371
SUM (Query By Example), 148
SUM (SEQUEL), 132
Summers, R. C., 393
Sundgren, B., 25
surrogate, 176
Svensson, P., 198
Swenson, J. R., 168, 174, 175
symbolic pointer, 42–43
symmetric exploitation, 448
symmetry, 445, 446
Symonds, A. J., 199
synchronization point, 412
synthesis of 3NF relations, 175, 176
system journal, 408
system log, 409
*System R, 123, 382–384, 401–403,
    407–408, 427, 453
*System 2000, 66, 208

table, 52–53
target list (DSL ALPHA), 86
Taylor, E., 112
Taylor, R. W., 314, 347
*TDMS, 22, 66
ternary relation, 74
third normal form, 162
    revised definition, 163
Thomas, J. C., 152
threat monitoring, 378
TIMES (relational algebra), 114
Titman, P. J., 199
Todd, S. J. P., 176, 198
TOP (DSL ALPHA), 101
TORUS (natural language system), 195
*TOTAL, 22, 23, 67
TOTAL (DSL ALPHA), 100
Tozer, E. E., 422
Traiger, I. L., 135, 190, 199, 419, 421
*TRAMP, 192, 197
transaction, 400, 406

TRANSIENT (DBTG), 359
transitive dependency, 161
tree-structured index, 38, 44
tree-structured relation, 143
Tsichritzis, D. C., 175, 198, 199, 208,
    347, 458
tuple, 53, 74
Turn, R., 378, 389, 392, 394
twin pointer (IMS), 249
    logical, 284
    physical, 249–251
twin segment (IMS), 212
    logical, 274
    physical, 274

UDL, see Unified Database Language
Uhrowczik, P. P., 25
*UL/I, 22
unary relation, 74
Unified Database Language, 429–443
UNION (relational algebra), 114
UNION (SEQUEL), 130
union-compatible, 114
UNIQUE (Query By Example), 148
UNIQUE (SEQUEL), 125
UNIQUE (integrity constraint),
    164, 397
unnormalized relation, 76
UP (DSL ALPHA), 87, 97
UPDATE (Query By Example), 146
UPDATE (SEQUEL), 131
UPDATE (DSL ALPHA), 96
USAGE-MODE (DBTG), 415
    EXCLUSIVE, 415
    PROTECTED, 415
USE FOR ACCESS CONTROL
    (DBTG), 386
USE FOR DB-EXCEPTION (DBTG),
    357
user, 15
user interface, 21
user profile, 378
User Work Area (DBTG), 312–313
utility programs, 20–21, 408–410
UWA, see User Work Area

validation, 8
VALUES (integrity constraint), 398
view (SEQUEL), 182, 383–384
violative operation, 172
VIRTUAL (DBTG), *see*
    ACTUAL/VIRTUAL
virtual data-item (DBTG), *see*
    ACTUAL/VIRTUAL
virtual domain, 184
virtual field, 12
virtual pairing (IMS), 283–286
virtual segment (IMS), 284
Virtual Storage Access Method
    (OS/VS), 241
Vorhaus, A. H., 68
Vose, M. R., 47
VSAM, *see* Virtual Storage Access
    Method

Wade, B. W., 135, 393
Waghorn, W. J., 346, 453
Wagner, R. E., 48
Wang, C. P., 176
Warburton, C. R., 45
Watson, V., 135

Wedekind, H. H., 176
Wee, R. S. S., 419
Wehr, L. A., 314
Whitney, V. K. M., 198
Wiktorin, L., 198
Williams, S. B., 69
window set (UDL), 430
wiretapping, 389
Wong, E., 47, 109, 112, 393
workspace, 15
    in DSL ALPHA, 84

XD field (IMS), 295ff.
*XDMS, 314
*XRM, 196
X3J4, 310

Young, J. W., Jr., 46
Younger Committee, 392
Youssefi, K., 112
Yuen, P. S. T., 46

Zaniolo, C. A., 168, 177
*ZETA, 195
Zloof, M. M., 137, 152